The Reformers and the Theology
of the Reformation

The Reformers and the Theology of the Reformation

William Cunningham

THE BANNER OF TRUTH TRUST

THE BANNER OF TRUTH TRUST
3 Murrayfield Road, Edinburgh EH12 6EL
P.O. Box 621, Carlisle, Pennsylvania 17013, U.S.A.

First published 1862
First Banner of Truth Trust edition 1967
Reprinted 1979

ISBN 0 85151 013 2

Reprinted by photolithography and
bound in Great Britain by
Billing & Sons Limited, Guildford, London and Worcester

PREFACE.

In introducing the present volume to the Public, the Editors feel that a few words of explanation may be desirable, in regard to the trust assigned to them, and the manner in which they have, in so far, attempted to discharge it.

In the interview which, at Dr Cunningham's request, they had with him within a few hours of his death, he committed to them the charge of his whole writings and manuscripts connected with the College, to be deposited in the Library, and to be used and applied to any purpose they judged right; stating, that he gave them absolute power to do in the matter as they considered to be best for his character, and the good of the Church. The charge thus verbally intrusted to them was formally and legally confirmed by the Trustees acting under Dr Cunningham's settlement; so that the Editors became invested with the character of his Literary Executors, and with the full powers and responsibilities attaching to such an office.

On examining his writings, they found that,—with respect to an important portion of them,—some little delay must occur before they could be properly prepared for the press, owing to their being required for the work of the Class during the present session of College; and that the wide-spread desire, throughout the Church, for the early publication of some of his valuable contributions to Theology, could be best met by giving to the Public the present volume in anticipation of the rest. It is made up of a number of Articles, contributed by Dr Cunningham to the "British and Foreign Evangelical Review," with a few additions from his manuscript Lectures, on Church History. The substance of these Articles originally formed a series of carefully prepared Lectures, delivered to his Class, on the leading Reformers and the character of their Theology; and they were subsequently transferred to the pages of the Review in which they appeared, with almost no alteration beyond extensive enlargements and additions, and such references to the more recent criticisms upon the Reformers as were suggested by the books reviewed. They were written upon a plan, and as an orderly series of discussions, embracing the leading historical characters, and the great developments of scriptural truth at the time of the Reformation; and were intended by their Author for separate publication as a connected whole. Happily the series was completed before Dr Cunningham's death; and it now exhibits a full and systematic view of the leading agents, and of the spiritual principles, of that great theological and ecclesiastical movement in the sixteenth century, which constitutes the greatest event in the history of the Church of Christ since the Apostolic Age, and which has bequeathed to us, in the present day, both our Church creeds and our Church polity.

The alterations which the Editors—in the exercise of their discretion—have made on the original text, have been more numerous than important, and in no case have affected the substance of the thought or reasoning. They have been guided in these alterations, sometimes by the manuscript corrections made by Dr Cunnningham himself; sometimes by the desire to avoid those repetitions and references to passing events, which naturally occur in a series of Articles, appearing at intervals in the pages of a Periodical; and sometimes, by a conviction—which many years of confidential intercourse with the Author on the subjects handled, as well as his own last instructions to them, enabled and warranted them to act upon,—of what he himself would have done had he been permitted to revise, with his own eye, the sheets before publication.

The quotations and references have been verified and corrected, with the kind assistance of the Rev. John Laing, Librarian to the New College.

The Editors expect to be enabled, in a short time,
to issue two other volumes similar to the present,
and comprising a full review of the leading theological
discussions that have taken place in the Christian
Church since the Apostolic Age.

JAMES BUCHANAN.

JAMES BANNERMAN.

New College,
Edinburgh, *April* 1862.

CONTENTS.

———◆———

LEADERS OF THE REFORMATION.*

THE Reformation from Popery in the sixteenth century was the greatest event, or series of events, that has occurred since the close of the Canon of Scripture; and the men who are really entitled to be called the "Leaders of the Reformation" have a claim to more respect and gratitude than any other body of un-inspired men that have ever influenced or adorned the church. The Reformation was closely connected in various ways with the different influences which about that period were affecting for good the general condition of Europe, and, in combination with them, it aided largely in introducing and establishing great improvements in all matters affecting literature, civilisation, liberty, and social order. The movement, however, was primarily and fundamentally a religious one, and all the most important questions that may be started about its character and consequences, should be decided by tests and considerations properly applicable to the subject of true religion. The Reformers claimed to be regarded as being engaged in a religious work, which was in accordance with God's revealed will, and fitted to promote the spiritual welfare of men; and we are at once entitled and bound to judge of them

* *British and Foreign Evangelical Review*, April 1860.   "LEADERS OF THE REFORMATION, by JOHN TULLOCH, D.D." 1859.

and their work, by investigating and ascertaining the validity of this claim.

There are two leading aspects in which the Reformation, viewed as a whole, may be regarded; the one more external and negative, and the other more intrinsic and positive. In the first aspect it was a great revolt against the see of Rome, and against the authority of the church and of churchmen in religious matters, combined with an assertion of the exclusive authority of the Bible, and of the right of all men to examine and interpret it for themselves. In the second and more important and positive aspect, the Reformation was the proclamation and inculcation, upon the alleged authority of Scripture, of certain views in regard to the substance of Christianity or the way of salvation, and in regard to the organization and ordinances of the Christian church. Many men have approved and commended the Reformation, viewed merely as a repudiation of human authority in religion, and an assertion of the right of private judgment, and of the exclusive supremacy of the Scriptures as the rule of faith, who have not concurred in the leading views of the Reformers in regard to Christian theology and church organization. In this sense, rationalists and latitudinarians have generally professed to adopt and act upon what they call the principles of the Reformation, while they reject all the leading doctrines of the Reformers. Men of this class usually attempt to pay off the Reformers with the credit of having emancipated mankind from ecclesiastical thraldom, established the right of private judgment, and done something to encourage the practice of free inquiry. But while giving the Reformers credit for these things, they have often rejected the leading doctrines of the Reformation upon theological and ecclesiastical subjects, and have been in the habit of claiming to themselves the credit of having succeeded, by following out the principles of the Reformation, in educing, either from Scripture or from their own speculations, more accurate and enlightened doctrinal views than the Reformers ever attained to. There has been a great deal of this sort of thing put forth both by rationalists and latitudinarians who professed to admit the authority of the Christian revelation, and by infidels who denied it. Dr Robertson in his life of Charles V. spoke of some doctrinal discussions of that period in such terms as justly to lay himself open to the following rebuke of Scott, the son of the commentator, in his excellent continuation of Milner's "History of the Church of Christ."

"It is manifest what is the character that Dr Robertson here affects, which is that of the philosopher and the statesman, in preference, if not to the disparagement, of that of the Christian divine. This is entirely to the taste of modern times, and will be sure to secure to him the praise of large and liberal views among those who regard a high sense of the importance of revealed truth, and all 'contending earnestly for the faith once delivered to the saints,' as the infallible mark of narrow-mindedness and bigotry."*

Dr Campbell of Aberdeen, too, who was a very great pretender to candour, has, in the last of his lectures on ecclesiastical history, made it manifest that he considered the chief benefits which the Reformers had conferred upon the world, to be the setting an example of free inquiry, and the exposing of church tyranny, superstitious and idolatrous practices, and clerical artifices, and that he despised all their zealous efforts and contendings in restoring the pure gospel of the grace of God, the true system of Christian theology, as conversant only, according to the common cant of latitudinarians, with metaphysical subtleties and scholastic jargon.

But the climax, perhaps, of this practice of paying off the Reformers with some commendation of their services in promoting free inquiry, while all their leading doctrines are rejected, is to be found in the facts, that in our own day such a man as Bretschneider wrote a "Dissertatio De Rationalismo Lutheri," and that Wegscheider dedicated his "Institutiones Theologiæ Christianæ Dogmaticæ," which is just a system of Deism in a sort of Christian dress, "Piis Manibus Martini Lutheri," mainly upon the ground, that he had opened up liberty of thought, and encouraged posterity to advance much further in the path on which he had entered.

A somewhat different aspect of this matter has been presented by certain writers, who are not disposed to allow to the Reformers even the credit of having encouraged and promoted free inquiry. It has been alleged that there is little or nothing said in the writings of the Reformers about the right and duty of private judgment, and that the absence of this, combined with their great zeal for what they reckoned truth, and their strenuous and vehement opposition to what they reckoned error, proved that after all they were nothing better than narrow-minded bigots. Hallam, in his "Literature of Europe during the 15th, 16th, and 17th centuries,"

---

* Vol. i. p. 270.

has some statements to this effect; and the facts on which he founds are in the main true, though they certainly do not warrant his conclusions.* It must, however, we fear, be conceded to Hallam and others who take this view: 1st, that the Reformers were not much in the habit of formally and elaborately discussing, *as a distinct and independent topic*, what has since been called the right and duty of private judgment; and 2d, that they ever professed it to be their great object to find out the actual truth of God contained in His word, that they were very confident that in regard to the main points of their teaching they had found the truth, and that they were very strenuous in urging that other men should receive it also upon God's authority. And these facts are amply sufficient to secure for them, in certain quarters, the reputation of being narrow-minded bigots.

The Reformers did not discuss at much length, or with any great formality, the subject of the right of private judgment as a general topic, but they understood and acted upon their right as rational and responsible beings to reject all mere human authority in religious matters, to try everything by the standard of God's word, and to judge for themselves, on their own responsibility, as to the meaning of its statements. And by following this course, by acting on this principle, by setting this example, they have conferred most important benefits upon the church and the world.

The fundamental position maintained by the Reformers was this, that the views which they had been led to form, as to what should be the doctrine, worship, and government, of the church of Christ, were *right*, and that the views of the church of Rome upon these points, as opposed to theirs, were *wrong*. This was the grand position they occupied, and they based their whole procedure upon the ground of the paramount claims of divine truth, *its* right as coming from God and being invested with His authority, to be listened to, to be obeyed, and to be propagated. When the papists opposed them in the maintenance of this position, and appealed on their own behalf to tradition, to ecclesiastical authority, to the decisions of popes and councils, the Reformers in reply pushed all this aside, by asserting the supremacy of the written word as the only standard of faith and practice, by denying the legitimacy of submitting to mere human authority in religious matters, and by

---

* Part I., chap. iv., sec. 60, 61.

maintaining that men are entitled and bound to judge for themselves, upon their own responsibility, as to what God in His word has required them to believe and to do.   They asserted these positions more or less fully as circumstances required, but still they regarded them as in some sense subsidiary and subordinate. The primary question with them always was, What is the *truth* as to the way in which God ought to be worshipped, in which a sinner is saved, and in which the ordinances and arrangements of the church of Christ ought to be regulated? They were bent upon answering, and answering aright, *this* important question, and they brushed aside everything that stood in their way and obstructed their progress.

There can be no doubt that the only satisfactory explanation of the conduct of the Reformers is, that they regarded themselves as fighting for the cause of God; and it is creditable to Hallam that, unable, as he admitted, to understand their theology, and having no predilection on their behalf, he should have seen and asserted this, in opposition to the ordinary calumnies of the papists.*   But the great, the only really important, question is, Was it indeed the cause of God? or in other words, was it indeed the truth of God which they deduced from His word, and which they laboured to promote and to enforce?   If it was not so, then they have deserved little gratitude, and they can have effected little good. In estimating the value of what God gave to them, and what they have transmitted to us, almost everything depends upon the truth, the Scriptural truth, of the doctrines which they taught and

---

* Hallam's statements about Luther and the Reformers are certainly very defective and erroneous, but they have much the appearance of being chiefly traceable to what may be called honest ignorance.   He seems to have intended to be fair and candid in his statements regarding them, and he probably was about as much so as could reasonably be expected of a man who was very imperfectly acquainted with theological subjects.   He admits (P. 1, c. iv., s. 61), that "every solution of the conduct of the Reformers must be nugatory, except one—that they were men absorbed by the conviction that they were fighting the battle of God." He describes Luther (s. 59), as a man "whose soul was penetrated with a fervent piety, and whose integrity, as well as purity of life, are unquestioned." He admits (c. vi., s. 26), that he had but a " slight acquaintance" with Luther's writings, and that he had " found it impossible to reconcile or understand his tenets concerning faith and works."   After all this, it was scarcely to be expected, from Hallam's usual good sense and fairness, that he should have charged Luther with Antinomianism.   There is a thorough exposure of the incompetency of Hallam, as well as of Sir William Hamilton in this matter, in Archdeacon Hare's admirable " Vindication of Luther."

laboured to advance. The highest honour of the Reformers, or rather the principal gift which God gave them, viewed as public teachers who have exerted an influence upon the state of religious opinion and practice in the world, was that, in point of fact, they did deduce from the word of God, the *truths* or *true doctrines* which are there set forth, and that they brought them out, and expounded and enforced them in such a way as led, through God's blessing, to their being extensively received and applied. Christian theology, in some of its most important articles, had for a long period been grossly corrupted in the Church of Rome, which then comprehended the largest portion of Christendom. The Lord was pleased, through the instrumentality of the Reformers, to expose these corruptions, to bring out prominently before the world the true doctrines of His word, in regard to the worship which He required and would accept, the way in which He had provided and was bestowing, and in which sinners were to receive, the salvation of the gospel, and the way in which the ordinances and arrangements of His church were to be regulated ; and to effect that these true Scriptural doctrines should be extensively disseminated, should become powerfully influential, and should be permanently preserved over a considerable portion of His church. The Lord did this by His Spirit at the era of the Reformation, and He employed in doing it the instrumentality of the Reformers. He guided them not only to the adoption of the right method, the use of the appropriate means for detecting error and discovering divine truth, but what was of primary and paramount importance, He guided them to a right judgment—that is, right in the main and with respect to all fundamental points, as to what particular doctrines were true and false, according to the standard of His own written word. Their unquestionable sincerity and integrity, their unwearied zeal and activity, their great talents and their undaunted courage, would only have shed a false glare around a bad cause, if it was not indeed the cause of God which they were maintaining. Their other good qualities would have tended rather to evil than to good results, if it had not been really error which they opposed and God's truth which they supported. We believe nothing *because* the Reformers believed it, and we approve of nothing *because* they practised it ; but, judging of them by the same standard which they applied to the church of Rome, and by which they professed to regulate their own opinions and conduct, *because* we believe with them that it is the right standard, we are firmly persuaded that what they opposed was error—grievous and dangerous error—and that what they maintained was in the main truth—God's own truth—taught in His word, and applied to them by the teaching of His own Spirit.

There is so much unanimity among the Reformers, so much harmony in the confessions of the Reformed churches, as to entitle us to speak of the *theology of the Reformation*, as conveying a pretty distinct idea of a particular system of doctrine upon the leading articles of the Christian faith; and we think it can be proved, not only that this theology was sound and scriptural, as compared with what had previously prevailed in the church of Rome, but that the deviations which Protestants have since made from it have been in the main retrogressions from truth to error. We do not set up the Reformers as guides or oracles; we do not invest them with any authority, or believe anything because they believed it. There is, indeed, no authority in religion but that of God, and authority, in its strict and proper sense, does not admit of degrees. The fact that certain doctrines were taught by some particular class or body of men, is either at once and of itself a sufficient reason why we must embrace them, or else it is of no real weight and validity in determining what we should believe. It is entitled to be received as authoritative and determining, only when the men in question can produce satisfactory evidence that they have been commissioned and inspired by God. There is a sense, indeed, in which some respect or deference is due to the opinions of others. But this respect or deference should never be transmuted into anything like authority or obligation. It may afford a valid call for careful attention and diligent investigation, but for nothing more. It should have no determining or controlling influence. The Reformers, with respect to all points in which they were substantially of one mind, may be regarded as being upon the whole entitled to more respect and deference than any other body of men who could be specified or marked out at any one period in the history of the church. But it holds true universally, that God has never given to any uninspired man, or body of men, to rise altogether above the influence of the circumstances in which they were placed, in the formation and expression of their opinions upon religious subjects. And even the greatest admirers of the Reformers readily admit that they, all of them, though not in the main features of their theological system, yielded more or less to the various sources of error which prevail among men, and more particularly, that they exhibited, on the one hand, traces that they had not wholly escaped from the corrupting influence of the system in which they had been educated, and on the other hand, what is equally natural, that they were sometimes in danger in avoiding one extreme of falling into the opposite one.

These obvious views about the position and services of the Reformers have been suggested to us by the perusal of Principal Tulloch's work on the "Leaders of the Reformation." It is intended as a popular sketch of the main features in the history of Luther, Calvin, Latimer, and Knox; and regarded in this light, it is fairly entitled to very considerable commendation. We cannot say that the work displays any great power of thought, or any great extent of research. We have no idea that Dr Tulloch is familiar with the writings of the Reformers, or that he is qualified to appreciate them in connection with the highest departments of the work which they performed. But he has given a very intelligent, interesting, and candid survey of the principal features of the life and the general character and position of the men whom he has selected as the leaders of the Reformation. He has taken considerable pains to understand and to state accurately most of the points he has discussed. He has shown a large measure of fairness and candour in the principal views he has put forth; and he has presented them generally in a very pleasing and interesting style.

Dr Tulloch's book, as a whole, would have been entitled to very considerable commendation, if it had not put forth some very objectionable and dangerous views in regard to the theology of the Reformers, by far the most important feature in their history. The object of the work did not require of Dr Tulloch to enter into theological exposition or discussion, and we might have passed over the work with commending what was commendable in it, if he had entirely ignored theological subjects. But he has not done this. He has put forth certain views in regard to the theology of the Reformers which we believe to be unsound and dangerous, and which we think it incumbent upon us to expose.

The Reformers themselves reckoned it the great duty which they were called upon to discharge, the great work which God

gave them to do, to bring out from the sacred Scriptures right
views of Christian theology and of church organization, in opposition to those which generally prevailed in the church of Rome.
They believed that they were enabled, by God's grace, to succeed
to a large extent in doing this; and all who have since concurred
with them in this belief have also, as a matter of course, regarded
their success *in this respect* as a very great service rendered to the
church and the world, as, indeed, the greatest service which they
rendered, or could render. We believe that the theology of the
Reformation, in its great leading features, both as it respects doctrine in the more limited sense of the word, and as it respects the
organization of the church as a society, is the unchangeable truth
of God revealed in His word, which individuals and churches are
bound to profess and to act upon. Dr Tulloch, we fear, has come
to a different conclusion upon this important question, and has
plainly enough given the world to understand that, in his judgment, the theology of the Reformation, though a creditable and
useful thing in the sixteenth century, and a great improvement on
the state of matters that then prevailed in the church of Rome,
has now become antiquated and obsolete, and quite unsuitable to
the enlightenment which characterizes this age.

He does not adduce any specific objections against the theology of the Reformation ; but having attained to a much greater
elevation, a far higher platform, than the Reformers ever reached,
he coolly but conclusively sets aside the results of all their investigations of divine things, as now scarcely worthy of being seriously examined. This not only, as we have already explained,
deprives the Reformers of what all who have in the main adopted
their principles, have regarded as the greatest honour which God
conferred upon them, the greatest service they were enabled to
render ; but it bears, and, as we believe, bears injuriously, upon
a matter of infinitely greater importance than any question affecting the reputation of any body of men, even the accurate exposition
of the system of revealed truth. Dr Tulloch does not profess to
discuss any theological questions ; and his views upon these points
are brought out very vaguely and imperfectly. But he has said
enough to show that he has given up the theology of the Reformation as untenable and unsatisfactory ; and he evidently thinks
that all liberal men who are abreast of this enlightened age must
do the same. It is quite evident that men's whole views and

impressions in regard to the history of the Reformers must be
greatly influenced by the admission or the denial, that they were
God's instruments in bringing out to a large extent the permanent
truth revealed in His word, and in restoring the church to a large
measure of apostolic purity; and it is highly creditable to Dr Tulloch that, denying this, he should have treated them with so large
a measure of justice and fairness in most other respects. But it
was scarcely possible that one who withholds from them their
highest and most peculiar honour should be perfectly just and
fair to them in everything else; and there are indications, though
not many or important, of his depreciating them even in matters
not much connected with their theology. There is not much to
complain of in what he says of Luther and Knox, barring their
theology, except that he underrates their intellectual powers, when
he says of the former[*] that, "as a theological thinker he takes no
high rank, and has left little or no impress upon human history;"
and of the latter[†] that, "as a mere thinker, save perhaps on political subjects, he takes no rank."[‡]

Few, we think, who have read the principal works of Luther
and Knox will concur in this opinion of these men, and even in
some of the things which Dr Tulloch himself has recorded about
them, there is enough to convince discerning men that they did take
high rank as thinkers on theological subjects. Luther, notwithstanding his great mental powers, and the great light he has
thrown upon many important topics of discussion, had yet such
defects and infirmities, as to unfit him very much for being
appealed to as a guide or oracle on theological subjects; and
Knox, overshadowed by Calvin, is not so frequently contemplated
as a theologian, though his treatise on Predestination proves, we
venture to think, that he is entitled to take high rank as a thinker.
For the reasons now referred to, neither Luther nor Knox seems
to have strongly excited Dr Tulloch's anti-theological zeal, and he

---

* P. 72.   † P. 317.

‡ This somewhat supercilious way
of disposing of eminent men is in great
favour with Dr Tulloch. He applies
it to Beza likewise, calling him (p.
145) "a lively, meddlesome, service-
able, but by no means great man."
Sir William Hamilton, who when he
condescends to praise any of the Reformers, and particularly when the

question respects their talents and
acquirements, must be regarded as a
somewhat higher authority than Dr
Tulloch, has pronounced such an eulogium on Beza as plainly implies that
he reckoned him a great man, and he
expressly describes him as "this great
thinker and illustrious divine." (Be
not Schismatics, etc., p. 30, 35.)

certainly deals out to them a large measure of justice and candour, though he does not appreciate fully either their talents or their services.

Calvin, however, as might be expected, does not fare so well in Dr Tulloch's hands. He was so thoroughly the great representative of all that Dr Tulloch seems most heartily to disapprove and dislike, viz., a distinct and definite system of theological doctrine, and a church organisation upon the model of apostolic precept and practice, that it was scarcely to be expected that the great Reformer would get justice from him. He does not, indeed, so far as we remember, make any direct attempt to depreciate Calvin's intellectual powers, or to dispute *his* right "to take high rank as a thinker." But we have a strong impression that he comes far short of a just appreciation even of Calvin's mental powers and capacities. And it should not be forgotten, that it has become very much the fashion now-a-days, even among Romanists, as a matter of policy, to praise Calvin's talents. Even Audin, his latest popish biographer, who is just as thoroughly unprincipled as the champions of popery usually are, has given the appearance of something like candour to his "Life of Calvin," by strong statements about his great talents, his literary excellencies, and his commanding influence. Dr Tulloch, while he makes no direct attempt to depreciate Calvin's talents, does injustice, we think, in several respects to his general character. He says nothing, indeed, against him which has not been said often before. He just repeats what has been so frequently alleged against Calvin, his want of the more amiable and engaging qualities, his pride and coldness, his sternness and cruelty. He does not seem to appreciate the purity and elevation of the motives by which Calvin was animated, and of the objects he aimed at. He does not appear to have turned to good account the greater accessibility now-a-days of Calvin's Letters, which are so admirably fitted to counteract some of the prevailing misconceptions of his character, and to show that there was nearly as much about him to love as to admire, as much to excite affection and confidence as veneration and respect. Dr Jules Bonnet, who has done so much to make Calvin's Letters more widely known, describes, in the preface to the English translation, his letters to Farel, Viret, and Beza, as exhibiting "the overflowings of a heart filled with the deepest and most acute sensibility." It might have been supposed that no one who had really read the two volumes of Calvin's Letters, to which this statement is prefixed, would have any doubt of its truth and accuracy. But Dr Tulloch it seems has not been able to find anything of this sort, and, accordingly, he disposes of Dr Bonnet's statement in this way*—" Overflowing of any kind is exactly what you never find in Calvin, even in his most familiar letters." We fear that Dr Tulloch must understand the word "overflowing" in a different sense from other men ; for if we had space we could easily produce plenty of extracts from his Letters, which most men, we are confident, would, without any hesitation, declare to be overflowings of the warmest and tenderest feeling, outpourings of the most hearty and cordial kindness and sympathy, and of the purest and noblest friendship. Calvin's character, intellectual, moral, and religious, has been most highly appreciated by the most competent judges ; and the collection of testimonies in commendation of him and his works, published in one of the last volumes of the Calvin Translation Society, containing his Commentary on Joshua, is probably unexampled in the history of the human race. But we are not sure if a more emphatic tribute to his excellence and his power is not furnished by the hostility of which he has been the object ; often breaking out into furious rancour, and frequently, even when assuming a greatly modified aspect, indicating a strong disposition to depreciate him, and to bring him down to the level of ordinary men. But we cannot dwell longer upon this topic. We must hasten to notice the position which Dr Tulloch has assumed in regard to the theology of the Reformation ; and here it will be necessary in fairness to give him an opportunity of speaking for himself. His views are brought out pretty fully in the following extracts :—

" The spiritual principle is eternally divine and powerful. It is a very different thing when we turn to contemplate the dogmatic statements of Luther. So soon as Luther began to evolve his principle, and coin its living heart once more into dogma, he showed that he had not risen above the scholastic spirit which he aimed to destroy. It was truly impossible that he could do so. Not even the massive energy of Luther could pierce through those intellectual influences which had descended as a hoary heritage of ages to the sixteenth century."†

" The Reformation, in its theology, did not and could not escape the deteriorating influences of the scholastic spirit, for that spirit survived it, and lived on in strength, although in a modified form, throughout the seventeenth

---

* P. 153.   † P. 88.

century. In one important particular, indeed, the scholastic and Protestant systems of theology entirely differed : the latter began their systematising from the very opposite extreme to that of the former—from the divine and not from the human side of redemption—from God and not from man. And this is a difference on the side of truth by no means to be overlooked. Still the spirit is the same—the spirit which does not hesitate to break up the divine unity of the truth in Scripture into its own logical shreds and patches, which tries to discriminate what in its moral essence is inscrutable, and to trace in distinct dogmatic moulds the operation of the divine and human wills in salvation, while the very condition of all salvation is the eternal mystery of their union in an act of mutual and inexpressible love. This spirit of ultra-definition—of essential rationalism—was the corrupting inheritance of the new from the old theology ; and it is difficult to say, all things considered, as we trace the melancholy history of Protestant dogmas, whether its fruits have been worse in the latter or in the former instance. The mists, it is true, have never again so utterly obscured the truth, but that dimness, covering a fairer light, almost inspires the religious heart with a deeper sadness."*

"While thus claiming for Calvinism a higher scriptural character, it would yet be too much to say that Calvinism, any more than Lutheranism, or latterly Arminianism, was primarily the result of a fresh and living study of Scripture. Calvin, no doubt, went to Scripture. He is the greatest biblical commentator, as he is the greatest biblical dogmatist, of his age ; but his dogmas, for the most part were not primarily suggested by Scripture ; and as to his distinguishing dogma, this is eminently the case. Like Luther, he had been trained in the scholastic philosophy, and been fed on Augustine ; and it was no more possible for the one than for the other to get beyond the scholastic spirit or the Augustinian doctrine. An attentive study of the ' Institutes' reveals the presence of Augustine everywhere ; and great even as Calvin is in exegesis, his exegesis is mainly controlled by Augustinian dogmatic theory."†

"This appeal to an earlier catholicity on the part of the reformed theologies—this support in Augustine—beyond doubt greatly contributed to their success in their day. For few then ventured to doubt the authority of Augustinianism, and the theological spirit of the sixteenth century hardly at any point got beyond it. It was a natural source of triumph to the great Protestant confessions against the unsettled unbelief or more superficial theologies which they encountered, that they wielded so bold and consistent a weapon of logic, and appealed so largely to an authoritative scriptural interpretation. Calvinism *could not but* triumph on any such modes of reasoning or of biblical exegesis as then prevailed ; and so long as it continued to be merely a question of systems, and logic had it all its way, this triumph was secure.

"But now that the question is changed, and logic is no longer mistress of the field ; now, when a spirit of interpreting Scripture, which could have

---

* Pp. 84–5.   † P. 166.

hardly been intelligible to Calvin, generally asserts itself—a spirit which recognises a progress in Scripture itself—a diverse literature and moral growth
in its component elements, and which at once looking backward with reverence and forward with faith, has learned a new audacity, or a new modesty,
as we shall call it, according to our predilections, and while it accepts withal
the mysteries of life and of death, refuses to submit them arbitrarily to the
dictation of any mere logical principle ; now that the whole sphere of religious
credence is differently apprehended, and the provinces of faith and of logical
deduction are recognised as not merely incommensurate, but as radically distinguished—the whole case as to the triumphant position of Calvinism, or
indeed any other theological system, is altered.   An able writer in our day
(Mansel, in his Bampton Lectures), has shown with convincing power what
are the inevitably contradictory results of carrying the reasoning faculty with
determining sway into the department of religious truth.   The conclusions of
that writer, sufficiently crushing as directed by him against all rationalistic
systems, are to the full as conclusive against the *competency* of all theological
systems whatever.   The weapon of logical destructiveness which he has used
with such energy, is a weapon of offence really against all religious dogmatism.
What between the torture of criticism, and the slow but sure advance of moral
idea, this dogmatism is losing all hold of the most living and earnest intelligence everywhere.   And it seems no longer possible, under any new polemic
form, to revive it.   Men are weary of heterodoxy and of orthodoxy alike, and
of the former in any arbitrary and dogmatic shape still more intolerably than
the latter.   The old *Institutio Christianæ Religionis* no longer satisfies, and a
new *Institutio* can never replace it.   A second Calvin in theology is impossible.
Men thirst not less for spiritual truth, but they no longer believe in the
capacity of system to embrace and contain that truth, as in a reservoir, for
successive generations.   They must seek for it themselves afresh in the pages of
Scripture, and the ever-dawning light of spiritual life, or they will simply
neglect and put it past as an old story." *

These extracts fully justify the statements we have made in
regard to the scope and tendency of this book, and in commenting
upon them in order to show this, we shall speak of the theology of
the Reformation and Calvinism as substantially identical, not
meaning by Calvinism the personal opinions of Calvin, but the
leading features of the Calvinistic system of theology, as distinguished from the Arminian and Socinian systems.   In this sense
Calvinism may be fairly called the theology of the Reformation,
as it was certainly, though with different degrees of accuracy and
fulness, maintained by the great body of the Reformers, and professed in most of the Confessions of the Reformed churches.   We

---

* Pp. 167–9.

never hesitate to call ourselves Calvinists, though there are some of Calvin's opinions which we reckon erroneous; and in adopting this designation, we mean simply to convey the idea that we are firmly persuaded that the fundamental principles of the Calvinistic system of theology, as generally set forth in the symbolical books of churches usually reckoned Calvinistic, are taught, and can be proved to be taught, in Scripture, as the revealed truth of God. And here a practical difficulty at once arises in dealing with Dr Tulloch. If we were to judge of him solely from the statements contained in this book, we would have little hesitation in saying, that he is not a Calvinist, in the sense above explained. But of course we are aware that he has, like ourselves, subscribed a Calvinistic creed, and that he holds an office, the chief duty of which may be said to be to expound this creed. We have, therefore, scarcely a right to say that he is not a Calvinist, unless he had said so more explicitly, perhaps, than he has done. And in anything we may say bearing on this point, we wish it to be understood that we make no categorical assertion as to what Dr Tulloch's theological opinions in point of fact are, and that we intend merely to set forth what seem to us to be the scope and tendency of the views indicated in this book. With this explanation, we have no hesitation in saying that we are unable to comprehend how any intelligent Calvinist could have published the statements we have quoted; and that they are plainly fitted to lead to the conclusion that the author has renounced, if he ever held, the theology of the Reformation. It is a significant fact, that Dr Tulloch, though a professor of theology, has not, from the beginning to the end of his book, given any distinct indication that he is a Calvinist, or made any profession of regarding the Reformers as having succeeded in the main in bringing out God's truth from His word. There are several statements which look like a profession of Calvinism, but which, when carefully examined, are clearly seen to come short of this. But we are not confined to negative materials. We are plainly told that Calvinism once triumphed, but that this triumph was temporary, and is long since over, that no theological system can now occupy a triumphant position, since we have at last reached a demonstration of the incompetency of *all* theological systems whatever.

Dr Tulloch's position is pretty distinctly indicated in the somewhat enigmatical deliverance, "The old 'Institutio Christianæ Reli-

gionis' no longer satisfies, and a new Institutio can never replace it."
There is a sense in which we could assent to the notions suggested
by this quotation. But in the sense in which Dr Tulloch ·evi-
dently understands it, we regard it as unsound and dangerous.
"The old 'Institutio Christianæ Religionis' no longer satisfies."
Every Calvinist will admit this to be true, if it be understood to
mean merely, that there are views set forth in the "Institutes" of
Calvin which can be proved from Scripture to be erroneous, and
that the progress of discussion since his time has indicated defects
existing in that work and improvements that might be made upon
it, as to the arrangement of the subjects, the mode in which several
topics are presented, singly or in their relation to each other, the
comparative prominence assigned to them, and the validity of all
the proofs by which they are supported. There are points coming
under these various heads, in which the "Institutes" do not now
satisfy, and we hold it to be a mark of the respect to which Calvin
and the "Institutes" are entitled, to be prepared to specify the
grounds of our dissatisfaction. But those things about the "Institutes," which do not satisfy us, are few and unimportant, and do
not materially affect the present and permanent value of that great
work. It is plainly in an entirely different sense from this, that
it no longer satisfies Dr Tulloch and other men of progress in the
present day. He evidently regards it as having proved an entire
failure in regard to its main substance, its principal contents or
materials, and its leading design. The materials of which the
"Institutes" are composed are, of course, just the leading doctrines
of Scripture, according to the view which Calvinists, from Augustine to the present day, have always taken of their meaning and
import. And the main question in judging of any work which
professes to exhibit in a scientific or systematic form the leading
principles of Christian theology must of necessity be,—Are the
materials of which it is composed, or the doctrines which it expounds and defends, accordant, in the main, with Scripture? Are
they as a whole the views which Scripture teaches, and which it
warrants and requires us to believe, as immutable truth resting
upon divine authority? Every Calvinist who has read Calvin's
"Institutes," of course, believes that the materials of which that
work is composed, are in the main the doctrines of God's word,
and therefore possessed of unchangeable verity. Most Calvinists
have also been of opinion, that the great doctrines of Christian

theology are upon the whole about as well arranged, as ably and accurately expounded, and as satisfactorily and conclusively defended in Calvin's "Institutes" as they ever have been or can be. We do not exact of every Calvinist that he must concur in this commendation of Calvin's "Institutes." But, of course, no man can call himself a Calvinist, unless he believe that the leading doctrines set forth in the "Institutes" are indeed taught by God in His word. And it is not very likely that any man could be found, who, while professing to hold the Calvinistic doctrines taught in the "Institutes," should, at the same time, assert that either he himself, or any one else, could expound them more ably and defend them more conclusively than Calvin has done.

But it is of comparatively small importance in what light the "Institutes" ought to be regarded, viewed merely as a specimen of Calvin's powers and achievements. The only vital question is this—Are the leading doctrines taught in the "Institutes" true and scriptural? Was the theology of Calvin, in its fundamental principles, correctly derived from the word of God? This is a vital question. We answer it in the affirmative, and we consider ourselves warranted in asserting that Dr Tulloch has answered it in the negative. There is, as was natural in the circumstances, a good deal of vagueness and confusion in his statements upon this subject. It was scarcely to be expected that he would at first speak out in an explicit and manly way. Men of progress in theology usually require to grope their way for a time, through hedges and along bye-ways. But with all the vagueness and confusion which characterise his statements, he has, we think, afforded sufficient grounds for charging him with maintaining,

1st, That the main features of the theology of the Reformation, the leading doctrines of the Calvinistic system, are not revealed to us in the word of God.

2d, That the Reformers erred in their whole theological system, because they had erroneous notions of the true province of logic, of the object and design of the sacred Scriptures, and of the way and manner in which they ought to be interpreted and applied in the formation of our religious opinions.

3d, That the crude and erroneous notions of the Reformers in regard to the province of logic, and the method of explaining and applying Scripture being corrected and taken away, it is now a fixed and settled thing that all theological systems are incompetent.

We believe that these three propositions exhibit accurately the sum and substance of Dr Tulloch's teaching upon the most important subject touched on in his lectures. It would afford us sincere gratification if Dr Tulloch could and would repudiate these views, and show that we had no sufficient grounds for imputing them to him. But this we fear is hopeless, and the next best thing would be, that he should plainly admit that he holds these positions in substance; and having thus come into the open arena, should boldly and manfully defend his convictions. The reputation of the Reformers, the settlement of any questions that may be started about the amount of the commendation that should be bestowed upon them, and about the grounds on which it should be based, all this is insignificant. But the question of the truth or falsehood of the theology of the Reformation is too important to be trifled with. There may turn out to be nothing formidable in the attack now made upon it, but from the magnitude of the interests involved, we like always to see who are the assailants, and what means of assault they have provided.

A combination seems to exist at present for the purpose of undermining and exploding the theology of the Reformation, without meeting it fairly and openly in the field of argument. A man of higher standing than Dr Tulloch has yet reached, one who has rendered many important services to the cause of Christian truth, Mr Isaac Taylor, has lent a helping hand to this object, by publishing (anonymously) the following statement:—

"The creeds and the confessions of the Reformation era were, indeed, with scrupulous care based upon the authority of Holy Scripture, and looking at them simply as they stood related to the manifold corruptions of the twelve centuries preceding, they might well claim to be scriptural. But in what manner had they been framed? *A certain class of texts* having been assumed as the groundwork of Christian belief, then a scheme of theology is put together accordingly, whence by the means of the *deductive logic*, all separate articles of faith are to be derived. As to any passages of Scripture which might seem to be of another class, or which do not easily fall into their places in this scheme, they were either ignored, or they were controlled, and this to any extent that might be asked for by the stern necessities of the syllogistic method."*

Dr Tulloch has not put forth anything against the Reformers so discreditable as this, but he evidently occupies ground the same

---

* *North British Review*, No. li. p. 60.

in substance, so far as concerns the erroneousness, both of the process by which they investigated divine truth, and of the results which they reached. He cannot, indeed, be so forgetful of the history and writings of the Reformers as to be capable of believing what Mr Taylor has said about a " certain class of texts." But in all other respects there is a wonderful harmony between them. They concur not only in the belief that the theology of the Reformation is fundamentally unsound and untenable, but also in their leading views of the errors attaching to the process by which this erroneous result was reached. They both think that it was the " deductive logic" that was the main cause of all the mischief, combined with certain erroneous notions of the way in which the Scriptures ought to be used and applied, meaning by this, apparently, just the doctrine of inspiration, as it has been usually held by the Christian church, and its immediate consequences. They both expect an entirely new theology, which is to replace the superannuated logical theology of the Reformation. They expect this first from abandoning the deductive logic, and then from the introduction of new modes of biblical exegesis. Mr Taylor, indeed, held out to the world the prospect of a new " exegetical method," which was to work wonders in reforming theology. We are not aware that this exegetical method has yet made its appearance. But Dr Tulloch speaks as if the new and improved process of investigating divine truth, and of explaining and applying the Bible, were already in operation, and had already succeeded, not only in bringing down Calvinism to the dust, but even in doing something to introduce a simpler and sounder theology. In the quotation we have given from him, he calls it a certain " spirit of interpreting Scripture," which he describes in terms very magniloquent, but not such as to convey to us any very definite idea of what this spirit is, or where it is to be found. We would like to know something about this " spirit of interpreting Scripture," which is to work such wonders, and to effect such improvements in theology. But as Dr Tulloch assures us that it " could hardly have been intelligible to Calvin," we fear we must renounce all hope of ever catching a glimpse of its import.

Dr Tulloch's work contains no theological discussion, and therefore we are not called upon to engage in theological discussion in reviewing it. There is no distinct specification of what it is in the theology of the Reformation, or in the system of Calvinism, which is unsound and untenable. There is no specification of what it was that was erroneous in those old modes of reasoning or of biblical exegesis, which led to the temporary triumph of Calvinism, or of what are the grounds of that new "spirit of interpreting Scripture," which has demolished Calvinism and introduced a sounder, that is, a more scanty and obscure, theology. We do not refer to the absence of anything of this sort, as if it were a defect in a book, which does not profess to discuss theological topics. We refer to it for the purpose, first, of expressing a doubt whether it was quite right and fair in Dr Tulloch to introduce what has so unfavourable a bearing upon the theology generally professed in Scotland, *without entering into theological discussion*, or setting forth with some fulness the grounds of the views expressed; and, secondly, of showing that we are not called on, in reviewing Dr Tulloch's book, to engage in theological discussion, since he has not given us anything distinct and substantial to answer.

The nearest approach to anything like definiteness which Dr Tulloch makes under this general head of the theology of the Reformation, is an allegation to the effect that the Reformers formed their system of doctrine by carrying to an unwarranted length the practice of drawing inferences from Scripture statements, and by exercising greatly too much their logical faculties in classifying, combining, and expanding the materials which Scripture affords. But even this is only a vague generality of no real value or use, apart from its proved applicability to actual processes of investigation which have been adopted by individuals or bodies of men, and to actual theological results which have been brought out. No one can well dispute, that men are entitled and bound to use their intellectual powers, not only in investigating the meaning of particular statements, but in classifying and combining a number of statements, in order to bring out as the result the full teaching of Scripture upon the subject to which the statements relate, and that we are to receive, as resting upon divine authority, not only what is " expressly set down in Scripture," but also what "may, by good and necessary consequence, be deduced from Scripture." It is admitted, on the other hand, that men have often gone too far in making deductions from scriptural statements, and especially what is with many a great bugbear in the present day, in making deductions from doctrines assumed to be already established, upon the principle of what is sometimes called the analogy of faith. But though these are dangers to be guarded against, we fear that no rules can be laid down, marking out distinctly what is warrantable and legitimate in these respects, and what is not; and, therefore, no decision upon these points can be founded upon mere vague general declamation about dangers and excesses. Each case in which error, either in the process adopted, or in the result brought out, is alleged, must be judged of and decided upon its own merits. The theology of the Reformers is not to be set aside, merely because men have often gone to an extreme in making deductions from scriptural statements, nor even because they themselves have sometimes erred in this respect. We insist that their theology, as a whole, and every doctrine which enters into their system, shall be judged of fairly and fully by the standard of Scripture, and of Scripture used and applied according to its real character and design. We embrace the theology of the Reformation just because we think we can prove, that all the particular doctrines which constitute it are taught in Scripture, rightly interpreted and applied; and while, on the one hand, we undertake the responsibility of asserting and proving this, we must, on the other hand, insist that any one who repudiates the theology of the Reformation, shall distinctly specify what the errors of the system are, and bring forward the evidence from Scripture that they are errors.

But Dr Tulloch assures us* that Mr Mansel, in his "Bampton Lectures," has conclusively established the incompetency of all theological systems whatever. Mr Mansel has not proved, and has not professed to prove, this. The fundamental principle of Mr Mansel's book is really and in substance just the doctrine which has always been a familiar commonplace with orthodox divines, viz., that the human faculties are unable adequately to comprehend all truths and all their relations, and that men have therefore no right to make their full comprehension of doctrines, or their perception of the accordance of doctrines with each other, the test or standard of their truth. And the principal merit of the work is, that it brings out this very important but very obvious and familiar principle in a philosophic dress, establishes it upon philosophic grounds, and connects it with the best philosophy of

---

* P. 169.

the age. The most legitimate and valuable application of Mr Mansel's principles, so far as theological subjects are concerned, is to expose the unwarrantable presumption of the objections commonly adduced against the leading doctrines that seem to be taught in Scripture, on the ground of their alleged contrariety to reason. We admit that his principles would also preclude the competency of founding a positive argument in support of the mysterious doctrines of theology, on what may be called rationalistic grounds derived from their intrinsic nature or mutual relation. But this is not sufficient to warrant Dr Tulloch's allegation that they establish the incompetency of all theological systems, *because it is not by any such unwarrantable rationalistic process that theological systems are formed.* The advocates of every theological system profess to find in Scripture all the materials of which their system is composed, and to be prepared to defend every doctrine they hold, and their system as a whole, by the authority of Scripture. The Reformers professed to derive their whole theology from Scripture, and undertook to produce evidence from Scripture for every doctrine they inculcated. And so do all Calvinists still. They may find some confirmation of their doctrines individually, and of their system as a whole, in considerations derived from natural reason and the exercise of their logical faculties. But they refer to Scripture as affording the chief direct positive proof of all they teach, and they undertake to show that the materials which Scripture furnishes, rightly and rationally used and applied, establish every part of their theological system. Calvinists do not pretend, that when they have proved some one of their doctrines from Scripture, they can derive all their other doctrines from this one, by mere logical deduction. They profess to produce direct positive proof from Scripture sufficient to establish every one of them, and to have recourse to rational considerations only for confirming the proof, and, especially for answering, or rather disposing of objections. In regard, then, to every one of the doctrines which enter into our theological system, we profess to show, that it accurately expresses or embodies the sum and substance of what is asserted or indicated in Scripture upon the point. There is nothing in Mansel's "Bampton Lectures," or anywhere else, which proves, or even appears to prove, that there is anything in this process which is incompetent or unwarrantable, or involves a transgression of the

just "limits of religious thought." If there be men who mainly
rest the truth of their doctrines individually, or of their systems
as a whole, upon any other ground than this reasonable and competent application of scriptural materials, they cannot plead on
their behalf, the example of the Reformers, or any of the best
defenders of Calvinism. We base all the doctrines of our system
upon statements contained in Scripture, we undertake to prove
them by a fair and rational application of the materials which
Scripture furnishes, and there is no ground for alleging that the
processes required in doing this, whether conducted so as to lead
in point of fact to a correct result in any particular case or not,
go beyond the fair and legitimate exercise of men's mental powers.
We are entitled to demand that our scriptural proofs shall be
fairly faced and disposed of, in place of the whole subject being
set aside as incompetent, upon the ground of a piece of palpably
irrelevant metaphysics.

These remarks may be illustrated by selecting an instance of
a particular doctrine, and we shall choose with this view the great
doctrine of justification, which, in some aspects, may be regarded
as the great distinguishing feature of the theology of the Reformation.

Dr Tulloch has given* a statement of this great doctrine of
Luther in a somewhat mystical and not very intelligible style, to
which it is not worth while to advert. What we have to do with
at present is this, that he complains, that Luther and the defenders of the theology of the Reformation, in place of being
contented with some vague generalities upon this subject, should,
by definition and exposition, have drawn it out into precise and
definite propositions, alleging in substance, that the whole process
by which this is done is unwarrantable and incompetent, and that
the result is not truth, but error. Let us take one of these precise and definite descriptions of justification, and see how the case
stands; and in order to give Dr Tulloch every advantage, we
shall select it from a period when the odious process of what he
calls "ultra-definition" had been carried somewhat farther than
was done by the Reformers, and when, of course, all that he
reckons so objectionable was most fully developed. About the
middle of the seventeenth century, an assembly of divines put

---

* P. 82.

forth the following statement of what they believed to be taught in Scripture on the subject of justification :—

"Those whom God effectually calleth, he also freely justifieth ; not by infusing righteousness into them, but by pardoning their sins and by accounting and accepting their persons as righteous ; not for anything wrought in them, or done by them, but for Christ's sake alone ; not by imputing faith itself, the act of believing, or any other evangelical obedience to them as their righteousness, but by imputing the obedience and satisfaction of Christ unto them, they receiving and resting on Him and His righteousness by faith, which faith they have not of themselves—it is the gift of God."*

Every one acquainted with the history of theological discussion, knows that this remarkable statement not only affirms, positively and explicitly, certain great truths, but, by plain implication, denies certain errors opposed to them, which have been held by Papists and Arminians to be taught in Scripture ; and the question raised by it is this, Are the doctrines asserted, or the doctrines denied, here, revealed to us in Scripture as true? It is quite possible that some men may refuse to adopt either of these alternatives, and may contend that Scripture teaches a third doctrine upon the subject of justification, different from either,—or that it does not teach any definite doctrine whatever upon the points here brought under consideration, and furnishes no materials for an intelligent and rational decision among the contending creeds. Our position upon the subject is clear and decided, and we wish to understand distinctly the position of any one whose views upon these matters we may be called upon to consider. We believe that the statement quoted from the "Confession of Faith" presents an accurate embodiment of the sum and substance of what Scripture warrants and requires us to believe upon the subject of justification ; and we hold ourselves bound to produce, in suitable circumstances, the Scripture proof that all the Protestant Calvinistic doctrines there asserted are true, and that all the Popish and Arminian doctrines there denied are false. In what precise way Dr Tulloch would define his position in regard to this matter, we can scarcely venture to say. We presume he will not affirm, that he believes either the one or the other set of opinions to be taught in Scripture, and to be binding upon men's consciences. He is not likely, we should suppose, to put forth a third set of opinions upon these points,

---

* Westminster Confession of Faith, c. xi.

different from the other two. The ground which, it would seem, he must take, in order to escape from the degradation of professing, in this nineteenth century, a precise set of opinions upon justification, is to maintain that Scripture does not furnish materials for laying down any such definite doctrines upon the subject. And this can be established only in one or other of two ways, either by producing some direct general proof of it *à priori*, as an abstract position, or by following the method of exhaustion and proving in detail, that not one of the attempts which have been made to deduce a definite doctrine of justification from scriptural materials has succeeded. There is thus a vast deal to be done beyond what has ever yet been attempted, before the great doctrine of justification, as set forth in the confessions of the Reformed churches, can be exploded, and the way opened up for restoring that obscurity and confusion, in regard to the way of a sinner's justification, which the Reformers did so much to dissipate, and which the men of progress in the present day seem so anxious to bring back.

There is one theological topic on which Dr Tulloch has given something like a deliverance, and it may be worth while to advert to it as a specimen of the new or advanced theology. In treating of the controversy between Luther and Erasmus on the subject of the bondage or servitude of the will, he gives the following sage and satisfactory deliverance regarding it :—

" It would be idle for us to enter into the merits of this controversy ; and, in truth, its merits are no longer to us what they were to the combatants themselves. The course of opinion has altered this as well as many other points of dispute, so that under the same names we no longer really discuss the same things. There are probably none, with any competent knowledge of the subject, who would care any longer to defend the exact position either of Luther or of Erasmus. *Both are right, and both are wrong. Man is free, and yet grace is needful ;* and the philosophic refinements of Erasmus, and the wild exaggerations of Luther, have become mere historic dust, which would only raise a cloud by being disturbed." *

And in referring to the same point as controverted between Calvin and Pighius, he disposes of it in this way :—

" So far as the merits of the controversy are concerned, it cannot be said that he is any more successful than the German Reformer. He is here and everywhere more simple and cautious in his statements, but his cold reiterations and evasions really no more touch the obvious difficulties, than Luther's heated paradoxes." †

* P. 52.   † P. 123.

The great controversy, then, about the bondage of the will, to which the Reformers attached so much importance in their discussions with the Romanists, and the Calvinists in their discussions with the Arminians, Dr Tulloch pronounces to have been a mere logomachy,—a question of no practical importance whatever, unworthy, it would seem, of receiving any serious consideration. Here, again, we fear that Dr Tulloch's deliverance must be held to imply a denial, that the doctrine taught by the Reformers is really revealed to us in Scripture. That doctrine, as set forth by the Westminster divines is, that " man, by his fall into a state of sin, hath wholly lost all ability of will to any spiritual good accompanying salvation." Luther, in defending this doctrine, in reply to Erasmus, has made some rash and exaggerated statements, which no one adopts. But Calvin, in defending the same doctrine, in reply to Pighius, has, as Dr Tulloch admits, avoided these excesses. And, independently of all peculiarities of individuals, we would like to know how Dr Tulloch would deal with the doctrine as stated by the Westminster divines. Is that, too, a mere logomachy, which is just as true and as false as the opposite doctrine taught by Papists and Arminians? Are there really no materials in Scripture for deciding either for or against the great Reformation doctrine of the bondage or servitude of the will of fallen man to sin? Is the whole of the process of investigating the meaning of Scripture for the decision of that question, as it has been conducted on both sides, unwarrantable and illegitimate? Or is there really an utter want of materials in Scripture for determining the question, either on the one side or on the other? The way in which Dr Tulloch has spoken in regard to this important doctrine of the Reformation, suggests and warrants such questions as these; and we would like to see him meet them, as well as those formerly proposed in regard to justification, openly and manfully, in order that we might, if possible, learn something about that " spirit of interpreting Scripture," of which Dr Tulloch discourses so magniloquently and unintelligibly, and by which Scripture seems to be rendered so inadequate to be " a light unto our feet and a lamp unto our path."

There is another important subject, in regard to which the Reformers have been generally regarded as having rendered good service to mankind, viz., the right organization of the Christian Church. This, in one aspect, might be comprehended under the general head of theology or doctrine, as it consists essentially in bringing out a portion of the mind and will of God, as revealed in His word. But it is common, and in some respects useful, to distinguish them, and Dr Tulloch has given them a separate treatment. The questions to be entertained and settled upon this subject are these: Has God given us, in His word, any indications of His will with respect to the worship and government of His church, which are binding in all ages? and if He has, What are they?

It is generally conceded that the Reformers restored the church to a large measure of apostolic purity and simplicity with respect to worship and government. But it cannot be said that they reckoned this matter so important as the restoration of sound doctrine, or that they were to so large an extent of one mind in the conclusions to which they came. In this, as well as in theology, more strictly so called, Calvin was the great master-mind, who stamped his impress most distinctly upon the church of that and of every subsequent period. His own contributions to the establishment of principle and the development of truth, were greater in regard to church organization than in regard to any other department of discussion,—of such magnitude and importance, indeed, in their bearing upon the whole subject of the church, as naturally to suggest a comparison with the achievements of Sir Isaac Newton in unfolding the true principles of the solar system. The Christian church is mainly indebted to Calvin, much more than to any other man, for bringing out distinctly, pressing upon general attention, and establishing the following great principles :—

1st, That it is unwarrantable and unlawful to introduce into the government and worship of the church anything which has not the positive sanction of Scripture.

2d, That the church, though it consists properly and primarily only of the elect or of believers, and though, therefore, visibility and organization are not *essential*, as papists allege they are, to its existence, is under a positive obligation to be organized, if possible, as a visible society, and to be organized in all things, so far as possible,—its office-bearers, ordinances, worship, and general administration and arrangements,—in accordance with what is prescribed or indicated upon these points in the New Testament.

3d, That the fundamental principles, or leading features, of what is usually called Presbyterian church government, are indicated with sufficient clearness in the New Testament, as permanently binding upon the church.

4*th*, That the church should be altogether free and independent of civil control, and should conduct its own distinct and independent government by presbyteries and synods, while the civil power is called upon to afford it protection and support.

5*th*, That human laws, whether about civil or ecclesiastical things, and whether proceeding from civil or ecclesiastical authorities, do not, *per se*—*i.e.* irrespective of their being sanctioned by the authority of God,—impose an obligation upon the conscience.

Calvin professed to find all these principles more or less clearly taught in Scripture; and we have no doubt that he succeeded in proving that they are all sanctioned by the word of God, and that thus they may be said to embody the permanent, binding, constitution of the Christian church. We do not say that none of these principles had ever been enunciated till Calvin proclaimed them. But some of them had never before been so clearly and explicitly set forth. None of them had ever before been so fully brought out in their true meaning, and in their complete evidence. And the presentation of them all in combination, expounded and defended with consummate ability, and at the same time with admirable moderation and good sense, furnishes a contribution to the right permanent organization of the Christian church such as no man ever made before, and no man could have an opportunity of making again. Calvin may be said, in a sense, to have settled permanently the constitution of the Christian church, not by assuming any jurisdiction over it, or by any mere exercise of his own talents and sagacity, but simply because God was pleased to make him the instrument of bringing out from the sacred Scriptures the great leading principles, bearing upon the organization of the church, which till that time had been very much overlooked, and had been far from exerting their proper influence. We believe that the leading principles which Calvin inculcated in regard to the organization of the church, never have been, and never can be, successfully assailed; while there is certainly no possibility of any one being able again to bring out from Scripture a contribution of anything like equal value.

Of course, everything depends upon the settlement of the question, whether or not these principles are taught in Scripture, as truth revealed for the permanent guidance of the church. The general process by which this is to be investigated and ascertained, is perfectly competent and legitimate in all its features, though opposite conclusions have been brought out by different parties who professed to follow it.   It has been contended,

1st, That Scripture sanctions the great principles above stated, as the permanent constitution of the church.

2d, That Scripture teaches something which is different from, or exclusive of, or opposed to, these principles, upon all or most of the points to which they relate.

3d, That little or nothing bearing upon matters of worship and government is prescribed to, or imposed upon, the church, and that there are no adequate materials for deciding upon the truth or falsehood of the two preceding positions.

Something plausible may be adduced in support of each of these three positions. But the question is, Which of them is true? which has really the sanction of Scripture? We embrace the first of them, and profess to be able to establish it by an accurate exposition and a reasonable application of materials which Scripture furnishes. The third of these positions is in substance that which is maintained by Dr Tulloch and other latitudinarians. He seems to think, that except, perhaps, in regard to some great general principles, so evident as scarcely to leave room for a difference of opinion, the church is left at liberty to settle questions about government and worship for herself, in the way which she may think best at the time and in the circumstances; that the views upon these subjects brought out by Calvin and the Reformers, though improvements upon the previous condition of things, and well suited to the times, furnish nothing like a pattern of what ought to be the permanent state of the church : and that Scripture cannot be shown to afford materials for deciding those controversies which have been carried on between different churches about questions of government and worship. These are the sort of notions which he indicates plainly enough in such passages as the following :—

" There are two distinct views that may be taken of this part of Calvin's work. It presents itself, on the one hand, as a moral influence—a conservative spiritual discipline suited to the time, as it was called forth by it ; and, on the other hand, as a new theory, or definite reconstitution of the church. In the first point of view, it is almost wholly admirable ; in the second, it

will be found unable to maintain itself any more than the Catholic theory which it so far displaced."* " It is a very different subject that is before us when we turn to contemplate the theocracy of Calvin, in its formal expression and basis as a new and definite outline of church government. In this respect he made more an apparent than a real advance upon the old Catholic theocracy. He took up the old principle from a different and higher basis, but in a scarcely less arbitrary and external manner. There is a kingdom of divine truth and righteousness, he said, and Scripture, not the priesthood, is its basis. The Divine word, and not Roman tradition, is the foundation of the spiritual commonwealth. So far all right; so far Calvin had got hold of a powerful truth against the corrupt historical pretensions of popery. But he at once went much farther than this, and said, not tentatively, or in a spirit of rational freedom, but dogmatically, and in a spirit of arbitrariness, tainted with the very falsehood from whose thraldom he sought to deliver men, ' this is the form of the divine kingdom presented in Scripture.'"†
" Presbyterianism became the peculiar church order of a free Protestantism, carrying with it everywhere, singularly enough, as one of the very agencies of its free moral influence, an inquisitorial authority resembling that of the Calvinistic consistory. It rested, beyond doubt, on a true divine order, else it never could have attained this historical success. But it also involved from the beginning a corrupting stain in the very way in which it put forth its divine warrant. It not merely asserted itself to be wise and conformable to Scripture, and therefore divine, but it claimed the direct impress of a divine right for all its details and applications. This gave it strength and influence in a rude and uncritical age, but it planted in it from the first an element of corruption. The great conception which it embodied was impaired at the root by being fixed in a stagnant and inflexible system, which became identified with the conception as not only equally but specially divine."‡ " But were not these ' elements,' some will say, really biblical? did not Calvin establish his church polity and church discipline upon Scripture? and is not this a warrantable course? Assuredly not, in the spirit in which he did it. The fundamental source of the mistake is here. The Christian Scriptures are a revelation of divine truth, and not a revelation of church polity. They not only do not lay down the outline of such a polity, but they do not even give the adequate and conclusive hints of one; and for the best of all reasons, that it would have been entirely contrary to the spirit of Christianity to have done so; and because, in point of fact, the conditions of human progress do not admit of the imposition of any unvarying system of government, ecclesiastical or civil. The system adapts itself to the life, everywhere expands with it, or narrows with it, but is nowhere in any particular form the absolute condition of life. A definite outline of church polity, therefore, or a definite code of social ethics, is nowhere given in the New Testament, and the spirit of it is entirely hostile to the absolute assertion of either the one or the other."§

* P. 175.   † P. 179.   ‡ P. 181.   § Pp. 182–3.

In order to establish his position, Dr Tulloch is bound either to produce Scripture evidence in support of the general notions or maxims on which he bases it, or else to prove in detail the utter inadequacy of all the attempts which have been made to show, that any definite views in regard to government and worship ought permanently to guide the churches of Christ. We profess to establish our position by both these classes of argument. In so far as we profess to lay down any general rules, whether of an imperative or of a prohibitory character, and in so far as we urge any specific arrangements as permanently binding, we undertake to produce sufficient evidence from Scripture for all we assert or require. Dr Tulloch has not entered upon any defence of the ground he has taken upon this subject; and, therefore, we are not called upon to discuss it. But as the loose and dangerous views which he has put forth are very prevalent in the present day, and as they are by no means destitute of plausibility, while, at the same time, we are persuaded that a large share of the favour they have met with is to be ascribed to ignorance and misapprehension, we shall take the opportunity of making a few explanatory observations regarding them.

Of the views generally held by the Reformers on the subject of the organization of the church, there are two which have been always very offensive to men of a loose and latitudinarian tendency,—viz., the alleged unlawfulness of introducing into the worship and government of the church any thing which is not positively warranted by Scripture, and the permanent binding obligation of a particular form of church government. The second of these principles may be regarded, in one aspect of it, as comprehended in the first. But it may be proper to make a few observations upon them separately, in the order in which they have now been stated.

The Lutheran and Anglican sections of the Reformers held a somewhat looser view upon these subjects than was approved of by Calvin. They generally held that the church might warrantably introduce innovations into its government and worship, which might seem fitted to be useful, provided it could not be shown that there was anything in Scripture which expressly prohibited or discountenanced them, thus laying the *onus probandi*, in so far as Scripture is concerned, upon those who opposed the introduction of innovations. The Calvinistic section of the Reformers, following their great master, adopted a stricter rule, and were of opinion, that there are sufficiently plain indications in Scripture itself, that it was Christ's mind and will, that nothing should be introduced into the government and worship of the church, unless a positive warrant for it could be found in Scripture. This principle was adopted and acted upon by the English Puritans and the Scottish Presbyterians; and we are persuaded that it is the only true and safe principle applicable to this matter.

The principle is, in a sense, a very wide and sweeping one. But it is purely prohibitory or exclusive; and the practical effect of it, if it were fully carried out, would just be to leave the church in the condition in which it was left by the apostles, in so far as we have any means of information; a result, surely, which need not be very alarming, except to those who think that they themselves have very superior powers for improving and adorning the church by their inventions. The principle ought to be understood in a common sense way, and we ought to be satisfied with reasonable evidence of its truth. Those who dislike this principle, from whatever cause, usually try to run us into difficulties by putting a very stringent construction upon it, and thereby giving it an appearance of absurdity, or by demanding an unreasonable amount of evidence to establish it. The principle must be interpreted and explained in the exercise of common sense. One obvious modification of it is suggested in the first chapter of the " Westminster Confession," where it is acknowledged "that there are some circumstances, concerning the worship of God and government of the church, common to human actions and societies, which are to be ordered by the light of nature and Christian prudence, according to the general rules of the word, which are always to be observed." But even this distinction between things and circumstances cannot always be applied very certainly; that is, cases have occurred in which there might be room for a difference of opinion, whether a proposed regulation or arrangement was *a distinct thing* in the way of innovation, or merely *a circumstance* attaching to an authorised thing and requiring to be regulated. Difficulties and differences of opinions may arise about details, even when sound judgment and good sense are brought to bear upon the interpretation and application of the principle; but this affords no ground for denying or doubting the truth or soundness of the principle itself.

In regard to questions of this sort there are two opposite extremes, into which one-sided minds are apt to fall, and both of which ought to be guarded against. The one is to stick rigidly and doggedly to a general principle, refusing to admit that any limitations or qualifications ought to be permitted in applying it; and the other is to reject the principle altogether, as if it had no truth or soundness about it, merely because it manifestly cannot be carried out without some exceptions and modifications, and because difficulties may be raised about some of the details of its application which cannot always be very easily solved. Both these extremes have been often exhibited in connection with this principle. Both of them are natural, but both are unreasonable, and both indicate a want of sound judgment. The right course is to ascertain, if possible, whether or not the principle be true, and if there seem to be sufficient evidence of its truth, then to seek to make a reasonable and judicious application of it.

With regard to the Scripture evidence of the truth of the principle, we do not allege that it is very direct, explicit, and overwhelming. It is not of a kind likely to satisfy the coarse, material, literalists, who can see nothing in the Bible but what is asserted in express terms. But it is, we think, amply sufficient to convince those who, without any prejudice against it, are ready to submit their minds to the fair impression of what Scripture seems to have been intended to teach. The general principle of the unlawfulness of introducing into the government and worship of the church anything which cannot be shown to have positive scriptural sanction, can, we think, be deduced from the word of God by good and necessary consequence. We do not mean, at present, to adduce the proof, but merely to indicate where it is to be found. The truth of this principle, as a general rule for the guidance of the church, is plainly enough involved in what Scripture teaches, concerning its own sufficiency and perfection as a rule of faith and practice, concerning God's exclusive right to determine in what way He ought to be worshipped, concerning Christ's exclusive right to settle the constitution, laws, and arrangements of His kingdom, concerning the unlawfulness of will worship, and concerning the utter unfitness of men for the function which they have so often and so boldly usurped in this matter. The fair application of these various scriptural views taken in combination, along with the utter want of any evidence on the other side, seems to us quite sufficient to shut out the lawfulness of introducing the inventions of men into the government and worship of the Christian church.

There is no force in the presumption, that, because so little in regard to the externals of the church is fixed by scriptural authority, therefore much was left to be regulated by human wisdom, as experience might suggest or as the varying condition of the church might seem to require. For, on the contrary, every view suggested by Scripture of Christianity and the church, indicates, that Christ intended His church to remain permanently in the condition of simplicity as to outward arrangements, in which His apostles were guided to leave it. And never certainly has there been a case in which it has been more fully established by experience, that the foolishness of God, as the apostle says, is wiser than men, that what seems to many men very plausible and very wise, is utter folly, and tends to frustrate the very objects which it was designed to serve. Of the innumerable inventions of men introduced into the government and worship of the church, without any warrant from Scripture, but professedly as being indicated by the wisdom of experience, or by the Christian consciousness of a particular age or country, to be fitted to promote the great ends of the church, not one can with any plausibility be shown to have had a tendency to contribute, or to have in fact contributed, to the end contemplated; while, taken in the mass, and of course no limitation can be put to them unless the principle we maintain be adopted, they have inflicted fearful injury upon the best interests of the church. There is a remarkable statement of Dr Owen's on this subject, which has been often quoted, but not more frequently than it deserves; it is this—" The principle that the church hath power to institute any thing or ceremony belonging to the worship of God, either as to matter or manner, beyond the observance of such circumstances as necessarily attend such ordinances as Christ Himself hath instituted, lies at the bottom of all the horrible superstition and idolatry, of all the confusion, blood, persecution, and wars, that have for so long a season spread themselves over the face of the Christian world." It is no doubt very gratifying to the pride of men to think that they, in the exercise of their wisdom, brought to bear upon the experience of the past history of the church, or (to accommodate our statement to the prevalent views and phraseology of the present day), in the exercise of their own Christian consciousness, their own spiritual tact and discernment, can introduce improvements upon the nakedness and simplicity of the church as it was left by the apostles. Perhaps the best mode of dealing with such persons, is to call upon them to exemplify their own general principle, by producing specific instances from among the innumerable innovations that have been introduced into the church in past ages, by which they are prepared to maintain that the interests of religion have been benefited;—or if they decline this, to call upon them for a specimen of the innovations, possessed of course of this beneficial character and tendency, which they themselves have devised and would wish to have introduced; and then to undertake to show, what would be no very difficult task, that these innovations, whether selected or invented, have produced, or would produce if tried, effects the very reverse of what they would ascribe to them.

There is a strange fallacy which seems to mislead men in forming an estimate of the soundness and importance of this principle. Because this principle has been often brought out in connection with the discussion of matters which, viewed in themselves, are very unimportant, such as rites and ceremonies, vestments and organs, crossings, kneelings, bowings, and other such *ineptiæ*, some men seem to think that it partakes of the intrinsic littleness of these things, and that the men who defend and try to enforce it, find their most congenial occupation in fighting about these small matters, and exhibit great bigotry and narrow-mindedness in bringing the authority of God and the testimony of Scripture to bear upon such a number of paltry points. Many have been led to entertain such views as these of the English Puritans and of the Scottish Presbyterians, and very much upon the ground of their maintenance of this principle. Now, it should be quite sufficient to prevent or neutralize this impression to show, as we think can be done, 1st, That the principle is taught with sufficient plainness in Scripture, and that, therefore, it ought to be professed and applied to the regulation of ecclesiastical affairs. 2d, That, viewed in itself, it is large, liberal, and comprehensive, such as seems in no way unbecoming its Divine author, and in no way unsuitable to the dignity of the church as a divine institution, giving to God His rightful place of supremacy, and to the church, as the body of Christ, its rightful position of elevated simplicity and purity. 3d, That, when contemplated in connection with the ends of the church, it is in full accordance with everything suggested by an enlightened and searching survey of the tendencies of human nature, and the testimony of all past experience. And with respect to the connection above referred to, on which the impression we are combating is chiefly based, it is surely plain that, in so far as it exists *de facto*, this is owing, not to anything in the tendencies of the principle itself or of its supporters, but to the conduct of the men who, in defiance of this principle, would obtrude human inventions into the government and worship of the church, or who insist upon retaining them permanently after they have once got admittance. The principle suggests no rites or ceremonies, no schemes or arrangements; it is purely negative and prohibitory. Its supporters never devise innovations and press them upon the church. The principle itself precludes this. It is the deniers of this principle, and they alone, who invent and obtrude innovations; and they are responsible for all the mischiefs that ensue from the discussions and contentions to which these things have given rise.

Men, under the pretence of curing the defects and short-comings, the nakedness and bareness, attaching to ecclesiastical arrangements as set before us in the New Testament, have been constantly proposing innovations and improvements in government and worship. The question is, How ought these proposals to have been received? Our answer is, There is a great general scriptural principle which shuts them all out. We refuse even to enter into the consideration of what is alleged in support of them. It is enough for us that they have no positive sanction from Scripture. On this ground we refuse to admit them, and, where they have crept in, we insist upon their being turned out, although, upon this latter point, Calvin, with his usual magnanimity, was always willing to have a reasonable regard to times and circumstances, and to the weaknesses and infirmities of the parties concerned. This is really all that we have to do with the mass of trumpery that has been brought under discussion in connection with these subjects. We find plainly enough indicated in Scripture a great comprehensive principle, suited to the dignity and importance of the great subject to which it relates, the right administration of the church of Christ,—a principle "majestic in its own simplicity."

We apply this principle to the mass of paltry stuff that has been devised for the purpose of improving and adorning the church, and thereby we sweep it all away. This is all that we have to do with these small matters. We have no desire to know or to do anything about them ; and when they are obtruded upon us by our opponents, we take our stand upon a higher platform, and refuse to look at them. This is plainly the true state of the case ; and yet attempts are constantly made, and not wholly without success, to represent these small matters, and the discussions to which they have given rise, as distinctively characteristic of English Puritans and Scottish Presbyterians; whereas, in all their intrinsic littleness and paltriness, they are really characteristic only of those who contend for introducing or retaining them.

It was a great service, then, that Calvin rendered to the church when he brought out and established this principle, in correction of the looser views held by the Lutheran and Anglican Reformers. If all the Protestant churches had cordially adopted and faithfully followed this simple but comprehensive and commanding principle, this would certainly have prevented a fearful amount of mischief, and would, in all probability, have effected a vast amount of good. There is good ground to believe, that, in that case, the Protestant churches would have been all along far more cordially united together, and more active and successful in opposing their great common enemies, Popery and Infidelity, and in advancing the cause of their common Lord and Master.

There is another principle that was generally held by the Reformers, though not peculiar to them, which is very offensive to Dr Tulloch and other latitudinarians, viz., the scriptural authority or *jus divinum* of one particular form of church government. This general principle has been held by most men who have felt any real honest interest in religious matters, whether they had adopted Popish, Prelatic, Presbyterian, or Congregational views of what the government of the church should be. The first persons who gave prominence to a negation of this principle, were the original defenders of the Church of England in Queen Elizabeth's reign, Archbishop Whitgift and his associates, who scarcely ventured to claim a scriptural sanction for the constitution of their church. They have not been generally followed in this by the more modern defenders of the Church of England, who have commonly claimed a divine right for their government, and not a few of whom have gone the length of unchurching Presbyterians and Congregationalists. But they have been followed by some men in every age who seemed anxious to escape from the controlling authority of Scripture, that they might be more at liberty to gratify their own fancies, or to prosecute their own selfish interest.

From the time of Whitgift and Hooker down to the present day, it has been a common misrepresentation of the views of *jure divino* anti-prelatists, to allege, that they claimed a divine right—a positive Scripture sanction—for the *details* of their system of government. Dr Tulloch seems to have thought it impossible to dispense with this misrepresentation, and accordingly he tells us that Presbyterianism "not merely asserted itself to be wise and conformable to Scripture, and therefore divine, but it claimed the direct impress of a divine right for all its details and applications." This statement is untrue. There may be differences of opinion among Presbyterians as to the extent to which a divine right should be claimed for the subordinate features of the system, and some, no doubt, have gone to an extreme in the extent of their claims. But no Presbyterians of eminence have ever claimed "the direct impress of a divine right for *all* the details and applications" of their system. They have claimed a divine right, or scriptural sanction, only for its fundamental principles, its leading features. It is these only which they allege are indicated in Scripture in such a way as to be binding upon the church in all ages. And it is just the same ground that is taken by all the more intelligent and judicious among *jure divino* Prelatists and Congregationalists.

Dr Tulloch, in the last of the quotations we have given from his book, endeavours to prove that no form of church government was or could have been laid down in Scripture, so as to be permanently binding upon the church. His leading positions are embodied in this statement:—

"The Christian Scriptures are a revelation of divine truth, and not a revelation of church polity. They not only do not lay down the outline of such a polity, but they do not even give the adequate and conclusive hints of one. And for the best of all reasons, that it would have been entirely contrary to the spirit of Christianity to have done so; and because, in point of fact, the conditions of human progress do not admit of the imposition of any unvarying system of government, ecclesiastical or civil."

Dr Tulloch admits that the Scriptures are "a revelation of Divine truth;" and since the truth revealed in them is not the theology of the Reformation, we hope that some time or other he will enlighten the world as to what the "Divine truth" is which they do reveal. As to the position that "the Scriptures are not a revelation of church polity," we venture to think, that it is possible that something may be taught in Scripture on the subject of church polity for the permanent guidance of the church; and if there be anything of that nature taught there, then it must be a portion of the "divine truth" which the Scriptures reveal. Whether anything be taught in Scripture on the subject of church polity, must be determined, not by such an oracular deliverance as Dr Tulloch has given, but by an examination of Scripture itself, by an investigation into the validity of the scriptural grounds which have been brought forward in support of the different theories of church government. Dr Tulloch will scarcely allege, that there is nothing whatever taught in Scripture as to what should be the polity of the church; and if there be anything taught there upon the subject, it must be received as a portion of divine truth. He is quite sure, however, that the sacred Scriptures "not only do not lay down the outline of such a polity, but they do not even give the adequate and conclusive hints of one." Here we are directly at issue with him. We contend that not merely "hints," but what may be fairly called an "outline" of a particular church polity, are set forth in Scripture in such a way as to be binding upon the church in all ages.

We admit, indeed, that when this position is discussed in the abstract as a general thesis, a good deal of the argument often adduced in support of it is unsatisfactory and insufficient, as well as what is adduced against it. When the position we maintain is put in the shape of an abstract proposition, in which the advocates of all the different forms of church government—Papists, Prelatists, Presbyterians, and Congregationalists—may concur; in other words, when the general position is laid down, that a particular form of church government, *without specifying what*, is sanctioned by Scripture, we admit that the materials which may be brought to bear in support of this position are somewhat vague and indefinite, and do not tell very directly and conclusively upon the point to be proved.

The strength of the case is brought fully out only when it is alleged that some one particular form of church government specified, as Prelacy or Presbyterianism, is sanctioned and imposed by Scripture. The best and most satisfactory way of establishing the general position, that the Scripture sanctions and imposes a particular form of church government, is to bring out the particular principles, rules, and arrangements in regard to the government of the church which are sanctioned by Scripture, and to show that these, when taken together, or viewed in combination, constitute what may be fairly and reasonably called a form of church government. By this process not only is the general proposition most clearly and directly established, but, what is of much more importance, the particular form of church government which Scripture sanctions, and which, therefore, the church is under a permanent obligation to have, is brought out and demonstrated.

Attempts, indeed, have been made to prove and to disprove the general thesis in the abstract by *à priori* reasonings, but most of these reasonings appear to us to possess but little force or relevancy. It is contended on *à priori* grounds, on the one hand, that there *must* have been a particular form of church government laid down in Scripture; and it is contended on similar grounds, on the other hand, that this *could not* be done, or that it was impossible consistently with the general nature of the Christian church, and the circumstances in which it was, and was to be, placed. But the truth is, that nothing which can be fairly regarded as very clear or cogent can be adduced in support of either of these abstract positions, unless the idea of a form of church government be taken, in the first of them, in a very wide and lax, and in the second, in a very minute and restricted sense. On the one hand, while there is a large measure of *à priori* probability, that Christ, intending to found a church as an organised, visible, permanent society, very different in character from the previously subsisting church of God, especially in regard to all matters of external organization and arrangement, should give some general directions or indications of His mind and will as to its constitution and government, we have no certain materials for making any assertion as to the extent to which He was called upon to carry the rules He might prescribe as of permanent obligation, or for holding that He might be confidently expected to give rules so complete and minute as to constitute what might with any propriety be called a form of church government. And, on the other hand, while it is evident that the Christian church was intended to be wholly different in external organization from the Jewish one, and to have no such minute and detailed system of regulations, as being intended for all ages and countries; and while on these grounds, but little as compared with the Jewish system, was to be subjected to precise and detailed regulations, and something might thus be left to the church to be determined by the light of nature and providential circumstances, there is no antecedent improbability whatever, arising from any source or any consideration, in the idea that Christ might give such general directions on this subject as, when combined together, might justly have the designation of a form of church government applied to them. On these grounds we do not attach much weight to those general *à priori* considerations, by which many have undertaken to prove, on the one hand, that Christ *must* have established a particular form of government for His church, or, on the other hand, that He *could not have* done so; and we regard the case upon this whole subject as left in a very defective and imperfect state, until the advocates of the principle of a scripturally sanctioned or *jure divino* form of church government, have shown what the particular form of church government is which the Scripture sanctions, and have produced the evidence that Scripture does sanction *that* form, and, of course, *a* form—which will be a sufficient answer to the allegation that He *could not have done so*.

We think we can prove from Scripture statement and apostolic practice, the binding obligation of certain laws or rules, and arrangements, which furnish not only " hints," but even an " outline of church polity," and which, when combined together, may be fairly said to constitute *a form of church government*. In this way, we think we can show that there is a particular form of church government which, in its fundamental principles and leading features, is sanctioned and imposed by Scripture, viz., the Presbyterian one.

If the general *à priori* considerations which have been frequently brought into the discussion of this subject are insufficient to establish the true position, that Scripture does sanction one particular form of church government, much less are they adequate to establish the false position that it does not. Dr Tulloch, as we have seen, asserts that we have " the best of all reasons" to show that the Scriptures do not lay down even an " outline" of a church polity. But his "best of all reasons" are not likely to satisfy any but those who are determined beforehand to be convinced. His reasons are two :—1st, " It would have been entirely contrary to the spirit of Christianity to have done so ;" 2d, "The conditions of human progress do not admit of the imposition of any unvarying system of government, ecclesiastical or civil." This is the whole proof which he adduces ; and these he calls "the best of all reasons." This, forsooth, is to prove that it is impossible that even the "outline" of a church polity could have been set forth in Scripture as permanently binding. Even Divine Wisdom, it would seem, could not have devised an outline of a church polity which would have been accordant with "the spirit of Christianity and the conditions of human progress." Our readers, we presume, will not expect us to say anything more for the purpose of refuting and exposing this. "The spirit of Christianity and the conditions of human progress" might have had some bearing upon the question in hand, if there had been on the other side the maintenance of the position, that the Scriptures imposed upon the church a full system of minute and detailed prescription of external arrangements, similar in character and general features to the Jewish economy. But when it is considered how entirely different from everything of this sort is all that is contended for by intelligent defenders of the divine right of a particular form of church government, most men, we think, will see that Dr Tulloch's appeal, for conclusive evidence against its possibility, to the spirit of Christianity and the conditions of human progress, is truly ridiculous.

The disproof of the position, which has been received so generally among professing Christians, that Scripture does sanction and prescribe the outline of a church polity, cannot be effected by means of vague and ambiguous generalities, or by high-sounding declamation. It can be effected, if at all, only by the method of exhaustion, that is, by the detailed refutation of all the different attempts which have been made to establish from Scripture the divine right of a particular form of church government. And this species of work is much more difficult, requires much more talent and learning, than declaiming about "the spirit of Christianity and the conditions of human progress."

At the same time, we must admit that it has become somewhat common and popular in modern times, to scout and ridicule the advancing of a claim to a divine right on behalf of any particular form of church government. This has arisen partly, no doubt, from the ignorant and injudicious zeal with which the claim has been sometimes advocated, even by those whose views upon the subject of church government were, in the main, sound and scriptural; but principally, we are persuaded, from certain erroneous notions of the practical consequences that are supposed to follow necessarily from the establishment of this claim.

All Papists and many Prelatists, in putting forth a claim to a divine right on behalf of their respective systems of church government, have openly, and without hesitation, deduced from their fancied success in establishing this claim, the conclusion, that professedly Christian societies which had not *their* form of government were, for this reason, to be refused the designation and the ordinary rights of Christian churches, or even to be placed beyond the pale within which salvation is ordinarily possible. This mode of procedure, in applying the claim to a divine right, universal among Papists, and by no means uncommon among a certain class of Prelatists, must .appear to men who know anything of the general genius and spirit of the Christian system, and who are possessed of any measure of common sense and Christian charity, to be absurd and monstrous; and by many the disgust which has been reasonably excited by this conduct, has been transferred to the general principle of claiming a *jus divinum* on behalf of a particular form of church government, from which it was supposed necessarily to flow. All this, however, is unwarranted and erroneous. Presbyterians and Congregationalists have as generally set up a claim to a divine right on behalf of their systems of church government as Papists and Prelatists have done; but we do not remember that there has ever been a Presbyterian or a Congregationalist of any note who unchurched all other denominations except his own, or who refused to regard and treat them as Christian churches merely on the ground that they had adopted a form of government different from that which he believed to have, exclusively, the sanction of the word of God.

But many seem to suppose that Presbyterians and Congregationalists, in not unchurching other denominations on the ground of rejecting what they believe respectively to be the only scripturally sanctioned form of church government, are guilty of an

amiable weakness, and fall into inconsistency, by declining to follow out their assertion of a *jus divinum* in judging of others, to its
natural and legitimate consequences. This notion is erroneous
and unjust, as will appear by attending to the true state of the
case. All that is implied in claiming a divine right for Presbyterianism, for instance, is that the person who does so believes, and
thinks he can prove, that Christ has plainly enough indicated in
His word His mind and will, that the fundamental principles of
Presbyterianism should always and everywhere regulate the
government of His church. Prelatists and Congregationalists,
professing equally to follow the guidance of the sacred Scriptures and to submit to the authority of Christ, have formed a
different and opposite judgment as to the true bearing and import of the materials which Scripture furnishes upon this subject,
and have in consequence set up a different form of government
in their churches. This being the true state of the case, the sum
and substance of what any candid and intelligent Presbyterian,
even though holding the *jus divinum* of presbytery, has to charge
against them is just this, that they have mistaken the mind and
will of Christ upon this point, that they have formed an erroneous judgment about the import of the indications he Has given in
His word, as to how He would have the government of His church
to be regulated. And this, which is really the whole charge, does
not, upon principles generally acknowledged, afford of itself any
sufficient ground for unchurching them, or for refusing to recognise and treat them as Christian churches. It is a serious matter
to adopt and to act upon erroneous views in regard to any portion
of divine truth, anything which God has made known to us in His
word, and we have no wish to palliate this in any instance. But
let the case be fairly stated, and let the principles ordinarily and
justly applied to *other errors* be applied to this one. There can
be no possible ground for holding, that the adoption and maintenance of an error on the subject of the government of the church,
by words or deeds, involves more guilt, or should be more severely
condemned, than the adoption and maintenance of an error upon
a matter of doctrine in the more limited sense of that word; and
on the contrary, there is a great deal in the nature of the subject,
viewed in connection with the general character, spirit, tendency,
and objects of the Christian economy, and in the kind and amount
of the materials of evidence which Scripture affords us for forming

a judgment upon such questions, which indicates that errors in regard to government should be treated with less severity of condemnation, and should less materially affect the intercourse of churches with each other, than errors (within certain limits) with regard to doctrine, which are not usually considered to warrant the unchurching of other denominations, or to form an insuperable obstacle to the maintenance of friendly relations with them.

These grounds on which we establish the unwarrantableness and unfairness of the common allegation, that claiming a divine right for one particular form of church government, implies the unchurching of other denominations who may have come to a different conclusion as to the bearing of the Scripture testimony upon this subject, apply equally to the wider and more comprehensive principle, formerly explained, of the unlawfulness of introducing anything into the government and worship of the church which is not positively sanctioned by Scripture. Lutherans and Anglicans generally contend that this principle is not taught in Scripture, and, on this ground, refuse to be so strictly tied up in regard to the introduction of ceremonies and regulations. We believe that, in denying this principle, they have fallen into an error in the interpretation and application of Scripture, and that the ceremonies and regulations which, in opposition to it, they may have introduced, are unlawful, and ought to be removed. But we never imagined, that because of this error in opinion, followed to some extent by error in practice, these denominations were to be unchurched, or to be shut out from friendly intercourse, especially as the scriptural evidence in favour of the principle, though quite sufficient and satisfactory to our minds, is of a somewhat constructive and inferential description, and as differences sometimes arise among those who concur in holding it about some of the details of its application.

If these views, which are in manifest accordance with the dictates of common sense, and with principles generally recognised in other departments of theological discussion, were admitted, there would be much less disinclination to yield to the force of the Scripture evidence in support of the two principles which we have explained, and which form, we are persuaded, the only effectual security for the purity of church administration, and the authority of church arrangements.

But there are, in every age, some men who seem anxious to

have the reputation of being in advance of all around them in the enlightened knowledge of theological subjects, and who, with this view, are very desirous to escape from the trammels of implicit deference to the authority of Scripture. The great source of error in religious matters is, that men do not fully and honestly take the word of God as their rule and standard. They may profess to do so, and they may do so to some extent; but there have been many contrivances, by which men have laboured to undermine the authority of Scripture as a rule of faith and practice, while professing to respect it, and have virtually set up themselves or their fellow-men as the ultimate standard of truth. Papists and Quakers, Rationalists and Traditionalists, Fanatics and Mystics, all undermine the supreme authority of Scripture, and substitute something else in its room; and the elements of the leading notions of these various parties, singly or in combination, are now in extensive operation amongst us. Indeed, one of the most remarkable features of the present age, is the extent to which these different, and apparently opposite, elements are combined even in the same persons, and co-operate in producing the same result. There are persons of some influence in the religious world, in the present day, in regard to whom it would not be easy to determine under which of the heads above mentioned they might most fairly be ranked—men who seem to be at once traditionalists, rationalists, and mystics, and who, under the influence of a combination of the elements of these different systems, set aside, to a considerable extent, the authority of Scripture, and pervert the meaning of its statements, or, at least, come far short in turning the Scriptures to good account, or in deriving from them the amount of clear and definite knowledge of divine things which they are fitted and intended to convey.

It might be a useful and interesting subject of investigation, to bring out a view of the way in which these different and opposite tendencies are, in the present day, combined in producing error and unsoundness, and especially indefiniteness and obscurity, on religious subjects. The great bugbear, indeed, now-a-days, is the inculcation of clear and definite doctrines upon theological topics. Men seem now quite willing to employ any pretence, derived from any quarter, for discountenancing definite and systematic views of Christian truth, and for bringing back again over the church all the confusion and obscurity of the dark ages. The men of progress in the present day seem to have resolved to gain distinction by extinguishing light, and plunging back into darkness; and they evidently hope that in this way they will acquire the reputation of being very advanced and very profound.

In every age since the revival of letters, there has been a class of men who were anxious to distinguish themselves from those around them by going ahead, by turning aside from the path which most of their friends and associates were pursuing, and by taking what they reckon a more advanced and elevated position. What they may happen to regard as constituting the advancement and elevation which minister to their self-complacency, may depend upon a great variety of causes and influences. But it has not usually been found very difficult to discover something or other which might be made to appear advanced and elevated, although it really was not so when tried by any standard reasonably and legitimately applicable. In this way, men of a certain stamp have usually found it easy enough to get up some plausible grounds for regarding and representing themselves as liberal and enlightened, and the generality of those around them as narrow-minded and bigoted; and at present, the greatest credit in theological matters is to be gained, it seems, by taking as little as possible from Scripture, by repudiating all clear and definite views upon doctrinal subjects, and by displaying a "voluntary humility" in striving to get back to the primeval condition of ignorance and obscurity. This condition of comparative ignorance and obscurity might be harmless and innocent before errors were broached and controversies were waged, but it has now become for ever unattainable on the part of •intelligent and educated men, and if it were attainable, could be realised only through a sinful refusal to improve the opportunities which God has given us of acquiring an accurate knowledge of His revealed will. There is, indeed, a bigotry which is despicable and injurious, the bigotry of those who refuse to practise any independent thinking, who slavishly submit to mere human authority, who never venture to entertain the idea of deviating in any point from the beaten track, and denounce as a matter of course all who do so, who can see only one side of a subject, or perhaps only one corner of one side of it, who are incapable of forming a reasonable estimate of the comparative importance of different truths and different errors, who contend for all truths and denounce all errors with equal vehemence, who never modify or retract their opinions, who have no difficulties themselves and no sympathy with the difficulties of others. We meet occasionally with bigots of this sort, and they are very despicable and very mischievous. There is also a species of progress, which is creditable and praiseworthy, exhibited by men who are thoroughly conversant with, and reasonably deferential to, the attainments of the churches and the achievements of the great theologians of former times, who can comprehensively survey and judiciously estimate the past, who can read the lessons "of doctrine, reproof, and correction" which it is fitted to suggest, who are thus by the study of the past qualified in some measure to anticipate and to guide the course of discussion in the future, and who, while, it may be, only confirmed by their researches and meditations in the soundness of their own leading convictions, have learned, at the same time and by the same process, a larger measure of friendly forbearance for those who differ from them. This is a kind of progress which should ever be regarded with approbation and respect, and in which all of us, according to our capacities and opportunities, should be seeking to advance. But this is a very different kind of thing from the latitudinarianism which finds its representatives in every age, and which at bottom is little better than a desire of notoriety, and an affectation of superior wisdom where no superior wisdom exists. We believe that the general run of latitudinarians, or men of progress, to be found in every generation of theologians from the Reformation to the present day, have upon the whole been as ignorant, as narrow-minded, and as self-conceited, as the bigots. We have no respect for any of the "men of latitude" and progress in the present day regarded as theologians; we have a very decided conviction, that the leading views in which the generality of the Reformers concurred, both with respect to the substance of Christian theology and the organization of the Christian church, can be fully established from Scripture; and we certainly never shall be shaken in this conviction by vague generalities, high-sounding pretensions, or supercilious declamation. But we have no wish to remain in darkness while the light is shining all around us. And we promise that, if Mr Isaac Taylor or Dr Tulloch will abandon the vague and equivocal declamation which they have put forth on this subject, if they will plainly and explicitly declare what are the Reformation doctrines on theological and ecclesiastical subjects which must now be dismissed as untenable, producing at the same time the detailed proof that these doctrines are not sanctioned by Scripture rightly interpreted and applied, we shall give them a careful and deliberate hearing ; and we shall examine their statements with the more earnestness and respect, if they not only refute the theology of the Reformation, but at the same time expound and establish a different theology that may be entitled to take its place.

The really vital questions which all men are called upon to solve as well as they can, are these :—What ought we believe concerning God and ourselves, concerning Christ and the way of salvation, concerning the church and the sacraments ? We have long held, that men who made a thorough and adequate, an accurate and comprehensive, use of the materials furnished by Scripture, would be constrained to admit, that the true answer to all these questions is, in substance, what is set forth in the confessions of the Reformed churches, the most important body of uninspired documents in existence. But the subject is too vitally important to be set aside as altogether beyond the pale of farther investigation, and we would not refuse to attend to any feasible attempt to show that these questions ought to be answered in a different way.

Dr Tulloch rejects the views which the Reformers derived from Scripture upon these points. But he has not told us what other views Scripture requires us to adopt, and he has given us nothing but some dark, mysterious hints, as to the nature of the process by which it may be shown that the theology of the Reformation will not do for the nineteenth century. We know something of the process by which Arminians and Socinians, rationalists and latitudinarians, have laboured to show that the theology of the Reformation is not taught in Scripture. We are well satisfied that nothing more formidable can be adduced against it than has been brought forward, consistently with an honest admission in any sense of the divine authority of Scripture ; and we are confirmed in this conviction by the fact, that some of the most learned modern German critics have admitted that the apostles believed and taught the leading doctrines of the Reformers, while they of course refuse to believe anything so irrational upon the authority of apostles. Surely it is high time that Mr Isaac Taylor should develop his new " exegetical method" which is to revolutionise theology, and that Dr Tulloch should unfold his " spirit of interpreting Scripture," which could have "hardly been intelligible to Calvin," but which, it seems, is quite adequate to demolish Calvinism. Whatever this mysterious method or spirit may be, we are not afraid of it. Let it be brought freely out to the open field of conflict, and let it do its best to overturn the theology of the Reformation. We have no anxiety about the result.

One of the worst passages in Dr Tulloch's book is the conclusion of his sketch of Luther. It is so bad that we must quote it at length :—

"They were consistent in displacing the Church of Rome from its position of assumed authority over the conscience, but they were equally consistent, all of them, in raising a dogmatic authority in its stead. In favour of their own views, they asserted the right of the private judgment to interpret and decide the meaning of Scripture, but they had nevertheless no idea of a really free interpretation of Scripture. Their orthodoxy everywhere appealed to Scripture, but it rested in reality upon an Augustinian commentary of Scripture. They displaced the mediæval schoolmen, but only to elevate Augustine. And having done this, they had no conception of any limits attaching to this new tribunal of heresy. Freedom of opinion, in the modern sense, was utterly unknown to them. There was not merely an absolute truth in Scripture, but they had settled, by the help of Augustine, what this truth was; and any variations from this standard were not to be tolerated. The idea of a free faith holding to very different dogmatic views, and yet equally Christian—the idea of spiritual life and goodness apart from theoretical orthodoxy —had not dawned on the sixteenth century, nor long afterwards. Heresy was not a mere divergence of intellectual apprehension, but a moral obliquity—a statutory offence—to be punished by the magistrate, to be expiated by death. It is the strangest and most saddening of all spectacles to contemplate the slow and painful process by which the human mind has emancipated itself from the dark delusion, that intellectual error is a subject of moral offence and punishment, as if even the highest expressions of the most enlightened dogmatism were or could be anything more than the mere gropings after God's immeasurable truth—the mere pebbles by the shore of the unnavigable sea—the mere star dust in the boundless heaven, pointing to a ' light inaccessible and full of glory, which no man hath seen, neither indeed can see.' It required the lapse of many years to make men begin to feel—and it may still require the lapse of many more to make them fully feel—that they cannot absolutely fix in their feeble symbols the truth of God; that it is ever bursting with its own free might the old bottles in which they would contain it; and that, consequently, according to that very law of progress by which all things live, it is impossible to bind the conscience by any bonds but those of God's own wisdom (word) in Scripture—a spiritual authority addressing a spiritual subject

—a teacher, not of ' the letter which killeth, but of the Spirit which giveth life.'"*

We have not now space for exposing, as it deserves, this remarkable and significant passage. We can only suggest a few hints as to its import and bearing.

1. Dr Tulloch makes the statement absolutely and without qualification, that heresy is not a " moral obliquity,"—that it is " a dark delusion that intellectual error is a subject of moral offence and punishment." Is this anything different from what Warburton, a century ago, denounced as " the master sophism of this infidel age, the innocence of error ?"

2. When Dr Tulloch intimates his approbation of " the idea of a free faith, holding to very different dogmatic views, and yet equally Christian," we presume he just means, in plain English, to tell us, that Calvinism, Arminianism, and Socinianism, are all equally Christian.

3. In this passage he seems to confound or mix up together all interference with heresy or " intellectual error" in religious matters, whether by the civil or the ecclesiastical authorities, as if all exercise of ecclesiastical discipline on such grounds, were just as unwarrantable and offensive as persecution, in the shape of the infliction of civil pains and penalties on the ground of error in religion. This confounding of things that differ, was one of the leading artifices of the infidels and semi-infidels, who discussed these subjects in the early part of last century, the Tindals and Collinses, the Hoadleys and Sykeses.

4. Dr Tulloch seems here to employ another sophism derived from the same not very respectable source, when, upon the grounds, that creeds and confessions are human productions, and of course exhibit indications of human imperfections, and that they are not fitted to serve all the purposes to which they have been sometimes applied, he would intimate that they are of no worth or value whatever, and are not fitted to serve any good or useful purpose. His views upon this point are certainly not brought out clearly and explicitly, but what has now been stated, seems, so far as we can judge, to be the substance of what he intended to indicate, especially in the last sentence of the quotation. There is a notion which seems to be pretty prevalent in

---

* Pp. 87–8.

the present day, though as yet in a somewhat latent and undeveloped form, and which produces some sympathy in the minds of many with what is said in disparagement of creeds and confessions. It is a doubt, at least, whether creeds and confessions, which are to be made terms of ministerial communion, and, of course, grounds of division among churches, should be so long and so minute as some of them are. We have noticed of late some indications of this feeling in men who are far superior to the vulgar aversion to creeds, and whom there is no reason to suspect of unfaithfulness to their own confession. We admit that this is a fair and reasonable topic for discussion, and we are not aware that, as distinguished from some of the other branches of the controversy about confessions, it has ever yet been subjected to so thorough, deliberate, and comprehensive an investigation as its importance deserves. We have no wish to encourage the raising of a discussion upon this subject. But we see symptoms which seem to indicate, that it is likely to be pressed upon the attention of the churches, and it may be well that men should be turning their thoughts to it.

5. Men who are familiar with the common cant of latitudinarians, will easily see that some of the statements contained in this passage, especially those which speak of the influence of Augustine, and of an "Augustinian commentary of Scripture," are intended to convey such notions as these—that the Reformers derived their leading theological views, not from the word of God but from the writings of Augustine; that they adopted Augustine's views, not because they had satisfied themselves of their accordance with Scripture, but from deference to his authority, or from some other adventitious, or accidental, or, it may be, unworthy, cause; that having adopted Augustinian views for some other reason than their accordance with Scripture, they then did what they could to bend and twist Scripture to the support of Augustinianism, and that in this way they brought out of Scripture what is not to be found there, what it does not sanction. All this Dr Tulloch's statements seem to us to imply. It would have been more creditable to him to have openly and explicitly asserted it. But as he has produced no evidence in support of these notions, we could only meet even an assertion of them, by a denial of their truth. We assert, that the notions which Dr Tulloch here indicates with regard to the theological views of the

Reformers are not true, and in flat contradiction to them we assert, that the Reformers adopted Augustine's views because satisfied, as the result of careful and deliberate investigation, that they were in accordance with the teaching of Scripture; *that they were right in entertaining this conviction;* that they brought out the evidence of the scriptural authority of the doctrines of Augustine much more fully and satisfactorily than he himself had done; in short, that they proved conclusively and unanswerably, that Augustinianism or Calvinism is revealed to us by God in His word.

The substance of what he seems to allege here against the Reformers, we have no doubt he would direct equally against those benighted men who in this nineteenth century are willing to acknowledge themselves Calvinists. He perhaps thinks that we too have been led to profess Augustinian or Calvinistic doctrines, not from an intelligent and honest study of the sacred Scriptures, but from some adventitious, irrelevant, inadequate, perhaps unworthy, motive or influence, and that we are perverting, or in some way or other misapplying, the materials furnished by Scripture, in order to procure support to our opinions. Dr Tulloch has no right to expect that any mere assertion of his on such a subject will carry much weight or excite much feeling. But since he has not hesitated to set aside the theology of the Reformation, the theology which has generally been professed in Scotland from the Reformation to the present day, and to do this in circumstances which did not admit of theological discussion, we think it probable that he is willing and ready to bring forward the grounds on which his views upon this subject are based. We must presume after what he has said, that he is prepared to give to the world a detailed exposure of the theology of the Reformation, a new "Refutation of Calvinism." He can scarcely avoid attempting something of this sort, and we venture to assure him, beforehand, that he will not succeed.

LUTHER.*

It is admitted by all Christians that the church is, in some sense, the organ and the representative of Christ upon earth. This principle, true in itself, is very liable to be abused and perverted. It is perverted grossly in the hands of Romanists, when it is represented as implying that the church, as a visible society, has virtually the same power and authority, the same rights and pre-rogatives, as its Master in heaven. The general principle about the church, understood in this sense, and combined with the assumption that the church of Christ upon earth is the church which acknowledges the authority of the Bishop of Rome as Christ's vicar, is the foundation of the papal claims to supremacy and infallibility. The same principle is also employed largely to defend or palliate some of the more offensive consequences of these claims, and some of the more offensive modes of enforcing them. On the ground of this identification of Christ and the church, the opponents of the church come to be regarded as the enemies of Christ, and His vicar is held to be entitled to deal with them, so far as he can, just as Christ may deal with those who continue finally obstinate and impenitent enemies to His cause. In this way papists come to subordinate everything, in the mode in which they regard and deal with their fellow-men, to the fancied honour and interests of the church, and to look upon the opponents of the church not as their fellow-men, whom they are bound to love, but simply as the enemies of Christ, whom they are entitled to injure. It is deeply engrained on the minds of Romanists, that those who are beyond the pale of the true church forfeit the

---

* *British and Foreign Evangelical Review*, April 1856.

1. Vindication of Luther against his recent English Assailants, by Julius Charles Hare. 1855.

2. Discussions on Philosophy and Literature, Education and University Reform, chiefly from the *Edinburgh Review*, by Sir William Hamilton, Bart. 1853.

ordinary rights of men and members of society; and that, especially when they take an active and prominent part in opposing and injuring the church, they ought to be treated as outlaws or as wild beasts.

It is this identification of the church and its visible head, the pope, with Christ Himself, that produces and accounts for that extraordinary subordination of everything to the interests of the church which is so remarkable a feature of popery; and that explains the persecutions which Romanists have at all times been quite willing to perpetrate. All this may be regarded as exhibiting the natural and appropriate result of popish principles, and as, in some sense, rather helping, when viewed in connection with certain tendencies of human nature, to palliate the cruelties which have disgraced the history of the Church of Rome. But there is an abuse of the principle which has been often acted upon by papists, though not often openly avowed, and which is altogether destitute of any appearance of excuse; it is that of acting as if it were held that men who oppose and resist the Church of Rome not only forfeit thereby the ordinary rights and privileges of men, of neighbours, and of relatives, but lose all right even to claim that the ordinary rules of integrity and veracity should be observed in regard to them. It has been no uncommon thing for papists to act as if not only the social and domestic affections, and the duties connected with them, but even the laws of immutable morality were to be subordinated to the interests of the church. This is the principle involved in the decision of the Council of Constance, and often acted upon in the Church of Rome, about keeping faith with heretics. That decision was intended to sanction the doctrine that heretics, the open enemies of the church, have no right to demand the fulfilment of engagements and promises, and that no pledges given to such persons should ever be allowed to stand in the way of any scheme for promoting the church's objects. These notions exert a constant and abiding influence upon the minds of most Romanists, even of many who would shrink from embodying them in formal propositions. The consummation of what is most discreditable in this matter is to be found in the fact, that some Jesuit writers have openly proclaimed the lawfulness of putting forth deliberate and intentional slanders for the purpose of injuring their enemies,—a fact established by Pascal in the fifteenth of his "Provincial Letters," and one that ought to be remembered and applied in judging of the reliance to be placed upon the statements of Romish controversialists.

With such views and impressions prevailing among Romanists, it was not to be expected that the Reformers, who did so much damage to the Church of Rome, would be treated with justice or decency. Accordingly, we find that a most extraordinary series of slanders against the character of the leading Reformers, utterly unsupported by evidence, and wholly destitute of truth and plausibility, were invented and propagated by Romish writers. Luther and the other Reformers were charged, in popish publications, with heinous crimes, of which no evidence was or could be produced; and these accusations, though their falsehood was often exposed, continued long to be repeated in most popish books. With respect to the more offensive accusations that used to be adduced against the Reformers, a considerable check was given to the general circulation of them, by the thorough exposures of their unquestionable falsehood which were put forth by Bayle in his Dictionary, a work which was extensively read in the literary world. Papists became ashamed to advance, in works intended for general circulation, allegations which Bayle's Dictionary had prepared the reading public to regard, without hesitation, as deliberate falsehoods, though they continued to repeat them in works intended for circulation among their own people. Scarcely any Romish writers who pretended to anything like respectability, have, for a century and a half, ventured to commit themselves to an explicit assertion of the grosser calumnies which used to be adduced against the Reformers. Some of them, however, have shown a considerable unwillingness to abandon these charges entirely, and like still to mention them as accusations which were at one time adduced, and which men may still believe if they choose.

But while Romanists have now ceased wholly or in a great measure to urge the grosser charges which they used to bring against the Reformers, their general principles and spirit continue unchanged : the outward improvement in their conduct being owing solely to fear or policy, and not to any real advancement in integrity and candour. It is emphatically true of almost all the defenders and champions of popery, that they fear nothing but a witness and a judge, and do not scruple to misrepresent and slander their enemies, so far as they think they can do this with impunity to themselves and benefit to their cause. They confine themselves now, in a great measure, to charges of a less heinous nature than those which before Bayle's time they were in the habit of adducing, and to charges which have some appearance at least of evidence to rest upon. But these lighter and more plausible accusations are in general almost as unfounded as the others. Protestants, of course, do not regard the Reformers as either infallible or impeccable. They believe that most of them held views, upon some points, more or less erroneous, and that all of them gave abundant evidence that they were stained with the common infirmities of humanity. But they regard them as men who were specially qualified and raised up by God for the advancement of His own cause, for bringing out the buried truth and reforming the corrupted church, who were guided by God's word and Spirit to views, in the main accurate, of the leading principles of Christian doctrine, and who, in the habitual tenor of their lives, furnished satisfactory evidence of acting under the influence of real religion and genuine piety. Believing this concerning the Reformers, Protestants feel it to be both their duty and their privilege to defend them from the assaults of adversaries, and especially to refute any thing that may seem to militate against the truth of the statement now given, of what they believe as to the general character and position of these illustrious men.

The great general position which Romanists are anxious to establish by all they can collect against the Reformers, from their writings or their lives, from their sayings or their doings, is this, that it is very unlikely that God would employ *such* men in the accomplishment of any special work for the advancement of His gracious purposes. In dealing with this favourite allegation of Romanists, Protestants assert and undertake to prove the following positions:—1st, That the allegation is irrelevant to the real merits of the controversy between us and the Church of Rome, which can be determined only by the standard of the written word; 2d, That the allegation is untrue,—in other words, that there is nothing about the character of the Reformers as a whole which renders it in the least unlikely that God employed them in His own special gracious work; and, 3d, That the general principle on which the allegation is based can be applied in the way of retort, with far greater effect, to the Church of Rome. Protestants, by establishing these three positions, effectually dispose of

the Romish allegation. It is with the second of them only that
we have at present to do, and even on it we do not mean to
enlarge.

Romanists have taken great pains to collect every expression
from the writings of the Reformers, and to bring forward every
incident in their lives, that may be fitted—especially when they
are all presented nakedly and in combination—to produce an unfavourable impression as to their motives and actions. In the
prosecution of this work, they are usually quite unscrupulous
about the completeness of their quotations and the accuracy of
their facts, and in this way they sometimes manage to make out,
upon some particular points, what may appear to ignorant or
prejudiced readers to be a good case. In dealing with the
materials which papists have collected for depreciating the character of the Reformers, and thus establishing the improbability
of God having employed them as His instruments in restoring
divine truth, and in reforming the church, there are three steps in
the process that ought to be attended to and discriminated, in
order to our arriving at a just and fair conclusion :—

1st, We must carefully ascertain the true facts of the case as
to any statement or action that may have been ascribed to them or
to any one of them; and we will find, in not a few instances, that
the allegations found in ordinary popish works on the subject are
inaccurate, defective, or exaggerated,—that the quotation is
garbled and mutilated, or may be explained and modified by the
context,—or that the action is erroneously or unfairly represented
in some of its features or accompanying circumstances.

2d, When the real facts of the case are once ascertained, the
next step should be to form a fair and reasonable estimate of what
they really involve or imply, taking into account, as justice demands, the natural character and tendencies of the men individually, the circumstances in which they were placed, the influences
to which they were subjected, the temptations to which they were
exposed, and the general impressions and ordinary standard on
such subjects in the age and country in which they lived.

3d, There is a third step necessary in order to form a right
estimate of the common popish charges against the Reformers,
and of the soundness of the conclusion which they wish to deduce from them, viz., that we should not confine our attention to
their blemishes and infirmities, real or alleged, greater or smaller,

but take a general view of their whole character and proceedings, embracing, as far as we have materials, all that they felt, and said, and did, and endeavour in this way to form a fair estimate of what were their predominating desires, motives, and objects, of what it was that they had really at heart, and of what was the standard by a regard to which they strove to regulate their conduct.

A careful application of these obviously just and fair principles will easily dispose of the materials which papists have so assiduously collected for the purpose of injuring the character of the Reformers, and convince every intelligent and honest inquirer, that there is not one of the leading men among them who has not, with all his errors and infirmities, left behind him sufficient and satisfactory evidence, so far as men can judge of their fellowmen, that he had been born again of the word of God through the belief of the truth, that he had honestly devoted himself to God's service, and that in what he did for the cause of the Reformation he was mainly influenced by a desire to promote the glory of God, to advance the prosperity of Christ's kingdom, and to secure the spiritual welfare of men.

But Romanists are not the only persons who have misrepresented and calumniated the Reformers. Many have sympathised with and abetted the efforts of Romanists to damage the character of the Reformers, who had not the palliation, such as it is, which they can plead of avenging the damage done to their church, and who seem to care nothing about Popery and Protestantism as such. What Dr M'Crie said of John Knox holds equally true of the other Reformers, and has been perhaps more fully realised in the case of those of them who exerted a still wider and more commanding influence :—

" The increase of infidelity and indifference to religion in modern times, especially among the learned, has contributed in no small degree to swell the tide of prejudice against our Reformer. Whatever satisfaction persons of this description may express or feel at the Reformation from popery, as the means of emancipating the world from superstition and priestcraft, they naturally despise and dislike men who were inspired with the love of religion, and in whose plans of reform the acquisition of civil liberty, and the advancement of literature, held a subordinate place to the revival of primitive Christianity."*

There has scarcely ever been an infidel or semi-infidel declaimer

---

* Life of Knox, p. 357. 6th Ed.

against bigotry and intolerance, however insignificant, who has
not attempted something smart about " Calvin burning Servetus."
Both Lord Brougham and Mr Macaulay have sunk to the level
of rounding off a sentence in this way. And Luther, from his
peculiar position and history, and from his special weaknesses and
infirmities, has furnished very copious materials to so-called Protestant, as well as to Popish, calumniators. A combination of
circumstances has had the effect of late years of bringing out, in
this country, from different classes of writers, a good deal of
matter fitted and intended to damage the character of the Reformers. Those who laboured long to un-Protestantise the
English Church before they left it to join the Church of Rome,
were, of course, anxious to depreciate the Reformers; and Newman and Ward, who are now both Romanists, did what they
could in this way. Moëhler, a Romish divine of learning and
ability, whose Symbolism has been much commended and read,
has laboured skilfully to excite strong prejudices against the theological views of the Reformers, and has succeeded all the better
because of the appearance of candour and moderation which he
presents, as compared with the generality of popish controversialists. Mr Hallam, in his " History of the Literature of Europe
during the Sixteenth and Seventeenth Centuries," was naturally
led to speak of the writings of the Reformers, but having only a
very partial acquaintance with their works, and not being able, as
he candidly enough admits, to understand much of their theology,
he very seriously misrepresents them, and especially Luther.
Hallam's great learning, accuracy, and impartiality upon general
and ordinary topics, are universally admitted; but he was very
imperfectly acquainted with the writings of the Reformers; and
experience seems to afford abundant evidence that men may be
candid and impartial on most questions of a historical, political,
and literary kind, and yet be strongly prejudiced on religious subjects. This we believe to be the case with Mr Hallam, while, as
might be expected, his depreciatory criticisms upon the Reformers
and the Reformation are now triumphantly quoted by Popish controversialists as the concessions of " an eminent Protestant authority." And, lastly, Sir William Hamilton, whose reputation stands
so deservedly high as a philosopher and a man of erudition, has
thought proper to go out of his way in order to indulge in some
attacks upon the character of the Reformers, first in an article in

the *Edinburgh Review** for 1834, on the Admission of Dissenters
to English Universities; and again, in 1843, in a pamphlet on the
controversy about the appointment of pastors, which produced in
that year the Disruption of the Church of Scotland.

In consequence of these things, the late lamented Archdeacon
Hare undertook the defence of Luther in a very elaborate and
admirable dissertation, bearing the form of a note to his work on
the " Mission of the Comforter," published in 1846. In this note,
marked by the letter W, which extended to above 300 pages,
Mr Hare, with great ability, with admirable scholarship, and a
thorough knowledge of the subject, defended Luther from the
misrepresentations of Hallam, Newman, Ward, Moëhler, and Sir
William Hamilton. Soon after, Sir William published his still
incomplete edition of the works of Reid, with notes and supple-
mentary dissertations, and subjoined to it an advertisement, dated
November 1846, in which he promised to publish soon, and previously to any other work, a production entitled, " Contributions
towards a True History of Luther and the Lutherans. Part I.,
containing notice of the Venerable Archdeacon Hare and his
Polemic." These " Contributions" have not yet appeared; but
in 1852, Sir William gave to the world "Discussions on Philosophy
and Literature, Education and University Reform," in which, in
republishing the article from the *Edinburgh Review* containing his
original attack upon Luther, he added to it some notes, taking
"notice of Archdeacon Hare and his Polemic." Mr Hare had
been requested by many, who were satisfied and delighted with
his defence of the Reformers, to publish his note as a separate
work, and accordingly, after the publication, in 1852, of his
" Contest with Rome," which we regard as upon the whole the
ablest, and, in some respects, the most valuable of his works, his
time, we believe, was chiefly occupied, amid the interruptions of
declining health, in preparing materials for subjoining to his
defence of Luther abundant proofs and illustrations, with an
exposure of Sir William's recent notes.

It is a great loss to theological literature that Mr Hare's health
and life were not spared to enable him to complete this work.
The " Vindication of Luther," published nearly a year ago, soon
after his death, and now lying before us, is merely a revised re-

* Vol. lx.

publication of the note W in the "Mission of the Comforter,"
though forming by itself a goodly 8vo. All that was available of
what he had been preparing for the new edition is the mere references to above 80 notes, which we have no doubt would have
contained a treasure of interesting and valuable materials. Sir
William's notes to his Discussions do not contain, or profess to
contain, the evidence of his most offensive charges against Luther
—charges made nine years before—evidence which he has been
repeatedly challenged to produce. With the exception, indeed, of
a grand theological display, abounding in blunders, on the doctrine of Assurance, Sir William's new matter consists chiefly of an
attack upon Mr Hare. Mr Hare might very easily have repelled
and retorted Sir William's charges against him, without producing
any great amount of valuable matter; but, from the number and
character of the references which have been preserved and published, there is every likelihood that the notes would have been an
enduring monument of his talents and scholarship, and of his
many noble and beautiful qualities of character. We, therefore,
deeply lament that he was not spared to complete this work, while
we estimate very highly what he has done, and regard his "Vindication of Luther" as a very valuable contribution to theological
literature, and an important service rendered to the cause of that
Protestant evangelical truth which Luther was honoured to be
the great instrument of reviving.

We believe that on some important points Mr Hare's doctrinal
views were defective and erroneous; but he had certainly imbibed
very thoroughly both the general spirit and the specific theology of
Luther. He was firmly established, both theoretically and practically, in Luther's great article of a standing or a falling church,—
the doctrine of justification by faith alone. His cordial appreciation
of this great doctrine, and his hearty love and esteem for Luther,
whose qualities as a man were in many respects so very different
from his own, are among the things which satisfy those who know
him only from his writings, that he lived by faith on the Son of
God, that he had a claim to the love of all Christ's people for the
truth's sake that was in him; while he combined, in no ordinary
degree, almost all those claims to respect and affection which are
inferior only to this one. We are convinced that Mr Hare's reputation, like Dr Arnold's, will grow and extend after his death,
and that even those who differed most widely from some of his

doctrinal views, will be more and more persuaded that his early death was, humanly speaking, a serious loss to the cause of Christ.

Mr Hare's thorough knowledge of Luther, and cordial affection for him, admirably fitted him for defending the Reformer from the numerous attacks which have recently been made upon him from a variety of quarters. We do not say that all that he has written in vindication of Luther is characterised by strict impartiality and by rigid accuracy. Love may operate in perverting men's judgments as well as hatred. But still love is the right state of mind to cherish in forming a judgment of our fellow-men, and its presence will pervert the judgment much less widely, and much less injuriously, than the opposite feeling. In regard to many subjects, indeed, it may be said that the prevalence of love in the heart is necessary to forming a sound and accurate judgment; and the character of the Reformers is one of the subjects to which this observation applies. Mr Hare's love to Luther has on one or two occasions led him to judge more favourably, or rather, less unfavourably, of Luther's conduct than perhaps a review of the whole circumstances would warrant, and to soften or slur over some of his rash and offensive expressions. But while this may be conceded, it is not the less true that his representation of the character and opinions of Luther is immeasurably more just and accurate than that given by his opponents; and that in his "polemic" with them, he has established a most decided superiority.

There is a great deal about Luther's character and history to call forth admiration and love; while there is also a good deal about him to afford an excuse to those who, from whatever cause, whether as papists or on some other ground, are disposed to regard him with opposite feelings. With many high and noble endowments, both from nature and grace, both of head and heart, which in many respects fitted him admirably for the great work to which he was called, and the important services which he rendered to the church and the world, there were some shortcomings and drawbacks both about his understanding and his temperament; the results and manifestations of which have afforded many plausible handles to his enemies, and have occasioned corresponding annoyance and difficulty to his friends.

Luther occupied a position, and exerted an influence in the history of the church, and altogether manifested a character, well

fitted to secure for him the admiration of all who are interested
in the advancement of Christian truth, or qualified to appreciate
what is noble, magnanimous, fearless, and disinterested. We have
abundant evidence of his continuing to retain the common infirmities of human nature, aggravated in some respects by the system
in which he had been originally educated, by the condition of society in the age and country in which he lived, and the influences
to which, after he commenced the work of Reformation, he was
subjected; but we have also the most satisfactory evidence of his
deep piety, of his thorough devotedness to God's service, of his
habitual walking with God, and living by faith in the promises of
His word. No one who surveys Luther's history and writings,
and who is capable of forming an estimate of what piety is, can
entertain any doubt upon this point.

The leading service which Luther was qualified and enabled
to render to the church, in a theological point of view, was the
unfolding and establishing the great doctrine of justification,
which for many ages had been grossly corrupted and perverted;
and bringing the truth upon this subject to bear upon the exposure
of many of the abuses, both in theory and practice, that prevailed
in the Church of Rome. His engrossment, to a large extent, with
this great doctrine, combined with the peculiar character of his
mind, led him to view almost every topic chiefly, if not exclusively,
in its relation to forgiveness and peace of conscience, to grace and
merit; and thus fostered a certain tendency to exaggeration and
extravagance in his doctrinal statements. Besides this defect in
Luther's theology, giving it something of one-sidedness, he had
some features of character which detract from the weight of his
statements, and from the deference to which otherwise he might
have appeared entitled, and which we feel disposed to accord to
such a man as Calvin. He was naturally somewhat prone to indulge in exaggerated and paradoxical statements, to press points
too far, and to express them in unnecessarily strong and repulsive
terms. And this tendency he sometimes manifests not only in
speaking of men and actions, but even in theological discussions.
He was not characterised by that exact balance of all the mental
powers, by that just and accurate perception of the whole relations
and true importance of things, and by that power of carefully and
precisely embodying in words just what he himself had deliberately
concluded, and nothing more, which, in some men, have so strong

a tendency to persuade us to give ourselves up to their guidance, under a sort of intuitive conviction that they will not lead us often or far astray from the paths of truth. In Luther's works, with a great deal to admire, to interest and impress, we often stumble upon statements which remind us that we must be on our guard, that we must exercise our own judgment, and not follow him blindly wherever he may choose to lead us. The leading defects of his character may be said to be,—1st, The impetuosity of his temperament, leading often to the use of exaggerated and intemperate language, both in conversation and in writing; though, as has been frequently and truly remarked, very seldom leading him into injudicious or imprudent *actions*, amid all the difficulties in which he was involved : and, 2d, A certain species of presumption or self-confidence, which, putting on the garb of better and higher principles, sometimes made him adhere with great obstinacy to erroneous opinions, shutting his understanding against everything that could be brought forward in opposition to them; and made him indulge sometimes in rather ridiculous boasting. The result of all these qualities was, that he has left many statements of an intemperate and exaggerated description; which have afforded a great handle to his enemies, and which, when collected and set off by being presented in isolation from accompanying statements and circumstances, and in combination with each other, are apt to produce a somewhat uncomfortable impression.

And then consider how this extraordinary man, of so peculiar a mental character and general temperament, was tried and tested. He occupied a very singular position, and was subjected to very peculiar influences. He was tried in a very unusual measure, with almost everything fitted to disturb and pervert, to elevate and to depress, with fears and hopes, with dangers and successes. Let it be further remembered, that of this man, who was so constituted and so circumstanced, there have been preserved and published no fewer than about 2300 letters, many of them private and confidential effusions to his friends; and that a great deal of his ordinary conversation or table talk has been recorded and transmitted to us, without our having any good evidence of its being accurately reported.

It is surely not to be wondered at that it should be easy to produce many rash, extravagant, inconsistent, and indefensible sayings of Luther. And if, notwithstanding the tests to which he

has been subjected, he still stands out as unquestionably a man of
high religious principle, of thorough and disinterested devotedness
to God's service, and of many noble and elevated qualities,—all
which most even of his depreciators, except the Popish section of
them, will probably concede,—how thoroughly base and despicable
is it in any man to be grasping at opportunities of trying to
damage his character and influence, by collecting and stringing
together (perhaps exaggerating and distorting), his rash and inconsistent, or it may be extravagant and offensive, sentiments and
expressions.   Papists, of course, are labouring in their proper
vocation in trying, *per fas aut nefas*, to damage Luther's character.
Popish controversialists are ever ready to sacrifice conscience, and
every manly and honourable feeling, to the interests of the
church ; and Tractarians, following in their footsteps, have imbibed
a large portion of their spirit.

Of Mr Hare's " Vindication of Luther," about 90 pages are
devoted to an exposure of the Tractarian attacks upon him by
Newman and Ward, who have since joined the Church of Rome ;
about 40 to an exposure of a popish attack upon him by Moehler ;
and the remaining 170 pages are occupied with an answer to the
assaults of " the great Protestant authorities," Mr Hallam and
Sir William Hamilton.

Newman had attacked Luther only incidentally, and somewhat cautiously, in his book on " Justification ; and though he
is convicted of several misrepresentations of Luther's opinions,
he is upon the whole let easily off.   Newman had spoken slight-
ingly of Luther, as not being, like Augustine, a father of the
church, but merely the founder of a school.   This has given
occasion to Mr Hare to indite the following very fine and striking
passage ·—

" But though Luther was not what was technically termed *a father*, and
could not be so, from the period when, for the good of mankind, it was ordained that he should be born, yet it has pleased God that he, above all other
men since the days of the apostles, should, in the truest and highest sense, be
a father in Christ's church, yea, the human father and nourisher of the spiritual life of millions of souls, for generation after generation.   Three hundred
years have rolled away since he was raised, through Christ's redeeming grace,
from the militant church into the triumphant ; and throughout those three
hundred years, and still at this day, it has been and is vouchsafed to him,—
and so, God willing, shall it be for centuries to come,—that he should feed the
children of half Germany with the milk of the gospel by his Catechism ; that

he should supply the poor and simple, yea, and all classes of his countrymen, with words wherewith to commend their souls to God when they rise from their bed, and when they lie down in it; that in his words they should invoke a blessing upon their daily meals, and offer up their thanks for them; that with his stirring hymns they should kindle and pour out their devotion, both in the solemn assembly and in the sanctuary of every family, that by his German words, through the blessed fruit of his labours, they should daily and hourly strengthen and enlighten their hearts, and souls, and minds, with that Book of Life in which God's mercy and truth have met together, His righteousness and peace have kissed each other, and are treasured up for the edification of mankind unto the end of the world. If this is not to be a father in Christ's church, I know not what is. Nay, more, his spiritual children are not confined to his own country. The word of truth, which he was sent to preach, has sounded from land to land, and was heard in our land also, coming as it did from the home of our forefathers, for the purification of the church, and for the guiding of numberless souls away from a vain confidence in the works of the flesh, to a living trust in their Saviour."*

Mr Ward's assaults, originally published in the *British Critic*, and afterwards collected in his book entitled "Ideal of a Christian Church," are likewise based chiefly upon Luther's doctrine of justification, which is grossly misrepresented, in order to afford materials for accusing him of Antinomianism. Mr Ward is conclusively convicted of gross incompetency and unfairness, nay, of bitter spite. But, really, the allegation that Luther was an Antinomian is so thoroughly contradicted by the whole tenor of his writings, and by the whole course of his life, and is so utterly destitute of all evidence, except some rash, unbecoming, and exaggerated statements about the law, the real meaning of which is evident enough to every candid inquirer, that we do not think it necessary to dwell upon this topic.

Mr Hallam's attack upon Luther rests chiefly upon the same general ground, and is directed to show that he has made statements of an Antinomian tendency. His mode of dealing with this subject has more the appearance of honest ignorance than Mr Ward's. He is certainly, as Mr Hare has proved, and as indeed he himself acknowledges, very imperfectly acquainted with Luther's works. He is also, from whatever cause, pretty strongly prejudiced against him. He plainly enough indicates that he had been somewhat influenced, in judging of Luther, by the representations of Bossuet; and as this is a topic to which

---

* Pp. 83–84.

we shall have occasion afterwards to advert, in pointing out
Sir William Hamilton's obligations to the great popish cham-
pion, we quote an interesting passage from this section of the
Vindication :—

"An explanation, however, of this, and of much more, seems to be afforded
by the first sentences in Mr Hallam's remarks on Luther: 'It would not be
just, probably, to give Bossuet credit in every part of that powerful delinea-
tion of Luther's theological tenets, with which he begins the History of the
Variations of Protestant Churches. Nothing, perhaps, in polemical eloquence,
is so splendid as this chapter. The eagle of Meaux is there truly seen, lordly
of form, fierce of eye, terrible in his beak and claws. But he is too determined
a partisan to be trusted by those who seek the truth without regard to persons
and denominations. His quotations from Luther are short, and in French.
I have failed in several attempts to verify the references.' Mr Hallam, who
here and elsewhere expresses such fervent admiration for Bossuet's eloquence,
says of Luther's Latin works,—'Their intemperance, their coarseness, their
inelegance, their scurrility, their wild paradoxes that menace the foundations
of religious morality, are not compensated, so far at least as my slight acquaintance with them extends, by much strength or acuteness, and still less
by any impressive eloquence.' To me, I own, in the face of this mild verdict,
Luther,—if we take the two masses of his writings, those in Latin and those
in his own tongue, which display different characters of style, according to
the persons and objects they are designed for, in the highest qualities of
eloquence, in the faculty of presenting grand truths, moral and spiritual ideas,
clearly, vividly, in words which elevate and enlighten men's minds, and stir
their hearts and control their wills,—seems incomparably superior to Bossuet ;
almost as superior as Shakspeare to Racine, or as Ullswater to the Serpentine.
In fact, when turning from one to the other, I have felt at times as if I were
passing out of a gorgeous, crowded drawing-room, with its artificial lights and
dizzying sounds, to run up a hill at sunrise. The wide and lasting effect which
Luther's writings produced on his own nation and on the world, is the best
witness of their power.

"I should not have touched on this point unless it were plain that Mr
Hallam's judgment on Luther had been greatly swayed by the 'Histoire des
Variations.' It is somewhat strange, to begin one's account of a man with
saying that ' it would not be just, probably, to give credit in every part' to what
a determined, able, and not very scrupulous enemy says of him, writing with
the express purpose of detecting all possible evil in him and his cause. In
truth, what could well be less just than this supererogatory candour ? In no
court of law would such an invective be attended to, except so far as it was
borne out by the evidence adduced. Mr Hallam says he had failed in several
attempts to verify the references. If he had succeeded, he would probably
have found that the passages cited are mostly misrepresented. How far the
misrepresentation is wilful I do not take upon myself to pronounces. Bossuet's
mind was so uncongenial to Luther's, so artificial, so narrow, sharing in the

national incapacity for seeing anything except through a French eye-glass; his conception of Faith, as I have had occasion to remark elsewhere, was so meagre, so alien from Luther's; and the shackles imposed upon him by his church so disqualified him for judging fairly of its great enemy; that we need not be surprised at any amount of misunderstanding in him when he came forward as an advocate in such a cause. Still, however fiercely the 'eagle of Meaux' may have desired to use his beak and claws, he might as well have pecked and clawed at Mount Ararat as at him whom God was pleased to endow with a mountain of strength, when He ordained that he should rise for the support of the church out of the flood of darkness and corruption.

"Here, as the assertion I have made concerning Bossuet's misrepresentations should not be made unsupported by proofs, I will cite two or three examples, showing how the quotations from Luther, which in his pages seem very reprehensible, become innocent when viewed along with the context in their original home. Nor shall these examples be culled out from the six books employed in the attack on Luther. They shall be taken from the first sections of that attack; thus they will better illustrate the manner in which it is carried on."*

This is followed up by what is certainly very conclusive proof that both Bossuet and Mr Hallam have put forth some gross misrepresentations of Luther's sentiments.

Mr Hallam and Mr Ward are about equally incompetent to form a correct estimate of Luther's theological views; but Mr Hallam is much the more fair and honest of the two. Mr Ward labours to collect evidence from all quarters against Luther, and Mr Hare gives the following summary of the results of his researches:—

"The evidence which Mr Ward's learning has collected in this matter, is a quotation taken from the English translation of 'Audin's Life of Luther;' two quotations from the English translation of ' Moëhler's *Symbolik*;' a quotation from an article of his own in the *British Critic*, which appears there to have been borrowed from the French translation of Moëhler; and certain extracts from an article in the *Edinburgh Review*, and from a pamphlet on the recent schism in the Church of Scotland. Verily, a formidable array of witnesses, picked out with a due recognition of the judicial maxim, that secondhand testimony is to be rejected! To one point, however, they do bear conclusive testimony, which is confirmed by all the rest of the volume, namely, to Mr Ward's utter incompetency for pronouncing an opinion on any question relating to the German Reformation."†

The quotations from Audin are not of much importance; but Mr Hare subjects to a thorough scrutiny the materials which

---

* Pp. 12–14.   † P. 165.

Ward has borrowed from Moëhler and Sir William Hamilton ; and the investigation of these things forms the most important portion of his Vindication. Moëhler's Symbolism has been so much praised of late, having been even pronounced to be the most formidable attack on Protestantism since the time of Bossuet, that it may be interesting to our readers to know something of the general character of this work, and of the answers it has called forth. On these points Mr Hare writes as follows :—

" Here,—as Moëhler's work has been translated into English, as it has been much bepraised by our Romanisers, and has evidently exercised a great deal of influence among them, and as it is well calculated to foster most delusive prejudices against the Reformation, and in favour of the Church of Rome, in readers prepared by visions about the glories of the middle ages, and who are ready to regard the Protestant churches as outcasts from the pale of Christianity, because, through whatever cause, they have adopted a different form of government,—let me be allowed to remark, that, able as the *Symbolik* certainly is, considering the cause it has to maintain, and plausible as it must needs seem to such as have nothing more than a superficial acquaintance with the topics which it discusses, still, in addition to the errors already spoken of, its value in the service of truth is destroyed by two pervading fallacies. In the first place, while the author's professed object, as is intimated by his title, is to compare the Protestant Symbolical Books with those of the Romish church, in order to ascertain and examine the doctrinal antitheses between them, he soon finds out that if he confines himself to these deliberate dogmatical expressions of doctrine he shall not be able to make out a case ; therefore he scrapes together all sorts of passages, not merely out of professedly dogmatical treatises—which, under certain restrictions, would be allowable— but out of occasional pamphlets, out of sermons, out of private letters, nay, even out of Luther's ' Table Talk,' to kindle and fan an odium which he cannot otherwise excite. Yet it is plain that such a procedure can only mislead and dupe the reader with regard to the great subject-matter of the controversy ; which is not, whether such and such individual Protestants may not at times have written extravagantly or unadvisedly, but is instituted to determine the relative value of the body of truth set forth by each church in the solemn confession of its faith. Strange, too, it may seem, that the thought of the ' Lettres Provinciales' did not come across him, and warn him of the tremendous retribution he might provoke. Moreover, after he has thus craftily shifted the whole ground of the contrast, so that, while it is nominally between the symbolical declarations of doctrine recognised by the opposite churches, in lieu of the Protestant symbolical declarations, he is continually slipping in whatever errors he can pick up in the most trivial writings of the Reformers, and these too not seldom aggravated by gross misrepresentations, —even this does not content him : a like trick must be played with the other scale. As the one side is degraded below the reality, the other is exalted

above it. The fallacy spoken of above, in p. 32, runs through the whole book.
The opposition of the Reformers is represented as having been directed not
against the gross corruptions and errors which prevailed when they began **the**
conflict, but against the modified exposition of Romish doctrine, drawn up
with such singular adroitness at the semi-reformation of Trent : nay, even this
is often refined and spiritualised by the interpolation of views belonging to the
theology and philosophy of the nineteenth century. Hence it is not to be
wondered at that Moëhler's work should impose on such readers as do not see
through these fallacies, but suppose his representations of the opposite parties
to be correct.

" Yet its influence ought to have been exploded long ago. For never in the
history of controversies was there a completer victory than that gained by
the champions of Protestant truth who replied to it. Indeed, the attack, **in-**
stead of being injurious, was eminently beneficial to the German Protestants.
It led them to examine the foundations of their strength,—to bring out the
divine armour of truth stored up in the writings of the Reformers. Among
the answers which Moëhler called forth, some, which are highly spoken of,—
for instance, Hengstenberg's and Marheineke's—I have not seen ; but the two
that I have read are triumphant. That by Nitzsch is a masterly assertion and
vindication of the great Protestant principles which Moëhler assailed, and its
calm and dignified tone and spirit, its philosophic power and deep Christian
wisdom, render it one of the noblest among polemical works. Baur, on the
other hand, takes up his Herculean club and smashes Moëhler's book to atoms.
Immeasurably superior to his adversary, through his vast learning and wonderful dialectic power, he pursues him through sophism after sophism, unravels
fallacy after fallacy, and strips off mis-statement after mis-statement, till he
leaves him at last in a condition of pitiable nakedness and forlornness. In
several of Baur's other works, the Hegelian predominates over the Christian,
to the great disparagement and sacrifice of Christian truth ; and his criticism
has of late years become extravagantly destructive : even in his answer to
Moëhler, his philosophy at times is too obtrusive. But his vindication of the
doctrines of the Reformation, and his exposure of the Tridentine fallacies, as
well as of Moëhler's, is complete." *

Moëhler has produced and given prominence to what is certainly the worst and most offensive passage that has yet been found
in Luther ; and Mr Hare has carefully considered it, and conclusively defended it,—not certainly from the charge of great rashness,
extravagance, and offensiveness, in point of phraseology, but from
that which the words, taken by themselves, seem at first view to
suggest, viz., of embodying a deliberate exhortation to the practice
of immorality. As this will probably continue for some time to
be a favourite topic of invective with Romanists and Romanisers,

----

* Pp. 169–172.

it is proper that we should give some general idea of the point, while we must refer to the Vindication for particulars.* The passage from Luther, as given in the English translation of Moëhler's Symbolism† is this : " Sin lustily (*pecca fortiter*), but be yet more lusty in faith, and rejoice in Christ, who is the conqueror of sin, of death, and of the world. Sin we must, so long as we remain here. It suffices, that through the riches of the glory of God, we know the Lamb which taketh away the sins of the world. From Him no sin will sever us, though a million times in a day we should fornicate or commit murder." The question here naturally occurs, To whom was this startling statement addressed ?   And it is no unimportant point in Luther's defence, that these words form part of a letter addressed to Melancthon, in 1521, when Luther was living in concealment in the Wartburg.   Mr Hare refers to this topic in this way :—

" Verily it does seem here as though hell were casting up its spray into heaven. Still, after our ample experience of the manner in which words may be misrepresented, and after the thousand thousand proofs afforded by Luther's writings and life that he did know something of the gospel, we will not be disheartened. At all events, we will try to make out what these awful words can mean,—to whom they can have been said,—for what purpose. Were they said to Simon de Montfort when he marched against the Albigenses ? or to Alva when he entered on his government in the Netherlands ? or to Louis XIV. when he revoked the edict of Nantes ? or to poor Mary, when she mounted the throne after the death of her brother Edward ? Were they a dram administered to Charles IX. and to Catherine of Medicis on the eve of St Bartholomew ? or a *billet doux* sent to Charles II. during the progress of his conversion ? or were they a motto written up in the halls of the Inquisition ? or can it be that Luther was once engaged in a friendly correspondence with Munzer ? or with Alexander VI. ?   No ; but to Melancthon, of all men that ever lived ! Not to Munzer ; not to Alexander VI.; not to Leo X. ; not to Clement VII. ; but to Melancthon ! A strange person, truly, to choose as the confidant of such a doctrine,—as the recipient of such an exhortation ! The tempter, against whom Luther so often battled, must for once have gained complete possession of him, and turned him into an instrument for destroying the soul of his younger friend."‡

Mr Hare then proceeds to show, from a careful consideration of the circumstances in which, and the objects for which, the letter was written, and from an accurate analysis of the train of thought that runs through it, how it was that Luther came to use such

---

* Pp. 178–194.   † Vol. i., p. 183.   ‡ Pp. 179, 180.

words, without, of course, having had the remotest intention of
teaching that sin was a light matter, or encouraging Melancthon
to commit it.　We must refer to the Vindication for the details of
all this, but we will quote the concluding passage :—

"Now in the passage of Luther which we are considering, the real offensiveness lies in the monstrous exaggeration of the language.　The indignation
bestowed upon him might, indeed, have been bestowed most deservedly upon
the truly atrocious and blasphemous proposition whereby the venders of indulgences, whom he assailed, tried to lure purchasers for their trumpery,—*Venias
papales tantas esse, ut solvere possint hominem, etiamsi quis per impossibile Dei
Genitricem violasset.*　Such a proposition is indeed an abomination in the sight
of God and man ; yet this doctrine, which Mr Ward might well call *too bad
for the devils*, the flagitious hierarchy encouraged ; or at least they would not
repress and condemn their emissaries for proclaiming it, even when called
upon and earnestly implored to do so.　Luther's proposition, on the other
hand, is fundamentally true ; his words render it probable that he was thinking of David's crimes ; the addition of *millies, millies*, as everybody acquainted
with his writings will recognise at once, is a mere Lutheranism.　Most readers
will remember his answer to Spalatin, with regard to the advice of his friends,
who would have dissuaded him from venturing to Worms, that *even if there
were as many devils in Worms as there were tiles on the house-tops, still he would
go thither.*　So, again, in his grand letter to the Elector from the Wartburg,
when he declares his resolution of returning to Wittenberg, he says he will not
be withheld by fear of Duke George.　*This I know full well of myself, if affairs
at Leipsic were in the same case as now at Wittenberg, I would ride thither even
though (your Electoral Grace must forgive my foolish speech) it were to rain
pure Duke Georges for nine days, and each one of them were nine times more
furious than this.*　These instances are notorious ; a multitude of similar ones
might be cited from Luther's writings, especially from those belonging to this
critical period of his life, when all his powers were stretched beyond themselves
by the stress of the conflict.　To our nicer ears such expressions may seem in
bad taste.　Be it so.　When a Titan is walking about among the pigmies, the
earth seems to rock beneath his tread.　Mount Blanc would be out of keeping
in Regent's Park ; and what would be the outcry if it were to toss its head
and shake off an avalanche or two ?　Such, however, is the dulness of the
elementary powers, they have not apprehended the distinction between force
and violence.　In like manner, when the adamantine bondage in which men's
hearts, and souls, and minds had been held for centuries, was to be burst, it
was almost inevitable that the power which was to burst this should not measure its movements by the rules of polished life.　Erasmus did so ; Melancthon
did so : but a thousand Erasmuses would never have effected the Reformation ;
nor would a thousand Melancthons, without Luther to go before him and to
animate him."*

---

* Pp. 191, 192.

We now proceed to consider Sir William Hamilton's attacks
upon Luther and the other Reformers. These Mr Hare has exposed fully and with severity—great, but not greater than they
deserve. Sir William entered upon the work of assailing the
character of the Reformers spontaneously and without call. In
an article in the *Edinburgh Review* for 1834, on the Admission of
Dissenters to English Universities, he laid hold of an excuse for
making the averment,* "That there is hardly an obnoxious doctrine to be found among the modern Lutherans (the Rationalists)
which has not its warrant and example in the writings of Luther
himself;" and proceeded to establish this position by what he calls
a "hasty anthology of some of Luther's opinions, *and in his own
words, literally translated.*" He then gives quotations from
Luther, under the three heads of speculative theology, practical
theology, and biblical criticism. Under the first head, his quotations consist *only* of four short passages upon the one subject of
the procedure of God in regard to sin and sinners. Under the
second, he *merely* gives some extracts from a single document,
setting forth the grounds on which Luther and Melancthon gave
their consent to the Landgrave of Hesse marrying a second wife,
while, at the same time, he continued to live with the first. He
has thus brought forward only one topic under the head of speculative theology, and only one topic under the head of practical
theology. And on neither of these two topics can it be said that
the modern Lutherans follow the "warrant and example in the
writings of Luther himself," though it was *professedly to establish
this* that Sir William collected his "hasty anthology." Nine
years afterwards—at the era of the disruption of the Church of
Scotland—Sir William published a pamphlet on the election of
pastors, entitled, "Be not Schismatics, be not Martyrs by Mistake;
a Demonstration that the principle of non-intrusion, so far from
being fundamental in the Church of Scotland, is subversive of
the fundamental principles of that and every other Presbyterian
Church Establishment." In this pamphlet he again, without any
provocation, assailed the character of the Reformers, though this
had nothing more to do with the election of pastors than with the
admission of Dissenters into English universities. In this pamphlet, indeed, he retracted the charge which, nine years before, in

---

* Vol. lx. p. 225.

the *Edinburgh Review*, he had brought against the Reformers in connection with the Landgrave's second marriage, that they were guilty in that affair of a "skulking compromise of all professed principle." But he retracted this charge only to substitute another in its room,—viz., that they approved of polygamy as good and lawful, nay, that they wished to have polygamy sanctioned by the civil law, and did something, though unsuccessfully, in order to bring about this result. And to this new form of the charge under the head of practical theology, he added the offensive allegation, that Luther publicly preached in recommendation of incontinence, adultery, and incest. As some of these charges against Luther had not been broached before by any of his opponents, it will be proper to give the very terms in which they were, for the first time, promulgated to the world, by Sir William Hamilton, at Edinburgh, in the year of grace 1843 :—

" Look, then, to the great author and the great guide of the great religious revolution itself,—to Luther and Melancthon ; even they, great and good as they both were, would, had they been permitted by the wisdom of the world to carry their theological speculations into practice, have introduced a state of things which every Christian of every denomination will now confess, would not only have turned the Reformation into a curse, but have subverted all that is most sacred by moral and religious law.

" Among other points of papal discipline, the zeal of Luther was roused against ecclesiastical celibacy and monastic vows ; and whither did it carry him ? Not content to reason against the institution within natural limits and on legitimate grounds, his fervour led him to deny explicitly, and in every relation, the existence of chastity, as a physical impossibility,—led him publicly to preach (and who ever preached with the energy of Luther !) incontinence, adultery, incest even, as not only allowable, but, if practised under the prudential regulations which he himself lays down, unobjectionable, and even praiseworthy. The epidemic spread,—a fearful dissolution of manners throughout the sphere of the Reformer's influence was, for a season, the natural result. The ardour of the boisterous Luther infected, among others, even the ascetic and timorous Melancthon. Polygamy awaited only the permission of the civil ruler to be promulgated as an article of the Reformation ; and had this permission not been significantly refused (whilst, at the same time, the epidemic in Wittenberg was homœopathically alleviated, at least, by the similar but more violent access in Munster), it would not have been the fault of the fathers of the Reformation if Christian liberty has remained less ample than Mahometan license. As it was, polygamy was never abandoned by either Luther or Melancthon as a religious speculation ; both, in more than a single instance, accorded the formal sanction of their authority to its practice,—by those who were above the law ; and had the civil prudence of the imprudent Henry VIII. not restrained him, sensual despot as he was, from carrying their spontaneous counsel into effect, a plurality of wives might now have been a privilege as religiously contended for in England as in Turkey."*

" I do not found merely or principally upon passages known to Bossuet, Bayle, etc., and, through them, to persons of ordinary information. These, I admit, would not justify *all* I have asserted in regard to the character of the doctrine *preached* by Luther.

" I do not found my statement of the general opinion of Luther and Melancthon in favour of polygamy on their special allowance of a second wife to Philip the Magnanimous, or on any expressions contained in their Consilium on that occasion. On the contrary, that Consilium, and the circumstances under which it was given, may be, indeed always have been, adduced to show that, in the case of the Landgrave, they made a sacrifice of eternal principle to temporary expedience. The reverse of this I am able to prove, in a chronological series of testimonies by them to the religious legality of polygamy, as a general institution, consecutively downwards from their earliest commentaries on the Scriptures and other purely abstract treatises. So far, therefore, was there from being any disgraceful compromise of principle in the sanction accorded by them to the bigamy of the Landgrave of Hesse, that they only, in that case, carried their speculative doctrine (held, by the way, also by Milton) into practice; although the prudence they had by that time acquired rendered them, on worldly grounds, averse from their sanction being made publicly known. I am the more anxious to correct this general mistake touching the motives of these illustrious men, because I was myself, on a former occasion, led to join in the injustice."†

It was in these circumstances, and with such a case before him, that Mr Hare prepared and published, in 1846, his elaborate and most valuable Note in defence of Luther in the second volume of the "Mission of the Comforter," and revised it for republication in a separate form previously to his death in 1855, notwithstanding Sir William's threat of an answer in 1846, and his attempt at self-defence, or rather at retaliation, in the notes to his "Discussions," published in 1852. When a man in Sir William's position comes forward ultroneously, and without call adduces such charges as these against Luther and his fellow-reformers, he must lay his account with his allegations being narrowly scrutinised, and his evidence, if he produce any, being carefully sifted. Sir William's acknowledged eminence as a philosopher and a man of erudition, gives a certain influence to any thing he may choose to aver, and makes it the more necessary that such statements as those we have

---

* " *Be not Schismatics, etc.*, pp. 7, 8.   † *Ibid*, p. 59 of 2d Ed.

quoted from him should be scrutinised with care, and, if found erroneous, exposed with all plainness.

The facts, that Sir William brought forward such charges, couched in such a tone and spirit, first in an article in the *Edinburgh Review*, on the Admission of Dissenters to English universities, and then again, nine years after, in a pamphlet on non-intrusion, or the election of pastors, indicate very plainly a certain *animus* with respect to the men so assailed : which is not disproved by his calling Luther and Melancthon " great and good men ;" and by his assuring us* that, " so far from disliking Luther, we admire him with all his aberrations (for he never paltered with the truth), not only as one of the ablest, but as one of the best of men." On the same page where this profession occurs, Sir William has made the following statements about the Reformer, —statements, it should be noticed, published for the first time in 1852 :—" Luther was betrayed into corresponding extravagances by an assurance of *his personal inspiration;* of which, indeed, he was no less confident than of his *ability to perform miracles.* He disclaimed the pope, he spurned the church, but, varying in almost all else, he *never* doubted of his own *infallibility*." The man who made these statements knows, and every man who has ever read anything concerning Luther knows, that in 1545, the year before his death, the great Reformer wrote a preface to a collected edition of his works, which began with these words :—" I have long and earnestly resisted those who wished my books, or rather the confusions of my lucubrations, to be published; both because I was unwilling that the labours of the ancients should be covered up by my novelties, and the reader hindered from reading them, and because now, by God's grace, there are many methodical books, among which the Commonplaces of Philip excel, by which the theologian and the bishop may be beautifully formed, especially since the sacred Scriptures may now be had in almost every language; while my books, as the want of method in the events occasioned and necessitated, are, indeed, but a rude and indigested chaos, which it is not easy now even for myself to bring into order. Induced by these considerations, I wished all my books to be buried in perpetual oblivion, that there might be room for better ones." This preface also contains the following state-

---

* Discussions, 2d Edit., p. 506.

ments :—"But, before all things, I beseech the pious reader, and
I beseech him for our Lord Jesus Christ's sake, that he would
read these productions with judgment, nay, with much compas-
sion;" "I narrate these things, excellent reader, for this reason,
that, if you are about to read my little works, you may remember
that I have been one of those who, as Augustine writes of himself,
have made progress by writing and teaching, and that I am not
one of those who from nothing suddenly become great, though
they have done, or tried, or experienced nothing, but with one
glance at Scripture exhaust its whole spirit." Sir William knows
that in the same year, 1545, Melancthon, with Luther's consent,
published a collection of the "Disputations or Propositions," put
forth and discussed by him in the theological school at Wittenberg, from 1519 to 1545; and that Luther wrote a preface to
them, which began with these words :—"I permit these 'Disputations or Propositions' of mine, handled from the beginning of my
cause in opposition to the papacy and the kingdom of the Sophists,
to be published, chiefly in order that the greatness of the cause,
and the success therein divinely granted to me, may not exalt me.
For in these is clearly shown my ignominy,—that is, my weakness
and ignorance, which led me at first to try the matter with the
greatest fear and trembling."

Sir William knows, and even "persons of ordinary information" know, that innumerable statements, similar in substance and
spirit to what have been quoted from these two prefaces, are found
in Luther's writings ; and yet, knowing all this, he ventures to
assert, that Luther had "an assurance of his personal inspiration,
and "never doubted of his own infallibility." Every one knows,
that on some occasions Luther showed a dogged obstinacy in
maintaining errors, and an unwarranted confidence that they were
truths, and that he occasionally talked about himself in a style
that somewhat resembled presumptuous, self-complacent boasting.
Sir William, we daresay, could easily produce a copious anthology
of this sort. But this would be no sufficient proof of the truth of
the charge, that Luther "was assured of his personal inspiration,"
and "never doubted of his own infallibility," even though it were
not contradicted by the passages we have quoted, and by many
others of similar import. These passages conclusively disprove
the charge, unless, indeed, it be alleged that they were altogether
hypocritical, and expressed feelings which Luther never enter-

tained; and no human being but a thorough-bred papist could be base enough to believe this.

The adduction of this baseless charge against Luther, and the adduction of it for the first time in 1852, six years after Mr Hare had exposed the charges of 1834 and 1843, must satisfy every intelligent man, that Sir William's statements about the character of the Reformer are entitled to no weight or deference, and ought to be received with the strongest suspicion.

Sir William has turned over a good many books, and picked up a good deal of information of a miscellaneous and superficial, though often recondite, description, upon some theological subjects, and evidently thinks that he is entitled to treat with contempt all the existing professional cultivators of theological literature. The eminence he has reached in his own department, the confidence with which he dogmatises on theological and ecclesiascal topics, and the real extent of his knowledge regarding them, though it is much less than he claims credit for, are fitted to give weight to his statements with a certain class of the community; while, at the same time, as we are persuaded, and think we can prove, he has gone astray in almost all the instances in which he has meddled with that class of subjects. Sir William resembles Bayle in many respects,—in the vigour and versatility of his intellect, in the variety and extent of his erudition, and in his propensity to deal with ecclesiastical questions; but he is greatly inferior to that famous sceptic in real love for historical accuracy, in patient and deliberate investigation of the materials of proof, and, above all, in that sound judgment, strong sense, and practical sagacity, which, in dealing with historical evidence, are far more valuable than metaphysical depth or subtilty. Sir William has some of Bayle's bad qualities, without his good ones; and this furnishes an explanation of the position which we do not hesitate to lay down, viz., that in all the leading instances in which he has taken up theological or ecclesiastical questions, he has exhibited not only blundering and inaccuracy, but a state of mind and feeling offensive to the real friends of truth and righteousness. We think the time has come when this position should be openly and explicitly laid down and pressed upon public notice, in order to prevent the mischief which the influence of Sir William's name is fitted to do, in matters in which no deference whatever is due to him, and which no man must be permitted to misrepresent; and we willingly avail ourselves of the assistance of Mr Hare's admirable Vindication, in order to establish this, so far as concerns his offensive attack upon Luther and his fellow-reformers.

We have already mentioned that Sir William's original attack upon Luther, published in the *Edinburgh Review* for 1834, and repeated in the "Discussions" in 1852, consisted chiefly of an ascription to him of erroneous and dangerous opinions; 1st, On speculative theology; 2d, On practical theology; and, 3d, On biblical criticism; and that he promised to give Luther's opinions "in his own words literally translated," thereby professing to have himself translated Luther's words from a personal examination of the original. The whole of what he produces as a specimen of Luther's speculative theology, consists of four short sentences, amounting in all to eight lines, and bears upon the one point of the purposes and procedure of God in regard to sin and sinners. Now Mr Hare has proved that these eight lines, given originally in the *Review* without any references, and as if they were one continuous extract, are made up of four scraps from different parts of the treatise, "De Servo Arbitrio;" and that they were taken not from the original, but from Bossuet's "History of the Variations of the Protestant Churches," where they are given with some deviations from the original that are fitted to make them rather more offensive. Mr Hare's proof that Sir William's extracts had been taken mediately or immediately from Bossuet was so perfectly conclusive, that it could not possibly be answered or evaded, and Sir William was under the necessity of having recourse either to confession or to silence. He chose the former and more honourable alternative; though to a man of his peculiar temperament such a confession must have been very painful and mortifying, especially as in the interval between the commission of the offence and Mr Hare's public exposure of it, he had disclaimed founding "upon passages known to Bossuet, Bayle, etc., and through them to persons of ordinary information." As confession is not an exercise in which Sir William often indulges, and as our readers, who are probably more familiar with his boastings, may be anxious to see how he performs it, we give it in his own words :—

"In regard to the testimonies from Luther under this *first* head, but under this *alone*, I must make a confession. There are few things to which I feel a greater repugnance than relying upon quotations at second-hand. Now those under this head were not taken immediately from Luther's treatise, 'De

Servo Arbitrio,' in which they are all contained. I had indeed more than once read that remarkable work, and once attentively, marking, as is my wont, the more important passages; but at the time of writing this article, my copy was out of immediate reach, and the press being urgent, I had no leisure for a reperusal. In these circumstances, finding that the extracts from it in *Theoduls Gastmahl* corresponded, so far as they went, with those also given by Bossuet, and as, from my own recollection (and the testimony, I think, of Werdermann), they fairly represented Luther's doctrine; I literally translated the passages, *even in their order*, as given by Von Stark (and in Dr Kentsinger's French version). Stark, I indeed now conjecture, had Bossuet in his eye. I deem it right to make this avowal, and to acknowledge that I did *what I account wrong*. But, again, I have no hesitation in now, *after full examination*, deliberately saying, that I do not think these extracts, whether by Bossuet, or by Stark and Bossuet, to be unfairly selected, to be unfaithfully translated, to be garbled, or to misrepresent in any way Luther's doctrine; in particular his opinions touching the divine predestination and the human will." *

Sir William's defence, in substance, is, that he, or rather Bossuet, had not really misrepresented Luther; and that the statements as they stand in the original are as strong and startling as in Bossuet's French or in his own English. This of course has nothing to do with the matter, in so far as it involves a question of scholar-like acting. But as, in this aspect of the affair, Sir William has frankly confessed that he acted wrong, we shall say nothing more about it. We cannot, however, concede that Bossuet and Sir William have correctly exhibited Luther's actual statements. Mr Hare has proved their incorrectness, though perhaps he has somewhat overrated the magnitude of the differences in point of substance between the original and the translations. There is only one of the four scraps to which Sir William in his defence refers specifically or with any detail; and a brief notice of what he says about it will prove that even in what he says " now, after full examination, deliberately," he has not reached complete accuracy. The second of the four sentences given in the *Review*,—and given as if it were part of one and the same passage along with the other three, this of itself being fitted to convey an unfair impression, even though the whole had been correctly translated,—is in these words: " All things take place by the eternal and invariable will of God, who blasts and shatters in pieces the freedom of the will;" and he now, " after full

---

* Discussions, 2d. Ed. pp. 506–7.

examination," gives it in his " Discussions,"* in the same words,
except that he substitutes "which" for "who." Bossuet's French
—Sir William's original—is this:† "Que sa prescience et la
providence divine fait que toutes choses arrivent par une
immuable, éternelle, et inevitable volonte de Dieu, qui foudroie
et met en pieces tout le libre arbitre." Sir William's remark
upon this passage is as follows: "I must not, however, here forget to acknowledge an error, or rather an inadvertence of mine,
which has afforded a ground for Mr Hare to make, as usual, a
futile charge against Bossuet. In the second of the above
extracts, not having Luther's original before me, I had referred
the relative pronoun to 'God,' whereas it should have been to
'the will of God.' In the versions of Stark and Bossuet it is
ambiguous, and I applied it wrongly."‡ Now it is not true, as
Sir William here asserts, that it was his error or inadvertence in
translating Bossuet's "qui" by "who," while it might equally
mean "which," that led Mr Hare to charge Bossuet with misrepresenting Luther's meaning. Mr Hare has said nothing
suggesting or implying this, and he has made statements plainly
precluding it. But the strange thing is, that while Sir William's
statement necessarily implies that in Luther's original there is a
relative pronoun, on the right application and translation of which
the sense somewhat depends, the fact is, *that no such relative
pronoun exists except in Bossuet;* that Sir William has not yet,
"after full examination," fulfilled his promise to give us "Luther's
opinions in his own words literally translated;" and that the
difference between what Luther said and what Sir William
continues to ascribe to him is not wholly unimportant. The
original passage in Luther consists of two sentences as follow:
"Est itaque et hoc in primis necessarium et salutare Christiano
nosse, quod Deus nihil præscit contingenter, sed quod omnia
incommutabili et æterna, infallibilique voluntate et prævidet et
proponit et facit. Hoc fulmine sternitur et conteritur penitus
liberum arbitrium. Ideo qui liberum arbitrium volunt assertum,
debent hoc fulmen vel negare, vel dissimulare, aut alia ratione à
se abigere."‖

* Pp. 507, 508.
† Liv. ii. sect. 17.
‡ P. 512.
‖ Luther's Latin Works, Jena,

1557, tom. iii. folio 170. We have
added the next sentence, to exhibit
the meaning more fully.

Now there is no relative pronoun here, to connect the crushing of the free-will either with the *Deus* or the *voluntas*, as Bossuet and Sir William represent it. Sir William originally ascribed it to the *Deus*, he now ascribes it to the *voluntas*; whereas Luther *ascribes it to neither*, but breaks off from them into a new sentence, and ascribes it to *hoc fulmen*. What this *fulmen* was must be ascertained from the general scope of the passage; and when this is taken into account, it becomes perfectly manifest that the crushing of free-will is ascribed neither to the *Deus* nor to the *voluntas*, strictly speaking, but to the great truth or fact, that God certainly foresees and governs all things. Even if this difference were more insignificant than it is, this would be no excuse for giving so garbled an extract from Luther, and so incorrect a translation of his words. Bossuet did not promise to translate literally, and yet he has given Luther's words more fully and correctly than Sir William, who did. Bossuet has acted unfairly, indeed, in over-leaping the barrier of the sentence, in extinguishing the *fulmen*, and in ascribing the crushing of the free-will directly to the *voluntas*, if not to the *Deus*. Sir William adopts this inaccuracy from him, and he continues to adhere to it even " after full examination" of the original; while he also perpetrates the *additional* unfairness of leaving out the first part of the sentence, by the introduction of a portion of which even Bossuet indicated, that it was the foreknowledge and providence of God about which Luther was here discoursing.

This is a very curious specimen of blundering. But its importance, we admit, lies chiefly in its bearing upon Sir William, and the question of the reliance to be placed upon the accuracy of his statements. That rash and exaggerated sentiments and expressions may be produced from Luther's writings upon a variety of subjects, is quite well known, and no intelligent Protestant would think of disputing this. That statements of this sort are to be found in his treatise " De Servo Abitrio," in reference to the decrees and providence of God, has always been abundantly notorious. That some of the statements quoted by Bossuet and Sir William do, even as they stand in the original, express Calvinistic doctrines in an unnecessarily and unwarrantably harsh and offensive form, we do not hesitate to admit. Indeed, it is a very remarkable fact, that not only the rash and impetuous Luther, but also the cautious and timid Melancthon, did, in their earlier works, make more unwarrantable and startling statements about the decrees and the agency of God, in their bearing upon men's actions, than Calvin ever uttered. When the Lutherans, in the next generation, abandoned the Calvinism of their master, they were very much at a loss what to make of his treatise "De Servo Arbitrio," which, in its natural and obvious meaning, seemed to be the production of one who, as was said of Beza, was Calvino Calvinior. The most devoted admirers of the *Megalander*, as they usually called him, admitted, of course, that there are some rash and exaggerated statements in the work. But that is very little to their purpose; for Calvinists, too, admit the truth of this, and contend that, even abstracting from everything that might rank under this head, the treatise plainly and explicitly asserts the fundamental principles of the Calvinistic system of theology. In the year 1664 Sebastian Schmidt, an eminent Lutheran divine, and professor of theology at Strasburg, published an edition of Luther "De Servo Arbitrio," copiously provided with annotations, "quibus," as is set forth in the title-page, "B. Vir ab accusatione, quasi absolutum Calvinianorum, vel durius aliquod Dei decretum in libro ipso statuerit, præcipue vindicatur." The annotations, of course, are utterly unsuccessful in effecting the object to which they are directed, viz., proving that Luther did not, in this work, teach Calvinistic doctrines. No amount of straining or perversion is adequate to effect *that*. Schmidt's annotations resemble very much a Socinian commentary upon the beginning of John's Gospel; and it is rather a curious coincidence, that those scraps which Sir William has paraded are duly provided by Schmidt with annotations, intended to show, not that they present Calvinism in a harsh and offensive form, but that they do not go so far as to teach Calvinism at all.

The compelling Sir William to confess publicly, that, in giving a view of Luther's opinions on speculative theology, he had got his whole materials at second hand, was an offence not to be forgiven; and accordingly he brings out, in connection with this topic, an assault, or rather a series of assaults, upon the Archdeacon, evidently intended to be murderous. This great philosopher, when he engages in theological controversy, exhibits *odium plusquam theologicum*. Our readers, we are sure, will not wonder at any little severity we have exhibited in dealing with him, when they read the following choice specimens of invective, culled from a few pages of the notes to the "Discussions."* "Mr Hare's observations under this head of speculative theology exhibit significant specimens of *inconsistency, bad faith*, and *exquisite error*. I shall adduce instances of each. But his baseless abuse—that I shall overpass." " He is only a one-sided advocate, an advocate from personal predilection and antipathies ; and even as such, his arguments are weak as they are wordy." " Lord Bacon says of some one, '—— has only two small wants ; he wants knowledge and he wants love.' But with the Archdeacon, we cannot well restrict his wants to two ; for he lacks logic besides learning and love ; and a fourth—withal a worse defect—is to be added, but a defect which it is always painful to be forced to specify." " Mr Hare is not the champion for Luther ; and if he be effectually counselled, the farrago will not again see the light" (this refers to Mr Hare's intimated purpose to republish Note W,—a purpose accomplished in the volume now lying before us), " for it is simply a verbose conglomeration of what I shall refrain from characterising ; the author making more mistakes or misrepresentations than the note—however confessedly prolix and garrulous—exhibits paragraphs. But the Archdeacon of Lewes neither learns nor listens. He is not content to enjoy his ecclesiastical good fortune in humility and silent thankfulness. He *will* stand forward ; he *will* challenge admiration ; he *will* display his learning ; he *will* play the polemic ; and thus exposes to scorn not merely himself," but also, as Sir William goes on to assert, with some detail, the church of which he was a dignitary. Now what is the cause, and what the ground of this violent outbreak, of this alarming exhibition of a philosopher in a fury ? The cause of it is simply this, that Mr Hare has laid before the public conclusive proof that much, we do not say all, of what Sir William has here alleged against his antagonist, is true of himself. And the ground of it is nothing more than this, that Mr Hare's work, when carefully scrutinized, exhibits a few instances of the oversights, errors, and partialities, which may be pointed out, more or less, in nineteen twentieths of the most respectable controversial works that ever were produced, and in which Sir William's polemic specially superabounds. No man with a sound head and a sound heart can read Sir William's onslaught on Mr Hare, of which we have given some specimens,

* 2d Edit. pp. 508, 524.

without seeing that the charges are grossly exaggerated, and have
really no solid foundation to rest on. We would not go so far as
to allege that *all* that Sir William charges upon Mr Hare is true
of himself; but we have no hesitation in saying, that any one who
might choose to allege this, could, without difficulty, produce a
much more plausible piece of pleading in support of his allegation
than Sir William has done. This is so manifestly the true state
of the case, that we do not think it necessary to go into detail to
defend Mr Hare against an assault which was evidently intended
to destroy him, but which, from its very recklessness, has proved
perfectly powerless.

It was very natural that Sir William should take under his protection Bossuet, to whom, in common with " persons of ordinary
information," he had been indebted for his specimen of Luther's
speculative theology; and, accordingly, he says of him, " In this
note I have spoken of Bossuet, signifying my reliance upon the
accuracy of his quotations; and I am as fully convinced of his
learning and veracity as of his genius."* As Mr Hare had adduced satisfactory evidence of Bossuet's unscrupulous unfairness,
Sir William could scarcely do less than guarantee his veracity;
and he could do this the more easily, as, in all probability, he never
had carefully investigated the subject. But the truth is, that
Bossuet's character for veracity was conclusively settled, in the
estimation of all intelligent and competent judges, before the
publication of his " History of the Variations of the Protestant
Churches," by the tremendous exposures made of him by Dr Wake,
afterwards Archbishop of Canterbury, in his " Exposition of the
Doctrine of the Church of England," and his two Defences of it.
We have no doubt that in these works, which have been republished in Bishop Gibson's " Preservative against Popery," Wake
has conclusively convicted Bossuet of deliberate lying, in repeated
instances; and these not bearing merely on the primary subject of
controversy between them, viz., the original publication of Bossuet's " Exposition of the Doctrine of the Catholic Church," but
also on several other topics unconnected with it. And in regard
to the " History of the Variations," though it is characterised by
extraordinary skill and dexterity, and is indeed in all respects one
of the most plausible and effective pieces of special pleading ever

---

* P. 506.

produced, and though it generally avoids gross and palpable false-hoods, yet it, too, has, we think, been proved to be utterly destitute of fairness and candour.   We think it scarcely possible for any man to read with care and discrimination, Basnage's " Histoire de la Religion des Eglises Reformées,* without being satisfied of the truth of this statement.   Papists still boast of his "History of the Variations," as unanswerable.   We believe that it has been most thoroughly answered by Basnage, in so far as it is argumenta-tive, that every thing like argument in it has been completely demolished, and that its author has been sadly exposed; while we cannot but admit, that even when every thing needful to satisfy the understanding has been provided, the admirable skill and adroiteness of the advocate of error has not only made the best of a bad cause, but may probably have left some painful doubts and uncertainties upon the minds of a considerable class of readers.

The argument of Bossuet's work lies within a very narrow compass.   It is this.   Variations in doctrine afford an evidence of error; Protestants have from the first been constantly varying in the doctrines they professed to hold : and, therefore, their views are erroneous.   In opposition to this, it has been proved, 1st, That the maxim about variations proving errors is not true, or is only partially true, in the sense in which alone it can serve Bos-suet's purpose in argument; 2d, That some of the variations which he ascribes to Protestants are produced, and that many more are greatly swelled in importance and magnitude, by his own misrepresentations ; and, 3d, That the argument, in so far as it has any weight, may be retorted with far greater force upon the Church of Rome.   These positions have been proved by Basnage in the most satisfactory and conclusive manner ; so that, so far as argument is concerned, the book has been thoroughly demolished. But Bossuet's great art throughout the whole work is, that he has contrived to bring in, in the most skilful and dexterous way, a great deal that is fitted to damage the characters of the Refor-mers, and thus to leave an uncomfortable impression upon men's minds, even when his argument, properly so called, is seen to be wholly untenable.   Bossuet's want of integrity, so far as this work is concerned, is exhibited chiefly in producing and magnifying

---

* Last Edit., 2 vols. 4to, 1725.

variations, by misrepresenting the views of the Reformers and other Protestants; and we think it scarcely possible for any one to read Basnage carefully, without being convinced, that it was only policy that restrained him from practising the grosser and more palpable frauds in which most popish controversialists indulge, and that with admirable skill he has systematically carried his misrepresentations just as far as he thought, upon the whole, to be safe or expedient.

We have really no pleasure in making such statements about Bossuet, who, in spite of his want of integrity in matters in which the interests of his church were concerned, was not only possessed of splendid mental endowments, but even of something like a certain elevation and nobility of general character. Integrity in matters in which the interests and reputation of the church are concerned, it is hopeless to expect of almost any popish controversialist. Arnauld and Nicole, the famous Jansenists, were the two other great contemporary champions of popery; and they have certainly furnished far better evidence that they were really men of religious and moral principle than can be produced in favour of Bossuet. And yet we have great doubts whether they held fast their integrity. We greatly admire all these men, though we do not put them in the same category; and while we would not pervert or explain away any matters of fact as to what they said or did, we feel strongly disposed to palliate their aberrations, by laying a portion of the responsibility upon the demoralizing and conscience-searing system to the influence of which they were subjected. It always deepens our indignation against the Man of Sin, the Mystery of Iniquity, when our attention is called to any thing which reminds us that that system reduced a man so noble in many respects as Bossuet was, to such artifices, and imperiled, at least, the integrity of such men as Arnauld and Nicole. We dismiss this subject with the following admirable remarks of Mr Hare on the famous " History of the Variations,' which we believe to be just and sound :—

"Indeed, if anything were surprising among the numberless παράλογα of literature, one should marvel at the inordinate reputation which the 'Histoire des Variations' has acquired, not merely with the members of a church glad to make the most of any prop for a rotten cause, but among Protestants of learning and discernment. One main source of its celebrity may lie in that spirit of detraction which exercises such a baneful power in all classes of mankind, ever since Cain slew his brother on account of his righteousness ; in the eagerness with which all listen to evil-speaking and slander, finding little diminution of their pleasure though it be strongly seasoned with lying ; in that want of sympathy with heroic and enthusiastic spirits which is so prevalent among men of the world, and the great body of men of letters, and their consequent satisfaction at seeing what towers beyond their ken cast down to the ground. Able as the ' Histoire des Variations' doubtless is, if regarded as the statement and pleading of an unprincipled and unscrupulous advocate, it is any thing but a great work. For no work can be great unless it be written with a paramount love of truth. This is the moral element of all genius, and without it the finest talents are worth little more than a conjuror's sleight-of-hand. Bossuet, in this book, never seems even to have set himself the problem of speaking the truth, as a thing to be desired and aimed at. He pretends to seat himself in the chair of judgment, but without a thought of doing justice to the persons he summons before him. He does not examine to ascertain whether they are guilty or not. His mind is made up beforehand that they are guilty ; and his only care is to scrape together whatever may seem to prove this, that he may have a specious plea for condemning them. Never once, I believe, from the first page to the last, did he try heartily to make out what the real fact was. He is determined to say all possible evil of the Reformers, to show that they went wrong at every step, in every deed, in every word, in every thought : to prove that they are all darkness, with scarcely a gleam of light. Hence his representation of Luther is no more like him than an image made up of the black lines in a spectrum would be like the sun. Bossuet picks out all the bad he can find, and leaves out all the good. But as even this procedure would poorly serve his purpose, the main part of his picture consists of sentences torn from their context ; which, by some forcible wrench, some process of garbling, by being deprived of certain limiting or counterbalancing clauses, by being made positive instead of hypothetical, or through some of the other tricks of which we have seen such sad instances in these pages, are rendered very offensive. With regard to the Landgrave's marriage, his treatment of Luther is more like the ferocity of a tiger, tearing his prey limb from limb, and gloating over it before he devours it, than the spirit which becomes a Christian bishop." *

This leads us to advert to Sir William's charges against Luther under the head of practical theology. We have already mentioned that the only materials originally produced under this head were extracts from the document in which Luther, Melancthon, and some other divines of that period, gave their permission or consent to the Landgrave of Hesse marrying a second wife while his first wife continued to live with him. This story is, of course, a great

---

* Pp. 272-274.

favourite with popish controversialists. It is an especial favourite with Sir William. He produced it in the *Edinburgh Review* in 1834; and again, a second time, nine years later, in his pamphlet in favour of the intrusion of ministers, though he now changed materially the nature of the accusation which, in connection with this matter, he adduced against the Reformers. In the notes to the original article, as republished in the " Discussions" in 1852, he has not brought forward much additional matter, so far as Luther and Melancthon are concerned; the chief fruits of his continued researches into this apparently congenial subject being, that he is at last able to boast*—whether truly or not we do not know—that he is now acquainted, he believes, with all the publications relative to this story, and that he has collected a considerable quantity of additional matter (certainly unknown before to " persons of ordinary information"), in order to blacken the character of Melander and Lening, two Protestant ministers who signed the document about the marriage along with Luther and Melancthon, and who might, without any detriment to the public, have been left in the obscurity from which Sir William's *extraordinary* information has dragged them.

It is unpleasant to have to discuss such a subject as this, and it is not easy to see what benefit the public can derive from the discussion of it; but if Sir William Hamilton persists in dwelling upon it, and in pressing it upon public attention, and if he is resolved to employ it for unjustly damaging the character of the Reformers, he thereby imposes upon others a necessity of dealing with it, instead of leaving it wholly in his hands, and allowing him to use it for purposes which many believe to be unjust and injurious. Sir William may probably allege that he is merely bringing out what is true, and that all truth ought to be proclaimed and made known. We do not admit that all that he has put forth upon this subject is true; and if it were, we would still take the liberty of regarding it as not creditable to any man to manifest a special anxiety to press such truths upon public attention without any apparent call to do so, and to labour to bring them out in their most offensive and aggravated form. Circumstances may occur in which anything that is really true may be brought out and proclaimed without impropriety by parties concerned in,

---

* P. 515.

or called to meddle with it; but it is not the less true that we are entitled to judge of men by the *selection* they make of the topics which they seem most anxious to press upon our notice. Sir William, no doubt, will claim to himself the credit of having been influenced in all he has done in this matter by pure love of truth; but we think we can venture to assure him, that his character would have stood much higher this day in the estimation of honourable men, if he had never meddled with the second marriage of the Landgrave of Hesse, and had left it to be handled by Romanists and Romanisers. We do not mean to go into details upon this painful subject. We can merely suggest a few hints, as to what ought to be thought of this affair, and of Sir William's mode of dealing with it.

Luther's conduct in this matter has not been approved of by Protestants, but, on the contrary, has been given up as indefensible. They have differed somewhat in the severity of their censures, and in the grounds on which they rest their condemnation of his conduct, but they have not undertaken to vindicate it. Basnage, in his reply to Bossuet's "History of the Variations," at once admits that Luther's conduct was wrong; and so does Seckendorff, in his great work, "De Lutheranismo." This, undoubtedly, is the right and honest course to pursue in the matter; though it is no doubt quite fair to see that the case is fully and correctly stated, and not exaggerated or perverted. Mr Hare has successfully exposed several unfair and malicious misrepresentations of Bossuet in his commentaries upon this subject; and has also pointed out the unfairness of the selection of the passages by Sir William from the principal document connected with this affair. Upon this last point he says :—

"When we compare them with the whole body from which they are torn, they who admire ingenuity, in whatsoever cause it may be displayed, will be struck with the dexterity shown in garbling the opinion of the divines, so as to render it as offensive as possible. The main part of it, wherein they perform their duty of spiritual advisers honestly and faithfully, telling the Landgrave of the evils likely to arise from his conduct, and of the Divine wrath which he was provoking by his sinful life, is wholly left out; so that it seems as if they had had no thought of their pastoral responsibility, but readily consented to do just what the Landgrave wished, and were solely deterred by fear of the shame it might bring on themselves and on their cause."*

* P. 241.

The proper antidote to this unfairness of Sir William's, is to give the document in full. This Mr Hare has done, and to his pages we must refer for it.* Mr Hare has brought out fully the leading features of this transaction, and has suggested almost everything that could be said in palliation of the conduct of the Reformers in this matter. He goes rather farther than we are prepared to do in palliation of what they did. We cannot but admit that his love for Luther has somewhat perverted his judgment,—has made him judge rather too favourably. At the same time, he has proved conclusively, that there were some material palliations of their conduct; and has shown that it involves gross ignorance or injustice to judge of the bare facts of the case by the notions and feelings of our own age and country, without taking into account the views that prevailed on such subjects in the sixteenth century, and the way in which they were then often discussed. This is of itself sufficient to establish the injustice and unfairness of the course which Sir William has pursued in the matter. But let us briefly advert to his more formal charges, based upon this transaction. Originally he accused them of the "skulking compromise of all professed principle;" meaning, of course, that in giving their consent to the Landgrave's bigamy, they sanctioned what they knew to be sinful, under the influence of selfish and secular motives, connected with the general interests of the Reformed cause, to which the good-will and the support of the Landgrave were very important. This is the view usually given of the transaction by popish controversialists. But Sir William, in his pamphlet in favour of intrusion, withdraws this charge, and substitutes another in its room; alleging that they approved of polygamy as lawful and warrantable, and, of course, acted in the matter in accordance with their own convictions,— their anxiety for the concealment of the marriage arising, on this second theory, not from the belief that it was sinful, but merely from prudential considerations to avoid scandal. He adheres to this latter view in his "Discussions." According to the former view of the matter, the conduct of the Reformers in consenting to the Landgrave's second marriage was a sin, being produced by the operation of sinful motives, and tending directly to bring about the commission of sin. According to the latter view, it was an

* Pp. 235–241.

error of opinion, or what, from its heinous and offensive character, might be called a heresy. But though the charge, as originally put, involved a sin, and in its second form was merely an error, most people in modern times will probably regard it as being quite as damaging to the character of Luther and Melancthon to have inculcated the lawfulness of polygamy, as to have been tempted, upon a particular occasion, to have given consent to the doing of what was sinful.

Mr Hare concurs in the general idea involved in Sir William's second deliverance upon the subject, viz., that the conduct of the Reformers is to be regarded rather as an error than as a sin, though he reaches that conclusion by a different course, and maintains the incorrectness of several of Sir William's positions, especially of his leading one, which ascribes to Luther and Melancthon a belief in the lawfulness of polygamy under the Christian dispensation. The leading features in his view of the case are exhibited in the following quotations :—

" When we examine the whole opinion connectedly, we are compelled to reject the excuse which Sir W. Hamilton so kindly proposes, in order to rescue Luther from the fangs of the Edinburgh Reviewer. For, from first to last, it is plain that the license, which the divines declare themselves unable to condemn, is meant by them to be regarded as a dispensation, and not as authorising or sanctioning polygamy ; and this is the main reason why they are so earnest in requiring that the second marriage, if entered upon, should be kept secret, lest it should be looked upon as the introduction of a general practice. Polygamy, as a general practice, they altogether condemn ; because they conceive that our Lord's words in the passage referred to re-establish the primary, paradisiacal institution of monogamy. At the same time, while they see that polygamy, though contrary to the original institution, is sanctioned in the Old Testament, both by the practice of the patriarchs and by the express recognition of it in the Book of Deuteronomy, they do not find any passage in the New Testament directly and absolutely forbidding it. Here we should bear in mind what their rule, especially Luther's, was. When the word of God seemed to him clear and express, then everything else was to bow to it : heaven and earth might pass away, but no tittle of what God had said. On the other hand, where no express Scripture could be produced, he held that all human laws and ordinances, and every thing enjoined by man's understanding on considerations of expediency, however wide that expediency might be, is so far flexible and variable, that it may be made to bend to imperious circumstances in particular cases.

" Thus the document itself forces us to decline Sir W. Hamilton's plea, that Luther was merely giving his sanction in a single instance to that which he desired at heart to establish generally, the patriarchal practice of polygamy."*

Then follows a careful investigation of Luther's general views on the subject of polygamy, as indicated in his writings, and of his presumed concurrence in the suggestion which Melancthon made to Henry VIII. of England, that it would be less objectionable to take a second wife than to divorce his first; after which he states thus the ground on which he thinks Luther acted in sanctioning the Landgrave's second marriage:—

"But though we must reject the plea that the advice given to the Landgrave is an instance of the predilection which the Reformers, on principle, entertained for polygamy, the evidence adduced abundantly proves, that, in sanctioning a dispensation in what appeared to them a case of pressing need, they were not acting inconsistently, but in thorough consistency with the principles which they had avowed for years before. To us, indeed, the notion of such a dispensation will still be very offensive; but we must beware, as I have already remarked, of transferring the moral views and feelings of our age to Luther's. The canon law admitted the necessity of dispensations; which, in matrimonial cases, were especially numerous. One of the main objects of the scholastic casuistry was to determine under what limitations they are admissible, as may be seen in our own authors on this branch of practical theology, such as Taylor; and the great importance of casuistry is beginning to be recognised anew by recent writers on ethics. The ignorant prater may cry, that Luther ought to have thrown all such things overboard, along with the other rubbish of Romanism. But it was never Luther's wont to throw things overboard in a lump. His calling, he felt, was to preach Christ crucified for the sins of mankind,—Christ, of whose righteousness we become partakers by faith. Whatever in the institutions and practices of the church was compatible with the exercise of this ministry, he did not assail unless it was flagrantly immoral. The sale of dispensations, the multiplication of cases for dispensations, in order to gain money by the sale of them, he regarded as criminal; and the abolition of such dispensations, where they have been abolished, the reprobation they lie under, are owing, in no small measure, to him. But the idea of law which manifested itself to him, convinced him that positive laws can only partially express the requirements of the supreme law of love, for the sake of which they must at times bend; and when he consulted his one infallible authority, he found that his heavenly Master's chief outward conflict during His earthly ministry, was to assert the supremacy of the law of love, which the Pharisees were continually infringing, while they stickled pertinaciously for the slightest positive enactment."†

* Pp. 242–3.   † Pp. 256, 257.

He sums up the matter in this way :—

"Such, then, is the amount of Luther's sin, or rather error—for sin I dare not call it—in this affair, in which the voice of the world, ever ready to believe evil of great and good men, has so severely condemned him, without investigation of the facts; although the motives imputed to him are wholly repugnant to those which governed his conduct through life. He did not compromise any professed principle, as the reviewer accuses him of doing : he did not inculcate polygamy, as the pamphleteer charges him with doing. But inasmuch as he could not discover any direct, absolute prohibition of polygamy in the New Testament, while it was practised by the patriarchs and recognised the law, he did not deem himself warranted in condemning it absolutely, when there appeared, in special cases, to be a strong necessity, either with a view to some great national object, or for the relief of a troubled conscience. Here it behoves us to bear in mind, on the one hand, what importance Luther attached, as all his writings witness, to this high ministerial office of relieving troubled consciences ; and it may mitigate our condemnation of his error,— which, after all, was an error on the right side, its purpose being to substitute a hallowed union for unhallowed license,—if we remember that Gerson had said openly, a century before, expressing the common opinion of his age, that it was better for a priest to be guilty of fornication than to marry. Such was the moral degradation of the church under the Egyptian bondage of ordinances, that even so wise and good a man could deem it expedient to sacrifice the sacred principles of right and purity, the sense of duty, and the peace of the soul, for the sake of upholding the arbitrary enactment of a tyrannical hierarchy. Indeed, the clamour which has been raised against Luther for this one act by the Romish polemics, is perhaps, among all cases of the beam crying out against the mote, the grossest and the most hypocritical.

"Nor should we forget what difficulties have in all ages compassed the settlement of special matrimonial cases. They may perhaps be less now in England than in other countries, notwithstanding the grievous scandals which attend them even here ; and there is always a prejudice inclining men to suppose that their own condition is the normal one for the whole human race : but if we compare the laws of marriage which prevail in the various branches of Christendom, and know any thing of their moral effects as manifested in family life, we shall perceive how hard it is to lay down any one inviolable rule. What the obscurity and uncertainty of the law was in Luther's time, we may estimate from the conflicting answers which were returned to the questions mooted with reference to Henry VIII.'s divorce. On the other hand, we should try to realise what the Bible was to Luther,—the source of all wisdom, the treasure-house of all truth, the primordial code of all law, the store-room from which, with the help of the Spirit, he was to bring forth every needful weapon to fight against and to overcome the world and the devil,—how, if the Bible had been put in the one scale, and all the books of all the great thinkers of the heathen and Christian world had been piled up in the other, they would not have availed, in his judgment, to sway the balance so much as

a hair'sbreadth. It was not much the practice of his age—least of all was it
Luther's—to estimate the lawfulness and propriety of an act by reference to
its general consequences. He did, indeed, bethink himself of the evil that
would ensue, if the dispensation were regarded as a precedent, and therefore
did he insist on its being kept secret : but he did not duly consider how impossible it was that such a step, taken by a man of so impetuous a character,
should be kept secret ; nor how terrible the evils would be if every pastor were
to deem himself authorised to give similar counsel; nor how perilous it is to
take the covering of secrecy for any acts, except such as are sanctioned by the
laws of God and man, while the moral feeling of society throws a veil over
them." *

Since it is necessary to discuss such painful and delicate topics,
in consequence of Sir William's offensive conduct, in forcing
them upon public attention, we prefer employing the words of
another to our own. We are very thankful to Mr Hare for vindicating Luther so well, and we shrink from enlarging upon the
subject. But justice demands one or two observations.

Sir William alleges that Luther maintained the lawfulness, or,
as he says, " the religious legality," of polygamy, even under the
Christian dispensation ; and he has been threatening the world for
nearly thirteen years with the publication of what he calls " an
articulate manifestation," " a chronological series of testimonies,"
in support of this charge. There is nothing new, certainly, in this
allegation. It was brought forward by Bellarmine,† who has been
followed in this by the generality of popish controversialists. It
has also been adduced by the defenders of polygamy, that they
might have some respectable countenance to their abominations,
as may be seen in the famous, or rather infamous, " Polygamia
Triumphatrix " of Lyser. We do not suppose that Sir William's
" articulate manifestation," if it ever see the light, will contain
any thing but what has been known and discussed before. There
is, indeed, some difficulty in ascertaining precisely and certainly
what Luther's views were on some points connected with polygamy.
There is some confusion and inconsistency in his statements. At
one time he certainly drew somewhat wide and incautious inferences
from the practice of the patriarchs in this respect, extending to
polygamy what our Saviour said of divorce, that, under the old
economy, God permitted it because of the hardness of men's hearts.
But he seems at length to have become quite settled in the con-

---

* Pp. 269–271.   † De Matrimonii Sacramento, c. x.

viction, that under the Christian dispensation polygamy was for-
bidden by the authority of our Saviour ; and if so, Sir William's
allegation that "polygamy was never abandoned by Luther as a
religious speculation," is unfounded.

But it must be noticed and remembered that Sir William has
gone farther than this, and asserted * that Luther and Melancthon
wished polygamy to be sanctioned by the civil authorities, and did
something, though unsuccessfully, directed to bring about this
result. All this is fairly implied in the language he has employed ;
and this involves a new charge, one which, so far as we know and
remember, has not before been advanced against them either by
papists or polygamists. This point specially needs to be proved ;
and when Sir William produces his "articulate manifestation,"
this special discovery of his own must be duly commended and
established, by an exhibition of the proof which has eluded the
researches of all previous depreciators of the Reformers.

We are not quite satisfied, as we have hinted, with some of the
grounds on which Mr Hare has based his vindication of Luther in
this matter. We do not see that anything short of Sir William's
position, that Luther believed in "the religious legality" of
polygamy, is altogether adequate to take his conduct out of the
category of a sin, and to invest it with the character of an error.
We believe that the transaction involved both an error in judgment
and a sin in conduct, the error, indeed, somewhat palliating the
sin. Luther and Melancthon held, as Mr Hare has shown, that
this was a matter on which dispensations might sometimes be
granted for special reasons, on extraordinary emergencies. And
this belief may be said, in a sense, to have palliated their conduct,
by bringing the subject of a dispensation before them as what
might be lawfully entertained. But even if this opinion had been
true, instead of being erroneous, the question would still remain,
whether or not this was a case for a dispensation to marry a second
wife ; and, at this point, we fear it must be admitted that the
element of direct and palpable sinfulness comes in. Even supposing that dispensations may be lawful in some cases of this sort,
there seems to be no fair ground for holding that the Landgrave's
was a case warranting a dispensation ; and what is specially pertinent to the point in hand, *there is no sufficient ground to believe*

---

* See quotation, pp. 75, 76.

that Luther and Melancthon really believed it to be a case warranting a dispensation. We cannot but conclude, from a deliberate survey of the whole case, that Luther and Melancthon were substantially satisfied that the Landgrave, in marrying a second wife, was guilty of sin; and that, therefore, in giving their consent to his doing this, they were themselves sinning. It was a solitary offence, with much to palliate it on a variety of grounds, but still it was a sin, committed under the influence of temptation; and as such it ought to be condemned.

It is an interesting and instructing circumstance, that one spot, in some respects similar, stains the character of John Knox; and we could not possibly find words that would, in our judgment, describe Luther's conduct in this matter more correctly than those in which Dr M'Crie has described a transaction in the life of our own Reformer :—

"In one solitary instance, the anxiety which he felt for the preservation of the great cause in which he was so deeply interested, betrayed him into an advice, which was not more inconsistent with the laws of strict morality, than it was contrary to the stern uprightness and undisguised sincerity, which characterised the rest of his conduct."*

The third head of Sir William's original attack upon Luther was Biblical Criticism; and under this head he collected, *chiefly from the " Table Talk,"* some rash and offensive statements ascribed to Luther, in which he is represented as speaking disparagingly of some of the books of Scripture. Mr Hare has here again convicted Sir William of several blunders, and one of them Sir William has been constrained to confess in the notes to his "Discussions."† But this topic is not worth dwelling upon. To collect and parade an "anthology" of rash and exaggerated statements from Luther, and especially to take materials for doing this from the "Table Talk," is about as unfair an occupation as can well be conceived; and if Sir William had confined himself to this, we would not have thought it worth while to have given him any disturbance, beyond denouncing his conduct in the terms it deserved.

But it must not be forgotten that there is one other very gross and heinous charge which Sir William has brought against Luther, a charge never, so far as we know, adduced before, and of which,

---

* P. 360.　　　　　　† P. 517, 6th Ed.

though it was fabricated by himself, and published to the world nearly thirteen years ago, he has not yet attempted to produce any evidence. It is stated and disposed of by Mr Hare in the following brief extract:—

"The other charges, that Luther 'publicly preached incontinence, adultery, incest even, as not only allowable, but, if practised under the prudential regulations which he himself lays down, unobjectionable, and even praiseworthy,' cannot be refuted in the same summary manner. I might cite a number of passages against incontinence from his writings: I might show that he often expressed a wish that adultery were punished capitally. But I will not waste words upon such accusations, proceeding from a witness whose testimony has been proved again and again to be utterly worthless. When a dear friend, whose faith and righteousness have been approved during a long life, under many severe trials, is said to have committed unheard-of enormities, without any specification of when, where, how, or what, one is fully warranted in replying that the assertions cannot possibly be true. Therefore I will merely defy Sir W. Hamilton to bring forward evidence in support of these atrocious charges. Should he attempt to do so, and adduce any passages beyond those which have been satisfactorily explained by Harless in the seventh volume of his Journal, I shall deem myself bound to use my best endeavours to set them on a right footing. At the same time, let me remark, that I trust he will not have the assurance to quote certain sayings, which explicitly refer solely to cases of impotence, as substantiating his allegations. Should he shrink from this test, finding that he cannot stand it, what can a generous, nay, what can an honest man do in his place, but come forward with an open recantation and a humble acknowledgment of the wrong he has done to one of the noblest pillars of Christianity, one of the greatest benefactors of mankind?"*

Sir William has certainly brought himself under very peculiar obligations to prove, if he can, his own special charges against Luther, viz., that he wished to have polygamy sanctioned by the civil authorities, and that he recommended, under certain restrictions, incontinence, adultery, and incest. And these, after all, are the most important points involved in this controversy, whether as affecting the character of Luther or Sir William Hamilton. If Sir William cannot conclusively establish these charges, there are no words too strong to characterise his conduct in adducing them. And yet we do not suppose that his friends will advise him to attempt to establish his accusations. He is sure to fail in the attempt. We do not pretend to possess a very thorough acquaintance with Luther's writings; but, from what we do know

---

* Pp. 286, 287.

of his works and of his character, we are very confident that these
odious charges cannot be established; while we are well aware
that, if the attempt is made, this will involve the bringing forward
of a great deal of matter most unsuitable to be made the subject of
public discussion. Sir William, indeed, has placed himself in such a
situation that he can neither speak nor be silent without justly incurring discredit and reproach. He has been much better employed
since 1843 than in defending his extraordinary pamphlet of that
year. He has, since that time, rendered most important services to
the world in the highest departments of philosophical speculation.
He has yet much to do in developing and promulgating his philosophical views; and we trust he will be spared to do this. We
are not in the least afraid of him. We have perfect confidence
in the goodness of our cause, and in the imprudence of our
opponent. We have exposed, with all plainness, his attack upon
the character of the Reformers, undeterred by the warning which
the very peculiar complexion of his assault upon Archdeacon Hare
seems fitted and intended to convey; and we have done so because
we believed this to be the discharge of an important public duty.
But we would rather avoid incurring, unnecessarily, the responsibility of calling him out again on theological and ecclesiastical
questions; *because* we are very certain that this is a field where
he can gain no credit to himself and confer no real benefit on his
fellow-men, and where he might exhaust time and strength that
may be employed more honourably for himself, and more beneficially for the world.

We have been, of necessity, so much engrossed with the
weaknesses and infirmities of Luther,—with the defects of his
character,—that it would be an act of injustice to him if we were
to conclude, without reminding our readers, of his strong claims to
our esteem and affection as a man, and of the invaluable services
which he was made the instrument of rendering to the church and
the world. The first of these points is beautifully touched upon
by Mr Hare, in the conclusion of his "Vindication:"—

"To some readers, it may seem that I have spoken with exaggerated admiration of Luther. No man ever lived whose whole heart, and soul, and life,
have been laid bare as his have been to the eyes of mankind. Open as the
sky, bold and fearless as the storm, he gave utterance to all his feelings, all
his thoughts: he knew nothing of reserve: and the impression he produced on
his hearers and friends was such, that they were anxious to treasure up every

word that dropped from his pen or from his lips. No man, therefore, has ever been exposed to so severe a trial : perhaps no man was ever placed in such difficult circumstances, or assailed by such manifold temptations. And how has he come out of the trial? Through the power of faith, under the guardian care of his heavenly Master, he was enabled to stand through life ; and still he stands, and will continue to stand, firmly rooted in the love of all who really know him. A writer quoted by Harless* has well said, ' I have continually been more and more edified, elevated, and strengthened, by this man of steel, this sterling soul, in whom certain features of the Christian character are manifested in their fullest perfection. His image, I confess, was for some years obscured before my eyes. I fixed them exclusively on the ebullitions of his powerful nature, unsubdued as yet by the Spirit of the Lord. But when, on a renewed study of his works, the holy faith and energy of his thoroughly German character, the truth of his whole being, his wonderful childlikeness and simplicity, revealed themselves to my sight in their glory ; then I could not but turn to him with entire, pure love, and exclaim, *His weaknesses are only so great, because his virtues are so great.*" †

These are the feelings which every rightly constituted and adequately informed mind will cherish towards Luther as a man ; and the services which he was enabled to render to the church and the world were such as to entitle him to be ever regarded with the profoundest admiration and gratitude. His great leading service, in so far as the highest of all interests are concerned, was the entire destruction of the doctrine of human merit, and the thorough establishment of the great scriptural truth of a purely gratuitous justification, through faith alone as the means or instrument of uniting men to Jesus Christ, and of applying to them all that He did and suffered in their room ; together with the vigorous and unshrinking application of these great principles to the exposure of all the mass of erroneous doctrines and of unauthorised and sinful practices, by which the Church of Rome had been leading men, formally or virtually, theoretically or practically, to pervert the gospel of the grace of God, and to build their hopes for eternity upon a false foundation. Under this general description may be comprehended, more or less directly, most of the theology which the writings of Luther contain. This was the work which God raised him up and qualified him to achieve ; and a more important work, one more fraught with glory to God and benefit to man, was probably never committed to any one who had not been endowed with the gift of supernatural inspiration. Luther's pre-

---

* vii. 2.   † Pp. 293-4.

vious training and experience before he appeared publicly as a
Reformer, were manifestly fitted and intended to lead him to
understand practically the true way of a sinner's acceptance and
deliverance from guilt and bondage; for, after being awakened to
some sense of divine things, and of his own relation to God, he
went long about to establish his own righteousness, before he was
brought into the glorious liberty of God's children. This was
evidently the best preparation for the work to which he was
destined. He had tried all other methods of obtaining deliverance
and peace, with the utmost earnestness, and in circumstances in
many respects favourable. He had been driven from every refuge
of lies, and shut up to an absolute submission to the righteousness
of God,—the righteousness which is of God by faith. He had
been compelled, and he had been enabled, to fight his way through
all the formidable obstacles which the current doctrines and
practices of the Church of Rome interposed to men's rightly discerning and appreciating their true condition as helpless sinners,
and the scriptural method of their deliverance, and was thus
eminently fitted for opening up to the miserable victims of Romish
delusion, the danger to which they were exposed, and the only
sure way in which deliverance and enlargement were to be obtained. This object he zealously and faithfully prosecuted during
the remainder of his life, keeping it principally in view in his
exposition of divine truth, and in his interpretation of the word of
God.

The doctrine of justification, notwithstanding the peculiarly
full, formal, and elaborate exposition which the Apostle Paul was
guided by the Spirit to make of it, became very soon involved in
obscurity and error; and though some, no doubt, in every age—
apparently decreasing, however, in number, in every succeeding
century—were practically, and, in fact, led by God's grace to
rest for their own salvation upon the one foundation laid in Zion,
yet it is, to say the least, somewhat doubtful whether, after the
age of the men who had held personal intercourse with the apostles
(from none of whom have we anything like detailed expositions of
Christian doctrine), any man can be produced who has given, or
who could have given, a perfectly correct exposition of the whole
of Paul's doctrine upon this vitally important subject. Confusion
and error upon this point continued to increase and extend,—even
Augustine giving the weight of his deservedly high authority to

views defective and erroneous regarding it,—until, by the admirable skill with which the doctrines and practices of the Church of Rome were adapted to foster and satisfy those notions, upon this subject, to which depraved men are naturally disposed, all scriptural views of the method of justification had, for many centuries before the Reformation, disappeared from the world; and while there was still a vague, unmeaning, and inoperative acknowledgment of Christ as a Saviour, the great body of His professed followers were practically and in reality relying upon their own works and merits, and upon the works and merits of other sinful creatures like themselves, for the salvation of their souls.

This was the condition in which Luther found the professing church in regard to theology and religion. He was guided, by the work of the divine Spirit upon his own understanding and heart, through the word, to appreciate aright men's utter helplessness and inability to do anything to merit or deserve the forgiveness of their sins and the enjoyment of God's favour; to see that salvation, and all its blessings, are purchased for men by Christ, and are freely imparted to them individually by God's grace through the instrumentality of faith; and to feel that the practical reception of these doctrines is the only sure provision for producing holiness of heart, and peace and joy in believing. And his life was mainly devoted to the exposition of these fundamental principles of Christian truth, and the application and enforcement of them in opposition to all the corruptions and abuses, theoretical and practical, of the Church of Rome. He was enabled to bring out his views on these subjects so clearly and convincingly, and to establish them so firmly upon the basis of scriptural authority, that in substance they were adopted by all the other Reformers, embodied in the confessions of all the Reformed churches, including the Church of England, and that they were always held with peculiar clearness and steadiness in the Lutheran Church, until the rationalism of last century swept away all regard to the authority of God's word, and all right conceptions of men's actual relation to God and the gospel method of salvation. There is little else in Luther's theological works than what may be said to be involved, more or less directly, in the exposition and application of these great truths; but there is all this set forth with much clearness and vigour, and applied with much energy and success. He scarcely seems ever to have proposed it to himself as an object, to open up the whole system of scriptural truth in its connection and details, and to unfold it in its various aspects. Human merit and ability on the one hand, and on the other full and purely gratuitous justification, as indispensably necessary for men, and actually provided and offered by God through Christ, are at once the points from which he ever starts, and the centres around which he ever moves; and by thoroughly establishing the one upon the ruins of the other, he has thrown a flood of light upon the most fundamental articles of Christian truth, and upon the interpretation of the most important portions of the word of God.

Luther* can scarcely be said to have investigated, with much care, or to have discussed, with much success, any department of divine truth, which was not more or less directly connected with these fundamental points; but then, both from the nature of the case and the forms which the corruption of the divine method of justification had assumed in the Church of Rome, the exposition and application of these topics led him to traverse a much wider field of divine truth than might at first sight be supposed. Still, as he certainly did not possess the comprehensive far-reaching intellect of Calvin, he views most topics only in their bearings on a sinner's acceptance, without always taking in all the different aspects in which they are presented to us in Scripture. It may be worth while to illustrate this by an example.

Luther, especially during the earlier part of his career (and the same holds true, in some measure, of his immediate followers), in treating of the worship of God, and the load of ceremonies with which the Church of Rome had encumbered and disfigured it, manifests an inadequate sense of the sinfulness of idolatry, viewed simply as such, or as a direct offence against God, and scarcely any sense of the sinfulness of man's introducing rites and ceremonies into the worship of God, simply upon the ground that God had not authorised or required them. He seems to think that the great evil of the Romish rites and ceremonies,—even those which, upon scriptural principles, should be chiefly and primarily denounced as idolatrous, and therefore directly and immediately involving a sin against God, independently of all other considerations and consequences,—*lay in the notion of merit that was conjoined*

---

* The remainder of this Essay is taken from Dr Cunningham's MS. Lectures on Church History, and did not appear in the *Review*.—EDS.

with them,—in the idea which the church inculcated, that through these rites and ceremonies men were either meriting God's favour, or at least securing for themselves an interest in the merits of other creatures. No doubt this view might be justly regarded as being the crowning iniquity of the popish system, that which most directly and immediately brought it to bear injuriously upon the salvation of men. But Luther seems to have seen little evil in these rites and ceremonies, except for the opinion of their meritoriousness, inculcated along with their observance; and would probably have been little disposed to object to them had they not been formally and explicitly represented by the church in this light, which, of course, brought them into collision with the Scripture doctrine of justification. But this view, though true, so far as it went, and very important, did not go to the root of the matter; and it was assigned to Zwingle, and still more fully to Calvin, to bring out the guilt of idolatry, as directly and immediately, in every instance, a sin against God, irrespective of all other consequences,—and to establish further the important principle, that God has given sufficiently clear indications in His word, that it is His will that no rites and ceremonies are to be introduced into His worship, except those which He himself has sanctioned,— a principle which might have been commended to Luther's approbation, if not by its direct and appropriate scriptural evidence, though that is clear enough, at least through an appeal to experience, which clearly proves, that whenever unauthorised rites and ceremonies are introduced into the worship of God, there is a strong and never failing *tendency* in men to regard the observance of them as meritorious in God's sight.

So far as concerns the exposition of those fundamental truths, on which he chiefly dwelt, the main grounds on which, with some show of reason, he has been charged with exaggerated and paradoxical statements, are his indiscriminate abuse of the law, his seeming to deny that it has any legitimate bearing upon regenerate men, and to deny also, that there is anything really good or holy, even in believers. The way in which Luther sometimes speaks of the Law, especially in his Commentary on the Epistle to the Galatians, is certainly unbecoming and indecent; but it is plain enough, from a fair and impartial survey of his whole doctrine upon this subject, that he really meant nothing more in substance than to shut it out, as Paul does, from all direct share in the justification of a sinner, and to illustrate its utter unfitness to serve the purposes of those who are seeking justification by deeds of Law. Some of his incautious statements about the relation of believers to the Law, gave rise afterwards to a controversy in the Lutheran Church, which was settled at length, along with many of those other internal disputes, in the Formula Concordiæ, in 1588, under the title, " De tertio usu Legis ;" but Luther certainly never really gave any countenance to Antinomian principles, and strenuously inculcated the necessity and obligation of holiness of heart and life.* And his declarations about the non-existence of anything truly good or holy in regenerate persons, though some-what strongly and incautiously expressed, did not really mean more than what we all believe to be a great scriptural truth, viz., that the best actions of believers are stained with such imperfec-tion and sin, that they can have nothing justifying, and nothing properly and intrinsically meritorious, about them.

But the great error of Luther, that which gives the most unfa-vourable impression of his character and mental structure, and which, in its influence, most extensively injured his usefulness and obstructed the cause of the Reformation, was his obstinate adherence to the unintelligible absurdity, commonly called Consubstantiation, —the real presence, not of Christ but of Christ's body and blood in the Lord's Supper, or the co-existence, in some way, of the real flesh and blood of Christ, in, with, or under, *in, cum,* or *sub,* the bread and wine in the Eucharist. This was a real remnant of Popery, to which, after throwing off almost everything in the doctrine of the Papists upon this subject that makes it valuable to them and offensive to us, viz., transubstantiation, or the change of the sub-stance of the one into that of the other, as implying the annihilation of the substance of the bread and wine,—the sacrifice of the Mass, —and the adoration of the host founded on this transubstantiation, he adhered with an obstinacy and intolerance most discreditable and most injurious to the Reformed cause. This was the chief subject of controversy, among the Reformers, in the earlier period

---

* Epitome, sect. vi. Tittmann Libri Symbolici Ecclesiæ Evangelicæ. The first use of the Law, was to restrain the open outbreakings of depravity ; the second, to convince men of sin, and to lead them to Christ ; and the third, respected its bearing on believers as a rule of life. This subject, of the use of the Law under the Gospel dispen-sation, is stated with admirable clear-ness and precision, accuracy and fulness, in our own Confession, c. xix., especially sects. 5 and 6.

of their labours. The controversy upon this point occupied a great deal of time and attention that might have been much better employed in opposing the common enemy; it produced, at length, an entire separation and much alienation of feeling among them; it thus led to other disputes and contentions, and tended at last to fix down the Lutheran Church in a much wider deviation from the scriptural orthodoxy of Calvin upon other points than Luther himself could have consistently approved of, or than, without this separation or alienation, would probably have been exhibited. The chief responsibility of controversies, and of all the evils that flow from them, lies upon those who take the wrong side on the merits of the points in dispute, because, if *they* had taken the right side of the question, as *they ought to have done*, there would have been no controversy. And in this Sacramentarian Controversy, as it was called, Luther certainly appeared to as little advantage in the moral character of the spirit which he manifested, as in the soundness of the doctrine which he maintained.

Papists have been accustomed to dwell, with great complacency, on the changes which took place in Luther's views during several years after he published his thesis upon Indulgences; and on this ground to taunt him with his inconsistencies, and to taunt Protestants with being blind followers of the blind. Audin says,[*] "What is the Lutheran doctrine? Is it faith minus indulgences, as in 1518; faith minus the priesthood, as in 1519; faith minus the sacraments of orders and extreme unction, as in 1520; faith with only two sacraments, as in 1521; or faith minus the mass and the worship of the saints, as in 1522." So far as the charges here referred to affect Luther himself, they merely indicate the gradual progress of an honest mind, following the guidance of the Spirit and word of God from darkness to light; and as to Protestants, even those of them who are commonly called Lutherans from their adopting the leading views of divine truth, in which Luther soon settled, they do not affect them at all. But these men seem determined to make Luther a Pope, whether he himself, and those who have adopted his leading principles solely because they believe them to be sanctioned by Scripture, will or not. They are so prepossessed with the duty of receiving their own opinions implicitly from the mouth of a fellow sinner, that

---

* P. 93.

they seem to be incapable of conceiving of such a thing as other men deriving theirs from the word of God, and believing only what they are persuaded is sanctioned by its statements. Protestants do not regard Luther as a Pope; they ascribe to him no infallibility, they receive no doctrine *because* he taught it; and as to Luther himself, he always fully confessed, that when he first raised his voice against indulgences, he was little better than a blind papist; that he was involved in great ignorance and error; that he had yet a great deal to learn, and that he learned slowly and gradually. He retracted his errors fully and frankly, whenever he was convinced of them, and during the whole progress of his views, gave the most satisfactory evidence of thorough integrity and love of truth. And it should further be noticed, that before he appeared publicly as a Reformer, he had already adopted, in substance, upon the testimony of God's word, all those fundamental principles in regard to the natural condition of man, and the way of his acceptance and deliverance, which he continued to hold through life; and that the changes which his opinions underwent after that period, arose mainly, as is evident from even Audin's statement, from his gaining progressively a deeper insight into the mystery of popish iniquity, from the expansive influence of the vital principles of Christian truth which God had implanted in his heart, in throwing off, one after another, the foul incrustations in which Popery wraps men's spirits, and from his applying fully and fearlessly, the touchstone of the word of God, and of the great doctrine of a free justification purchased by Christ and imparted through the faith that unites with Him, to all the fearful mass of corruptions by which the Romish system has perverted the principles of God's oracles and the gospel of His grace.* Luther's opinions seem to have become settled within five or six years after the publication of his thesis; and we do not find any evidence, that after that period they received any material modification.

It may be proper to allude, in conclusion, to a question which has been much discussed in subsequent times, viz., whether Luther held the peculiar opinions on doctrinal points which are usually associated with the name of Calvin. When Luther's followers, in a subsequent generation, openly deviated from scriptural

---

* Luther's *Confessions and Retractations*.

orthodoxy on these points, they set themselves to prove that Luther had never held Calvinistic principles; and for several succeeding generations, Lutheran authors, in general, indulged in the most bitter and malignant vituperation of Calvin and his doctrines, more even than that which generally prevailed among writers of the Church of England during last century. But we have no hesitation in saying, that it can be established beyond all reasonable question, that Luther held the doctrines which are commonly regarded as most peculiarly Calvinistic, though he was never led to explain and apply, to illustrate and defend some of them, so fully as Calvin did. We need go no further in proof of this, than to his famous work, " De Servo Arbitrio," published in 1525, in reply to Erasmus, in which he has unequivocally asserted the most peculiar and generally obnoxious tenets of Calvinism, in respect to God's sovereign agency in preordaining all things; in conferring, according to the unsearchable counsel of His own will all spiritual blessings; and in thus determining, according to His own good pleasure, the eternal destinies of men; and has asserted them with an unshrinking boldness, and, we might say, with a rashness and offensiveness of statement which can certainly not be paralleled in the works of Calvin himself. There is no ground for alleging that Luther ever retracted the sentiments contained in this work. Indeed, at a much later period of his life, in 1537, he expressly declared that of all his works, his treatise " De Servo Arbitrio," and his larger " Catechism," were the only ones which he now regarded as written with due care and accuracy. The Lutherans are, therefore, obliged to attempt to explain away the strong statements of this very valuable work, and to extract out of them their manifestly Calvinistic sense, under the cover of admitting, that the work does contain some rash and incautious declarations; and in perusing some of their attempts of this sort, one is often reminded, by the boldness of their perversions, of a Socinian commentary upon the first chapter of John's Gospel. It has also been asserted, that in his commentary upon Genesis,* the last work he published, he substantially though not formally, retracted any peculiarly Calvinistic principles which he might previously have taught. But there is no good ground for this allegation; for, upon a fair examination of the passages in the

* C. 26.

commentary, it appears plain, that they do not contain, even in substance, any retractation of his former views, but merely cautions to guard against the abuse of them,—against their being applied in an erroneous and injurious way; while, it is certain, that cautions to the same effect as full and strong, and in every respect as judicious and practical, abound in the writings of Calvin himself. It is highly creditable to Luther, that while he was not led to dwell at much length upon the illustration and defence of some of the doctrines which are commonly reckoned Calvinistic peculiarities, he yet had the sagacity to see, that without including in his system these peculiar doctrines, it was impossible to maintain and to expound fully and consistently, the sovereign agency of God in the salvation of sinners, or to give to the Sovereign Ruler and Disposer of all things, the place which He claims to Himself. *

----

* *Hottinger's Historia Ecclesiastica*, tom. viii., p. 640-50.

THE REFORMERS

AND

THE DOCTRINE OF ASSURANCE.*

———————

Sir William Hamilton,† in the course of his attack upon Archdeacon Hare, introduces a lengthened and elaborate historico-theological statement, chiefly upon the subject of Assurance. We quote the passage as it is the text of our present discourse :—

" *Assurance,* Personal Assurance, Special Faith (*the feeling of certainty*) that God is propitious to *me,* that *my* sins are forgiven,—(*Fiducia,' Plerophoria Fidei, Fides Specialis*),—Assurance was long universally held in the Protestant communities to be the criterion and condition of a true or *saving faith.* Luther declares that ' he who hath not assurance spews faith out ;' and Melancthon, that ' assurance is the discriminating line of Christianity from Heathenism.' Assurance is, indeed, the *punctum saliens* of Luther's system, and an unacquaintance with this, his great central doctrine, is one prime cause of the chronic misrepresentation which runs through our recent histories of Luther and the Reformation. Assurance is no less strenuously maintained by Calvin; is held even by Arminius; and stands, essentially, part and parcel of all the confessions of all the churches of the Reformation, down to the Westminster Assembly. In that synod *assurance* was, in Protestanism, for the *first,* indeed *only* time, formally declared ' *not to be of the essence of faith ;*' and,

———————

* British and Foreign Evangelical Review. October 1856.
Discussions on Philosophy and Literature, Education and University Reform, etc. By Sir WM. HAMILTON, Bart. 1853.

† In the interval between the publication of the former article and the present one, Sir William Hamilton died, and Dr Cunningham, in his introductory remarks, thus refers to the event :—" The knowledge, if we had possessed it, that he was to die so soon, would assuredly have modified somewhat the tone in which the discussion was conducted,—would have shut out something of its lightness and severity, and imparted to it more of solemnity and tenderness ; and the knowledge which we did possess, that he, as well as ourselves, was liable every day to be called out of this world and summoned into God's presence, *ought* to have produced this result."—Eds.

accordingly, the Scottish General Assembly has subsequently, once and again, condemned and deposed the holders of this, the doctrine of Luther, of Calvin, of all the other churches of the Reformation, and of the older Scottish church itself. In the English, and more articulately, in the Irish establishment, assurance still stands a necessary tenet of ecclesiastical belief. (See *Homilies*, Book I., Number iii., Part 3, specially referred to in the eleventh of the *Thirty-nine Articles*; and Number iv., Parts 1 and 3; likewise the sixth *Lambeth Article*.) Assurance was consequently held by all the older Anglican churchmen, of whom Hooker may stand for the example; but assurance is now openly disavowed without scruple by Anglican churchmen, high and low, when apprehended; but of these, many, like Mr Hare, are blissfully incognisant of the opinion, its import, its history, and even its name.

" This dogma, with its fortune, past and present, affords, indeed, a series of the most *curious contrasts*. For it is curious that this cardinal point of Luther's doctrine should, without exception, have been constituted into the fundamental principle of all the churches of the Reformation; and, as their common and uncatholic doctrine, have been explicitly condemned at Trent. Again, it is curious that this common and differential doctrine of the churches of the Reformation should now be abandoned virtually in, or formally by, all these churches themselves. Again, it is curious that Protestants should now generally profess the counter doctrine, asserted at Trent in condemnation of their peculiar principle. Again, it is curious that this, the most important *variation* in the faith of Protestants, as, in fact, a gravitation of Protestantism back towards Catholicity, should have been overlooked, as indeed, in his days, undeveloped, by the keen-eyed author of ' The History of the Variations of the Protestant churches.' Finally, it is curious that, though now fully developed, this central approximation of Protestantism to Catholicity should not, as far as I know, have been signalised by any theologian, Protestant or Catholic; whilst the Protestant symbol (' *Fides sola justificat*,'—' Faith alone justifies'), though now eviscerated of its real import, and now only manifesting an unimportant difference of expression, is still supposed to mark the discrimination of the two religious denominations. For both agree that the three heavenly virtues must *all* concur to salvation; and they only differ, whether faith, *as a word*, does or does not involve hope and charity. This misprision would have been avoided had Luther and Calvin only said, ' *Fiducia sola justificat*,'— ' Assurance alone justifies;' for on their doctrine assurance was convertible with true faith, and true faith implied the other Christian graces. But this *primary* and *peculiar* doctrine of the Reformation is now harmoniously condemned by Catholics and Protestants in unison." *

We hope to be able to prove that this elaborate statement contains about as large an amount of inaccuracy as could well have been crammed into the space which it occupies; and, if we succeed in doing this, we may surely expect that Sir William's

---

* Discussions, 2d Ed., pp. 508-9.

authority upon theological subjects will henceforth stand at least as low as zero.

It may help us to form an estimate of the accuracy of Sir William's history of this subject, if we begin with a brief statement of what were the views of the Reformers and the Romanists upon this point, and of what was the general course which the discussions regarding it followed. That the Reformers generally held very high views upon the subject,—that they were in the habit of speaking very strongly of the importance and necessity of men being personally assured about their own salvation, —is of course well known to every one who has the slightest acquaintance with their history and writings. The causes that tended to produce a leaning towards what may be regarded as exaggerated views and statements upon this subject, were chiefly these two :—1st, Their own personal experience as converted and believing men ; and, 2d, The ground taken by the Romanists in arguing against them.

The Reformers, speaking of them generally as a body, and with reference to their ordinary condition, seem to have enjoyed usually an assurance of being in a state of grace and of being warranted to count upon salvation. God seems to have given to them the grace of assurance more fully and more generally than He does to believers in ordinary circumstances. And this is in accordance with the general course of His providential procedure. The history of the church seems to indicate to us two positions as true, with reference to this matter, viz.,—1st, That assurance of salvation has been enjoyed more fully and more generally by men who were called to difficult and arduous labours in the cause of Christ, than by ordinary believers in general. And, 2dly, That this assurance, as enjoyed by such persons, has been frequently traceable to special circumstances connected with the manner of their conversion as its immediate or proximate cause. So it certainly was with the Reformers. The position in which they were placed, and the work they were called upon to do, made it specially necessary that they should enjoy habitually the courage and the strength which spring from a well-grounded assurance of salvation. This, accordingly, God gave them ; and He gave them it in many cases, as He has often done in subsequent times, by so regulating the circumstances which preceded and accompanied their conversion, as to satisfy them, almost as if by a perception of their senses, that they had passed from death unto life. The Reformers having been in general, for these reasons and by such processes, assured, ordinarily, of their own salvation, were not unnaturally led, from this cause, to give great prominence to the subject of assurance, and to regard and to represent it as in some way or other necessarily connected with the Christian faith, and as an indispensable constituent element of the Christian character.

But, in the second place, the Reformers were the more induced to adhere to this view, and to exert themselves to establish and defend it, in consequence of the ground that was taken up by their popish antagonists. The Romanists then, as well as now, were accustomed to allege that it was impossible for Protestants to have any *certainty* of the soundness of their views, or of the safety of their position,—that though they might be able to produce plausible and apparently satisfactory pleadings in support of what they taught, they could have no adequate ground for perfect assurance of its truth ; while Romanists had a firm ground for absolute certainty in the testimony or authority of the church. There were three important subjects to which chiefly the Romanists were accustomed to apply this alleged point of contrast between their position and that of the Reformers. They were accustomed to allege that Protestants, upon Protestant principles, could have no certainty, and nothing more than a probable persuasion, 1st, That the books generally received, or any particular books specified, were possessed of divine authority; or, 2d, That *this* and not *that* was the meaning of a scriptural passage, or the substance of what Scripture taught upon a particular topic; or, 3d, That any particular individual was now in a state of grace and would be finally saved. The more reasonable Romanists did not deny that there were rational considerations bearing upon the establishment of the divine authority of the books of Scripture, sufficient to silence and confute infidels ; or that, by the ordinary rules and resources of exegesis, something might be done towards settling the meaning of many scriptural statements; or that men, by a diligent and impartial use of scriptural materials, combined with self-examination, might attain to good hope with respect to their ultimate salvation. But they denied that Protestants could ever attain to full and perfect certainty upon any of these points,—could ever reach such thorough and conclusive assurance as the authority of the church furnished to those who received it. Protestants, in dealing with this allegation, were not unnaturally led to maintain, that upon all these subjects they had, or might have, not merely a probable persuasion, but a strict and absolute certainty, and to labour to unfold the grounds of the certainty to which they laid claim. It was here that many of the Reformers were led to propound views which appear to have been somewhat extreme and exaggerated, both in regard to the kind and degree of the certainty they contended for, and the grounds on which they professed to establish its reality and legitimacy. Protestants are not infallible any more than papists. Neither the great Reformers of the sixteenth century, nor the great systematic divines of the seventeenth, are to be implictly followed. The truth is, that God has never yet given to any body of uninspired men to rise altogether, and in every respect, in their mode of dealing with the doctrines of His word, above the influence of their circumstances. There has never been any uninspired man, or any company of uninspired men, that has not given some indication of the imperfection of humanity, in their mode of dealing with some portion or other of divine truth. The Reformers, as a body, are unquestionably more entitled to deference in matters of theological doctrine than any other body of men who have adorned the church since the apostolic age. But there can be no reasonable doubt that there are some doctrinal points on which many of them have gone astray, either from retaining something of the corruption of the popish system which they had abandoned, or, what is about equally natural and probable, in consequence of the imperfection of human nature, from running into an extreme opposite to that which they had forsaken.

It is pretty evident that the papists, by taunting the Reformers with their want of certainty on the three points to which we have referred, drove them into the assertion of extreme and untenable positions. The Reformers claimed for their convictions and conclusions, on these questions, a kind and degree of certainty which the nature of the subject did not admit of, and they fell into further errors in endeavouring to set forth the grounds or reasons of the certainty or assurance for which they contended. They contended that they had, or might have, a perfect and absolute certainty in regard to all those matters,—a certainty resting not only upon rational grounds and a human faith, as it was called, but upon supernatural grounds and a divine faith, such as their popish opponents were accustomed to ascribe to the authority of the church, when it set forth any doctrine and called upon men to believe it as revealed by God. And as a substitute for the authority of the church, the popish ground for an absolute assurance and divine faith, the Reformers were accustomed to bring in the agency of the Holy Spirit, as producing certainty or assurance; and they did this not unfrequently in a way that seemed to be liable to the charge at least of confusion and irrelevancy.

The Reformers ought not to have allowed the Romanists to drag them into perplexed metaphysical discussions as to the nature and grounds of the certainty with which they held their convictions upon the important topics to which we have referred. They would thus have escaped the temptation to which, we think, it must be admitted, they sometimes yielded, of straining matters in order to get something like a ground for a kind and measure of certainty which the nature of the case did not admit of.

It was enough that they could produce adequate rational grounds for all their convictions,—grounds which fully satisfied their own minds, and which they could defend conclusively against the objections of gainsayers, as being sufficient and satisfactory reasons of assent. This was all that their opponents had a right to demand; and this was all that could legitimately come into a controversial discussion. The *vividness and efficacy* of these convictions might be somewhat affected by the kind and degree of evidence bearing upon the particular topic under consideration, or by the qualities of their mental constitution and habits, or by other collateral and adventitious influences. But a real conviction or assent, based upon rational grounds, which were perfectly satisfactory to their own minds, and the relevancy and validity of which they could triumphantly defend against all opponents, was quite sufficient, whether this might be called a certainty of faith or not; and if this conviction did not produce, in their minds, such a sense or feeling of assurance as they desired,—if it did not prove so practically efficacious as they wished,—it would be quite reasonable that they should ask the special blessing of God, the agency of the Holy Spirit, to bring about these results. And their prayers might be answered, the Spirit might be given, and the strongest, the most vivid, and the most efficacious certainty or assurance might be produced, without anything like a special revelation, and without the introduction of any new or additional grounds or reasons for the conviction. The Reformers, however, in their eagerness to claim for their convictions the very highest certainty or assurance, and to assign an adequate cause for this, by substituting the Holy Spirit instead of the church, went sometimes to the unwarrantable extreme of ascribing to the Holy Spirit not merely a subjective influence upon men's understandings and hearts, but an objective presentation of new and additional grounds and reasons for belief.

These general observations apply to the way in which the Reformers met the allegations of the Romanists about their want of certainty or assurance in regard to all the three subjects formerly mentioned, viz., the divine authority of the books of Scripture, the meaning of scriptural statements, and the certainty of personal salvation. In order to have a sure, and at the same time a compendious way of getting the highest assurance, even the certainty of faith, upon all these subjects, they substituted the Holy Spirit instead of the church; and to make this serve the same purpose in argument as the church does among Romanists, they were led to employ some modes of statement about the Spirit's operation which are not sanctioned by Scripture, though exhibiting perhaps rather confusion of thought than positive error. But we cannot dwell upon this general topic, and must return to the special subject of the assurance of personal salvation, with which alone we have at present to do.

The Reformers in general enjoyed ordinarily the assured belief that they were in a state of grace, and would be finally saved. They felt the importance of this grace in the arduous work in which they were engaged. They saw abundant ground in Scripture for the general position, that believers might be and should be assured of their own salvation. They inculcated this position upon their followers, persuaded that personal assurance would at once tend to preserve them from the perverting influence of popish sophists, and fit them for doing and bearing all God's will concerning them. The Romanists, on the other hand, laboured to show that believers could have no full and well-grounded assurance that they had attained to a condition of safety, except either by special revelation, or by the testimony of the church; their object of course being to make men feel themselves entirely dependent upon the church for security or certainty on all subjects of interest and importance, and to deprive them of the energy and confidence which a well-founded assurance of personal salvation was fitted to produce, in contending against the prestige of ecclesiastical authority and influence. The Reformers, in order to show that the assurance which might be attained without either a special revelation or the testimony of the church, was full and perfect, were led to identify it with our belief in the doctrines of God's word, and to represent it as necessarily included or implied in the act or exercise of justifying and saving faith; nay, even sometimes to give it as the very definition of saving faith, that it is a belief that our own sins have been forgiven, and that we have been brought into a state of grace. This seemed to be an obvious and ready method of giving to the belief of our personal safety for eternity the very highest degree of certainty, and hence many of the Reformers were tempted to adopt it.

This view was certainly exaggerated and erroneous. It is very evident that no man can be legitimately assured of his own salvation simply by understanding and believing what is contained or implied in the actual statements of Scripture. Some additional element of a different kind must be brought in, in order to warrant such an assurance; something in the state or condition of the man himself must be in some way ascertained and known in order to this result. It may not, indeed, always require any lengthened or elaborate process of self-examination to ascertain what is needful to be known about men themselves, in order to their being assured that they have been brought into a state of grace. The circumstances that preceded and accompanied their conversion may have been such as to leave them in no doubt about their having passed from darkness to light. Their present consciousness may testify at once and explicitly to the existence in them of those things which the Bible informs us accompany salvation. But still it is true, that another element than any thing contained in Scripture must be brought in as a part of the foundation of their assurance. And when they are called upon to state and vindicate to themselves or to others the grounds of their assurance, they must of necessity proceed, in substance, in the line of the familiar syllogism, "Whosoever believeth in the Lord Jesus Christ shall be saved; I believe, and therefore," etc.

There is no possibility of avoiding, in substance, some such process as this; and while the major proposition is proved by Scripture, the minor can be established only by some use of materials derived from consciousness and self-examination. There are no positions connected with religion which can be so certain as those which are directly and immediately taught in Scripture, and which are usually said to be believed with the certainty of faith or of divine faith. The introduction of an element, as necessary to the conclusion, derived from a different source, viz., from the knowledge of what we ourselves are, must be admitted in fairness to complicate the evidence, and to affect the kind, if not the degree, of the certainty or assurance that may result from it. It is unwarrantable to give as the definition of saving faith, the belief that my sins are forgiven; for it is not true that my sins are forgiven until I believe, and it holds true universally, that God requires us to believe nothing which is not true before we believe it, and which may not be propounded to us to be believed, accompanied at the same time with satisfactory evidence of its truth; and if so, the belief that our sins are forgiven, and that we have been brought into a state of grace, must be posterior in the order of nature, if not of time, to the act of faith by which the change is effected, and cannot therefore form a necessary constituent element of the act itself, cannot be its essence or belong to its essence.

It is not very surprising that Luther should have made rash and exaggerated statements upon this subject as he did upon others. But it is certainly strange, that a man of such wonderful soundness and penetration of judgment as Calvin should have said, as he did say,* "We shall have a complete definition of faith, if we say that it is a steady and certain knowledge of the divine benevolence towards us, which, being founded on the truth of the gratuitous promise in Christ, is both revealed to our minds and confirmed to our hearts by the Holy Spirit;" and that this in substance should have been pretty generally, though not universally, received as a just definition or description of saving faith, both by Lutheran and Calvinistic divines, for the greater part of a century. We cannot but look upon this as an illustration of the pernicious influence of men's circumstances upon the forma-

---

* Instit. l. iii., c. ii. sec. 7.

ion of their opinions—a view of the matter decidedly confirmed
by the fact that neither Luther nor Calvin, nor the other eminent
divines who have sanctioned this notion of the nature and import of faith, have been able to carry it out in full consistency,
but have become entangled in contradictions. Luther, indeed,
contradicted himself very explicitly upon this point; for while
there are passages in his works which very unequivocally represent personal assurance as necessarily involved in saving faith,
and while this doctrine is taught in the Confession of Augsburg,* and in the Apology for it,†—both which works are symbolical in the Lutheran Church—it is easy enough to produce
from his writings passages in which a broader and more correct
view is given of the nature of saving faith, as having respect
directly and primarily only to truths and promises actually contained in Scripture, and, of course, only secondarily and infe-
rentially to anything bearing upon our personal condition and
prospects. Calvin never contradicted himself so plainly and
palpably as this. But in immediate connection with the definition above given from him of saving faith, he has made
statements, with respect to the condition of mind that may exist
in believers, which cannot well be reconciled with the formal definition, except upon the assumption that the definition was intended
not so much to state what was essential to true faith and always
found in it, as to describe what true faith is, or includes, in its
most perfect condition and in its highest exercise. As the passage
is valuable in itself, and is well fitted to throw light upon the real
views of the Reformers, and to illustrate the danger of judging of
what these views were from a superficial examination of their
writings or of isolated extracts from them, we shall quote it at
some length, though we fear most men will be of opinion that
Calvin has not very fully solved the difficulty which he started :—

"But some one will object that the experience of believers is very different
from this; for that, in recognising the grace of God towards them, they are
not only disturbed with inquietude which frequently befalls them, but sometimes also tremble with the most distressing terrors. The vehemence of temptations to agitate their minds is so great that it appears scarcely compatible
with that assurance of faith of which we have been speaking. We must, therefore, solve this difficulty, if we mean to support the doctrine we have advanced.

* Art. iv.
† Tittmann's *Libri Symbolici Ec-* | *clesiæ Evangelicæ*, pp. 13 and 58.

When we inculcate that faith ought to be certain and secure, we conceive not of a certainty attended with no doubt, or of a security interrupted by no anxiety; but we rather affirm that believers have a perpetual conflict with their own diffidence, and are far from placing their consciences in a placid calm never disturbed by any storms. Yet, on the other hand, we deny, however they may be afflicted, that they ever fall and depart from that certain confidence which they have conceived in the divine mercy. The Scripture proposes no example of faith more illustrious or memorable than David, especially if you consider the whole course of his life. Yet that his mind was not invariably serene appears from his innumerable complaints, of which it will be sufficient to select a few. . . . . To render this intelligible, it is necessary to recur to that division of the flesh and the spirit which we noticed in another place, and which most clearly discovers itself in this case. The pious heart, therefore, perceives a division in itself, being partly affected with delight through a knowledge of the divine goodness, partly distressed with sorrow through a sense of its own calamity; partly relying on the promise of the gospel, partly trembling at the evidence of its own iniquity; partly exulting in the knowledge of life, partly alarmed by the fear of death. This variation happens through the imperfection of faith; since we are never so happy during the present life as to be cured of all diffidence, and entirely filled and possessed by faith. Hence those conflicts, in which the diffidence which adheres to the relics of the flesh rises up in opposition to the faith formed in the heart. But if in the mind of the believer assurance be mixed with doubts, do we not always come to this point, that faith consists not in a certain and clear, but only in an obscure and perplexed knowledge of the divine will respecting us? Not at all. For if we are distracted by various thoughts, we are not therefore entirely divested of faith; neither, though harassed by the agitations of diffidence, are we therefore immerged in its abyss; nor if we be shaken, are we therefore overthrown. For the invariable issue of this contest is, that faith at length surmounts those difficulties from which, while it is encompassed with them, it appears to be in danger."*

Other proofs might be adduced that the Reformers, when judged of as they should be, by a deliberate and conjunct view of all they have said upon the subject, did not carry their doctrine of assurance to such extremes as we might be warranted in ascribing to them because of some of their more formal statements, intended to tell upon their controversies with Romanists regarding this matter. And more than this, the real difference between the Reformers and the Romanists upon the subject of assurance, when calmly and deliberately investigated, was not quite so important as the combatants on either side imagined, and did not really respect the precise questions which persons imperfectly acquainted with

* B. iii. c. ii. s. 17, 18.

the works on both sides, might naturally enough regard it as involving.

With respect to the nature of saving faith, the principal ground of controversy was this, that the Romanists held that it had its seat in the intellect, and was properly and fundamentally assent (*assensus*), while the Reformers in general maintained that it had its seat in the will, and was properly and essentially trust (*fiducia*). The great majority of eminent Protestant divines have adhered to the views of the Reformers upon this point, though some have taken the opposite side, and have held faith, properly so called, to be the mere assent of the understanding to truth propounded by God in His word; while they represent trust and other graces as the fruits or consequences, and not as constituent parts and elements, of faith. This controversy cannot be held to be of very great importance, so long as the advocates of the position, that faith is in itself the simple belief of the truth, admit that true faith *necessarily and invariably* produces trust and other graces,— an admission which is cheerfully made by all the Protestant defenders of this view, and which its popish advocates, though refusing in words, are obliged to make, in substance, in another form. There is an appearance of greater simplicity and metaphysical accuracy in representing faith as in itself a mere assent to truth, and trust and other graces as its necessary consequences. But the right question is, What is the meaning attached in Scripture to the faith which justifies and saves? Upon this question we agree with the Reformers in thinking, that in Scripture usage faith is applied, in its highest and most important sense, only to a state of mind of which trust in Christ as a Saviour is a necessary constituent element. *This* question about the nature of justifying faith is not determined in the Westminster Confession, the leading symbol of the great body of Presbyterians throughout the world; and it is well that it is left in that condition, for if it had been settled there in accordance with the views of the Reformers and the compilers of the Confession, this would have excluded from the Church of Scotland Dr John Erskine and Dr Thomas Chalmers.

There was not among the Reformers, and there has not been among modern Protestants, unanimity, as to what is involved in the *fiducia* which is included in justifying faith. The generality of modern divines and some of the Reformers held that this *fiducia* was just trust or confidence in Christ's person, as distinguished from mere belief of the truth concerning Him, and as involving some special application or appropriation to ourselves of the discoveries and provisions of the gospel, but not, directly and immediately, any opinion or conviction as to our actual personal condition; while the generality of the Reformers, and some modern divines, especially those known in Scotland as Marrow men, have regarded it as comprehending this last element also, and have thus come to maintain that personal assurance is necessarily and directly included in the exercise of saving faith, or belongs to its essence.

But though a considerable number of the Reformers held this view, and although, as we have explained, they were probably led into the adoption of it by their controversy with the Romanists, yet the truth or falsehood of this view did not form the real or main subject of controversy between them. The leading topic of discussion was this, Whether, without any special revelation, believers could and should (*possent et deberent*) be assured of their justification and salvation? This was *practically* the question that was controverted. It is one of great practical importance, and orthodox Protestant divines, in general, have continued ever since to concur with the Reformers in answering it in the affirmative. But though this was practically the real point controverted,—though the papists were most anxious to persuade men that they could attain to no certainty upon this point, except either by a special revelation or by the testimony of the church,—yet this was not just the precise form which the question assumed in the controversy; and the reason of this was one which we have already hinted at, viz., that the more reasonable Romanists shrank from meeting the question, *as thus put*, with a direct negative, and fell back upon the topic of the *kind or degree* of the assurance or certainty that was ordinarily attainable by believers. Into this discussion of the nature and grounds of the certainty that might attach to this matter, the Reformers were unfortunately tempted to follow their opponents. In the heat of controversy many of them were led to lay down the untenable position, that the certainty or assurance ordinarily attainable by believers was of the highest and most perfect description,—that it was the certainty of faith, or, as they sometimes expressed it, the certainty of divine faith, the same certainty with which men believe in the plainly revealed doctrines of God's word. And then, again, *it was as an argument or proof in support of this extreme and untenable position as to the kind or degree of certainty*, that they were led on to assert, that this personal assurance was necessarily involved in justifying faith,—nay, was its distinguishing characteristic, and belonged, of course, to its essence.

That the account now given of the subordinate, and as we might call it, accidental, place held in the doctrinal system of the Reformers by their extreme views of the nature of the certainty or assurance which they asserted, and of the argument which they advanced in support of it, is well founded, may be shown by the important fact, that while many of them taught these views in their private writings, and in some of their polemical and practical treatises, they did not introduce them into their Confessions of Faith, into compositions intended to be symbolical and to define the terms of ministerial communion. They are taught, indeed, as we have mentioned, in the Confession of Augsburg, and the Apology for it. They are also set forth pretty explicitly in the Saxon and Wirtemberg Confessions, which are both Lutheran documents,—the first having been composed by Melancthon, and the second by Brentius.* But they are not taught in the Confessions of the Reformed or Calvinistic Churches. The earliest Confessions of the Reformed Churches are the two Confessions of Basle, and there is no statement of them to be found there. Calvin had undoubtedly taught in his " Institutes," and also in his " Catechism" of Geneva, that saving faith necessarily includes or implies personal assurance. But he did not introduce any statement to this effect into the Confession of the French Protestant Church. It is doubtful, indeed, whether Calvin composed the French Confession, or only revised and sanctioned it. But this latter view is enough for our present purpose ; and besides, if the Confession was not originally composed by Calvin, it was composed by Antony Chandieu or Sadeel, and he had taught in his own writings the same views as Calvin upon this subject, though neither he nor Calvin seems to have thought of introducing them into the Confession. In the Palatine or Heidelberg Catechism, which was not originally intended to be symbolical, but was rather adapted for popular instruction, faith is described as necessarily com-

---

* *Harmonia Confessionum Fidei*, Genevæ, 1581, p. 154–5, 160, 207–9.

prehending assurance.* The Belgic Confession, composed in 1563, contains no assertion of these views, though its authors probably believed them, as they afterwards added the Heidelberg Catechism to their Confession as symbolical. The latter Helvetic Confession, composed in 1566, and approved of by most of the Reformed Churches, gives no countenance to these peculiar opinions. And lastly, the Synod of Dort, in 1618, representing almost all the Reformed Churches, not only gave no sanction to these views, but made statements which can scarcely be reconciled with them, and which form part of the evidence by which it may be shown, that a more careful and exact analysis of these matters was leading men's minds rather in a direction opposite to the views of the Reformers upon this subject, and thus paving the way for the more explicit rejection of them by the Westminster Assembly.

Now, let it be remembered that we do not assert that the authors of these documents did not hold the same views as Luther and Calvin upon the subjects of faith and assurance, and the relation subsisting between them. We concede that, generally speaking, they did hold the same views as these leading Reformers. We concede, too, that in some of these Confessions there are expressions employed which indicate, plainly enough, to competent judges, that they held these views. But these concessions being made, we still think it a consideration of great importance, that

---

* (Q. 21.) It seems to have been chiefly the Geneva and the Heidelberg Catechisms that Perkins had in view in an interesting passage in his "Reformed Catholic," published in 1598. Perkins was a very eminent divine, a thorough Calvinist, and a man of distinguished piety. The passage we refer to may be regarded as an evidence that, before the end of the sixteenth century, some of the most competent judges were seeing that the language of the Reformers upon this subject required some modification. It is as follows :— " This doctrine (that of implied or infolded faith) is to be learned for two causes : First of all, it serves to rectify the consciences of weak ones, that they be not deceived touching their estate. For if we think that no faith can save but a full persuasion, such as the faith of Abraham was, many truly bearing the name of Christ must be put out of the roll of the children of God. We are, therefore, to know that there is a growth in grace as in nature; and there be differences and degrees of true faith, and the least of them all is infolded faith. Secondly, this point of doctrine serves to rectify and in part to expound sundry *catechisms*, in that they seem to propound faith unto men at so high a reach as few can attain unto it,—defining it to be a certain and full persuasion of God's love and favour in Christ ; whereas, though every faith be from its nature a certain persuasion, yet only the strong faith is the full persuasion. Therefore faith is not only in general terms to be defined, but also the degrees and measures thereof are to be expounded, that weak ones, to their comfort, may be truly informed of their estate."—*Perkins' Reformed Catholic*, pp. 274-5.

they did not distinctly embody them in their Confessions of Faith, as this proves that they did not really occupy any such place in their system of theology as some of their statements, made in the heat of controversy, might lead us to suppose.

The account we have given of the views of the Reformers and the Romanists upon the subject of faith and assurance, and of the course which the discussion regarding it took, is sufficient, at once and of itself, if it be well-founded, to overturn some of Sir William's leading positions in his history of this matter. But we must now look at his statements more closely and directly. His first leading position is this :—

" *Assurance,* Personal Assurance, Special Faith (*the feeling of certainty* that God is propitious to *me,* that *my* sins are forgiven, —*Fiducia, Plerophoria Fidei, Fides Specialis*), Assurance was long *universally* held in the Protestant communities to be the criterion and condition of a true or *saving faith.*" Here the first thing to be noted is the assumption, that "*personal assurance, special faith,* —*fiducia, plerophoria fidei, fides specialis,*" do, in the writings of the Reformers, all mean one and the same thing; and that this one thing is " the feeling of certainty that God is propitious to *me,* that *my* sins are forgiven." We could easily show that this assumption involves great ignorance of the *usus loquendi* of the Reformers, that the different words are used in different senses, and that the same word is used in different senses by different authors. But it is not worth while to dwell upon this point. The statement, that "assurance was long *universally* held in the Protestant communities to be the criterion and condition of a true and saving faith" is not correct. For it has been proved, that Peter Martyr, Musculus, and Zanchius, three of the most eminent divines at the period of the Reformation, did not hold this view of the nature of saving faith. The allegation, that "assurance is the *punctum saliens* of Luther's system" is one which no man, acquainted with Luther's writings, can believe. The assertion, that "assurance stands, essentially, part and parcel of *all* the Confessions of *all* the churches of the Reformation, down to the Westminster Assembly," is utterly untrue. We have already explained how this matter stands as a question of fact, in regard to the earliest and most important Confessions. If Sir William's assertion had any foundation in truth, the passages teaching the doctrine of assurance might easily be produced. But no such passages have been, or can be, produced, because they have no existence.

Sir William is, in substance, right in saying, that in the Westminster Assembly assurance was formally declared not to be of the essence of faith; and he is right also in saying, that this was then done for the first time by an ecclesiastical synod, though, as we have already remarked, the Synod of Dort paved the way for it. It is of more importance to remark, that this decision of the Westminster Assembly has been generally acquiesced in ever since by the great body of Calvinists and Presbyterians over the world.

Sir William's next statement, viz., that on the ground of this deliverance of the Westminster Assembly, " the Scottish General Assembly has once and again deposed the holders of this, the doctrine of Luther and Calvin, of all the other churches of the Reformation, and of the older Scottish Church itself," is a curious mixture of truth and error, though the error preponderates. If the doctrine that assurance is not of the essence of faith be plainly asserted in the standards of a church, and be thus explicitly assented to by every minister as a condition of his ordination, it does not appear why it should be held up as something monstrous, that men who may come afterwards to reject this doctrine, should forfeit their office as ministers in that church, though it would no doubt be a very painful thing to have to cut off a brother who held no erroneous views except upon this one point. Sir William's statement is plainly fitted and intended to convey the impression that cases of *this* kind have occurred in the Church of Scotland, or, that men have been deposed merely because they held the views of the Reformers upon this point, while they were not charged with any other doctrinal errors. This impression is erroneous. No such cases have ever occurred. In the only instances, and they have been very few, in which ministers holding that assurance is of the essence of saving faith, have been subjected to ecclesiastical discipline, this error was held in conjunction with the much more serious one of universal atonement, or universal pardon, which it naturally tends to introduce; and it was no doubt the maintenance of this second and more serious error that reconciled the heart and conscience of the church to the infliction of censure.

Sir William's assertion, that the doctrine of assurance being of the essence of faith was that " of the older Scottish Church itself," has an appearance of truth about it, but it is fitted likewise to convey a false impression of the facts of the case. There is sufficient evidence that the older Scottish Church, or the first generation of Protestant ministers in Scotland, held in general the same views of faith and assurance as were taught by Luther and Calvin. But they had not embodied these views in any public symbolical documents, or required the belief of them as a term of ministerial communion; and yet this is plainly the impression which Sir William's statement is fitted to produce. In the old Scottish Confession of Faith, prepared by John Knox, and adopted by the General Assembly in 1560, these views are certainly not asserted. It contains nothing on this, or any other subject, which might not be assented to by men who had subscribed the Westminster Confession. The only thing bearing upon these views that can, in any sense, be regarded as a deliverance of the church, is, that the National Covenant of 1581 contains a condemnation of the " general and doubtsome faith of the Papists;"—a statement which, whatever we may know otherwise of the opinions of its authors, is far too vague to commit the church, or any who subscribed the document, to the definite doctrine, that assurance is of the essence of saving faith.

Sir William's next statement is an astounding one: "In the English, and more articulately in the Irish Establishment, *assurance still stands a necessary tenet of ecclesiastical belief.*" This, we presume, will be a piece of news to the clergy of the English and Irish Establishments. We venture to assert, that not one of the 18,000 or 20,000 clergymen who represent the United Church of England and Ireland, has ever imagined that he had come under an obligation to believe and to teach "assurance;"—by which, of course, Sir William means, as the whole scope of the passage shows, notwithstanding the obscurity and confusion of his language, the doctrine that assurance of personal salvation is essential to, and is necessarily included or implied in, justifying faith. But Sir William has referred to proofs and authorities upon this point, and what are they? He gives them thus:—" See Homilies, book i., number iii., part 3, specially referred to in the eleventh of the Thirty-nine Articles; and number iv., parts 1 and 3; likewise the sixth Lambeth Article." The authorities here referred to are two, viz., the first Book of the Homilies, and the Lambeth Articles.

Now, in regard to the Books of the Homilies, we think it can be shown, 1st. That they are not properly symbolical books of the Church of England, so that the clergy are to be held bound to maintain and teach every thing contained in them; and, 2d. That though the Homilies contain plain enough indications that the views entertained by most of the Reformers were held also in the Church of England, they do not exhibit distinct and definite statements of these peculiar opinions.

The extent to which the Church of England is committed to the Homilies is this, that in her 35th Article she has declared that " the second Book of Homilies doth contain a godly and whole-some doctrine, and necessary for these times, as doth the former Book of Homilies; and therefore we judge them to be read in churches by ministers, diligently and distinctly, that they may be understood by the people,"—and that the 11th Article refers to one of the Homilies for a fuller setting forth of the doctrine of justi-fication. Now this does not necessarily imply, and has never been regarded as implying, that the Church of England took her ministers bound to believe and to teach every thing contained in these books. The Homilies were intended to furnish materials for popular instruction, and not to regulate the terms of mi-nisterial communion. A conscientious man, who had subscribed the Articles, would not, indeed, consider himself at liberty, without first renouncing his position, to oppose the general scope and main substance of the views of doctrine and duty contained in the Homilies; for, by subscribing the Articles, he has declared this to be godly and wholesome: but the most conscientious men would deny that they were committed to all and every thing contained in the Homilies. And they would take this ground, not from loose views of what subscription to symbols implies, but because they have never subscribed the Homilies, or done any thing equivalent to this. In short, what is said in the Articles about the Homilies does not make the Homilies Articles, does not raise them to the same level, does not incorporate them with that primary and fundamental symbol. The statement in the 7th Article, that " the three Creeds ought thoroughly to be received and believed, for they may be proved by most certain warrants of holy writ," no doubt incorporates the Creeds with the Articles, and makes them equally binding; but nothing like this is said about the Homilies, and therefore they stand upon a different footing. On these grounds

we contend, that an incidental statement of the doctrine of assurance in the Homilies, would not have afforded an adequate ground
for Sir William's allegation, that this doctrine "still stands a
necessary tenet of ecclesiastical belief."

We have now to remark, in the second place, that anything
said about this doctrine in the Homilies is not only incidental, but
indefinite. The principal passages bearing upon the point are
these:—"For the right and true Christian faith is, not only to
believe that the Holy Scriptures and all the foresaid articles of
our faith are true, but also to have a sure trust and confidence in
God's merciful promises, to be saved from everlasting damnation
by Christ; whereof doth follow a loving heart to obey His commandments." And again: "And this [a quick or living faith] is
not only the common belief of the articles of our faith, but is also
a true trust and confidence of the mercy of God through our Lord
Jesus Christ, *and a stedfast hope of all things to be received at His
hands*." While these statements are quite explicit in rejecting
the idea that saving faith is the mere belief of the truth, they do
not definitely decide in favour of any one precise view of the
nature, object, and grounds of the *fiducia*, or trust, which they
describe. When these matters came to be more exactly and
elaborately discussed in the seventeenth century, distinctions were
introduced and applied, which tended to throw much light upon
the subject, and which now require to be known and kept in view,
in order that we may form a right estimate of the true import
even of the vague and indefinite statements of former writers.
It may be proper to illustrate this point by a specimen or two, as
it admits of extensive application. Le Blanc, professor of theology at Sedan to the French Protestant Church, of whom we
shall have afterwards occasion to speak more fully, gives the following statements of the differences which have been exhibited
among Protestant divines upon this subject:—

"Hic observandum est, *fiduciam* apud doctores Reformatos pluribus modis
sumi, adeoque plures eorum qui hac in parte diverse loquuntur, idem reapse
inter se sentire; alios vero qui videntur eodem modo loqui, revera tamen
quoad sensum inter se discrepare."

If this be so, it would require a great deal more of careful and
patient research than Sir William ever gave to this or to any
other theological subject, to enable him to thread his way through

its intricacies, and to entitle him to speak with confidence of his success in doing so.   Again, Le Blanc says, more particularly—

"Præcipui vero scholæ Reformatæ theologi de fiducia varie loquuntur, dum quidam dicunt fiduciam esse partem fidei primariam, et proprium illius actum, alii vero istud negant et docent fiduciam esse quidem fidei prolem atque effectum, sed non tamen actum ejus proprie dictum; ac practerea fiduciæ nomine, alii quidem istud, alii vero aliud, intelligunt."

He then mentions four different senses in which this *fiducia*, trust or confidence, has been understood by Protestant divines, the first two of which are thus described:—

"Primum ergo, fiduciæ nomine intelligitur actus ille per quem in Deum recumbimus, illi innitimur, et ei adhæremus, tanquam fonti et authori salutis, ut vitam et salutem ab eo consequamur.   Secundo, fiducia apud multos designat firmam persuasionem de gratia et venia a Deo impetrata et de nostra cum eo reconciliatione."*

Turretine explains the distinctions applicable to this matter with his usual masterly ability, in this way:—

"Diversitas quæ inter orthodoxos occurrit oritur ex diversa acceptione *fiduciæ*, quæ trifariam potest sumi. 1. Pro fiduciali assensu seu persuasione quæ oritur ex judicio practico intellectus de veritate et bonitate promissionum evangelicarum, et de potentia, voluntate, ac fidelitate Dei promittentis. 2. Pro actu refugii et receptionis Christi, quo fidelis, cognita veritate et bonitate promissionum, ad Christum confugit, illum recipit et amplectitur et in illius meritum unice recumbit. 3. Pro confidentia seu acquiescentia et tranquillitate animi quæ oritur ex refugio animæ ad Christum et ejus receptione. Primo et secundo significatu fiducia est de essentia fidei et bene a theologis dicitur ejus forma; sed tertio, recte ab aliis non forma sed effectus fidei dicitur, quia nascitur ex ea, non vero eam constituit."†

We have made these quotations chiefly for the purpose of illustrating the position, that as these distinctions were not present to the minds of the Reformers, but were the growth of later speculation, we should not attribute to them any one of these distinct and definite opinions, without specific evidence bearing upon the precise point to be proved, and should not allow ourselves to be carried away by the mere words, *trust* and *confidence*, *certainty* and *assurance*, without a full and deliberate consideration of the whole evidence bearing upon the meaning of the statements.   The statements may be so definite as to indicate what of the views that were subsequently developed were held by the parties under consideration or they may not. The statements of the Catechisms of Geneva and Heidelberg are so expressed, as to convey the doctrine that personal assurance is of the essence of saving faith; the Confessions of the Reformed churches do not in general teach this doctrine; and the Homilies of the Church of England resemble more the Confessions than the Catechisms. Even if they were symbolical and authoritative, they would not make " assurance," in the precise and definite sense in which Sir William here uses the word, " a necessary tenet of ecclesiastical belief."

Sir William's second proof of his position is the " sixth Lambeth Article." The history of the Lambeth Articles affords an irrefragable proof that Calvinism was the generally received doctrine of the great body of the highest authorities in the church and universities of England, and of the mass of the English clergy, in the latter part of the reign of Elizabeth and of the sixteenth century: while nothing is more certain and notorious than that they never received the sanction of the church in its public, official character; that they never were imposed by any authority, civil or ecclesiastical; and that there is not a shadow of ground for alleging, that any Anglican clergyman is, or ever was, under any appearance of obligation to believe or teach anything contained in them, the sixth Article or any of the other eight.

But even if the Lambeth Articles were symbolical and authoritative, they would not impose an obligation to teach the precise and definite doctrine which is the subject of Sir William's allegation. The sixth Article is in these words:—" Homo vere fidelis, id est, fide justificante præditus, certus est plerophoria fidei, de remissione peccatorum suorum et salute sempiterna sua per Christum." It would manifestly require something much more definite than this, to tie down men to the maintenance of the position, that personal assurance is necessarily included in saving faith and belongs to its essence. It simply says, " A true believer is certain with the assurance of faith." It does not say that every believer is so, at all times; it defines nothing about the nature of the process by which the certainty is produced, or the ground on which it rests; it specifies nothing of the relation subsisting between faith and assurance: and on these grounds it is totally unfit for the purpose for which Sir William referred to it. The truth is, that a man might honestly subscribe this Lambeth Article, without being thereby committed to more than the position which, as we have explained, formed the real subject of controversy between the Reformers and the Romanists, viz., that the believer may and should be assured of his forgiveness and salvation.

Sir William, however, not only asserts that assurance, in the sense in which it has been so often explained, "still stands a necessary tenet of ecclesiastical belief" in the English Establishment, but he further says, that it does so "more articulately" in the Irish. He gives no other references than those we have examined, to the Homilies and the Lambeth Articles, and of course none bearing upon the alleged greater "articulateness" of the Irish Church in this matter. The truth probably was this: Sir William must have known that the Lambeth Articles are not, and never were, of any authority in the Church of England; and he would scarcely have ventured to refer to them as establishing anything about the obligations of the clergy of that church. But he had probably read somewhere that the Lambeth Articles, though never imposed upon the Church of England, were, through Archbishop Usher's influence, sanctioned and adopted in the Church of Ireland,—a statement which is true in substance, though not strictly correct; and this was probably the whole of the knowledge on the ground of which he thought himself entitled to assert the greater articulateness of the Irish Church, and to refer to the sixth Lambeth Article. In "the Articles of Religion agreed upon by the archbishops and bishops, and the rest of the clergy of Ireland, in the Convocation holden at Dublin in the year of our Lord God 1615," the whole of the Lambeth Articles are embodied, though with some additions and verbal alterations. The subject of assurance is thus stated in No. 37, under the head "Justification and Faith:"—

"By justifying faith, we understand not only the common belief of the articles of Christian religion, and a persuasion of the truth of God's word in general, but also a particular application of the gracious promises of the gospel to the comfort of our own souls; whereby we lay hold on Christ with all His benefits, having an earnest trust and confidence in God, that He will be merciful to us for His only Son's sake. So that a true believer may be certain by the assurance of faith of the forgiveness of his sins, and of his everlasting salvation by Christ."*

* *Hardwick's History of the Articles*, Appendix, No. vi., pp. 347, 348.

It is somewhat difficult to say whether this could, with truth, be said to be more "articulate" than the statements quoted from the "Homilies." The first sentence does seem to embody rather more of the tone and spirit of the Catechisms of Geneva and Heidelberg, though it is very far from being explicit in declaring their peculiar views upon this point. But then, in the second sentence, which is in substance a translation of the sixth Lambeth Article, there is an alteration which rather tells on the other side,—"may be certain," instead of "*certus est;*" a change which confirms the view above given of the real meaning of the Article, and brings it nearer to the great fundamental Protestant position, *vere fidelis potest et debet certus esse.* There is nothing, then, in these Irish Articles of 1615 to commit any one who may receive and adopt them, to the doctrine that assurance is of the essence of faith. Sir William, however, probably meant the greater articulateness, which he predicated of the Irish Church, to refer to the more formal ecclesiastical sanction given to these statements in the Irish than in the English Establishment; and our answer to this is, that for two centuries past neither the Irish Church nor any of its bishops or clergymen, have furnished any ground whatever for the allegation, that they were under any obligation to teach the doctrine of assurance, beyond what is implied in subscription to the English Articles. There was a period, indeed, when the Irish Articles, and, of course, the Lambeth Articles, were invested with some authority in Ireland, but that period was brief, and has long since gone by. An investigation into the history and standing of the Irish Articles can now possess a merely historical value, and determines no question of present duty. It is curious and interesting, however; and we would refer those who desire full information upon this subject to Hardwick's "History of the Articles of Religion,"—a book which, notwithstanding its strong anti-Calvinistic prejudices, we cannot but commend most highly for ability and learning and general fairness.* We must again request our readers to notice and remember what is suggested by the fact, that Sir William made this assertion about the Churches of England and Ireland.

But perhaps Sir William's grandest display is to be found in the second paragraph of the passage on which we are commenting,

---

* C. viii. and Appendix vi.

where he brings out the "series of the most curious contrasts" which "this dogma, with its fortunes, past and present, affords." He swells the number of these curious contrasts, by repeating what is really one and the same idea, in two or three different forms. He gives five "curious contrasts," but the first three turn upon a single point, and the substance of them may be embodied in one position, which, indeed, is the sum and substance of what Sir William is most anxious to establish, viz., that the whole of the Reformed churches have not only abandoned the doctrine of assurance, the fundamental doctrine of the Reformation, but have all adopted the opposite popish doctrine, which was taught by the Council of Trent when it condemned the doctrine of the Reformers.

Before adverting to this leading position, we must notice his fourth and fifth specimens of "curious contrasts." He states them thus :—

"Again, it is curious, that this, the most important‾variation in the faith of Protestants,—as, in fact, a gravitation of Protestantism back to Catholicity, —should have been overlooked, as, indeed, in his days undeveloped, by the keen-eyed author of 'The History of the Variations of the Protestant Churches.' Finally, it is curious, that, though now fully developed, this central approximation of Protestantism to Catholicity should not, as far as I know, have been signalised by any theologian, Protestant or Catholic."

If this variation was "undeveloped" in Bossuet's time, it does not seem "curious" that it should have been overlooked by him, even though he was "keen-eyed;" while we admit that it is "curious," if true, that "it should not have been signalised by any theologian, Protestant or Catholic," until Sir William Hamilton discovered and promulgated it. But the truth is, that this variation,—for there was a doctrinal variation upon this point, though certainly it was not of such magnitude as Sir William alleges,— was developed in Bossuet's time, and was not overlooked by him, but was distinctly set forth, though not much enlarged upon, in his "History of the Variations." Indeed, all Sir William's assertions upon these points are wholly untrue. That this variation was *not* overlooked by Bossuet, is proved by the following extract from his "History of the Variations."*

"Les ministres qui ont écrit dans les derniers tems, et entr'autres, M. de Beaulieu (Le Blanc), que nous avous vu à Sedan, un des plus savans et des plus pacifique de tous les ministres, *adoucissent* le plus qu'ils peuvent le dogme

* Liv. xiv. s. 90.

de l'inamissibilité de la justice *et même celui de la certitude de salut :* et deux
raisons les y portent : la première est l'eloignement qu'en ont eu les Luthériens,
à qui ils veulent s'unir à quelque prix que ce soit : la seconde est l'absurdité
et l'impiété qu'on decouvre dans ces dogmes, pour peu qu'ils soient pénétrés.
. . . . Toutes les fois que nos Réformés *désavouent* ces dogmes impies, louons-
en Dieu, et, sans disputer davantage, prions les seulement de considérer que le
Saint Esprit ne pouvait pas être en ceux qui les ont enseignés, et qui ont fait
consister une grande partie de la Réforme dans de si indignes idées de la justice
Chrétienne."

So far from this variation not having been signalised before,
it actually formed one leading subject of a controversy that was
carried on between theologians of distinguished eminence, both
Protestant and Romanist, before the publication of Bossuet's
"History of the Variations;" and as this topic not only conclusively disproves Sir William's assertions, but is fitted to throw
light upon the general subject under consideration, we will give a
brief notice of the controversy referred to.

In 1665, Louis le Blanc, Lord of Beaulieu, Professor of
Theology in the College of the French Protestant Church at
Sedan, a man of great ability and learning, published "Theses
Theologicæ de Certitudine quam quis habere possit et debeat de
suâ coram Deo justificatione." In these Theses, he described it
as a misrepresentation of papists, to allege that Protestants held,
among other things, that personal assurance was necessarily comprehended in justifying faith and belonged to its essence; and
explained what he held to be the doctrine generally taught by
Protestants úpon this subject. He represented their doctrine as
being substantially this, that believers can and should be assured
of their being forgiven and being in a state of grace, and that the
want of this assurance was faulty and sinful; but that this assurance was not the proper act of justifying and saving faith,
and did not belong to its essence, since faith might exist for a
time without it; that it was a result or consequence of faith,
posterior to it in the order of nature, and frequently also of time;
that though this assurance might be called an act of faith, it was
but a secondary and reflex, not a primary and direct act of faith;
and that while the certainty attaching to this personal assurance
might be called a certainty of faith, it was so named in an improper sense, since it did not rest immediately and exclusively
upon what was actually contained in God's word, but partly
also upon a reflex act concerning ourselves. These are, in sub-

stance, the views, in regard to faith and assurance, which are set
forth in the Westminster Confession, prepared twenty years before; and Le Blanc, without any parade of proofs or authorities,
declared them to be then generally prevalent among Protestants.
The prevalence of these views, of course, implied, and was seen
and admitted to imply, a variation, or a departure from those held
by the generality of the Reformers.

About seven years after, in 1672, the famous Antony Arnauld,
Doctor of the Sorbonne, the friend and associate of Pascal and
Nicole, published his work entitled, "Le Renversement de la
Morale de Jesus Christ, par les Erreurs des Calvinistes touchant
la Justification;" and as he meant to make the doctrine of assurance play an important part in proving that the Calvinists overturn the morality of Jesus Christ, he adduced at length* the
evidence that Calvinists teach that "every believer is assured
with the certainty of divine faith of his own justification and
salvation;" and† he gives "a refutation of a professor of Sedan,
who had abandoned the common sentiments of his sect, concerning the certainty of divine faith, which they think that every
believer has of his justification and salvation." Arnauld's evidence in support of the ascription of this opinion to Protestants is
derived chiefly from the writers of the sixteenth century, and ter-
minates with the Synod of Dort, in 1618, which, he alleges,
sanctioned it; and as Le Blanc in his Theses had not produced
any authority, Arnauld, in refuting him, just referred to the evidence he had already adduced. In 1674, Le Blanc published
"Theses Theologicæ de fidei justificantis natura et essentia, in
quibus variæ Protestantium sententiæ referuntur et expenduntur,
et breviter refelluntur quæ super eâ re quidam liber recens Scrip-
tori harum Thesium imputat." These Theses as well as the
former ones were afterwards embodied in his great work commonly called "Theses Sedanenses," of which the third edition
was published at London in 1683. In these Theses concerning
the nature and essence of justifying faith, he goes very fully into
the whole subject, examines the authorities bearing upon it, and
defends himself from the charges which Arnauld, in his "Renversement," had brought against him, of abandoning the common
views of Protestants, and of concealing and misrepresenting their

---

* Liv. ix. c. iii. and iv.   † Liv. x. c. iv.

true doctrines. Le Blanc, of course, did not deny that there had been many eminent Protestant divines who taught that personal assurance was necessarily included in saving faith. But he contended and proved, that from the time of the Reformation downwards, there had always been some eminent Protestant writers who had taken a broader and more correct view of the nature of saving faith and of the relation between it and assurance,—that, in recent times, the number of divines who held this view had been progressively increasing,—that, nearly thirty years before this, it had obtained a great triumph, by being distinctly set forth in the Westminster Confession, whose sentiments upon this point had been generally approved of by Protestant writers; and that, on all these grounds, Arnauld and the papists were acting unwarrantably in asserting that the opposite view was that which had always been and still was, held by Protestants. He claims in support of his views the concurrence of Zanchius, Peter Martyr, Musculus, Perkins, Bishop Davenant, and the other English divines who attended the Synod of Dort, Ames, Du Moulin, Walæus, Wittichius, Mestrezat, etc. He expresses his concurrence in the statements of the Westminster Confession of Faith, and repeatedly refers to it* in disproof of the allegation of the Romanists, that opposite views had up till that time been generally maintained among Protestants. Le Blanc admitted that, in the earlier period, views different from his and from those of the Westminster Confession, were more generally prevalent; but he contended that, in later times, matters had changed, and the balance had turned to the other side. He, of course, did not deny that there had been a variation here in the history of Protestant doctrine, though he did not think the change which had been brought about was one of great intrinsic importance, and maintained that, from the beginning, there had been some Protestants who held the views which had ultimately gained the ascendency.

This elaborate dissertation of Le Blanc was not only approved of in general by Protestant divines, but it convinced an eminent Romish theologian of that period, Le Fevre, a doctor of theology of the Faculty of Paris, that Arnauld had misrepresented Protestants, in ascribing to them generally the doctrine of assurance. He

---

* Pp. 211, 216, 221, 222, 229.

expressed this opinion in a work written against Protestantism; and this again called forth the redoubtable Jansenist, who published, in 1682, "Le Calvinisme Convaincu de nouveau de Dogmes Impies contre ce qu'en on ecrit, M. Le Fevre, etc., et M. Le Blanc," etc. In this work Arnauld went over the ground again without throwing much additional light upon it, or shaking any of Le Blanc's main positions.

In the meantime a new combatant had entered the field. This was the famous Peter Jurieu, a man of singular talents and activity, who had formerly been professor at Sedan. In 1675, he published his " Apologie pour la Morale des Reformés, ou Defense de leur doctrine touchant la Justification, la perseverance des vrais saints, et la certitude que chaque fidéle peut et doit avoir de son salut," in reply to Arnauld's " Renversement." This work Claude, the most distinguished defender of Protestantism in France, pronounced to be "one of the finest books that had appeared since the Reformation." The first two books of it treat of justification and perseverance, and the third and last of certitude or assurance. He takes very much the same ground as Le Blanc, denying that Arnauld was entitled to charge upon Protestants in general the doctrine that assurance is of the essence of faith, though admitting that this doctrine was extensively taught among them in the sixteenth century. He adduces a portion of the evidence of this, referring to Le Blanc's Theses for additional testimonies, and shows very ably and ingeniously, that neither the earlier nor the later doctrine was chargeable with the odious consequences which Arnauld had laboured to fasten upon them. He takes some pains to bring out the difference between the belief men have in articles of faith, and the assurance they have of their own forgiveness, and to show that men might doubt about their salvation without ceasing to be true believers. He exposes very ably and conclusively the futility of the attempt of Arnauld to draw an argument in favour of popery from the concessions made by Le Blanc and others, as to the variations in the doctrine of Protestants, and even an approximation again in some minor doctrinal matters to the Church of Rome; and points out the folly of making so much ado about differences of so little intrinsic importance as those which had been exhibited, or might still subsist, among Protestants on the subject of assurance.

Le Blanc and Jurieu were both men of very fine talents and

of extensive learning. Both have rendered important services to the cause of truth, and both have also done it some injury. Le Blanc had a great desire to reconcile the differences of contending sects and parties, and laboured to show that the points of difference among them, when calmly and deliberately examined, were not of great importance, and resolved many of them into mere logomachies. He applied this principle to some of the topics controverted between Protestants and Papists, and not merely to topics so unimportant, comparatively, as assurance, but even to some branches of the great doctrine of justification,—a circumstance of which Nicole has skilfully availed himself in his work entitled, " Prejugés Legitimes contre les Calvinistes." As Le Blanc brought extensive theological learning, and a singularly ingenious and discriminating mind, to bear upon this subject, his " Theses Sedanenses" must be regarded as a dangerous book for the young student of theology, who might be in danger of being misled by it into an under-estimate of the importance of having clear views and definite convictions upon many topics usually discussed in polemic divinity ; while it is certainly a work of the very highest value to the more mature theologian.

Jurieu is probably very much under-estimated by those whose knowledge of him has been derived, not from the perusal of his own writings, but from other sources. His reputation has suffered greatly in consequence of his having quarrelled with Bayle, who, after having formerly praised him and his writings in the highest terms, pilloried him through the whole of his Dictionary, making frequent occasions for assaulting him. Jurieu had some qualities which laid him open to such assaults. With great ability and penetration, and great mental energy and activity, he had a rashness and recklessness about him that often led him into scrapes, and afford many a handle to his enemies,—to personal enemies, as Bayle,—or to opponents in controversy, as Bossuet. He threw himself with such eagerness into every one of the many controversies in which he engaged, that he seemed for the time to see everything through that medium, appeared to contend for victory quite as much as for truth, and was ever anxious to turn every thing to the account of the present controversial occasion. All this produced sometimes a carelessness and rashness both in the statement of facts and in the employment of arguments, which his friends could not defend, and which his enemies skilfully improved. This was just the kind of man whom Bayle was peculiarly qualified to expose; and he has done his best to turn his opportunities to good account. But all who are acquainted with Jurieu's works, know that he was a man of very fine powers, that he has rendered very valuable services to truth in the discussion of some important questions, and has inflicted some deadly wounds even upon such opponents as Bossuet, Arnauld, and Nicole. Though his reputation has been damaged by Bayle's Dictionary, yet the mischief has been in some measure repaired by a very full, elaborate, and interesting life, in which justice is done him, in Chauffepie's Supplement to Bayle.*

Arnauld, Le Blanc, and Jurieu, are all first-class names in theological literature. Their labours ought to have been known to a man of Sir William's pretensions, and yet we have seen that he has asserted, that a topic which formed a subject of formal and lengthened controversy between them, was unnoticed and unknown until it was " signalised" by himself. We could easily prove that this variation has been " signalised" by many theologians. But it is unnecessary to dwell upon this point. We shall quote one specimen, as it embodies at the same time a good summary of the chief reasons that tended to produce the change. It is taken from a common work of an eminent divine, published in the latter part of the seventeenth century, " Marckii Compendium Theologiæ." †

" Non diffitendum interim, de hac ipsâ fiduciali applicatione diversum sentire quoque nostros. Dum *antiquiores* juxta catachesim nostram faciunt hunc Actum fidei essentialem, ad justificationem et salutem necessarium, sed non absque antecedenti amplexu et connexa resipiscentia concipiendum; *Recentiores* vero plures volunt potius esse eam fidei ipsius et justificationis consequens, quod abesse possit, fide et salute manente, 1. Tum ob multorum verè Christum apprehendentium perpetuas dubitationes ; 2. Tum ad vitandas magis Pontificiorum, Arminianorum, et schismaticorum strophas, qui vel homines ad securitatem hoc fidei actu duci, vel obligari ad falsum credendum cum remissio fidem sequatur, vel prò omnibus juxta hoc officium credendi mortuum esse Christum, clamant ; 3. Tum denique, quod hæc fiducia magis Dei beneficium speciale paucioribus proprium, quam officium commune sit."

We should now proceed to the more formal consideration of the leading position which, as we have seen, forms the substance of Sir William's first three " curious contrasts,"—viz., that the whole of the Reformed churches have not only abandoned the

* Vol. iii.   † C. xxii. sec. 23.

doctrine of assurance, the fundamental doctrine of the Reformation, but have all adopted the popish doctrine which was taught by the Council of Trent, when it condemned the doctrine of the Reformers. But we are prevented from going so fully into the discussion of this position as we would have liked to have done, and had collected materials for doing. We have now only space for a few hints.

Sir William calls the doctrine of assurance—that is, of course, the doctrine that assurance of personal salvation is necessarily included in saving faith—the "fundamental principle of all the churches of the Reformation," "the common and differential," "the primary and peculiar," doctrine of the Reformation. Some of the Reformers made strong and exaggerated statements about the importance of their peculiar opinions upon this point; and Nicole, and other old popish controversialists, in dealing, as with a known and familiar thing, with that variation, which was unknown to all theologians until Sir William "signalised" it, have endeavoured to show that a change upon a topic so important should have led men to return to the Church of Rome. Yet neither Reformers nor Romanists, even in the heat of controversy, have ever put forth such extravagant exaggerations upon this point as those we have quoted from Sir William. To represent the doctrine of assurance as "the fundamental principle of all the churches of the Reformation," carries absurdity upon the face of it. From the very nature of the case, no doctrine upon such a subject could be the fundamental principle of the Reformed churches. If the Reformers had been contented, as they should have been, with asserting the general position that believers can and should be assured of their own salvation, and if the Romanists had ventured to meet this general position with a direct and unqualified negative, even in that case, no soundminded man, whatever he might have been tempted to say in the heat of controversy, could have deliberately regarded this difference as fundamental. But while this was really and practically the controversy between them, yet, as we have explained, the formal or technical ground of contention was reduced within still narrower limits,—the papists professing to deny the doctrine of their opponents only with this explanation, that by assurance they meant the infallible certainty of divine faith, by which men believed the great doctrines of religion; and many of the Reformers, injudiciously and incautiously accepting this explanation, and bringing forward the notion that personal assurance is necessarily included in saving faith, as an argument in support of it. The controversy thus turned in form upon the kind or measure of the certainty attaching to men's convictions on the subject of their own state and prospects, and the grounds on which the actual certainty contended for might be established. It is impossible that any particular doctrine upon such points as these could "have been constituted into the fundamental principle of all the churches of the Reformation;" and, therefore, Sir William's position might be safely and reasonably rejected, even by those who have no great knowledge of these matters.

Sir William plainly asserts, that a precise and definite doctrine upon this subject was, in opposition to the Reformers, laid down by the Council of Trent, and that this popish doctrine has now been adopted by all the Protestant churches. But this notion, though not altogether destitute of an apparent plausibility, has no real foundation in truth. It is no doubt true that in so far as there has been a deviation from the views generally held by the Reformers, it has proceeded in a direction which tends to diminish the differences between Protestants and papists. But, indeed, it can scarcely be said with truth, that either the Reformed Churches or the Church of Rome were formally and officially committed to any very definite doctrine upon this subject. There is nothing, as we have seen, precise and definite upon this topic in the Confessions of the Reformed churches. There is nothing so definite in any of the Calvinistic Confessions of the sixteenth century, in favour of assurance being of the essence of saving faith, as there is in the Westminster Confession on the other side. With respect to the deliverances of the Council of Trent upon this subject, we have to remark, 1st, That they condemned several positions which had not been laid down by the Reformed churches, but merely put forth by individual Reformers, and which Protestants, both at the time and since, have thought untenable and exaggerated; 2d. That a difference of opinion existed in the council itself, and that this prevented their giving any very definite, positive deliverance. Catharinus, one of the most eminent divines of that period, maintained in the council views upon the subject of assurance substantially the same as those held by the generality of the Reformers; he continued to hold these views; and after all the

deliverances of the council had been passed, he maintained that
none of his positions had been condemned, and that he was still at
liberty to profess them.   Indeed, while the whole tone and spirit
of the deliverances of the council upon this subject is adverse to
the views of the Reformers, its chief formal deliverance is just this,
"Nullus scire valet certitudine fidei, *cui non potest subesse falsum,*
se gratiam Dei esse consecutum;"* where the matter is thrown
back very much upon the point, that the certainty claimed is the
certainty of faith, and where some additional materials for metaphysical speculation are provided, by the clause we have put in
italics.

The view we have given of these points, in their bearing upon
the state of the question, is fully confirmed by what we find in
Cardinal Bellarmine when treating of this topic.†   After admitting
the existence of different opinions on the subject in the Council
of Trent and in the Church of Rome, he gives this as the doctrine
held by the great body of Romish theologians in opposition to the
errors both of Protestants and Romanists, " Non posse homines
in hac vitâ habere certitudinem fidei de suâ justitiâ, iis exceptis
quibus Deus speciali revelatione hoc indicare dignatur ; " and in
giving more formally the state of the question, he puts it in this
way, "Utrum debeat aut possit aliquis sine speciali revelatione,
certus esse *certitudine fidei divinae, cui nullo modo potest subesse
falsum,* sibi remissa esse peccata."   Here we see the controversialist
stands intrenched behind the " certitudo fidei divinae cui nullo
modo," etc., and calls upon his opponent to prove that the certitude
or assurance to which he lays claim, is possessed of such qualities,
and is based upon such grounds, as these phrases are understood
to indicate.   But while the great popish controversialist takes
care at first to intrench himself behind these safeguards, he
afterwards brings out somewhat more fully and freely, though
still not without precaution, what he and Romish writers in general
have inculcated upon this point.‡   He lays down and undertakes to prove the four following positions : " 1. Non posse
haberi certitudinem fidei de propriâ justitiâ,"—a denial of the
Protestant "potest ;" 2. "Neminem teneri ad illam habendam
etiamsi forte posset haberi,"—a denial of the Protestant " debet ;"
3. "Non expedire ut ordinarie habeatur ;" 4. "Reipsâ non haberi

---

* Sess. vi. c. ix.   † De Justific. lib. iii., c. ii. et iii.   ‡ C. viii.

nisi a paucis, quibus a Deo specialiter justificatio propria reve-
latur." These positions formed then, and in substance they form
still, the real points of divergence between Protestants and Papists
upon the subject of assurance. *The technicalities of the controversy
are somewhat altered, while its substance remains the same.* The
grand question still is, as it has always been, Is it practicable,
obligatory, and expedient, that believers should be assured of their
justification and salvation? Upon this question the Reformed
churches have always maintained, and still maintain, the affirmative; while the Romanists, for obvious reasons, have always taken
the other side. Modern Protestants, as the result of a more careful,
deliberate, and unembarrassed examination of the subject, than
the Reformers were able to give to it, have become indifferent
about the question, whether this assurance should be called *the
certainty of faith*, or have plainly admitted that this designation
was an improper one; and they have modified also an extreme
view about the precise relation subsisting between assurance and
saving faith,—a view which seems to have been suggested by a
desire to establish the warrantableness of this designation. This
is really the sum and substance of the variation,—of the change
which has taken place.

We are confident that no one who is competently acquainted
with this subject, and who surveys the history of the discussions
regarding it, with calmness and deliberation, can fail to see that
this is the true state of the case. And if this, or anything like
this, be indeed the true state of the case, what an extraordinary
misrepresentation must be the view given of the matter by Sir
William Hamilton! His view is to be exposed and overthrown
by establishing these two positions: 1st, That, from the nature of
the case, no doctrine upon the subject of assurance could have
been the fundamental principle of the Reformers; and, 2d, That
the difference between the Reformers and the generality of modern
Protestant divines is not one of fundamental importance, even
when regarded merely in its relation to this non-fundamental subject, and, of course, sinks into insignificance when viewed in its
relation to the general system of Protestant doctrine.

Sir William seems to have been half conscious of this; and
therefore he makes an attempt, in conclusion, to involve the great
Protestant doctrine of justification in one common ruin with the
comparatively small doctrine of assurance. He represents it as a

consequence of the change which he alleges has taken place in the views of Protestants in regard to assurance, that "the Protestant symbol ('Fides sola justificat,—Faith alone justifies'), though now eviscerated of its real import, and now only manifesting an unimportant difference of expression, is still supposed to mark the discrimination of the two religious denominations. For both agree that the three heavenly virtues must all concur to salvation, and they only differ, whether faith, *as a word*, does or does not involve hope and charity." This would be the most dangerous of all Sir William's misrepresentations, were it not rendered innocuous by its extravagance. Even if the deviation from the views of the Reformers, and the return to popish notions upon the subject of assurance, had been as great as Sir William represents it, this would not have affected the differences between Protestants and Romanists upon anything really involved in the doctrine of justification. Sir William's statement, though applied only to the doctrine that faith alone justifies, seems fitted and intended to convey the impression, that the whole Protestant doctrine of justification has been exploded and abandoned; and, therefore, the first remark we have to make upon it is this,—that there are some important differences between Protestants and Romanists on the subject of justification which are not directly touched even by the position, that faith alone justifies. We refer, of course, to the vitally important questions, 1st, as to the meaning and import, and, 2d, as to the cause, or ground, or foundation, of justification. Even though the doctrine that faith alone justifies were "eviscerated," Protestants might and should maintain their whole controversy with Romanists upon these fundamental points. We remark, in the second place, that all that is important in the Protestant doctrine, as comprehended under the head that faith alone justifies, is untouched by any change that has taken, or could, take place, in regard to assurance. The two main questions usually discussed between Protestants and Romanists *under this head* are these : 1st, Is there anything else in men themselves which stands in the same relation to justification as faith does ?—Protestants answering this question in the negative, and Papists contending that there are six other virtues, as they call them, including, of course, hope and charity, which stand in the very same relation to justification. Protestants admitted that all these virtues do and must exist in justified men, and might thus, in a sense, be said, to use Sir William's phrase, " to concur to salvation;" but they wholly denied that they have any such bearing as faith has upon the justification of a sinner. 2d, In what capacity or respect is it that faith justifies ? Is it as an instrument, or as a condition, or as a meritorious cause ? Surely it is quite plain, that, even if a man had come to believe all that is taught by the Council of Trent upon the subject of assurance, he might still, without any inconsistency, maintain all the doctrines of the Reformers upon these important points.

Sir William adverts to the fact, that the deviation from the views of the Reformers upon the subject of assurance, which he represents as an abandonment of " the fundamental principle of all the Reformed churches," is embodied in the Westminster Confession; and yet there can be no doubt that the whole doctrine of the Reformers upon the subject of justification is set forth with most admirable fulness and precision in the 11th chapter of that document, while no ingenuity, however great, could devise even a plausible pretence for alleging that there is any inconsistency in this.

We have some apprehension that the controversial spirit is rising and swelling in our breast, and therefore we abstain from making any reflections upon the extraordinary inaccuracies which we have considered it our duty to unfold. But we would like to attempt something in the way of expounding and inculcating the great truth taught in Scripture, and set forth in the Westminster Confession, upon the subject of assurance. That it is practicable, obligatory, and expedient, that believers should be assured of their justification and salvation, was, not certainly, " the fundamental principle of all the Reformed churches," but the fundamental principle of the teaching of the Reformed churches *on the subject of assurance.* It is fully and clearly declared in the Westminster Confession. It has been held professedly by the whole body of Calvinistic divines, both before and since the variation which Sir William has signalised. And yet we fear it has at all times been too much neglected, both theoretically and practically, viewed both as declaring a truth and enforcing a duty. We believe that the prevailing practical disregard of the privilege and the duty of having assurance, is, to no inconsiderable extent, at once the cause and the effect of the low state of vital religion amongst us—one main reason why there is so little of real communion with God as our reconciled Father, and so little of real, hearty devotedness to His cause and service. Some sense of the sin and danger of neglecting this subject occasionally arises in men's minds, and is, from time to time, pressed upon the notice of the church, but in many cases such attempts have only led to controversial discussions, and have failed in producing any beneficial practical results. It is not easy to keep the exact high road of truth ; and men, filled with some one important idea or object, are very apt to run into exaggerations and extremes. Upon no subject has this been more conspicuously the case than on that of assurance ; partly, perhaps, because of the influence of Luther, Calvin, and their associates. It has happened repeatedly in the history of the church, that pious and zealous men, impressed with the importance of getting a larger share of attention to the subject of assurance, have been led into the adoption of untenable and erroneous positions concerning it. Then the champions of orthodoxy have buckled on their armour, and have demonstrated by irrefragable logic, that these positions are characterised by, it may be, confusion, inconsistency, and error ; and then men, satisfied upon this point, settle down again upon their lees, and think no more of the importance of coming to a decisive adjustment upon the question as to what is their present relation to God, and what are their future prospects. This is the abuse, not the use of controversy. The uses of theological controversy are, to expose error, and to produce and diffuse clear and correct opinions upon all points of doctrine. It is the church's imperative duty to aim at these objects, and controversy seems to be as indispensable with a view to the second as to the first of them. But it is an evil and an abuse, when the exposure of error is made to serve as a *substitute* for the realization and application of what is admitted to be true. This has repeatedly, in the history of the church, taken place in regard to the subject of assurance ; and this result, again, has, we are persuaded, been productive of injurious consequences to the interests of true religion, and tended to keep the church at a low point in the scale of devotedness and efficiency.

MELANCTHON

AND THE

THEOLOGY OF THE CHURCH OF ENGLAND.*

———◆———

THESE are two great works, of permanent value, and must be regarded as most important accessions to the theological literature of the present age. They are, indeed, almost wholly republications of books which have been in existence for nearly three centuries. But many of the books of which they are composed were so scarce as to be practically inaccessible, and they are now brought within the reach of all, and provided fully with every necessary literary apparatus. Bretschneider of Gotha started the idea of editing and publishing a complete Corpus Reformatorum, and began with putting forth, in 1834, the first volume of the whole writings of Melancthon. The work proceeded very slowly, one volume only being usually published annually. Bretschneider died during its progress, and the work has very recently been brought to a close under the superintendence of Bindseil, who is professor of philosophy and librarian at Halle. The last volume, the twenty-eighth, was just ready in time to admit of its being deposited in the foundation-stone of the pedestal of a brazen statute of Melancthon, erected at Wittemberg, on the 19th of April last, the tricentenary anniversary of his death. We do not know whether the works of any more of the Reformers are to be brought out in the same style,

* *British and Foreign Evangelical Review*, Jan. 1861.
PHILIPPI MELANTHONIS OPERA QUÆ SUPERSUNT OMNIA. 1834-1860.

THE WORKS OF THE PARKER SOCIETY. 1841-1855.

and with similar completeness and apparatus. It would certainly be an inestimable service to theological literature to produce such an edition of the whole works of the other leading Reformers. But the length of time that has been occupied with the publication of Melancthon is somewhat discouraging. It is a great boon, however, to have given us such an edition of the whole works of the "Preceptor of Germany."

The Parker Society was instituted in 1840, "for the publication of the works of the fathers and early writers of the Reformed English Church;" and in the course of fourteen years gave to the world fifty-five volumes of most interesting and valuable matter, including a most important collection of Letters not before published, which had been written by the English Reformers to their continental correspondents, and have been preserved in different libraries, but especially in that of Zurich. The Parker Society was instituted, and its proceedings were conducted, under the influence of decidedly anti-Tractarian views. It was intended to bring out the predominance of the doctrinal and evangelical element, as opposed to the sacramental, the hierarchic, and the ritualistic, among the founders of the Church of England,—the thoroughly anti-popish character of the whole position they assumed,—their full sympathy in spirit and feeling, and their substantial identity in opinion, with the continental Reformers; in short, to make it palpable that the Church of England, as settled in the time of Edward and Elizabeth, was very different, in the most important respects, from what it was made by Charles and Laud, and from what the Tractarians have again attempted to make it. The works of the Parker Society contain a great storehouse of matter of the highest value and importance, viewed both historically and theologically. As a whole, they thoroughly establish the true historical position of the Church of England, as settled by its fathers and founders; and, at the same time, furnish materials amply sufficient to prove, that the great leading anti-Popish, anti-Tractarian, evangelical features of its constitution, in so far as they agreed with those of the continental Reformed churches, are truly scriptural and primitive.

A similar work was attempted, and to a considerable extent executed, in the early part of this century, by the Rev. Leigh Richmond, whose pastoral labours and popular writings were so largely blessed. When it was attempted to put down the piety and orthodoxy that grew up so remarkably in the Church of England, in the end of the last and the beginning of the present century, by the allegation, that those who held evangelical and Calvinistic views might indeed be Methodists and Dissenters, but could not be regarded as true Churchmen, it was thought proper to bring out the evidence, that the fathers and founders of the Church of England,—the great body of the most influential divines of that church during the reigns of Edward and Elizabeth,—not only held what are commonly reckoned evangelical views concerning the doctrines of grace, but were chiefly decided, though moderate, Calvinists. With this view Mr Richmond undertook, with the assistance of some friends, to edit a republication of "The Fathers of the English Church." This work was published in portions from 1807 to 1812, it was completed in eight volumes, and exerted an extensive and wholesome influence. It is, of course, greatly inferior in extent and completeness, and in its literary apparatus, to the works of the Parker Society. But there is one point in which it has the advantage of its successor, viz., in going back to the men who suffered for their Protestanism in the reign of Henry VIII. The Parker Society restricted itself, with the exception of Tyndale, to works published after the accession of Edward, whereas Richmond's "Fathers of the English Church" gives us the works of Frith, Barnes, Lancelot Ridley, and others, who were confessors or martyrs under Henry, who are on every account deserving of the highest respect and esteem, and who have left behind them unequivocal evidence that they had embraced the whole substance of the theological views of Augustine and Calvin.

The Parker Society, by its invaluable series of publications, may be said to have finally established beyond the possibility of answer, the true theological views and position of the great body of the fathers and founders of the Church of England; to have proved conclusively, that nearly all the Anglican Protestant divines who flourished during the reign of Edward and Elizabeth were, like the Reformers of the continent, Calvinistic in their doctrinal views, and that they did not reckon of much importance, or defend confidently and on high grounds, the points on which the Church of England differed, as to government and worship, from the continental churches. Men who have been trained up in the denial of these positions may continue to adhere to their old prejudices;

but we scarcely think it possible that another generation can grow up in the disbelief of them, unless great care be taken to shut out everything like intelligent, independent, and candid investigation.

In the discussions which have taken place in regard to the theological views that prevailed among the founders of the Church of England, and might, therefore, be supposed to be embodied in her public symbols, Melancthon has usually had much prominence assigned to him, and has been turned to great account, especially by those who were anxious to disprove the opinion upon this subject which we have represented as now fully established. He has been employed, as a sort of medium of probation, for showing that the founders of the Church of England were not Calvinists. It has been strenuously contended, that the men who prepared and established the Anglican symbols had adopted the theological views of Melancthon, and that his views were opposed to those of Calvin and the other Reformers. It is in this way that the republication of Melancthon's works, and the series of works by the Parker Society, are historically connected with each other; so that we must take them both into account in seeking to form a right estimate of the original theology of the Church of England, and especially of its accordance with that of the generality of the Reformers. Before attempting some explanation of this matter, it may be proper to point out somewhat fully the position, influence, and tendencies of Melancthon, in a theological point of view.

For nearly the whole of Luther's public life, Melancthon, who was one of his colleagues in the University of Wittemberg, was closely and intimately associated with him in all his labours, and undoubtedly rendered important services to the cause of the Reformation and the interests of Protestant truth. It would be easy enough to point out how much benefit resulted to the Church, from the influence upon each other and upon their common cause, of these two men, acting together with the utmost harmony during a long period, though so strikingly different from each other both in talents and character, both in gifts and graces. But we cannot dwell upon this. Melancthon's actions and writings do not afford nearly such abundant materials as Luther's do, that furnish a handle to his enemies to depreciate his character; though his friends, that is, the friends of the Reformation, have been perhaps more perplexed as to the way in which they ought to estimate and represent it. In many respects he was a perfect contrast to

Luther. He had none of Luther's vehemence and impetuosity of temperament, none of his presumption and self-confidence. He had less, not only than Luther, but than the generality of men, of irritability and pugnacity; and on all these accounts he both incurred less personal enmity, and has left scarcely any materials in the way of violent invective, intemperate language, rash and exaggerated statements, to be collected by his enemies, and paraded to the injury of his character. There is scarcely anything that gives so much advantage to a man's enemies as the use of intemperate language, or that affords more ready and more plausible materials for exciting a prejudice against him. And as Melancthon did not indulge in this practice, his reputation has not been exposed to the same rude assaults which have been so often directed against Luther's.

A recent popish publication says that all the Reformers, "with *perhaps* the exception of Melancthon, were coarse hypocrites," while the fact is, that there are much more plausible grounds for charging Melancthon with hypocrisy than any one of them,—if by that be meant keeping back his real opinions, and acting as if they were different from what they were.

The character of Melancthon is one which it is indeed very difficult to describe with fairness and accuracy; and, with the materials we possess, it would be an easy matter for an ingenious person to draw two different sketches of him, which might represent him in very different lights, and which yet might both possess not only plausibility, but a considerable portion of truth. Bossuet has devoted the 5th book of his "History of the Variations" to Melancthon, and has exerted his great skill and ingenuity in exaggerating and aggravating all his weaknesses and infirmities, in putting the worst construction upon all his shortcomings in word and deed, and thus producing the most unfavourable impression of his character and motives; and the various features which he has introduced into the picture, can be all supported by a certain amount of plausible evidence. On the other hand, Scott, in his very valuable continuation of "Milner,"* gives his general opinion of Melancthon in the following words :—"On the whole, after reading nearly two thousand of his letters and numerous others of his papers and writings, I confess that I cannot but regard him as one of the

* Vol. ii. p. 150.

loveliest specimens of the grace of God ever exhibited in our fallen
nature." And though this may surely be regarded as somewhat
of an exaggerated statement, yet we have no doubt that Scott has
given such explanations of what seems at first sight most objectionable in Melancthon's public conduct, especially in regard to
the Interim, and has produced such abundant and satisfactory
materials in proof of his personal excellence, as to afford conclusive evidence to any person of candour and impartiality, that he
was not only a man of genuine piety and decided Christian principle, but that he was eminently distinguished by the unusual degree in which he possessed and exhibited some, though certainly
not all, of the graces of the Christian character.

But our object is not to settle what Melancthon's character
was, or to describe it and show it forth. It is rather to indicate
some of the lessons which a survey of his character and history
may be fitted to suggest to students of theology and to ministers
of the gospel. And this, were it to be done at length and in detail,
would be a task of considerable difficulty. It brings us at once
into contact with what is by far the most serious and important
difficulty, in surveying the history of the church and of theological
discussions, viz., hitting the right medium in judging of men and
actions, between bigotry on the one hand, and latitudinarianism on
the other; between sanctioning, on the one side, a contentious and
pugnacious spirit, leading men unnecessarily to disturb the peace
of the church by fighting for points which are unimportant in
themselves, which divide the friends of Christ's cause, and which
there may be no very obvious and urgent call to contend for in
existing circumstances; and sanctioning, on the other, the selfish
and cowardly disposition, combined with an inadequate sense of
the claims of truth, which so often leads men to decline contending
when contending is a duty even at all hazards, under pretence that
the matters in dispute are unimportant. Both tendencies have
been very fully exhibited in the history of the church, and in their
practical operation have been fraught with the greatest mischief.

The tendency to latitudinarian indifference is usually exhibited
when religion is in a low or declining condition. The tendency
to unnecessary contention about matters unimportant in themselves, or not coming home to our circumstances, and not requiring
at the time to be contended for, is usually a symptom of a somewhat more healthy condition of things—a condition in which Satan

scarcely ventures to attempt, in the first instance, to seduce men into latitudinarian indifference to truth, but seeks rather to take advantage of their zeal for truth, combined, of course, as it is in all men, with the operation of inferior motives, to involve them in unnecessary contentions about unimportant matters, that waste their strength and energy, that lead the love of many to wax cold; and thus tend to bring on that low and declining state of religion in which the opposite policy of tempting men into latitudinarian indifference to truth may be tried with success, and tried with the more success, because of the natural reaction from the low-minded and offensive bigotry that preceded it. On this general ground, we are persuaded that unnecessary contentions about matters which do not deserve, or do not at the time require, to be contended for, is the temptation with which good and pious men, occupying public situations, are most apt to be beset, and against which, therefore, they ought most carefully to guard. Latitudinarian indifference to truth does not very easily find its way into the hearts of men, who have any real sense of divine things and of their own responsibility to God, and who are raised by Christian principle above the influence of selfish and worldly motives in their grosser and more palpable forms; whereas there are many worldly and selfish motives, neither so low in themselves, nor so palpable in their ordinary operation, as the love of money, which are very apt to mingle with men's zeal for truth, and tend to involve them in the guilt of being wanton disturbers of the peace, or obstructors of the unity and harmony, of the church. And the instances have always been, and still are, numerous and deplorable, in which a few men, influenced probably in the main by pious and creditable motives, but generally possessing somewhat less than the ordinary share of good sense and sound judgment, and more than the ordinary share of vanity and self-conceit, by taking up and fighting some point, perhaps unimportant in itself, or not lying within the sphere of their responsibility, have gained for themselves some notoriety, and have succeeded in doing a good deal of mischief.

These reflections, of course, have suggested themselves rather in the way of contrast with those which the case of Melancthon is more directly and immediately fitted to call forth. Melancthon unquestionably exhibited the opposite, or latitudinarian, extreme of compromising or sacrificing the claims of truth; and it is as a warning against this danger, that his example ought to be chiefly and most directly applied.   But we have thought it proper to make these observations, that it might not be supposed that the danger of imbibing his spirit, and of following his example, is the only one against which men are called upon to guard, or that there is no risk of good men being tempted to engage in unnecessary contention, or in wanton disturbance of the peace and harmony of the church.   The great error and sin of Melancthon was, that in order to put an end to contention, and to promote peace and union, he was tempted, upon a variety of occasions, to do or to give his consent to what plainly amounted to a compromise or sacrifice of scriptural doctrine,—to a sinking or abandoning of a testimony which he was called upon to bear for God's truth.   This appeared chiefly in the form of his being willing to slur over important truths in vague and general expressions, which might be adopted by different parties who were not really agreed ; and this not for the purpose of ascertaining how far parties who confessedly differed, and who still meant to keep up a distinct testimony upon the points in which they differed, agreed with each other,—for this, in certain circumstances, might be both lawful and expedient, nay, even obligatory,—but with the express and avowed object of the parties uniting together upon the footing of abandoning any other public testimony for truth than the very vague and general one in which they might have come to agree.   This, of course, was the object aimed at in all the conferences and negotiations which he had with the Romanists, and in all the discussions which took place with regard to the Interim.   And this is a course that is generally full of peril and beset with temptation—temptation to be unfaithful to the truth to which men have been enabled to attain, and which it is still incumbent upon them to hold fast and to set forth.

No one, indeed, would deny, as an abstract truth, that individuals and churches may have been led in providence to assert and to embody, in their public profession, truths which, though it was *at the time* a duty to contend for them because they were openly impugned, are yet not of so much intrinsic importance as to authorise their being made permanently grounds of division and separation ; and that, therefore, it is an open question for individuals and churches to consider occasionally, as they may seem called in providence, whether the maintenance of some particular doctrine, as a part of their public profession, should continue to prevent their union with others with whom, on other points, they are agreed. But though it would be manifestly absurd to deny this as a general position, its practical application is attended with great difficulty, and requires much care and caution, much prudence and circumspection.   The practical question in such cases will usually turn mainly upon the point, whether the dropping a truth from a public profession, or wrapping it up in more vague and general terms, really amount, in the circumstances, to a virtual denial of it, or involve, in any way, a dereliction of the duty which men owe to it.   And when the question is brought to this point, there are usually strong temptations, covered over with plausible pretences, which are likely to lead men to compromise truths which they ought to have maintained.

Melancthon, probably, would never have been prevailed upon to renounce or deny, in words, any of the doctrines of the Augsburg Confession, but he was tempted, again and again, to do what, in all fair and honest construction, amounted to a virtual renunciation or denial of them, though, no doubt, he did not regard it in that light.   And, indeed, the great lesson which his conduct is fitted to impress upon us is this, that in certain combinations of circumstances, there is great danger that even good men may be tempted, from a desire of peace and unity, to compromise the truth of God which had been committed to them, and that against this danger, and everything that might lead to it, we are required most carefully to guard.   There can be no doubt that an unscriptural longing for peace and unity—for there is such a thing, springing, of course, not from pure Christian love, but from the infusion of some carnal and worldly motives and influences, or from mere natural temperament—has, on a variety of occasions, led to corruption and compromise of God's truth, on the part both of individuals and churches.   And we are thus reminded that, in so far as concerns the discharge of the duty which we owe to God's truth, we are surrounded with dangers upon the right hand and the left, and that we have much need to examine carefully the motives by which we may be influenced in these matters, and to seek and depend upon divine guidance and direction—practising, indeed, because of the abounding difficulties of the subject, much forbearance in judging of others, and exercising much rigour in judging of ourselves.

The grievous shortcomings of Melancthon in this matter, his being so often led into what amounted to a virtual betrayal or

compromise of truth, have been usually ascribed to the timidity of
his disposition. But this is to be taken with some explanation.
There is no reason to believe that Melancthon dreaded any temporal consequences to himself, or that he was influenced by a regard to any selfish or worldly considerations in the gross and open
form in which they usually present themselves to men's minds—
in other words, by anything really inconsistent with moral integrity. He was afraid of the evils of contention, and he was afraid
of injuring the cause which he loved; and these motives, good
in themselves, but operating with unreasonable and undue force,
and leading to an inadequate sense of the claims of divine truth,
and of the responsibility connected with its full and honest
maintenance, and tending to exclude a due measure of reliance
upon God's providence and promises, led him into those compro-
mises by which he grievously injured truth and damaged his own
reputation. In this way he has become useful to the church,
partly, at least, by exhibiting to future generations a striking
warning, that even good men, who are raised above the influence
of fear and selfishness in their gross and palpable forms, may yet,
through certain weaknesses and infirmities, be led to do much
injury to the cause which they sincerely desire, and would be willing at all merely personal sacrifices, to promote.

Luther has given a most interesting testimony to Melancthon's
superiority to fear and worldliness, in all matters that concerned
himself personally, while he thought him unnecessarily and weakly
anxious about the public cause; and we have also a similar testimony from Calvin, in a letter addressed to Melancthon himself,
while faithfully expostulating with him about his conduct in the
adiaphoristic controversy—a letter which is most honourable to
its author, while it does ample justice to him to whom it was addressed. "Though I am confidently persuaded you never were
driven by the fear of death to turn aside a hairbreadth from the
line of duty, yet it is possible your mind may be open to the influence of fear of a different description. I know how you shrink
from the charge of a repulsive rigidity and stiffness. But remember the servant of Christ must make light when duty requires it
of his reputation, as well as his life. Not that I am so little
acquainted with you, or so unjust to you, as to think you like
vainglorious and ambitious men, dependent upon the breath of
popular applause. But I doubt not you are sometimes subject to

compunctious visitings of this kind:—'Is it the part of a wise and considerate man to divide the church for trifles? Is not peace so precious, that it deserves to be purchased at the price of some inconveniences? What madness is it so tenaciously to hold to every punctilio as to risk the whole substance of the gospel?' I suspect that you were formerly too much affected by such suggestions urged upon you by artful persons, and I candidly state my apprehensions to prevent the divine greatness of soul which I know belongs to you being now restrained from freely exerting itself. I would rather suffer along with you a thousand deaths, than see you survive a surrender of the truth. Perhaps my fears are vain, but you cannot too carefully guard against giving the wicked any occasion of triumph through the faults of your temper." *

Melancthon's weaknesses and infirmities originated partly in his intellectual tendencies and capacities, though even these, it should ever be remembered, are very much under the control of moral causes, and are, therefore, comprehended within the sphere of moral responsibility. He seems to have had considerable difficulty in making up his own opinion, clearly and decidedly, upon great questions, especially those which were fraught with important practical bearings; and this appeared very clearly in the history of his theological sentiments. Melancthon adopted, generally speaking, the theology of Luther; and, perhaps, it may be said that the chief, if not the only real service which he rendered to the cause of sound Christian theology, was,—that he explained and defended the leading tenets of Luther with much dexterity, perspicuity, and elegance, abstaining commonly from those exaggerated and paradoxical statements, by which Luther sometimes gave unnecessary offence and called forth needless prejudice,—and that he thus contributed largely to their reception among the educated and intelligent classes. This was the service for which Melancthon was specially fitted; this was the work which he performed; and, in performing it, he became the instrument of conferring important benefits upon the church, and greatly advancing the cause of scriptural truth. This statement, however, must be restricted in its application to the doctrines which Melancthon continued decidedly and permanently to hold, among those great

---

* Scott, vol. iii. pp. 393-4.

truths which Luther was chiefly instrumental in restoring to the church.   And there *are* some points in Luther's system of theology, in regard to which it is not easy to determine with certainty whether Melancthon continued really to hold them or not.   There is, indeed, good reason to fear that his dubious and uncertain course in regard to some doctrinal points, tended, in the long run, to favour the introduction into the Lutheran Church of a much more lax and unsound system of theology.   He seems to have attained at length to sound and scriptural views on the sacramentarian controversy, and to have abandoned Luther's doctrine of consubstantiation, or the corporal presence of Christ in the Eucharist.   But he never had the courage and manliness, even after Luther's death, to make a public and explicit declaration of his change of sentiment, though Calvin faithfully expostulated with him on the impropriety of his conduct.   Though, however, his opinions upon this point tended to a much closer approximation to the standard of truth, the tendency upon other points of still greater importance seems rather to have been in the opposite direction.

His principal works, of a more strictly theological kind, are the "Apology for the Confession of Augsburg," and the "Loci Communes."   The Apology may be justly regarded as a very valuable and satisfactory vindication of the leading Protestant doctrines, in so far as they occupied a prominent place in Luther's teaching, and had been set forth in the Augsburg Confession, not directly including, however, what are usually reckoned the peculiarities of the Calvinistic system; though Luther certainly held these peculiar doctrines, and there is no good reason to think that he ever abandoned them.   Melancthon, so far as we can judge from his Apology, seems for the time to have been benefited rather than injured by the perilous negotiations in which he was involved at the diet of Augsburg in 1530, and in which he showed such deplorable weakness ; and this work contains no evidence of what has sometimes been alleged, viz., that Luther's controversy with Erasmus led Melancthon to modify some of the views which he had formerly held, but which Luther continued to maintain, as to the natural bondage or servitude of the human will in reference to everything spiritually good.*

---

* Scott is very anxious to make out that the two letters which Melancthon | is alleged to have addressed to the Cardinal Legate Campeggio at the Diet

The first edition of his Loci Communes was published in 1521, when he was only twenty-four years of age. He published a second, greatly enlarged and altered, in 1535; and again a third with considerable, though less important, changes, in 1543; and it is the alterations introduced into these different editions, that have occasioned the chief difficulties and discussions as to the real sentiments of Melancthon upon some doctrinal questions.* In the first edition he had maintained the very highest predestinarian and necessitarian tenets. He there asserted, that " since all things happened necessarily according to the divine predestination, there is no such thing as liberty in our wills;" " that the Scriptures teach that all things happen necessarily;" " they take away liberty from our wills by the necessity of predestination." This was a doctrine which Calvin never taught, and which forms no necessary part of the Calvinistic system, though it has been held by some Calvinistic theologians.   Calvin held, and the Westminster Standards expressly teach, that man, as originally created, had a liberty of will, which fallen man has not; and consequently, he held, that any necessity or bondage which he ascribed to the human will *as it is*, was based, not upon man's mere relation to God as a dependent creature,—not upon God's predestination, or His foreordaining whatsoever comes to pass and His certainly executing His decrees in providence, although He does so,—but upon the entire depravity which has been superinduced upon his nature by the fall.   The high doctrine, which Melancthon originally taught, he seems to have soon abandoned, as it is wholly expunged from the two subsequent editions of the Commonplaces.   But there is good reason to doubt, whether in abandoning this doctrine, which Calvin never held, he did not cast off along with it some principles which are plainly taught in the word of God, and which have been generally held by Calvinistic divines.   Melancthon, indeed, asserted in all the editions of his Commonplaces, and seems, upon the whole, to

of Augsburg, must have been forgeries (vol. i. App. ii. p. 537). But we fear there is no sufficient ground to deny their genuineness, which is admitted by Dr Merle D'Aubigné, vol. iv. p. 258, and by Bretschneider, tom ii. p. 168.

* Scott has given a brief summary of the differences among the various editions of this work, of which the earlier ones have become extremely scarce (vol. ii. c. xii. p. 182-9). A complete collection of the whole materials bearing upon the history of this work, including a reprint of the three different editions entire, and a vast amount of literary information, occupies the whole of the 21st and 22d volumes of the works of Melancthon.

have maintained consistently through life, the doctrine which was held in common by Luther and Calvin, as to the entire depravity of human nature and the utter impotency of the will of man, *as he is*, to any spiritual good; although (for there is scarcely anything about Melancthon in which we are not annoyed with deductions and drawbacks) there are not wanting some expressions in the later editions, which have afforded plausible grounds to those who took the unscriptural side in what was called the Synergistic controversy that disturbed the Lutheran Church chiefly after his death, for alleging,—that he was not wholly opposed to some sort of co-operation or synergism of the human will with the gracious agency of God, even in the *first* movements towards regeneration. Calvin published, in 1543, cotemporaneously with the last edition of Melancthon's Commonplaces, his "Defensio sanæ et orthodoxæ doctrinæ de Servitute et liberatione humani arbitrii," and prefixed to it a dedication to Melancthon, in which he spoke of him in the most friendly and eulogistic terms; and Melancthon, in acknowledging it,[*] says that he agreed with Calvin's views upon these subjects, but still with a qualification, which, with a man of his temperament, so unwilling on some occasions to speak out his mind fully and openly, might cover or conceal differences not immaterial. After giving a brief summary of his opinions upon these subjects, he adds, "et quidem scio hæc cum tuis congruere, sed sunt παχυτερα et ad usum accommodata." We do not estimate the authority of Melancthon so highly as to be very anxious to get his testimony in favour of Calvin's views; but it is only fair to Melancthon himself, to give due weight to a statement of agreement which is creditable to him, especially as nothing has been produced from his works sufficiently explicit to prove, that he ever materially deviated from scriptural truth upon *these* important points.

There *is* reason to fear that he abandoned, or, at least, that he became utterly afraid to state distinctly and explicitly, the doctrine of predestination, or unconditional personal election to eternal life, as taught in Scripture, and held and expounded by Augustine and Calvin. The section upon predestination in the later editions of his Commonplaces, may be regarded, with some plausibility, either as a specimen of great confusion, or of studied

---

* Scott, iii. p. 376.

and careful reticence; but in no *other* light can it be justly represented.   And in *either* case, considering what he had taught upon
this subject in the first edition, there is reason to fear that his
timidity, his tendency to shrink from decided views upon great
and difficult questions involving important practical bearings, had
led him, in his heart, to abandon an important scriptural truth,
though he had not the courage openly and fully to admit and
proclaim the conclusion to which he had come, if, indeed, he *had*
come to any very definite conclusion regarding it.

With respect to the great doctrine of justification by faith
through the imputed righteousness of Christ,—the establishment
of which was the distinguishing service which Luther was honoured to render to the cause of truth and religion,—it is but
justice to Melancthon to say, that in whatever vague, general,
and ambiguous terms he might have been tempted to express it,
in order to promote peace, and effect an adjustment with the
Church of Rome, his own actual sentiments regarding it seem
never to have varied, or to have been turned aside from scriptural
truth.   It was asserted, indeed, by a body of Lutheran theologians,
in 1569, a few years after his death,[*] that on one occasion he had
used this expression, " quod *præcipue* fide justificamur," which was
certainly a deplorable and shameful compromise of the *sola fides*,
for which Luther and he had so long and so strenuously contended;
but then, it is added in the way of palliation, that this was done
"tempore magnæ angustiæ et metus," and that he afterwards
condemned it himself.   His works, however, steadily and consistently maintain the scriptural doctrine of justification, and he
has rendered no unimportant service to the cause of Christian
truth by his defence of this fundamental doctrine of the Reformation.   Bossuet, indeed, after having laboured to prove that Melancthon's opinions upon most points were loose and fluctuating,
held with no firmness and stability, is candid enough to admit,
that there was one point on which he did not vary, and which
formed an impassable barrier between him and the Church of
Rome,—the only thing, indeed, as Bossuet alleges, which fixed him
firmly upon the Protestant side,—and this was the doctrine of justification by imputed righteousness.[†]

---

[*] Weisman Historia Ecclesiastica,   [†] Histoire des Variations, lib. v.
vol. ii. p. 201.   sect. 29, 30.

Whatever, then, may have been Melancthon's personal excellencies as a man and a Christian, and whatever his services to the cause of Protestant truth, we see about him very plain indications of tendencies, which should impress us with a sense of the great danger of imbibing his spirit and following his example, in matters connected with the public interest of God's cause. He had about him weaknesses and infirmities which tended to lead him, first, to adopt erroneous and defective views of divine truth; and second, to fail in doing full justice in the face of dangers and difficulties, even to what he still believed to be true. Our first duty, so far as concerns the public interest of God's cause in the world, is to find out the truth which is sanctioned by His word,—and then to assert, maintain, and defend it, so far as we have any call or opportunity to do so,—guarding with special care against any course of action which might be fairly held to involve, directly or by implication, a renunciation or denial of any part of it. And these are not duties in which the example of Melancthon is fitted to afford us much direct assistance, though it may serve as a beacon to warn us against dangers and temptations that might lead us to come short in the discharge of them. There is much about Melancthon, the influence of which is fitted to add grace and beauty to our Christian profession, to lead us to adorn the doctrine of our God and Saviour, and to commend it to the favourable acceptance of others; but these things, however valuable, are of less intrinsic importance, than the great duty of ascertaining and holding up the whole truth of God, and of contending earnestly for the faith once delivered to the saints.

The question as to the precise views of Melancthon upon some of the theological topics to which we have now referred, has been pretty fully discussed in this country, in connection with the controversy as to the doctrinal sense of the articles of the Church of England, and the opinions of those who framed them. It is very certain that, during the whole of the long reign of Elizabeth,—in many respects the most important and interesting period in the history of the Church of England,—the great body of her divines, and of her ecclesiastical authorities, including every name of eminence to be found in her communion, were Calvinists. It is equally certain that, for the last two centuries, a decided majority of her clergy have been anti-Calvinists, while there has always been a respectable minority who adhered to the theology of Augustine and the Reformers. As the articles have continued unchanged for 300 years, while the theological views that prevailed in the church have varied so much, this has led at different times to a great deal of discussion as to what the articles really mean, or were intended to mean, and as to what subscription to them may be fairly held to imply. Calvinists generally have contended that the natural, obvious sense of the articles is Calvinism,—moderate Calvinism indeed, cautiously and temperately expressed,—that the great body of those who prepared the articles in Edward's time, as well as of those who adopted and established them in the beginning of Elizabeth's reign, with very little change, and exactly as they now stand, were Calvinists,—and that, on all these grounds, Calvinists need have no hesitation in subscribing them. The more timid and charitable Calvinists have been disposed to admit, that there is an opening left for men subscribing the articles who had not embraced the peculiarities of Calvinism; while many profess their inability to conceive how this can be done, without puting the articles to a degree of straining and torture that is unwarrantable and dangerous. The Arminians, of course, labour to show, that there is nothing in the articles to preclude them from subscribing them; and the more intelligent, conscientious, and modest among them, scarcely venture to take higher ground than this,—not presuming to deny the perfect warrantableness of Calvinists entering the ministry of the Church of England, and undertaking all the obligations which this implies. Some of the more reckless among them, as for instance Bishop Tomline, Archdeacon Daubeny, and Archbishop Laurence, have ventured to assert that the articles explicitly contradict the Calvinistic doctrine, and of course should shut out all who adhere to it. But the more moderate Arminians have generally leant rather to the side of merely asking admission for themselves without pretending to exclude their opponents. Bishop Burnet was preeminently qualified to judge on such a question, both in its historical and theological aspects; and he, though himself a decided Arminian, has candidly admitted, that " the 17th article seems to be framed according to St Austin's doctrines," that "it is very probable that those who penned it meant that the decree was absolute;" and that " the Calvinists have less occasion for scruple (in subscribing it than the Arminians) since the article does seem more plainly to favour them."*

The aspects in which this subject obviously presents itself are not such as to reflect much credit upon the Church of England. It is a very awkward and painful thing to see so much controversy going on among themselves, as to what those articles which they have all subscribed really mean, or were intended to mean. Some contend that they teach Calvinism ; others, that they teach Arminianism ; others, that they teach both ; and others again, that they teach neither, but some other scheme of doctrine different from both. Sometimes they denounce one another as dishonest in subscribing the articles in a sense of which they do not fairly admit ; and sometimes they unite in lauding the wisdom and moderation of their church, in leaving an open door for the admission of men of different and opposite opinions. It is quite possible that churches may carry to an unwise and unreasonable extent, the number and minuteness of the doctrinal definitions, which they embody in their symbolical books, and to which they require conformity. But there is no ground whatever to believe that the framers of the English articles were in the least influenced by any such wise and moderate views as have been sometimes ascribed to them ; the articles were expressly and avowedly intended "for avoiding diversities of opinions, and for the establishing of consent touching true religion ;" and a considerable number of them are occupied with topics which are comparatively unimportant in a general summary of Christian doctrine.

The way in which the controversy has been conducted upon the anti-Calvinistic side, has certainly not been creditable to most of those who have taken part in it. In general, those who have denied the Calvinism of the English articles have displayed a low standard, both of knowledge of the subject, and of fair dealing. The study of systematic theology has always been greatly neglected in the Church of England, partly, perhaps, because of the equivocal character of the theology of her articles, and of the earnest desire of many of her clergy to make her theology more equivocal than it is ; and, without a thorough acquaintance with systematic theology, both in its substance and its history, men are very incompetent to discuss the questions, whether the articles are

---

* Exposition of Articles, art. 17, p. 165.

Calvinistic or Arminian, or both, or neither. Such questions cannot of course be intelligently or satisfactorily handled, except by men who thoroughly understand what Calvinism is, and what Arminianism is ; and this cannot be attained without a real familiarity with the works of the ablest men who have discussed these subjects on both sides, and at different periods. A man may be an Arminian though he is not aware of it, and even honestly, though ignorantly, denies it; and this ignorance and confusion as to what Calvinism is, and as to what Arminianism is as opposed to it, are plainly exhibited by the late Mr Stanley Faber, and by Mr E. Harold Browne, the present Norrisian Professor of Divinity at Cambridge. There is, indeed, good reason to believe, that there prevails among the clergy of the Church of England, a great want of intelligent acquaintance even with the *status quæstionis* in the controversy between the Calvinists and the Arminians. We would not hesitate to undertake to prove, that the same charge might be established against almost all who have at any time professed to show that the English articles are not Calvinistic.*
We are not, indeed, inclined to speak with much severity of those who merely plead, that, while they cannot see satisfactory grounds for embracing the peculiar doctrines of Calvinism, they, at the same time, do not see that these doctrines are so plainly and explicitly set forth in the articles, as to make it impossible for them to subscribe them. This ground may be maintained with considerable plausibility, and when maintained without any palpable violations of integrity and propriety, would not exclude its supporters from a fair claim to respect. But we cannot make the same admission in regard to those men who boldly aver that the articles shut out Calvinism, and that they cannot be honestly subscribed by Calvinists.

Before proceeding to make some observations upon the subject

---

* We are glad to be able to shelter ourselves in making these statements, which might seem invidious and presuming, under the high authority of the late Dr M'Crie. In one of the notes to his admirable and delightful work, the " Life of Andrew Melville," he says, " The publications against Calvinism which have lately appeared in England, are in their statement of the question unfair, in their reasoning shallow, and in respect of the knowledge which they display of the history of theological opinions contemptible." (C. x. p. 332, edit. of 1856.) We take the liberty of adopting this statement, and of adding, that it is equally applicable to " the publications against Calvinism which have appeared in England " during the forty years which have intervened since the appearance of Dr M'Crie's work.

of the theology of the Church of England, it may be proper to give some notices of the literature of the question, or of the leading features in the history of the very interesting controversial discussions which have been carried on regarding it.

That during the whole reign of Elizabeth, and the greater part of that of James, Calvinism prevailed almost universally among the men of ability and learning, of station and influence, in the Church of England, and was then generally regarded as being most fully accordant with its authorised symbols, has been incontrovertibly established, by evidence multifarious in kind and superabundant in degree. This is proved by the whole history of the proceedings connected with the Lambeth articles and the cases of Baro and Barret in 1595, the Irish articles in 1615, and the Synod of Dort in 1618–19. The discussion of this topic as a subject of public controversy, seems to have commenced with the proceedings in the case of Dr Richard Montague, one of the leading agents of Archbishop Laud, in introducing Tractarianism and Arminianism. His work entitled "Appello-Cæsarem" was published in 1625. It was intended to defend himself against the charge, founded upon a previous work, of leaning towards Arminianism and Popery; and it attempted to show that the Arminian and semi-Popish views objected to, were not contradicted by anything in the authorised formularies of the church. The House of Commons, which at that time was very theological and very sound in its theology, passed a vote condemning his Appeal, as tending to bring in Popery and Arminianism, in opposition to the religion by law established. But what was of more importance so far as the interests of truth are concerned, the work was formally and elaborately answered by Dr George Carleton, then Bishop of Chichester, who had been a few years before the head of the English delegates sent to the synod of Dort, and had proved himself fully worthy of so honourable a position. Dr Carleton's work was published in 1626, and is entitled "Examination of those things wherein the author of the late Appeal taketh the doctrines of the Pelagians and Arminians to be the doctrines of the Church of England." The work is one of much interest and value, both from its author and the position it occupies in the controversy. It is remarkable, among other things, for the distinct assertion, that there had been, up till that time, no real difference in doctrinal matters between the Conformists and the

Puritans.   Carleton died in 1628, and through Laud's influence Montague was appointed to succeed him in the see of Chichester.

Arminianism continued to advance, and, in 1630, Prynne, the famous lawyer, published his " Anti-Arminianism, or the Church of England's old antithesis to new Arminianism." This is a vast collection of documentary evidence to prove, that from the earliest times, and especially since the commencement of the Reformation in the time of Henry VIII., the Church of England had been decidedly opposed to Arminian views, and had professed the great principles of Augustinian or Calvinistic doctrine. This work gave mortal offence to Laud and his faction, who were now all-powerful, and was understood to be the principal cause of the barbarous punishment which was soon afterwards inflicted upon Prynne, though his Histriomastix was made the pretence for it. It is a remarkable instance of providential retribution, that Prynne became ultimately the chief instrument of accomplishing " Canterbury's Doom," as he called one of his books against Laud, and bringing him to the scaffold. Prynne was a man of great research and industry, as well as thorough integrity. But he had not a well-balanced or discriminating mind. He had a much greater power of swallowing than of digesting. He was in the habit rather of numbering than weighing his proofs and testimonies. His " Anti-Arminianism," therefore, like his other works, contains a prodigious storehouse of materials, in the way of quotations and references, much more than sufficient in the gross to establish his leading position, but requiring some caution and sifting in the particular application of them. He declares that up till the time when he wrote he could mention only five men who had come forward publicly to defend Arminianism. These were Barret and Baro,—whose cases were mixed up with the history of the Lambeth articles, and the proceedings against whom sufficiently proved that, in the last decade of the sixteenth century, the whole learning and influence of the Church of England were Calvinistic,—Thompson, who, he says,* was " a dissolute, ebrious, profane, luxurious, English-Dutchman," and who, in 1614, published a treatise against the perseverance of the saints, which was answered by Dr Robert Abbot, Bishop of Salisbury,—Montague, already men-

---

* P. 260.

tioned, successively Bishop of Chichester and Norwich,—and Dr
Thomas Jackson, a man of a much higher class than any of them.
Prynne's testimonies certainly require to be winnowed, but we
have no doubt that he has produced and indicated materials,
which, taken *in cumulo*, are amply sufficient to prove ten times
over, that during the whole century intervening between the time
when he wrote and the first dawning of the Reformation under
Henry VIII., the prevailing current of opinion with all competent
judges among the clergy of the Church of England was Calvinistic, as opposed to Arminian,—and that the fundamental principles
of Calvinism, though cautiously and temperately expressed, were
embodied, and were intended to be embodied, in the church's
authorised formularies.

The next work in the order of time is the great storehouse of
materials on the Arminian side. It is by Dr Peter Heylin, a wor-
shipper and tool of Laud, whose life he wrote, under the designation of Cyprianus Anglicus. Heylin's work was published in
1659, and is entitled "Historia Quinqu-Articularis, or a Declaration of the Judgment of the Western Churches, and more particularly of the Church of England, in the five controverted points
reproached in these last times by the name of Arminianism." It
contains an elaborate discussion of most of the materials bearing
upon the question, as to the original theology of the Protestant
Church of England. The materials are discussed and applied
with a good deal of ingenuity and boldness, and the work is in
many respects well fitted to make an impression, because of its
author's apparently full knowledge of the subject, and the confidence with which he takes up his positions. Heylin had very
much the same intellectual defects as Prynne, and in addition, we
fear, he laboured under more serious infirmities as a thorough
and unscrupulous partizan. He had read a great deal, but he was
very imperfectly acquainted with theology properly so called, and
Archbishop Usher once said of him that he should be sent to
learn his catechism. He has been convicted of having exhibited
in this and in his other works a great deal of blundering and misrepresentation. So certain and notorious is this, that Archdeacon
Blackburne, in the "Confessional,"* did not hesitate to describe
him as "a man lost to all sense of truth and modesty whenever

---

* P. 153, 2d Edition.

the interests or claims of the church came in question;" and that the late Dr M'Crie, after exposing a strange display of ignorance made by Bishop Coplestone, adds, "a modern writer who could trust Heylin as an authority deserved to fall into such ridiculous blunders."*

This work of Heylin was answered by Henry Hickman, a man of very superior learning and ability, and one of the ministers ejected by the Bartholomew Act of 1662. His reply was published in 1673, and entitled, "Historia Quinqu-Articularis Exarticulata, or Animadversiones on Dr Heylin's Quinquarticular History." This work of Hickman's is a very masterly and effective exposure of Heylin's incompetency, especially in the more theological departments of the argument, and it contains within a short compass a large amount of accurate and important information, embodied in a very terse and vigorous, though unpolished, style. It ought to have deprived Heylin of all respect and influence, and must have done so if it had been read. But it does not seem to have ever attained any considerable circulation, and, in consequence, the great body of the English clergy continued, like Coplestone, to believe Heylin, and to "trust in him as an authority."

The next occasion on which the question of the Calvinism of the English articles was discussed, was when it was brought, somewhat incidentally, into the Arian controversy. In 1721 Dr Waterland published a work entitled, "The Case of Arian Subscription Considered," in answer to the attempt which had been made by Dr Samuel Clarke to show, that those who, like himself, denied the true and proper divinity of the Son, could honestly assent to the formularies of the church. Dr Sykes, who was one of Clarke's leading supporters, and who showed himself ever ready and willing to defend any bad cause that needed support, published a reply to this, called, "The Case of Subscription to the Thirty-nine Articles considered." In this pamphlet he laid down the position, that the articles are, and were intended by their compilers to be, Calvinistic; and that Dr Clarke and his friends could as clearly prove, that Arians could honestly subscribe them, as Dr Waterland and his friends could prove, that Arminians could do so. This was rather galling as an *argumentum ad*

---

* *Life of Melville*, p. 333.

hominem, and Waterland published a "Supplement to the Case of Arian Subscription," in which he attempted to answer this and the other arguments of Sykes, while Sykes rejoined in a Reply to the Supplement. Waterland certainly has not made much of the point raised by Sykes about the Calvinism of the articles; he has done little more than give a brief summary of the materials collected by Heylin; and this was rather low work for a man of Waterland's high and well-merited reputation. Sykes, who was no more a Calvinist than a Trinitarian, has certainly not proved that an Arian subscriber can make out as plausible a case as an Arminian one; but he has proved, and in this he has defeated his antagonist, that the fathers and founders of the Church of England were Calvinists, and intended the articles to be taken in a Calvinistic sense. Waterland, indeed, in discussing this point, gives plain indications of not knowing well what to say, or where to plant his foot. He sets out with boldly averring—"For my own part I think it has been abundantly proved that our articles, liturgy, etc., are not Calvinistical." But after giving a summary of this *abundant* proof, and having had to face the 17th article, he winds up with this very lame and impotent conclusion—"the presumption rather lies against Calvinism;" "I am rather of opinion that the article leans to the anti-Calvinian persuasion."*

This is not very encouraging, but most who have since discussed this subject on the same side, have referred to and commended Waterland's pamphlet, apparently for the purpose of giving their cause the prestige of his well-earned reputation for great ability and learning, and for invaluable services to truth in defending the proper and supreme divinity of our Saviour.

About fifty years after this, a variety of causes led to the renewal of discussions concerning the meaning and object of the English articles, such as, the publication of "Blackburne's Confessional," advocating very loose and unsound views on the general subject of creeds and confessions, but at the same time maintaining, that Sykes had conclusively established against Waterland the Calvinism of the articles,—the application to Parliament in 1772 by many clergymen to be released from the obligations of subscription,—and the expulsion of the "Methodist" students from Oxford. Sir Richard Hill, brother of Rowland, defended the

---

* *Works by Bishop Van Mildert,* vol. ii. pp. 341, 352-3.

expelled students, by showing that their opinions on doctrinal subjects were the same as those of the founders of the Church of England, in a pamphlet entitled, " Pietas Oxoniensis ;" and when Dr Nowell published a reply to this, it called forth, in 1769, from Toplady, then a young man, but of very fine talents and of great promise, a crushing answer, entitled, " The Church of England vindicated from the charge of Arminianism, and the case of Arminian subscription particularly considered." This, he afterwards expanded into a regular treatise, which he published in 1774, in two volumes, entitled, " Historic proof of the Doctrinal Calvinism of the Church of England." This work is highly creditable to his talents and learning, and is perhaps, upon the whole, the most complete and satisfactory book we have, devoted to this subject. He is perfectly conclusive in discussing all the main topics that bear upon the settlement of the question, but he gets rather beyond his depth in dealing with what he calls the Arminianism of the Church of Rome, a subject with which he was evidently acquainted very imperfectly.

The only work of that period, on the other side, which has attained to any standing, or is now known, is Dr Winchester's " Dissertation on the 17th Article," published in 1773, a temperate and sensible work, though not displaying much either of strength or ingenuity in managing the cause. It was republished in 1803, both separately and in the " Churchman's Remembrancer."

We have already had occasion to refer to the revival of the discussion about the historic Calvinism of the Church of England, in the end of the last century and the beginning of the present, in consequence of the great advance which then took place in Christian piety and orthodoxy. In reply to the numerous and virulent attacks then made on the evangelical clergy, Mr Overton published, in 1801, a volume entitled, "The True Churchman Ascertained, or an apology for those of the regular clergy of the Establishment, who are sometimes called Evangelical Ministers." This is an able and elaborate work, and certainly establishes satisfactorily, that those of the evangelical clergy who were moderate Calvinists held the same doctrinal views as the fathers and founders of the Church of England. In 1803, Archdeacon Daubeny, some of whose statements in his previous publications, had been refuted by Overton, produced a bulky reply to the "True Churchman," in an octavo volume of nearly 500 pages, to which he gave a title, framed after a model which was common enough among the older controversialists, but which modern civilisation has exploded. It was called "Vindiciæ Ecclesiæ Anglicanæ, in which some of the false reasonings, incorrect statements, and palpable misrepresentations, in a publication entitled, etc., are pointed out." Overton's "True Churchman" is singularly free from "false reasonings, incorrect statements, and palpable misrepresentations," while Daubeny's Vindiciæ superabounds in these beauties, as was conclusively proved in two works published in 1805, the one entitled, " Candid Examination of Daubeny's Vindiciæ," republished from the *Christian Observer*, and the other by Mr Overton, entitled, "Four Letters to the Editor of the *Christian Observer*."

In 1802, a pamphlet was published, chiefly occasioned by Overton's work, entitled, "The Articles of the Church of England proved not to be Calvinistic," by Dr Kipling, Dean of Peterborough, and Deputy Regius Professor of Divinity in the University of Cambridge. This production has been very highly commended, but it is, we think, a singularly poor affair. Its leading feature is the adduction of statements and quotations, as anti-Calvinistic, which no intelligent Calvinist would hesitate to adopt. As this is really a prominent characteristic of most of the works on the same side, it may be proper to signalise it, by quoting Overton's description of it as exhibited by Kipling, and in contrast with the applause with which his work was received.

" No reasoning can be more futile than that of Dr Kipling upon this subject. It is capable of the fullest demonstration, that, by the same process, the learned Dean might prove the complete anti-Calvinism of Calvin himself. It is a fact, which nothing but the most perfect disingenuity or ignorance of the subject can controvert, that nine-tenths at least of the arguments extracted from our Articles and Liturgy, by which the Dean endeavours to prove the *utter repugnancy* of these forms to the theology of Calvin, may also be extracted from Calvin's own writings. Yet this reasoning of Dr Kipling is continually represented as ' *demonstrative and incontrovertible ;*' as possessing ' *uncommon merit ;*' as ' *invincible,*' and not less clear than ' *mathematical demonstration itself ;*' as having ' *proved to demonstration*' the point he had to establish ; as ' *decisive*' on the question, and such as ought to ' *set it at rest for ever.*' These verdicts, too, the reader will perceive, are pronounced by the professed guardians of truth and religion, by writers who highly extol each other as learned divines !" *

All the expressions here quoted were actually applied to Dr Kipling's production by the reviewers and pamphleteers of the period.

The "Bampton Lecture" for 1804 was preached by Dr Richard Laurence, then Regius Professor of Hebrew in Oxford, and afterwards Archbishop of Cashel, and it is entitled, "An Attempt to illustrate those Articles of the Church of England which the Calvinists improperly consider as Calvinistic." Dr Laurence was a man of superior learning and ability; he has made some valuable contributions to our theological literature; his "Bampton Lecture" contains a great deal of interesting and valuable matter, it has been republished repeatedly—the fourth and last edition having come out in 1853—and it is now justly regarded as the standard work on the Arminian side. On these grounds, it will be needful for us to notice it more fully. At present we merely mention it in its chronological order.

The controversy was renewed by the publication, in 1811, of Bishop Tomline's well-known work, "The Refutation of Calvinism." He had given, in a previous work, "Elements of Christian Theology," the common Arminian interpretation of the Articles; and in the "Refutation" he gives fully the argument against Calvinism, not only from Scripture and the Fathers, but also from the history and formularies of the Church of England. This work was at one time prodigiously commended. Indeed, we have a recollection of having once looked into a book by an Episcopalian clergyman, in which it was extolled as one among the four or five greatest works ("Butler's Analogy" being mentioned as one) the Church of England has produced. The book has long since found its level, and is now regarded as a very mediocre production, displaying considerable diligence in the collection of materials, but an utter want either of ability or of fairness in the application of them. Scott's "Remarks" upon it are a full and conclusive, though, from the plan pursued of following his opponent step by step, a somewhat tedious exposure of the "Refutation;" and they establish the great superiority, in all respects, of the rector over his bishop, of the inmate of the humble parsonage of Aston Sandford over the occupant of the venerable palace of Buckden.

The "Inquiry into the Doctrines of the Reformation, and of the United Church of England and Ireland, respecting the ruin and recovery of Mankind," published in 1814, by the Rev. W. B.

Mathias of Dublin, is a valuable compilation, consisting almost wholly of extracts, and turning to good account, so far as the " United Church" is concerned, the writings of its fathers and founders, which had been made accessible by Leigh Richmond's work formerly referred to.

This brings us down to the present day, when the discussion about the theological views of the founders and the formularies of the Church of England has been renewed, and in a somewhat different aspect, in connection with the controversy about baptismal regeneration. Dr Goode, now Dean of Ripon, to whose great learning and ability as an opponent of Tractarianism, and a defender of evangelical truth, we have repeatedly borne a cordial testimony, published, in 1849, a most valuable and important work on this subject, entitled, " The Doctrine of the Church of England as to the Effects of Baptism in the case of Infants,"—the great general object of which was to show, that those who rejected the Tractarian doctrine of baptismal regeneration, might conscientiously undertake all the obligations connected with the ministry of the church, including, of course, the use of the baptismal service. One leading argument which he employs, in order to establish this general position, is in substance this : No one who embraces the Calvinistic system of theology can consistently believe the high church doctrine of baptismal regeneration; the great body of the fathers and founders of the Church of England, the men who prepared her formularies, her articles and liturgy, in the reign of Edward, and established them, with scarcely any change and almost precisely as we now have them, in the reign of Elizabeth, were Calvinists; and, consequently, there can be no inconsistency between a reception of these formularies and a rejection of the Tractarian doctrine of baptismal regeneration.

The different positions which go to make up this argument, Dr Goode has discussed with great talent and erudition. We are not called upon to express an opinion upon the question, whether he has fully established his general conclusion. We have not, indeed, examined the whole matter with sufficient care, to entitle us to pronounce a judgment upon the main question involved. But we have no doubt that he has conclusively established the position, that the great body of the leading English divines, both during the short reign of Edward and the long reign of Elizabeth, were Calvinists, and, of course, would not admit any-

thing into the public formularies of the church which was inconsistent with Calvinism. To the proof of that position he has
devoted the third chapter of his work, consisting of above one
hundred pages, "on the school of theology to which our reformers
and early divines belonged." He has not contented himself, as
most controversialists on such questions do, with merely borrowing
the materials provided by his predecessors, but has subjected the
whole of the old materials to a fresh and independent examination;
and has also turned to good account some very important new
materials, furnished by the "Zurich Letters," now, for the first
time, published by the Parker Society. He has not spent much
time in refuting the attempts of the Arminians to establish their
position. He is occupied mainly with adducing the direct positive
evidence on the other side; and that evidence is such as to be
plainly and palpably unanswerable. With all competent and fair-
minded men, it must now be held to be settled, that the reformers
and the early divines of the Church of England belonged to the
Calvinistic school of theology. It follows from this that there can
be nothing in her formularies which does not admit, at least, of a
Calvinistic interpretation; while it may still be a question, to what
extent they have introduced their Calvinism into the formularies,
and thus, in a sense, imposed it upon the church.

Archdeacon Wilberforce, who had not then joined the Church
of Rome, published an answer to Dr Goode's book, under the
title of "The Doctrine of Holy Baptism," displaying, as all his
works do, very considerable learning and ingenuity. He does
not give much prominence to the consideration of the question,
whether the founders of the Church of England were Calvinists
or not. He, in a great measure, evades this question, and considers
it his best policy to rest directly and immediately upon the position,
that the formularies, as they stand, do clearly and certainly teach
baptismal regeneration—teach it so clearly and certainly, that
no indirect or collateral evidence can affect the proof of this doctrine being taught in them. He asserts, indeed, that the formularies of the Church of England were not drawn up by Calvinists;
but for the proof of this, so far as the articles are concerned,
he just refers to Laurence's "Bampton Lectures;" and in regard
to the mass of conclusive evidence adduced by Dr Goode on the
other side, he can scarcely be said even to look at it. He protests
" against the injustice with which Goode treats Archbishop

Laurence,* and opposes to his "hostile judgment" a high eulogium pronounced upon the "Bampton Lectures" by Mr Stanley Faber, in his work on "Primitive Election." Mr Faber has not shown such a discriminating judgment, or such a full and comprehensive knowledge of the bearings and relations of the subject of which he treats, as to entitle his opinion, upon any topic involved in the discussion, to much respect. But still Laurence was a man of very superior learning and ability. His "Bampton Lecture" is the most learned and elaborate attempt that has ever been made to show, that the articles of the Church of England are not Calvinistic, and it seems to be now generally regarded by the Arminians as their standard defence. In addition to the commendations of it by Faber and Wilberforce, it is represented as satisfactory and conclusive, along with Winchester's Dissertation on the 17th Article, by one quite entitled to be ranked with these men, the late Archdeacon Hardwicke, whose striking and premature death, a year or two ago, among the Pyrenees, was universally regarded as a great loss to our theological literature.† On these accounts it will be proper to give a somewhat fuller notice of Laurence's work; and this will lead us into the merits of the subject.

The injustice with which Wilberforce alleges that Goode treated Laurence, is brought out in the following passage :—

"I cannot but enter my humble protest against the remarkable partiality and superficial character of the work above referred to (Archbishop Laurence's "Bampton Lectures"), and, consequently, the erroneous nature of the view it gives of the subject of which it treats; and I trust that the few facts I am about to mention will be sufficient to put the reader on his guard against its statements."‡

We give only one specimen of the facts by which Goode has established the truth of this charge :—

"And here, again, I must notice the remarkable partiality displayed by Archbishop Laurence in his "Bampton Lectures." From a perusal of these Lectures, one might suppose that Melancthon was the only one of the foreign Reformers invited to this country by Cranmer, and the invitations addressed to *him* are very carefully recorded; while the fact is that, with this single exception, almost all, if not all, who were invited to this country by Cranmer,

---

* P. 235.   ‡ Effects of Baptism, p. 55, 2d
† History of the Articles, p. 372.   Edit.

to aid him in the work of Reformation, were of the Reformed churches, and therefore of Zwinglian or Calvinistic views."*

In addition to the facts adduced by Goode, we may mention some specimens of Laurence's mode of discussing this subject, which will convince most men that, to whatever cause it is to be ascribed, he was incapable of exercising discrimination or of manifesting ordinary fairness, when he had Calvin or Calvinism to deal with.

He thus announces his general opinion of Calvin, which will probably be received by most people as a novelty. "No man, perhaps, was ever less scrupulous in the adoption of general expressions, but perhaps no man ever adopted them with more mental reservations, than Calvin."† The man who could believe and assert this would assuredly scruple at nothing.

"'Horribile quidem decretum fateor!' were the precise expressions which he used when shuddering at his own favourite idea of irrespective reprobation."‡ The quoting Calvin's words, in order to convey to English readers the idea, that he confessed that his doctrine concerning the divine decree was *horrible*—when it is notorious and unquestionable that he only intended to represent it as awful, fitted to call forth deep emotions of awe and solemnity, as an inscrutable and alarming mystery, just as he speaks of the "horribilis Dei majestas," ‖ is merely an instance of the universal unfairness exhibited by the Anglican Arminians. There is not a man among them, from the highest to the lowest, who has been able to deny himself the pleasure and the triumph of quoting Calvin's alleged confession about the "horrible decree." Thus far Laurence stands on the same level with a crowd of associates —*defendit numerus*; but in the way in which he has brought out this point, there is a special unfairness which has not often been equalled. "Irrespective reprobation" (an expression which of itself conveys a misrepresentation) is not the subject of which Calvin is speaking. He is treating only of the implication of the human race in the penal consequences of Adam's first sin, and of the purpose and agency of God in relation to the fall and its results. It is surely time that anti-Calvinists, who profess any regard for truth or decency, should drop this topic of the "horrible decree," after having made it do duty for a couple of centuries.

---

* P. 65.
† Sermon viii., Note 4, p. 375.
‡ Sermon ii., p. 45.
‖ Inst. lib. iii., c. 20, s. 17.

In his destitution of solid proof to show that the compilers of the English articles did not embrace the theological views of Calvin, he has recourse to the following curious piece of evidence :— " If Calvin's system had been adopted by our Reformers, *never surely* would they have inserted among our articles that of Christ's descent into hell, which seems to have been directly levelled against one of his peculiar opinions, and one which he thought important." *
What connection there can be between the grounds for believing either that the English Reformers had, or that they had not, adopted Calvin's system of theology, and the mode in which they dealt with a topic so irrelevant and so unimportant, comparatively, as Christ's alleged descent into hell, it would puzzle most men of common sense to discover. But, besides, the statement of Laurence about the descent into hell, in its relation to Calvin's opinions, is quite inconsistent with the notorious facts of the case. The English article (the 3d) is simply an adoption of the article in what is commonly called the Apostle's Creed, which is just the creed of the Roman Church. This topic of the descent into hell, did not find its way into the Roman creed till the fifth century, and it certainly ought never to have been introduced into any creed or confession. What tempted the compilers of the English articles to devote one of them to this topic, it is not easy to understand, even though there were some at the time who denied it. But Laurence's notion, that it is " directly levelled against one of Calvin's peculiar opinions," is simply preposterous. It is perfectly notorious that Calvin rejoiced and exulted in the article in the creed about the descent into hell, as explicitly *sanctioning* " one of his peculiar opinions;" and he even seems to have so far yielded to a common infirmity of human nature, as to have been disposed, because of its containing this article, to think more favourably of the claim put forth by the Church of Rome, on its behalf, to an apostolic origin.†
Laurence takes great pains to make out, as affording a presumption against the English articles being Calvinistic, that in 1553, when they were first established, Calvin was not much known in England,—that his peculiar theological system had not then attracted much notice, and was not generally received even in the continental Reformed churches; and Faber has followed

---

* P. 245.   † *Inst.* lib. ii. c. xvi. s. 8 and 18.

him in this course of argument.*   The alleged facts are greatly overstated; and though they were all true, they would not furnish even a presumption in favour of the conclusion deduced from them.   Calvin had fully set forth his system of theology in the first edition of his "Institutes" in 1536; and from the time of his return to Geneva in 1541, he occupied a position of prominence and influence in the Protestant world, certainly inferior to that of no other man, instructing the churches everywhere by his writings, and guiding them by his counsels.   Cranmer had repeatedly sought his advice, and urged him to correspond with King Edward. In the beginning of 1552, before proceeding to draw up articles for the Church of England, Cranmer's mind was much set upon the preparation of a general confession of faith for the Protestant churches, and with this view he invited to England Calvin, Bullinger, and Melancthon.   Calvin's great work, the Consensus Genevensis, or treatise de Æterna Dei Predestinatione, was published in 1551, or very early in 1552, and we have direct and explicit evidence that it did exert an influence on the deliberations and consultations which were going on in England in the course of that year, in connection with the preparation of the articles.   It is but fair to mention, that this evidence was unknown to Laurence, having been published for the first time, by the Parker Society, in 1846, in the third series of the "Zurich Letters;" but it affords a good illustration of the truth, that a just cause is always advanced by the progress of research and discovery.   It is found in a letter of Traheron, Dean of Chichester, and Librarian to King Edward, written to Bullinger in September 1552, while the articles were under consideration, and undergoing the revision of various parties, civil and ecclesiastical, but not yet published.

"THE GREATER NUMBER AMONG US, *of whom I own myself to be one, embrace the opinion of John Calvin*, as being perspicuous and most agreeable to Holy Scripture.   And we truly thank God, that that excellent treatise of the very learned and excellent John Calvin, against Pighius and one Georgius Siculus, should have come forth at the very time when the question *began* to be agitated among us; for we confess that he has thrown much light upon the subject, or rather so handled it, as that we have never before seen anything more learned or more plain."†

---

* *Laurence*, pp. 44, 144, 236; *Faber on Primitive Election*, p. 356.

† *Zurich Letters*, 3d series, p. 325. Since writing this, we happened to notice that this, and some other extracts from Traheron's letters to Bullinger, had been published by Hottinger, from the original in Zurich, in

But, in truth, this discussion about Calvin is, to a considerable extent, irrelevant,—at least the proof of the Calvinism of the English Reformers and their formularies is not dependent upon the settlement of this point, and, indeed, cannot be materially affected by it. No one ascribes the Calvinism of the English Reformers to the personal influence of Calvin and his writings. It is to be traced chiefly to the study of the word of God and of the writings of Augustine. To the study of the writings of Augustine, is to be traced, instrumentally, a large proportion of the piety and orthodoxy that adorned the church for above 1000 years before the Reformation. The great body of the Reformers, on the continent, embraced Calvinism, even those who published their views before Calvin's name was known, and almost all of them ascribed much influence to Augustine's works in the formation of their opinions. This holds true also of the earliest English Reformers. Tyndale, Frith, and Barnes, who suffered martyrdom in the time of Henry VIII., were evidently familiar with the writings of Augustine, and from the study of his works and of the word of God they had become Calvinists. Calvinism, indeed, was not a new or unknown thing in England even before the Reformation. The three greatest men the church of that country had produced were Anselm and Bradwardine, both Archbishops of Canterbury, and Wycliffe, professor of theology at Oxford; and these men were all Calvinists—Anselm, indeed, in a less developed form, but Bradwardine and Wycliffe most fully and explicitly. These things are all well known, and in this state of matters it is mere unworthy trifling to seek, as Laurence does, to find even a presumption bearing upon the subject of the Calvinism of the English Reformers, in a minute investigation of the question how far Calvin and his writings were known to them or consulted by them in the year 1552.

We have said enough, we think, to show that, on this question at least, Archbishop Laurence is entitled to no deference whatever; and that in point of accuracy of statement and solidity of argument, he has sunk to the level of the generality of those who, from Heylin downwards, have undertaken the defence of the same cause.

---

his Hist. Eccles., tom. viii. p. 721–4; but they were certainly very little known in this country till published by the Parker Society. The apology for Lawrence was suggested to us by a statement to the same effect, made by Wilberforce, in attempting to defend him against Goode, p. 237.

But it is quite possible, notwithstanding all we have seen, that the book may contain sufficient materials to prove that the articles are not Calvinistic. The leading feature of the book,—determining, however, rather the form into which the materials are thrown than the substance of the materials themselves,—is, that it professes to bring out fully and precisely the doctrines that generally prevailed in the Church of Rome before the Reformation ; and, since the doctrines of the articles were very much directed against the errors that prevailed, to employ a knowledge of the errors for ascertaining the precise import of the correctives applied. This process is in its general character fair and reasonable, but it requires a more thorough knowledge of the whole subject, and a larger amount both of ability and candour, than Laurence possessed, to turn it to good account, and to bring out of its application results that can be relied upon. The way in which he applies his general principle is to this effect. He brings out fully the thoroughly unsound and Pelagian character of the views which generally prevailed in the church, and especially among the schoolmen, the leading divines of the period, on the subjects of original sin, free will, merit, justification, and predestination. He then assumes, that from the extreme unsoundness of the popish doctrine, no very large amount of soundness, nothing of an Augustinian or Calvinistic character in the Protestant corrections of it, need be supposed to be necessary or even probable,—that there might probably be a full and ample repudiation of the popish error without any leaning towards the other extreme. The practical application he makes of this notion, is to establish it as a sort of general rule, that there is a presumption in favour of the lowest and most moderate interpretation of the doctrinal statements of the Reformers, provided they are still held so sound and evangelical as to convey a condemnation of the grossly Pelagian views which generally prevailed before the Reformation. But there is really no weight in all this. The general position, that a knowledge of the precise opinions which prevailed before the Reformation may be usefully applied in ascertaining the exact import and bearing of the statements adopted by the Reformers upon the same points, is certainly well founded. But there is no ground for the notion which constitutes Laurence's peculiar principle, viz., that there is a general presumption in favour of the Protestant deviation from ante-Reformation Pelagianism being

the smallest which the words used will admit of. We know of
no ground for any such presumption, and we cannot admit it.
Our conviction is, that the great glory of the Reformation, in a
doctrinal point of view, is that the Reformers, and especially
Calvin, saw and proclaimed that it was necessary, as the only
thorough and permanent counteractive to the gross Pelagianism
of the Church of Rome and to all the practices based upon it, to
go back, decidedly and avowedly, even above and beyond the
Calvinism of Augustine to the Calvinism of the New Testament.
This certainly was the ground taken by the great body of the
continental Reformers, though Melancthon, whose weaknesses and
infirmities were so great and palpable, partially abandoned it.
And if it is alleged that the Reformers of England took lower and
narrower ground than this, and contented themselves with merely
condemning and lopping off some of the grosser and more offensive
developments of the prevailing Pelagianism, this must be established, not by vague and baseless presumptions, but by direct
and positive proof, by a deliberate and detailed examination of the
actual doctrines they have propounded on every topic of importance.   Laurence has no difficulty in showing, that the doctrines
which generally prevailed before the Reformation on the subjects
of original sin, free will, justification, and merit, were of a
thoroughly Pelagian complexion, and, of course, might have been
contradicted and excluded by statements, upon the part of the Reformers, which did not go beyond the standard of what might now
be called Arminianism.   But this is of no real value in proving
that they stopped there, and did not go on to bring out, as the
only complete and effectual antidote to the Pelagianism of the
schoolmen, at least the whole Calvinism of Augustine.

It is chiefly, however, with Laurence's discussion of the subject
of predestination that we have to do at present.   And this differs
in several respects from the other topics introduced.   On the
subjects of original sin, free will, grace, justification, and merit,
while there is but one doctrine that is true, there is room for a
considerable variety of opinions, more or less plausible, and more
or less nearly approximating to the truth, the difference being in
degree rather than in kind.   But in regard to predestination,
there are really' just two sides, clearly and distinctly defined, and
every man who has formed an intelligent judgment upon the
matter must be either a Calvinist or an anti-Calvinist,—that is, he

must either assert or deny, that God has from eternity chosen some
men, certain persons of the human race individually, to salvation,
through Christ, and has determined to effect and secure *their*
salvation in accordance with the provisions of the covenant of
grace.   Another difference is, that Pelagian or Arminian views in
regard to predestination were not so generally prevalent in the
Church of Rome as in regard to the other topics.   Some of the
most eminent of the schoolmen, while supporting Pelagian views
on depravity, justification, and grace, continued to hold, in substance, Augustinian views in regard to predestination.   Their
unsoundness in regard to the one class of topics, was owing to the
want of a careful and humble study of the Bible, and to the low
state of personal religion, and their comparative soundness on
the other, was to be ascribed to the strength and vigour of their
intellects, and their fondness for prosecuting profound speculations; while the Calvinism of the Reformers indicated at once
and in combination, the deepest sense of divine and eternal things,
in regard to those matters which bear more immediately upon
personal duty and experience, and the most profound and elevated
conceptions about the deep things of God.

Ignorance, or disregard of these points of difference, and of
the facts connected with them, has led to a thorough failure in
Laurence's attempt to apply his general principle to the subject
of predestination.   He misrepresents the views that generally
prevailed in the church before the Reformation, describing them
as more anti-Calvinistic than they were, and he utterly fails ,to
bring out any substantial difference, though he professes to have
done so, between the doctrine which he ascribes to the schoolmen,
and that which he ascribes to Melancthon and the Lutherans, and
which he represents as the doctrine of the English Reformers.
Mr Mozley, a man of a far higher order of intellect, and much
more profoundly versant in the subjects of which he treats, has
proved, in his work on Predestination,* that Laurence has misunderstood and misrepresented the views of Thomas Aquinas, the
greatest and most influential of all the schoolmen, and has shown
that the angelic Doctor, instead of being a low Arminian, as
Laurence alleges, was in substance an Augustinian and a Calvinist.   Mozley, like most men who have intellect enough and

---

* C. x. p. 280-5.

erudition enough to understand this matter, believes and maintains, that there is "no substantial difference between the Augustinian and Thomist and the Calvinist doctrine of predestination."* Laurence evidently did not understand the *status quæstionis* in the controversy between Calvinists and Arminians. He had no clear and definite conception of what Calvinism is, and of what Arminianism is, as opposed to it. Laurence ascribes a certain doctrine on the subject of predestination to the schoolmen and to the Church of Rome; and then he alleges that the Lutherans, with whose theological views he identifies those of the Church of England, "differed from the Church of Rome in several important particulars;" nay, that "they were entirely at variance with her upon the very foundation of the system."† The doctrine which he ascribes to the Church of Rome is simply Arminianism, in the form of an alleged election of individuals to salvation, founded on a foresight of their faith, holiness, and perseverance; and the doctrine of the Lutherans and Anglicans, alleged to differ from this, "upon the very foundation of the system," just consists of the very same Arminianism, that is, of the same denial of the fundamental principle of Calvinism, put in the form or based upon the ground of an assertion, that election is merely a choice of men in the mass, or taken collectively, to the enjoyment of outward privileges, which they may improve or not as they choose. Laurence's argument is, that since there existed this *fundamental* difference between the Church of Rome and the Lutheran and Anglican Reformers, it is probable that the latter did not deviate further from the Romish doctrine than this difference indicates. There is a deplorable amount of ignorance and confusion in all this, and though it has not much connection with the argument upon the subject immediately under consideration, it may be proper to give some explanations concerning it, especially as we find some additional blundering on the same subject, and in a different direction, among some of those who have taken part in this controversy on the same side with Laurence.

Dr Tucker, Dean of Gloucester, in his Letters to Dr Kippis, published in 1773, in adverting to the alleged Calvinism of the Church of England, ventured upon the assertion, that, " at the time just preceding the Reformation, the Church of Rome, in

---

* Note xxi. p. 413.   † P. 163, 164.

respect to predestination, grace, free will, and perseverance, was truly Calvinistical." This idea tickled the Anglican Arminians greatly. They chuckled over it as a proof that the Church of England must be anti-Calvinistic; while, at the same time, they must have felt somewhat doubtful about the accuracy of the statement as to the matter of fact. Dr Winchester, whose Dissertation on the seventeenth Article was published very soon after, adopted it as true, and founded an argument upon it,* and he was followed in this both by Bishop Tomline, in his Elements of Christian Theology,† and by Archdeacon Daubeny, in his Vindiciæ.‡ Laurence knew too much of the subject to swallow this; and, besides, his argument led him to take the opposite tack, to found much upon the opposite position, that the Church of Rome was thoroughly Arminian. The argument of Tucker and his followers was this, the Church of Rome was Calvinistic, and therefore the Church of England is probably Arminian. The argument of Laurence was, the Church of Rome was grossly Arminian, and therefore there is a strong probability that the Church of England, in reforming herself, would not go so far away as to embrace Calvinism, but would be contented with adopting a less gross and more refined Arminianism. The common conclusion is false, the argument in both cases is weak and untenable, and the main fact asserted is, in both cases, altogether inaccurate. Before the Reformation, the Church of Rome could not be said to be either Calvinistic or Arminian, that is, she had not formally and officially committed herself to either side in this great controversy. She had always professed great respect for the opinions of Augustine, and for the decisions of the African Synods and the Council of Orange in the Pelagian controversy; and she had never, as a church, formally and officially given any doctrinal decision inconsistent with that profession. Thus far she might be said to be Calvinistic. But on the other hand, it is certain, that doctrines of a Pelagian and semi-Pelagian cast had been long sanctioned by a very large portion of her most influential authorities, and especially by many of the schoolmen; so that, before the Reformation, Pelagianism might be said to pervade nearly the whole of the ordinary teaching of the church, though it had never been formally sanctioned as authoritative and

---

* P. 79.   † Vol. ii. p. 320.   ‡ P. 80.

binding.   In these circumstances, the Church of Rome could not
with propriety be said to be either Augustinian or Pelagian,
although, in somewhat different senses and aspects, both designations might be applied to her.   The Reformers, both in England
and on the continent, were led, almost to a man, by the study of
the Bible and of the works of Augustine, and, as we believe,
under the guidance of the Spirit of God, to repudiate the Pelagianism or Arminianism which prevailed all around them in the
ordinary teaching of the church, and to fall back upon the Calvinism of the New Testament and of the Bishop of Hippo.   But,
as the church officially was not at the time committed to oppose
Augustinian, or to support Pelagian, views, the topics involved in
that controversy did not form any proper part of the dispute between the Reformers and the Church of Rome; and, in consequence, they were not subjected to a full, searching, and exhaustive
discussion, until they came to form the subject of disputes among
Protestants themselves, in contending first with the Lutherans,
when they had thrown off the Calvinism of their master, and
afterwards with the Arminians.

It was on this ground that the doctrine of predestination was
not formally discussed and decided on in the Council of Trent.
It was, however, incidentally brought under the consideration of
the Council in connection with the subject of free will and justification; and the account which Father Paul has given of the
debate that took place, decidedly confirms the impression, which
the whole history of all the discussions that ever have taken place
upon these matters is fitted to produce, viz., that there is a clear
line of demarcation between the fundamental principle of the
Augustinian or Calvinistic, and the Pelagian or Arminian, systems
of theology,—that the true *status quæstionis* in the controversy between these parties can be easily and exactly ascertained,—that it
can, without difficulty, be brought to a point where men may and
should say either Aye or No, and, according as they say the one
or the other, may be held to be, and may be warrantably called,
Calvinists or Arminians.*   But, though the doctrine of predesti-

---

* It is not difficult to show, that it
is one and the same great controversy
in its main substance and leading features, which has been carried on, in
every age, by the Augustinians, Tho-
mists, Dominicans, Jansenists, and
Calvinists on the one side, and by
Pelagians, Scotists, Franciscans, Jesuits, and Arminians, on the other.

nation was discussed in the Council of Trent, and discussed on the same grounds on which it always has been and must be discussed, between Calvinists and Arminians who understand what they are about, no decision was pronounced upon the subject in any of the leading aspects of the question, and the members of the church were left quite free, as the Jansenists always contended, to maintain, if they chose, the whole theological system of Augustine. The Church of Rome has since, indeed, become more deeply tainted with Pelagianism by the doctrinal decisions pronounced in the cases of Baius, Jansenius and Quesnel. But we are not aware that there is even now any decision of that church, which stands in the way of her members maintaining the whole substance of the Calvinistic doctrine of predestination.

While it is certain that the great body of the Reformers adopted in substance the theological system of Augustine, and while it is certain that the system of Augustine was in its fundamental characteristic features, just the system of Calvin,—the differences between the views of Augustine and Calvin being greatly less in point of intrinsic importance than the differences between Augustine's views *and any form whatever of anti-Calvinism,*—it is not disputed that there were considerable differences among individuals and sections of the Reformers, in the way and manner in which their theological views were developed and applied. Constitutional capacities and tendencies, intellectual and moral, peculiar habits of thought and feeling, specialities occurring in the course of their studies and occupations—all these variously modified, no doubt, operated in different ways, and to a considerable extent, in influencing their mode of conceiving, representing, and applying doctrines which were in substance the same. And these causes of diversity amid unity ought to be taken into account, and fairly estimated and allowed for, not in judging of truth, but in judging of the men, and in exhibiting towards them due forbearance and fairness.

The men among the Reformers who exhibited the highest mental powers, and exerted the largest amount of influence as individuals in their different spheres, viz., Luther, Zwingle, Calvin, and Knox, were all unequivocal, decided, outspoken Calvinists, and did not hesitate to bring out, defend, and apply their principles. Melancthon went from one extreme to another, and the cause of his deviations, both from sound doctrine and sound practice on

public questions, is plainly to be traced to weaknesses and infirmities, palpably discernible both in his mental and moral constitution.   There is no evidence that Luther ever abandoned or
retracted his Calvinism, but there are indications that, in the latter
part of his life, he became, probably through Melancthon's influence, less anxious to give it prominence, and more concerned
about guarding against the abuse of it.   No other leading man
among the Reformers went so far astray in doctrinal matters as
Melancthon.   Bullinger was a Calvinist, though a very cautious
and moderate one, shrinking from some of the more precise and
stringent statements of Calvin on particular points.   He became
more decided and outspoken in maintaining Calvinistic principles
as he advanced in life, and as some indications appeared of differences among Protestants themselves, of deviations tending in an
anti-Calvinistic direction.   We believe that Bullinger had more
influence with the English Reformers, and upon the Reformation
they effected, than either Melancthon on the one side, or Calvin
on the other ; and whether it was because of influence exerted by
him or not, the actual theological views adopted by Cranmer and
embodied in the articles, more nearly resembled, in point of fact,
the opinions of Bullinger than those of any other eminent man of
the period.

It is quite true that Cranmer and his associates, who mainly
determined the character of the English Reformation, were a good
deal Melancthonian in their general character, tendencies, and sym-
pathies.   Cranmer resembled Melancthon both in his excellencies
and his defects, and would, we fear, in similar circumstances, have
gone as far in sacrificing principle and in compromising truth, as
Melancthon was ready to have done at the Diet of Augsburg in
1530.   Indeed, it is, and will always remain, something of a
mystery, how Cranmer contrived to thread his way through the
rocks and quicksands of Henry's reign, without sacrificing his integrity.   The English Reformers were, upon the whole, cautious
and timid men, who leaned decidedly to the side of peace, quiet-
ness, compromise, and who were trained by their peculiar, and in
many respects unfavourable, circumstances, to the habit of avoiding, as far as possible, to give offence.   There was a decided want
of men among them who were possessed of a high and commanding
order of intellect, or of the capacity of bold, vigorous, and independent thinking.   There was not one man among them qualified

by a combination of intellectual and moral qualities, to stamp his image, as an individual, upon his age or country. There is not one of them who has taken a high place or exerted a lasting influence as a theologian, in the exposition and discussion of important doctrinal questions. There was no native Englishman of the period equal in point of ability and learning, as a theologian, to either of the two men, Martin Bucer and Peter Martyr, whom Cranmer succeeded in getting over from the continent,—whom he placed in the most influential situations, the divinity chairs of Cambridge and Oxford,—with whom, during almost the whole reign of Edward, he was intimately associated,—who must have exerted a great influence over his mind,—and who were decided Calvinists. There is not one of those who acquired distinction in the church before the accession of Elizabeth who can be regarded as a first-class theologian. Bishop Jewel is the first Anglican churchman to whom we would be disposed to concede that title, and he, as was said by Froude, one of the founders of Puseyism, wrote " very much like an irreverent dissenter." Latimer and Hooper were excellent and most valuable men, great preachers, and eminently practical and useful, but they had neither capacity nor taste for the higher departments of theological speculation. Bishop Ridley had probably more influence with Cranmer, and was perhaps an abler man, than either of them, but he was not a man of a high order of intellect, and it was probably to this and to the want of any great familiarity with theological discussions, and not merely to a feeling of reverential modesty, that we owe his well-known statement about predestination and cognate topics—" In these matters I am so fearful that I dare not speak further, yea, almost none otherwise, than the very text doth, as it were, lead me by the hand." There is an element of truth and beauty in this sentiment. But it is thoroughly one-sided, it is wholly unsuitable to what has long been the actual condition of the church, and in its practical application, it is chiefly to favour the supporters of error, those who find their advantage in confusion and obscurity. Ridley's notion sounds well, and is apt to make an impression at first upon the minds of men who have not examined the subject or studied its history. It might have been practicable and safe to act upon it, if errors and heresies had never arisen to disturb the peace and purity of the church. The great controversies of the fourth and fifth centuries against the Arians and Pelagians put an end to the condition of things in which it might have been possible to act upon Ridley's notion.   This condition of things can never return, and it is now the church's imperative duty to seek, by turning Scripture to the fullest possible account, by bringing out and combining all that it teaches, explicitly or by good and necessary consequence, to unfold plainly and distinctly the whole scheme of divine truth, and to refute and expose the errors and heresies which may still be striving to gain an ascendency.

The character and tendencies of Cranmer and Ridley, determined, to a large extent, the general type of the English Reformation.   It was in the main cautious, timid, compromising.   This applies to some extent even to its theology, but not to such an extent as to have made the theology Arminian, or even neutral, but only so far as to have made it moderate Calvinism.   The proof that the great body of those who were concerned in preparing the English articles in the reign of Edward, and in establishing them again in the reign of Elizabeth, were in their own personal convictions Calvinists in doctrine, though averse to all extreme views, and to all strong and incautious statements, and anxious to guard against the practical abuse of their doctrines, is, we are persuaded, perfectly conclusive and unanswerable.   As a whole, it cannot be touched; and the evidence in support of this position is gaining in strength, and has gained in our own day, by the progress of research and investigation.   We cannot, of course, pretend either to adduce the evidence, or to answer what has been brought forward on the other side.   Those who wish to see this evidence fully adduced and cleared from objection, will find all this in the books already mentioned, by Prynne, Hickman, Toplady, Overton, and Goode; and if they are capable of estimating evidence, and possessed of a reasonable measure of impartiality and candour, they will not be moved by anything that has been produced upon the other side by Heylin, Winchester, Daubeny, Tomline, and Laurence.

The Calvinism, however, of the fathers and founders of the Church of England, does not at once and *ipso facto* settle the Calvinism of the articles and the liturgy.   It proves, indeed, that there is nothing anti-Calvinistic in the formularies of the church, and that no Calvinist need have any hesitation about approving of them, unless they could be shown to be palpably self-contradictory.   But still it is possible, that, though Calvinists themselves, they may have abstained from making an explicit profession of Calvinism a term of communion. They may have intended to leave an open door both for Calvinists and Arminians, and with this view may have prepared their public symbols in such indefinite and ambiguous terms as would exclude neither, because they might be assented to by both. This is about as much as the more respectable Arminians venture to assert, and it is all to which they can manage to give anything like plausibility. We are not concerned to prove that Arminians cannot honestly subscribe the articles. This is a question not so much for strangers, as for themselves and for their fellow-churchmen. But the ground taken by such men as Daubeny, Tomline, and Laurence, that the articles are inconsistent with Calvinism, and must exclude all honest Calvinists, we cannot but protest against as an outrage upon historic truth. We have never been able to understand how any one but a Calvinist could comfortably subscribe the 17th article. But we have no wish to press this. We admit that it is very cautiously and temperately expressed, and that it would have been easy if its compilers had so intended, to have made it more stringently, explicitly, and undeniably, Calvinistic. What we maintain is, that its most natural and obvious meaning is Calvinistic,—that there is no evidence, internal or external, fitted to lead us to doubt, that it teaches, and was intended to teach, Calvinism,—and that all the attempts which have been made to show that it is positively anti-Calvinistic, have been mere exhibitions of incompetency or of something worse.

We can only make a few observations upon the 17th article. The most important parts of the article, the beginning and the end, are as follow:—

"Predestination to life is the everlasting purpose of God, whereby, before the foundations of the world were laid, He hath constantly decreed by His counsel, secret to us, to deliver from curse and damnation those whom He hath chosen in Christ out of mankind, and to bring them by Christ to everlasting salvation, as vessels made to honour. Wherefore, they which be endued with so excellent a benefit of God, be called according to God's purpose by His Spirit working in due season: they through grace obey the calling: they be justified freely: they be made sons of God by adoption: they be made like the image of His only-begotten Son Jesus Christ: they walk religiously in good works, and at length, by God's mercy, they attain to everlasting felicity.

"Furthermore, we must receive God's promises in such wise, as they be generally set forth to us in holy Scripture, and in our doings that will of God is to be followed which we have expressly declared unto us in the word of God."

Now the first reflection that occurs on reading this is, that there is not one word or phrase in it to which any Calvinist can object, or ever has objected. Every Calvinist sees in it a plain and explicit statement of his fundamental principle, that God hath from eternity chosen some men in Christ, and resolved to deliver and save them, and that, in consequence of this election, these men, so chosen, are enabled to believe in Christ, are justified and regenerated, are enabled to lead holy lives, and are preserved unto salvation. This is plainly what the article states, and this is just a simple unequivocal declaration of the fundamental, the only fundamental, principle of Calvinism. Calvinists could easily introduce certain expressions, *suggested by later controversies and the sophisms and evasions to which they gave rise*, which would make the article more undeniably and exclusively Calvinistic; but no one has ever felt the slightest difficulty about the statements, as plainly and obviously, without comment or explanation, teaching the Calvinistic doctrine of election.

It has been strongly alleged by Arminians, that the caution or caveat contained in the last sentence is inconsistent with Calvinistic opinions, and was intended to exclude them. But this is a sheer misrepresentation. No Calvinist has ever had the slightest difficulty about approving of this caveat, because it is quite notorious, that this mode of speaking is universal among Calvinistic divines in unfolding the practical application of their doctrine, —that the second part of the statement is given in the very words of Calvin himself,—and that the first part of it, too, is found in substance, though not *verbatim*, in his writings. No Calvinist can have any difficulty in showing the perfect consistency of this caveat with his doctrine concerning predestination. But no Arminian can give any intelligible reason why such a caveat should have been introduced, except in connection with a previous statement of Calvinistic predestination. It is only the Calvinistic, and not the Arminian, doctrine that suggests or requires such guards or caveats; and it is plainly impossible that such a statement could ever have occurred to the compilers of the articles as proper and necessary, unless they had been distinctly aware, that they had just laid down a statement which at least included the

Calvinistic doctrine. Calvinists have always regarded it as a strong confirmation of their doctrine, that the Apostle Paul so plainly intimates, that he expected that almost as a matter of course, men would adduce against his doctrine the same objections which have, in every age, been adduced against Calvinism, but which nobody would ever think of adducing against Arminianism. Upon the same principle, the caveat introduced into the end of the 17th article, is a plain proof that the Calvinistic doctrine was at least included in the preceding statements. The common allegation, that this caveat excludes Calvinism, is purely ridiculous.

While Calvinists find nothing in the 17th article but what is in full accordance with their ordinary train of thinking, and with the usual language of their most eminent writers, Arminians are obliged to distort and pervert it. Bishop Tomline, in his Elements of Christian Theology, does it in this way.*

" Those whom He hath chosen in Christ out of mankind, are that part of mankind to whom God decreed to make known the gospel; and it is to be observed, that this expression does not distinguish one set of Christians from another, but Christians in general from the rest of mankind; and, *consequently*, ' to bring them by Christ to everlasting salvation,' does not mean actually saving them, but granting them the means of salvation through Christ."

This surely ought to repel and disgust honest men, and yet it is in substance the interpretation which must be put upon the article, as well as upon the statements of Scripture, by the Arminians. Sometimes the idea is put in a more gross and offensive form, as when Dean Kipling, in discussing this subject, lays it down as the doctrine of the founders of the Church of England, that " every person is an elect, whom some duly authorised minister of the gospel has baptized in the Christian faith ;"† and sometimes it is glossed over with more skill and plausibility, as by Archbishop Laurence in his "Bampton Lectures." But the leading idea is the same, " chosen in Christ" means, chosen as Christians, *i.e.*, chosen to enjoy the outward privileges of the church; and as to God's having decreed to deliver them from curse and damnation, and to bring them by Christ to eternal salvation, this just means that God decreed to give to them the enjoyment of the outward means of grace, the final result being left entirely

---

* Vol. ii. p. 301.   † P. 86.

dependent upon themselves, upon their improvement of their privileges.

Laurence dwells at considerable length upon the expression "chosen *in Christ*," and labours to show that this was intended to support Arminianism, and to exclude Calvinism, alleging that the expression was selected for the purpose of intimating that "God predestinated His elect in Christ, *or the Christian Church*, to salvation,"—that the only election is, "the election of a collective mass on account of Christ,"—and that He "predestinates to the adoption of children, those who duly receive and apply the means of salvation which He has thus gratuitously provided for them." * The argument founded upon the expression "chosen *in Christ*," the only thing in the leading section of the article alleged to have the appearance of being anti-Calvinistic, can be easily disposed of.

1st. In the clause "whom He hath chosen in Christ out of mankind," the words "*in Christ*" alleged to teach the Arminian notion of the election of the visible church to the outward means of grace as being the only election, were added on the revision of the articles in Elizabeth's reign, in 1562, having formed no part of the article as it was prepared in Edward's reign. But the insertion of these words could not have been intended to serve an Arminian purpose, for it is notorious, and is generally conceded by our opponents, that most of those who had the management of the ecclesiastical affairs in Elizabeth's reign, were decided Calvinists, even when this is not conceded in regard to Cranmer and his associates. This concession indeed could not decently be refused, when it is notorious that, in 1562, immediately after the articles as they now stand had been passed in convocation, Bishop Jewel wrote to Peter Martyr, then at Zurich, in the following terms :— "As to matters of doctrine, we have pared every thing away to the very quick, and do not differ from your doctrine by a nail's breadth."†

2d. The phrase "chosen in Christ," is a scriptural expression ;

---

* P. 161, 168-9. Goode has distinctly charged Laurence with asserting that "the doctrine of our church is, that the elect people of God are all the baptized," and with making the "monstrous statement, that all in the visible church are to be considered as the elect " (p. 54, 90) ; and this charge is undoubtedly true, in substance, though Laurence has not perhaps brought out his notion quite so fully and explicitly.

† *Zurich Letters*, 1st series, p. 59.

and as the Calvinists of course think that they can interpret it in
entire accordance with their theological views, it is just as unwarrantable to infer Arminianism, as it would be to infer Calvinism, from the mere adoption of it.

3d. The expression is used in the whole series of undeniably
Calvinistic confessions, both in those prepared before and after
the Arminian controversy—in the Scottish Confession of 1560, as
well as in the Westminster one, in the French, Belgic, and Helvetic, and in the canons of the synod of Dort.

All these things are quite notorious, and they are perfectly
conclusive against Laurence's argument; but the Anglican anti-
Calvinists seem to be ignorant enough of theology, to look upon
him as an oracle, and to believe such statements as these because
he makes them. The truth is, that the first attempt to employ this
expression in a controversial way for Arminian purposes, was
made by the Lutherans, when, in the latter part of the sixteenth
century, they were shuffling out of the Calvinism of their master.
They wished still to maintain, if they could, that election was gratuitous,—a position which even Melancthon held to the last,—and
that it was not to be traced to anything in men themselves. These
positions of course cannot be held intelligently and consistently
by any but Calvinists. But first the Lutherans, and afterwards
Arminius, attempted to involve this whole matter in obscurity
and confusion, by representing Christ as the cause and foundation
of election, and by trying to show that this implied, that men were
elected as Christians, or because of their relation to Christ.
Calvinists had no difficulty in showing the sophistical and evasive
character of this attempt, and proving that under a profession of
honouring Christ, it assigned to Him a place in the scheme of
salvation which Scripture does not sanction ; and that in so far as
men are concerned, it plainly implied, when stripped of the
vagueness and confusion thrown around it, either, that election is
only to the outward privileges of the church, or that, if it be
supposed to refer to eternal life, it is based upon a foresight of
men's faith,—that is, that it is not gratuitous, but really founded
upon something in men themselves. The exposure of this
Lutheran and Arminian sophistry produced some interesting,
though occasionally rather intricate, discussion, on topics which
seem to be utterly unknown among the Anglican Arminians, but
which are now quite indispensable to a thorough acquaintance

with the subject, and of which a masterly summary is given in Turretine's Theolog. Elenct.*

There is nothing, then, in the 17th article, but what in its natural and obvious meaning is most fully accordant with Calvinism, and seems to have been intended to teach the fundamental principle of that system of theology, while the attempts which have been made to disprove this, and to bring in an Arminian interpretation of it, can be shown to be utterly unsuccessful.

This is quite sufficient to establish the Calvinism of the article, especially when viewed in connection with the known sentiments of its compilers. But the evidence is further strengthened by comparing it with the section on predestination in the later editions of " Melancthon's Commonplaces." All who deny the Calvinism of the article maintain that it was derived from Melancthon's writings, and was intended to embody the views which he came ultimately to adopt. But we think it scarcely possible for any one at all versant in these matters, to compare the article with Melancthon's section on predestination, without seeing a marked contrast between them. We cannot give quotations, or go into any detail upon this point; but we think it manifest, that the 17th article is much more clearly and explicitly Calvinistic, or rather, is much more like, and comes much more near to, Calvinism, than anything to be found in Melancthon's later writings. If the compilers of the articles had really meant to leave the only question of fundamental importance on the subject of predestination undecided,—and this, as we have said, is about as much as the more respectable defenders of Arminianism usually venture to allege,— they had before them, in the section upon this subject in the later editions of " Melancthon's Commonplaces," a very fair attempt at saying nothing—that is, at professing to explain the matter without decidedly and explicitly taking either side. But they did not take this course; for the 17th article is, to say the very least, not nearly so obscure and ambiguous as the exposition of Melancthon; from which the inference is plain, that though on some points they may have followed Melancthon, they here put themselves under the surer and steadier guidance of Calvin, or, at least, of Bullinger.

Arminians, in discussing this subject, usually try to take advantage of the concession, which we cannot withhold from them,

---

* Loc. iv. Qu. x.

that the founders of the Church of England were moderate, as distinguished from extreme, or ultra-Calvinists, and that the doctrine of the article is moderate Calvinism. They are disposed to scout the idea of moderate Calvinism as an inconsistency and absurdity,—to insinuate that men should not be held to be Calvinists at all unless they have embraced all the points of the system in its most detailed and developed form,—and to allege that since this is not true of the Anglican Reformers, they should not be regarded as Calvinists. This whole notion is plainly exaggerated and untenable, and confounds things that differ. It is quite warrantable and fair to press men with the consequences or results of the principles they profess, in order to show them that, in right reason, they ought either to abandon their principles, or else embrace the ulterior views to which they can be shown legitimately to lead. But it is unwarrantable to draw inferences as to what, in point of fact, men's principles are, from our views of what consistency would seem to require of them. Men are not to be disbelieved when they tell us, as a matter of fact, that in their convictions they have come thus far, but that they stop here, merely because we think that either they should not have come so far, or that, if they did, they should have advanced farther. The subject we are at present considering is essentially a matter of fact—a question as to what views certain men did embrace and profess—and it should be determined by the ordinary evidence applicable to such a matter of fact, viz., the statements and procedure of the parties themselves, and not by any inferences and deductions of ours, in the soundness of which they do not acquiesce. These Anglican Arminians, most of whom have given abundant evidence that they do not understand what Calvinism is, presume to set up an arbitrary standard of Calvinism; and if men do not come up to this standard, they infer, not merely that they are not Calvinists, but that they do not, in point of fact, hold, whatever they may profess, any of the leading doctrines usually regarded as Calvinistic. All this is utterly unwarrantable and extravagant, and it is the more so when we have to deal, as in this case, not merely with the personal convictions of individuals, but with the public formularies which they prepared for the church. The same qualities and influences which made Cranmer and his associates only moderate Calvinists, in their own personal convictions, were likely to operate still more powerfully when they were preparing public documents

for the church, to which other men were to be required to assent.
Here it is quite natural to expect, that they would be still more
moderate Calvinists than they were in their own individual convictions.* All this is quite natural and intelligible, and it affords
no reasonable ground for doubting that, as individuals, they
honestly and sincerely held all the Calvinism which, by their
statements and actions, they have professed, or that they really
meant to embody, in the formularies of the church, all the Calvinism
which is there indicated. Moderate Calvinism, as distinguished
from Calvinism of a more definite and detailed description, may
be an indication of something defective in men's mental and moral
capacities or tendencies, or, it may be traceable to some qualities
and feelings, good and creditable in the main, but carried out to
an unwarrantable excess. But this is no reason why men should
have ascribed to them inferences and deductions from their principles which they do not themselves perceive or admit, or should
have any doubt thrown upon the trustworthiness of their professions as to what they do hold.

For ourselves, we do not affect the designation of moderate
Calvinists. We believe the whole Calvinism of the canons of
the synod of Dort, and of the Confession of the Westminster
Assembly, and we are willing to attempt to expound and defend,
when called upon, the whole doctrine of these symbols, to show
that it is all taught or indicated in Scripture. We have been only
confirmed in our Calvinism by all the study we have given to this
subject. But while our own personal convictions of the truth of

---

* It is common in works intended
to disprove the Calvinism of the 17th
article, to give numerous and lengthened extracts from Calvin. One-
fourth part of the whole of Winchester's pamphlet upon the subject, and
one-third of Kipling's, is made up in
this way. This has a great appearance of fairness, but it is really a controversial artifice. It is intended to
deepen the impression of the discrepancy between Calvin and the article,
though there is no fair comparison
between a brief, summary statement
of a doctrine intended for a public
formulary, and the minute details,
perhaps incautious and exaggerated
expressions, that are to be expected
in elaborate expositions and defences
of the doctrine, prepared by an individual, and intended merely for general
perusal. The question is not, whether
the compilers of the articles agreed in
all respects with Calvin, as an individual, but whether they professed the
fundamental principles of the system
of theology usually called after his
name. The only fair comparison is
between the 17th article and the statements on predestination contained in
the Calvinistic confessions prepared
about the same time; and here certainly there is no inconsistency,
scarcely even an apparent discrepancy.

a fully-developed Calvinism have become confirmed by continued study, we have, at the same time, and by the same process, been taught a larger measure of forbearance towards those who differ from us on some of the questions connected with these profound and mysterious subjects,—and especially, towards those who do not see their way to go so far as we think warrantable, in explaining and defining some points, and who, while, it may be, not explicitly denying what we believe to be true, yet rather shrink from the more detailed and definite explanations which we regard as true and warrantable.   The more we have studied these subjects, the more have we become convinced, that the one fundamental principle of Calvinism,—*that* the admission or denial of which constitutes the real line of demarcation between Calvinists and anti-Calvinists, is the doctrine of predestination in the more limited sense of the word, or of election, as descriptive of the substance of the teaching of Scripture with regard to what God decreed or purposed from eternity to do, and does or effects in time, for the salvation of those who are saved ; and that every man ought to be held by others, and ought to acknowlege himself, to be a Calvinist, who believes that God from eternity chose some men, certain persons of the human race, absolutely and unconditionally to salvation through Christ, and that He accomplishes this purpose, or executes this decree in time, by effecting and securing the salvation of these men in accordance with the provisions of the covenant of grace.   Of all the doctrines usually discussed between Calvinists and Arminians, and commonly held by Calvinists to be taught in Scripture, this doctrine of election is at once the most important in itself, and the most clearly revealed in God's word.   In regard to the other doctrines of the Calvinistic system of theology, as set forth by the synod of Dort and the Westminster Assembly, we believe, 1*st*, That they can be all sufficiently and satisfactorily established by scriptural evidence bearing directly upon each particular topic ; and 2*d*, That they may be all legitimately and conclusively deduced in the way of consequence or inference from the great doctrine of election.   It is men's duty to ascertain what God has revealed upon all these matters in His word, and to exercise their rational faculties in estimating and developing the logical relations of these doctrines with each other.   And, for ourselves, we have no doubt that the full legitimate use and improvement of the word of God and of our rational faculties, ought to lead men to the firm belief and the open maintenance of the doctrines generally held by Calvinists, with regard to what is commonly, though improperly, called reprobation, the nature and extent of the atonement, the certain and insuperable efficacy of grace, and the final perseverance of all believers. We believe that when men deny, or even decline or refuse to profess, the doctrines generally held by Calvinists upon these subjects, they are, in so far, to be held as coming short in the discharge of their duty and the improvement of their privileges in regard to the truth of God. But we are disposed to practise more of indulgence and forbearance towards perplexities and confusions, or even positive errors, on these questions, than on the great fundamental principle of election, partly because of the difference among them in respect of intrinsic importance, and partly because of the difference in the clearness and fulness of the Scripture evidences by which they are supported.

At present, however, we have to do, not with abstract speculations, but with the construction of evidence bearing upon a matter of fact, viz., what opinions were actually held by certain parties. The general allegation here is, that the founders of the Church of England were not Calvinists; and one reason adduced in support of it is, that while there may be some ground for holding that they believed in the Calvinistic doctrine of election, they did not believe in certain other doctrines which have been usually regarded as necessary parts of the Calvinistic system of theology. And our general answer, based upon the grounds already referred to, is, that it is unwarrantable to draw inferences as to what men's opinions in point of fact are, from what consistency on their part, seems to us to require; and that we not only acknowledge, but must claim, every man as a Calvinist who believes in the Calvinistic doctrine of election, even though, from disadvantages and drawbacks in some of the features of his mental and moral constitution, or of his position and opportunities, he may be involved in perplexity and confusion, or even positive error, in regard to some of the other doctrines usually held by Calvinists. This is a sufficient answer to the argument in general; and when we examine the special grounds by which the general position is commonly supported, we find that they can be shown to be irrelevant, inaccurate, and inconclusive. We can only refer to them, and that only in their purely historical aspects, as bearing upon the matter of fact which we have been investigating.   They are chiefly these :—

I. The 17th article, it is said, cannot be Calvinistic, because it contains nothing whatever about reprobation, which is alleged to be an essential part of the Calvinistic system.   Reprobation properly means a statement of the doctrine of Scripture as to what God purposed from eternity, and does in time, in regard to those men who ultimately perish.   Now, every Calvinist admits, that there is comparatively little indicated in Scripture concerning this awful and mysterious subject, and that what can be known about it must be partly learned in the way of inference and deduction, from the much clearer and fuller information given in Scripture concerning God's purposes and procedure in regard to those who are saved.   This consideration shows the unworthy and dishonourable character of the efforts usually made by Arminians to thrust in the discussion of reprobation before that of election, notwithstanding that the latter is both much more important in itself, and much more fully revealed in Scripture, than the former.   But this consideration also shows how probable it is, that men of a timid and cautious temperament, though firmly believing in the doctrine of election, might not hold themselves called upon to say anything about reprobation, especially when preparing public formularies. This idea was acted upon at that period by men who were undoubtedly Calvinists.   There is no statement of reprobation in the Scottish Confession of 1560, or in the Second Helvetic of 1566, which was approved of by almost all the Reformed churches, though the authors of these documents were decided Calvinists, and the documents themselves are undoubtedly Calvinistic.   This topic is stated very briefly and compendiously even in the French and Belgic Confessions; and it was only the perverse, offensive, and discreditable conduct of the Arminians at the synod of Dort, in thrusting this topic into prominence and priority, that rendered it necessary for the church to put forth a somewhat fuller statement of its nature and position.   It is indeed the proceedings of heretics that have all along, and in every age, produced and necessitated the more full and detailed explanations and definitions which the church has been led to put forth.   And one reason why heretics have such a bitter hatred of these explanations and definitions is, because they feel that in this way their errors are exposed, and grave suspicions are sometimes excited as to their integrity.

But we have said more than enough to show that the omission of any mention of reprobation affords no presumption against the Calvinism of the 17th article.

II. Another favourite allegation of the Arminians upon this subject is, that the articles and liturgy cannot be Calvinistic, because they teach the doctrine of universal redemption, and this entirely precludes Calvinism. This topic is thus put by Waterland, in a passage which has been often quoted or referred to since by controversialists on the same side, and which is a fair enough specimen of the accuracy of the facts and the conclusiveness of the reasonings prevalent in that class of writers :—" In the year 1618, our divines, at the synod of Dort, had commission to insist upon the doctrine of universal redemption as the doctrine of the Church of England, which one doctrine, pursued in its just consequences, is sufficient to overthrow the whole Calvinian system of the five points." *

Now, the assertion that the English divines, at the synod of Dort, had commission to insist upon the doctrine of universal redemption, is not true, though it is not wholly destitute of a colourable pretext. No such commission or instruction was given to them, or was acted on by them, though some of them were favourable to that doctrine. And Waterland, we believe, could have produced, if called upon, no direct authority for the statement, except an unsupported assertion of Heylin's. The futility of the argument drawn from this doctrine against the Calvinism of the Church of England, will appear from the following considerations :—.

1. This doctrine of universal redemption is of such a nature that, as experience proves, it is easy to produce abundance of quotations that seem to assert it, and that do assert something like it, from authors who did not believe it, and never intended to teach it.

2. A great variety of doctrines pass currently under the general name of universal redemption, graduating from the grosser form, which would exclude not only all Calvinistic principles, but all right conceptions of a vicarious atonement, even as held professedly by Arminians themselves, to the comparatively harmless form, in which it seems to be little else than an unwarranted and exaggerated mode of embodying the truth, that the offers and

---

* Supplement to the Case of Arian Subscription Works, vol. ii. p. 348.

invitations of the gospel are to be addressed to all men, to men indiscriminately without distinction or exception.

3. It is perfectly certain that a considerable number of eminent divines, who undoubtedly believed the whole of what is usually held by Calvinists, both in regard to election and reprobation, have professed to maintain the doctrine of universal redemption. This does not afford a presumption that the doctrine is true, but it furnishes a proof, that the fact that men hold it is no evidence that they are not Calvinists. This statement applies to Cameron and Amyraut, to Daillee and Claude, to Davenant and Baxter, and to come down to our own times, to Thomas Scott and Ralph Wardlaw. We have never been at all impressed with the reasonings of these men in favour of universal redemption, but we cannot, because of what we reckon their error upon the subject, consent to their being handed over to the Arminians.

Waterland's statement is peculiarly inexcusable, because the mention of the synod of Dort ought to have suggested to him the name of Bishop Davenant, and he ought to have known that we have a work of Davenant's, entitled, " Dissertationes Duæ prima de Morte Christi, altera de Prædestinatione et Reprobatione," and that, while the first of these is a very able defence of the doctrine of universal redemption, as it has been usually held by men who professed Calvinistic views upon other points, the second is a most thorough and masterly exposition and defence of the views ordinarily held by Calvinists in regard to election and reprobation. Indeed, we do not believe that there exists a better or more satisfactory vindication of the Calvinistic doctrine of predestination, in both its branches of election and reprobation, than the second of these two Dissertations.*

III. The third and last of the positions sometimes taken up by those who deny the Calvinism of the English articles and liturgy is, that these formularies are opposed to the doctrine of the certain perseverance of all believers or saints, and that this

---

* Davenant's "Animadversions" on Hoard's " God's Love to Mankind" is better known, and displays the same high qualities. But so far as general impression and effect are concerned, it has the great disadvantage of being literally a reply to Hoard's treatise, the whole of which is inserted, and then answered step by step; whereas the " Dissertation on Predestination and Reprobation" is a formal discussion, scientifically and scholastically digested and arranged, and taking up the different branches of the subjects in their due logical order.

doctrine is a necessary part of Calvinism. It is certainly a necessary part of Calvinism, that all those whom God has absolutely chosen to salvation shall be saved; and no man ever held the Calvinistic doctrine of election without believing this. But this is not the question that is discussed in connection with the views of some of the early English divines about perseverance or apostasy. They all admitted that all the elect would certainly persevere, and could not fall away, but some of them seem to have held that some men, though not elected to salvation, might attain to faith and conversion, and yet, because not elected, might fall away and finally perish.

It has been alleged that the 16th article of the Church of England sanctions this view, and we admit that there is a good deal to countenance it in Augustine. There is no real difficulty in the 16th article, which Calvinists have always subscribed without hesitation, as being true so far as it goes, and as not contradicting any of their principles. Augustine's error and confusion upon this subject seems to be traceable in some measure to his having embraced, more or less fully and explicitly, the mischievous heresy of baptismal regeneration; and it is probably owing to the same cause, that there have always been, from the time of Bishop Overall down to the present day, some highly respected Anglican divines who preferred the opinion of Augustine to that of Calvin in regard to the possible apostasy of some who had been brought to faith and repentance, while agreeing with them both in maintaining the great principle, that God from eternity chose some men, certain persons, to salvation, and that in carrying out this electing purpose He effects and secures the salvation of every one of those whom He has chosen in Christ.* It is quite unwarrantable to represent this as a difference of vital importance between Augustine and Calvin, in relation to the great distinctive features of the theological system which they held in common, and which they have done more than any uninspired men to commend to the acceptance of the people of God And it is deserving of special notice, that on this particular point, Cranmer followed Calvin, and not Augustine;† so that we have the fullest and most direct

* A very good specimen of this may be found in a work entitled "The Union between Christ and His People, four Sermons preached before the University of Oxford," by Dr Heurt- ley, the present able, excellent, and accomplished Margaret Professor of Divinity there.

† Goode, p. 52.

authority for maintaining, that nothing of an anti-Calvinistic complexion upon the subject of perseverance or apostasy is, in so far as the intention of the compilers is concerned, to be found in the Anglican formularies.

We have spoken strongly as to the futility of the arguments derived from these subjects of reprobation, universal redemption, and perseverance, in support of the alleged matter of fact of the anti-Calvinism of the Anglican formularies; for it is, we think, very clear and certain, that no considerations deduced from these topics can be of any avail in weakening the evidence for, or in strengthening the evidence against, the position, that these symbols teach, and were intended to teach, the fundamental principles of the Calvinistic system of theology. But while we cannot allow that there is any difficulty whatever in disposing of the attempts to refute the historical proof of the doctrinal Calvinism of the Church of England, by inferences derived from these doctrines, we willingly admit that these doctrines in themselves, viewed in their nature and meaning, in their evidence and application, and in their relation to each other, and to the scheme of divine truth as a whole, involve profound and inscrutable mysteries. They lead at once into the most arduous and difficult questions with which the mind of man has ever grappled. The investigation of the doctrines of reprobation, universal redemption, and perseverance, requires us to grapple with the most arduous and difficult of all topics in the fields both of scriptural exegesis and theological speculation; and no one has ever prosecuted this investigation in a right and becoming spirit without having been impressed with a sense of the profound difficulties attaching to it, and without being led, in consequence, to regard differences of opinion on some points with forbearance and kindly consideration, however decided may have been the conclusions to which he himself has come.

Still men should ascertain and profess the whole of what is taught or indicated on these subjects in Scripture, and they should not allow mere caution or timidity, or any other feeling or motive, even though it should assume the form of reverence or modesty, to interfere with the discharge of this duty. While reticence, perplexity, confusion, and even positive error upon some of the features of these profound and solemn subjects may be treated with forbearance, all due allowances being made for peculiarities in men's constitution and circumstances, they should never be approved of or encouraged. Men should be warned of these shortcomings and infirmities, and exhorted to guard against them. We are persuaded that there are many of the evangelical clergy in the Church of England, who come far short of doing justice to God's truth in these matters, nay, come far short even of what their own convictions, defective and confused as they often are, should lead them to do. There are not a few of the evangelical clergy, men of genuine and elevated piety, and faithful and devoted ministers, who, while really believing in the Calvinistic doctrine of election, seem to shrink from making an explicit public profession of their judgment, or from giving it anything like prominence. We suspect that in some instances they are half afraid to think or read, or speak about the subject of election, lest they should be led to form, or should be suspected of having formed, definite or decided opinions on what are reckoned the higher or more mysterious departments of the subject, connected with reprobation, the extent of redemption, and the certainty of perseverance. Whatever may be the precise cause of this mode of acting, and whatever the precise forms it may assume in different individuals, it is a great weakness and infirmity, and it involves or produces a neglect or disregard of the duty they owe to God's truth, and to God's cause on earth as virtually identified with the proclamation or diffusion of His truth. From the number and variety of the grounds on which men of this class, who are substantially Calvinists at heart and in their own convictions, labour to excuse themselves from openly and explicitly admitting and proclaiming this,—ranging from the elevated sophistry of men of high intellect and learning like Mr Mozley, down to the mawkish sentimentality of the weakest of the brethren,—it would almost seem as if an open profession of Calvinism still led, in the Church of England, to something like martyrdom. We fear that some of the evangelical clergy, who are really Calvinists in substance and at heart, are deficient in the manly, outspoken independence and courageous integrity of the Newtons and Scotts of a former generation. We believe that it would advance the peace of mind of many of these excellent men, and increase their efficiency and usefulness as preachers of the gospel and defenders of God's truth, if they would bring out their theological convictions more definitely and prominently—if, by a deeper study of these subjects, they were led to form, and if, by a deeper sense of the responsibility connected with this department of the duty of Christian ministers, they were led to profess more detailed and definite views of doctrine, and thus to identify themselves more cordially and avowedly with the leading principles of that system of theology, which has been embraced in substance by a large proportion of the ablest and best men that have ever adorned the Church of Christ,—which was adopted by the whole body of the Reformers, with scarcely a single exception, and even by those timid and cautious men who presided over the Reformation of the Church of England, and prepared her authorised formularies.

We believe that one reason why so many of the evangelical clergy rest contented with very obscure and indefinite views upon many theological subjects is, that, from a variety of causes, they are led to shrink from investigating them; and that their Calvinism, such as it is, is to be traced, not to a careful study of the subject, or the exercise of their mental powers, but rather to their own personal experience.   There is not a converted and believing man on earth, in whose conscience there does not exist at least the germ, or embryo, of a testimony in favour of the substance of the Calvinistic doctrine of election.   This testimony may be misunderstood, or perverted, or suppressed; but it exists in the ineradicable sense which every converted man has, that if God had not chosen him, he never would have chosen God, and that if God, by His Spirit, had not exerted a decisive and determining influence in the matter, he never would have been turned from darkness to light, and been led to embrace Christ as his Saviour.   This is really the sum and substance of Calvinism.   It is just the intelligent and hearty ascription of the entire, undivided glory of their salvation, by all who are saved, to the sovereign purpose, the infinite merit, and the almighty agency of God,—the Father, the Son, and the Holy Ghost.   And all that Calvinists ask is, that men who have been constrained to believe, and feel this to be true in surveying the way by which God has led them, would embody their convictions in distinct and definite propositions; and that finding these propositions fully supported by the sacred Scriptures, they would profess and proclaim them as a portion of God's revealed truth.

There is, indeed, a vast amount of evidence that can be adduced in favour of the Calvinistic doctrine of election, when this doctrine is looked at nakedly and by itself—evidence from Scripture, reason, and experience,—evidence which is fitted to impress, and has impressed, equally men of the highest and most soaring intellect, and of the most devoted and childlike piety. But at present we have to do not with arguments and proofs, but only with authorities and testimonies; and on this subject the general position we are anxious to impress is this, that in favour of the Calvinistic doctrine of election, as descriptive of the substance of what Scripture teaches with respect to the divine purposes and procedure in regard to the salvation of those who are saved, there is a mass of testimonies in the experiences, convictions, and impressions of religious men, greatly superior both in amount and value, to what may appear upon a superficial view of the matter. These testimonies, indeed, are often clouded and obscured, brought out in a very vague and imperfect way, and enveloped in much darkness and confusion. But still, viewed collectively and in the mass, and estimated fairly in a survey of the history of the church and of the experience of God's people, they do furnish a powerful confirmation to the proper proofs from Scripture and reason, for the Calvinistic representation of what God purposes and does for the salvation of His chosen.

And with respect to that department of the general subject on which not Calvinists but Arminians are so fond of enlarging, viz., the purposes and procedure of God in regard to those of the human race who ultimately perish, Calvinists undertake to show —1st, That they only follow, humbly and reverentially, the imperfect indications given us in Scripture on this profoundly mysterious subject; 2d, That while desirous to dwell chiefly upon the subject of election, as being both more important in itself, and more fully and clearly set before us in Scripture, they have been compelled, by the perverse and vexatious importunity of their opponents, to give more prominence to the subject of reprobation than they had themselves any desire to give it; and 3d, That the inscrutable mysteries attaching to this subject, apply in reality not to the Calvinistic representation of it, but to the actual realities of the case,—to facts which all parties admit, and which all are equally bound, and equally unable, to explain,—the facts, viz., of the fall of the whole human race into an estate of sin and misery, and of this fearful state becoming permanent in regard to a portion of the race; in other words, the one great fact of the existence and the permanence of moral evil among God's rational and responsible creatures.

The Bible assumes or asserts, while it scarcely professes to explain, these two great facts of the fall of the whole human race into a state of sin and misery, and of the result that a portion of the race is to be left for ever in that condition. But its leading primary object is to unfold the great scheme of mercy, by which God has effectually provided for the salvation from this state of sin and misery of an innumerable multitude, which, for anything that has been made known to us, may, in the ultimate result of things, comprehend a great majority of the descendants of Adam. God has devised such a scheme as this, to the praise of the glory of His grace. He has made it known to us, that we may share in its blessings,—that we may attain to salvation ourselves,—may assist, as the instruments, in His hand, in promoting the salvation of our fellow-men,—and may be prepared for ascribing, with all our hearts, in time and through eternity, glory, and honour, and blessing to Him that loved us, and washed us from our sins in His own blood, and made us kings and priests unto God and His Father.

ZWINGLE,

AND THE

DOCTRINE OF THE SACRAMENTS.*

It is a very common practice of popish writers to represent
Protestantism and the Reformation as thoroughly identified with
Luther, with his character, opinions, labours, and achievements.
Protestantism, according to a mode of representation in which
they are fond of indulging, and which is not destitute of a certain
measure of plausibility, is a new religion never heard of till it was
invented by Luther, and traceable to him alone as its source and
origin. Having thus identified the Reformation and Protestantism
with Luther, they commonly proceed to give an account of him
whom they represent as the author of our faith, bringing out,
with great distortion and exaggeration, everything about his
character and history, about his sayings and doings, which may
be fitted to excite a prejudice against him, especially as contemplated in the light in which *they*, not *we*, represent him, viz., as
the author and founder of a new religious system. Independently
of the utterly unfounded and erroneous assumptions in point of
principle and argument, on which this whole representation is
based, it is altogether untrue, as a mere historical fact, that Luther
occupied any such place in regard to the Reformation and Protestantism, as Papists,—for controversial purposes,—are accustomed
to assign to him. He was not the only person who was raised up
at that period to oppose the Church of Rome, and to bring out

* *British and Foreign Evangelical Review*, October 1860.

from the word of God other representations of apostolic Christianity than those which the papacy inculcated and embodied. It is quite certain that, in different parts of Europe, a considerable number of persons, as early as Luther, and altogether independently of him, had been led to deduce from the sacred Scriptures doctrines substantially the same as his, even the doctrines which may be said to constitute the fundamental principles of Protestantism. In France, Lefevre and Farel, of whom so very interesting an account is given by Dr Merle D'Aubigné in the 12th book of his "History of the Reformation,"* had been led to adopt, and to promulgate, to a certain extent, the leading doctrines of the Reformation before Luther appeared publicly as a Reformer; and they certainly stand much more in the relation of something like paternity to Calvin, and to all that he was honoured to achieve, than Luther does. And if an open breach with the Church of Rome, and the organisation of a Protestant Church, previously to and independently of Luther, are insisted upon as necessary to the character and position of a Reformer, we cán point to Zwingle and his associates, the Reformers of German Switzerland.

Zwingle, indeed, was honoured to perform a work both as a reformer and as a theologian, which entitles him to special notice; and we intend at present giving a brief account of the doctrines which he taught, the place which he occupied, and the influence which he exerted, in regard to theological subjects.

The important movement of which Zwingle might be said to be the originator and the head, was wholly independent of Luther; that is to say, Luther was in no way whatever, directly or indirectly, the cause or the occasion of Zwingle being led to embrace the views which he promulgated, or to adopt the course which he pursued. Zwingle had been led to embrace the leading principles of Protestant truth, and to preach them in 1516, the year before the publication of Luther's Theses; and it is quite certain, that all along he continued to think and act for himself, on his own judgment and responsibility, deriving his views from his own personal and independent study of the word of God. This fact shows how inaccurate it is to identify the Reformation with Luther, as if all the Reformers derived their opinions from him,

* Vol. iii.

and merely followed his example in abandoning the Church of Rome, and organizing churches apart from her communion. Many at this time, in different parts of Europe, were led to study the sacred Scriptures, and were led further to derive from this study views of divine truth substantially the same, and decidedly opposed to those generally inculcated in the Church of Rome. And, more particularly, it is certain that Luther and Zwingle,—the two men who, in different countries, may be said to have originated the public revolt against Rome and the organisation of Protestant churches,—were wholly independent of, and unconnected with, each other, in the formation of their opinions and their plans, and both derived them from their own separate and independent study of God's word.

We need not dwell upon Zwingle's general character as distinguished from his theological opinions, for, indeed, it has never been subjected to any very serious or formidable assaults. He was, in a great measure, free from those weaknesses and infirmities which have afforded materials for charges, in some degree true, and to a much greater extent only plausible, against both Luther and Melancthon. He usually spoke and acted with calmness, prudence, and discretion, and, at the same time, with the greatest vigour, intrepidity, and consistency. He gave the most satisfactory evidence of being thoroughly devoted to God's service, and of acting under the influence of genuine Christian principle; and his character was peculiarly fitted, in many respects, to call forth at once esteem and affection.

He has been sometimes charged, even by those who had no prejudice against his cause or his principles, with interfering too much in the political affairs of his country, and connecting religion too closely with political movements. And, indeed, his death at the battle of Cappell has been held up as an instance of righteous retribution,—as an illustration of the scriptural principle, that "he that taketh the sword shall perish by the sword." Though this view has been countenanced by some very eminent and influential names in the present day, we are by no means sure that it has any solid foundation to rest upon. We do not know any scriptural ground which entitles us to lay it down as an absolute rule, that the character of the citizen and the patriot must be entirely sunk in that of the Christian minister,—anything which precludes ministers from taking part, in any circumstances, in promoting the political wellbeing of their country, or in seeking, in the use of lawful means, to have the regulation of national affairs directed to the advancement of the cause and kingdom of Christ. Ministers certainly show a spirit unworthy of their office, and indicate the low state of their personal religion, when they ordinarily give much time or attention to anything but the direct and proper business of their office, and when they act as if they believed that the success of Christ's cause was really dependent upon political changes, upon results to be accomplished by human policy and human laws; and scarcely anything short of downright immorality tends more powerfully to injure their usefulness, than engaging keenly in the ordinary contentions of political partizanship which may be agitating the community.   But since they are not required to abandon wholly the discharge of the duties, or the exercise of the rights, which devolve upon them as citizens, or to become indifferent to the temporal welfare or prosperity of their country; and since it can searcely be disputed that, in point of fact, the way in which national affairs have been regulated and national laws framed, has often materially contributed to the obstruction or the advancement of Christ's, cause, it seems scarcely fair at once to condemn the conduct of those who may have done something directed to the object of securing the right regulation of national affairs, by means of vague allegations about the spirit of Christianity and the use of carnal weapons, etc., etc., without a careful examination of the particular things done, viewed in connection with the whole circumstances in which they took place. Many countries were so situated at the time of the Reformation, that it was scarcely possible to keep political and religious matters entirely distinct, and scarcely practicable for men who were interested in the welfare of true religion, to abstain from taking part in the regulation of national affairs; and the narrower the sphere of action, the more difficult, or rather impracticable, did such separation and abstinence often become.   What John Knox did, was compelled to do, and did with so much advantage to his country, in Scotland, it was at least equally warrantable and necessary for Zwingle to do in the small canton of Zurich, and in the Helvetic confederation.   And while this may be said generally of his taking some part in the regulation of the public affairs of his country, we are not aware that any evidence has been produced, that he either recommended or approved of any of the public proceedings of Zurich and her confederate cantons, which were clearly objectionable on grounds of religion, equity, or policy. It is well known that he disapproved, and did what he could to prevent, the steps that led to the war in which he lost his life; and it was in obedience to the express orders of the civil authorities, and in the discharge of his duties as a pastor, that, not without some melancholy forebodings, he accompanied his countrymen to the fatal field of Cappell. We cannot dwell upon this subject, but we have thought it proper to express our doubts, whether the disapprobation which some eminent men in the present day have indicated, of Zwingle's conduct in this respect, is altogether well founded. We confess we are inclined to regard this disapprobation as originating rather in a narrow and sentimental, than in an enlarged and manly, view of the whole subject; and to suspect that it may have been encouraged by an unconscious infusion of the erroneous and dangerous principle of judging of the character of Zwingle's conduct by the event,—of regarding his violent death upon the field of battle as a sort of proof of his Master's displeasure with the course he had pursued. But we cannot dwell upon historical and biographical matters, and must proceed to notice Zwingle's theology.

Though he preached the gospel, and inculcated the leading principles of Protestantism in 1516, it was not till 1519 that he was called to come forth publicly in opposition to the Church of Rome, and it was in 1522 that his first works were published; so that, as his death took place in 1531, when he was only forty-seven years of age, his public labours as a Reformer extended only over a period of twelve, and as an author over a period of nine, years. And when we attend to the multiplicity and abundance of his public labours, and the character of the four folio volumes of his works produced in this brief space, we are constrained to form the highest estimate both of his ability and his industry. His works are chiefly occupied with the exposition of Scripture, and with unfolding and defending the doctrines which he had deduced from the word of God, in opposition to the errors of the Papists and the Anabaptists,—or, as he commonly called them, the Catabaptists,—and in opposition to Luther and his followers, on the subject of the presence of Christ's flesh and blood in the Eucharist. It is deplorable, indeed, to find, that through Luther's error and obstinacy, so large a portion of the brief but most valuable life of

Zwingle was of necessity occupied in exposing the unintelligible absurdity of consubstantiation.

Zwingle was not endowed with the fire and energy, with the vigorous and lively imagination, or with the graphic power of Luther, but his understanding, upon the whole, was sounder, and his mental faculties were better regulated and more correctly balanced. He had not been led either by the course of his studies, or by his spiritual experience,—that is, God's dealings with his soul in leading him to the knowledge and belief of the truth,—to give such prominence as Luther did, to any particular departments or aspects of divine truth. He ranged somewhat more freely over the whole field of Scripture for truths to bring out and enforce, and over the whole field of popery for errors to expose and assail; and this has given a variety and extent to his speculations, which Luther's works do not perhaps exhibit in the same degree. And as he was eminently distinguished for perspicacity and soundness of judgment, he has very generally reached a just conclusion, and established it by judicious and satisfactory arguments from Scripture. There are errors and crudities to be found in Zwingle's works, but they are not perhaps so numerous as in Luther's; and several instances occur in which, on points unconnected with the sacramentarian controversy, and without mentioning Luther's name, he has corrected some of the extravagancies and over-statements in which the great Saxon Reformer not unfrequently indulged. Indeed, considering the whole circumstances in which Zwingle was placed, the opportunities he enjoyed, the occupations in which he was involved, and the extent to which he formed his views from his own personal independent study of the sacred Scriptures, he may be fairly said to have proved himself quite equal to any of the Reformers, in the possession of the power of accurately discovering divine truth, and establishing it upon satisfactory scriptural grounds.

His theology upon almost all topics of importance, derived from his own independent study of the word of God, was the same as that which Luther derived from the same sacred and infallible source, as was fully proved by the articles agreed upon at the conference at Marburg, in the year 1529. This conference is one of the most interesting and important events in the history of the church, both in its more personal and in its more public aspects. It was a noble subject for the graphic pen of Dr Merle

D'Aubigné, who has certainly done it ample justice, and whose narrative of it, in the thirteenth book of the "History of the Reformation,"* is singularly interesting, and admirably fitted to exert a useful and wholesome influence. We do not know that ever, on any other occasion in the history of the church, four such men as Luther and Melancthon, Zwingle and Œcolampadius, met together in one room, and sat at the same table discussing the great doctrines of theology. Luther's refusal to shake hands with Zwingle, which led that truly noble and thoroughly brave man to burst into tears, was one of the most deplorable and humiliating, but at the same time solemn and instructive, exhibitions of the deceitfulness of sin and of the human heart, the world has ever witnessed.

The importance of the Marburg conference, in its more public aspects, lies in this, that it was the first formal development, both of the unity and the divergence of the two great sections of the first Reformers, who had, independently of each other, derived their views of divine things from the study of the word of God. At this conference, the leading doctrines of Christianity were embodied in fifteen articles, and both parties entirely agreed with each other in regard to fourteen and two-thirds of the whole—comprehending almost everything that could be regarded as fundamental in a summary of Christian truth. Even in regard to the Lord's Supper, they agreed upon most matters of importance, and differed only on this question, " Whether the true body and blood of Christ be corporally present in the bread and wine ?" and in regard to this question of the corporal presence, they promised to cherish Christian love towards one another "as far as the conscience of each will allow"—" quantum cujusque conscientia feret." Luther's conscience, unfortunately, would not allow him to go far, in the way of Christian love, towards those who denied the unintelligible dogma which he defended so strenuously; and the mischiefs that arose from this controversy, and from the way in which it was conducted, especially by Luther and his followers, including its indirect and remote consequences, have been incalculable in amount, and are damaging the cause of Protestantism, and benefiting the cause of popery, down to the present day. Luther and his followers are the parties responsible for this controversy, and for all the mischief which, directly and indirectly,

* Vol. iv.

immediately and remotely, it has occasioned, 1st, and principally, because they were palpably and wholly wrong on the merits of the question ; and, 2d, because they also displayed a far greater amount of the injurious influences which controversy usually exerts upon the spirit and conduct of men, than their opponents did.   How many have there been in every age who, while destitute of all Luther's redeeming qualities, have displayed largely the grievous infirmities which he exhibited in the sacramentarian controversy, and, like him, have laid all the responsibility of this upon their *conscience,* which compelled them to stand fast for the truth ; and how great the mischief which persons of this stamp have done to the church, by their number and audacity, notwithstanding their insignificance individually !*

The subjects on which the orthodoxy of Zwingle has been chiefly assailed are the doctrine of original sin and the salvation of the heathen ; and, on the ground of statements which he made on these subjects, the papists have been accustomed to accuse him of Pelagianism and Paganism.   In regard to the first of these topics, viz., the doctrine of original sin, on which Bossuet and other papists have adduced heavy charges against Zwingle's orthodoxy, as if he denied it altogether, it has, we think, been proved that when a full and impartial view is taken of his whole doctrine, he does not materially deviate from the standard of scriptural orthodoxy on the subject of the natural and universal depravity of man; and that the peculiarities of his statements, upon which the charge is commonly based, really resolve into differences chiefly about the precise meaning and the proper application of words.   He seems to have been anxious to confine the proper meaning of the word *peccatum* to an actual personal violation of God's law, and to have been disposed to call the natural depravity of man, the source or cause of actual transgression, by the name of a disease, *morbus,* rather than of a sin or peccatum.   But though he attached unnecessary importance to this distinction, he has clearly defined his meaning, explained in what sense men's natural propensity to violate God's law is, or is not, *peccatum;* he has fully expressed his

---

* The articles of the Conference at Marburg are given entire in Hospinian's "Historia Sacramentaria," Pars altera, p. 77 ; Hottinger's " Historia Ecclesiastica," tom. viii. p. 444. They are also given, but not quite so fully and accurately, in Melchior Adam's Vitae Germanorum Theologorum, Vita Zwinglii, p. 32.

accordance in the great scriptural doctrine, that all men do, in point of fact, bring into the world with them a depravity of nature, a diseased moral constitution, which certainly, and in every instance, leads them to incur the guilt of actual transgressions of God's law, and which, but for the interposition of divine grace, would certainly involve them in everlasting misery. The Marburg Articles were prepared by Luther, who had been led to entertain suspicions of Zwingle's orthodoxy upon other points than the real or corporal presence, and among others on original sin, and were no doubt intended by him to test Zwingle's soundness in the faith. Yet Zwingle had no hesitation in subscribing the proposition which Luther prepared upon this point, viz., "credimus peccatum originis, ab Adamo in nos carnali generatione propagatum, tale peccatum esse, quod omnes homines condemnet, et nisi Christus opem nobis suâ morte et vitâ tulisset, æternâ morte nobis in eo moriendum fuisset, neque unquam in regnum dei et beatitudinem æternam pervenire potuissimus."* This in all fairness must be held to establish Zwingle's substantial orthodoxy in regard to the universality, and the fatal consequences, of man's natural depravity; and the suspicion *afterwards* expressed by Luther as to Zwingle's soundness upon this subject, without any new cause having been afforded for the suspicion, should be regarded merely as a specimen of the unjust and ungenerous treatment which he too often gave to the sacramentarians and others who opposed him. It is proper to mention that Milner has given a very defective and unfair representation of Zwingle's views upon this subject, as if he were anxious to establish a charge of error against him, and that the unfairness of Milner's statements has been pointed out, and Zwingle satisfactorily vindicated from the imputation, by Scott, in his excellent continuation of Milner.

Zwingle's adoption of this article upon original sin also proves, that he did not deviate quite so far from sound doctrine, in his views about the salvation of the heathen, as might at first sight appear from some of his statements upon this point. He has, indeed, plainly enough intimated, as some of the fathers have done, his belief that some of the more wise and virtuous heathen were saved and admitted to heaven; and in specifying by name some of the individuals among them whom we might expect to meet there,

* Art. iv.

such as Hercules and Theseus, he has certainly not shown his usual good sense.   But he never meant to teach (and his subscription to the above-quoted article, as well as the whole tenor of his writings, proves it) that men may be saved "by framing their lives according to the light of nature, and the law of the religion they profess."*   On the contrary, he constantly taught that men, if saved at all, were saved only on the ground of Christ's atonement, and by the operation of God's grace.   But he thought, without any sufficient scriptural warrant, that the benefits of Christ's death might be imparted to men, and that their natures might be renewed by God's agency, even though they were not acquainted with any external supernatural revelation, and that some of the heathen did manifest such moral excellence as to indicate the presence of God's special gracious agency.   This was certainly seeking to be wise above what is written.   We are not called upon to be making any positive affirmations as to what God can do or may do, in extending mercy to individuals among men. But the principle is clearly revealed to us in Scripture, that the general provision which God has made for saving men individually from their natural guilt and depravity, is by communicating to them, through the medium of an external revelation, and impressing upon their hearts by His Spirit, some knowledge of the only way of salvation through a Redeemer and a sacrifice; and this truth, solemn and awful as it is, we are bound to receive as the ordinary rule of our opinions and practice, abstaining from all unwarranted speculations, and resting satisfied in the assurance, that the Judge of all the earth will do right.   Still there may be said to be less of error and presumption in the notion, that a knowledge of divine truth has been communicated extraordinarily to some men who were not acquainted with an external supernatural revelation, than in the notion, that men may be saved merely by framing their lives according to the light of nature, and the particular religion, whatever it may be, with which they may happen to have been acquainted; and, to the benefit of this difference in degree, such as it is, Zwingle is entitled, though his mode of discussing the subject cannot be vindicated.

    There is nothing in the articles of Marburg bearing very directly and explicitly upon the doctrines which are usually re-

---

* *Westminster Confession*, c. x.

garded as the peculiarities of the Calvinistic system, though we
are persuaded that none but Calvinists can hold, with full intelligence and thorough consistency, the great scriptural doctrines
which are there set forth, concerning the natural guilt and depravity of man, the way of salvation through Christ, gratuitous
justification, and the production of faith and regeneration by God's
immediate agency. Still, as some men do not perceive and admit
the necessary connection between these great doctrines and what
they call the peculiarities of Calvinism, the question may still be
asked, whether Zwingle agreed with Calvin in those peculiar doctrines with which his name is usually associated? And in answer
to this question, we have no hesitation in saying,—what is equally
true of Luther,—that though Zwingle was not led to dwell upon
the exposition, illustration, and defence of these doctrines, so fully as
Calvin, and although he has not perhaps given any formal deliverance on the irresistibility of grace and the perseverance of the
saints, in the distinct and specific form in which these topics came
to be afterwards discussed, yet in regard to the universal foreordination and efficacious providence of God, and in regard to election
and reprobation, he was as Calvinistic as Calvin himself.

It is rather singular that both Mosheim and Milner have denied
this position, though it can be most fully established. Mosheim
says, that "The celebrated doctrine of an absolute decree respecting the salvation of men, *which was unknown to Zwingle*, was inculcated by Calvin;"* and Milner says, "On a careful perusal
of Zwingle's voluminous writings, I am convinced that certain
peculiar sentiments afterwards maintained by Calvin, concerning
the absolute decrees of God, made no part of the theology of the
Swiss Reformer."† This statement of Milner's is very cautiously
expressed, and contains no specification of the precise points upon
which Zwingle and Calvin are said to have differed. But it is
quite plain, from the whole scope of the passage where this extract
occurs, that Milner just means, in substance, to say, as Mosheim
does, that while Luther, as he admits, though Mosheim denies this
too, was, on the subject of predestination and the decrees of God,
a Calvinist, Zwingle was not. Scott, however, whose representations of the theological sentiments of the Reformers are very full

---

* Murdock's Translation by Reid, | † Century xvi. c. 12.
p. 664.

and accurate, and whose Continuation of Milner is, on this account, peculiarly valuable and deserving of the highest commendation, has fully proved that the representations of Mosheim and Milner upon this point are perfectly erroneous. It is indeed scarcely possible that they could ever have read Zwingle's "Elenchus in Strophas Catabaptistarum," or his treatise, "De Providentia Dei." In these treatises he has clearly and unequivocally expressed his sentiments upon this subject, in full conformity with those afterwards taught and expounded by Calvin, while it cannot be alleged that he has contradicted them in any part of his writings. It may be worth while to give one or two brief extracts from these works in confirmation of this position. In his "Elenchus,"* he gives the following statement as a summary of Paul's argument in the Epistle to the Romans:—" Fide servamur, non ex operibus. Fides non est humanarum virium sed dei. Is ergo eam dat iis quos vocavit, eos autem vocavit quos ad salutem destinavit, eos autem ad hanc destinavit quos elegit, elegit autem quos voluit, liberum enim est ei hoc atque integrum, perinde atque figulo, vasa diversa ex eadem massa educere. Hoc breviter argumentum et summa est electionis a Paulo tractatæ." And, in his commentary upon this summary of Paul's argument, he makes it clear beyond all possibility of reasonable doubt, that he believed, upon Paul's authority, that God, by an absolute decree, chose some men to everlasting life, and made effectual provision that *they* should be saved,—a choice or election made without regard to anything foreseen in them, but solely according to the counsel of His own will. And in his treatise, " De Providentia Dei," he has a chapter, the 6th, on " Election," in which he fully explains his views in such a way as to leave no room for doubt as to their import, and makes some statements even about reprobation, quite as strong as any that ever proceeded from Calvin. Indeed he here expressly tells us that, in his early life, when he was engaged in the study of the Schoolmen, he held, as most of them did, what we should now call the common Arminian doctrine of God's electing men to life because He foresaw that they were to repent and believe the gospel, and that they would persevere in faith and good works. " Quæ mihi sententia, ut olim scholas colenti placuit, ita illas deserenti et divinorum oraculorum puritati adhærenti,

---

* Opera, tom. ii. p. 34, a.

maxime displicuit."* And then he proceeds to show, with a clearness and a force not unworthy of Calvin himself, that this Arminian doctrine is utterly inconsistent with the perfections and moral government of God, and necessarily makes men, whatever its supporters may profess to maintain about the divine sovereignty, the absolute arbiters of their own everlasting destiny,—the true authors of their own salvation.

Many other extracts of a similar kind will be found in Hottinger and Scott.† They are amply sufficient to establish, that Zwingle concurred with Luther in teaching those great doctrines which have brought so much odium on the name of Calvin, before that great man had been led even to form his views of divine truth; for Luther's treatise "De Servo Arbitrio" was published when Calvin was seventeen, and Zwingle's treatise "De Providentia Dei" when Calvin was twenty years of age.

These misstatements of Mosheim and Milner about the theological views of Zwingle, are rather remarkable specimens of the "humanum est errare," and are fitted to remind us of the little reliance that should be placed upon second-hand authorities. Mosheim further lays it down, that Zwingle and Calvin differed from each other, not only in regard to predestination, but also in regard to the power of the civil magistrate in religious matters, and the doctrine of the sacraments. On the first of these points, Mosheim is right in saying of Calvin, " that he circumscribed the power of the magistrate in matters of religion within narrow limits, and maintained that the church ought to be free and independent, and to govern itself by means of bodies of presbyters, synods, or conventions of presbyters, in the manner of the ancient church, yet leaving to the magistrate the protection of the church, and an external care over it." These were the views of Calvin, and they have been the views ever since of the great body of those who have usually been ranked under his name, as opposed to Erastianism on the one hand, and to Voluntaryism on the other. But Mosheim falls into inaccuracy and exaggeration when, in contrast with these views of Calvin, he alleges, that "Zwingle assigned to civil rulers full and absolute power in regard to religious matters, and, what many censure him for, subjected the

* Opera, tom. i. p. 366, b. | Scott, vol. iii. p. 142–152, and 194–
† Hottinger, tom. viii. p. 616–650. | 231.

ministers of religion entirely to their authority." There is no warrant for ascribing such extreme views upon this subject to Zwingle, who, though he did not restrain the power of the civil magistrate within such narrow bounds as Calvin assigned it, was not nearly so Erastian as Mosheim himself and the generality of Lutheran writers. There is no ground, indeed, for believing that Zwingle ever attained to a distinct conception of the great scriptural principle, which has been generally held by Calvinists, viz., that Christ has appointed in His church a government in the hands of ecclesiastical office-bearers, distinct from, independent of, and not subordinate in its own sphere to, the civil magistrate. But he certainly showed that he was decidedly in advance of Luther and Melancthon on this question, and that he was altogether opposed to the leading principle which chiefly Erastus laboured to establish, by ascribing fully and unequivocally the power of excommunication solely to the church itself, and not to the civil magistrate. And with respect to the wider and more general subject of the province and function of the civil magistrate in regard to religion, Zwingle may perhaps be regarded as holding the main substance of what sound principle demands, in maintaining, as it can be proved that he did, that all the powers conceded to the civil authorities of Zurich in religious matters, were exercised by them as representing the church, and only with the church's own consent. We do not believe that the church can lawfully concede or delegate to the civil authorities any power which Christ has conferred upon her. But still there is a fundamental difference between this principle of Zwingle's and the proper Erastian tenet, which ascribes to the civil magistrate jurisdiction or authority, not merely *circa sacra*, but *in sacris*, as inherently attaching to his office."*

But, perhaps, the most interesting topic of discussion connected with the investigation of the opinions of Zwingle, is his doctrine on the subject of the sacraments. A very general impression prevails, and it is certainly not altogether without foundation, that Zwingle held low and defective views upon this subject. He is usually alleged to have taught, that the sacraments are just

---

* On this subject, see Zwingle, De vera et falsa Religione. De magistratu, tom. ii. p. 232–3, and Subsidium sive Coronis de Eucharistia, p. 248. | Gerdes's Historia Reformationis, tom. i. p. 286–7, and Supplement to Preface. Scott iii. pp. 32 and 91.

naked and bare signs or symbols, emblematically and figuratively representing or signifying scriptural truths and spiritual blessings; and that the reception of them is a mere commemoration of what Christ has done for sinners, and a profession which men make before the church or one another, of the views which they have been led to entertain upon the great doctrines of Scripture concerning the way of salvation, as well as a public pledge to follow out consistently the views thus professed; and there are undoubtedly statements in Zwingle's writings which seem fairly enough to imply, that this was the whole doctrine which he taught concerning the sacraments. This doctrine was generally regarded by Protestants, especially after Calvin had published his views upon the subject, as being defective, and, though true so far as it went, yet coming far short of bringing out the whole truth taught in Scripture regarding it. And as the papists were accustomed to bring it as a serious charge against the Reformers, that they explained away the whole mystery and efficacy of the sacraments, the Protestant churches became anxious to disclaim the view which Zwingle had seemed to sanction. Accordingly, in the original Scottish Confession, prepared by John Knox, and adopted by the church in 1560, it is said, "We utterly condemn the vanity of those who affirm sacraments to be nothing else but naked and bare signs."* Similar disclaimers are to be found in many of the other Confessions of the Reformed churches, and in the writings of the generality of the Protestant divines of that period; though there is some good reason to doubt, whether there be adequate grounds for alleging that Zwingle held the sacraments to be nothing else but naked and bare signs, and though there is considerable difficulty in ascertaining, in some cases, what those meant to affirm who were anxious to repudiate this position. It is very manifest that Zwingle, disgusted with the mass of heresy, mysticism, and absurdity, which had prevailed so long and so widely in the church on the subject of the sacraments, leant very strongly to what may be called the opposite extreme of excessive simplicity and plainness. It is not wonderful that he did not succeed perfectly in hitting the golden mean, or that the reaction against the monstrous and ruinous system which had been wrought out and established in the Church of Rome, tempted him to try to simplify the sub-

---

* C. 21.

ject of the sacraments beyond what the Scripture required or sanctioned. We believe that he did, to some extent, yield to this temptation; but we are persuaded, at the same time, that he rendered services of the very highest value to the church, by the light which he threw upon this important and intricate subject.

There is some difficulty in ascertaining precisely what Zwingle's views upon the subject of the sacraments were, and there is some ground to think that, towards the end of his life, he ascribed a higher value and a greater efficacy to these ordinances than he had once done. In his great work, "De Vera et Falsa Religione," published in 1525, he admits that he had spoken of the sacraments somewhat rashly and crudely, and indicated that his views were advancing in what Protestants generally would reckon a sound direction. It is true, indeed, that, in a later work published in 1530, his "Ratio Fidei," he continued to assert, "sacramenta tam abesse ut gratiam conferant, ut ne adferant quidem aut dispensent." But many Protestants who were far enough from regarding the sacraments as naked and bare signs, have denied that the sacraments confer grace;* and, indeed it is only in a very limited and carefully defined sense, that any persons, intelligently opposed to the doctrine of the Church of Rome, admit this position. In a work published in the same year, in defence of his "Ratio Fidei," he declared, that he was quite willing to concur in anything that might be said in commending and exalting the sacraments, provided that what was spoken symbolically was understood and applied symbolically, and that the whole honour of whatever spiritual benefit was derived, was ascribed to God, and not either

---

* We may give a specimen of what is a common mode of speaking among Protestant authors, from Willet's Synopsis Papismi, Cont. xi., q. ii., p. 463:—"The sacraments have no power to give or confer grace to the receiver, neither are they immediate instruments of our justification; instrumental means they are to increase and confirm our faith in the promises of God; of themselves they have no operation, but, as the Spirit of God worketh by them, our internal senses being moved and quickened by those external objects. Neither do we say that the sacraments are bare and naked signs of spiritual graces, but they do verily exhibit and represent Christ to as many as by faith are able and meet to apprehend Him. So to conclude; look how the word of God worketh, being preached, so do the sacraments; but the word doth no otherwise justify us but by working faith at the hearing thereof, so sacraments do serve for the increase of our faith; faith is not a servant and handmaid to the sacraments, but faith is the more principal, and the sacraments have no other use or end than as they are helps for the strengthening of our faith. Grace of themselves they can give or confer none."

to the person administering them, or to any efficacy of the outward elements or actions. And in the last work which he wrote,
and which was not published till after his death, the " Expositio
Fidei," he gave some indications, though perhaps not very explicit,
of regarding the sacraments not only as signs but as seals,—as signs
and seals not only on the part of men, but of God,—as signifying and
confirming something then done by God through the Spirit, as well
as something done by the receiver through faith. This is the great
general principle which has been usually held by Protestants upon
the subject, and is commonly regarded as constituting the leading
point of difference between what is often represented as the
Zwinglian doctrine of the sacraments being only naked and bare
signs, and that generally held by the Protestant churches. We
cannot assert that Zwingle has brought out very distinctly and
explicitly this important principle, that the sacraments are signs
and seals on the part of God as well as of men ; and, therefore,
we cannot assert that his doctrine, though it is true so far as it
goes, brings out the whole of what Scripture teaches upon this
subject, or deny that he leant unduly and excessively to the side
of plainness and simplicity in the exposition of this topic. But
we are persuaded that he manifested very great strength and
vigour of mind in his speculations upon this matter, and that he
aided greatly the progress of scriptural truth in regard to it.

It was in the highest degree honourable to Zwingle that he so
entirely threw off the huge mass of extravagant absurdity and
unintelligible mysticism which, from a very early period, had been
gathering round the subject of the sacraments, and which had
reached its full height in the authorised doctrine of the Church
of Rome. This was an achievement which Luther never fully
reached, either in regard to baptism or the Lord's Supper.
Zwingle's rejection of the whole of the erroneous and dangerous doctrine in regard to the sacraments which had been inculcated by the schoolmen, and sanctioned by the Church of Rome,
was, in the circumstances in which he was placed, one of the
most arduous and honourable, and, in its consequences, one of
the most important and beneficial achievements which the history of the church records. The great general principles by
which Zwingle was guided in the formation and promulgation of
his views in regard to the sacraments were these :—1st, That
great care should be taken to avoid anything which might appear

to trench upon the free grace of God, the meritorious efficacy of Christ's work, and the almighty agency of His Spirit in bestowing upon men all spiritual blessings; and, 2d, That whatever external means of grace may have been appointed, and in whatever way these means may ordinarily operate, God must not be held to be tied or restricted in the communication of spiritual benefits to the use of anything of an external kind, though He has Himself appointed and prescribed it; and, 3d, That the most important matter connected with the subject of the sacraments, is the state of mind and heart of the recipient; and that, with reference to this, the essential thing is, that the state of mind and heart of the recipient should correspond with the outward act which, in participating in the sacrament, he performed. Zwingle was deeply persuaded, that the right mode of investigating this subject was not to follow the example of the Fathers, in straining the imagination to devise unwarranted, extravagant, and unintelligible notions of the nature and effects of the sacraments, for the purpose of making them more awful and more influential, but to trace out plainly and simply what is taught and indicated in Scripture regarding them. By following out this course conscientiously and judiciously, he was led, in the first place, to repudiate the whole huge mass of absurdity and heresy which the fathers and the schoolmen had accumulated around this subject; and, in the second place, to lay down and to apply the three great general principles above stated, which were fitted not only to exclude much grievous error, but to bring in much important and wholesome truth. Zwingle, in these ways, rendered valuable service to the church, and has done much to put the general subject of the sacraments upon a sound and safe footing.

Zwingle's mental constitution gave him a very decided aversion to the unintelligible and mystical, and made him lean towards what was clear, definite, and practical. He had a strong sense of the great injury that had been done to religion by the notions which had long prevailed in regard to the sacraments. And under these influences, it is not surprising that, while discarding a great deal of dangerous error, he should have left in abeyance some portion of wholesome truth. He leant to the side of what was clear, palpable, and safe, and, in the circumstances in which he was placed, this was the right side to lean to. It is not surprising that he did not stop precisely at the right point, and that he carried the work of demolition somewhat too far. And when we consider what a mass of unintelligible and incredible absurdities, to the deep degradation of the human intellect,—and what a mass of heresies, perverting the way of salvation and tending to ruin men's souls,—had been invented by the fathers and the schoolmen, and sanctioned by the Church of Rome on the subject of the sacraments, we cannot but sympathise with Zwingle's general spirit and tendencies in regard to this matter, and rejoice in the large measure of success which attended his investigations. It is indeed a matter of fundamental importance, and perhaps more indispensable than anything else towards preparing men for a rational, intelligent, and beneficial reception of the sacraments, and guarding against self-deceit and danger in the use of them, that they have distinct and accurate conceptions of what the outward elements and actions signify or represent, and of what is professed or implied in the reception of them; that is, of what is the state of mind and heart on the part of the recipient which the reception of them indicates or proclaims. It is in a great measure from inattention to this fundamental point, that so many in every age have been led to participate in the sacraments, who were thereby making a false profession, and of course injuring their own souls; while they were entertaining unfounded expectations of getting spiritual blessings without having any anxiety or concern about what is ordinarily necessary with a view to that result. Zwingle rendered a most important service, by bringing out this great principle, which had been almost entirely buried, and pressing it upon the attention of the church. He came short indeed of the truth in his doctrine as to the nature and efficacy of the sacraments, by not bringing out fully what God does, or is ready and willing to do, through their instrumentality, in offering to men and conferring upon them, through the exercise of faith, spiritual blessings. But he laid a good foundation, on which the whole truth taught in Scripture might be built, when he directed special attention to the true significance and import of the outward elements and actions; and pressed upon men the paramount necessity of seeing to it, that the state of their mind and heart corresponded with the outward signs which they used,—with the outward actions which they performed.

To all this amount of commendation in connection with the

exposition of the sacraments, we believe Zwingle to be well entitled, while the true amount of his shortcoming or deficiency it is not very easy to estimate. Indeed, in regard to this latter point, it should not be forgotten, that of the important document commonly called the "Consensus Tigurinus,"—in which was embodied a state-ment of the fundamental principles about the sacraments, which were held in common by the churches of Geneva and Zurich, as represented by Calvin and by Bullinger the successor of Zwingle, —Calvin declared his conviction, that "if Zwingle and Œcolam-padius, these most excellent and illustrious servants of Christ, were now alive, they would not change a word in it." *

We do not consider it necessary to dwell longer upon the examination of the opinions of Zwingle in regard to the sacraments. Indeed we do not intend to bring forward anything farther that is connected with the personal history of the great Reformer of German Switzerland.† We propose now to give some exposition of the general doctrine or theory of the sacraments, as it has been held by the Reformed churches,—and especially as it has been

---

* Niemeyer's "Collectio Confes-sionum," p. 201.

† There are lives of Zwingle in Melchior Adam's "Vitae Germanorum Theologorum," p. 25, and in Chauf-fepie's Continuation of Bayle's Dic-tionary, tom. iv. Hess's "Life of Zwingle," which was translated into English, and published in this country in the early part of this century, is not a work of much value. Much better is "Ulrich Zwingli et son Epoque," translated from the German of J. J. Hottinger, and published at Lausanne, in 1844; and still better and much more complete is Christoffel's "Zwingli, or the Rise of the Reforma-tion in Switzerland," translated from the German, by John Cockran, Esq., and published by Messrs Clark at Edin-burgh, in 1858. There is a full discus-sion of the principal charges which have been adduced against Zwingle, and of the leading misrepresentations which have been put forth of his life and doc-trines, in the "Apologia pro Zwinglio et ejus Operibus," prefixed by his son-in-law Gualther, to the folio edition of his works, published in 1581, and in "Hottingeri Historia Ecclesiastica," tom. viii. p. 285–400. Much interest-ing matter concerning Zwingle's life and labours will be found in Ruchat's "Histoire de la Reformation de la Suisse," tom. i. and ii., Gerdes's "Historia Reformationis," tom. i. and ii., and Scott's "Continuation of Mil-ner," vols. ii. and iii. Of Zwingle's own works, several, having a symboli-cal character, are given in Niemeyer's "Collectio Confessionum," viz., "Ar-ticuli sive Conclusiones," lxvii., occu-pying a similar place to Luther's "Theses," but exhibiting a much fuller view of scriptural antipapal truth, his "Ratio Fidei" presented to the Em-peror at the diet of Augsburg, in 1530, and his "Expositio Christianae Fidei" written in 1531 and published after his death. Of his other works those which are perhaps the most important, as giving within a comparatively brief compass most information as to his doctrines upon points which are still interesting, are the Explanation of the sixty-seven Articles, the "Commen-tarius de vera et falsa Religione," and the treatise "De Providentia Dei."

set forth in the Confession of Faith and Catechisms which were prepared by the Assembly of Divines at Westminster, and which are still received as symbolical by the great body of Presbyterians over the world.

A grievous corruption of the scriptural doctrine of the sacraments appeared very early in the church; it spread far and wide, and exerted a most injurious influence upon the interests of true religion. Confusion and exaggeration very early appeared in speaking of these ordinances, or the "tremendous mysteries," as some of the Fathers called them; and this confusion and exaggeration soon led to a substitution of the mere observance of outward rites for the weightier matters of the law,—for the essential features of Christian character and conduct. Even in the second century, we find plain indications of a tendency to speak of the nature, design, and effects of the sacraments, in a very inflated and exaggerated style,—a style very different from anything we find in the New Testament. We have a striking instance of this in the famous passage on the Eucharist, occurring near the end of the first Apology of Justin Martyr, the very earliest of the fathers who was not cotemporary with the Apostles. Romanists contend that this passage teaches the doctrine of transubstantiation; Lutherans, that it teaches consubstantiation; and most other men, that it teaches neither the one nor the other. All men of candour admit that the passage is obscure and ambiguous, and all men of sense should have long ago come to the conclusion, that it was not worth while to spend any time in investigating its meaning.* It holds true of this, as of many other passages in the writings of the fathers, which have given rise to much learned discussion in modern times, that it really has no definite meaning; and that if we could call up its author, and interrogate him on the subject, he would be utterly unable to tell us what he meant when he wrote it. This tendency to exaggeration and extravagance, to confusion and absurdity, upon the subject of the sacraments, increased continually, in proportion as sound doctrine upon matters of greater importance disappeared and vital religion decayed, until, in the middle ages, Christianity came to be looked upon by the great body of its professors, as a system which consisted in, and the whole benefits of which were connected with,

---

* Semisch's *Justyn Martyr*, vol. ii.   *Biblical Cabinet*, No. 44.
pp. 339, 340.

a series of outward ceremonies and ritual observances. The nature, design, and effects of the sacraments occupied a large share of the attention of the schoolmen; and, indeed, the exposition and development of the Romish and Tractarian doctrine upon this subject, may be justly regarded as one of the principal exhibitions of the antiscriptural views and the perverted ingenuity of the scholastic doctors. An exaggerated and unscriptural view of the value and efficacy of the sacraments was too deeply engrained into the scholastic theology, and was too much in accordance with the general policy of the Church of Rome, and the general character and tendency of her system, to admit of the Council of Trent giving any sanction to the sounder views which had been introduced by the Protestants, especially by that section of them who have been called the Reformed, to distinguish them from the followers of Luther.

The doctrine of the Church of Rome upon this subject is set forth in the first part of the decree of the 7th Session of the Council of Trent, which treats *de Sacramentis in genere*, and in statements made in treating of some of the other sacraments individually. The leading features of their doctrine on the general subject of the sacraments are these, that "through the sacraments of the church all true righteousness either begins, or, when begun, is increased, or, when lost, is repaired;" "that men do not obtain from God the grace of justification by faith alone without the sacraments, or, at least, without a desire or wish to receive them; "that the sacraments contain the grace which they signify or represent, and confer it always upon all who receive them, unless they put a bar or obstacle in the way" (*ponunt obicem*); that is (as they usually explain it), unless they have at the time of receiving the sacrament a deliberate intention of committing sin; and that they confer or bestow grace thus universally *ex opere operato*, that is, by some power or virtue given to them and operating through them. The application of these principles, which constitute the general doctrine or theory of the sacraments in the Romish theology, to the sacrament of baptism, and to the fundamental blessings of forgiveness and regeneration which it signifies or represents, plainly implies,—what indeed the Council of Trent expressly teaches—viz., that baptism is the instrumental cause of justification, which with Romanists comprehends both forgiveness and regeneration,—that all adults receive when baptized, unless they put a bar in the way, these great blessings,—that all infants, being unable to put a bar in the way of the efficacious operation of the sacrament, receive in baptism the forgiveness of original sin and the renovation of their moral natures,—and that no sin of unbaptized persons, not even the original sin of those who die in infancy, is forgiven without baptism. This is in substance the doctrine in regard to the sacraments, which is taught by the modern Tractarians of the Church of England, and which, indeed, in its main features, may be said to have been always held by High Churchmen. Some of them shrink, indeed, from speaking so plainly on some points as the Council of Trent has done, especially on the *opus operatum;* but there is no difficulty in showing that all High Churchmen must concur in substance with the general sacramental theory of the Church of Rome. The essential idea of the Popish and Tractarian doctrine upon this subject is, that God has established an invariable connection between the sacraments as outward ordinances, and the communication by Himself of spiritual blessings, of pardon and holiness; with this further notion, which naturally results from it, that He has endowed these outward ordinances with some sort of intrinsic power or inherent capacity of conveying or conferring the spiritual blessings with which they are respectively connected. This is what is, and, indeed, must be, meant by the sacramental principle, about which High Churchmen in the present day prate so much; and, notwithstanding their efforts to wrap it up in vague and indefinite phraseology, it is plainly in substance just the doctrine which was established by the Council of Trent. It is a necessary result of this principle, that the want of the outward ordinance—not the neglect or contempt of it, but the mere want of it—from whatever cause arising, deprives men of the spiritual blessings which it is said to convey or confer. Romanists have found it necessary or politic to make some little exceptions to this practical conclusion; but this is the great general result to which their whole scheme of doctrine upon the subject leads, and which ordinarily they do not hesitate to adopt and to apply.

In opposition to all these views, Protestants have been accustomed to maintain the great principle, that the only thing on which the possession by men individually of the fundamental spiritual blessings of justification and sanctification is, by God's arrangements, made necessarily and invariably dependent, is union to Jesus Christ, and that the only thing on which union to Christ may be said to be dependent, is faith in Him; so that it holds true, absolutely and universally, that wherever there is faith in Christ, or union to Him by faith, there pardon and holiness—all necessary spiritual blessings—are communicated by God and received by men, even though they have never actually partaken in any sacrament, or in any outward ordinance whatever. Scripture, we think, plainly teaches this great truth, that as soon as, and in every instance in which, men are united to Christ by faith, they receive justification and regeneration; while without or apart from personal union to Christ by faith, these indispensable blessings are never conferred or received. Every man who is justified and regenerated is certainly admited into heaven, whether he have been baptised or not; and there is no ground in Scripture for maintaining, either, that every one who has been baptised has been forgiven and regenerated, or that those who have not been baptised have not received these great blessings.

If this great general principle can be established from Scripture, it must materially affect some of the views which Romanists and Tractarians hold in regard to the sacraments, and especially in regard to their necessity and importance. Romanists, indeed, are in the habit of charging Protestants with holding that the sacraments are unnecessary or superfluous. But this is a misrepresentation. In perfect consistency with this great doctrine, which represents the possession of spiritual blessings and the ultimate enjoyment of heaven, as dependent absolutely and universally upon union to Christ through faith and upon nothing else, we maintain, that the sacraments which Christ instituted are of imperative obligation, and that it is a duty incumbent upon men to observe them when the means and opportunity of doing so are afforded them; so that it is sinful to neglect or disregard them. Upon the subject of the necessity of the sacraments, Protestant divines have been accustomed to employ a distinction, which, like many other scholastic distinctions, brings out very clearly the meaning it was intended to express, viz., that the sacraments are necessary, *ex necessitate præcepti non ex necessitate medii;*—necessary *ex necessitate præcepti,* because the observance of them is commanded or enjoined, and must therefore be practised by all who have in providence an opportunity of doing so, so that the voluntary neglect or disregard of them is sinful; but not necessary *ex necessitate medii*, or in such a sense, that the mere fact of men not having actually observed them, either produces or proves the non-possession of spiritual blessings,—either excludes men from heaven, or affords evidence that they will not in point of fact be admitted there. Regeneration or conversion, as implying a thorough change of moral nature, is necessary, both *ex necessitate præcepti* and *ex necessitate medii*. It is necessary, not merely because it is commanded or enjoined, so that the neglect or omission of it is sinful, but also because, from the nature of the case, the result cannot be attained without it; inasmuch as it holds true, absolutely and universally, in point of fact and in the case of each individual of our race, that except we be born again we cannot enter the kingdom of heaven. No such necessity can be established with respect to the sacraments, though Romanists and Tractarians assert this, and must do so in order to carry out their principles consistently.

But while this great general principle about spiritual blessings and eternal happiness being dependent upon union to Christ, and upon nothing else, is inconsistent with the Popish and Tractarian notions of the necessity of the sacraments, and furnishes a strong presumption against the higher views of the importance and efficacy of these ordinances, it does not of itself give us any direct information as to what the sacraments are, as to their nature, objects, and effects. Protestants profess to have a certain theory or doctrine in regard to the sacraments as well as Romanists and Tractarians. A definition of the sacraments,—or throwing aside the technical scholastic meaning of the word definition,—a description of the leading features of the sacrament, or a statement of the main positions held concerning them, is properly the sacramental principle; although that phrase has been commonly employed in the present day in a more limited and specific sense. At the time of the Reformation the name Sacramentarian was applied by Luther to Zwingle and his followers, to convey the idea that they explained away or reduced to nothing the value and efficacy of the sacraments; while Zwingle, throwing back the nickname, protested that it might be applied with more propriety to those who made great mysteries of the sacraments, and ascribed to them a value and importance beyond what Scripture warrants. The justice of this statement of Zwingle has been confirmed by the aspect which the discussion of this topic has assumed in the present day. The Tractarians seem to think that none ought to be regarded as really believing in sacraments, except those who concur with the Church of Rome in holding, that there is an invariable connection between the outward sign and the spiritual blessing signified, and that the outward ordinance exerts a real efficacious influence in producing the internal result. This, accordingly, is what they mean by the sacramental principle, on which they are fond of enlarging, and of which they claim to themselves a sort of monopoly. And this is the sense in which the phrase is now commonly used. But the sense in which the expression ought to be employed, is just to designate the fundamental idea of the general doctrine of Scripture on the subject of the sacraments; and in this sense, of course, Protestants have their sacramental principle as well as Romanists and Tractarians.

We believe that Scripture furnishes sufficient materials for giving a general definition or description of the sacraments, or of a sacrament as such; and we call this the sacramental principle, or the true doctrine of Scripture concerning the sacraments. The Reformers put forth their sacramental principle, or their general doctrine concerning the sacraments, in opposition to the views which prevailed at the time in the Church of Rome, and which were afterwards established by the Council of Trent. Definitions and descriptions of the sacraments were in consequence introduced into all the Confessions of the Reformed churches; and the investigation of the nature, the objects, and the effects of the sacraments has continued ever since to hold a place in theological discussions. Since the time when Calvin succeeded in bringing the churches of Geneva and Zurich to a cordial agreement upon this subject, in the adoption of the Consensus Tigurinus in 1549, there has been no very great difference of opinion concerning it among Protestant divines, although there have occasionally been individuals who showed an inclination, either towards the popish and superstitious, or towards the Socinian and Rationalistic, doctrine; and although the Church of England, from her unfortunate baptismal service, has been repeatedly placed in a most difficult and deplorable position. But though there is no great difference of opinion among the Reformed churches, and among Protestant divines, concerning the general doctrine of the sacraments, there seems to have sprung up, in modern times, a great deal of ignorance and confusion in men's conceptions upon this subject. While the sacraments individually, baptism and the Lord's Supper, have been a good deal discussed in some of their aspects, the general doctrine of sacraments, as equally applicable to both, or to any other ordinances for which the designation of a sacrament might be claimed, has been very much overlooked. Even the boasting of the Tractarians about the sacramental principle, has not led to much discussion about the nature and design of the sacraments in general. The two latest works, so far as we know, which have been published under the title of the Doctrine of the Sacraments, contain nothing whatever on the general questions to which we have adverted. In the year 1838 a work was published, entitled, " The Doctrine of the Sacraments," extracted from the " Remains of Alexander Knox," who was the friend and correspondent of Bishop Jebb, and whose writings seem to have contributed, in no small degree, to the rise and growth of Tractarianism; and this work discusses, with no little ability, many questions about baptism and about the Lord's Supper, but it contains nothing about the sacraments in general, or about sacraments as such. This statement likewise applies to a recent work of Archbishop Whately, the latest we believe, he has published. In 1857, he put forth a work, entitled, "The Scripture doctrine concerning the Sacraments, and the Points connected therewith;" and it contains an able discussion on some points connected with baptism, and on some points connected with the Lord's Supper, but nothing whatever on the general nature, objects, and effects of the sacraments.

The disregard of this topic has tended to produce a great deal of confusion and error in men's conceptions upon the whole subject. We are in the habit of seeing baptism and the Lord's Supper administered in the church, and are thus led insensibly and without much consideration, to form certain notions in regard to them, without investigating carefully their leading principles and grounds,—and especially without investigating the relation in which they stand to each other, and the principles that may apply to both of them. We believe that there is scarcely any subject set forth in the Confessions of the Reformed churches, that is less attended to and less understood than this of the sacraments; and that many even of these who have subscribed these Confessions, rest satisfied with some defective and confused notions on the subject of baptism, and on the subject of the Lord's Supper, while they have scarcely even a fragment of an idea of a sacramental principle, or of any general doctrine or theory on the subject of sacraments.

We are persuaded that it would tend greatly to enable men to understand more fully, what we fear many subscribe without understanding, if they took some pains to form a distinct and definite conception of what is taught in the Confessions of Faith in regard to sacraments in general, and then applied these views to the two sacraments of baptism and the Lord's Supper separately. It is quite true that the Scriptures can scarcely be said to contain any statements which bear very directly and formally upon the topics usually set forth in Confessions of Faith, and discussed in systems of theology, under the head *de Sacramentis in genere*, or to give us anything like full and systematic information about the general subject of the sacraments as such.   But the New Testament plainly sets before us two outward ordinances, and two only, the observance of which is of permanent obligation in the Christian church, and which manifestly resemble each other in many respects, both in their general character as emblematic or symbolical institutions, and in their general purpose and object as means of grace—that is, as connected in some way or other with the communication and the reception of spiritual blessings.   As these two ordinances evidently occupy a peculiar place of their own, in the general plan of the Christian system and in the arrangements of the Christian church, it is natural and reasonable to inquire, whether there are any materials in Scripture for adopting any general conclusions as to their nature, design, and efficacy, that may be equally applicable to them both.   And, accordingly, what is usually given as the definition or description of the sacraments, or of a sacrament as such, is just an embodiment of what it is thought can be collected or deduced from Scripture, as being equally predicable of baptism and the Lord's Supper.   Of course nothing ought to be introduced into the definition or description of the sacraments, which cannot be proved to be equally and alike applicable to all the ordinances to which the designation of a sacrament is given; and the less men find in Scripture that seems to them equally applicable to both ordinances, the more meagre is their sacramental principle, or their general doctrine in regard to the nature and design of the sacraments.

The Reformed Confessions and Protestant divines, in general,

have agreed very much in the definition or description of the
sacraments, though there is a considerable diversity in the clearness and distinctness with which their doctrine upon this subject
is unfolded.   It can scarcely, we think, be denied that the general
tendency, even among the Reformers, was to exaggerate or over-
state the importance and efficacy of the sacraments.   Zwingle's
views were a reaction against those which generally prevailed in
the Church of Rome ; but the extent to which he went rather
reacted upon the other Reformers, and made them again approximate somewhat in phraseology to the Romish position.   This
appears more or less even in Calvin, though in his case there was
an additional perverting element—the desire to keep on friendly
terms with Luther and his followers, and with that view to
approximate as far as he could to their notions of the corporal
presence of Christ in the Eucharist.   We have no fault to find
with the substance of Calvin's statements in regard to the sacraments in general, or with respect to baptism; but we cannot deny
that he made an effort to bring out something like a real influence
exerted by Christ's human nature upon the souls of believers, in
connection with the dispensation of the Lord's Supper—an effort
which, of course, was altogether unsuccessful, and resulted only
in what was about as unintelligible as Luther's consubstantiation.
This is, perhaps, the greatest blot in the history of Calvin's labours
as a public instructor ; and it is a curious circumstance, that
the influence which seems to have been chiefly efficacious in
leading him astray in the matter, was a quality for which he
usually gets no credit—viz., an earnest desire to preserve unity
and harmony among the different sections of the Christian
church.

   But, independently of any peculiarity of this sort, we have no
doubt that the general tendency among Protestant divines, both
at the period of the Reformation and in the seventeenth century,
was to lean to the side of magnifying the value and efficacy of the
sacraments, and that some of the statements even in the symbolical
books of some churches, are not altogether free from indications
of this kind.   But while this is true, and should not be overlooked,
there is not nearly so much ground for the allegation, and in so
far as there is ground for it, it does not apply to points of nearly
so much importance, as persons imperfectly and superficially
acquainted with the history of theological discussion have some-

times supposed. Indeed, blunders have occurred in connection
with this subject which are perfectly ludicrous.

Dr Phillpotts, the present Bishop of Exeter, a man of very
considerable skill and ability in controversy, and respectably
acquainted with some departments of theological literature; asserted,
in a charge which he published in 1848, that several of the Confessions of the Reformed churches—specifying " the Helvetic, that
of Augsburg, the Saxon, the Belgic, and the Catechism of
Heidelberg"—agreed with the Church of Rome and the Church
of England in teaching the doctrine of baptismal regeneration.
Dr Goode, now Dean of Ripon,—who has done most admirable
service to the cause of Christian Protestant truth, by his crushing
and unanswerable exposures of Tractarianism, and who, in point
of learning and ability, is one of the most creditable and successful
champions the Evangelical party in the Church of England has
ever had,—thoroughly exposed this " astounding statement,"—
"this most extraordinary blunder." He showed that it arose from
a very imperfect and superficial acquaintance with their theology
as a whole ; and proved that the construction thus put upon some
of their statements was, in the first place, not required by anything
they had said ; and, in the second place, was precluded, not only
by the views set forth in some of these documents on the subject
of election, but by the views taught in all of them on the general
character and objects of the sacraments, and the persons for whom
they are intended, and in whom alone they produce their appropriate effects. The exposure was so conclusive, that Dr Phillpotts
felt himself constrained to withdraw the statement in the second
edition of his charge ; but tried to cover his retreat by an unfounded
allegation, that the documents to which he had referred were self-
contradictory.*

It was upon the same grounds which misled the Bishop of
Exeter, that the same allegation of teaching baptismal regeneration has recently been adduced against " the deliverance of the
Westminster divines in the "Shorter Catechism," on the subject of
baptism." It is very certain that the Westminster divines did
not intend, in this deliverance, or in any other which they put
forth, to teach baptismal regeneration. A contradiction is not to be
imputed to them, if by any fair process of construction it can be

---

* See Goode's " Vindication of the | p. 9 ; and his " Effects of Infant
Defence of the Thirty-nine Articles," | Baptism," chap. iv. pp. 143 and 160.

avoided; and it is in the highest degree improbable that they should have contradicted themselves upon a point at once so plain and so important. The doctrine of baptismal regeneration, whatever else it may include, is always understood to imply, that all baptized infants are regenerated. Now there is nothing in the "Shorter Catechism" which gives any countenance to this notion, or, indeed, conveys any explicit deliverance as to the bearing of baptism upon infants. The notion that the "Shorter Catechism" teaches baptismal regeneration, must, we presume, be based upon the assumption, that the general description given of the import and object of baptism, is intended to apply to every case in which the outward ordinance of baptism is administered. But there is no ground for this assumption. The general description given of baptism must be considered in connection with the general description given of a sacrament, and it is the disregard of this which is one main cause of the ignorance and confusion so often exhibited upon this whole subject. In accordance with views which we have already explained, the description of a sacrament is intended to embody the substance of what is taught or indicated in Scripture, as being true equally and alike of both sacraments. Of course, all that is said about a sacrament not only may, but must, be applied both to baptism and the Lord's Supper, as being in all its extent true of each of them.

The definition or description given of a sacrament in the "Shorter Catechism," is that it "is a holy ordinance instituted by Christ, wherein, by sensible signs, Christ and the benefits of the new covenant are represented, sealed, and applied to believers." In order to bring out fully the teaching of the catechism on the subject of baptism, we must, in the first place, take in the general description given of a sacrament, and then the special description given of baptism, and we must interpret them in connection with each other as parts of one scheme of doctrine. Upon this obvious principle, we say, that the first and fundamental position taught in the "Shorter Catechism" concerning baptism is this, that it (as well as the Lord's Supper) "is an holy ordinance instituted by Christ, wherein, by sensible signs, Christ and the benefits of the new covenant are represented, sealed, and applied to believers." It is of fundamental importance to remember, that the catechism does apply this whole description of a sacrament to baptism, and to realize what this involves. In addition to this general

description of baptism as a sacrament, common to it with the
Lord's Supper, the catechism proceeds to give a more specific
description of baptism as distinguished from the other sacrament.
It is this,—" baptism is a sacrament, wherein the washing with
water, in the name of the Father, the Son, and the Holy Ghost,
doth signify and seal our ingrafting into Christ, our partaking
of the benefits of the covenant of grace, and our engagement to
be the Lord's." Now the only ground for alleging that this
teaches baptismal regeneration, must be the notion, that it applies, in point of fact, to all who have been baptized, and that all
who have received the outward ordinance of baptism are warranted to adopt this language, and to apply it to themselves.
But the true principle of interpretation is, that this description
of baptism applies fully and in all its extent, only to those who are
possessed of the necessary qualifications or preparations for baptism,
and who are able to ascertain this. And the question as to who
these are, must be determined by a careful consideration of all
that is taught upon this subject. Much evidently depends upon
the use and application of the pronoun *our* here,—that is, upon
the question, who are the persons ·that are supposed to be speaking, or to be entitled to speak, that is, to employ the language in
which the general nature and object of baptism are here set forth ?
The *our*, of course, suggests a *we*, who are supposed to be the
parties speaking, and the question is, Who are the *we?* Are they
all who have been baptized ? or only those who are capable of
ascertaining that they have been legitimately baptized, *and who,
being satisfied on this point, are in consequence able to adopt the
language of the catechism intelligently and truly ?* Now this
question is similar to that which is often suggested in the interpretation of the apostolical epistles, where the use of the words
we, us, and *our*, raises the question, who are the *we* that are
supposed to be speaking ? that is, who are the *we*, in whose name,
or as one of whom, the apostle is there speaking ? And this
question, wherever it arises, must be decided by a careful examination of the whole context and scope of the passage. In the
catechism, we have first a general description given of a sacrament,
intended to embody the substance of what Scripture is held to
teach or indicate, as equally and alike applicable to both sacraments.
One leading element in this description is, that the sacraments are
for the use and benefit of believers, and this principle must be

kept in view in all the more specific statements afterwards made about either sacrament. This consideration, as well as the whole scope of the statement, clearly implies, that the description given of baptism proceeds upon the assumption, that the persons who partake in it are possessed of the necessary qualifications,— that is, that they are believers, and do or may know that they are so.

This principle of construction is a perfectly fair and natural one. It has always been a fundamental principle in the theology of Protestants, that the sacraments were instituted and intended for believers, and produce their appropriate beneficial effects, only through the faith which must have previously existed, and which is expressed and exercised in the act of partaking in them. This being a fundamental and recognised principle in the Protestant theology of the sacraments, it was quite natural that it should be assumed and taken into account in giving a general description of their objects and effects. And the application of this principle of interpretation to the whole deliverances of the Westminster divines upon the subject of the sacraments, in the Confession of Faith and in the Larger Catechism as well as in the Shorter, introduces clearness and consistency into them all, whereas the disregard of it involves them in confusion, and inconsistency.

On the grounds which have now been hinted at, and which, when once suggested, must commend themselves to every one who will deliberately and impartially examine the subject, we think it very clear and certain, that the *we*, suggested by the *our* in the general description of baptism, are only the believers who had been previously set forth as the proper and worthy recipients of the sacraments; and that consequently the statement that "baptism signifies and seals *our* ingrafting into Christ," etc., must mean, that it signifies and seals the ingrafting into Christ OF THOSE OF US who have been ingrafted into Christ by faith. This construction, of course, removes all appearance of the catechism teaching baptismal regeneration.

The truth is, that the only real difficulty in the case is precisely the reverse of that which has been started. The difficulty is, not that the catechism appears to teach, that infants are all regenerated in baptism ; but that it appears to teach, that believers are the only proper recipients of baptism, as well as of the Lord's Supper; while yet at the same time it also explicitly teaches, that the infants of such as are members of the visible church are to be baptized. This will require some explanation, while at the same time the investigation of it will bring us back again to the main subject which we wished to consider, viz., the true doctrine of the Reformed churches, and especially of the Westminster standards, in regard to the nature, objects, and effects of the sacraments in general.

The general view which Protestants have commonly taken of the sacraments is, that they are signs and seals of the covenant of grace, that is, of the truths which unfold the provisions and arrangements of the covenant, and of the spiritual blessings which the covenant provides and secures,—not only signifying or representing Christ and the benefits of the new covenant, but sealing or confirming them, and in some sense applying them, to believers. As the sacraments are the signs and seals of the covenant, so they belong properly to, and can benefit only, those who have an interest in the covenant, the *fœderati ;* and there is no adequate ground for counting upon their exerting their appropriate influence in individual cases, apart from the faith which the participation in them ordinarily expresses, and which must exist before participation in them can be either warrantable or beneficial. These are the leading views which Protestant divines have usually put forth in regard to the sacraments in general, that is, their general nature, design, and efficacy. In looking more closely at the doctrines of Protestant churches upon this subject, it is necessary to remember, not only that, as we have already explained, they usually assume, in their general statements, that the persons partaking in the sacraments are duly prepared, or possessed of the necessary preliminary qualifications, but also that, when statements are made which are intended to apply equally to baptism and the Lord's Supper ; or, when the general object and design of baptism are set forth in the abstract, they have in their view, and take into their account, only *adult* baptism, the baptism of those who, after they have come to years of understanding, ask and obtain admission into the visible church by being baptized.

This mode of contemplating the ordinance of baptism is so different from what we are accustomed to, that we are apt to be startled when it is presented to us, and find it somewhat difficult to enter into it. It tends greatly to introduce obscurity and confusion into our whole conceptions on the subject of baptism, that

we see it ordinarily administered to infants, and very seldom to
adults.   This leads us insensibly to form very defective and erroneous conceptions of its design and effects, or rather to live with
our minds very much in the condition of blanks, so far as concerns any distinct and definite views upon this subject.   There is
a great difficulty felt,—a difficulty which Scripture does not afford
us adequate materials for removing, in laying down any distinct
and definite doctrine as to the bearing and efficacy of baptism in
the case of infants, to whom alone, ordinarily, we see it administered.   A sense of this difficulty is very apt to tempt us to remain
contentedly in great ignorance of the whole subject, without any
serious attempt to understand distinctly what baptism is and
means, and how it is connected with the general doctrine of
the sacraments.   And yet is quite plain to any one who is capable of reflecting upon the subject, that it is *adult* baptism
alone which embodies and brings out the full idea of the ordinance, and should be regarded as the primary type of it,—*that*
from which mainly and principally we should form our conceptions of what baptism is and means, and was intended to accomplish.   It is in this aspect that baptism is ordinarily spoken
about, and presented to our contemplation, in the New Testament, and we see something similar in tracing the operations of
our missionaries who are engaged in preaching the gospel in
heathen lands.

Adult baptism, then, exhibits the original and fundamental
idea of the ordinance, as it is usually brought before us, and as it
is directly and formally spoken about in the New Testament.
And when baptism is contemplated in this light, there is no more
difficulty in forming a distinct and definite conception regarding
it than regarding the Lord's Supper.   Of adult baptism, we can
say, just as we do of the Lord's Supper, that it is in every instance,
according to the general doctrine of Protestants, either the sign
and seal of a faith and a regeneration previously existing, already
effected by God's grace,—or else that the reception of it was a
hypocritical profession of a state of mind and feeling which has no
existence.   We have no doubt that the lawfulness and the obligation of infant baptism can be conclusively established from Scripture; but it is manifest that the general doctrine or theory just
stated, with respect to the import and effect of the sacraments,
and of baptism as a sacrament, cannot be applied fully in all its

extent to the baptism of infants. The reason of this is, because Scripture does not afford us materials, either, for laying down any definite position as to a certain and invariable connection between baptism and spiritual blessings,—that is, for maintaining the doctrine of baptismal regeneration ; or, for stating such a distinct and definite alternative with respect to the efficacy of the ordinance in individuals, as has been stated above in the case of adult baptism and the Lord's Supper. But notwithstanding these obvious considerations, we fear it is a very common thing for men, just because they ordinarily see infant, and very seldom see adult, baptism, to take the baptism of infants, with all the difficulties attaching to giving a precise and definite statement as to its design and effect in their case, and to allow this to regulate their whole conceptions with respect to this ordinance in particular, and even with respect to the sacraments in general. This is a very common process ; and we could easily produce abundant evidence, both of its actual prevalence, and of its injurious bearing upon men's whole opinions on this subject. The right and reasonable course is plainly just the reverse of this,—viz., to regard adult baptism as affording the proper fundamental type of the ordinance,—to derive our great leading conceptions about baptism from the case, not of infant, but of adult, baptism, viewed in connection with the general theory or doctrine applicable to both sacraments ; and then, since infant baptism is also fully warranted in Scripture, to examine what modifications the leading general views of the ordinance may or must undergo, when applied to the special and peculiar case of the baptism of infants.

These views were acted upon, though not formally and explicitly stated, by the Reformers in preparing their Confessions of Faith, and in their discussions of this subject. It is impossible to bring out, from their statements about the sacraments, a clear and consistent sense, except upon the hypothesis, that, in laying down their general positions as to the nature, objects, and effects of the sacraments, they proceeded upon the assumption, that those partaking in these ordinances were duly qualified and rightly prepared ; and more particularly, that the persons baptized, in whom the true and full operation of baptism was exhibited, were adults,—adult believers. The Council of Trent, in their decrees and canons on the subject of justification, which in the Romish system comprehends regeneration, and of which they asserted baptism, or the sacrament of faith, as they call it, to be the instrumental cause,* dealt with the subject on the assumption, that they were describing the process which takes place in the case of persons who, after they have attained to adult age, are led to embrace Christianity and to apply for baptism. And we find that the Reformers, in discussing these matters with their Romish opponents, accommodated themselves to this mode of putting the case; and having thus adult baptism chiefly in their view, were led sometimes to speak as if they regarded baptism and regeneration as substantially identical. They certainly did not mean to assert or concede the popish principle, of an invariable connection between the outward ordinance and the spiritual blessing, for it is quite certain, and can be conclusively established, that they rejected this. They adopted this mode of speaking, which at first sight is somewhat startling, 1st, because the Council of Trent discussed the subject of justification chiefly in its bearing upon the case of those who had not been baptised in infancy, and with whom, consequently, baptism, if it was not a mere hypocritical pretence, destitute of all worth or value, was, in the judgment of Protestants, a sign and seal of a faith and regeneration previously wrought and then existing; and 2dly, because it was, when viewed in this aspect and application, that their great general doctrines, as to the design and efficacy of the sacraments in their bearing upon the justification of sinners, stood out for examination in the clearest and most definite form. This was the true cause of a mode of speaking sometimes adopted by the Reformers, which, to those imperfectly acquainted with their writings, and with the state of theological discussion at the time, might seem to countenance the doctrine of baptismal regeneration.

It was very important to bring out fully and distinctly the nature and character of the sacraments as signs and seals of the covenant of grace and its benefits, the import of the profession implied in partaking in them, and the qualifications required for receiving them rightly; *and then to connect the statement of their actual effects with right views upon all these points.* This process was at once the most obvious and the most effectual way, of shutting out the erroneous and dangerous notions upon the subject of the sacraments that prevailed in the Church of Rome. It

---

* Session vi. c. 8.

was very important with this view, to give a compendious and summary representation of what was set forth in Scripture as the sacramental principle or theory, as being equally applicable to both sacraments; and to keep steadily before men's minds the consideration, that this could be held to be fully realized and exhibited only in those for whom the sacraments were mainly intended, and who were duly prepared for receiving and improving them aright. Their minds were filled with these principles, and they were anxious to set them forth, in opposition to the great sacramental system which had been excogitated by the schoolmen, and sanctioned by the Church of Rome. And it was because their minds were filled with these principles that, though strenuously opposing the tenets of the Anabaptists, they yet saw clearly and admitted the somewhat peculiar and supplemental position held by infant baptism. They held it to be of primary importance to bring out fully the sacramental principle as exhibited in its entireness in adult baptism and the Lord's Supper; and in aiming at accomplishing this, they were not much concerned about putting forth definitions or descriptions of the sacraments or even of baptism, which could scarcely be regarded as comprehending infant baptism, or as obviously and directly applying to it. They never intended to teach baptismal regeneration, and they have said nothing that appears to teach it, or that could be supposed to teach it, by any except those who were utterly ignorant of the whole course of the discussion of these subjects as it was then conducted. They never intended to discountenance infant baptism; on the contrary, they strenuously defended its lawfulness and obligation. But they certainly gave descriptions of the general nature, design, and effects of the sacraments, which, if literally interpreted and pressed, might be regarded as omitting it, or putting it aside.

It is impossible to deny, that the general description which the "Shorter Catechism" gives of a sacrament teaches, by plain implication, that the sacraments, so far as regards adults, are intended only for believers; while no Protestants, except some of the Lutherans, have ever held that infants are capable of exercising faith. It also teaches, by plain implication, in the previous question, the 91st, that the wholesome influence of the sacraments is experienced only by those who "by faith receive them." All this is applied equally to baptism and the Lord's Supper. Its general import, as implying a virtual restriction of these ordinances to believers, is too clear to be misunderstood or to admit of being explained away. And then, again, the apparent discrepancy between this great principle, and the position that " the infants of such as are members of the visible church are to be baptized," is too obvious to escape the notice of any one who deliberately examines the catechism with a view to understand it. These considerations would lead us to expect to find, that the discrepancy is only apparent, and that there is no great difficulty in pointing out a mode of reconciliation. The mode of reconciliation we have already hinted at. It is in substance this, that infant baptism is to be regarded as a peculiar, subordinate, supplemental, exceptional thing, which stands, indeed, firmly based on its own distinct and special grounds, but which cannot well be brought within the line of the general abstract definition or description of a sacrament, as applicable to adult baptism and the Lord's Supper.

The Westminster divines, then, have given a description of a sacrament, which does apply fully to adult baptism and the Lord's Supper, but which does not directly and *in terminis* comprehend infant baptism. This, which is the plain fact of the case, could only have arisen from their finding it difficult, if not impossible, to give a definition of the sacraments in their great leading fundamental aspects, which would at the same time apply to, and include, the special case of the baptism of infants. This, again, implies an admission that the definition given of a sacrament does not apply fully and in all its extent to the special case of infant baptism; while it implies, also, that the compilers of the catechism thought it much more important, to bring out fully, as the definition of a sacrament, all that could be truly predicated equally of adult baptism and the Lord's Supper, than to try and form a definition that might be wide enough and vague enough to include infant baptism, a topic of a peculiar and subordinate description. This is the only explanation and defence that can be given of the course of statement adopted in the catechism.

It may possibly occur to some, that since it is certain that the compilers of the catechism held, that it was the children of believers only that were to be baptized, and that they were to be baptized on the ground of their parents' faith, and the general principle of

covenant relationship based upon this, the word *believers*, in the
definition of a sacrament, might include infants, viewed as one
with their believing parents, and virtually comprehended in them.
But, besides that this leaves untouched the statement which implies, that spiritual benefit is derived from the sacraments only by
"those who by faith receive them," we think it quite plain and
certain, from the whole scope of the statement given in answer to
the question, What is a sacrament? that the *believers* to whom
the sacraments represent, seal, and apply Christ and His benefits,
are those only who themselves directly and personally partake in
the sacraments, and not those also who, though not believers
themselves, may be admitted to one of the sacraments because of
their relationship to believers.

A similar doubt might be started about the meaning and application of the parallel passage in the "Larger Catechism."* A sacrament is there described as " an holy ordinance instituted by Christ,
in His church, to signify, seal, and exhibit *unto those that are within
the covenant of grace*, the benefits of His mediation, to strengthen
and increase their faith," etc. Now there can be no doubt that,
according to the prevailing opinions and the current *usus loquendi*
of the period,—and, as we believe, in accordance with Scripture,—
the expression, "those that are within the covenant of grace," might
include the children of believers, who were regarded as *fœderati*,
and as thus entitled to the "*signa et sigilla fœderis*." But it is quite
certain that the expression is not used here in this extended sense,
or as including any but believers. For this sentence goes on immediately, without any change in the construction, and without
any indication of alteration or restriction in regard to the persons spoken of, to say, that the sacraments were instituted " to
strengthen and increase THEIR faith,"—implying, of course, that
the persons here spoken of had faith before the sacraments came
to bear upon them, or could confer upon them any benefit.

There can, then, be no reasonable doubt that the " Shorter
Catechism" in defining or describing a sacrament restricts itself
to the case of adult believers; and the only way of reconciling
the definition with its teaching on the subject of infant baptism is
by assuming that it is not to be applied absolutely and without
all exception in other cases; and that infant baptism, though

* Q. 162.

fully warranted by Scripture, does not correspond in all respects with the full sacramental principle in its utmost extent and clearness, as exhibited in adult baptism and the Lord's Supper, and must therefore be regarded as occupying a peculiar, and supplemental position. We know no other way of showing the consistency with each other of the different statements contained in the catechism. The principle we have explained refutes the allegation of inconsistency or contradiction, and resolves the whole difficulty into a certain concession on the subject of infant baptism,—a concession not affecting the scriptural evidence for the maintainence of the practice of baptizing infants, but merely the fulness and completeness of the doctrinal explanation that should be given of its objects and effects.

The explanation we have given upon this point is in full accordance with the views set forth in the " Westminster Confession of Faith," and in the Confessions of the Reformed churches generally. They all of them assert the scriptural authority of infant baptism, while at the same time most of them, though with different degrees of clearness, present statements about the sacraments or about baptism, which do not very fully and directly apply to the baptism of infants.* We have been the more disposed to give some time to the explanation of the peculiar position and standing of the topic of infant baptism, because it is not merely indispensable to the intelligent and consistent exposition of the " Shorter Catechism," but also because ignorance or disregard of it produces much error and confusion in men's whole views with respect to the sacraments in general. Men who have not attended to and estimated aright this topic of the peculiar and subordinate place held by the subject of infant baptism are very apt to run into one or

---

* Strange as it may seem, this holds true, to some extent, even of the articles of the Church of England, though, perhaps, somewhat less fully and explicitly than in the case of any other of the Reformed churches. In the general statements about the sacraments in the 25th article, and in the chief portion of the 27th, on baptism, there is nothing to suggest that infant baptism is comprehended in the description ; and, indeed, the general scope and spirit of the statements rather seem to ignore or pretermit it, though there is not the same explicit and restricting reference to *believers* and *faith* which occurs in the "Shorter Catechism." And then, again, the only express mention of infant baptism, which occurs in the end of the 27th article, and which simply asserts that it " is in anywise to be retained in the church as most agreeable to the institution of Christ," brings it in very much in the same supplemental, exceptional sort of way, in which the Westminster standards deal with it.

other of two extremes,—viz., 1st, that of lowering the true sacramental principle, as brought out in the general definition of a sacrament, and as exhibited fully in the case of adult baptism and the Lord's Supper, to the level of what suits the special case of infant baptism; or, 2d, that of raising the explanation propounded of the bearing and effect of infant baptism, up to a measure of clearness and fulness which really attaches only to adult baptism and the Lord's Supper. And, as error is generally inconsistent, and extremes have a strong tendency to meet, cases have occurred in which both these opposite extremes have been exhibited by the same persons, in connection with that one source of error and confusion to which we have referred. The truth, as well as the importance, of some of the points which have been referred to in the course of the preceding statements, will appear more clearly, as we proceed to explain more fully and formally the general doctrine of the sacraments, as set forth in the Westminster symbols, in accordance with the other Confessions of the Reformed churches.

The doctrine of the sacraments, or the sacramental principle, in the proper import of that expression, is intended, as we have explained, to embody the sum and substance of what is taught or indicated in Scripture, as equally and alike applicable to both the ordinances to which the name of a sacrament is commonly given. Of course, nothing ought to be introduced into the definition or description of a sacrament, but what there is sufficient scriptural ground, more or less direct and explicit, and more or less clear and conclusive, for holding to be predicable equally and alike of baptism,—that is, adult baptism and the Lord's Supper. Besides the scriptural statements that bear directly upon these two ordinances separately, there are views suggested by their general character and position, taken in connection with general scriptural principles, to which it may be proper, in the first instance, to advert. There is not a great deal in Scripture that can be said to bear very directly upon the question, What is a sacrament? but there is a good deal that may be deduced from Scripture by good and necessary consequence.

There are two different aspects in which the sacraments are to be regarded, 1st, Simply as institutions or ordinances whose appointment by Christ stands recorded in Scripture, and whose celebration in the church, according to His appointment, may be contemplated or looked at by spectators,—and, 2a, as acts which men perform, transactions in which men individually take a part;—that is, they may be regarded either as mere instituted symbols, or also, and in addition, as symbolic actions which ·men perform.

Viewed, in the first of these aspects, as symbols, they merely signify or represent (these two words are generally used synonymously in this matter) spiritual blessings, Christ and the benefits of the new covenant, and the scriptural truths which make known, unfold, and offer these blessings to men; while, in regard to the second aspect of them, this much at least must be evident in general, that the participation in the sacraments by men individually, is on their part an expression or profession of a state of mind and feeling, with reference to the truths which the outward symbols represent, and the blessings which they signify. Viewed, in the first of these aspects, as mere symbols which have been instituted and described in Scripture, and which may be contemplated or looked at, it is evident that the sacraments are merely, to use an expression which Calvin and other Reformers applied to them, appendages to the gospel,—that is, merely means of declaring and bringing before our minds in another way, by a different instrumentality, what is fully set forth in the statements of Scripture. In baptism, viewed in this light, God is just telling us, by means of outward symbols instead of words, that men, in their natural condition, need to be washed from guilt and depravity, and that full provision has been made for effecting this, through the shedding of Christ's blood and the effusion of His Spirit. In the Lord's Supper, in like manner, He is just telling us that Christ's body was broken, and that His blood was shed, for men; and that, in this way, full provision has been made, not only for restoring men to the enjoyment of God's favour, and creating them again after His image, but for affording them abundance of spiritual nourishment, and enabling them to grow up in all things unto Him who is the Head. The sacraments, as symbols, thus teach, by outward and visible representations, the leading truths which are revealed in Scripture concerning the way of salvation; and teach them in a manner peculiarly fitted, according to the principles of our constitution, to bring them home impressively to our understandings and our hearts.

And it is important to notice that, even in this simplest and most elementary view of the sacraments, they may truly and reasonably be called seals as well as signs,—they may be said not only to signify or represent, but to seal. A seal is something external, usually appended to a deed or document, or impressed upon a substance which forms the subject of negotiation or arrangement, and it is intended to strengthen or confirm conviction or faith, expectation or confidence. A seal, in this sense, the only sense in which it can apply to the sacraments, is a thing of no real intrinsic value or importance apart from the engagement ratified. Its use and efficacy are purely conventional. Seals are based, indeed, upon a natural principle in our complex constitution, in virtue of which external objects or actions connected with, or added to, declarations, engagements, or promises, are regarded as tying or binding more strongly those from whom these deeds or documents proceed, and as thus tending to strengthen and confirm the faith and the hope of those to whom they are directed. It is this principle in our constitution which is the source and origin, the *rationale* and defence, not only of the sealing of deeds and documents,—that is, of the practice of appending a seal to the signature of the names attached to them,— but of the whole series of outward significant rites and ceremonies, which in all ages and countries have been associated with covenants and treaties, with bargains and barterings. These sealings, and other similar rites and ceremonies, which in such variety have prevailed in all ages and countries in connection with transactions of this sort, have been always regarded and felt as somehow binding the parties more strongly to their respective statements and engagements, and as thus strengthening their reliance upon each other, in reference to everything that had been declared or promised. And yet it is quite plain, that these sealings and other rites and ceremonies usually connected with compacts and bargains, can scarcely be said to possess any value apart from the engagement sealed, or to exert a real influence in effecting any important result. The only essential things in transactions of this sort, are the deeds or documents, embodying a statement of the things arranged or agreed upon with all their circumstances and conditions, and the signatures of the parties, binding themselves to the terms set forth in the deed.

Applying these obvious principles to Christianity and salvation, it is plain that the essential things as bearing on the practical result, are arrangements and proposals, made and revealed by God, understood and accepted by men. It is indispensable that men understand the import of the offers and proposals made to them, be satisfied that they come from God, and then accept and act upon them. The covenant of grace is thus substantially a proposal made by God to men, which is accepted by them ; and the essential things are, the substance of the proposal set forth as in a deed or document, and the concurrence of the parties, as if attested by their signatures. The sacraments, according to the views which have generally prevailed among Protestants, are signs and seals of this covenant,—that is, as signs they embody in outward elements (for we are not speaking at present of the sacramental actions) the substance of what is set forth more fully and particularly in the written word ; and this additional, superadded, external embodiment of the provisions and arrangements, is regarded as occupying the place, and serving the purpose of a seal appended to a signature to a deed ; not certainly as if it could very materially affect the result, so long as we had the deed and the signatures, but still operating, according to the well-known principles of our constitution, in giving some confirmation to our impressions, if not our convictions, of the reality and certainty, or reliability of the whole transaction.

But we proceed to advert to the second and higher view that must obviously be taken of the sacraments. They were intended not so much to be read about or to be looked at, as to be participated in. Men are individually to be washed with water, in the name of the Father, the Son, and the Holy Ghost, and they are individually to eat bread and to drink wine at the Lord's table, in remembrance of Christ. This being the case, the questions naturally arise, What is the meaning and what the object of those acts which they perform ? Why did God require these things at their hands ? What is the effect which the doing of these things is intended to produce ? and, What are the principles which regulate and determine the production of the resulting effects ? Now, as bearing upon the answer to these questions, there are some positions which are generally admitted, and are attended with no difficulty. The two leading aspects in which the sacraments, viewed as actions which men perform, are represented in Scripture are,—first, as duties which God requires of us, and, second, as means of grace or privileges which he appoints and bestows. And again, under the first of these heads, viz., commanded duties, there are two views that may be taken of them, 1st, as acts of worship; and 2d, as public professions of Christianity. It is, of course, men's duty to render to God the acts of worship, and to make the professions, which He requires of them. The sacraments seem plainly to possess these two characters. In participating in them, we are rendering an act of worship to God, and we are making a public profession by an outward act, and all this He has required at our hands, or imposed upon us as a duty. If this be so, then it follows that any general principles which are indicated in Scripture, or involved in the nature of the case, as being rightly applicable to acts of worship and to public professions, must be applied to them. Whatever is necessary to make an act of worship reasonable and acceptable to God, and whatever is necessary to make a public profession intelligent and honest, must be found in men's participation in the sacraments, in order to make it fitted to serve any of its intended purposes. And this most simple and obvious view of the general nature and character of the sacramental actions ought not to be overlooked or forgotten, as it is well fitted, when remembered and applied, to guard us both against error in doctrine and delusion in practice.

It is the second of these views of them, however,—that which represents them as outward public professions,—which bears more immediately upon their mode of operation and their actual effects, as privileges or means of grace. All admit that the sacraments embody or involve a public profession of a certain state of mind and feeling. Indeed, this is plainly implied in their character as symbolical or emblematical ordinances. We cannot conceive that it should have been required as a duty of those to whom the gospel is preached, that they should be baptized and should partake in the Lord's Supper, unless this washing with water, and this eating bread and drinking wine, symbolized and expressed some state of mind, some conviction, or feeling, or purpose, bearing upon their relation to God, and the salvation of their souls. That participation in the sacraments is a discriminating mark or badge of what may be called, in some sense, a profession of Christianity, and that it involves an engagement to perform certain duties, is admitted by all, even those who take the lowest views of their nature and design. And all orthodox divines hold that this constitutes one end and object of the institution of these ordinances, though they regard it only as a subordinate one. In the very important document formerly referred to, called "Consensus Tigurinus," prepared by Calvin, and embodying the agreement among the Swiss churches on the whole subject of the sacraments, while it is admitted that there are various ends and objects of the sacraments, such as, that they may be marks and badges of a Christian profession and union or brotherhood—that they may be incitements to thanksgivings and exercises of faith and a pious life, and engagements binding to this—it is laid down, "that the one principal end of these ordinances is, that God, by them, may attest, represent, and seal His grace to us." * This mode of statement is in accordance with the views generally entertained by the Reformed divines, and it is adopted in the Westminster Confession,† where, after describing it as the end or object of the sacraments "to represent Christ and His benefits, and to confirm our interest in Him," it adds, evidently in the way of suggesting some additional points of less fundamental importance, "as also to put a visible difference between those that belong unto the church and the rest of the world, and solemnly to engage them to the service of God in Christ." These subordinate ends of the sacraments, connected with their character and functions as badges of a public profession and solemn engagements to duty, do not in themselves require lengthened explanation, as they are simple and obvious, and have not given rise to much discussion, except in so far as the question has been raised, as to the precise import and amount of the profession which participation in the sacraments involves.

This is a question of some difficulty and importance; and it is intimately connected with the investigation of the great primary end or object of the sacraments, and with their character and function as means of grace. It is generally admitted by Protestant divines, that the sacraments are signs and seals of the covenant of grace, that is, of the truths and promises setting forth the provisions and arrangements which may be said to constitute the covenant, and of the spiritual blessings which the covenant offers and secures; and these terms, accordingly, are applied to them in almost all the Confessions of the Reformed churches. But even where there is a concurrence in the use of these epithets, there is still room for error and confusion on some important topics connected with this matter. The leading questions connected with

---

* Niemeyer, p. 193.   † C. 27, s. 1.

the sacraments may be ranked under two heads—1st, What are their objects or ends, comprehending the purposes for which they were instituted, and the effects which they actually produce? And 2d, Who are their proper subjects, the parties for whom they were intended, those who are qualified to partake in them lawfully and beneficially? These two heads of investigation, which may be briefly described, as respecting, the first the objects, and the second the subjects, of the sacraments, are very closely connected with each other. The settlement of either of these questions would go far to determine the other. If we had once ascertained what is the leading primary object of the sacraments, there would be no great difficulty in deducing from this, viewed in connection with other doctrines plainly taught in Scripture, what kind of persons ought to partake in them; and if we once knew who are the parties that ought to partake in them, we might from this infer a good deal, positively as well as negatively, in regard to the purpose they were intended to serve. On some grounds it would seem to be more natural and expedient to begin with examining the objects or ends of the sacraments. But as we have been led, in the arrangement we have adopted, to advert to the view of the sacraments as badges of a public profession, and as the consideration of this topic, which has not yet been completed, is connected rather with the examination of the subjects than the objects of the sacraments, we shall consider, in the first place, in contemplating them as means of grace, the question, who are the parties for whom they were intended? We are the less concerned about following what might seem to be the more strictly logical order, because our object is rather explanation than defence;—it is rather to bring out what the doctrine of the Reformed Confessions, and especially of the Westminster symbols, on the general subject of the sacraments, is, than to establish its truth and to vindicate it from objections;—as we have in view chiefly the case of those who have professed to believe these symbols, but who still exhibit a great deal of ignorance in regard to their meaning and import.

We have mentioned, as the first and most general division that obtains on the subject of the sacraments, that they may be regarded either, first, as duties which God requires; or, second, as means of grace. The difficulties which have arisen, and the discussions which have been carried on respecting them, have turned chiefly upon their character and functions as means of grace. It is universally admitted that the sacraments are means of grace; and the great general idea involved in this position is this, that they are institutions which God intended and appointed to be, in some sense, the instruments or channels of conveying to men spiritual blessings, and in the due and right use of which men are warranted to expect to receive the spiritual blessings they stand in need of. In this wide and general sense, even those who hold the lowest view of the sacraments, admit that they are means of grace; while it is also true that the great differences in doctrine which have been maintained by different churches on the whole subject of the sacraments resolve very much into the different senses in which the position, that they are means of grace, may be explained. In the wide sense above stated, the position that the sacraments are means of grace, may be conclusively inferred from the fact, that God has appointed them, and required the observance of them at our hands. As the outward acts which constitute the observance of the sacraments are in themselves not moral, but merely positive or indifferent, we are warranted to believe that God appointed them solely for our benefit, and because He intended them to be in some way instruments or channels of conveying to us spiritual blessings.

The Romish doctrine upon this subject is, that the sacraments contain the grace which they signify; that they confer grace always and certainly, where men do not put an obstacle in the way; that they do this *ex opere operato*, or by some sort of physical or intrinsic power bestowed upon them, apart from the state of mind of the recipient; that baptism is the instrumental cause of justification as including both remission of sin and regeneration; and that the Lord's Supper invariably conveys spiritual nourishment. There are some points, however, involved in the exposition of these doctrines, which have not been explicitly settled by the authority of the church, and in regard to which some latitude is left for a difference of opinion. Among Protestants, again, high churchmen, and men disposed to exalt the value and efficacy of the sacraments, have generally adopted, or, at least, approximated to, the Romish doctrine as explained by its more reasonable defenders, and have been disposed to allege that the controversies with the Church of Rome upon this subject, resolve very much into disputes about words or points of no great importance; while sounder Protestants have, in general, met the Romish doctrines with decided opposition. At the same time, it must be admitted, that it is not easy to fix upon any definite modes of statement, which can be said to be distinctly Protestant as opposed to Romanism, about the true character and functions of the sacraments as means of grace, viewed apart from the doctrine held with regard to their subjects and objects. It is generally supposed that the strongest statement to which the Church of Rome is pledged on this point, is, that the sacraments "contain the grace which they signify or represent," implying, that the grace resides or is laid up in them, and that they give it out; and yet Calvin, in his "Antidote to the Council of Trent," seventh sessioɪ, admits that there is a sense in which it is true "sacramentis contineri gratiam quam figurant." He asserts also that those who allege, that by the sacraments grace is conferred upon us when we do not put an obstacle in the way, overturn the whole power of the sacraments; while he distinctly admits that the sacraments are instrumental causes of conferring grace upon us, though the power of God is not tied to them, and though they produce no effect whatever apart from the faith of the recipient. And, moreover, we find, upon a principle formerly explained, that in dealing (sixth session) with the position, that baptism is the instrumental cause of justification, he rather objects to the omission of the Gospel or the truth, and to the high place assigned to baptism, than meets the position of the Council with a direct negative. His statement is this—"It is a great absurdity to make baptism alone the instrumental cause. If this be so, what becomes of the gospel? Will it not even get into the lowest corner? But, they say, baptism is the sacrament of faith. True; but when all is said, I will still maintain that it is nothing but an appendage to the gospel (*evangelii appendicem*). They act preposterously in giving it the first place; and this is just as if one should say that the instrumental cause of a house is the handle of the workman's trowel. He who, putting the gospel in the background, numbers baptism among the causes of salvation, shows thereby that he does not know what baptism is or means, or what is its function and use."* It would be easy to show, that there are many other eminent divines who have differed from each other as to the phraseology that ought to be employed in explaining the position, that the sacraments are means of grace, some asserting and others denying, that they are

---

* Calvin—Tractatus Theologici omnes, Amstel 1667, p. 242.

causes of grace,—that they confer, or convey, or bestow spiritual blessings,—while yet there is no very material difference of opinion among them; as is evident from their agreement in regard to the two important questions, as to the persons for whom the sacraments are intended, and the purposes they were instituted to serve. And on this ground we shall now, as has been intimated, consider—1st, the subjects, and, 2d, the objects, of the sacraments; assuming only, in the meantime, that the position, universally admitted, that the sacraments are means of grace, implies that, in some way or other, they are employed by God as instrumental or auxiliary in bestowing upon some men some spiritual blessings.

1. Let us first advert, then, to the subjects of the sacraments, or the persons for whom they were intended. We have already seen that, both in the Larger and the Shorter Catechism, the Westminster Assembly have distinctly laid down the position, that the sacraments, baptism and the Lord's Supper, are intended for believers, for men who had already and previously been led to embrace Christ as their Saviour; and that they were not in the least deterred from the explicit assertion of this great principle by its appearing to exclude or ignore the practice of infant baptism, which they believed to be fully sanctioned by Scripture. This great principle is not set forth in the Confession of Faith quite so explicitly as it is in the Catechisms, but it is taught there by very plain implication. The Confession* lays it down as the first and principal end or object of the sacraments, of both equally and alike, " to represent Christ and His benefits, and to confirm our interest in Him,"—this last clause implying, that those for whom the sacraments were intended, have already and previously acquired a personal interest in Christ, which could be only by their union to Him through faith. It further† in speaking still of the sacraments, and, of course, of baptism as well as the Lord's Supper, asserts that " the word of institution contains a promise of benefit to worthy receivers;" and worthy receivers, in the full import of the expression, are, in the case of adult baptism, believers. In the next chapter, the twenty-eighth, the description given of baptism manifestly applies only to believing adults. It is there described as a " sacrament of the New Testament, ordained by Jesus Christ, not only for the solemn admission of the party bap-

---

* Ch. xxvii. sec. 1.   † Sec. 3.

tized into the visible church, but also to be unto him a sign and seal of the covenant of grace, of his ingrafting into Christ, of regeneration, of remission of sins, and of his giving up unto God, through Jesus Christ, to walk in newness of life." It is quite true that infants, as well as adults, though incapable of faith, must be ingrafted into Christ, and must receive regeneration and remission; and that without this, indeed, they cannot be saved. But the statement in the Confession plainly assumes, that each individual baptized not only should have the necessary preliminary qualifications, but should be himself exercised and satisfied upon this point; and should thus be prepared to take part, intelligently and consciously, in the personal assumption of the practical obligations which baptism implies.

This is sufficient to show that the teaching of the Confession is quite in harmony with that of the Catechisms, though upon this particular point it is not altogether so explicit. It holds true, indeed, generally—we might say universally—of the Reformed churches, as distinguished from the Lutheran, and of almost all the Reformed theologians, that though firm believers in the divine authority of infant baptism, they never hesitate to lay down the general positions, that the sacraments are intended for believers; that participation in them assumes the previous and present existence of faith in all who rightly receive them; and that they produce their appropriate, beneficial effects only through the operation and exercise of faith in those who partake in them. The Reformed divines, not holding the doctrine of baptismal regeneration, did not regard the baptism of infants as being of sufficient importance to modify the general doctrine they thought themselves warranted to lay down with respect to the sacraments, as applicable to adult baptism and the Lord's Supper. And it is interesting and instructive to notice, that the adoption, by the Lutherans, of the doctrine of baptismal regeneration led them to be much more careful of laying down any general statements, either about the sacraments or about baptism, which virtually ignored the baptism of infants. They are much more careful than the Reformed divines, either expressly and by name to bring in infant baptism into their general definitions or descriptions, or, at least, to leave ample room for it, so that there may be no appearance of its being omitted or forgotten. It may be worth while to give a specimen of this. Buddæus, one of the best of the

Lutheran divines, a man whose works exhibit a very fine combination of ability and good sense, learning and evangelical unction,
in treating of the effect of baptism, which, he says, may also be
regarded as the end or object of the ordinance, lays it down, that
it is "with respect to infants, regeneration, and with respect to
adults, the confirming and sealing (*confirmatio et obsignatio*) of the
faith of which they ought to be possessed before they are admitted
to baptism."* In contrast with this, many of the Reformed
divines asserted, without any hesitation, that the great leading object and effect of the sacraments, and, of course, of baptism as
well as of the Lord's Supper, was just the *confirmatio fidei*, that is,
the confirming and strengthening of the faith, which must, or, at
least, should, have existed in the case of adults before either sacrament was received.

This, however, bears rather upon the objects than the subjects
of the sacraments. And in returning to the latter of these topics,
we would lay before our readers, what we regard as a very complete and comprehensive summary of the doctrine of the Reformed
churches upon this point, in the words of Martin Vitringa, in
his "Adnotationes" to the "Doctrina Christianæ Religionis per
Aphorismos summatim descripta" of Campegius Vitringa.

"From these quotations, it clearly appears, that the common doctrine of our
divines concerning the proper subjects of the sacraments amounts to this:—

1st. That the sacraments have been instituted only for those who have
already received the grace of God—the called, the regenerate, the believing,
the converted, those who are in covenant with God; and also that it is proper
for those to come to them who have true faith and repentance.

2d. That they who receive the sacraments are already, before receiving
them, partakers through faith of Christ and His benefits, and are therefore
justified and sanctified before they take the sacraments.

3d. That faith is the medium, the mouth, and the hand, by which we
rightly receive and perceive the sacraments.

4th. That the faith of those who lawfully receive the sacraments is confirmed and increased by them, and that they are more closely united to
Christ.

5th. That those only who receive the sacraments in faith have, in the use
of them, the promise of the remission of sins and of eternal life bestowed,
sealed, and applied in a singular way, just as if God were addressing them individually, and were promising and sealing to them remission of sins and
eternal life; and thus believers are rendered more certain about their com-

---

* "Theologia Dogmatica," lib. v. c. i. s. 7.

munion with Christ and His benefits, so that they can certainly determine that Christ belongs to them with His gifts.

6th. That by the sacraments the promises of the covenant of grace are offered and sealed, under the condition of true faith and penitence.

7th. That only true believers and true penitents, using the sacraments worthily, receive not only the signs, but also the things signified, which are sealed to them, and also that they only receive them with benefit and advantage.

8th. That God wishes the sacraments to be administered to those who are possessed of true faith and unfeigned repentance, but that the ministers of the church ought to admit to the sacraments those who make a profession of faith and penitence, and do not openly contradict it by their life and conduct, and that they, before coming to the sacraments, ought to be admonished to try themselves, whether they have true faith and repentance, lest being destitute of faith and repentance, they should receive the sacraments to their condemnation.

9th. That unbelieving and impenitent persons receive only the naked signs but not the things signified; that nothing is sealed to them; that, moreover, they profane and contemn the sacraments; and that from this profanation and contempt the sacraments not only do not benefit but hurt them, and bring to them condemnation and destruction; and then, that the sacraments, when administered to unbelieving and impenitent persons, remain sacraments so far as God is concerned, but so far as concerns the unbelieving and impenitent, lose the nature and power of a sacrament.

10th. That the sacraments do not, in the first instance, bestow grace, faith, and penitence, and are not the instruments of producing the beginnings of faith and penitence, but only confirm, increase, and seal them."*

It will be observed, that all these important doctrinal statements are made concerning *the sacraments*, and of course are intended to apply equally and alike to baptism and the Lord's Supper; and that the sum and substance of what is here asserted of both these ordinances is, that, in the case of adults, they were intended only for persons who have already been enabled to believe and repent, and that it is believers only who do or can derive any benefit from partaking in them, all others using them only to their own condemnation. We do not adopt every expression in this summary just as it stands. But, we have no doubt, that in its substance, it is in full accordance with the teaching of Scripture, and of the Reformed as distinguished from the Lutheran churches. Upon the second of these points, indeed,—the historical question of the identity of these views with those of the Reformed churches and of the leading Reformed divines of the sixteenth and seventeenth centuries,—Vitringa has produced his evidence at length.

---

* C. xxiv. tom. vi. p. 489.

His quotations fill about twenty pages, and are certainly amply sufficient to establish his position. They prove that the quotation we have produced, contains a correct summary of the doctrine of the Reformed churches in regard to the proper subjects of the sacraments. Vitringa gives extracts from eight or ten of the Confessions of the Reformation period, and from above fifty of the most eminent divines of that and the succeeding century. He has thus brought together a vast store of materials, abundantly sufficient to establish his position, so far as authority is concerned; and we think it may be worth while to give the names of the divines from whom he produces his extracts. They are Zwingle, Œcolampadius, Bucer, Musculus, Bullinger, Calvin, Beza, Zanchius, Ursinus, Olevianus, Sadeel, Whitaker, Aretus, Sohnius, Polanus, Chamier, Junius, Perkins, Bucanus, Kuchlinus, Acronius, Trelcatius, Scharpius, G. J. Vossius, Maccovius, Walaeus, Rivetus, Amyraldus, Altingius, Forbes, Voetius, Wendelinus, Cocceius, Hottinger, Heidanus, Maresius, Venema, Burman, Mastricht, Witsius, Turretine, Heidegger, Leydecker, Braunius, Marckius, Roell, Meyer, Gerdes, Wyttenbach; in short, all the greatest divines of the sixteenth and seventeenth centuries. Here is a storehouse of names and quotations, which might enable any one to set up as an erudite theologian by means of a stock of second-hand authorities.

We are dealing at present only with the historical and not with the scriptural view of the case; but we may briefly advert to the kind of proof by which it can be shown, that the proper subjects of the sacrament are only believing and regenerated men. The general place or position of the sacraments seems plainly to indicate that they were intended only for those who had already been led to embrace Christ, and had been born again of His word. It is evident, from all the representations given us on this subject in the inspired account of the labours of the apostles, that men first of all had the gospel preached to them, were warned of their guilt and danger as sinners, and were instructed in the way of salvation through Christ; and that thus, through the effectual working of God's Spirit, they were enabled to believe what they were told, to embrace Christ freely offered to them, and to receive Him as their Lord and Master. They were told, among other things, that it was Christ's will that they should be baptized, and should thereby publicly profess their faith in Him, and be formally admitted into the society which He had founded. When, in these or in similar circumstances, and upon these grounds, a man asks and obtains the administration to him of baptism (of course we speak at present only of adults, for, upon grounds formerly explained, we *must* form our primary and leading conceptions of the import and object of this ordinance from the baptism of adults, and not of infants), the application seems plainly to carry upon the face of it, a profession or declaration, that he has been led to choose Christ as his Saviour and his Master, and is determined in every way to follow out this profession of entire dependence and of implicit subjection. If faith and regeneration are necessary preparations and qualifications for baptism, they must of course exist in all who come to the Lord's table, which, from its nature, and from the place it occupies in the apostolic history, must manifestly come after baptism.

These obvious general considerations tell in favour of the position, that the sacraments were instituted and intended only for believers, and this view is confirmed by a closer examination of the particular features and provisions of the ordinances themselves. In regard to the Lord's Supper, it is generally admitted, that it is intended for, and can be lawfully and beneficially partaken of only by, those who have already been received into God's family, and are living by faith in His Son. An attempt, indeed, was made in the course of the Erastian controversy, as conducted at the time of the Westminster Assembly, to set up the notion, that the Lord's Supper is a converting ordinance, and may therefore be rightly partaken of by those who have not yet believed and been regenerated. But this notion, manifestly got up merely for the purpose of undermining ecclesiastical discipline, was unanswerably exposed by George Gillespie, in the 3d Book of his " Aaron's Rod Blossoming." And when a similar notion was, with a similar purpose, promulgated about a century later among the Congregationalists of New England, it was again put down, with equal ability and success, by Jonathan Edwards, in his " Inquiry into the Qualifications for Communion." The notion has not again, so far as we are aware, been revived in any such circumstances as to entitle it to notice. It is otherwise in regard to baptism. Some men seem to shrink from laying down the position, either that the sacraments, or that baptism, should be held to be intended for believers, and, of course, to require or presuppose faith and regeneration, because this leaves out and seems to exclude the case of infant baptism,—a difficulty which neither the Reformers nor the compilers of the Westminster standards, though decided pædo-baptists, allowed to influence or modify their statements. Others take wider and more definite ground, and endeavour to establish a great disparity between baptism and the Lord's Supper as to their import and objects, and to disprove the equal applicability to both these ordinances, of the definition and description usually given of a sacrament. No one, indeed, can deny, that there are some points in which baptism and the Lord's Supper stand alone and resemble each other. All admit that both these ordinances are emblems or symbolical representations of scriptural truths, fitted and intended to embody and to exhibit the great doctrines revealed in the word of God concerning the salvation of sinners. This description is undoubtedly true of these ordinances so far as it goes. It is admitted by all Protestants, that this description applies equally and alike to baptism and the Lord's Supper, and that there are no other institutions under the Christian economy to which it does apply. But the question is, Can we not get materials in Scripture for giving a more complete and specific account of what is equally true of these two ordinances, and may, therefore, be set forth as the full and adequate description of the sacraments? and more especially, have we not materials for making statements of a more precise and specific kind, both about the subjects and the objects of these ordinances, that shall apply equally to both of them? This, at least, is what has been generally maintained and acted upon by Protestant divines. They have embodied the substance of these materials in their description of a sacrament, and the leading features of this description, as set forth in the Westminster standards are, that both ordinances equally and alike are intended for believers, and represent, seal, and apply, to believers Christ and His benefits.

So far as concerns the subjects of the sacraments, the topic with which at present we have more immediately to do, it is generally admitted, that partaking in the Lord's Supper implies a profession of faith in Christ, and is, therefore, warrantable and beneficial only to believers. But many, and, we fear, a growing number, refuse to admit this principle as applicable to baptism. It is contended, not only that infants who are incapable of faith ought to be baptized (a position which all the Reformers and all the Confessions of the Reformed churches decidedly maintained, though they did not allow it to affect their general definition of a sacrament), but also that adults may be admitted to baptism, though they are not, and do not profess to be believers and regenerate persons,—baptism, it is alleged, not expressing or implying a profession of believing in Christ, but only a profession of a willingness to be instructed in the principles of Christianity.   This notion is flatly opposed to the leading views with respect to the sacraments, which have always prevailed in the Protestant churches, and been embodied in the Reformed Confessions.   But it seems now to prevail to a considerable extent among the Congregationalists of this country.   And we fear that it is likely to continue to prevail, because while it can be defended with considerable plausibility in argument, it has also this important practical advantage, that it furnishes a warrant, or an excuse, for baptizing the infants of persons who could not be regarded as qualified to be members of the Christian church in full standing, or as admissible to the Lord's table.   There is a very elaborate and ingenious defence of this view of the import and object of baptism, and of the absence of all similarity in these respects between it and the Lord's Supper, in Dr Halley's work, entitled, " Baptism, the designation of the Catechumens, not the symbol of the members, of the Christian Church," which Dr Wardlaw, in reply to whom chiefly it was written, did not answer, and which Dr W. Lindsay Alexander has pronounced to be unanswerable.   We think it can, and it certainly should, be answered.   But this we cannot attempt at present, our object being chiefly explanation rather than defence.   The attempt to make so wide a gulf between baptism and the Lord's Supper, and to extend the application of baptism beyond the range of the membership of the church, so as to include all who are placed, by their own voluntary act, or that of their parents, under the church's superintendence and instruction, while neither in connection with their own baptism nor that of their children, are they held to make a profession of faith and regeneration, is, of course, flatly opposed to the definition or description of a sacrament, given in the Confessions of the Reformed churches as applicable to both ordinances.   It is also, we are persuaded, inconsistent with every consideration suggested by the symbolic or emblematic character of the ordinance as an outward act, implying a declaration or profession of a certain state of mind and feeling on the part of the person baptized, and with all that is asserted

or indicated in Scripture as to the connection between baptism on
the one hand, and remission and regeneration on the other.

It is, as we have explained, of fundamental importance in
judging of these symbolical ordinances, to attend to the profession
implied in the outward act, and to the correspondence between the
outward act and the state of mind and heart of the recipient.
When a man asks, in obedience to Christ's commands, to be
solemnly washed with water, in the name of the Father, the Son,
and the Holy Ghost, and when, in compliance with this request,
he has baptism administered to him, he seems as plainly and as
explicitly to make a profession of faith in Christ, as when he applies for and obtains admission to the Lord's table. Baptism,
indeed, may be said to be a formal and solemn entering into
Christ's service, implying a promise to be thereafter governed and
guided by Him. And it surely is this, *at least;* that is, this is
just about as low a view as can be taken of the ordinance, and of
the act of engaging in it. But even this view of it implies, that
in the honest and intelligent reception of baptism, such views of
Christ are professed as presuppose the existence of saving faith.
Men cannot honestly and intelligently enter Christ's service and
profess their unreserved submission to His authority, unless and
until they have been led to adopt such views of what is revealed
in Scripture concerning Him, as imply and produce true faith in
Him as a Saviour. Why should any man desire and ask to be
washed with water in the name of the Father, the Son, and the
Holy Ghost, unless he has already been led to adopt such views
of the three Persons of the Godhead, and of the way of salvation,
as must have led him to embrace Christ as all his salvation and
all his desire? In short, an application to be baptized, and the
being actually baptized as the result of the application, plainly
imply a profession, that the person so acting has been already led
to believe in Christ, to receive and accept of Him as his Saviour
and his Master; and that he intends to profess or declare, by being
baptized, the views he has been brought to entertain concerning
Christ, and the relation into which he has been led to enter with
respect to Him, and to pledge himself to the discharge of all the
obligations which these views and that relation impose. When
this state of mind and feeling has not been produced, we cannot
conceive that the baptism of an adult can be an honest and intelligent act. The nature of the act itself, and the almost universal

consent of the Christian church, in every age and country down till the present day, attach this meaning and significance to the baptism of an adult ; and, if so, the baptism of any one who has not believed and been born again, must be a hypocritical form.

This view of the matter is confirmed, we think, by all that is said in the New Testatment, whether in explicit statement or in indirect allusion, concerning the relation between baptism and the great spiritual blessings which are invariably connected with faith in Christ, viz., remission and regeneration.   The relation subsisting between baptism and these fundamental blessings involves a discussion of the whole topics comprehended in the controversy about baptismal justification and regeneration; and on this we cannot enter.   It seems to us pretty plain, that the scriptural statements which are usually brought to bear upon the settlement of this controversy, and which are founded on by the advocates of baptismal regeneration, imply, that some connection subsists between baptism, in the legitimate use of it, and these fundamental blessings; while the view which has been devised by modern Congregationalists, and is defended by Dr Halley, seems to deny any connection whatever between them.   The texts referred to seem to imply *either*, that baptism, in the right and legitimate use of it, is a sign or symbol, a seal and a profession of remission and regeneration, *as previously conferred and then existing in the party baptised; or else* that regeneration is produced or bestowed in baptism, and through the instrumentality of that ordinance.   The first of these views is, we are persuaded, that which is sanctioned by Scripture, and certainly it has been generally taught by the Reformed churches.   The latter is the common Popish and Tractarian doctrine; and though it has no solid scriptural ground to rest upon, it can be defended from Scripture with some plausibility, and this is more, we think, than can be said, so far as concerns this branch of the argument, in favour of the notion, that baptism may be rightly and honestly applied for and received by men who have not already and previously received faith in Jesus Christ, the forgiveness of their sins, and the regeneration of their natures.   We would only say, before leaving this subject, that we cannot but regard the serious error to which we have adverted, as affording another illustration of a danger formerly mentioned, that, viz., of allowing the notions or impressions which the special exceptional case of infant baptism, is apt to suggest, to influence unduly our views about baptism in general, and even about the sacraments as a whole. The giving undue prominence to the special case of infant baptism, is very apt to blind men's eyes to the strength of the evidence, that baptism in its general import and object,—that is, adult baptism in its legitimate use,—implies a profession of faith in Christ, and can therefore be rightly received and improved only by believers; while, at the same time, the temptation to reject this great scriptural principle, which is so explicitly set forth in almost all the Confessions of the Reformed churches, is strengthened by the opening thus made, for giving baptism to the children of those who do not make a profession of faith, and who would not, or should not, have been admitted to the Lord's Supper.

2. We must now proceed to advert to the second leading division of the subject, viz., the objects of the sacraments, or the purposes for which they were institued, and which they are fitted and intended to serve,—or what is virtually the same thing, the beneficial effects which men are warranted to expect, and do receive, from the right use of them. There is, as we have mentioned, a very close connection between this topic and that which we have already considered. If the sacraments were intended for believers, —if their proper subjects are those only who have already been united to Christ, and been born again of His word, then it follows, that they could not have been fitted or intended to be auxiliary or instrumental in bestowing or producing anything which is implied in the existence of saving faith, or in effecting anything which is involved in, or results from, saving faith, wherever it exists. Upon the ground, then, of what has been already set forth under the former head, it follows, not only that justification and regeneration are not bestowed or produced in or by baptism, but that they must have been already bestowed and produced before baptism can be lawfully or safely received. This is a principle of fundamental importance, and it is confirmed by all that is taught us in Scripture, both with respect to the subjects and the objects of the sacraments. There is, indeed, no principle more important with reference to this whole matter, whether viewed theoretically or practically, whether regarded as an exposition of truth, or as a security against corruption and abuse, than that the sacraments are intended for believers, and of course must have been fitted to aid them in some way or other, in the great work of carrying on the life of God in their souls, in promoting their growth in knowledge,

righteousness, and holiness. The sacraments are means of grace,
that is, they are ordinances or appointments of God, which are
intended to be in some way auxiliary or instrumental in conveying to men spiritual blessings. The blessings conveyed by the
sacraments, and to be expected from the right use of them, cannot
of course be those which, according to God's arrangements, are
conveyed to men, and must exist in and be possessed by them,
before the sacraments can be lawfully and honestly received. It
is a fundamental principle of scriptural doctrine, that justification
and regeneration are necessarily and invariably connected with
faith, and that they are cotemporaneous with it, whatever may be
the precise relation subsisting among them in the order of nature.
Whoever has been enabled to believe in Jesus Christ has been
justified and regenerated ; he has passed through that great ordeal
on which salvation depends, and which can occur but once in the
history of a soul. And if these principles are well founded, then
the spiritual blessings which the sacraments may be instrumental
in conveying, can be those only which men still stand in need of,
with a view to their salvation, after they have been justified and
regenerated by faith. And these are the forgiveness of the sins
which they continue to commit, a growing sense of God's pardoning mercy, and grace and strength to resist temptation, to discharge duty, to improve privilege, and to be ever advancing in
holiness ;—or, to adopt the language of the " Shorter Catechism,"
in describing the blessings which accompany or flow from justification, adoption, and sanctification, they are " assurance of God's
love, peace of conscience, joy in the Holy Ghost, increase of grace
and perseverance therein to the end." There is nothing asserted
or indicated in Scripture to preclude the conveyance of *any or
all of these blessings*, through the instrumentality of the sacraments, as well as of the other means of grace. On the contrary,
there is good scriptural ground, why believers should expect to
receive, in the right use of the sacraments, any or all of these
blessings, according as they may need them. And, accordingly,
it is the general doctrine of the Reformed Confessions, that
the great leading object of the sacraments,—the main purpose
which they were designed and fitted to accomplish,—is just to be
instrumental or auxiliary, in conveying these blessings, to those
who have believed through grace, in producing these results in
those who have already been renewed in the spirit of their minds,

and to do this mainly, if not solely, by strengthening and confirming their faith.

We have already had occasion to quote the principal passages in which this doctrine concerning the great leading object or design of the sacraments, is set forth in the Westminster symbols, but it may be proper to advert to them somewhat more formally in this connection. In the Confession of Faith,* the main position laid down regarding the sacraments is this, that they " are holy signs and seals of the covenant of grace, immediately instituted by God, to represent Christ and His benefits, and to confirm our interest in Him, as also," etc. Here the general nature and character of the sacraments is declared to be, that they are holy signs and seals of the covenant of grace; and the principal object, —the leading design, on account of which they were instituted by God,—is said to be " to represent Christ and His benefits, and to confirm our interest in Him." The " representing Christ and His benefits" applies more properly to the sacraments in their character and functions as signs; " the confirming our interest in Him," in their character and function as seals. The representing or signifying Christ and His benefits,—that is, the blessings of the covenant of grace, and the doctrines or promises which unfold and offer, and which, when believed and applied, instrumentally convey or bestow them,—applies more immediately to the mere symbols or elements, and to the preaching of the gospel to all without distinction or exception, which is involved in the selection and appointment of such symbols, as recorded in the New Testament. The " confirming our interest in Him " brings under our notice the more limited and specific object of the sacraments, as brought out in the actual individual participation in them by persons duly qualified and rightly prepared. This latter statement suggests, at once, as a fundamental point in the doctrine of the sacraments, and, of course, as true of baptism as well as the Lord's Supper, that they are intended only for those who have already obtained an interest in Christ by faith, and that they are designed to benefit these persons, mainly by confirming this interest in Christ, which they have already acquired, and which they must have possessed before they could lawfully and beneficially partake, even in the initiatory sacrament of baptism. This important principle

* C. 27.

is also explicitly declared in the 19th chapter of the Confession, which treats of Saving Faith. Concerning saving faith, it says, that " it is ordinarily wrought by the ministry of the word, by which also, and by the administration of the sacraments and prayer, it is increased and strengthened." Here the increasing and strengthening of saving faith, previously produced and already existing, is ascribed to the administration of the sacraments, and of course is predicated equally and alike of baptism and the Lord's Supper; and this incidental, though most explicit, assertion of the principle, that the sacraments were designed to increase and strengthen saving faith, shows how familiar the minds of the compilers of the Westminster Confession were with a doctrine, which is now very much ignored by many who profess to follow in their footsteps.

The same doctrine, as to the objects of the sacraments, is very explicitly set forth in the " Larger Catechism," where, in answer to the question,* What is a sacrament? it is said, that " a sacrament is an holy ordinance instituted by Christ in His church, to signify, seal, and exhibit unto those that are within the covenant of grace, the benefits of His mediation, to strengthen and increase their faith and all other graces, to oblige them to obedience, to testify and cherish their love and communion one with another, and to distinguish them from those that are without." We have already shown that, according to the strict grammatical construction of this sentence, the expression, " those that are within the covenant of grace," is used simply as synonymous with believers, and not in the wider sense in which it might include also the children of believers; and that, therefore, the "Larger Catechism" agrees with the Confession of Faith and the " Shorter Catechism," in setting forth this great doctrine in regard to the subjects of the sacraments, viz., that they are intended for believers, for those who have already received the gift of faith; not meaning to exclude the baptism of infants,—which was regarded as fully sanctioned by scriptural authority,—but virtually conceding, 1st, That the full and adequate idea of a sacrament, as exhibited in adult baptism and the Lord's Supper, does not directly and thoroughly apply to the case of infant baptism ; and 2d, That it is of more importance to bring out fully and explicitly, the sacramental principle,—the true

* Q. 162.

and full doctrine of the sacraments,—as applicable to adult baptism
and the Lord's Supper, than to attempt to lay down some more
vague and diluted view upon this subject, which might include
the special and peculiar case of the baptism of infants. This
being assumed, we see that the "Larger Catechism," in entire
accordance with the Confession of Faith, gives it as the true
account of the general nature and character of the sacraments,
that "they signify, seal, and exhibit" the benefits of Christ's
mediation to believers, and that their primary leading object is to
strengthen and increase faith and all other graces, where these
have been already produced. The three other objects here assigned
to the sacraments, viz., "to oblige them to obedience, to testify
and cherish their love and communion one with another, and to
distinguish them from those that are without,"—all, be it observed,
applicable only to believers,—are usually described by theologians,
and were, no doubt, regarded by the Westminster divines, as the
secondary or subordinate objects or ends of the sacraments. And
it is plain that,—in respect of intrinsic importance in their bearing
upon the salvation of sinners,—they do not stand upon the same
level with the great object and result of strengthening and increasing faith and all other graces, and thereby signifying, sealing,
and exhibiting the benefits of the covenant of grace.

The general definition or description of a sacrament, given in
the "Shorter Catechism" is very explicit in declaring, that the
proper subjects of the sacraments are believers, though it does
not bring out so formally and fully what are their objects or ends,
except in so far as the truth upon this point is implied in their
general nature and character. But as the statement in the
"Shorter Catechism" is that with which most people in Scotland are
familiar, though in many cases, we fear, familiar only with the
words, without understanding the meaning, it may be proper to
give a somewhat full and formal explanation of it, even though
this may involve some repetition. It is this : " A sacrament is
an holy ordinance instituted by Christ, wherein by sensible signs
Christ and the benefits of the new covenant are represented,
sealed, and applied to believers."

1. This statement explicitly asserts, as we have shown, that
the sacraments, baptism, as well as the Lord's Supper, are intended for believers, and produce their appropriate beneficial
results only in those who by faith receive them; while it assumes

or takes for granted, that those who partake in them are duly qualified for doing so, by the possession of that faith which, in receiving them, is professed or declared.

2. The things which are represented, sealed, and applied to believers in the sacraments are, " Christ and the benefits of the new covenant," not some of the benefits of the covenant, however important and fundamental, but these benefits as a whole,—everything, including both a change of state and of character, which is invariably connected with saving faith ; not the covenant of grace, regarded merely as a statement or exposition of a certain compact or transaction revealed in Scripture and bearing upon the salvation of sinners, but the grace of the covenant, or the blessings which the covenant offers, conveys, and secures. Any attempt to represent baptism, or the water the application of which constitutes baptism, as representing or signifying remission,—apart from regeneration, or regeneration apart from remission,—and any attempt to explain the difficulty about sealing by distinguishing between the covenant of grace and the grace of the covenant, and alleging that sacraments are seals of the covenant, but are only signs or symbols of spiritual blessings,—is precluded by the terms of this statement, and still more explicitly by the further explanation given in the Confession of Faith and Larger Catechism.

3. " Christ and the benefits of the new Covenant" are here declared to be equally and alike " represented, sealed, and applied ;" and this one complex position being predicated of them, it cannot, in consistency with this statement, be alleged, that these benefits, or any of them, are either represented and not sealed, or sealed and not represented, in reference to any one class or section of legitimate and worthy recipients. The admission of the accuracy of this description of a sacrament implies, that there is a sense in which Christ and His benefits are, in baptism and the Lord's Supper, not only represented and signified, but also sealed and applied to believers.

4. The " signify, seal, and exhibit" of the " Larger Catechism" are evidently identical with the " represented, sealed, and applied" of the Shorter,—" signify" being synonymous with " represent," —and " exhibit" with " apply." And in considering these expressions, we have first to advert to the question of the consistency of this account of the nature and character of the sacraments, with

the view which, as we have seen, is given in these symbols, of their
main object, their principal design. There is no difficulty in perceiving how the signifying and sealing here ascribed to the sacraments, accord with the doctrine which represents their leading
object to be, to confirm or strengthen a faith previously existing,
and thereby to contribute to convey the blessings which believers
still need. Signifying and sealing naturally suggest the idea, that
the things signified and sealed not only exist, but are actually possessed by those to whom they are signified and sealed. Whatever may be the precise kind of influence and effect indicated by
these words, they assume or imply, that the things of which they
are predicated have been already bestowed or conveyed, and are
now held or possessed. The sacraments are for believers. In
describing their general nature and character, it is usually
assumed that the persons who receive them are duly qualified by
the possession of faith; by receiving the sacraments, they express
and exercise their faith; they thus have all the great fundamental
blessings, the possession of which is invariably connected with the
existence of faith, signified and sealed to them; and the tendency
and effect of this are to strengthen and increase their faith, and
thereby to convey to them more fully and abundantly those other
blessings of which they still stand in need.

But while the signifying and sealing ascribed to the sacraments
are plainly, whatever may be their precise meaning and import,
quite accordant with the general doctrine taught concerning their
objects, there seems to be more difficulty about "exhibiting" or
"applying." Do not these words convey the idea of conferring
or bestowing what was not previously possessed? Do they not
thus sanction the notion, that Christ and His benefits are conveyed
or bestowed, not previously to the lawful reception of the sacraments, but in and by the use of them? Now, in opposition to
this notion, we take the position, that the doctrine that the sacraments are for believers, and assume the previous existence in
worthy recipients of the great spiritual blessings with which saving
faith is invariably connected, is far too explicitly and too fully set
forth in the Westminster symbols, in accordance with the general
doctrine of the Reformed churches, to admit of its being set aside
or involved in uncertainty, on the ground of a single vague and
ambiguous expression, even though there were greater difficulty
than there is, in interpreting that expression in harmony with the

general strain of their teaching. The proof of this in the state-ments of the Confession and Catechisms, is too clear to require the application of any collateral and subordinate evidence. But it so happens, that we have evidence of this sort, which would be conclusive as to what was the doctrine which the Westminster divines intended to teach upon this point, even though the lan-guage of their symbols, taken as a whole, had been much more ambiguous than it is. This evidence, we find in statements con-tained in Samuel Rutherford's "Due Right of Presbyteries," and in George Gillespie's "Aaron's Rod Blossoming." Rutherford and Gillespie are, literally and without any exception, just the two very highest authorities that could be brought to bear upon a question of this kind, at once from their learning and ability as theologians, and from the place they held and the influence they exerted in the actual preparation of the documents under consider-ation. That Rutherford held the views about the sacraments which we have ascribed to the Westminster standards, is quite certain, from the following quotations from the work above re-ferred to :—

"All believers as believers, *in foro Dei* before God, have right to the seals of the covenant; those to whom the covenant and the body of the charter belongeth, to those the seal belongeth; but *in foro ecclesiastico*, and in an orderly church way, the seals are not to be conferred by the church upon per-sons because they believe, but because they profess their believing; therefore the apostles never baptised pagans, but upon profession of their faith." "Cer-tainly, God ordaineth the sacraments to believers as believers, and because they are within the covenant, and their interest in the covenant is the only true right of interest to the seals of the covenant; profession doth but declare who believe and who believe not, and consequently who have right to the seals of the covenant, and who not; but profession doth not make right, but declareth who have right."*

There is no great difficulty connected with the Lord's Supper, so far as concerns the point now under consideration. The diffi-culty applies only to baptism, and in regard to baptism the follow-ing statements of Rutherford are conclusive :—

"1. Baptism is not that whereby we are entered into Christ's mystical and invisible body as such, for it is presupposed we be members of Christ's body, and our sins pardoned already, before baptism come to be a seal of sins par-doned. But baptism is a seal of our entry into Christ's visible body, as swear-ing to the colours is that which entereth a soldier to be a member of such an

---

* Pp. 185 and 258.

army, whereas, before his oath, he was only a heart friend to the army and cause.

"2. Baptism, as it is such, is a seal, and a seal—as a seal,—addeth no new lands or goods to the man to whom the charter and seal is given, but only doth legally confirm him in the right of such lands given to the man by prince or state. Yet this hindereth not, but baptism is a real legal seal, legally confirm-·ing the man in his actual visible profession of Christ, remission of sins, regeneration, so, as though before baptism he was a member of Christ's body, yet, *quoad nos*, he is not a member of Christ's body visible, until he be made such by baptism."*

Gillespie, in like manner, has the following explicit statement upon this subject:—

"The papists hold that the sacraments are instrumental to confer, give, or work grace, yea, *ex opere operato*, as the schoolmen speak. Our divines hold that the sacraments are appointed of God, and delivered to the church as sealing ordinances, not to give, but to testify what is given, not to make, but to confirm saints. And they not only oppose the papist's *opus operatum*, but they simply deny this instrumentality of the sacraments, that they are appointed of God for working or giving grace where it is not. This is so well known to all who have studied the sacramentarian controversies, that I should not need to prove it, yet, that none may doubt of it, take here some few, instead of many testimonies."†

Nay, what is somewhat remarkable, and singularly pertinent to our present purpose, we find that the same difficulty which we are now considering, is stated and answered by Gillespie, and that his answer to it is virtually a commentary upon the passage we are examining, and establishes the sense in which it was understood by those who may be regarded as its authors,—thus not only

---

* P. 211.

† B. iii. c. 12, p. 409. Gillespie's quotations in proof of his position are from the old Scotch Confession, the synod of Dort, and the Belgic Liturgy, Calvin, Bullinger, Ursinus, Musculus, Bucer, Festus Hommius, Aretius, Vossius, Paræus, Walæus, etc. We give one of his quotations from Ursinus, who was the principal author of the Heidelberg or Palatine Catechism, because it is a very brief, terse, and comprehensive statement of the substance of the doctrine of the Reformed churches, in regard both to the subjects and objects of the sacraments, as contradistinguished from the word or the truth; and because we wish to mention that there is no divine of the sixteenth century, who has brought out more clearly and fully the great principle, that the leading object of the sacraments is the *confirmatio fidei*. "Quasi non pueris jam notum verbum et conversis et non conversis esse annunciandum, quo illi quidem confirmentur, hi vero convertantur; sacramenta autem iis esse instituta qui jam sunt conversi et membra populi dei facti." Judicium de disciplina ecclesiastica. Oper. tom. iii. p. 809, and not p. 89, as it is printed in Gillespie.

proving that the doctrine we have asserted is to be maintained, notwithstanding its apparent discrepancy, with one expression, but at the same time showing in what way this apparent discrepancy is to be explained. The remarkable passage is as follows:—" You will say, peradventure, that Protestant writers hold the sacraments to be, 1, Significant or declarative signs; 2, Obsignative or confirming signs; and 3, Exhibitive signs, so that the thing signified is given or exhibited to the soul." Now these three points are manifestly identical with the three words employed in the catechisms,—"signify, seal, and exhibit," in the Larger,—and "represent, seal, and apply," in the Shorter. The main question is, What is meant by the third point, exhibit and apply, or exhibitive signs? and Gillespie's answer is this:—

" I answer, that *exhibition*, which they speak of, is not the giving of grace where it is not (as is manifest by the aforequoted testimonies), but an exhibition to believers, *a real, effectual, lively application of Christ, and of all His benefits, to every one that believeth, for the staying, strengthening, confirming, and comforting of the soul.* Our divines do not say that the sacraments are exhibitive ordinances, wherein grace is communicated to those who have none of it, to unconverted or unbelieving persons.

" By this time it may appear (I suppose) that the controversy between us and the papists, concerning the effect of the sacraments (setting aside the *opus operatum,* which is a distinct controversy, and is distinctly spoken to by our writers,—setting aside also the *causalitas physica* and *insita,* by which some of the papists say the sacraments give grace, though divers others of them hold the sacraments to be only moral causes of grace), is thus far the same with the present controversy between Mr Prynne and me, that Protestant writers do not only oppose the *opus operatum* and the *causalitas physica* and *insita,* but they oppose (*as is manifest by the testimonies already cited*) all causality or working of the first grace of conversion and faith in or by the sacraments, supposing always a man to be a believer and within the covenant of grace before the sacrament, and that he is not made such, nor translated to the state of grace in or by the sacrament."*

We think it of some importance to show, that these views of the sacramental principle, or of the doctrine of the sacraments, which, though so clearly and fully set forth in the Westminster standards, have been so much lost sight of amongst us, were openly maintained by the leading divines of the Church of Scotland during last century. Principal Hadow and Thomas Boston may be regarded as the heads of two different schools of theology

---

* Pp. 496-7.

in Scotland, in the early part of last century, and, as happens not unfrequently in theological discussions, they divided, we think, the truth between them in the points controverted. They have both left very explicit statements of their views upon this subject of the sacraments, especially in regard to baptism, about which alone there is any difficulty, so far as concerns the points we have been considering. Principal Hadow lays down this position, that the commonly received doctrine of the Reformed churches does not "ascribe any other virtue or efficacy to baptism, than what is moral and objective, in representing and signing the promises, confirming of faith, and exhibiting or applying the promised benefits of the covenant unto believers, by way of a sign and seal, which still supposeth grace already conferred on those in whom this sacrament hath its due operation;" and he supports this and one or two other positions of a similar import and tendency, by quotations from Zwingle, Bullinger, Peter Martyr, Musculus, Polanus, Wollebius, Aretius, Calvin, Beza, Spanheim, Turretine, Heidegger, Bucer, Zanchius, Ursinus, Paræus, Wendelinus, Rivet, Walæus, Hoornbeck, Essenius, Leydecker, Mastricht, Witsius, Alting, Maresius, Gomarus, Maccovius, Ames, Arnoldus, Danæus, Chamier, Amyraut, Du Moulin, thus furnishing, like Vitringa, a great storehouse of materials for a theological display.*

Boston's views are brought out in the following extract from his "Miscellany Questions in Divinity:"—†

"The sacraments are not converting but confirming ordinances; they are appointed for the use and benefit of God's children, not of others; they are given to believers as believers, as Rutherford expresses it, so that none other are subjects capable of the same before the Lord. Either must we say they have no respect at all to saving grace, or that they are appointed as means of the conveyance of the first grace,—that is, to convert sinners,—or finally, for confirmation of grace already received. If it be said they have no respect at all to saving grace, then baptism cannot be called the baptism of repentance, nor are persons baptized for the remission of sins, nor can it be looked on as a seal of the righteousness of faith, all which is evidently against Scripture testimony. If it be said they are appointed as means of the conveyance of the first grace, then, First, either there are none converted before baptism, which is manifestly false, or else baptism is in vain conferred on converts, which is no less false. But surely in vain are means used to confer on any that which

---

* *The Doctrine and Practice of the Church of Scotland anent the Sacra-* | *ment of Baptism,* p. 23. Published anonymously in 1704.
† Q. vi. Works in folio, p. 384.

they had before. Second, it were unfaithfulness to Christ and cruelty to men to withhold the sacraments from any person whatsoever. Were it not soul-murder to withhold the means of conveyance of the first grace from any, and unfaithfulness to Him who will have all men to be saved and come to the know-ledge of the truth. But that the sacraments, and particularly baptism, are not to be conferred on all promiscuously, none can deny. Wherefore it re-mains that they are indeed appointed for confirmation, which doth necessarily suppose the pre-existence of grace in the soul, seeing that which is not cannot, be confirmed."

These quotations confirm everything we have said as to the doctrine which has been regarded by the most competent judges as taught in the Westminster standards. We give only one other short quotation, from Dr John Erskine, probably the greatest divine in the Church of Scotland in the latter part of last century:—

" Scripture sufficiently proves that the sacraments of the New Testament are signs and seals of no other covenant than that covenant of grace which secures eternal happiness to all interested in it. And the partaking of them manifestly implies a partaking of covenant blessings on the one hand, and the exercise of faith on the other. To begin with baptism, John baptized for the remission of sins, and so did Christ's disciples. We are told that baptism saves us, and by baptism we are said to put on Christ, to die, to be buried, and to rise with Him, because the water in baptism represents and seals that blood of Jesus which cleanseth from the guilt of sin, and purchases for us the sanctify-ing influences of the Spirit, and all other needful blessings. Baptism, then, is a seal of spiritual 'blessings ; and spiritual blessings it cannot seal to the un-converted."*

We have now explained the doctrine taught in the Westminster standards concerning the subjects and the objects of the two sacraments of the Christian church,—that is, the persons who can lawfully and beneficially partake in them, and the purposes which, in these persons, they are fitted and intended to accomplish. Another question still remains to be considered, viz., Have we any further information as to the way and manner in which the sacraments produce their appropriate effects, or as to the principles which regulate the production of the results? So much mischief has been done to the souls of men by the perversion or abuse of the sacraments, that we consider it necessary, in connection with this branch of the subject, to state again distinctly what is, of course, obviously implied in the views we have explained, viz., that men who outwardly partake in the sacraments without having

* *Theological Dissertations*, Diss. ii. p. 94.

been previously led to believe in Christ Jesus, can derive from them no benefit whatever. Persons who are still unbelieving and impenitent, do not, in receiving baptism or the Lord's Supper, discharge a duty, or perform an acceptable act of worship, or enjoy and improve a privilege or mean of grace. On the contrary, they are only committing a sin, because they are presumptuously engaging in a sacred service, while destitute of the qualifications which God has required, and because, in the very act of outwardly receiving the sacraments, they are making a false and hypocritical profession ; they are declaring, by deeds, the existence of a certain state of mind and heart, corresponding to the outward act they are performing, while it has really no existence. The sacraments can be expected to become the means of grace, or the channels of conveying spiritual blessings, only when men rightly receive them, that is, when they are duly prepared for the reception of them, and when they faithfully improve them for their intended objects. With respect to the due preparation, there are required what the old divines used to call an habitual and an actual, or a general and a special, preparation. The habitual or general preparation is, of course, faith, without which already existing there can be no warrant for participating in the sacraments, and no capacity of benefiting by them ; and the actual or special preparation is just faith in exercise, under the influence of right views and suitable impressions of our own wants and necessities at the time, and of the nature, character, and objects of the ordinance, whether it be baptism or the Lord's Supper, in which we are about to engage. It is only in these circumstances that the sacraments can be expected to prove means of grace.

The question thus becomes limited to this, In what way, or through what process, do the sacraments become instrumental in conveying spiritual blessings to those persons, who, having pre-viously believed in Christ, and been justified and regenerated, receive these ordinances under a due sense of regard to Christ's authority, and from a sincere desire to share more abundantly in the blessings of which they still stand in need, and which are all treasured up in Him? Now as to the way and manner, the process and regulating principles, according to which these men derive benefit from receiving the sacraments, the word of God has certainly not given us much direct information. And this, indeed, is just a part or a consequence of a more general truth, viz., that Scripture does not ascribe to the sacraments any such prominence or influence in the way of contributing to men's salvation, by conveying to them spiritual blessings, as the Popish or Tractarian theory does. There are, indeed, some important negative truths bearing upon this subject, which are clear and certain, and which it is important to remember and to apply, as the great securities against error and abuse. Most of these have been referred to already, but it may be proper now to state them together, and in this connection. They are chiefly these—

1. That the sacraments do not occupy any such place in the scheme of God's arrangements, as to make the participation in them or in either of them, necessary to the possession and enjoyment of any spiritual blessing, or to entire meetness for heaven.

2. That no spiritual blessings are derived from the sacraments, without the previous existence and the present exercise of true saving faith.

3. That the sacraments become effectual means of grace and salvation, not from any virtue—that is, any power or worth, personal or official—in him who administers them, nor from any virtue in them—that is, from any intrinsic efficacy inherent in them, and resulting *ex opere operato*—and that they do not operate certainly and invariably in conveying any spiritual blessings.

4. That the sacraments are not seals of spiritual blessings, in any such sense as implies, that they are attestations to the personal character or spiritual condition of those who receive them, or, that the mere reception of the sacraments is to be held as of itself furnishing a proof, or even a presumption, that those receiving them are true believers, and may be assured that they have reached a condition of safety.

These truths, it will be observed, are to a large extent negative. They consist mainly of denials of certain notions, about the nature and necessity, the subjects, objects, and effects of the sacraments, which are very apt to spring up in men's minds, and which have been openly maintained by Romanists and High Churchmen. And when we reflect upon the extent to which these unwarranted and extravagant notions about the sacraments have prevailed, and upon the fearful amount of injury they have done to the souls of men, we reckon it about sufficient to know, that, in the case of adults, they are *not* intended for those who have not already faith and regeneration ; that they do *not* produce any beneficial results which may not be comprehended under the general head of aiding and assisting believers in carrying on the work of sanctification in their hearts ; and that they do *not* directly and of themselves furnish any evidence, that faith and regeneration have been produced, and that the work of grace has begun. Let men firmly believe and carefully apply these negative doctrines, and they will thus be preserved from error and delusion, and at the same time will be able, if they carefully improve what they know, and wait upon God for His blessing, to derive from the sacraments all the spiritual benefits they were ever fitted and intended to be the means of conveying.

There is really nothing more declared or defined upon this point in Scripture, or in the Westminster symbols, except what may be implied in, or deducible from, their general character as signs and seals of the covenant of grace. The general idea suggested by the word *seal* is that of *confirming;* and there is no great difficulty in seeing how this idea may be applied to the sacraments, without imagining that they are in themselves attestations, on God's part, to men's individual character and condition, or that they involve anything very exalted or mysterious. There is, first of all, the general consideration, that Christ having expressly appointed these two special ordinances to be instruments or channels of conveying to men spiritual blessings, in addition to what may be called the more ordinary means of grace, the word and prayer, we have in this very circumstance special grounds for confidently expecting His special blessing when we receive and use them aright. This consideration is well fitted to confirm us in our determination to improve the sacraments to the uttermost, and in our confident expectation of deriving spiritual benefit from doing so.

And when we look more particularly to the character of the sacraments as outward actions of a symbolic import, we see plainly, that they have an individualizing, appropriating bearing or tendency, which fits them specially for being made the instruments in the hand of the Spirit of guiding us to a personal application of divine truth to our own condition and circumstances, and thus sealing or confirming our faith, love, and hope. A believer, in partaking of the sacraments, stands forth, plainly and palpably, as making a personal profession of his faith in Christ, and giving a personal promise and pledge to persevere in faith and obedience. The natural tendency of this is to lead him to realize more fully his actual position, obligations, and prospects as a believer, and this warrants the confident expectation that the Spirit will actually employ it for accomplishing this result. But the sacraments are to be regarded as signs and seals on the part of God as well as of man. And in this aspect their sealing or confirming character comes out in this way : God, by giving to a believer, in the ordinary course of His providence, an opportunity of partaking in the sacraments, does not indeed thereby attest or indorse his personal character and standing as a believer, but He may be said to single him out and to deal with him in his individual capacity,—addressing to him personally, and in a manner and circumstances peculiarly fitted to come home with power to his understanding, heart, and conscience, the great truths of Scripture, with the knowledge, belief,—and application of which all spiritual blessings are connected; and thus intimating His readiness and willingness to bestow, in connection with these ordinances, all needful spiritual blessings, in accordance with all that He has revealed in His word, as regulating His conduct in such matters. Viewed as signs and seals on God's part, the sacraments may be fairly regarded as signifying or intimating this, and the declaration of all this in such circumstances, and with such accompaniments, is well fitted to exert a sealing or confirming influence upon the minds of believers.

The substance of this matter may be embodied in these two positions,—1st, That the Holy Spirit ordinarily employs the sacraments, when received by persons duly qualified and rightly prepared, as means or instruments of conveying to them clearer views and more lively and impressive conceptions of what He has done and revealed in His word, with respect to the provisions and arrangements of the covenant of grace, and their special application to men individually. And, 2d, That the Holy Spirit, acting in accordance with the principles and tendencies of our constitution, ordinarily employs the sacraments, as means or instruments of increasing and strengthening men's faith with reference to all its appropriate objects, and thereby of imparting to them, in greater abundance, all the spiritual blessings which are connected with

the lively and vigorous exercise of faith; that is, all those subordinate blessings,—as in a certain sense they may be called,
—which accompany and flow from justification and regeneration.*

We have now stated the substance of what is suggested by
Scripture, and set forth in the Westminster Standards, concerning the way and manner in which the sacraments become means
of grace and produce their appropriate beneficial effects; and,
indeed, more generally, concerning the nature and character, the
subjects and the objects, the end and the effect, of these ordinances. And we have done so under the influence of a strong
desire and determination to avoid the very common and very injurious tendency, either, directly to overrate the value and efficacy
of the sacraments, or to furnish facilities and encouragements to
others to overrate them, by leaving our statements on these subjects in a condition of great vagueness and confusion. Any
attempts to assign to them greater dignity, value, and efficacy
than we have ascribed to them, or to invest them with a deeper
shade of mystery, are, we are persuaded, not only unsanctioned
by Scripture, but inconsistent with the fair and legitimate consequences of what it teaches, and are fitted to exert an injurious
influence upon the interests of truth and holiness. The strong
natural tendency of men to substitute the tithing of mint, anise,
and cumin, for the weightier matters of the law,—to substitute the
observance of outward rites and ceremonies for the diligent cultivation of Christian graces and the faithful discharge of Christian
duties,—is strengthened by everything which, professedly upon
religious grounds, either adds to the number of the rites and ceremonies which God has prescribed, or assigns even to prescribed
rites and ceremonies an importance and an efficacy beyond what
He has sanctioned. In the second of these ways, as well as in the
first, the truth of God has been grievously perverted, and the interests of practical godliness have been extensively injured. Almost the only rites and ceremonies permanently binding upon the
Christian church are baptism and the Lord's Supper; and these

---

* Beza explains *sealing* in this way:
—*Q.* Quid *obsignationem* appellas? *R.*
Applicationem efficaciorem *per fidei
incrementum*, siquidem quo fides major
est, eo præstantius est ejus effectum,
ut Christus cum suis donis magis ac
magis nobis ipsis velut insculpatur.
(Quæstionum et Responsionum Chris-
tianarum, Pars Altera, quæ est de
Sacramentis, p. 24.)

have been in every age so distorted and perverted by exaggeration and confusion, as to have proved, in point of fact, the occasions of fearful injury to men's souls. It is true that men have some-times exhibited a tendency to go to the opposite extreme, to depre-ciate instituted ordinances, and to reduce their importance, value, and efficacy below the standard which the word of God sanctions. But the tendency to overvalue the sacraments, and to make the observance of them a substitute, more or less avowedly, for things of much greater importance, is far more common and far more dangerous; more dangerous, at once, because it is more likely to creep in, and to gain an ascendancy in men's minds, and because, when yielded to and encouraged, it exerts a more injurious influence upon the highest and holiest interests, by wrapping men in strong delusion in regard to their spiritual condition and prospects, and leading them to build their hopes of heaven upon a false founda-tion.

We have confined ourselves to an explanation of the sacra-mental principle, or the general doctrine or theory of the sacra-ments as applicable to both these ordinances—a subject greatly neglected and misunderstood. We have referred to baptism and the Lord's Supper, only, in so far as this was necessary, for illustrating something connected with the exposition of the general doctrine. We have had no occasion to dwell upon the Lord's Supper, because the application of the general doctrine of the sacraments to it is plain enough, and because there is no serious difficulty connected with it, unless we had gone into the discussion of the kind and manner of the presence of Christ in this ordinance, which we regard as one of the most useless controversies that ever was raised. We have been obliged to dwell at some length on baptism, and especially infant baptism, chiefly because of the peculiar place which infant baptism holds,—a peculiarity, the igno-rance or disregard of which has introduced much error and con-fusion into men's views upon this whole subject. The peculiarity is, that infant baptism really occupies a sort of subordinate and exceptional position; while, at the same time, this peculiarity being overlooked, and infant baptism coming much more frequently under our notice than adult baptism, we are very apt to allow the specialties of this peculiar case to modify unduly our views, not only of baptism, but even of the sacraments in general.

The views we have set forth upon this subject, may, at first sight, appear to be large concessions to the anti-pædobaptists,—those who deny the lawfulness of the baptism of infants; and to affect the solidity of the grounds on which the practice of pædobaptism, which has ever prevailed almost universally in the Christian church, is based.   But we are firmly persuaded, that a more careful consideration of the whole matter will show, that these views,—besides being clearly sanctioned by Scripture, and absolutely necessary for the consistent and intelligible interpretation of the Confessions of the Reformed churches, and especially of the Westminster symbols,—are, in their legitimate application, fitted to deprive the arguments of the anti-pædobaptists of the plausibility they possess. It cannot be reasonably denied, that they have a good deal that is plausible to allege against infant baptism.   But we are satisfied, that the plausibility of their arguments will always appear greatest, to men who have not been accustomed to distinguish between the primary, fundamental, and complete idea of this ordinance as exhibited in the baptism of adults, and the distinct and peculiar place which is held by infant baptism, with the special grounds on which it rests.   We cannot conclude without simply stating the following leading positions that ought to be maintained and set forth, in order to guard against error and delusion on the subject of infant baptism :—

1st. That Scripture, while furnishing sufficient materials to establish the lawfulness and obligation of infant baptism, does not give us much direct information concerning it,—does not furnish materials for laying down any very definite deliverances as to its proper effects in relation to individuals; and that the whole history of the church inculcates the lesson, that, upon this subject, men should be particularly careful to abstain from deductions, probabilities, or conjectures, beyond what Scripture clearly sanctions.

2d. That while believers are under the same obligation to present their infant children for baptism as to be baptized themselves, if they have not been baptized before, no infants ought to be baptized, except those of persons who ought themselves to be baptized as adults upon their own profession, and who, being thus recognised as believers, are not only entitled, but bound, to be habitually receiving the Lord's Supper.

3d. That while believers are warranted to improve the baptism of their children in the way of confirming their faith in the salvation of those of them who die in infancy, and in the way of encouraging themselves in a hearty and hopeful discharge of parental duty towards those of them who survive infancy, neither parents nor children, when the children come to be proper subjects of instruction, should regard the fact that they have been baptized, as affording of itself even the slightest presumption that they have been regenerated; that nothing should ever be regarded as furnishing any evidence of regeneration, except the appropriate proofs of an actual renovation of the moral nature, exhibited in each case individually; and that, until these proofs appear, every one, whether baptized or not, should be treated and dealt with in all respects as if he were unregenerate, and still, needed.to be born again of the word of God through the belief of the truth.

JOHN CALVIN.*

JOHN CALVIN was by far the greatest of the Reformers with respect to the talents he possessed, the influence he exerted, and the services he rendered in the establishment and diffusion of important truth. The Reformers who preceded him may be said to have been all men, who, from the circumstances in which they were placed, and the occupations which these circumstances imposed upon them, or from the powers and capacities with which they had been gifted, were fitted chiefly for the immediate necessary business of the age in which their lot was cast, and were not perhaps qualified for rising above this sphere,—which, however, was a very important one. Their efforts, whether in the way of speculation or of action, were just such as their immediate circumstances and urgent present duties demanded of them, while they had little opportunity of considering and promoting the permanent interests of the whole scheme of scriptural truth, or the whole theory and constitution of Christian churches. After all that Luther, Melancthon, and Zwingle had done, there was still needed some one of elevated and comprehensive mind, who should be able to rise above the distraction and confusion of existing contentions, to survey the wide field of scriptural truth in all its departments, to combine and arrange its various parts, and to present them, as a harmonious whole, to the contemplation of men.

* *British and Foreign Evangelical Review.*

The Works of Calvin in English, by the Calvin Translation Society. 52 vols. 8vo. 1843-1856.

Letters of John Calvin. By Dr JULES BONNET.

This was the special work for which God qualified Calvin, by bestowing upon him both the intellectual and the spiritual gifts necessary for the task, and this He enabled him to accomplish. God makes use of the intellectual powers which He bestows upon men, for the accomplishment of His own purposes ; or rather He bestows upon men those intellectual powers which may fit them naturally, and according to the ordinary operation of means, for the purposes which He in His sovereignty has assigned to them to effect. He then leads them, by His grace, to devote their powers to His glory and service, He blesses their labours, and thus His gracious designs are accomplished.

Calvin had received from God mental powers of the highest order. Distinguished equally by comprehensiveness and pene-tration of intellect, by acuteness and soundness of judgment, his circumstances, in early life, were so regulated in providence, that he was furnished with the best opportunities of improving his faculties, and acquiring the learning and culture that might be necessary with a view to his future labours. Led by God's grace early and decidedly to renounce the devil, the world, and the flesh, and to devote himself to the service of Christ, he was also led, under the same guidance, to abandon the Church of Rome, and to devote himself to the preaching of the Gospel, the exposi-tion of the revealed truth of God, and the organisation of churches in accordance with the sacred Scriptures and the practice of the apostles. In all these departments of useful labour his efforts were honoured with an extraordinary measure of success. Calvin did what the rest of the Reformers did, and, in addition, he did what none of them either did or could effect. He was a diligent and laborious pastor. He gave much time to the instruction of those who were preparing for the work of the ministry. He took an active part in opposing the Church of Rome, in promoting the Reformation, and in organising Protestant churches. Entering with zeal and ardour into all the controversies which the eccle-siastical movements of the time produced, he was ever ready to defend injured truth or to expose triumphant error. This was work which he had to do in common with the other Reformers, though he brought higher powers than any of them, to bear upon the performance of it. But in addition to all this, he had for his special business, the great work of digesting and systematising the whole scheme of divine truth, of bringing out in order and har-

mony, all the different doctrines which are contained in the word
of God, unfolding them in their mutual relations and various
bearings, and thus presenting them, in the most favourable aspect,
to the contemplation and the study of the highest order of minds.

The systematising of divine truth, and the full organisation of
the Christian church according to the word of God, are the great
peculiar achievements of Calvin. For this work God eminently
qualified him, by bestowing upon him the highest gifts both of
nature and of grace; and this work he was enabled to accomplish
in such a way as to confer the greatest and most lasting benefits
upon the church of Christ, and to entitle him to the commendation and the gratitude of all succeeding ages.

The first edition of his great work, "The Institution of the
Christian Religion," was published when he was twenty-seven
years of age; and it is a most extraordinary proof of the maturity
and vigour of his mind, of the care with which he had studied the
word of God, and of the depth and comprehensiveness of his
meditations upon divine things, that though the work was afterwards greatly enlarged, and though some alterations were even
made in the arrangement of the topics discussed, yet no change of
any importance was made in the actual doctrines which it set
forth. The first edition, produced at that early age, contained
the substance of the whole system of doctrine which has since
been commonly associated with his name,—the development and
exposition of which has been regarded by many as constituting a
strong claim upon the esteem and gratitude of the church of
Christ, and by many others as rendering him worthy of execration
and every opprobrium. He lived twenty-seven years more after
the publication of the first edition of the Institutes, and a large
portion of his time during the remainder of his life was devoted
to the examination of the word of God and the investigation of
divine truth. But he saw no reason to make any material change
in the views which he had put forth; and a large proportion of
the most pious, able, and learned men, and most careful students
of the sacred Scriptures, who have since adorned the church of
Christ, have received all his leading doctrines as accordant with
the teaching of God's word.*

---

* In a work published a short time before Calvin's death, Beza made the following statement upon this point,— a statement fully confirmed by all the

The "Institutio" of Calvin is the most important work in the history of theological science, that which is more than any other creditable to its author, and has exerted directly or indirectly the greatest and most beneficial influence upon the opinions of intelligent men on theological subjects. It may be said to occupy, in the science of theology, the place which it requires both the "Novum Organum" of Bacon, and the "Principia of Newton" to fill up, in physical science,—at once conveying, though not in formal didactic precepts and rules, the finest idea of the way and manner in which the truths of God's word ought to be classified and systematised, and at the same time actually classifying and systematizing them, in a way that has not yet received any very material or essential improvement. There had been previous attempts to present the truths of Scripture in a systematic form and arrangement, and to exhibit their relations and mutual dependence. But all former attempts had been characterized by great defects and imperfections; and especially all of them had been more or less defective in this most important respect, that a considerable portion of the materials, of which they were composed, had been not truths but errors,—not the doctrines actually taught in the sacred Scriptures, but errors arising from ignorance of the contents of the inspired volume, or from serious mistakes, as to the meaning of its statements. One of the earlier attempts at a formal system of theology was made in the eighth century, by Johannes Damascenus, and this is a very defective and erroneous work. The others which had preceded Calvin's "Institutes," in this department, were chiefly the productions of the schoolmen, Lombard's four books of "Sentences," and Thomas Aquinas's "Summa," with the commentaries upon these works; and they all exhibited very defective and erroneous views of scriptural truth. Augustine was the last man who had possessed sufficient intellectual power, combined with views, in the main correct, of the leading doctrines of God's word, to have produced a system of theology that might have been generally received, and he was not led to undertake such a work, except in a very partial way. The first edition of Melancthon's

facts of the case. "Hoc enin (Deo sit gratia) vel ipsa insidia Calvino tribuat necesse est, ut quamvis sit ipse ex eorum numero qui quotidie discendo consenescunt, nullum tamen dogma jam inde ab initio ad hoc usque tempus, in tam multis et tam laboriosis scriptis, ecclesiæ proposuerit, in quo illum sententiam mutare et a semetipso dissentire oportuerit."—Abstersio Calumniarum, p. 263.

Common Places,—the only one published before Calvin produced the first edition of his "Institutes,"—was not to be compared to Calvin's work, in the accuracy of its representations of the doctrines of Scripture, in the fulness and completeness of its materials, or in the skill and ability with which they were digested and arranged; and in the subsequent editions, while the inaccuracy of its statements increased in some respects rather than diminished, it still continued, to a considerable extent, a defective and ill digested work, characterised by a good deal of prolixity and wearisome repetition. It was in these circumstances that Calvin produced his "Institutes," the materials of which it was composed being in almost every instance the true doctrines really taught in the word of God, and exhibiting the whole substance of what is taught there on matters of doctrine, worship, government, and discipline,—and the whole of these materials being arranged with admirable skill and expounded in their meaning, evidence, and bearings, with consummate ability. This was the great and peculiar service which Calvin rendered to the cause of truth and the interests of sound theology, and its value and importance it is scarcely possible to overrate.

In theology there is, of course, no room for originality properly so called, for its whole materials are contained in the actual statements of God's word; and he is the greatest and best theologian, who has most accurately apprehended the meaning of the statements of Scripture,—who, by comparing and combining them, has most fully and correctly brought out the whole mind of God on all the topics on which the Scriptures give us information,—who classifies and digests the truths of Scripture in the way best fitted to commend them to the apprehension and acceptance of men,—and who can most clearly and forcibly bring out their scriptural evidence, and most skilfully and effectively defend them against the assaults of adversaries. In this work, and indeed in almost any one of its departments, there is abundant scope for the exercise of the highest powers, and for the application of the most varied and extensive acquirements. Calvin was far above the weakness of aiming at the invention of novelties in theology, or of wishing to be regarded as the discoverer of new opinions. The main features of the representation which he put forth of the scheme of divine truth, might be found in the writings of Augustine and Luther,—in neither singly, but in the two conjointly.

But by grasping with vigour and comprehensiveness the whole scheme of divine truth and all its various departments, and combining them into one harmonious and well-digested system, he has done what neither Augustine nor Luther did or could have done, and has given conclusive evidence that he was possessed of the highest intellectual powers, as well as enjoyed the most abundant communications of God's Spirit.

The two leading departments of theological science are the exegetical and the systematic. The two most important functions of the theologian are first, to bring out accurately the meaning of the individual statements of God's word, the particular truths which are taught there; and, second, to classify and arrange these truths in such a way as to bring out most fully and correctly the whole scheme of doctrine which is there unfolded, and to illustrate the bearing and application of the scheme as a whole, and of its different parts. And it is important to notice, that in both these departments, Calvin stands out pre-eminent, having manifested in both of them the highest excellence and attained the greatest success. He has left us an exposition of nearly the whole word of God, and it is not only immeasurablys uperior to any commentary that preceded it, but it has continued ever since, and continues to this day, to be regarded by all competent judges, as a work of the highest value, and as manifesting marvellous perspicacity and soundness of judgment. There is no department of theological study the cultivators of which, in modern times, are more disposed to regard with something like contempt the labours and attainments of their predecessors, and to consider themselves as occupying a much higher platform, than the exact and critical interpretation of Scripture; and we think it must be admitted that, in modern times, greater improvements have been made in this department of theological science than in any other. Yet, Calvin's Commentary continues to secure the respect and the admiration of the most competent judges, both in this country and on the continent, even of those who are disposed to estimate most highly the superiority of the present age over preceding generations in the department of scriptural exegesis. And it is perhaps the most striking illustration of the extraordinary gifts which God bestowed upon Calvin, and of the value of the services which he has rendered to Christian truth and to theological science, that he reached such distinguished excellence, and has exerted so extensive and per-

manent an influence, *both* as an accurate interpreter of Scripture,
and as a systematic expounder of the great doctrines of God's
word.*

Besides the Commentary upon Scripture and the "Institutes,"
the leading departments of Calvin's works are his "Tractatus"
and his "Epistolæ," both of which are much less known amongst
us than they should be. The "Tractatus" are chiefly controversial pieces, in defence of the leading doctrines of his system when
assailed by adversaries, and in opposition to the errors of the
Papists, the Anabaptists, the Libertines, the advocates of compro-
mises with the Church of Rome, and the assailants of the orthodox doctrine of the Trinity. His "Epistolæ" consist partly of
confidential correspondence with his friends, and partly of answers
to applications made to him from all parts of the Protestant world,
asking his opinion and advice upon all the most important topics
that occurred, connected with the administration of ecclesiastical
affairs in that most important crisis of the church's history. They
manifest throughout the greatest practical wisdom and the truest
scriptural moderation, as well as warm friendship and cordial
affection; and the perusal of them is indispensable to our forming
a right estimate of Calvin's character, and of the spirit and motives by which he was animated, while it is abundantly sufficient
of itself to dispel many of the slanders by which he has been
assailed.

In these different departments of his works, we have Calvin
presented to us as an interpreter of Scripture, as a systematic
expounder of the scheme of Christian doctrine, as a controversial

---

* In proof of the truth of this
statement of the high estimate of Calvin's qualifications and success in the
department of exegesis, formed by the
most competent judges in the present
day, it is enough to refer to Professor
Tholuck's elaborate Dissertation on
Calvin as an interpreter of the holy
Scripture. Tholuck has published editions of Calvin's Commentaries on the
Psalms, and on the New Testament;
and, in the dissertation referred to, he
has set forth the grounds of the high
estimate he had formed of the value of
these works, under the four heads of
Calvin's *doctrinal impartiality*, exegetical tact, various learning, and deep

Christian piety. Tholuck's very high
estimate of Calvin, as an interpreter of
Scripture, is the more to be relied on,
and has probably exerted the greater
influence in Germany, because he is
not himself a Calvinist, and, indeed,
brings out, in the conclusion of his
dissertation, his divergence from Calvin's views on predestination and
cognate topics. Bretschneider and
Hengstenberg also, critics of the highest reputation, and of very different
schools of theology, both from Tholuck
and from each other, have borne the
strongest testimony to Calvin's qualifications as an interpreter.

defender of truth and impugner of error, and as a friend and practical adviser in the regulation of the affairs of the church; and his pre-eminent excellence in all these departments are, we are persuaded, such as justly to entitle him to a place in the estimation and gratitude of the church of Christ, which no other uninspired man is entitled to share. Calvin certainly was not free from the infirmities which are always found in some form or degree even in the best men; and in particular, he occasionally exhibited an angry impatience of contradiction and opposition, and sometimes assailed and treated the opponents of the truth and cause of God with a violence of invective, which cannot be defended, and should certainly not be imitated. He was not free from error, and is not to be implicitly followed in his interpretation of Scripture, or in his exposition of doctrine. But whether we look to the powers and capacities with which God endowed him, the manner in which he employed them, and the results by which his labours have been followed,—or to the Christian wisdom, magnanimity, and devotedness, which marked his character, and generally regulated his conduct, there is probably not one among the sons of men, beyond the range of those whom God miraculously inspired by His Spirit, who has stronger claims upon our veneration and gratitude.

We believe that this is in substance the view generally entertained of Calvin by all who have read his works, and who have seen ground to adopt, in the main, the system of doctrine which he inculcated as based upon divine authority. Many men who were not Calvinists have borne the highest testimony to Calvin's great talents and his noble character, to his literary excellencies and his commanding influence. But those who are persuaded that he brought out a full, and, in the main, accurate view of the truth of God, with respect to the way of salvation and the organisation of the Christian church, must ever regard him in a very different light from those who have formed an opposite judgment upon these subjects. If Calvin's system of doctrine, government, and worship, is in the main scriptural, he must have enjoyed very special and abundant communications of God's Spirit in the formation of his convictions, and he must have rendered most important services to mankind by the diffusion of invaluable truth. Men who are not Calvinists may admire his wonderful talents, and do justice to the elevation of his general character, and the purity and disinterestedness of his motives. But unless they are persuaded that his views upon most points were, in the main, accordant with Scripture, they cannot regard him with the profound veneration which Calvinists feel, when they contemplate him as God's chosen instrument for diffusing His truth; nor can they cherish anything like the same estimate of the magnitude of the services he has rendered to mankind, and of the gratitude to which, in consequence, he is entitled.

The Calvin translation Society, which has done a great and useful work, by making almost all his writings accessible to English readers, translated and circulated Professor Tholuck's Dissertation formerly referred to; and subjoined to it a number of testimonies in commendation of Calvin's works, from eminent men of all classes and opinions, of all ages and countries, including not only Calvinists and theologians, but also infidels and Arminians, statesmen and philosophers, scholars and men of letters. These testimonies have been added to from time to time, and being now collected together, they fill above 100 pages in the last volume of his works, which contains the translation of his commentary upon Joshua. Many more testimonies to the value and excellence of Calvin's writings might have been produced.* But this collection, as it stands, could not probably be matched in the kind and amount of commendation it exhibits, in the case of any other man whose writings and labours were confined to the department of religion.

Indeed, it is probably true that no man whose time and talents were devoted exclusively to subjects connected with Christianity and the church, has ever received so large a share both of praise and of censure. He has been commended, in the strongest terms, by many of the highest names both in Christian and in general literature; and the strength of their commendation has been generally very much in proportion to their capacities and opportunities of judging. But if he has received the highest commendation, he has also been visited with a vast amount of censure,—the one

---

* There are some additional and very valuable testimonies to Calvin's character and writings given in his life in Haag's "La France Protestante," tom. iii. p. 109, especially from three of the most eminent literary men of the present age, Guizot, Mignet, and Sayous. Haag brings out also an interesting contrast between the candid admissions of some of the older Romish writers, and the unscrupulous mendacity of his latest popish biographer Audin.

being really, in the circumstances, just about as significant a testimony to his excellence and his influence as the other. The papists had the sagacity to see that Calvin—by his great talents and the commanding influence which he exerted—was really their most formidable adversary at the era of the Reformation. And in accordance with their ordinary principles and policy, they endeavoured to ruin his character by the vilest slanders. Most of these calumnies being utterly destitute of all evidence, and therefore disgraceful only to those who invented or repeated them, have long since been abandoned by every papist who retained even the slightest regard for character or decency, though they are still occasionally brought forward or insinuated. Some of the Lutheran writers of his own time, and of the succeeding generation, mortified apparently that Calvin's influence and reputation were eclipsing those of their master, railed against him with bitter malignity, and were even mean enough sometimes to countenance the popish slanders against his character. Specimens of this discreditable conduct, on the part of the Lutherans, may be seen in the answers made by Calvin himself, and by Beza, to the attacks of Westphalus and Heshusius.

During Calvin's life, and for more than half a century after his death, most of the divines of the Church of England adopted his theological views, and spoke of him with the greatest respect. But after, through the influence of Archbishop Laud and the prevalence of Arminian and Pelagian views, sound doctrine and true religion were, in a great measure, banished from that church, Calvin, as might be expected, came to be regarded in a very different light. During most of last century, the generality of the Episcopalian divines who had occasion to speak of him and his doctrines, indulged in bitter vituperation against him, and not unfrequently talked as if they regarded him as a monster who ought to be held up to execration. Indeed, we do not know that theological literature furnishes a more melancholy exhibition of ignorance, prejudice, and bitter hatred of God's truth, than the general mode of speaking about Calvin and his doctrines, that prevailed among the Episcopalian clergy of last century. Some of them write as if they were ignorant enough to believe that Calvinism and Presbyterianism were invented by Calvin, and were never heard of in the church till the sixteenth century; and when they speak of him in connection with his views about the divine sovereignty and decrees, we might be tempted to think, from the spirit they often manifest, that they looked upon him almost as if he himself were the author or cause of the fate of those who finally perish. It is but fair to say that this state of things has been greatly improved since the latter part of last century. This is owing, partly to the high commendation which Bishop Horsley gave to Calvin's writings, and to the public advice which he tendered to the Episcopalian clergy, as one of which they stood greatly in need,—viz., to see that they understood what Calvinism was before they attacked it;—but chiefly to that far greater prevalence of evangelical doctrine and true religion, which, though grievously damaged by Tractarianism, still forms so pleasing a feature in the condition of the English Church.

Calvin has also had the honour to receive, at all times, a very large share of the enmity of " the world of the ungodly,"—of men who hate God's truth, and all who have been eminently honoured by Him to be instrumental in promoting it. Such persons seem to have a sort of instinctive deep-seated dislike to Calvin, which leads them to dwell upon and exaggerate everything in his character and conduct that may seem fitted to depreciate him. It is not uncommon, even in our own age and country, to hear infidel and semi-infidel declaimers, who know nothing of Calvin's writings or labours, when they wish to say a particularly smart and clever thing against bigotry and intolerance,—meaning thereby honest zeal for God's truth,—bring in something about Calvin burning Servetus.

The leading charges commonly adduced against Calvin's character, as distinguished from his doctrines, are pride, arrogance, spiritual tyranny, intolerance, and persecution. Some of these are charges which, as universal experience shows, derive their plausibility, in a great measure, from the view that may be taken of the general character and leading motives of the man against whom they may be directed, and of the goodness and rectitude of the objects which he mainly and habitually aimed at. Those who have an unfavourable opinion of a man's general motives and objects, will see evidence of pride, obstinacy and intolerance, in matters in which those who believe that he was generally influenced by a regard to God's glory and the advancement of Christ's cause, will see only integrity and firmness, uncompromising vigour and decision, mixed, it may be, with the ordinary remains of hu-

man infirmity.   The piety and integrity of Calvin, his paramount
regard to the honour of God and the promotion of truth and
righteousness, to the advancement of Christ's cause and the
spiritual welfare of men, are beyond all reasonable doubt.   And
those who, convinced of this, examine his history with attention and
impartiality, will have no difficulty in seeing that, for most of these
charges, there is no real foundation; and that, in so far as evidence
can be adduced in support of any of them, it really proves nothing
more than that Calvin manifested, like all other men, the remains
of human infirmity, especially, of course, in those respects to which
his natural temperament and the influence of his position and circumstances, more peculiarly disposed him.   The state of his health,
the bent of his natural dispositions, and the whole influence of his
position, occupations, and habits, were unfavourable to the cultivation of those features of character, and those modes of speaking
and acting, which are usually regarded as most pleasing to others,
and best fitted to call forth love and affection in the ordinary intercourse of life.   The flow of animal spirits, the ready interest in
all ordinary commonplace things, and the play of the social feelings, which give such a charm to Luther's conversation and letters,
were alien to Calvin's constitutional tendencies, and to his ordinary
modes of thinking and feeling.   He had a great and exalted mission assigned to him ; he was fully alive to this, thoroughly
determined to devote himself unreservedly, and to subordinate
everything else, to the fulfilment of his mission, and not unconscious of its dignity, or of the powers which had been conferred
upon him for working it out.   With such a man, so placed, so
endowed, and so occupied, the temptation, of course, would be,
to identify himself and all his views and proceedings with the
cause of God and His truth,—to prosecute these high and holy
objects sternly and uncompromisingly, without much regard to the
opinions and inclinations of those around him,—and to deal with
opposition, as if it necessarily implied something sinful in those
from whom it proceeded, as if opposition to him involved opposition to his Master.   Calvin would have been something more than
man, if, endowed and situated as he was, he had never yielded to
this temptation, and been led to deal with opponents and opposition in a way which only the commission of the inspired prophets
would have warranted.

Calvin did occasionally give plain indications of undue self-confidence and self-complacency, and of a mixture of personal and carnal feelings and motives, with his zeal for the promotion of truth and righteousness. But there is nothing suggested by a fair view of his whole history that is fitted to throw any doubt upon the general excellence of his character, as tried by the highest standard that has ordinarily been exhibited among men; or on the general purity, elevation, and disinterestedness of the motives by which he was mainly and habitually influenced. There is sufficient evidence that he still had, like the apostle, " a law in his members warring against the law of his mind," and sometimes " bringing him into captivity to the law of sin." And, from what we know, from Scripture and experience, of the deceitfulness of the heart and the deceitfulness of sin, we cannot doubt that there was a larger admixture of what was sinful in his motives and conduct than he himself was distinctly aware of. But this, too, is characteristic of all men,—even the best of them,—and there is really no ground whatever for regarding Calvin as manifesting a larger measure of human infirmity than attaches, in some form or other, to the best and holiest of our race; while there is abundant evidence that, during a life of great labour and great suffering, he fully established his supreme devotedness to God's glory and service, his thorough resignation to His will, his perfect willingness to labour in season and out of season, to spend and to be spent, for the sake of Christ and His gospel. It was assuredly no such proud, arrogant, domineering, heartless despot as Calvin is often represented to have been, who composed the dedications which we find prefixed to his commentaries upon the different portions of the Bible, and many of his letters to his friends,—expressing often the warmest affection, the deepest gratitude for instruction and services received; and exhibiting a most cordial appreciation of the excellences of others, a humble estimate of himself, and a perfect willingness to be or to do anything for the sake of Christ and of His cause. It was certainly no such man as he is often described, who lived so long on such terms with his colleagues in the ministry, and held such a place, not only in their veneration and confidence, but in their esteem and affection, as are indicated by the whole state of things unfolded to us in Beza's life of him.

With reference to the principal charge which, in his own as well as subsequent times, was brought against his motives and temper, Calvin has put on record the following protestation, in a letter written towards the end of his life, in the year 1558 :—

"I can with reason boast, however much ungodly men call me inexorable, that I have never become the enemy of one human being on the ground of personal injuries. I confess that I am irritable; and, though this vice displeases me, I have not succeeded in curing myself as much as I could wish. But, though many persons have unjustly attacked me, an innocent, and, what is more, well-deserving man,—have perfidiously plotted all kinds of mischief against me, and most cruelly harassed me, I can defy any one to point out a single person to whom I have studied to return the like, even though the means and the opportunity were in my power."*

On a ground formerly adverted to, we have no doubt that there was sometimes, in Calvin's feelings and motives, a larger admixture of the personal and the imperfect than he was himself aware of, or than he here admits. We always shrink from men making professions about the purity of their motives, as we cannot but fear, that this indicates the want of an adequate sense of the deceitfulness of sin and of their own hearts, a disposition to think of themselves more highly than they ought to think. It would not, we think, have been at all unwarrantable or unbecoming, if Calvin, in the passage we have quoted, had made a fuller admission of sinful motives, which he would no doubt have acknowledged that the Searcher of hearts must have seen in him. And yet, we have no doubt, that his statement, strong as it is, is substantially true, so far as concerns anything that came fairly under the cognisance of his fellow-men,—anything on which other men were entitled to form a judgment. Whatever the Searcher of hearts might see in him, we believe that there was nothing in his ordinary conduct, in his usual course of outward procedure, that could entitle any man to have denied the truth of the statement which he here made about himself, or that would afford any materials for disproving it. And if this, or anything like it, be true, then the practical result is, that the common notions about Calvin's irritability, the extent to which he was ordinarily influenced by personal, selfish, and sinful motives, are grossly exaggerated; and that, though this might be said to be his besetting sin,—that to which his constitutional tendencies and the whole influence of his position chiefly disposed him,—there was really nothing in it, that entitled any of his fellow-men to reproach him, or that could be

---

* *Letters of John Calvin*, by Dr Bonnet, vol. iii. p. 429.

justly regarded as anything more than a display of that common human infirmity, which even the best men manifest in some form or degree.

Calvin's superiority to the influence of personal, angry, and vindictive feelings, is very fully brought out in the course he pursued, with respect to the men who filled the office of the ministry at Geneva after Farel and he had been driven into exile, in 1538, —a topic which has not been brought out in any of the histories of Calvin so prominently as it should have been. Calvin and Farel had been banished from Geneva, solely because of their integrity and boldness in maintaining the purity of the church in the exercise of discipline, by refusing to admit unworthy persons to the Lord's Supper. Their colleagues in the ministry who were not banished, and the persons appointed to succeed them, were of course men who submitted to the dictation of the civil authorities in the exercise of discipline, and admitted to the Lord's table indiscriminately without regard to character. These men were, no doubt, strongly tempted, in self-defence, to depreciate as much as possible the character and conduct of Calvin and Farel, and to this temptation they yielded without reserve. Three or four months after his banishment, Calvin wrote from Basle to Farel, who had been called to Neufchatel, in the following terms :—*

"How our successors are likely to get on I can conjecture from the first beginnings. While already they entirely break off every appearance of peace by their want of temper, they suppose that the best course for themselves was to tear in pieces our estimation, publicly and privately, so as to render us as odious as possible. But if we know that they cannot calumniate us, excepting in so far as God permits, we know also the end God has in view in granting such permission. Let us humble ourselves, therefore, unless we wish to strive with God when He would humble us."

A division soon arose at Geneva upon the question, whether or not the ministry of these men ought to be recognised and waited on. Many—and these, as might be expected, were the best men in the city in point of character and the most attached to Calvin —were of opinion that these men ought not to be treated as ministers, and that religious ordinances ought not to be received at their hands. Saunier, and Cordier (author of the "Colloquies"), men of the highest character and standing, regents in the college, refused

* "Letters," vol. i. pp. 50, 51.

to receive the Lord's Supper at the hands of these men, and were in consequence driven from their posts, and obliged to quit the city. Calvin,—who had now taken up his abode at Strasburg,—was consulted upon this important question of casuistry, and gave his decision on the side of peace and conciliation, advising them without any hesitation to recognise and wait upon the ministry of these men. And this may surely be regarded as a triumph of reason and conscience over personal and carnal feeling. In the whole circumstances of this case, as now adverted to, it is very plain that all the lower and more unworthy class of feelings, everything partaking of the character of selfishness in any of its forms or aspects, everything like wounded vanity or self-importance, everything like a tendency to indulge in anger or vindictiveness, must have tended towards leading Calvin to decide this question, in accordance with the views of those in Geneva whom he most respected and esteemed. If Calvin had been such a man as he is often represented, so arrogant and so imperious, so much disposed to estimate things by their bearing upon his own personal importance and self-complacency, and to resent opposition and depreciation, all that we know of human nature, would lead us to expect, that he would have encouraged his friends to refuse all countenance to the existing clergy and to the ecclesiastical system which they administered. The fact that he gave an opposite advice, may be fairly regarded as a proof, that the personal and the selfish (in the wide sense of undue regard to anything about self) had no such prominence or influence among his actuating motives as many seem to suppose,—that the lower and more unworthy motives were habitually subordinated to the purer and more elevated,—and that their operation, so far as they did operate, should not be regarded as distinctively characteristic of the individual, but merely as a symptom of the common human infirmity, which in some form or degree is exhibited by all men, even those who have been renewed in the spirit of their minds.

As Calvin's conduct in this matter illustrates not only his elevation above the influence of personal and selfish feeling, but also his strong sense of the importance of respecting constituted authorities, and preserving the peace of the church, it may be worth while to bring out somewhat more fully what he thought and felt regarding it. The great general principle on which he founded his judgment upon this question was to this effect, that the men in office preached the substance of scriptural truth, and administered the sacraments in accordance with scriptural arrangements, notwithstanding the promiscuousness of the admission to partake in them,—and that this being secured, everything else was, in the circumstances, of comparatively inferior importance, and should be subordinated, as a motive in determining conduct, to the respect due to the ministerial office and the persons who, in providence, held it, and to a regard to the peace of the community. He distinctly admits that the people were entitled to judge for themselves, on their own responsibility, whether or not the ministers preached the gospel, and unless satisfied upon this point, were fully warranted to abandon their ministry—recognising thus, the paramount importance which Scripture assigns to the truth and the preaching of it, as the great determining element on this whole subject.   It has been well said in regard to this matter, that preaching the truth is God's ordinance, but preaching error is not God's ordinance, and is therefore not entitled to any recognition or respect.   The ground taken by Calvin recognises this principle, and, therefore, though it is abundantly wide and lax,—more so, perhaps, than can be thoroughly defended,—it gives no countenance whatever to the views of those who advocate the warrantableness of waiting upon the ministry of men who do not preach the gospel, but who are supposed to have other recommendations, on the ground of their connection with some particular system or constitution, civil or ecclesiastical.   Calvin's first explicit reference to this subject occurs in a letter to Farel, written from Strasburg, in October 1538.   The question as there put was this, " Whether it is lawful to receive the sacrament of the Lord's Supper from the hands of the new ministers, and to partake of it along with such a promiscuous assemblage of unworthy communicants ?"   Calvin's deliverance upon it was this :—

" In this matter I quite agree with Capito.   This, in brief, was the sum of our discussion : that among Christians there ought to be so great a dislike of schism, as that they may always avoid it so far as lies in their power.   That there ought to prevail among them such a reverence for the ministry of the word and of the sacraments, that wherever they perceive these things to be, there they may consider the church to exist.   Whenever therefore it happens, by the Lord's permission, that the church is administered by pastors, whatever kind of persons they may be, if we see there the marks of the church, it will be better not to break the unity.   Nor need it be any hindrance that some points of doctrine are not quite so pure, seeing that there is scarcely any church which does not retain some remnants of former ignorance. It is sufficient for us if the doctrine on which the church of God is founded be recognised, and maintain its place. Nor should it prove any obstacle, that he ought not to be reckoned a lawful pastor who shall not only have fraudulently insinuated himself into the office of a true minister, but shall have wickedly usurped it. For there is no reason why every private person should mix himself up with these scruples. The sacraments are the means of communion with the church; they must needs therefore be administered by the hands of pastors. In regard to those, therefore, who already occupy that position, legitimately or not, and although the right of judging as to that is not denied, it will be well to suspend judgment, in the meantime, until the matter shall have been legally adjudicated. Therefore, if men wait upon their ministry, they will run no risk, that they should appear either to acknowledge or approve, or in any way to ratify their commission. But by this means they will give a proof of their patience in tolerating those who they know will be condemned by a solemn judgment. The refusal at first of these excellent brethren did not surprise nor even displease me."[*]

Calvin discussed the same subject more fully in a letter addressed in June 1539, "To the Church at Geneva;" and as it is most honourably characteristic of its author, while this topic has not received the prominence in his history to which it is entitled, we shall quote the greater part of it.

"Nothing, most beloved brethren, has caused me greater sorrow, since those disturbances which had so sadly scattered and almost entirely overthrown your church, than when I understood your strivings and contentions with those ministers who succeeded us. For although the disorders which were inseparably connected with their first arrival among you, might with good reason prove offensive to you; whatever may have given the occasion, I cannot hear without great and intense horror that any schism should settle down within the church. Wherefore, this was far more bitter to me than words can express;—I allude to what I have heard about those your contentions, so long as you were tossed about in uncertainty; since owing to that circumstance not only was your church rent by division quite openly, but also the ecclesiastical ministry exposed to obloquy and contempt. . . . . Now, therefore, when, contrary to my expectation, I have heard that the reconciliation between your pastors and the neighbouring churches, having been confirmed also by Farel and by myself, was not found to be sufficient for binding you together in sincere and friendly affection, and by the tie of a lawful connection with [your pastors, to whom the care of your souls is committed, I felt myself compelled to write to you, that I might endeavour, so far as lay in me, to find a medicine for this disease, which, without great sin against God, it was not possible for me to conceal. And although my

---

[*] Vol. i. pp. 77–8.

former letters had not been very lovingly received by you, I was nevertheless unwilling to be wanting in my duty, so that, should I have no further success, I would at least deliver my own soul.   Neither do I so much question your spirit of obedience (of which, indeed, I have proof) towards God and His ministers, as that I can at all fear that this my exhortation will have no weight with you, neither has my sincerity towards you lain concealed.   That my advice has not been taken by you, I consider is rather to be imputed to the circumstances of the time, when such was the state of disorder, that it was very difficult indeed to determine what was best.   Now at length, however, when your affairs, by the favour of God, are in a more settled and composed state, I trust that you will readily perceive that my only object is to lead you into the right way ; that being so persuaded with regard to me, you may show in reality by what motive you are brought into subjection to the truth. Especially, I ask you to weigh maturely, having put aside all respect of persons, of what honour the Lord accounts them worthy, and what grace He has committed to those whom He has appointed in His own church as pastors and ministers of the word.   For He not only commands us to render a willing obedience, with fear and trembling, to the word while it is proclaimed to us ; but also commands that the ministers of the word are to be treated with honour and reverence, as being clothed with the authority of His ambassadors, whom He would have to be acknowledged as His own angels and messengers. Certainly so long as we were among you, we did not try much to impress upon you the dignity of our ministry, that we might avoid all ground of suspicion ; now, however, that we are placed beyond the reach of danger, I speak more freely my mind.   Had I to do with the ministers themselves, I would teach what I considered to be the extent and measure of their office, and to what you also are bound as sitting under their ministry.   Since, of a truth, every one must render an account of his own life, each individual for himself, as well ministers as private persons, it is rather to be desired, that every one for himself may consider, what is due to others, than that he may require what may further be due to him from some one else.   Where such considerations have their due weight, then also this established rule will operate effectually, namely, that those who hold the office of ministers of the word, since the guidance and rule over your souls is intrusted to their care, are to be owned and acknowledged in the relation of parents, to be held in esteem, and honoured on account of that office which, by the calling of the Lord, they discharge among you.   Nor does the extent of their function reach so far as to deprive you of the right conferred on you by God (as upon all His own people), that every pastor may be subject to examination, that those who are thus approven may be distinguished from the wicked, and all such may be held back who, under the guise of shepherds, betray a wolfish rapacity.   This, however, is my earnest wish concerning those who in some measure fulfil the duty of pastors, so as to be tolerable, that you also may conduct yourselves towards them in a Christian spirit, and with this view that you may make greater account of that which may be due by you to others, than what others owe to yourselves.

" This also I will set forth plainly and in a few words. Two things here are to be considered. The one, that the calling of your ministers does not happen without the will of God. For although that change which took place upon our departure may have been brought to pass by the subtlety of the devil, so that whatever followed on that change may justly be suspected by you : in it, nevertheless, the remarkable grace of the Lord is to be acknowledged by you, who has not allowed you to be left altogether destitute ; nor let you fall back again under the yoke of Antichrist, from which He hath once rescued you already. But He rather wished that both the doctrine of the gospel should still exist, and that some appearance of a church should flourish among you, so that with a quiet conscience you might continue there. We have always admonished you that you should acknowledge that overturning of your church as the visitation of the Lord sent upon you, and necessary also for us. Neither ought you so much to direct your thoughts against the wicked and the instruments of Satan, as upon personal and individual sins, which have deserved no lighter punishment, but indeed a far more severe chastisement. I would now therefore once more repeat the same advice. For besides that such is the particular and suitable remedy for obtaining mercy and deliverance of the Lord from that just judgment which lies upon you, there is also another very weighty reason that ought to bring you to repentance ; lest peradventure we may seem to bury in oblivion that very great benefit of the Lord towards you, in not having allowed the gospel edifice to fall utterly to ruin in the midst of you, seeing that it has held so together, that as an instance of His direct interference it must be reckoned as a miracle of His power, by which alone you were preserved from that greatest of all calamity. However that may be, it is certainly the work of God's providence, that you still have ministers who exercise the office of shepherds of souls and of government in your church. We must also take into account, that those servants of God who exercise the ministry of the word in the neighbouring churches, have, in order to check such dangerous contests, themselves approved of the calling of those men ; whose opinions we also have subscribed, since no better method occurred to us by which we could consult your welfare and advantage. That you are well assured of our conscientious integrity we have no doubt, so that you ought at once to conclude, that we did nothing which was not sincere and upright. But putting out of view even all idea of kindly affection, the very discussion of that delicate point was a proof quite as sincere as could be given on my part, that you would have no obscure instruction from me. Therefore, you must seriously look to it, that you are not too ready to disapprove of what the servants of God judge to be essential to your advantage and the preservation of the church. The other point to be well considered by you is this, that there may be due inspection of their regular discharge of duty, that they may fulfil the ministry of the church. And here, I confess, discretion evidently (nor would I wish to be the author of bringing any tyranny into the church) is required, that pious men should esteem as pastors those who do not stand only on their calling. For it is an indignity not to be borne, if that reverence and regard is to be given to certain personages, which the Lord Himself desires may be assigned only to the ministers of the word. Consequently, I readily grant you concerning that minister who shall *not* have taught the word of our Lord Jesus Christ, whatever title or prerogative he may put forth as a pretence, that he is unworthy to be considered as a pastor, to whom due obedience can be shown in the ministry. Because, however, it is clear to me, in reference to our brethren who at present hold the office of the ministry among you, that the gospel is taught you by them, I do not see what can excuse you, as before the Lord, while you either neglect or reject them. If some one may reply, that this or that in their doctrine or morals is objectionable, I require you, in the first place, by our Lord Jesus Christ, that so far as may be, you will first of all weigh the matter in your mind, and without any hastiness of judgment. For since we all of us owe this on the score of charity to one another, that we may not rashly pass sentence against others, but rather, so far as lies in us, that we hold fast by clemency and justice, much more is that moderation to be practised towards those whom the Lord is pleased to peculiarly distinguish above others. And even although there may be somewhat wanting which might justly be required of them (as to which I am not able to speak definitively, since I have no certain knowledge), you must just consider, that you will find no person so thoroughly perfect as that there shall not be many things which are still to be desired. Wherefore, that rule of charity is not duly honoured by us, unless we uphold our neighbours, even with their very infirmities, provided we recognise in them the true fear of God and the sincere desire of following the very truth itself. Lastly, I cannot possibly doubt, in so far as concerns their doctrine, but that they faithfully deliver to you the chief heads of Christian religion, such as are necessary to salvation, and join therewith the administration of the sacraments of the Lord. Wherever this is established, there also the very substance of the ministry ordained by the Lord Jesus Christ thrives and flourishes; and all due reverence and respect is to be observed toward him who is the minister.

" Now, therefore, most beloved brethren, I entreat and admonish you, in the name and strength of our Lord Jesus Christ, that turning away from man your heart and mind, you betake yourselves to that one and holy Redeemer, and that you reflect, how much we are bound to submit entirely to His sacred commands. And if everything He has appointed among you ought deservedly to be held inviolate, no consideration whatever ought so to deflect you from the path of duty, that you may not preserve whole and entire that ministration which He so seriously commends to you. If already you dispute and quarrel with your pastors to the extent of brawls and railing, as I hear has occurred, it is quite evident, from such a course of proceeding, that the ministry of those very persons in which the brightness of the glory of our Lord Jesus Christ ought to shine forth, must be subject to contempt and reproach, and all but trampled under foot. It is therefore incumbent on you carefully to beware, lest while we seem to ourselves only to insult men, we in fact declare war on God Himself. Nor, besides, ought it to seem a light matter to you, that sects and divisions are formed and cherished within the church, which no one who has a Christian heart beating in his breast can, without horror, even drink in by the hearing of the ears.   But that the state of matters is indeed such where a separation of this kind exists, and as it were a secession between pastor and people, the thing speaks for itself.   In conclusion, therefore, accept this admonition, if you wish me to be held by you as a brother, that there may be among you a solid agreement, which may correspond with such a name ; that you may not reject that ministry which, for your advantage and the prosperity of the church, I have been forced to approve of without any fear or favour in respect of men. . . . . . Here, therefore, with the most fervent salutation written by my own hand, do I supplicate the Lord Jesus, that He protect you in His holy fortress of defence ; that He may heap on you His gifts more and more ; that He may restore your church to due order, and, specially, that He may fill you with His own spirit of gentleness, so that in true conjunction of soul we may every one bestow ourselves in the promoting of His kingdom."*

We are not prepared to adopt every statement made by Calvin in this letter to the church of Geneva, or in the one to Farel, formerly quoted ; but we think it very plain, that the decision which he gave upon the important practical question submitted to him, and the main grounds on which he rested it, conclusively disprove some of the more unfavourable prevalent impressions in regard to his character and motives,—especially the supposed undue predominance of pride and arrogance, and, more generally, of the irascible and vindictive tendencies of human nature.   Indeed, we cannot conceive how any one can read Calvin's letters with attention and impartiality without being satisfied of the injustice of these impressions.   Knowing how prevalent, and yet how unreasonable, was the impression of Calvin's coldness and heartlessness, and of his intemperate violence and imperious arrogance, we once took the trouble of running over the first·two volumes of the English translation of his Letters by Dr Bonnet, published at Edinburgh a few years ago, to collect proofs of the falsehood of these impressions, and we noted on the fly-leaf the pages which furnished materials fitted to serve this purpose.   We arranged the references under the two heads of—1st, Strong and hearty affection ; and 2d, Moderation and forbearance—*i.e.*, moderation in his own judgment upon interesting and important topics, and forbearance with those who differed from him.   Our references under both heads,—our evidences of the possession of both these features of character,—soon swelled to a large extent, and at length

---

* *Calvin's Letters*, by Bonnet, vol. i. pp. 118-125.

presented a body of proof which seems to us perfectly overwhelming. It may interest and gratify some of our readers, if we give as a foot-note the pages we noted in carrying out this design.* They will find in them abundant evidence of Calvin's strong and hearty affection, and also of his moderation and forbearance.

Every one knows that the favourite topic of declamation and invective with the enemies of Calvin, is the share which he had in the death of Servetus. All who, from whatever cause, hate Calvin, and are anxious to damage his reputation, are accustomed to dwell upon this transaction, as if it were one of the most disgraceful and atrocious which history records; until, from disgust at the shameless falsehood, injustice, and absurdity of the common misrepresentations regarding it, we are in some danger of being tempted to view it, and other transactions of a similar kind, with less disapprobation than they deserve.

Gibbon said, that he was "more deeply scandalized at the single execution of Servetus, than at the hecatombs which have blazed at the Auto-da-fés of Spain and Portugal." And Hallam has imitated the unprincipled infidel by saying, "The death of Servetus has perhaps as many circumstances of aggravation as any execution for heresy that ever occurred."† The latest writer we have seen upon this subject, Mr Wallace,—we presume a Unitarian minister,—in a work of very considerable research, entitled "Anti-Trinitarian Biography," in three vols., published in 1850, writes about it in the following offensive style :—"A bloodier page does not stain the annals of martyrdom than that in which in this horrible transaction is recorded;" he describes it as stamping the character of Calvin as that "of a persecutor of the first class, without one humane or redeeming quality to divest it of its criminality or to palliate its enormity," as "one of the foulest murders recorded in the history of persecution;" and he speaks "of the odium which his malignant and cruel treatment of Servetus has so deservedly brought upon him."‡ While men, who are

---

* Vol. i., p. 75, 79, 86, 89, 111, 119, 130, 133, 147, 151, 187, 195, 205, 208, 214, 222, 230, 242, 270, 283, 421, 434, 452 ; vol. ii., p. 43, 50, 53, 95, 123, 257, 260-1, 295, 323, 377, 386, 407 : and of his moderation and forbearance, Letters xxv. and xxvii., p. 78, 87, 90–92, 113, 117, 126, 135, 158–9, 163, 175, 188–9, 194, 204, 211, 243, 257, 266, 270, 290, 306, 315, 356, 380, 396, 409, 417, 430 ; vol. ii., p. 20–1, 47–9, 106, 177, 192, 212, 224, 233, 258, 270, 286, 315, 333, 346, 353, 394, 418, 428, 432.

† *Literature of Europe*, vol. i. pp. 547.

‡ Vol. i. pp. 442–6.

the avowed opponents of almost everything that has been generally reckoned peculiar and distinctive in the Christian revelation, speak on this subject in such terms, other men, whom it would be unfair to rank in this category, deal with this topic in a manner that is far from being satisfactory; and we could point to indications of this both in Dr Stebbing, the translator of Henry's admirable life of Calvin, and in Principal Tulloch. On these accounts it may be proper to make some observations upon this subject, though we cannot go into much detail.

It is common for those who discuss this subject, under the influence of dislike to Calvin, to allege that those who do not sympathise with them in all their invectives against him, are to be regarded as defending or apologising for his conduct in the matter. Mr Wallace, in the work just referred to,* says—" Among other recent apologists of the stern Genevese reformer, M. Albert Rilliet and the Rev. W. K. Tweedie (now Dr Tweedie of Edinburgh) stand conspicuous, but their arguments have been ably and triumphantly refuted by a well-known writer in the *Christian Reformer* for January, 1847."

Now it is not true, in any fair sense of the word, that M. Rilliet and Dr Tweedie are apologists for Calvin in this matter. They both decidedly condemn his conduct; and they merely aim at bringing out fully the whole facts of the case, in order that a fair estimate may be formed of it, and that the amount of condemnation may be, upon a full and impartial examination of all its features and circumstances, duly proportioned to its demerits. Rilliet has evidently no sympathy with Calvin's theological views, or with his firm and uncompromising zeal for truth. He has acted only the part of an impartial historian. He has brought out fully and accurately the whole documents connected with the trial of Servetus at Geneva, and he has pointed to some of the inferences which they clearly establish,—especially these, that Servetus's whole conduct during the trial was characterised by recklessness and violence, or by cunning and falsehood—that Calvin was at this time at open war with the prevailing party among the civil authorities of Geneva, on the important subject of excommunication— that they took the management of the trial very much into their own hands, without consulting with him—that Calvin's interposi-

---

* Vol. i. p. 444.

tion in the matter was much more likely to have brought about the acquittal than the condemnation of Servetus—that Servetus knew this and acted upon it, and that this was the explanation of the reckless violence with which, during one important stage in the trial, he publicly assailed Calvin. The only fair question is, Are these positions historically true? Have they been sufficiently established? M. Rilliet and Dr Tweedie answer in the affirmative, and are in consequence set down as apologists of Calvin. As to Mr Wallace's allegation, that M. Rilliet and Dr Tweedie have been triumphantly refuted in the *Christian Reformer* for January 1847, this is really little better than blustering. There is nothing in the article referred to, that refutes the above-mentioned positions of Rilliet, which must be regarded as now conclusively established. The article is mainly occupied with an attempt to prove, that the authorities of Geneva had no jurisdiction over Servetus, since the offence for which he was tried was not committed within their territory, and that there was no law then in force in Geneva attaching to heresy the penalty of death. The writer has failed in establishing these two positions; but even if he had succeeded in proving them, this would not materially affect the question, so far as concerns its bearing upon Calvin, or the estimate that ought to be formed of the part he took in it. There is more plausible ground for Mr Wallace's allegation that Dr Henry, in his "Life of Calvin," defends his conduct in this matter, although here, too, there is a great want of fairness manifested by not giving a full view of the biographer's sentiments.

No man in modern times defends Calvin's conduct towards Servetus. No one indeed can defend it, unless he be prepared to defend the lawfulness of putting heretics to death, and this doctrine has been long abandoned by all but papists. There is no other ground on which Calvin can be defended, for he has distinctly and fully assumed the responsibility of the death of Servetus, though he endeavoured, unsuccessfully, to prevent his being burned. Some injudicious admirers of Calvin have attempted to exempt him from the responsibility of Servetus's death; and it is quite true that other causes contributed to bring it about, and that it would, in all probability have been effected, whether Calvin had interfered in the matter or not. But there can be no doubt that Calvin beforehand, at the time, and after the event, explicitly approved and defended the putting him to death, and assumed the responsibility of the transaction.   Some of Calvin's admirers were at one time anxious to free him from the charge, founded on the letter which he was alleged to have written to Farel in 1546, and in which this passage occurs :—" Servetus wrote to me lately, and added to his letter a large volume of his delirious fancies. He intimates that he will come to this place, if agreeable to me. But I will not interpose my assurance of his safety, for if he shall come, if my authority is of any avail, I will not suffer him to depart alive."   There is no reason, however, to doubt the genuineness of this letter, which is preserved in the Imperial Library at Paris.   And there is nothing in it which is not covered by the notorious facts, that Calvin firmly believed and openly maintained that Servetus, by his heresy and blasphemy, had deserved death, —that it was a good and honourable work to inflict the punishment of death upon him, and professed that he was quite willing to aid in bringing about this result.   Entertaining these views, he acted a manly and straightforward part in giving expression to them.   If Calvin had been such a monster of cruelty and malignity as he is represented to have been, by his slanderers, from Bolsec and Castellio in his own time, to Audin and Wallace in the present day, he would have encouraged Servetus to come to Geneva, and then have got him tried and executed.   His letter, then, to Farel, is really no aggravation of what is otherwise known and unquestionable in regard to Calvin's views upon this subject.

The injustice usually exhibited by Calvin's enemies upon this whole matter should just make his friends the more anxious to take up no untenable position regarding it, to admit fully and at once everything that can be proved as a matter of fact, and to maintain no ground which cannot be successfully defended.   His enemies have little or nothing that is plausible to bring forward, beyond what is involved in the general charge of believing and acting on the lawfulness of putting heretics and blasphemers to death, except what is furnished to them, sometimes, by injudicious friends of the Reformer—taking up ground that cannot be maintained.

But while the conduct of Calvin, in the case of Servetus, must be judged of mainly and primarily by the truth or falsehood of the doctrine of the lawfulness of putting heretics and blasphemers to death,—and while every one now concedes that, tried by this test, it cannot be defended, it is quite possible that there may be other collateral views of the matter, which may materially affect our estimate of the different parties, and tell powerfully in the way either of palliation or of aggravation. Indeed, the only fair and honest question in regard to the case of Servetus, now that the lawfulness of putting heretics to death has been long abandoned, is this—Does Calvin's conduct in the matter furnish evidence that he was a bad or cruel man? Does it prove him to have been in any respect worse than the other Reformers—that is, worse than the best men of his age? This is the only question which is now entitled to consideration, and this question, we venture to assert, must be answered in the negative, by every one who is not perverted by hatred of the truth which Calvin taught, by every one who is possessed of impartiality and candour. The leading considerations which prove that this is the only answer that can be given to the question, we shall merely state, without enlarging upon them.

1. The doctrine of the lawfulness and duty of putting heretics and blasphemers to death, was then almost universally held, by Protestants as well as papists,—by men of unquestionable piety and benevolence, if there were any such persons,—and those who were zealous for God's truth were then not only willing but anxious to act upon this doctrine whenever an opportunity occurred. There is no need to produce evidence of this position; but it may be proper to advert here to a statement which seems to contradict it, made by Dr Stebbing, the translator of Henry's Life of Calvin, and adopted from him by Mr Wallace in his Anti-Trinitarian Biography. Dr Stebbing thinks that Henry has gone too far in defending Calvin, and in his anxiety to repudiate all concurrence in this, he makes the following statement, in his preface : " Henry has defended Calvin in the case of Servetus with admirable ability; but the translator believes still, as he has ever believed, that when men enjoy so large a share of light and wisdom as Calvin possessed, they cannot be justified, if guilty of persecution, because they lived in times when wicked and vulgar minds warred against the rights of human conscience." Now this statement obviously and necessarily implies, that in Calvin's time it was only " wicked and vulgar minds" who countenanced persecution, and that Calvin's conduct is indefensible, because he agreed on this point only with the wicked and vulgar, and differed from the better and higher class of minds, among his cotemporaries. This is what Dr Stebbing has said. But of course he could not mean to say this; for

he must have known, if he gave any attention to what he was saying, that the statement is unquestionably false. Every one knows that in Calvin's time the defence of persecuting principles was not confined to the "wicked and vulgar," but was almost universal, even among the best and highest minds. It is to be presumed that Mr Wallace did not perceive the folly or the falsehood of this statment of Dr Stebbing's, when he quoted it with so much gusto, and set it forth as a "well-merited censure from the pen of one of Calvin's most ardent admirers."*

2. Servetus was not only a heretic and a blasphemer, but one about whom there was everything to provoke and nothing to conciliate. More than twenty years before his death he had put forth views which led Bucer, one of the most moderate of the Reformers, to declare that he ought to be torn in pieces. He continued thereafter to lead a life of deliberate hypocrisy, living for many years in the house of a popish prelate, conforming outwardly to the Church of Rome, while, at the same time, he embraced every safe opportunity of propagating his offensive heresies and blasphemies against the most sacred and fundamental doctrines of Christianity. He repeatedly denied, upon oath, all knowledge of the books which he had published, and he conducted himself during his trial with reckless violence and mendacity. We do not mention these things as if they excused or palliated his being put to death, but merely as illustrating the unreasonableness and unfairness of attempting to represent the case as one of *peculiar* aggravation, or as *specially* entitled to sympathy. Chaufepié, whose article on Servetus in the 4th volume of his Continuation of Bayle's Dictionary is, perhaps, upon the whole, the best and fairest view of the subject that exists, says: "Unfortunately for this great man (Calvin) he is more odious to certain people than Servetus is. They cannot resolve to render him the justice, which no impartial person can refuse to him, without doing an injury to his own judgment."

3. Servetus had been convicted of heresy and blasphemy by a popish tribunal at Vienne, and had been condemned to be burned by a slow fire; and he escaped from prison and came to Geneva with that sentence hanging over him. During his trial at Geneva the popish authorities transmitted the sentence they

* Vol. i. p. 446.

had pronounced against him, and reclaimed him, that they might carry it into execution. It was then put to Servetus, whether he would go back to Vienne or go on with his trial at Geneva. He preferred to remain where he was, and there is good reason to believe that the determination of the civil authorities at Geneva to pronounce and execute upon him a sentence of death, was, in some measure, produced by the fear that the papists would charge them with being indifferent, if not favourable, to heresy, if they spared him. There is abundant evidence that this consideration operated, to some extent, as a motive, upon the conduct of the Protestant churches at the time of the Reformation.* As a specimen of this, we may refer to Bishop Jewel's " Apology of the Church of England," a work which was approved of by the Convocation, and thus clothed with public authority. In the third chapter of the Apology, sect. 2, Jewel boasts, that Protestants not only detested and denounced all the heretics who had been condemned by the ancient church, but also that, when any of these heresies broke out amongst them, " they seriously and severely coerced the broachers of them with lawful and civil punishments." If this was distinctly set forth and boasted of as an ordinary rule of procedure, in opposition to popish allegations, we cannot doubt that the consideration would operate most powerfully, in so very peculiar, and indeed unexampled, a case as that of Servetus, in which not only had a popish tribunal condemned him to the flames, but had publicly demanded his person that they might put that sentence in execution. In these circumstances, no Protestant tribunal could be expected to do anything else but pronounce a similar sentence, unless either the proof of the charge of heresy and blasphemy had failed, or they had believed it to be unlawful to put heretics and blasphemers to death.

4. Although Calvin, after having, notwithstanding extreme personal provocation, done everything in his power to convince Servetus of his errors, approved of putting him to death as an incorrigible heretic and blasphemer, he exerted his influence, but without success, to prevent his being burned, and to effect that he might be put to death by some less cruel and offensive process; so that to talk, as is often done, of Calvin *burning* Servetus, is simply and literally a falsehood.

* Augusti Corpus Lib. Symb. Diss. Hist., pp. 590-2.

5. The Reformers generally, and more especially two of the mildest and most moderate of them all, both in their theological views and in their general character,—Melancthon, representing the Lutherans, and Bullinger, representing the Zuinglians,—gave their full, formal, public approbation to the proceedings which took place in Geneva in the case of Servetus.

6. Archbishop Cranmer exerted all his influence with King Edward, and succeeded thereby, though not without great difficulty, in effecting the burning of two heretics—one of them a woman and the other a foreigner—whose offences were in every respect, and tried by any standard whatever, far less aggravated than Servetus's. *

As all these six positions are notorious and undeniable, it must be quite plain to every one who reflects, for a moment, on what these facts, individually and collectively, involve or imply, that the *peculiar* frequency and the *special* virulence with which Calvin's conduct in regard to Servetus has been denounced, indicate, on the part of those who have done so, not only an utter want of anything like impartiality and fairness, but a bitter dislike, to a most able and influential champion of God's truth.

It might be supposed that most men, knowing these facts, would admit that there are many palliations attaching to the death of Servetus, and to Calvin's conduct in the matter; and yet Mr Wallace, as we have seen, as if determined to outstrip in the virulence of his invective all that had been said by papists and infidels, describes it as being "without one humane or redeeming quality to divest it of its criminality or palliate its enormity." The ground on which men who are fond of railing at Calvin in this style, commonly excuse themselves, is an allegation to the effect that he was mainly influenced in this matter by personal and vindictive feelings,—that, under the influence of these feelings, he had been long plotting Servetus's death, and seeking an opportunity of cutting him off,—and that he gave information against him to the popish authorities at Vienne, and was thus the cause of

---

* Burnet, after narrating (*History of the Reformation*, P. II. B. I., under the year 1549) Cranmer's very prominent and influential share in bringing about these two burnings,—the one that of an Anabaptist woman, the other that of an Arian Dutchman, —adds, "One thing was certain, that what he did in this matter flowed from no cruelty of temper in him, no man being further from that black disposition of mind; but it was truly the effect of those principles by which he governed himself."

his being tried and condemned there. These assertions are, to a large extent, utterly destitute of proof; and, in so far as there is any appearance of evidence in support of them as matters of fact, they furnish no foundation for the conclusions which have been based upon them. The general allegation, that Calvin was mainly or largely influenced by personal and vindictive feelings towards Servetus, is destitute of all proof or even plausibility. There is no evidence of it whatever, and there is no occasion whatever to have recourse to this theory. All that Calvin ever said or did in the case of Servetus, is fully explained by his conviction of the lawfulness and duty of putting heretics and blasphemers to death; and by his uncompromising determination to maintain, in every way he reckoned lawful, the interests of God's truth, and to discharge his own obligations, combined with the too prevalent habit of the age to indulge in railing and abuse against all who were dealt with as opponents. There were very considerable differences in character and disposition between Cranmer and Calvin, but it is in substance just as true of the latter as of the former, that his conduct "was truly the effect of those principles by which he governed himself." Calvin, in his last interview with Servetus, on the day before his death, solemnly declared that he had never sought to resent any personal injuries that had been offered to him,—that many years ago he had laboured, at the risk of his own life, to bring Servetus back to the truth,—that, notwithstanding his want of success, he long continued to correspond with him on friendly terms,—that he had omitted no act of kindness towards him,—until at last Servetus, exasperated by his expostulations, assailed him with downright rage. To this solemn appeal Servetus made no answer, and there is no ground whatever to warrant any human being to call in question its truth or sincerity. The truth is, that there is at least as good evidence that Mr Wallace hates Calvin as that Calvin hated Servetus.[*]

We have seen some specimens of the rancorous abuse with which he assails the Reformer. But we have not exhausted his

---

[*] Armand de la Chapelle, whose review of Allwoerden's Historia Michaelis Serveti in the *Bibliotheque Raisonnée* for 1728-9, tom. i. and ii., is characterised by great ability and fairness, thus describes the conduct of some of Calvin's accusers in his time, and they do not seem to be much improved yet:—" Je soutiens qu'il n'y a que malice noire, et qu'aigre intolerance dans l'animosité personnelle que certaines gens font parôitre contre cet illustre Reformateur. — (*Bib. Rais.*, tom. i. p. 400.)

performances in this way. He assures us that Calvin formed a
plan for the destruction of Servetus, and that he prosecuted it for
thirteen years before he succeeded in accomplishing his object,—
that he "came to the deliberate determination of plotting his
destruction,"—that "he was always on the watch for something
by which he might criminate Servetus,"—that he "was on the
watch for him, and caused him to be apprehended soon after his
arrival" in Geneva.* These are statements for which no evidence
has been or can be produced. They can be regarded in no other
light than as mere fabrications. Mr Wallace also gives us to
understand that, in his judgment, the conduct of Calvin in this
matter showed him to be "a man who, under the guise of religion,
could violate every principle of honour and humanity."† *Under the
guise of religion!* We could scarcely have believed it possible,
that any man would have insinuated a doubt of the sincerity of
Calvin's conviction, that he was doing God service and discharging
a duty, in contributing to bring about the death of Servetus. The
sincerity and earnestness of this conviction do not, of course, furnish any proof that he was right, or supply any materials for
defending his conduct. Still this conviction is an important
feature in every case to which it applies, and it ought always to
be taken into account. We do not believe that Mr Wallace will
get much countenance, even from papists and infidels, in his insinuation, that Calvin is not entitled to the benefit of it.

His allegation about "violating every principle of honour and
humanity," is probably intended to bear special reference to what
has been charged against Calvin, in connection with the information against Servetus, given to the popish authorities at Vienne;
and this is, indeed, the only feature of the case, the discussion of
which is attended with any difficulty. Mr Wallace's statement
upon the point is this :—

"Calvin, who was always on the watch for something by which he might
criminate Servetus, soon gave out that this work" (his last work, the "Chris-
tianismi Restitutio," which he had got secretly printed without his name at
Vienne, and the substance of which he had sent to Calvin some years before)
"was written by him. And availing himself of the assistance of one William
Trie, a native of Lyons, who was at that time residing at Geneva, he caused
Servetus to be apprehended and thrown into prison on a charge of heresy.
Some of the friends and disciples of Calvin have attempted to free him from

<hr>

* Vol. i. pp. 432–4.   † Vol. i. p. 446.

this odious imputation, and he has himself represented it as a calumny; but the fact that Servetus was imprisoned at the sole instigation of Calvin is too well established to admit of dispute. Abundant proofs of it may be found in the accounts of De la Roche, Allwoerden, Mosheim, Bock, and Trechsel." [*]

We will advert first to Mr Wallace's references to authorities. He says that abundant proofs that Calvin was the author and originator of the whole proceedings against Servetus at Vienne, may be found in the accounts of De la Roche, Allwoerden, Mosheim, Bock, and Trechsel. We have not read Mosheim and Trechsel, but we are confident that the proofs to be found in the other three authors are not abundant, and are not even sufficient. De la Roche and Allwoerden published before Trie's three letters to his friend at Lyons, which Calvin is alleged to have instigated and dictated, were given to the public, and therefore were scarcely in circumstances to judge fairly on this question.

De la Roche [†] does not enter into anything like a full and formal investigation of this matter. The main evidence he adduces, that Calvin was the author or originator of Trie's letters, is a statement to that effect made by Servetus himself on his trial, coupled with the fact, that in his judgment Calvin's denial did not fully meet the precise charge as laid. Allwoerden, whose work is in reality just the first edition of Mosheim's, goes much more fully into this matter, and produces additional proofs, though they are not very "abundant" or satisfactory. His authorities are only Bolsec, in his Life of Calvin, and the anonymous author of the work entitled, " Contra Libellum Calvini," etc., in reply to Calvin's Refutation of the errors of Servetus. Bolsec, indeed, says that Calvin wrote to Cardinal Tournon to give information against Servetus,—that Trie wrote to many people at Lyons and Vienne, at the solicitation of Calvin, and that in consequence, Servetus was put in prison. [‡] But Bolsec's Lives both of Calvin and Beza have always been regarded, except by papists, whose church Bolsec had joined before he published them, as infamous libels, to which no weight whatever is due. The other work referred to has been ascribed to Laelius Socinus and to Castellio; and it is not improbable that both were concerned in the production of it, as is supposed also to have been the case with another work bearing upon this subject, and published under the fictitious

---

[*] Vol. i. p. 433.
[†] " Bibliotheque Anglaise," tom. ii. 1717.

[‡] " Bolsec," p. 11.

name of Martinus Bellius. The author of this work says, that those who had seen Trie's letters to his popish friend, "think that they were written by Calvin, because of the similarity of the style," and that they were of a higher order than Trie could have produced. This is all the evidence he adduces, and it plainly shows, that at the time the report rested merely upon conjecture or suspicion. This anonymous and unknown author says also, that "there are some who say, that Calvin himself wrote to Cardinal Tournon,"—a statement which shows how thoroughly the whole matter was one of mere hearsay. It is proper also to mention, that it is this work which contains the report, given, however, merely as a hearsay (sunt qui affirmant), that Calvin laughed when he saw Servetus carried along to the stake. This report even De la Roche, with all his prejudices against Calvin and Calvinism, denounces as an "execrable calumny," though it is really a fair enough specimen of the way in which Calvin has been often dealt with. De la Chapelle very happily ridiculed the manifest and palpable insufficiency of this evidence, in this way, "The cotemporary enemies of Calvin only suspected that he was the author of the letter, and behold now-a-days, 170 years after the event, De la Roche and Allwoerden are quite certain of it. Perhaps in another 100 years, it will be found out that it was Calvin himself who carried the letter to Lyons."*

But Trie's three letters have since been published, and may be expected to throw some light upon this subject. They were procured from Vienne, and published by Artigny in 1749, and they have since been commented upon by Mosheim, Bock, and many others. Bock is one of those referred to by Mr Wallace, as exhibiting "abundant proofs" that Calvin employed Trie to effect the apprehension of Servetus at Vienne. But the truth is, that Bock, though strongly prejudiced against Calvin, and though unfair enough to allege that he was somewhat influenced by personal and vindictive feelings in this matter, did not profess to produce "abundant proofs" of the point now under consideration; *nay, he expressly admits that it could not be proved*, though he was strongly inclined to believe it. The whole of what he says upon the subject is this:—"An. Gul. Trie homo, indoctus, proprio motu an Calvini instinctu et consilio hoc fecerit, *certo quidem statui nequit*

---

* "Bibl. Rais.," tom. i. p. 390.

non tamen vanæ videntur *conjecturæ* hanc illi dictasse epistolam, qua Servetus tanquam hæreticus exurendus, accusabatur."* We accept Bock's concession that there is no proof but only conjectures, but we do not admit that the conjectures are possessed of any real weight or probability. Mr Wallace could easily have found room, if he had chosen, for a summary of the "abundant proofs" of which he boasts. But it was more convenient just to make a flourish by a reference to Bock and other names, whose works few were likely to examine.

Trie's letters not only afford no evidence, but do not even furnish any plausible ground of suspicion, that Calvin was, in any way, connected with, or cognisant of, the origin of this matter,—that is, that it was at his instigation that Trie conveyed information to his popish friend about Servetus, and the book which he had recently published. So far as appears from the correspondence, Trie's statement about Servetus and his book seems to have come forth quite spontaneously, without being suggested or instigated by any one. It has every appearance of having come up quite naturally and easily, in the course of correspondence with a friend, who was urging him to return to the Church of Rome, on the ground of the unity and soundness of doctrine that prevailed there, as contrasted with the varieties and heresies that were found among Protestants. This naturally and obviously led Trie, as it would have led any one in similar circumstances who happened to be cognisant of Servetus and his book, to tell his friend of what had been going on of late, in the way of heresy, in his own neighbourhood, and in a place where popish authorities had entire control. In short, there is no ground to believe, or even to suspect, that Calvin was connected with originating or instigating the proceeding, which ultimately led to Servetus's apprehension by the popish authorities at Vienne. If men are determined to put the worst possible construction upon everything relating to Calvin, they may have some suspicion that he instigated Trie to write to Vienne about Servetus. But Mr Wallace's "abundant proofs" can really be regarded in no other light than as downright audacity.

And then it must not be forgotten, that we have from Calvin himself what must in all fairness be regarded as a denial of this

---

* *Historia Anti-trinitariorum*, tom. ii. p. 355.

charge. In his Refutation of the errors of Servetus, he intimates that it had been alleged against him, that it was through his agency (meâ operâ) that Servetus had been seized at Vienne. He scouted the idea as absurd and preposterous, as if he had been in friendly correspondence with the popish authorities; and then he concludes with saying, that if the allegation were true, he would not think of denying it, for he would not reckon it at all dishonourable to him, as he had never concealed that it was through his agency that Servetus had been seized and brought to trial at Geneva. Calvin evidently saw no material difference in point of principle, between doing what was practicable and necessary to bring him to trial at Vienne, and doing what was requisite with the same view at Geneva. He certainly could not mean by this statement to deny what he did do, in the way of furnishing materials to be used as evidence against Servetus at Vienne; for what he had done in this respect was quite well known, and was distinctly mentioned in the formal sentence of the popish authorities, which had been publicly produced in the subsequent trial. He never could have thought of denying this, and therefore he must have meant merely to deny, that he was the author or orginator of the proceedings; in other words, to deny that he had written himself, or that he had instigated Trie to write, although even of this he indicates that he would not have been ashamed if it had been true.

This leads us to advert to what it was that Calvin did in connection with the proceedings against Servetus at Vienne; and this topic may be properly connected with a statement of Principal Tulloch's on this subject. Dr Tulloch, as might be expected, seems disposed to press the more unfavourable views of this transaction. He describes it as a "great crime,"—he speaks of "the undying disgrace which, under all explanations, must for ever attach to the event,"—and assures us that "the act must bear its own doom and disgrace for ever."* Of his more specific statements, the only one to which we think it needful to advert, is the following:—

"The special blame of Calvin in the whole matter is very much dependent upon the view we take of his previous relation to the accusation and trial of Servetus by the Inquisition at Vienne. If the evidence, of which Dyer has made the most, were perfectly conclusive, that the Reformer, through a

* *Leaders of the Reformation*, pp. 101, 138, 144.

creature of his own of the name of Trie, was really the instigator, from the
beginning, of the proceedings against Servetus,—that from Geneva, in short,
he schemed, with deep-laid purpose, the ruin of the latter, who was then
quietly prosecuting his profession at Vienne,—and, from MSS. that had privately come into his possession, furnished the Inquisition with evidence of
the heretic's opinions,—if we were compelled to believe all this, then the
atrocity of Calvin's conduct would stand unrelieved by the sympathy of his
fellow-reformers, and would not only not admit of defence, but would present
one of the blackest pictures of treachery that even the history of religion discloses. The evidence does not seem satisfactory, although it is not without
certain features of suspicion. There can be no doubt, however, that Calvin
was so far privy, through Trie, to the proceedings of the Inquisition, and that
he heartily approved of them."*

This is a curious and significant passage, and seems to indicate,
that Dr Tulloch occupies the position of one who is "willing to
wound, but yet afraid to strike." Dyer's "Life of Calvin," the
authority here referred to by Dr Tulloch, was published in 1850,
and is got up with considerable care and skill. Its general object
manifestly is, to check and counteract the tendency to think more
favourably of Calvin, which had grown up in the community, in
connection with the labours of the Calvin Translation Society and
other causes. It was this, too, probably, that called forth the
special virulence of Mr Wallace, whose "Anti-Trinitarian Biography" was published in the same year. But Mr Dyer goes
about his work much more cautiously than Mr Wallace. He
abstains generally from violent invective and gross misrepresentation, and labours to convey an unfavourable impression by insinuation, supported by an elaborate and sustained course of special
pleading in the style of an Old Bailey practitioner, combined with
a considerable show of moderation and fairness. The reference
which Dr Tulloch, in the passage we have quoted, makes to Mr
Dyer, is fitted to convey the impression, that that author goes as
far as Mr Wallace in ascribing the whole proceedings connected
with Servetus's apprehension at Vienne to Calvin's agency or instigation. But this is not the case. Mr Dyer was too cautious
to assert this. He saw and admitted, that there is no evidence
that Calvin had anything to do with the origination of the matter,
—that is, no evidence that Trie's first letter was written at his
instigation or with his cognisance.

"The Abbé d'Artigny goes farther than the evidence warrants, in posi-

---

* Pp. 138–9.

tively asserting that Trie's letter was written at Calvin's dictation, and in calling it Calvin's letter in the name of Trie. It is just possible that Trie may have written it without Calvin's knowledge; and the latter is therefore entitled to the benefit of the doubt. He cannot be absolutely proved to have taken the first step in delivering Servetus into the fangs of the Roman Catholic Inquisition; but what we shall now have to relate will show, that he at least aided and abetted it."*

It is true, as Dr Tulloch says, that Mr Dyer has made the most of the evidence about Calvin aiding and abetting in the matter. But there is really no mystery or uncertainty about this. What Calvin did, in this respect, is well known and quite ascertained, though we do not deny that there is room for a difference of opinion, or rather of impression, as to how far it can be thoroughly defended.

The principal sentence in the quotation from Dr Tulloch is a piece of rhetorical declamation, and is characterised by the inaccuracy and exaggeration which usually attach to such displays. It is not alleged by Mr Dyer, or indeed even by Mr Wallace, that Calvin's conduct corresponded with the description which Dr Tulloch has here pictured of it; and yet his statement plainly implies that Mr Dyer has asserted all this to be true of Calvin—has undertaken to prove it, and has produced evidence in support of it, which though not, in Dr Tulloch's judgment, sufficient to establish it, is not destitute of weight. We cannot understand what could have tempted Dr Tulloch to dash off such an inflated and exaggerated description of Calvin's conduct, and to ascribe it, without warrant, to the cold and cautious Mr Dyer. He surely could not expect that his assertion, that Mr Dyer had undertaken to prove all this, and thought that he had proved it, would be sufficient to induce some people to believe it or to regard it as probable, even though it "would present one of the blackest pictures of treachery that even the history of religion discloses."

The first charge in this indictment against Calvin, given hypothetically, so far as Dr Tulloch is concerned, *but alleged by him to be adduced and believed by Mr Dyer*, is, that "the Reformer, through a creature of his own of the name of Trie, was really the instigator, from the beginning, of the proceedings against Servetus." Now Mr Dyer, as we have seen, expressly admits that this position cannot be proved, and Calvin himself has denied it, while declaring, at the same time, that he would not have been

---

* Dyer's *Life of John Calvin*, p. 314.

ashamed to acknowledge it, if it had been true. The second charge is merely a rhetorical expansion and amplification of the first, with a fine touch added in the end by Dr Tulloch's own hand, without any countenance from his authority, "that from Geneva he schemed, with deep-laid purpose, the ruin of the latter, *who was then quietly prosecuting his profession (as a physician) at Vienne.*" The clause which we have put in italics is fitted, and to all appearance was intended, to convey the impression, that Servetus had abandoned the work of propagating heresy and blasphemy, in which he had been engaged more or less, occasionally, for about a quarter of a century—that he had retired from the field of theology, and was *quietly* occupied with the practice of medicine, giving no ground of offence to any one, when Calvin devised and executed a plot for bringing him to trial and death. Now all this is palpably inconsistent with the best known and most fundamental facts of the case. *Every one knows*, that the whole proceedings against Servetus, both at Vienne and at Geneva, originated in, and were founded on, the fact of his having just succeeded in getting secretly printed at Vienne, a large edition of his work entitled "Christianismi Restitutio," in which all his old heresies and blasphemies were reproduced. Servetus had taken every precaution to guard against this work being known in his own neighbourhood, but a large number of copies had been sent to Frankfort and other places for sale, and one copy at least had reached Geneva. Indeed, the substance of the information which Trie's first letter conveyed to his popish friend at Lyons was just this, that this book had recently been produced and printed in his neighbourhood, and that Servetus was the author and Arnoullet the printer of it. So far is Mr Dyer from giving any countenance, as Dr Tulloch insinuates, to this rhetorical flourish, about Servetus "quietly prosecuting his profession at Vienne," that for a purpose of his own,—intending to damage Calvin in another way,—he calls special attention to the consideration, that Servetus's printing his book at this time "was an overt act, and furnished something tangible to the Roman Catholic authorities, who would have looked with suspicion on mere manuscript evidence, furnished by a man whom they considered to be a great heretic himself."*

---

* P. 362.

This leads us to advert to the third and last charge in the indictment, viz., that "from MSS. that had privately come into his possession, he furnished the Inquisition with evidence of the heretic's opinions." This charge, as here stated, is not put quite accurately, but we admit that in substance it is not only adduced, but established, by Mr Dyer. He puts it thus,—"But this (that is, the admission that there is no evidence that Trie's first letter was written with Calvin's knowledge) does not clear him from the charge of having furnished the evidence by which alone Trie's denunciation could be rendered effectual ; and of thus having made himself a partaker in whatever guilt attaches to such an act."*

Calvin did not perceive or admit that there was any guilt attaching, either to Trie's conduct or to his own, in this matter ; but he certainly did the substance of what is here ascribed to him. The facts are these. Trie, in his first letter to his popish friend,— in which he told him of the publication of Servetus's work, and gave the name of the author and printer,—enclosed also the first leaf of the book. His friend communicated this to the popish authorities, who made some investigation into the case. But so effectual had been the precautions taken by Servetus to secure secrecy, that they could get hold of nothing tangible. Trie's friend was in consequence requested to write to him again, and to urge him to furnish, if possible, any additional materials that might throw light upon the matter. In answer to this application, Trie sent about twenty letters, which, a good many years before, Servetus had addressed to Calvin, and which were to be used, not as Dr Tulloch says, "as evidence of the heretic's opinions," but as materials for establishing his identity. Trie's account of the way in which he procured the letters is this, and it is all we know of Calvin's procedure in this matter :—†

"But I must confess, that I have had great trouble to get what I send you from Mr Calvin. Not that he is unwilling that such execrable blasphemies should be punished ; but that it seems to him to be his duty, as he does not wield the sword of justice, to refute heresy by his doctrines, rather than to pursue it by such methods. I have, however, importuned him so much, representing to him that I should incur the reproach of levity, if he did not help me, that he has at last consented to hand over what I send."

Calvin had great hesitation in giving up these letters to be

* P. 361.   † Dyer, p. 316.

employed for this purpose, and it would have been better, perhaps, if he had declined to comply with the application. Not that the matter is one of any material importance, or that his conduct in this affair can affect injuriously his general character in the estimation of intelligent and impartial men; but that it is fitted to give a handle to enemies, and has been regarded with somewhat different feelings, even among those whose prepossessions are all in his favour. Calvin had no doubt as to the lawfulness of his giving up these letters for the purpose of establishing Servetus's identity. His views as to the way in which heretics ought to be dealt with, and the responsibility which, in consequence, he was quite willing to incur in such cases, prevented any doubt as to the warrantableness of the step proposed. His hesitation seems to have turned only on its becomingness or congruity,—on the propriety of a man in his position taking, in the circumstances, an active part in a criminal process, which might result in the shedding of blood. How far Calvin's conduct in this matter should be regarded as a violation of the confidence that ought to attach to friendly intercourse, must depend very much upon the circumstances in which the correspondence was begun, and carried on, and ended; and of all this we know nothing, and cannot judge. Taking even the most unfavourable view which any reasonable man can form of the transaction, there is really nothing in it,—apart of course from its assuming or implying the lawfulness of putting heretics to death,—that can be considered very heinous, or that is fitted to create any strong prejudice against Calvin's general character. There is not one of the leading Reformers, against whom more serious charges than this cannot be established.

It is satisfactory to know, that although these letters to Calvin are mentioned among the *pieces justificatives* in the sentence pronounced upon Servetus by the popish authorities, they had got, before the sentence was passed, direct and conclusive evidence from other sources, to prove, in the face of his deliberate perjury, that he was Servetus,—though he had lived for thirteen years in Vienne under a different name,—and that he had printed and published the heretical and blasphemous book which had been ascribed to him. Dyer has given a full, and, upon the whole, a fair view, of this branch of the case.*

---

* Pp. 319-325.

We did not intend to dwell so long on this matter of Servetus. But since so much has been put forth of late years, by Wallace and Dyer, by Stebbing and Tulloch, fitted to convey erroneous and unfair impressions upon some features of the case, we do not regret that we have been led to enlarge somewhat upon it, although confining ourselves strictly to what seemed to require explanation.[*]

The impression which the more temperate and reasonable opponents of Calvin's views chiefly labour to produce with respect to his character is this,—that he was a proud and presumptuous speculator upon divine things, very anxious to be wise above what is written, and ever disposed to indulge his own reasonings upon the deepest mysteries of religion, instead of seeking humbly and carefully to follow the guidance of God's word, without pressing any further than it led him.   Now it is perhaps not very unnatural that men *who have never read Calvin's writings*, and who are decidedly and zealously opposed to his doctrines, may have insensibly formed to themselves some such conception of his general character and spirit, or may have very readily believed all this when they saw it asserted by others.   This notion, however, has not only no foundation to rest upon, but it is contradicted by the whole spirit that breathes through the writings of Calvin.   We are not at present speaking of the actual truth of his doctrines, but merely of the general spirit in which his examination of God's word and his investigation of divine truth is conducted; and upon this point, we have no hesitation in saying, that there is nothing which is more strikingly and palpably characteristic of the general spirit in which Calvin ordinarily conducts his investigations into divine truth, and his speculations on the mysteries of religion, than his profound reverence for the word of God, the caution and sobriety with which he advances, and his

* We have already intimated that we consider the Art. " Servetus," in the 4th volume of Chauffepie's " Noveau Dictionnaire," or Continuation of Bayle, as giving the best and fairest view of the whole case. The fullest collection of the materials bearing upon his trial at Geneva, is to be found in Rilliets' work, entitled " Relation de Proces Criminel," etc., published in 1844; or, still better, in a translation of this work, published at Edinburgh, in 1846, under the title " Calvin and Servetus," with an excellent Introduction, consisting chiefly of a fine sketch of Calvin's life, by the Rev. Dr Tweedie, who has also contributed a valuable article to the " North British Review," vol. xiii., exhibiting a very successful appreciation of Calvin himself, and of his modern biographers, Henry, Dyer, and Audin.

perfect readiness at all times to lay aside or abandon every statement, or even mode of expression, that did not clearly appear to
him to have the sanction of the sacred Scriptures. And we think
it quite impossible for any man of fairness and candour to read
Calvin's writings without being constrained to feel that this was
the state of mind and the general spirit which he at least intended
and laboured to cherish and to manifest. Men of general fairness
and candour may continue, after reading Calvin's writings, to
think that he has brought out from the sacred Scriptures, doctrines upon some of the deeper mysteries of religion which are
not taught there; and some may even be disposed to allege that,
misled by the deceitfulness of the human heart, he did not always
know what manner of spirit he was of. But no person, we think,
of fairness and discernment can fail to see and admit, that he had
laid it down as a rule to himself, to follow humbly, implicitly, and
reverentially the guidance of God's word, that he carefully laboured
to act upon this rule, and honestly believed that he had succeeded
in doing so.

From the nature of the case, it is not easy to prove this by an
adduction of evidence. But there are one or two points of a
pretty definite description, which may be fairly regarded as confirming it. It was not Calvin's practice to attempt to strain the
particular statements of Scripture, in order to bring out more
abundant evidence of doctrines which he believed to be true. On
the contrary, he has incurred the suspicion of some of the more
unintelligent friends of truth, by occasionally admitting, that a
particular text gave no support to a sound doctrine, in support of
which it was commonly adduced. He showed no disposition, in
general, to sanction the use of unscriptural phrases and statements
in the exposition of scriptural doctrines; and it has been thought,
that in some cases,—as in regard to the doctrine of the Trinity for
instance,—Calvin, disgusted with the unwarranted and presumptuous speculations of the schoolmen upon this subject, even carried
to an extreme his anxiety to adhere to mere scriptural terms and
statements in the exposition of this mystery. Now whether he
was right or wrong in the particular cases to which these observations apply, his conduct in this respect indicates a state of mind, a
general spirit, and a habit of procedure, very different from what
are often ascribed to him; and may be fairly regarded as affording
evidence, that the great object of his desires and aims was just to

ascertain and bring out truly and accurately the mind of God in
His word; to submit his understanding and his opinions wholly
to the control of the inspired standard; to go as far as Scripture
led him, and no farther, in the exposition of divine mysteries.
Whether he has in every instance succeeded in this object which
he proposed to himself, is, of course, a different question; but we
confess we do not know where to find a finer model, in general,
of the spirit in which the examination of God's word and the investigation of divine truth ought to be conducted, than in the
writings of Calvin; and we are persuaded also, that the more
fully men imbibe his general spirit in this respect and faithfully
act upon it,—a spirit which will lead them equally to go without
fear or hesitation as far as Scripture goes, and to stop without
reluctance where Scripture stops,—the more firmly will they be
convinced that the great doctrines, with which Calvin's name is
commonly associated, are indeed the very truth of God, and do
most fully show forth the perfections of Him "by whom are all
things, and for whom are all things."

We do not mean to attempt anything like theological discussion; but we would like to make a few observations on Calvin's historical position, viewed in relation both to the system
of doctrine usually called by his name, and to his principles with
respect to the worship and government of the church. The sum
and substance of what Calvin aimed at, and to some extent
effected, was to throw the church back, for the cure of the evils
by which she was polluted and disgraced at the era of the Reformation, upon the Augustinianism (or Calvinism) in doctrine, and
the Presbyterianism in worship and government, which he believed
to be taught in the New Testament. He of course adopted these
views, because he believed that the word of God required this.
On the scriptural evidence of his views we are not called upon at
present to enter. We can merely advert to one or two features
of the aspects which they present historically, especially when
contemplated in their bearing upon the condition to which the
church had sunk at the time when the Reformation commenced.
Doctrine (viewed more especially as comprehending the exposition
of the way of life, or the method of the salvation of sinful men),
worship, and government,—in short, everything about the church
or professedly Christian society,—had fallen into a state of gross
corruption. There might be difficulties, from want of materials,

in pointing out precisely at what times particular corruptions in doctrine, worship, and government were invented and introduced. But it might be supposed that no one could fail to see and acknowledge, that the church of the fifteenth century, viewed both in its Eastern and Western branches,—though it is with the latter that we have more immediately to do,—was very different in all important respects from the church of the first century, as brought before us in the writings of the inspired apostles. The system, however, which had grown up, and which overspread the church in the fifteenth century, was too firmly rooted in men's passions, prejudices, and selfish interests, to admit of the light of truth, as to what the church should be, being easily let in. The Reformation of the sixteenth century became, in consequence, a severe and protracted struggle, requiring and giving scope for the highest powers and qualities on both sides, both in choosing the ground to be taken, and in keeping or maintaining it. And it is here that the pre-eminent grandeur and majesty of Calvin shine forth. A profound and penetrating survey of the existing condition and of the past history of the church, combined with the study of the word of God, in leading him to see, that the only thorough remedy, the only effectual cure,—for the deplorable state of matters that now prevailed,—the only process that would go to the root of the existing evils and produce a real and permanent reformation, was to reject all palliatives and half measures, and to fall back upon the thoroughness and simplicity of what was taught and sanctioned by our Lord and His apostles.

Perhaps the one most indispensable thing in order to the restoration of true Christianity in the world, was the bringing out from the sacred Scriptures of the whole doctrine of the Apostle Paul in regard to the justification of sinners, and this was the special work which God qualified and enabled Luther to effect. The history of this doctrine of justification is remarkable. In consequence of the particularly full and formal exposition of it which the Apostle Paul was guided by the Spirit to put on record in his Epistles to the Romans and Galatians, Satan seems to have felt the necessity of carrying on his efforts to corrupt it in an indirect and insidious way, of proceeding by sapping and mining, rather than by open assault. Accordingly, there was scarcely anything like direct and formal controversy on the subject of justification from the time of Paul to that of Luther. But yet the true doctrine of Scripture on the subject had been very thoroughly corrupted. All that is taught in Scripture in regard to it had been thrown into the back-ground and explained away, without being directly and explicitly denied. Notions of an adverse tendency had been introduced, diffused, and mixed up with the general series of ecclesiastical arrangements, connected especially with the efficacy of the sacraments, the conditions and merits of good works, and the interposition of other creatures in procuring the favour of God. By these processes quietly and insidiously carried on, the doctrine of justification had been greatly corrupted in the church, even before Augustine's time, and he did nothing to check the progress of corruption, or to introduce sounder views, upon this important subject. Indeed, his own views upon it always continued confused and to some extent erroneous. When Luther was honoured to bring out fully the true scriptural doctrine of justification, which had been concealed and buried so long, the Church of Rome rejected it, while all Protestant churches received it. Luther applied very fully the true scriptural doctrine of justification to all the corruptions of the papal system which were *directly* connected with it, but he did not do much in the way of connecting the doctrine of justification with the other great doctrines of the Christian system. It was reserved for the comprehensive master mind of Calvin to connect and combine the Scripture doctrine of justification as taught by Luther, with the large mass of important scriptural truth set forth in the writings of Augustine. And this combination of Lutheranism and Augustinianism is just Calvinism, which is thus the fullest, most complete, and comprehensive exposition of the whole scheme of Christian doctrine. It went to the root of the prevailing corruption of Christian truth, and overturned it from the foundation.

The grand heresy, which might be said to have overspread the church for many centuries, was in substance this,—that the salvation of sinful men, in so far as they might need salvation, was to be ascribed, not to the one true God, the Father, the Son, and the Holy Ghost, but to men themselves and to what they could do, or to what could be done for them by their fellow-men and other creatures. This, more or less fully developed, was the great heresy which lay under the whole elaborate externalism of the mediæval and Romish religion. Almost everything that is dis-

tinctive, either in the specific tenets and practices, or in the more
general features and tendencies, of the full-blown popery with
which the Reformers had to contend, might be traced back, more
or less directly, to this great principle; while, on the other hand,
almost all the particular features of the system tended to deepen
and strengthen in men's minds the comprehensive heresy in which
they had their root and origin.   Çalvin saw that the only effectual
way of dealing with this great perversion of the way of salvation,
—so well fitted to lead men to build upon a false foundation their
hopes of heaven,—the only way to overturn it root and branch, to
demolish at once the whole height of the superstructure and the
whole depth of the foundation,—was to bring out fully and definitely the whole doctrine of Scripture concerning the place held
in the salvation of sinners by the Father, by the Son, and by the
Holy Ghost.   He made it his great object to bring out and to
embody the whole doctrine of Scripture upon these subjects, and
accordingly Calvinism is just a full exposition and development of
the sum and substance of what is represented in Scripture as done
for the salvation of sinners by the three persons of the Godhead.
It represents the Father as arranging, in accordance with all the
perfections of His nature and all the principles of His moral government, and at the same time, with due regard to the actual
capacities and obligations of men, the whole provisions of the
scheme of redemption, choosing some men to grace and glory, and
sending His Son to seek and to save them.   It represents the Son
as assuming human nature, and suffering and dying as the Surety
and Substitute of His chosen people,—of those whom the Father
had given Him in covenant,—of an innumerable multitude out of
every kindred and nation and tongue,—as bearing their sins in
His own body, and bearing them away,—as doing and bearing
everything necessary for securing their eternal salvation.   It
represents the Holy Spirit as taking of the things of Christ and
showing them to men's souls, as taking up His abode in all whom
Christ redeemed with His precious blood, effectually and infallibly
determining them to faith and holiness; and thus applying the
blessings of redemption to all for whom Christ purchased them,
and finally preparing them fully for the inheritance of the saints.
These are in substance the views given us in Scripture of the way
in which sinners of the human race are saved.   They are views
which, as experience fully proves, are most offensive to the natural

tendencies and inclinations of men's hearts; and plainly as they are taught in Scripture, there is a constant and powerful disposition, —especially when true religion is in a low or languishing condition, —to reject them or explain them away, and to substitute in their room notions which, more or less directly, exclude or contradict them. They certainly had been thoroughly excluded from the practical teaching, and from the whole plans and arrangements of the church, at the period of the Reformation ; while it is true, on the other hand,—and it is this with which at present we have more immediately to do,—that these views, and these alone, overturn from the foundation the whole system of notions which then generally prevailed, and which so fearfully perverted the way of salvation.

We believe that it is impossible to bring out accurately, fully, and definitely, the sum and substance of what is taught in Scripture concerning the place which the Father, the Son, and the Holy Ghost hold in the salvation of sinners, without taking up Calvinistic ground,—without being in a manner necessitated to assert the fundamental principles of the Calvinistic system of theology. It is, we believe, impossible otherwise to do full justice, and to give full effect, to what Scripture teaches, concerning the sovereign supremacy of the Father in determining the everlasting destiny of His creatures,—concerning the death and righteousness of Christ, as of infinite worth and value, and as infallibly efficacious for securing all the great objects to which they are directed,—and concerning the agency of the Holy Spirit in certainly and infallibly uniting to Christ through faith all whom the Father had given to Him, and preserving them in safety unto His eternal kingdom. Those who reject or put aside the peculiar doctrines of Calvinism can, we think, be shown to be practically, and by fair construction, withholding from God, the Father, the Son, and the Holy Ghost, more or less of the place and influence which the Scripture assigns to them in the salvation of sinners; and to be giving to men themselves, or at least to creatures, a share in effecting their salvation which the Scripture does not sanction. And when Calvinistic principles are rejected or thrown into the back-ground, not only is something, more or less, of necessity taken from the Creator and assigned to the creature, but an opening is made,—an opportunity is left,—for carrying on this process of transferring to man what belongs to God to almost any extent, until the scriptural method of salvation is wholly set aside or overturned.

Men who profess to derive their opinions, in any sense, from the sacred Scriptures, must be substantially,—whether they will or not, and whether they are aware of it or not,—Socinians, or Arminians, or Calvinists. The distinctive characteristic of Socinianism is, that it virtually invests men with the power of saving themselves, of doing everything that is needful for effecting their own salvation.* Arminianism virtually divides the work of saving men between God and men, and is more or less Pelagian according to the comparative share and influence which it assigns to the Creator and the creature respectively. Calvinism, and that alone, gives to God the whole honour and glory of saving sinners,—making men, while upheld and sustained in the possession and exercise of all that is necessary for moral agency, the unworthy and helpless recipients at God's hand of all spiritual blessings. Calvinism not only withholds, in point of fact, from men, any share in the work of effecting their own salvation, and ascribes this wholly to God; but when rightly understood and faithfully applied, it prevents the possibility of any such perversion of the gospel scheme of redemption, of any such partition of the work of men's salvation. And it is upon this ground that it was so thoroughly adapted,—not only to overturn from the foundation the whole system of destructive heresy that had overspread the church at the time of the Reformation, but to prevent, in so far as it might be adopted and carried out, the possibility of the reintroduction of such a dangerous perversion of scriptural principles and arrangements.

Popery, if we view it in relation to the method of salvation, and have respect more to its general spirit and tendency than to its specific tenets, may be said to belong to the head of Arminianism. Papists concur with the Arminians in admitting the divinity and atonement of Christ and the agency of the Spirit; but they concur with them also in not giving to the Son and the Spirit the commanding and determining position and influence in the salvation of sinners which the Scripture assigns to them. Popery thus realises the general idea above indicated of Arminianism, viz., that it divides the work of saving sinners between God and sinners themselves. What may be called the Arminianism of popery,—in a sense which will be easily understood from the explanation that

---

* Coleridge tells us of a friend of his, " a stern humorist," who bound up a number of Unitarian tracts into a volume, and titled it upon the back, " Salvation made easy, or, Every man his own redeemer."

has now been given,—was, before the Reformation, of a very Pela-gian cast,—that is, the work of saving sinners was practically taken almost entirely from the Creator and assigned to the creature ;—not, indeed, that men in general were represented, according to the Socinian view, as able to save themselves, but, what is the special peculiarity of popery in regard to this subject, men were represented as on the one hand able to do a good deal for saving themselves, and then as dependent for the remainder, not merely upon the Saviour and the Spirit, but also upon fellow-men and fellow-creatures, upon saints and angels.   And for this complicated system of anti-scriptural perversion of the way of salvation, the only effectual cure, the only radical remedy, was the great Cal-vinistic principle, which distinctly, consistently, and unequivocally ascribes the whole salvation of sinners, from first to last, to the grace and the power of God, the Father, the Son, and the Holy Ghost.

This perversion of the way of salvation was most congenial to man's natural inclinations and tendencies.   Everything had been done which human and Satanic skill could devise, to give it a commanding influence over the whole current of men's thoughts and feelings.   It was firmly established over the whole of Chris-tendom at the Reformation ; and if it were to be dealt with at all, it would require the strongest appliances,—the most powerful and thoroughgoing influences,—to counteract it, to drive it out and to keep it out.   And this was what Calvinism, and Calvinism alone, —looking to the natural fitness of things, the ordinary operation of means,—was adequate to effect.   Calvin derived his system of doctrine from the study of the sacred Scriptures, accompanied by the teaching of the divine Spirit.   But there is nothing in the fullest recognition of this that should prevent us,—especially when we are comparing Calvin with the other Reformers who enjoyed the same privileges,—from noticing and admiring the grasp and reach of intellect, the discernment and sagacity, which God had given to Calvin in such large measure, and which fitted him so peculiarly for the station and the work that were assigned to him. And this view of the admirable suitableness of Calvinism, to go to the root of the evils that polluted the church and endangered the souls of men at the time of the Reformation, is confirmed by the consideration, that all subequent deviations from Calvinism in the Protestant churches,—whether leading in the direction of rational-

ism or traditionalism,—whether pointing towards Socinianism or
popery,—have tended to bring back, in some form or degree, the
great ante-Reformation heresy, the great heresy, indeed, of all
times, that of taking the work of men's salvation from the Creator
and assigning it to the creature.

With respect to Calvin's views in regard to the worship and
government of the church, we had an opportunity, in discussing
Principal Tulloch's "Leaders of the Reformation," to state briefly
what they were, and to point out their magnitude and importance,
as throwing a flood of light upon the whole subject to which they
relate. His great principle of the unlawfulness of introducing
anything into the worship and government of the church without
positive scriptural sanction, evidently went to the root of the matter, and swept away at once the whole mass of sacramentalism
and ceremonialism, of ritualism and hierarchism, which had grown
up between the apostolic age and the Reformation, which polluted
and degraded the worship of God, and which, in themselves and
in their connection with unsound views on the subject of justification, were exerting so injurious an influence on men's spiritual
welfare. Any other principle, or rule, or standard, that could
have been applied to this whole subject, must have been defective
and inadequate, and must have left at least the root of the evil
still subsisting, to be a source of continued and growing mischief.
The fair and full application of Calvin's great principle, would at
once have swept away the whole mass of corruption and abuse
which had been growing up for 1400 years ; would have restored
the purity and simplicity of the apostolic church ; and have prevented the introduction of unauthorised and injurious innovations into the Protestant churches, and saved a fearful amount of
mischief, occasioned by the efforts made to retain or reintroduce
such things.

A fact or two will illustrate the elevation of Calvin's position
in regard to this class of topics. Augustine bitterly deplored the
prevalence of rites and ceremonies in his time, and declared that
the condition of the Christian church in this respect, had become
more intolerable than that of the old dispensation. But having,
to some extent at least, abandoned the principle of the exclusive
authority of the written word in regard to rites and ceremonies,—
though he still held it fast in regard to matters of doctrine,—he had
no means of grappling with this giant evil,—he did not venture

to attempt to do so; and matters continued, at least, without any improvement in this respect for 1000 years. Luther objected to the mass of rites and ceremonies with which he found the worship of the Christian church overspread, mainly upon two grounds. 1st, That they had, from their number, become burdensome and distracting, tending to supersede and exclude other things of more importance; and 2d, That the idea of meritoriousness, which was commonly attached to them, more or less definitely, tended to pervert and undermine the great doctrine of justification. But these principles, though undeniably true, still left the whole subject on a very vague and unsatisfactory footing. Calvin grappled with it in all its magnitude and difficulty, by maintaining, 1st, That they were in the mass unlawful, simply because of their want of any positive scriptural sanction; and 2d, That many of them, independently of mere tendencies, were positively idolatrous, and were therefore directly and immediately sinful, as being violations of the first and second commandments of the Decalogue.

So much for worship; and then in regard to government, Calvin took the best practicable means both for putting an end to all existing corruptions and abuses, and preventing their recurrence. 1st, By putting an end to anything like the exercise of monarchical authority in the church, or independent power vested officially in any one man, which was the origin and root of the papacy; 2d, By falling back upon the combination of aristocracy and democracy, which prevailed for at least the first two centuries of the Christian era, when the churches were governed by the common council of presbyters, and these presbyters were chosen by the churches themselves, though tried and ordained by those who had been previously admitted to office; 3d, By providing against the formation of the spirit of a mere priestly caste, by associating with the ministers in the administration of ecclesiastical affairs, a class of men who, though ordained presbyters, were usually engaged in the ordinary occupations of society; and 4th, By trying to prevent a repetition of the history of the rise and growth of the prelacy and the papacy, through the perversion of the one-man power, by fastening the substance of these great principles upon the conscience of the church, as binding *jure divino*. These great principles, so well fitted to sweep away all the existing corruptions and abuses in the government of the church, and to prevent their recurrence, are evidently in accordance with the fundamental ideas on which the modern theory of representative government is based, and with the leading features of the provision, which has commended itself to all our best and wisest men, for the management of those religious and philanthropic associations which form one of the great glories of our age.

In looking back upon the last three centuries, whether we survey the history of speculative discussion or of the practical influence of Christian churches, we have no reason to be ashamed of our Calvinism or our Presbyterianism; but, on the contrary, are just confirmed in our admiration and veneration for Calvin, or rather in our gratitude to the great Head of the church for all the gifts and graces which He bestowed upon that great man, and for all that He did through Calvin's instrumentality.

CALVIN AND BEZA. *

WE have given some account of the doctrine promulgated, and of the influence exerted upon important theological questions, by the leading Reformers,—Luther, Zwingle, and Calvin,—keeping in view chiefly the object of furnishing materials for the formation of correct opinions in regard to those aspects of their doctrines, character, and influence, which have been made subjects of controversial discussion in more modern times. We have also given a view of the character and theological position of Melancthon, chiefly because of the influence he seems to have exerted in leading the Lutheran churches to abandon the Calvinism of their master, and even contributing eventually to the spread of Arminianism among the Reformed churches,—and because of the connection alleged to exist, historically and argumentatively, between his views and those of the Church of England. The only other man among the Reformers whom we propose to bring under the notice of our readers is Beza. Beza stood in a relation to Calvin very similar in some respects to that in which Melancthon stood to Luther; and there is this farther point of resemblance between him and the Preceptor of Germany, that they were the two great scholars of the Reformation, in the more limited sense in which that word is commonly employed,—that is, they possessed a thorough and critical knowledge of the classical writers of Greece and Rome, they had a great talent and predilection for philological expositions and discussions, and they exhibited, in an eminent degree, that cultivation and refinement both of thought

* *British and Foreign Evangelical Review.* July 1861.

and style, which a thorough acquaintance with classical literature is so well fitted to produce.

Beza was, during the latter years of Calvin's life, most intimately associated with him. He was one of the very ablest defenders of Calvin's system of theology. He succeeded to the high position which Calvin had long held, not only in Geneva, but in the Protestant world; and was, for a period of above forty years after Calvin's death, the most prominent and influential theologian in the Reformed, as distinguished from the Lutheran, Church. He was thirty years of age before he openly and thoroughly abjured the Church of Rome,—a step which involved exile from his native county, and the sacrifice both of a handsome private patrimony and lucrative ecclesiastical benefices. But after joining the Reformed church, and settling in Switzerland, first at Lausanne, and then at Geneva, he was spared, in providence, for considerably more than half a century in the full vigour of his powers; and during this long period he was enabled, by the excellence of his character, the strength of his intellect, the extent of his erudition and literary acquirements, and by his strenuous and unwearied exertions, to confer the most important benefits upon the church of Christ and the cause of Protestant truth.

He exerted great influence for a very long period in most of the Reformed churches, and in none more than in that of Scotland. He advised and encouraged our own great Reformer John Knox, in the whole course of his arduous struggle with the Church of Rome, and strenuously exhorted him to take care that Scotland should be delivered from prelacy as well as popery. He did much to form the character and to direct the views of Andrew Melville, who went to Geneva when a very young man,—who was for some years a professor in the university of that city over which Beza presided,—and who continued to carry on an intimate correspondence with Beza during the whole of his noble struggle in his native land against prelatic and Erastian usurpation.

Beza's character, as might have been expected, has been subjected, like that of his great coadjutors in the work of the Reformation, to the most unscrupulous popish slanders. The grosser charges which have been adduced against him are unsupported by any appearance of evidence, and are utterly unworthy of notice. They are still occasionally adverted to, as well as those of a simi-

lar kind against Calvin, by some of the obscurer class of popish
controversialists, though we are not aware that since the publication of Bayle's Dictionary, any papist, who wished to put on
even the appearance of a regard for candour or fairness has ventured to repeat them. There is, indeed, one charge against Beza's
character of a less heinous description, which has a foundation in
truth, and of which even the more respectable Romanists have
endeavoured to make the most. It is, that in early life he published a volume of poetical pieces, some of which were of a licentious description. The fact is true; but the circumstances of the
case, which popish writers, of course, usually conceal, were these:
—The poems were written before he was twenty years of age, and
before he joined the Protestant Church, though it appears that even
as early as his sixteenth year he had some religious convictions, and
some impression of the falsehood of popery. He afterwards repeatedly and publicly expressed his contrition for the offence. He
did what he could to suppress the circulation of the work, and he
at length published, by the advice of his friends, another edition
of the poems, in which all that was unbecoming and offensive was
omitted. He always, indeed, denied and defied his enemies to
prove, that at any time his conduct was such as his poems might
have led men to suspect. And it is certain, in point of fact, that
some measure of looseness and coarseness in conversation and in
writing was not uncommon then, among persons whose general
character and conduct were in other respects unobjectionable.

It may be worth while to quote one or two of his expressions
of contrition for this juvenile offence, which was at once a sin
against the law of God, and at the same time, by furnishing a
handle to his enemies, an obstruction, to some extent, to his future
usefulness. In 1560, soon after his settlement at Geneva, he
published one of the most important of his smaller works, entitled
" Confessio Christianæ fidei." He dedicated it to his early instructor, Melchior Wolmar, who had been professor of Greek in
the universities of Orleans and Bourges,—who had the singular
honour of being also, for a time, the preceptor of Calvin,—who
exerted an important and wholesome influence in the formation of
the character and views of his two illustrious pupils,—and who has
been immortalized by their grateful and affectionate eulogies. In
this dedication to Wolmar, Beza gives a brief but very interesting
summary of his past history, and refers to the publication of his

poems in the following terms;—"As to these poems, no one
condemned them earlier, or now detests them more, than I, their
unhappy author. I wish they were buried in perpetual oblivion,
and that God would grant me that, since what is done, cannot
become undone, those who read my other writings, so different
from these, would rather congratulate me on the Lord's kindness
to me, than continue to accuse one who, of his own accord, confesses and deplores this sin of his youth." Again, in his note upon
Matthew i. 19, having occasion to refer, in explanation of the
word παραδειγματισαι, to a statement of an ancient author, about
some one who had exposed himself to disgrace by publishing
"versus parum honestos," he introduces this reference to his own
case,—"Quod et mihi juveni, necdum in ecclesiam Dei adscito,
evenit, quam tamen maculam spero me tum dictis tum factis
eluisse." All this ought in fairness to have shut the mouths of
his enemies. But it had no such effect, and papists have continued ever since to dilate upon the "Juvenilia," as the poems
were called, and to make them much worse than they are, by
perverting some of their statements, which mean no such thing,
into actual confessions of heinous crimes. This is the only charge
that can be substantiated against Beza's character. It does not
affect his position or influence as a Reformer, as it was not till
about ten years after the publication of his poems, that he joined
the cause of the Reformation. And after he did take this important step, he was enabled, by God's grace, for more than half a
century, not only to maintain an unblemished public reputation,
but to afford, like his fellow-reformers, the most satisfactory
evidences of personal piety, of zeal for God's glory, and of
devotedness to the cause of truth and righteousness.

Beza's works are, to a large extent, controversial and occasional,
—that is, they arose very much out of the particular controversies
which at the time engaged the attention of the Reformers,—and
on this account perhaps they have been less read in subsequent
times than they deserved. They comprehend, however, full discussions of all the various topics which engaged the attention of
the Reformers, and affected the cause of the Reformation and the
interests of Protestant truth, during the whole of the latter half
of the sixteenth century. They thus occupy a very important
place in a survey of the history of theological speculation at that
important era; and in all of them certainly Beza has afforded

abundant proof, that he was possessed of great talents and extensive erudition, and that he was fully qualified in all respects to expound and discuss the most profound and difficult questions in theology.   The Church of Rome was still a formidable opponent; and Beza has made some valuable contributions to the popish controversy, especially in his "Antithesis Papatus et Christianismi," subjoined to his Confession of faith, in his "Apologia de Justificatione," and in his treatise on "the Notes or Marks of the True Church."   The controversy between the Lutheran and the Reformed Churches, which had been much embittered in the interval between the death of Melancthon in 1560, and that of Calvin in 1564, continued dring the remainder of the century; and Beza was thus under the necessity, as Zwingle had been, of spending a great deal of time and pains in exposing the absurdities of consubstantiation, and of the strange notion invented to explain and defend it, known by the name of the ubiquity or omnipresence of Christ's body.   The Lutherans became much more unsound in their general theological views after the death of their master; and they proceeded so far at length as to reject what are commonly reckoned the peculiarities of Calvinism, while they still continued, though very inconsistently, to repudiate, even in the "Formula Concordiæ," the semi-Pelagain or Arminian views about synergism or co-operation, to which Melancthon had given some countenance. This change, of course, widened the subjects of controversy between the Lutheran and Reformed Churches; and Beza in consequence was led to write much, and he did it with great ability, on predestination and cognate topics.   The fuller discussion which this important subject underwent after Calvin's death, led, as controversy usually does when conducted by men of ability, to a more minute and precise exposition of some of the topics involved in it.   And it has been often alleged that Beza, in his very able discussions of this subject, carried his views upon some points farther than Calvin himself did, so that he has been described as being Calvino Calvinior.   We are not prepared to deny altogether the truth of this allegation; but we are persuaded that there is less ground for it than is sometimes supposed, and that the points of alleged difference between them in matters of doctrine, respect chiefly topics on which Calvin was not led to give any very formal or explicit deliverance, because they were not at the time subjects of discussion, or indeed ever present to his thoughts.

The principal subjects in regard to which the allegation referred to has been made, are the question controverted between the sublapsarians and the supralapsarians about the order of the divine decrees in their bearing upon the fall of the human race,— the imputation of Adam's first sin to his posterity,—the extent of the atonement,—and the nature and import of justification. It may not be uninteresting to explain how the matter stands as to the views of Calvin and Beza respectively upon these important subjects. We mean to devote to this matter the principal portion of our present discussion ; and we think it will appear, from the survey, that there is really no very material difference between the theology of Calvin and of Beza, any apparent discrepancy arising chiefly from the usual tendency of enlarged controversial discussion to produce a greater amount of exactness and precision in details; while it may also appear that Beza, by his very able exposition and defence of the doctrines of Calvin, has rendered important services to the cause of scriptural theology and Protestant truth, and has to some extent anticipated that exactness and precision with respect to definitions and distinctions, which are characteristic of the great systematic divines, especially the Dutch and Swiss theological professors, of the seventeenth century. But we must first notice the services of Beza in some other departments of theological literature.

A class of subjects came to be discussed in the latter part of the sixteenth century which had not engaged so much of the attention of the earlier Reformers,—especially the Erastian and the Prelatic controversies,—and in the discussion of these matters Beza bore his part nobly as an able and faithful champion of the truth. The Erastian controversy, indeed, as conducted between Erastus and Beza, turned mainly upon the particular subject of the excommunication of church members ; and it was not till the following century, that the whole of the principles usually regarded by Presbyterian divines as comprehended in the Erastian controversy, were subjected to a full and thorough discussion. Still, even at that early stage, the question was mooted, on which the entire progress of the subsequent discussion, down even to our own day, has made it more and more manifest that the whole controversy hinges,—viz., whether or not Christ has appointed in His church a government, distinct from, independent of, and in its own province not subordinate to, civil magistracy ? And on this great question, as well as on the particular topic of excommunication comprehended under it, Erastus took the side which has always been supported by politicians, sycophants, and worldlings, while Beza ably defended that which has been adhered to by all intelligent and conscientious Presbyterians.

The subject of prelacy was more fully discussed during this period than that of Erastianism, mainly because the Church of England, differing in this from almost all the Reformed churches, adopted a prelatic constitution. Beza entertained very strong and decided views upon this subject, and his two books, the one, "De Triplici Episcopatu," and the other, a reply to Saravia's "Treatise de Ministrorum Evangelii Gradibus," are still important and valuable works in the contest between Presbytery and Prelacy; although Episcopalian controversialists have continued, down even to the present day, to produce garbled and mutilated extracts from Beza as well as from Calvin, to prove that these great men were favourable to the prelatic form of church government. Hadrian Saravia, his principal opponent upon this subject, had been a minister in the Low Countries, and was ultimately settled as a prebend of Canterbury, where he became intimate with Hooker. He, of course, knew well that Beza was a decided Presbyterian, and indeed he gives him the exclusive credit of preventing prelacy from being adopted in the Reformed churches. "Nam hoc audeo affirmare, si unus D. Beza episcopos retineri ecclesiæ judicasset utile, nullæ ab iis abhorrerent Reformatæ ecclesiæ, quæ hodie episcopos nullos admittere primum reformationis esse caput æstimant."* This is really doing Beza too much honour; for we may confidently assert, that Andrew Melville would have kept prelacy out of Scotland at least, even if Beza had been tempted to abandon the cause of Presbytery. It is, however, a fine testimony to the important and extensive influence which Beza exerted, in maintaining in the Protestant churches that form of government, which has the full sanction of apostolic practice as set before us in the New Testament,—confirmed by the testimony of the only genuine and authentic remains of apostolic men, the Epistles of Clement and Polycarp,—and which was decidedly approved of by the great body of the Reformers.

Beza was one of the very first who attempted anything in an

---

* Prologus ad Examen Tractatus de Triplici Episcopatu.

important department of theological literature, which has since his time received a great deal of attention. We mean what is now usually comprehended under the two heads of criticism and exegesis,—the former including every thing bearing upon the settlement of the true text of the Greek New Testament, or of the actual words which should be held to constitute it,—and the latter including every thing bearing upon the exact grammatical interpretation of all the words and phrases which are found to compose it. And Beza's labours in these departments, including his different editions of the Greek text from MSS. and his translation and annotations or commentary, were such as,—considering the circumstances in which he was placed, and the means and opportunities he enjoyed,—reflect great credit upon his scholarship and critical acumen. A very unjust and unfair attack has been made upon Beza's character and labours, through the medium of his translation of the New Testament into Latin, and his annotations or commentary upon it, by Dr Campbell of Aberdeen, in the tenth of his " Preliminary Dissertations to his Translation of the gospels; and as we remember receiving from the perusal of this Dissertation in our student days, an unfavourable impression of Beza, which we have been long satisfied was thoroughly unjust, we think it proper to make some observations upon it.

Dr Campbell's Preliminary Dissertations form a work which is in many respects very valuable,—one of the most important contributions, indeed, which have been made by Scotland to a department of theological study far too little cultivated among us,—the critical exposition of the New Testament. It is a work, however, which ought to be read with much caution, as there is not a little about it that is very defective and objectionable, and fitted to exert an injurious influence upon the minds of students of theology. Dr Campbell was a very great pretender to impartiality and candour. But it is very plain, that he had his blinding and perverting prejudices like other men, and that these were not in favour of what we have been accustomed to regard as the most important truths revealed in God's word, or of the men who were most zealous in defending them. We had formerly an opportunity of pointing out* how destitute Dr Campbell was of all adequate sense of the importance of sound doctrine,

---

* P. 3.

and how incompetent, in consequence, he was to appreciate aright the most important service rendered to the church by the Reformers. Such a man was not to be expected to have any liking to so able, faithful, and zealous a champion of Scripture truth as Beza was. And accordingly, in the Dissertation formerly referred to, he has made an attack upon Beza's Latin translation of the New Testament, and upon his character generally, which we think belies all his loud and frequent professions of fairness and candour.

The general charge which he adduces against Beza, and which he illustrates by a detail of instances, is that,—under the influence of theological prejudice and partisanship,—he mistranslates a number of passages, and even acknowledges that he had done this in order to promote his own theological views, or to deprive those of his opponents of some appearance of scriptural support. The case is put by Dr Campbell in a very unfair and exaggerated form, and in such a way as evidently to insinuate a charge against Beza's integrity in dealing with the word of God. He has adduced nothing, however, which,—even were it all true and correct, —would amount to a proof of anything like a want of integrity. For there is not the slightest ground to allege, that Beza either introduced into his translation, or brought out in his annotations, any thing but what he honestly believed to be the true and real mind of God in His word. The charge derives its whole plausibility from these two things—1st, That Beza was not always sufficiently careful to *keep distinct* the functions of the mere translator and those of the commentator, and did in consequence sometimes deviate in his translation from the literal meaning of the mere words, that he might bring out more plainly and distinctly what he believed to be the true scriptural sense of the passage ;— and 2d, that he sometimes assigned, as the reason for this deviation, that a more literal translation of the mere words would seem to contradict some other portion of Scripture, or some truth which he believed to be taught there—a statement on which, wherever it occurs, Dr Campbell puts an unfair and offensive construction, as if it were a confession of a dishonourable or fraudulent motive or purpose. Now, this conduct of Beza indicates, no doubt, a defective and erroneous conception of the precise and proper functions of the mere translator, as distinguished from the commentator ; but it should not be regarded as incon-

sistent with integrity, especially when we take into account the
circumstances in which the translation was put forth, and the relation between it and the commentary. Beza's translation of the
New Testament into Latin was not published, or intended to be
used, separately or by itself, but was printed alongside of the
original Greek, while the Vulgate Latin version was also inserted
in a third parallel column; and the annotations subjoined at the
foot of the page, were intended chiefly to explain the reasons of
the translation, which was thus virtually embodied in the commentary as a part of it.

The true state of the case will be better understood by adverting
to the instances which Dr Campbell founds upon; some of which
indeed are based upon misrepresentation, and others are mere
specimens of wire-drawn criticism and special pleading, illustrating nothing but his unfairness and anxiety to make out a case.
One is, that in Acts xiv. 23, Beza has translated the words
χειροτονησαντες δε αυτοις πρεσβυτερους, "quumque ipsis per suffra-
gia creassent presbyteros;"—and this Dr Campbell represents as an
unfair translation of the word χειροτονεω, in order to sanction the
doctrine of the popular election of ministers. That Beza believed
in the doctrine of the right of the Christian people to the substantial choice of their pastors, and that he regarded this passage as
a proof of it, is certain; and no man of good sense and sound
judgment, who has deliberately and impartially examined his
writings, can entertain any doubt of this.* But the unfairness of
the version cannot be established; for Beza certainly thought,
whether rightly or wrongly, and many other competent judges
have agreed with him, that he gave here *the most literal and exact*
rendering of the word χειροτονεω, and that any other version would
have come short of bringing out the whole meaning of what was
implied in it. On several occasions Beza has translated παντες
ανθρωποι, not by *omnes homines*, but by *quivis homines*,—that is,
men of all sorts and in all varieties of circumstances, without distinction or exception; and Dr Campbell represents every instance

---

* We are aware that the accuracy
of this view of Beza's sentiments upon
this subject was disputed by some of
the early defenders of the Church of
England,—by some of the champions
of patronage and moderatism about the
period of the secession from the Church
of Scotland in last century,—and more
recently, with much less knowledge
of the subject, by Sir William Hamilton; but we do not regard any of
these facts as requiring any modification of the statement made in the
text.

of this sort as an unfair perversion of Scripture to serve Calvinistic purposes. Beza, of course, honestly believed that *quivis* brought out more accurately the real mind of the inspired writer in these passages than *omnes* did, as it would have been generally understood; and in this we have no doubt that he was right. It would have been more accordant, however, with correct views of the precise functions of a translator, to have retained the word *omnes*, and explained its sense in the notes as a commentator. But, considering the circumstances, formerly adverted to, as to the object of his translation, and the relation in which it stood to his annotations, it is quite unfair to represent this as a violation of integrity. Perhaps the worst case for Beza which Dr Campbell has adduced is his translation of Heb. x. 38, and in this he has been followed by the authors of our authorised version. In this passage Beza has, without warrant from the original, inserted the word *quis*,— in our version *any man*,—to prevent the text from appearing to discountenance the doctrine of the perseverance of the saints. This was certainly an unwarrantable deviation from the proper functions of a translator; though it ought to be mentioned, in justice to Beza and our translators, that Grotius (in loc.), who did not believe in the Calvinistic doctrine of perseverance, agreed with Beza in thinking that some countenance is given to the insertion by the passage in Habbakuk, here quoted by the apostle ; and that, —as is noticed by Dean Trench, in his admirable work " On the Authorised Version of the New Testament, in connection with recent proposals for its Revision," *—the same sense is assigned to the passage upon purely philological grounds by De Wette and Winer, who had no Calvinistic predilections.

The most unwarranted and unjust of Dr Campbell's instances of Beza's alleged unfairness, is that founded on, and suggested by, his translation of 1 John iii. 9—πας ὁ γεγεννημενος ἐκ θεου ἁμαρ-τιαν ὁν ποιει—which he translated—*quisquis natus est ex Deo peccato non dat operam*. Of course Beza's reason for, and object in, translating the last words of the clause, *peccato non dat operam*, —instead of *peccatum non facit*, as the Vulgate has it,—was, as he states explicitly, to avoid the appearance of the passage teaching the doctrine of the sinless perfection of regenerate persons in this life, and thus contradicting many explicit declarations of Scripture.

---

* 2d Edition, p. 199.

So far, this instance is exactly similar to those already adverted to, in which the proper functions of the translator and the commentator are not kept sufficiently distinct. But Dr Campbell farther makes Beza's translation of this passage, combined with his annotations or commentary on two other passages—Matt. v. 20 and vii. 23—the foundation of a more general and more serious charge against his character and teaching. He distinctly accuses him of having for his object in these passages, "kindly to favour sinners, not exorbitantly profligate, so far as to dispel all fear about their admission into the kingdom of heaven," * and of endeavouring, with this view, to elude the force of our Lord's declaration, † and "reconcile it to his own licentious maxims." He supports this very heavy charge by perverting Beza's statements in these passages, in order to extract from them the sentiment, that men need have no doubt of getting to heaven unless they were, and continued to be, gross and heinous sinners. Now this is really, in plain terms, a misrepresentation and a calumny. The passages adduced *manifestly* afford no ground whatever for the allegation, that Beza intended to teach the doctrine ascribed to him ; and we can scarcely persuade ourselves that Dr Campbell himself believed that the proof which he adduced was sufficient to establish his charge. It is perfectly plain that Beza, in the passages quoted or referred to, intended to teach and did teach, this doctrine, *and no other*,—viz., that the fact that men are still sinners in God's sight,—sinning every day in thought, word, and deed,—was not of itself a sufficient reason why they should conclude, that they had not been united to Christ by faith, and why they might not enjoy good hope through grace ; while he has never said anything fitted, and much less intended, as is alleged, to lead men to remain at ease in their sins, because sure of heaven, if only they are "not exorbitantly profligate." Dr Campbell quotes, in the original Latin, a sentence from the middle of Beza's note on 1 John iii. 4, where this matter is most fully explained, and does so, for the purpose of showing that Beza acknowledged, that his object in giving the translation *peccato non dat operam*, instead of *peccatum non facit*, was to shut out the appearance of this statement countenancing the doctrine of sinless perfection in this life. But in the sentence *almost immediately preceding* that which he quotes for this purpose,

---

* Diss. x., p. v., s. 12.   † Matt. v. 20.

Beza expressly describes the kind of person to whom his statement applies, whom he regards as unregenerate, and therefore inadmissible into heaven, and shut out from the present hope of it,— not as one who is merely "not exorbitantly profligate," but as one "who does not strive after holiness, that is, in whom sin reigns,"— *qui sanctitati non studet, id est, in quo regnat peccatum*,—referring, of course, to the apostle's description of the distinction between the regenerate and the unregenerate, sin *reigning* in the latter, and still present and very manifest at least to themselves, though not reigning, in the former. And what makes the matter much worse is, that in the words *immediately succeeding* the extract quoted by Dr Campbell, Beza has expressly and solemnly *protested* against this very misinterpretation of his meaning, in the following scriptural and most striking and edifying statement :—

"Why do we say this? Is it to discountenance the earnest pursuit of holiness? is it to show that men should not every day be growing in grace? By no means ; for we teach that a perpetual progress in holiness is the certain and perpetual effect of faith. Why then do we say this? It is lest Satan should deprive us of our comfort. For if we can conclude that we are in Christ, only when we shall no longer need to offer the prayer, '*forgive us our debts*,' who does not see, who does not feel, who does not experience a thousand times every day, that it is quite in vain that this consolation is offered to us?"

Dr Campbell had no right to distort and pervert the plain meaning of Beza's statements, and to ascribe to him "licentious maxims," which he had not only never countenanced, but had expressly and solemnly disclaimed. Dr Campbell, it is to be feared, disliked Beza's Calvinistic doctrine, and probably disliked still more his strict Calvinistic morality and experimental godliness ; and the whole of his remarks upon Beza's translation of the New Testament are characterised by uncandid misrepresentation. It is quite unwarranted to represent Beza's general character as a controversialist, as marked by a want of fairness and candour. There are some controversialists who,—from strong prejudice and impetuosity, from rashness and recklessness, or from something like a sort of natural obliquity of understanding and a deficiency of sense and judgment,—manage their disputes in such a way, that we find some difficulty in determining whether a want of fairness and candour is the worst charge that can be justly adduced against them, and whether we are not warranted in accusing them of a positive want of integrity. But men who are acquainted with

Beza's writings, and who can judge of them with anything like
impartiality, will have no such difficulty in forming their estimate
of his character. They will not only reject the suspicion which
Dr Campbell has laboured to raise against his general integrity,
but they will be convinced, that,—though he sometimes indulged
most unwarrantably in the severity of invective against opponents,
which was then so common,—he showed no disposition to take unfair advantages, or to practise the mere artifices of controversy, but
manifested habitually no ordinary measure of impartiality and
candour; in short, they will probably conclude, that Beza possessed
a much larger amount of integrity and fairness than Dr Campbell
did, though he did not make so ostentatious a parade of these
qualities.*

The chief points, as we have mentioned, on which it has been
alleged, that Calvin and Beza differed in their theological sentiments, and that Beza was more Calvinistic than Calvin, are the
order of the divine decrees in their bearing upon the fall as controverted between the Sublapsarians and the Supralapsarians,—
the imputation of Adam's first sin to his posterity,—the extent of
the atonement,—and the nature and import of justification ; and
to each of these four points we now propose to advert in succession, contemplating them chiefly in their historical aspects.

I. The controversy between the Sublapsarians and the Supralapsarians is one of no great intrinsic importance, though it has

---

* As this is a grave matter, we give
Beza's note in full, putting in italics
the sentence which Dr Campbell quotes
from it, and quotes in the original
Latin. We are entitled to assume
that he had read the whole of what we
are about to quote.

"Quisquis operam dat peccato—πας
ὁ ποιων την ἁμαρτιαν (1 John iii. 4).
Dare operam peccato, et purificare se,
opponuntur. Itaque ποιειν ἁμαρτιαν
differt hoc loco ab ἁμαρτανειν simpliciter accepto. Sed de eo demum dicitur qui sanctitati non studet, id est,
in quo regnat peccatum. Idque ita
esse non modo liquet ex antithesi, sed
etiam ex eo quod supra commemoravit
(c. i. ver. 8 et c. ii. ver. 1), ex tota
denique Scriptura et rei experientia
perpetua. *Itaque non homines sed
monstra hominum sunt Pelagiani, Ca-*
thari, Cælestiani, Donatistæ, Anabap-
tistæ, Libertini, qui ex hoc loco perfec-
tionem illam somniant, a qua absunt
ipsi omnium hominum longissime. Quorsum autem hoc? An ut studium
sanctimoniæ damnemus? An ut homines doceamus quotidie non progredi? Minime profecto, quum perpetuum sanctificationis progressum
doceamus certum ac perpetuum esse
fidei effectum. Quorsum ergo? Nempe
ne Satan nobis hanc consolationem
nostram eripiat. Nam si tum demum
nos in Christo esse colligemus, quum
non amplius indigebimus illa preca-
tione, *et remitte nobis debita nostra,*
quis non videt, quis non sentit, quis
non millies quotidie experitur, frustra
nobis hanc consolationem proponi?"—
Theodori Bezæ Annotationes Majores
in Nov. Test. 1594, p. 609.

occasionally been discussed with considerable keenness. In modern times, indeed, it is much more frequently and fully dwelt
upon by Arminians than by Calvinists. They usually labour to
give prominence to this matter, as if it were a tópic of great importance, about which Calvinists were at irreconcileable variance
among themselves; insinuating, at the same time, that Supralapsarianism,—which is more likely to appear harsh and offensive to
man's natural feelings,—is the truest and most consistent Calvinism, though, in point of fact, it has been held by comparatively
few Calvinistic theologians. This artifice seems to have been first
tried by Baro, the Margaret Professor of Divinity at Cambridge,
who was compelled by the academical authorities to resign his
office, because of his anti-Calvinistic notions. It was adopted by
Arminius himself; and he has been followed in this by most of
those who have been called after his name, including even, though
in a less offensive form, Richard Watson, whose "Theological
Institutes" is the leading text-book of the evangelical Arminianism of the Wesleyan Methodists.

We do not intend to dwell at length upon the topics usually
introduced into this controversy, because they scarcely lie within
the line of legitimate discussion, and because, to give them much
prominence, is really to countenance the unfair use which the
Arminians have commonly made of this subject. It is usually
discussed in the works of the great systematic divines of the seventeenth century, under the heads of "The Object of Predestination," and "The Order of the Divine Decrees." The question is
usually put in this form, whether the object of the decree of predestination, electing some men to eternal life and leaving others
to perish, be man unfallen or man fallen; or, in other words,
whether we should conceive of God as in the act of electing some
men to life and passing by the rèst, contemplating men, or having
them present to His mind, simply as rational and responsible beings
whom He was to create, or as regarding them as fallen into a state
of sin and misery, from which He resolved to save some of them,
and to abstain from saving the rest. Those who go above and
beyond the fall, and regard the object of the decree of predestination as man or the human race, viewed as not yet created and
fallen but simply as to be created, are called Supralapsarians; while
those who stop as it were before the fall, and regard the object of
the decree of predestination as man or the human race, viewed as

already fallen into a state of sin and misery, are called Sublapsa-rians. It is evident that this question virtually resolves into that of the order of the divine decrees,—or the investigation of this topic, how we should conceive of the relation in point of time be-tween the different decrees, or departments of the one decree, of God in regard to the human race. The fundamental Supralapsa-rian position, as above stated, is virtually identical with this one,—that we ought to conceive of God as *first* decreeing to manifest His character in saving some men and in consigning the rest to misery; *then in sequence and subordination to this decree,* resolv-ing to create man, and to permit him to fall into a state of sin; while the fundamental Sublapsarian position is, that we ought to conceive of God as *first* decreeing to create man and to permit him to fall, and *then* as resolving to save some men out of this fallen and corrupt mass, and to leave the rest to perish. The whole history of the discussion which has taken place between Supralapsarians and Sublapsarians shows, that this really em-bodies the true state of the question; and this again shows, that the question runs up into topics which lie beyond the reach of our faculties, and which are not made known to us in Scripture. And this general position is confirmed by the fact, that both parties ad-mit, that there is not any real succession of time in the divine mind, and that the whole of the decree or decrees of God with respect to the human race are in truth one simple undivided act of the divine intelligence, exercised in accordance with all the perfec-tions of the divine nature.

The views which most naturally and obviously occur in sur-veying the discussions which have taken place on this subject, are such as these. It seems plainly enough to have been made the principal design of the revelation which God has put into our hands, to inform us of the fall of man from the estate in which he was created into an estate of sin and misery; and especially of the great and glorious scheme which God has devised and executed for saving some men from this condition of guilt, depravity, and wretchedness, and bringing them into an estate of salvation by a Redeemer. Accordingly Scripture tells us little or nothing that does not bear more or less directly upon these objects. It tells us very little of God's plans and purposes, except what we see actually being executed or carried into effect, in the process by which some men are saved from the death in sins and trespasses in which all men lie, and are prepared for everlasting blessedness. This is the substance of what God is now doing with the race of man, and this is the substance of what He has represented Himself in His word, as from eternity decreeing or purposing to do. In the absence of any definite scriptural information, we have no satisfactory materials for ascertaining more than this concerning the divine counsels and plans, and we should carefully abstain from precarious and conjectural speculations upon topics which lie so far beyond the reach of our capacities. We can scarcely frame a conception of any plans or purposes which God could have formed concerning the eternal salvation of men, which did not assume or imply, that they were regarded or contemplated as having all fallen into a state of sin and misery, from which some of them were to be rescued. And thus it appears, that, practically, any conception we can form of God's act in predestinating some men to life and in passing by the rest, must proceed substantially upon Sublapsarian principles. The Supralapsarian theory is founded rather upon abstract reasonings, by which we follow out the connection of doctrines in the way of speculation, than upon any direct information that is given us in Scripture. And however plausible, or even conclusive, some of these reasonings may appear to be, we can scarcely fail to feel that in prosecuting them, we are involved in matters which are too high for us, and with respect to which it is impossible for us to attain to anything like firm and certain footing.

It may be said that all Calvinists agree in every thing which almost any Calvinist regards as taught upon this subject in Scripture with clearness and certainty. They all believe that God, according to the eternal counsel of His own will, hath unchangeably foreordained whatsoever comes to pass; and they include the fall of Adam in God's eternal purpose, and in His sovereign execution of that purpose in providence. And this of course is the great difficulty, from which Sublapsarians cannot indeed escape, but which seems to be somewhat aggravated upon the Supralapsarian theory. For by that theory, God appears to be represented as more directly and positively decreeing and appointing the fall,—as a mean necessary for carrying into effect a purpose,—conceived of as already formed, of saving some men, and leaving others to perish. Although all Calvinists believe and admit that God foreordained the fall of Adam, and that He decreed to exercise, and did exercise, the same providence or agency in regard to that event, as in regard to the other subsequent sinful actions of men,—" having purposed to order it to His own glory," *—yet most Calvinists have thought it more in accordance with the general representations of Scripture, and with the caution and reverence with which we ought to contemplate the counsels and actings of Him who is incomprehensible, but of whom we know certainly that He is not the author of sin, to conceive of Him as regarding men as already fallen into a state of sin and misery, when He formed the purpose of saving some men and of leaving others to perish.

The difference, then, between Calvinists upon this subject is not of any material importance. It does not affect the substance of the doctrine which all Calvinists maintain in opposition to the Arminians. It is a point rather of abstract speculation upon the logical consequences of doctrines, than a matter of direct revelation ; and it is one on which many judicious Calvinists, in modern times, have thought it unnecessary, if not unwarrantable, to give any formal or explicit deliverance,—while they have usually adhered to the ordinary representations of Scripture upon the subject, which are at least practically Sublapsarian. Sublapsarians all admit that God unchangeably foreordained the fall of Adam, as well as every other event that has come to pass ; while they deny that this doctrine can be proved necessarily to involve the conclusion, that, to use the word of our Confession of Faith, " God is the author of sin," or " that violence is offered to the will of the creatures," or that " the liberty or contingency of second causes is taken away."† And Supralapsarians all admit that God's eternal purposes were formed in the exercise of all His perfections, and upon a full and certain knowledge of all things possible as well as actual,—that is, certainly future ; and more especially that a respect to sin does come into consideration in predestination, or, —as Turretine expresses it, in setting forth the true state of the question upon that point,—" in prædestinatione rationem peccati in considerationem venire, ut nemo damnetur nisi propter peccatum, et nemo salvetur nisi qui miser fuerit et perditus."‡ Even when

---

* *Westminster Confession*, c. vi. s. 1.
† C. iii. s. 1.
‡ Loc. iv. Q. ix. s. 7.—The Sublapsarians, while maintaining "lapsum hominem esse proprium subjectum tum electionis tum reprobationis," conceded to the Supralapsarians "lap- sum hominis non esse causam reprobationis," and held that the foresight of the fall was present to the divine mind in predestination, " non subratione causæ sed sub ratione connexæ conditionis, quam intuitus est in omnibus, sive electis sive reprobatis." (Dave-

this question used to be discussed among Calvinists, both parties, though occasionally betrayed into strong statements in the excitement of controversy, admitted that the difference involved nothing of material importance, and did not really affect the substance of any doctrine revealed in Scripture. The Supralapsarians have always been a small minority among Calvinistic divines, and have had to defend their views against the great body of their brethren. They have usually been men of high talent, with a great capacity and inclination for abstract speculation, and considerable confidence in their own powers. In these circumstances, it is quite in accordance with the well-known principles of human nature, that they should have been specially disposed to overrate the importance of their peculiar notions. And yet we find that they generally concurred with the Sublapsarians in representing the difference as one of no great moment. There never was a more able or more zealous Supralapsarian than Dr William Twisse, the prolocutor of the Westminster Assembly. No one has written in support of Supralapsarian views at greater length, or with greater keenness, and yet he, to his honour, has made the following candid admission as to the great importance of the points in which the opposite parties agreed, and the small importance of the one point in which they differed :—

" It is true there is no cause of breach either of unity or amity between our divines upon this difference, as I showed in my digressions (De Praedestination Digress. 1), seeing neither of them derogates either from the prerogative of God's grace, or of His sovereignty over His creatures to give grace to whom He will, and to deny it to whom He will; and, consequently, to make whom He will vessels of mercy, and whom He will vessels of wrath ; but equally they stand for the divine prerogative in each. And as for *the ordering of God's decrees* of creation, permission of the fall of Adam, giving grace of faith and repentance unto some and denying it to others, and finally, saving some and damning others, whereupon only arise the different opinions as touching the object of predestination and reprobation, it is merely *apex logicus*, a point of logic. And were it not a mere madness to make a breach of unity or charity in the church of God merely upon a point of logic ?"*

On this unnecessary, and now obsolete subject of controversy, it has been alleged that Calvin and Beza took opposite sides,

---

nant Determinationes, Qu. xxvi. pp. 122–3, and De Praedestinatione, p. 116.)

* *The Riches of God's Love unto the Vessels of Mercy*, etc., in answer to Hoard, p. 35.

that the former was a Sublapsarian, and the latter a Supralapsarian.
There is no doubt that Beza, in defending the doctrine of predestination, was led to assert Supralapsarian views; though he was
not, as has been sometimes alleged, the first who broached them,
for they had been held by some of the more orthodox schoolmen,
as has been shown by Twisse and Davenant. * But, while Beza's
opinion is clear enough, it is not by any means certain on which
side Calvin is to be ranked, and this question—viz., Whether
Calvin is to be regarded as a Sublapsarian or a Supralapsarian?
has been made the subject of formal and elaborate controversy.
The sublapsarians have endeavoured to show that they are entitled
to claim Calvin's authority in support of their views, while Supralapsarians and Arminians have generally denied this,—the former
of these two classes, that they might claim his testimony in their
own favour,—and the latter, that they might excite odium against
him, by giving prominence to all the strongest and harshest statements that ever dropped from him on the subject of predestination.
A specimen of the way in which this question, as to what Calvin's
views were, has been handled by Sublapsarians, will be found in
Turretine. † The case of the Supralapsarians is elaborately pleaded
by Twisse, in his "Vindiciæ Gratiæ, potestatis, ac providentiæ
Dei;"‡ while the Arminian view is brought out by Curcellæus, in
reply to Amyraldus, in his treatise "De jure Dei in creaturas
innocentes." §

All this, of course, implies that there is real ground for doubt
and for difference of opinion, as to what Calvin's sentiments upon
this subject were; and the cause of this is, that the question was
not discussed in his time,—that it does not seem to have been ever
distinctly present to his thoughts as a point to be investigated,—and
that, in consequence, he has not been led to give a formal and explicit deliverance regarding it. This is the cause of the difficulty
of ascertaining what Calvin's opinion upon this point was; and if
it be indeed true that this precise question he was never led
formally and deliberately to consider and decide, it is scarcely
worth while to spend time in examining the exact meaning of
statements which bear upon it only indirectly and incidentally.
At the same time, we are of opinion that the preponderance of evi-

---

* Davenant. *Determinationes*, p.
121.

† Loc. iv. Q. ix. s. 30.

‡ Lib. i. Digress. viii. c. 2.

§ C. x. Opera, p. 762.

dence here is in favour of the Sublapsarians,—that is, we think
that, on taking a fair and impartial view of Calvin's general character and principles, and of all that he has written connected with
this matter, it appears more probable that, if the question had been
directly and formally proposed to him, and he had been called
upon to give an explicit deliverance regarding it, he would have
decided in favour of Sublapsarian views.   But, as matters stand,
we do not think that either party is entitled to claim him as an
actual adherent.   There is a remarkable passage in Calvin's
"Tractatus de Æterna Dei Prædestinatione,"—which is published
in Niemeyer's "Collectio Confessionum," under the title of "Consensus Genevensis,"—containing, perhaps, about as near an approximation as anything he has written to a deliverance upon this question.   It cannot be reconciled with the Supralapsarian view; while,
at the same time, that view, or something very like it, is set aside
rather as unwarrantable and presumptuous, than as positively
erroneous.   We think it worth while to quote this passage, not
only because of its bearing upon the matter under consideration,
but also because it furnishes a good illustration of the injustice
often done to Calvin by men who have never read his writings,—
and a specimen of the abundant evidence that might be adduced
of his genuine moderation, his thorough good sense, his mature
wisdom, and of the profound reverence and caution with which he
usually conducted his investigations into divine things.   Having
occasion to refer to the difference between the two topics of the
bearing of God's foreordination and providence upon the fall of
Adam, on the one hand, and the bearing of foreordination and
providence upon the election and reprobation, the salvation and
final misery, of fallen men individually on the other,—and this
virtually involves the point controverted between the Supralapsarians and the Sublapsarians,—he expresses himself in the following words :—"Ceterum quæstionem hanc (*i.e.*, the bearing of divine
foreordination and providence upon Adam's fall) non ideo tantum
parcius attingere convenit, quod abstrusa est ac in penitiore sanc-
tuarii Dei adyto recondita, sed quia otiosa curiositas alenda non
est, cujus illa nimis alta speculatio alumna est simul ac nutrix.
Quamquam interim quæ Augustinus Libro de Genesi ad literam
undecimo disserit, quum ad Dei timorem et reverentiam omnia
temperet, minime improbo.   Altera autem pars (*i.e.*, the bearing
of divine foreordination and providence upon the fate and destiny

of fallen men individually), " quod ex damnata Adae sobole Deus quos visum est eligit, quos vult reprobat, sicuti ad fidem exercendam longe aptior est, ita majore fructu tractatur. In hac igitur doctrina, quæ humanæ nàturæ et corruptionem et reatum in se continet, libentius insisto, sicuti non solum ad pietatem propius conducit sed magis mihi videtur theologica ; (*i.e.,* more intimately connected with a full exposition of the scheme of Christian theology). Meminerimus tamen in ea quoque sobrie modesteque philosophandum, ne alterius progredi tentemus quam Dominus nos verbo suo deducit." * In this noble passage Calvin virtually puts aside Supralapsarian speculations, and insists only on that great doctrine of predestination, in the maintenance of which all Calvinists are agreed. Beza, then, in his explicit advocacy of Supralapsarianism, went beyond his master. We do not regard this among the services which he rendered to scriptural truth ; especially as we are bound in candour to admit that there is some ground to believe that his high views upon this subject exerted a repelling influence upon the mind of Arminius, who studied under him for a time at Geneva.

We may add some historical notices of the subsequent discussions connected with this subject, especially as the references we have made to Dr Twisse will naturally suggest the inquiry, how this matter was dealt with by the Westminster Assembly. In addition to Beza, the most eminent men who defended Supralapsarian views in the sixteenth century were Whittaker and Perkins. These were the greatest divines in the Church of England during the latter part of Queen Elizabeth's reign,—men quite entitled to rank with Jewel and Hooker in point of ability and learning, and superior to them in knowledge of the sacred Scriptures, and in acquaintance with the system of doctrinal theology. But, in the next generation, the Sublapsarian view was advocated by Dr Robert Abbot, Bishop of Salisbury, brother of Archbishop Abbot, a very able divine and a thorough Calvinist. His opinion upon this point was adopted by Bishop Davenant, and the other English delegates to the synod of Dort; and Supralapsarianism has not again been advocated by any very eminent theologian in England except Twisse. The eminent men who most elaborately and zealously defended Supralapsarianism in the seventeenth cen-

* Niemeyer, p. 269.

tury were Gomarus, Twisse, and Voetius,—all of them perhaps
more distinguished by their erudition, subtlety, and pugnacity,
than by their comprehensive ability, judgment, and discretion;
though they have all rendered very important services to theological literature.   Gomar, who, when a young man, had visited
England and studied theology under Whittaker at Cambridge, was
the zealous opponent of the views which his colleague Arminius
laboured, at first secretly, and afterwards more publicly, to introduce into the university of Leyden.   He resigned his chair when
Vorstius was chosen as his colleague upon the death of Arminius;
and after officiating for a few years at Saumur, he was settled at
Groningen, and laboured there as professor of theology and
Hebrew during the remainder of his life.   He was a member of
the synod of Dort as one of the Belgic professors, and there he
openly and strenuously maintained his Supralapsarian views; and
though he stood almost alone, he gave a great deal of annoyance
to the synod, by his vehemence and pertinacity.   There were five
Belgic theological professors members of the synod, and they
formed one collegium.   Three of them, Polyander, Thysius, and
Walaeus, entirely concurred in their Judicia on all the five points
on which the synod gave a deliverance.   The fourth, Sibrandus
Lubbertus, who, from Dr Balcanquhall's Letters, appears to have
exhibited a good deal of the temper and spirit of Gomar, gave in
a separate Judicium of his own, but subscribed also that of his
three colleagues.   Gomar gave in a separate Judicium, differing
from those of his colleagues and of the great body of the members
of the synod, in the one point of asserting the Supralapsarian
theory as to the object of predestination.

But the great question is, whether the synod of Dort gave any
deliverance upon this point, and, if so, what that deliverance was.
The synod of Dort, representing as it did almost all the Reformed
churches, and containing a great proportion of theologians of the
highest talents, learning, and character, is entitled to a larger
measure of respect and deference than any other council recorded
in the history of the church.   That the great body of the members
of the synod were Sublapsarians, is certain.   This appears clearly
from the Judicia of the different colleges, as they were called, of
the divines who composed it.   The collection of these Judicia
forms the second part of the important work, entitled, "Acta
Synodi Nationalis Dordrechti habitæ," and constitutes the most

interesting and valuable discussion that exists of all the leading
points involved in the controversy between Calvinists and Arminians.   These Judicia all take, more or less explicitly, Sublapsarian ground; except that of Gomar, and that of the divines of
South Holland, who leaned to the Supralapsarian side, but thought
that it was not necessary for the synod to decide this question, as
the difference was not very important in itself, and admitted of
being reconciled by explanations.   The synod seems to have
adopted this suggestion, and to have abstained from giving a
formal or explicit deliverance upon the point in dispute, though in
the general scope and substance of its canons it certainly takes
Sublapsarian ground.   It has been contended, however, that the
synod condemned Supralapsarian views; and this question gave rise
to a very keen controversy, which was carried on for a long time
by Gomar and Voet on the one side, and on the other by Maresius or Des Marets, who succeeded Gomar as professor of theology
at Groningen.   Voet, then a young man, was a member of the
synod, indeed one of the delegates from South Holland.   He lived
to a great age, surviving all the other members of the synod, and
having been for many years professor of theology at Utrecht.
He became a man of prodigious learning, published many valuable
works, and was well known beyond the bounds of theological
literature by the controversies he carried on with Des Cartes.
Gomar and Voet, who had subscribed the canons of the synod,
held their Supralapsarian views to the last; and, while they did
not deny that the great majority of the members of the synod
were Sublapsarians, they maintained that the synod, in its public
collective capacity, had done nothing to condemn the opposite
theory, while Maresius and others asserted that it had.   We are
satisfied, that on this point, Gomar and Voet have the superiority
in the argument, and have succeeded in proving, that the synod
did not intend to frame, and did not frame, their canons so as to
make it impossible for Supralapsarians honestly and intelligently
to subscribe them,—that they did not intend to make, and did not
make, any definite opinion upon this point a term of communion,
or a ground of exclusion.   The ground taken in the canons of the
synod is, indeed, practically and substantially Sublapsarian; but
the matter is not put in such a form as necessarily to exclude
Supralapsarians, who, without straining, can assent to all that is
in the canons as being true so far as it goes, though they do not

regard it as containing a full statement of the whole truth upon the subject.*

The course pursued by the synod of Dort upon this question was just that followed by the Westminster Assembly in the Confession of Faith which they prepared; and the mode of dealing with this matter adopted by these two most authoritative representatives of Calvinistic theology was, we are persuaded, marked by great Christian wisdom. Dr Twisse, the prolocutor or president of the Westminster Assembly, died before they had done much, if anything, in the way of preparing their confession. But there can be little doubt that his writings must have exerted a considerable influence upon the minds of many, in regard to a point which he had elaborated so zealously. Baillie tells us that they had some tough debates in the Assembly upon the subject of election, but that this matter was at length harmoniously adjusted. As the members were all decided Calvinists, these debates must have turned only upon such minute and unimportant points as those involved in the controversy between the Supralapsarians and the Sublapsarians about the object of the decree of predestination; and the adjustment was effected, *as the result proves,* by the omission in the Confession of any statement that might be fairly held to contain or to imply a denial of Supralapsarianism. There are two or three expressions in the canons of the synod of Dort, which Supralapsarians may require to explain, if not to qualify. But there is nothing in the Westminster Confession to which they would object, while it is also true that there is nothing in it that sanctions their peculiar position; and while it is equally true of it as of the canons of Dort, that in developing the scheme of salvation, it adopts practically and substantially Sublapsarian ground. We have no doubt that, as in the case of the synod of Dort, the great majority of the members of the Westminster Assembly were Sublapsarians in their own convictions; while, at the same time, they intended to leave this an open question, and framed their

---

* The discussions on this subject will be found in a Disputatio et Apologia, subjoined to the collected edition of the works of Gomar; in Voet's "Disputationes Selectæ," tom. i. p. 357, and tom. v. p. 602; and in Maresius's "Theologus Paradoxus," pp. 97-108. Turretine's assertion, tom. i.

p. 377, that the synod of Dort sanctioned the Sublapsarian doctrine as being the more true, and better fitted for quieting consciences, and for neutralising the objections of adversaries, is stronger than a fair view of the whole facts of the case, as brought out by Gomar and Voet, warrants.

statements in such a way as to exclude neither party. And this, we have no doubt, was the course of true Christian wisdom; because, while, on the one hand, Supralapsarians can adduce in support of their theory processes of argumentation which do not perhaps easily admit of being directly answered, so that some men of speculative capacities and tendencies would shrink from meeting the leading Supralapsarian position with a direct negation ; yet, on the other hand, it is plain that Scripture, in the ordinary current and complexion of its representations, assumes the fall of man, starts as it were from that point, and is chiefly directed to the object of unfolding the provision made for remedying the effects of the fall, and the way in which this provision is brought into full practical operation.

There has been no discussion upon this subject of any great importance since the controversy which was carried on so long and so angrily between Voet and Des Marets, about the middle of the seventeenth century. The "Formula Consensus Helvetica," adopted as a test of orthodoxy by the Swiss churches in 1675, the chief authors of which,—Heidegger and Turretine,—were decided Sublapsarians, contains a formal and explicit repudiation of Supralapsarianism, thus contrasting unfavourably in point of wisdom and good sense with the canons of the synod of Dort and the Confession of the Westminster Assembly. This injudicious procedure was the more inexcusable, because those Calvinistic divines who would have been most likely to shrink from a formal repudiation of Supralapsarianism, would have been the most strenuous opponents of the loose views of the Saumur divines about the imputation of Adam's sin to his posterity and the extent of Christ's atonement, against which principally the "Formula Consensus" was directed.* Some attention was called to this subject by a dissertation of Mosheim published in 1724, "De Auctoritate Concilii Dordraceni paci sacræ noxia," in which he adduced it as a serious charge against the synod that they had not condemned Supralap-

---

* This important document furnishes another and a worse instance of the want of wisdom and foresight which has been too often exhibited in connection with the preparation and imposition of symbolical books. Capellus was the colleague of Placæus and Amyraldus at Saumur, and in condemning the views of Placæus about imputation, and of Amyraldus about the extent of the atonement, they introduced into the Formula, and thereby made a term of communion, an explicit repudiation of the views of Capellus, now almost universally received, about the origin and authority of the Hebrew vowel points.

sarian views. An elaborate answer to this dissertation was published in 1726, by Stephanus Vitus, professor in the German Reformed Church at Cassel, entitled, "Apologia pro Synodo Dordracena," and containing a great deal of curious matter. The most important thing, however, in Vitus's "Apologia" is a proof, —the most full and elaborate with which we are acquainted,— that Luther, of whom Mosheim professed to be a follower, held as high Calvinistic doctrine as the Supralapsarians; that his followers, in renouncing his Calvinism, had sunk very much to the level occupied by Erasmus in his controversy with their master; and that all the attempts which have been made by Lutheran writers to disprove these positions have utterly failed. The question that had been agitated about the object of the decree of predestination continued to be discussed in systems of theology, though rather as a matter connected with the history of the past, than as a living, subsisting, subject of controversy; and for more than a century and a half it may be regarded as having become practically obsolete.*

II. The second topic to which we proposed to advert is the doctrine of the imputation of Adam's first sin to his posterity. It has been alleged that while Beza's views upon this subject were distinct and explicit, in full accordance with the higher and stricter tenets which have been generally held by Calvinistic divines, Calvin's were much more vague and indefinite. It has been contended that Calvin's views upon this doctrine were in substance the same as those which were put forth by Placæus or La Place at Saumur, and condemned by the National Synod of the Reformed Church of France in 1644-45; and which have been generally regarded by Calvinistic divines as amounting to a virtual denial of imputation in the fair and legitimate sense of the word. Almost all professing Christians, Romanists and Arminians as

* Those who wish to examine this subject upon its merits, will find very able expositions of it, and conclusive defences of Sublapsarianism, in Turretine, loc. iv. qu. ix., and in De Moor's Commentarius in Marckii Compendium, c. vii. sect. 17, 18, tom. ii. pp. 63-72. The great storehouse of materials on the Supralapsarian side, is Twisse's Vindiciæ Gratiæ, a folio volume of 800 pages of close printed Latin. Bishop Sanderson tells us that, having a great admiration for Twisse, and having begun to entertain doubts of the truth of the Calvinistic theology, in which he had been trained, he read this book through to a syllable. We think it somewhat doubtful whether any other man ever performed this feat.

well as Calvinists, admit what may in some sense or other be
called the imputation of Adam's sin to his posterity,—that is, they
all admit that mankind, the human race, suffer on account of
Adam's sin, or are placed in a worse position, both with respect to
character and circumstances, as the result or consequence of that
sin, and of the relation in which they stand to him who committed
it.   But there have been great differences of opinion among those
who professed to believe in divine revelation, both with respect to
the nature and amount of the deterioration that has taken place in
men's moral character and spiritual capacities through the fall ; and
with respect to the nature of the relation subsisting between
Adam and his posterity, with which this deterioration is admitted
to be in some way connected.   As we have at present to do only
with differences among men who are substantially Calvinists, we
may assume upon the first of these points,—the nature and amount
of the deterioration,—the truth of the doctrine which is held by
all Calvinists, and even by the more evangelical Arminians, viz.,
that all men bring with them into the world a thoroughly depraved
moral nature,—a universal and pervading proneness or tendency to
sin,—which certainly leads, in the case of every individual, to many
actual violations of the divine law,—which cannot be subdued or
taken away by any human or created power,—and which, but for
some special extraordinary divine interposition, must issue in consigning men to everlasting destruction from God's presence.   This
is the great fundamental doctrine in that department of theological science which is now commonly called anthropology, or the
investigation of what man is.   This doctrine is just the assertion
of a fact with respect to the moral character of human nature, or
the moral qualities, capacities, and tendencies of men as they come
into the world.   Its truth or falsehood ought to be investigated as
a matter of fact, by the examination of all the evidence, from any
quarter, that legitimately bears upon it.   This great doctrine or
fact is clearly revealed to us in the sacred Scriptures, but it is not
a matter of pure revelation.   Something may be learned concerning it from an examination of man's constitution, and from a
survey of the doings of men collectively and individually ; and all
that can be learned from these sources,—from psychology and
history, from observation and experience,—fully accords with, and
decidedly confirms, the information given us upon the subject in
Scripture.   Jonathan Edwards' work on "Original Sin" is

devoted to the investigation of this great doctrine or fact; and it certainly establishes its truth or reality, by evidence from Scripture, observation, and experience, which never has been, and never can be, successfully assailed.

Now this great doctrine as to what man is, or as to the actual moral character of human nature, is evidently from the nature of the case the fundamental and most important truth upon the whole subject to which it relates. It is plainly the most important thing that can be known in regard to the natural condition of man, the most important both theoretically and practically, in itself,—in its relation to the general scheme of Christian doctrine,—and in its bearing upon the duties which men are called upon to discharge. All the other questions which have been agitated with respect to the natural state and condition of man, may be said to be in some sense subordinate and inferior to this one. They respect chiefly the origin and cause, the explanation or *rationale*, of the great fact which this doctrine asserts; and therefore they cannot rise in point of intrinsic importance to the level of the question as to the reality of the fact itself. The matter of fact, when once established by its own appropriate evidence, must be admitted to be true, and must be dealt with and applied as a reality, even though we knew nothing, and had no means of knowing anything, about its origin or cause; and though we were unable to give any explanation or solution of difficulties that might be started upon the subject, viewed either in its relation to the moral government of God, or to the responsibility of man. Upon all these grounds it is of the last importance that men,—especially those who are called upon to instruct others in the way of salvation,—should be thoroughly established in the assured belief, that we all bring with us into the world a thoroughly depraved moral nature, which infallibly involves us in violations of the divine law, and subjects us to the divine wrath and curse; and familiar with the whole evidence by which the reality of this great fact can be established.

All Calvinists, many Arminians, and, indeed, we may say almost all of whatever name or denomination, who have given good evidence that they had honestly submitted their understandings to the authority of Scripture, and had cordially embraced the truth as it is in Jesus, have admitted the truth of this humbling and alarming doctrine with respect to the actual moral condition of mankind. There have been considerable differences, indeed, as to what was the most accurate way of stating and applying it. But among Calvinists at least,—and with them only we have at present to do,—the differences which have given rise to controversy, have turned, not upon the nature, import, and evidence of this great fact as to what man by nature is, but upon the explanations or theories which have been propounded as to its cause, ground, or origin; and especially as to the relation subsisting between the first sin of Adam, and the moral character and condition of his posterity. All who believe in the moral depravity of human nature as an actual feature of character, universally attaching to the race, admit, upon the authority of Scripture, that the origin of this is to be traced to Adam's sin, and to the connection subsisting between him and his posterity; and the leading controversies upon the subject may be said to resolve into these two questions—Have we any materials in Scripture that enable us to draw out this general idea, of some connection subsisting between the sin of Adam and the moral character of his posterity, into more distinct and definite positions? and, if so, What are the precise positions to which the fair application of these materials points? All the discussions which have taken place among Calvinists about the imputation of Adam's sin to his posterity may be ranked under these general heads. The doctrine which has been held upon this subject, by the great body of Calvinistic divines, is this, that in virtue of a federal headship or representative identity, established by God between Adam and all descending from him by ordinary generation, his first sin is imputed to them, or put down to their account; and they are regarded and treated by God as if they had all committed it in their own person, to the effect of their being subjected to its legal penal consequences, —so that, in this sense, they may be truly said to have sinned in him and fallen with him in his first transgression. Upon this theory, the direct and immediate imputation of Adam's first sin to his posterity, or the holding them as involved in the guilt or *reatus* of that offence, is regarded as prior in the order of nature and causality to the transmission and universal prevalence among men of a depraved moral nature; and as being, to some extent, the cause or ground,—the *rationale* or explanation,—of the fearful fact that man is morally what he is, a thoroughly ungodly and depraved being. The great body of Calvinistic theologians have believed, that Scripture sufficiently warrants this definite doctrine

about the imputation of Adam's sin to his posterity, or about the
true character of the relation subsisting between him and them,
and the bearing of the results of this relation upon their condition; and in this belief we are persuaded they are right. But
there have been some men who have held Calvinistic views in
regard to the actual depravity of human nature, and in regard to
the other departments of Christian truth, who have not been able
to find in Scripture a sufficient warrant for this doctrine, who
have in consequence rejected it, and have contented themselves
with very vague and indefinite views, or with no views at all,
upon this branch of the subject. And these men have generally
contended that Calvin himself was of their mind upon this question, and differed from the great body of those who, following
Beza in this matter, have been generally classed under the name
of Calvinists. It must be admitted that there is some plausible
ground for this allegation, though we believe that it cannot be
substantiated.

Before proceeding to consider how the case stands upon this
point, it may be proper to explain somewhat the grounds usually
taken by those Calvinists who have not concurred with the ordinary Calvinistic doctrine. In surveying the history of the discussions which have taken place upon this subject, we find even
among the minority of Calvinists who have rejected the generally
received doctrine of the direct and proper imputation of Adam's
sin, as the cause or explanation, *pro tanto*, of the universal prevalence of a depraved moral nature among his posterity, three
pretty well marked divisions—1st, Some simply refuse to receive
the ordinary Calvinistic doctrine, on the ground that they see no
sufficient warrant for it in Scripture,—abstain from all further
discussion,—and profess to receive the fact of universal moral
depravity, as fully established by its appropriate evidence, without attempting anything in the way of accounting for it. 2d,
There are others who, wishing to adhere to the common orthodox phraseology, profess to admit imputation, but evacuate
it or explain it away, by distinguishing between an immediate or
antecedent, and a mediate or consequent, imputation,—rejecting
the former, which is what Calvinists in general contend for, and
admitting only the latter, which is not imputation in any true and
proper sense. 3d, There are some who admit the substance of
the ordinary orthodox doctrine of the imputation of Adam's sin,

but who abstain or shrink from the use of the phraseology in which orthodox divines have been accustomed to express or embody it. There is no good ground for alleging that Calvin is to be ranked with either of the two first of these classes; but it may be contended, with some plausibility, that he might be ranked with the third. And, indeed, we are disposed to admit that this is not far from the truth, provided the admission be taken with these qualifications,—that there is no ground to believe that he denied or rejected any part of the doctrine which has been generally held by Calvinists on this subject,—and that his not employing very fully the phraseology commonly used by later Calvinists when treating of this matter, is not to be ascribed (as it is in the case of some of those whose writings have suggested to us this third head in our classification), to his having considered this phraseology, and having disliked or disapproved of it, but simply to its having never been present to his mind.

Beza brought out this doctrine of the imputation of Adam's sin to his posterity more fully and precisely than it had been before. He expounded and developed it more fully than any preceding theologian,—both as directly and in itself an element in the guilt or *reatus* of the condition into which the human race fell through Adam's transgression,—and as the cause, ground, or explanation of the actual moral depravity attaching to all men as they come into the world. These more precise and definite views had not occurred to Calvin, and do not seem to have ever been distinctly present to his thoughts. The course which the discussion of this whole subject took in his time, not only did not tend to lead his thoughts in that direction, but tended powerfully to lead them in what may be called an opposite one. This is the true and full explanation of the want of definiteness and precision which, it must be admitted, characterise many of Calvin's statements about the imputation of Adam's sin viewed as a distinct topic of discussion, as compared with the fulness and exactness with which it was brought out afterwards; while there is really no reason to doubt that he held the whole substance of the doctrine which has since been generally maintained by Calvinistic divines.

It may be worth while to give some account of the way in which this subject was usually discussed in Calvin's time; as this will not only furnish an explanation of the reason why he did not

usually give so much prominence as might have been expected
to the doctrine of imputation, and why he did not always treat it
with great exactness and precision, but will also expose the inaccuracy of a notion which seems to prevail, that this doctrine of
imputation is a mere Calvinistic peculiarity,—nay, even that it is
the most extreme, objectionable, and mysterious dogma of ultra
Calvinism.

The doctrine of the fall of the whole human race in Adam was,
from the beginning, a part of the creed of the universal church;
and, from Augustine's time, this had been generally spoken of
under the designation of the imputation of Adam's sin to his posterity.   Most of the schoolmen continued to use this language,
though in their hands the doctrine of Augustine was obscured
and corrupted.   The whole subject of original sin was discussed
at length in the Council of Trent, in the year 1546; and, through
the respect generally professed and entertained for Augustine,
the deliverance of the Council regarding it was in the main true
and sound so far as it went,—containing little of positive error,—
though chargeable with vagueness, obscurity, and much imperfection.   But the discussion brought out some of the errors which
had been broached by the schoolmen, and still prevailed extensively in the Church of Rome.   Albertus Pighius, who was one
of the leading opponents of Calvin, and against whom Calvin's
two most important controversial treatises—the one on Free-will
and the other on Predestination—were principally directed, and
Ambrosius Catharinus, another eminent divine of that period,
attended the Council of Trent, and took a prominent part in its
discussions.   In the debates on original sin, these two theologians
zealously maintained the imputation of Adam's sin to his posterity,
and Catharinus delivered a long address, the substance of which
is given by Father Paul in his History of the Council,* and in
which he laboured to establish this doctrine from the testimony of
Scripture and the authority of Augustine.   But then these men
also maintained that the guilt of Adam's first sin imputed constituted *the whole* of the sinfulness of the estate into which man fell;
and they denied the transmission of an actually corrupt or depraved moral nature from Adam to his descendants; and, as they
also held a doctrine which had been generally adopted by Romish

---

* Lib. ii. s. 65.

theologians, and has been formally sanctioned by the Council of Trent,—viz., that this imputation of Adam's sin was wholly done away in Christ, and that an actual deliverance from it, and all its consequences, is communicated to all men in baptism,—they thus practically reduced the sinfulness of man's natural condition to little or nothing, and deprived it of any great power to impress the minds of men.   Father Paul tells us that the doctrine of Pighius and Catharinus was very well received by many of the bishops; but that, as the authority of most of the theologians was opposed to it, they did not venture to adopt and sanction it.   The theologians, however, who opposed it, did not deny the imputation of Adam's sin to his posterity; this was universally admitted; they maintained that this imputation did not constitute the *whole* of original sin, but that there was also, in conjunction and in connection with this, the transmission from Adam to his descendants of a deteriorated moral nature.   And this view, which certainly could be just as conclusively established by testimonies both from the Bible and Augustine, prevailed in the Council.   Cardinal Bellarmine, accordingly,* says, that the doctrine of Pighius and Catharinus is partly true and partly false,—true, in so far as it admits the imputation of Adam's sin to his posterity,—and false, in so far as it maintained that this imputation was the whole of original sin, and that there was no transmission of a corrupted nature; and then he proceeds to show that this negative portion of their doctrine was a heresy, as being opposed to the decrees of the Council of Trent.

This doctrine of Pighius and Catharinus, which prevailed widely in the Church of Rome even after the deliverance of the Council, was dealt with by Calvin and the other Reformers very much in the same way as by Bellarmine.   Since the doctrine of the imputation of Adam's sin to his posterity was not denied by the Church of Rome, and was not rejected but sanctioned, though not defined and developed, by the Council of Trent; and since, on the contrary, some of those who were most zealous in maintaining it, employed it practically to soften and explain away the most important features of the sin and misery of men's natural condition, Calvin was naturally led to give more prominence, in his expositions and discussions of this subject, to the transmission

---

* De Amissione Gratiæ et Statu peccati, lib. v. c. 16.

and the actual universal prevalence of a depraved moral nature than to the imputation of Adam's sin, which was not then a subject of controversy. This was the true cause or explanation why Calvin was led to make occasionally statements upon this subject, which have induced some men to allege that he did not hold the imputation of Adam's sin to his posterity, but believed the sinfulness of men's natural condition to consist only in the want of original righteousness, and in the possession of a depraved moral nature, certainly and invariably producing actual transgressions.

The truth as to Calvin's sentiments upon this subject is, in substance, this : that he has never, directly or by implication, denied the imputation of the guilt of Adam's sin to his posterity, and that he has, on a variety of occasions, plainly enough asserted it ; though he has not, from the cause above stated, given it the prominence to which, if true, it is entitled, in a systematic exposition of the scheme of divine truth,—has not always introduced it where, perhaps, we might have expected it to be introduced,—and has not stated it with so much fulness and precision,—especially in the aspect of its being regarded as producing, and to some extent explaining, the universal prevalence of a depraved moral nature,—as was done by later Calvinists after this whole matter was subjected to a fuller controversial discussion. There is, we think, sufficient evidence that this is really the true state of the case to be found in the extracts from Calvin, quoted and referred to by Turretine ;* and there would be no difficulty in producing other passages quite as explicit, and some, perhaps, still more so, from his two treatises on Free-will and Predestination. There is no reason, then, to fear that, in maintaining the higher and more precise views upon the subject of the imputation of Adam's sin, which have been held by the great majority of the ablest and most accurate theologians, we may expose ourselves to the risk of having the venerable authority of Calvin adduced against us.

The question as to what were Calvin's views upon the subject of the imputation of Adam's sin, was first brought into prominence by Placæus, who broached sentiments upon this point differing from those which had been generally held by Calvinistic divines, and claimed Calvin himself as an authority upon his side. As the discussion raised by Placæus forms the most important era in the

---

* Loc. ix. q. ix. s. 41.

history of this subject, and as his peculiar opinions have received
some countenance in influential quarters in the present day, it
may be proper to give some notice of it. Placæus or La Place,
Amyraldus or Amyraut, and Cappellus or Cappel, were all settled
in the year 1633 as theological professors in the Protestant University of Saumur. They were all men of great learning and
ability, of great industry and activity, and though they did not
renounce the fundamental principles of the Calvinistic system of
theology, they exerted an extensive influence in diffusing loose and
unsound opinions upon some important doctrinal questions, not only
in France, but over the Reformed churches. Placæus, in a Dispu-
tation published in the " Theses Salmurienses,"—' De statu hominis lapsi ante gratiam'—put forth some views on the imputation of
Adam's sin, which were regarded by many as contradicting the doctrine which had been generally professed in the Reformed churches.
Accordingly, the National synod held at Charenton in December
1644 and January 1645, condemned his book, though without
mentioning his name, and prohibited the publication of the doctrines it advocated. This decree of the synod led to a good deal of
controversial discussion. Garisolles, the moderator of the synod,
defended it; and answered Placæus's " Disputatio" in a work
which we have never seen, but which is highly praised by Turretine. Andrew Rivet, perhaps the most eminent divine of the
period, published a defence of the synod, consisting chiefly of extracts from the Reformed Confessions, and from all the most
eminent divines, both of the Reformed and Lutheran Churches.
Most of these extracts were translated and published in the first
series of the " Princeton Essays." They are a very valuable body
of testimonies, but there are some of them which can scarcely be
regarded as sufficiently precise and definite to contradict Placæus's
position. Placæus defended himself in a very elaborate treatise,
published in 1665, " De imputatione primi peccati Adami." In
this work he laboured to show, that his opinion was not inconsistent with the generally received doctrine of the Reformed churches;
for that they merely asserted the imputation of Adam's sin to his
posterity, and that he had not denied this, but held it in a certain
sense. In this work, he developed fully the distinction, on which
chiefly he based his defence, between immediate or antecedent,
and mediate or consequent, imputation. He rejected the former
and maintained the latter, and contended that Calvin and other

eminent divines concurred in the substance of his doctrine, though they had not expressed it in this particular definite form. His doctrine is in substance this, that the guilt or *reatus* of Adam's first sin is not imputed to his posterity directly and immediately, as a distinct step in the process,—a separate and independent element in the sinfulness of the estate into which man fell,—having its own proper basis or warrant in the federal relation subsisting between Adam and his posterity, and affording, by its antecedence in the order of nature, a basis or explanation for the moral depravity which came upon men as a consequence, in the way of penal infliction through the withdrawal of divine grace. This is the doctrine which has been generally held by Calvinistic divines, but this doctrine Placæus openly and earnestly repudiated. He contended, that the imputation of Adam's sin is simply a consequence or result of the moral depravity which is admitted to attach to men, in consequence somehow of their connection with Adam, but of the existence and transmission of which no explanation is given or attempted; and that all that is meant by the imputation of Adam's sin is this, that God,—contemplating men as actually and already, in virtue of their connection with Adam, subject to moral depravity, and involved thereby in actual transgressions of His law,—resolves, upon this ground, to regard and treat them in the same way as Adam by his sin had deserved to be treated. God's act in regarding and treating men in the way in which Adam deserved to be treated, is thus based upon the medium of the previous existence of moral depravity as already an actual feature of men's condition, and is a consequence of its universal prevalence; instead of being viewed as an antecedent of this depravity in the order of nature, and the ground, and, in some measure, the explanation or rationale of it. And hence the name of mediate and consequent, as distinguished from immediate and antecedent, imputation, by which this notion has since Placæus's time been commonly designated.

Independently of the question, which of these doctrines has the sanction of Scripture?—though that of course is the only question of vital importance,—it is surely very manifest, that it is a mere abuse of language to call this notion of Placæus by the name of imputation,—that it is not imputation in any real honest meaning of the word,—and that he never would have thought of calling this imputation, unless he had been tied up by ecclesiasti-

cal authority and his own voluntary engagements, to maintain
that in some sense or other Adam's first sin was imputed to his
posterity. It is also very manifest that this doctrine does not
give, or attempt or profess to give, any account of the origin, or
any explanation of the cause, of the moral depravity of man, and
the universality of actual transgression proceeding from it. Nay,
it precludes any attempt to explain it, however partially, except
this, that God in mere sovereignty established a constitution, in
virtue of which it was provided, and did actually result, that all
men should have transmitted to them the same depraved moral
nature which Adam brought upon himself by his first sin. And
there certainly can be nothing which more directly and immediately than this resolves at once the sin and misery of the human
race into the purpose and the agency of God. Placæus, moreover, brings out very plainly in this work the true character and
tendency of his peculiar doctrine, and its palpable inconsistency
with the views which have been generally held by Calvinistic
divines, by explicitly denying that God made any covenant with
Adam, or that any federal relation subsisted between him and his
posterity; and makes it manifest that his doctrine of imputation,
falsely so called, at once results from, and produces,—at once
flows from and leads to,—an entire rejection of the principle of
Adam's federal or representative headship.*

This doctrine of Placæus was not adopted by almost any
divines of eminence who really believed in inherent depravity as
an actual feature of man's moral nature. It was explicitly condemned by the churches and divines of Switzerland in the "Formula Consensus." It has been made a question among the Presbyterians of the United States, though we do not remember that
the point has been mooted in this country, whether the Westminster Confession condemns the view of Placæus; and the general
opinion there seems to be, that there is nothing in the Confession
so precise and definite as to make it unwarrantable for one who
believes only in mediate and consequent imputation to subscribe
it. The leading statement upon the subject is this †—"They (our
first parents) being the root of all mankind, the guilt of this sin
was imputed, and the same death in sin and corrupted nature conveyed, to all their posterity descending from them by ordinary gene-

---

* Pp. 18, 22, 27, 170-2, 245, and 253.   † C. v. s. 3.

ration." Now this statement, *read in the light of the discussions
which Placæus occasioned,* is certainly vague and indefinite, and
resembles much more closely the deliverances given on this subject in the Confession of the sixteenth century than that embodied
in the Consensus of 1675. The Confession was completed about
the end of 1646, not quite two years after the National Synod of
Charenton. It is probable that the members of the Assembly
were not yet much acquainted with the discussions which had
been going on in France, and were in consequence not impressed
with the necessity of being minute and precise in their deliverance
upon this subject. It is a curious circumstance, that both in the
Larger and the Shorter Catechisms, there are statements upon
this point more full and explicit, and more distinctly exclusive of
the views of Placæus. The Larger Catechism* says, "The covenant being made with Adam, as a public person, not for himself
only, but for his posterity, all mankind descending from him by
ordinary generation sinned in him, and fell with him, in that first
transgression;" and both Catechisms, more distinctly than the Confession, represent the guilt of Adam's first sin as the first, and in
some sense the leading, element in the sinfulness of man's natural
condition. More than a year elapsed between the completion of
the Confession and that of the Catechisms; and we think it by no
means unlikely,—though we are not aware of any actual historical
evidence bearing upon the point,—that during this interval the
members of the Assembly may have got fuller information concerning the bearing of the discussions going on in France, and
that this may have led them to bring out somewhat more fully
and explicitly in the Catechisms the views which, in common with
the great body of Calvinistic divines, they undoubtedly entertained about the imputation of Adam's sin. Every one who has
read Placæus's book will see, that he would, without hesitation,
have subscribed the statement in the Confession, but that he
would have had extreme difficulty in devising any plausible pretence for concurring in what has been quoted from the Larger
Catechism.

In the seventeenth century this doctrine of Placæus received
some countenance from Vitringa and Venema. It was adopted
by Stapfer in his "Theologia Polemica," who, however, when

---

* Q. 22.

accused of error on this account, endeavoured to defend himself, by maintaining that both views of imputation were sound,—a position which, though in a certain sense it can be defended, was .in the circumstances a mere evasion of the charge.*   From Stapfer it was adopted by Jonathan Edwards in his great work on Original Sin.   Edwards' views, however, upon this point do not seem to have been clear or consistent, as he sometimes makes statements which manifestly imply or assume the common Calvinistic doctrine.†   It is, indeed, plain enough that Edwards had never subjected this particular topic of imputation to a careful investigation, —his work on Original Sin being devoted to the object of establishing the doctrine or fact of man's inherent native depravity, an object which he has thoroughly and conclusively accomplished. Dr Chalmers, in the first volume of his lectures upon the Epistle to the Romans, gives some indications that he had adopted this doctrine, though he does not bring it out with anything like fulness and explicitness.   He had evidently, when he published that volume, not examined this subject with much care and attention, and was probably altogether unacquainted with the discussions which had previously taken place among theologians concerning it,—which, in all likelihood, was the case also with Edwards.   It is most gratifying to notice that Dr Chalmers, upon a more careful and deliberate study of this subject, renounced the defective and erroneous view which he had imbibed from Edwards ; and that in his great work, the " Institutes of Theology," he, with the candour and magnanimity of a great mind, retracted his error, and supported the doctrine of the imputation of Adam's sin as it has been generally held by Calvinistic divines.‡

This doctrine of mediate or consequent imputation, which admits imputation only in this sense,—that, on account of our inherent, moral depravity, as an actual feature of our condition, we are regarded and treated by God in the same way as Adam had deserved to be treated, in the same way as if we had committed Adam's sin,—has also been maintained by one of the most powerful, brilliant, and valuable writers of the present day, Mr Henry Rogers, in a very interesting Essay on the " Genius and

---

* Tom. i. p. 236, tom. iv. pp. 513-14, pp. 561-6.
† " Princeton Essays," 1st Series, p. 151.

‡ " Institutes," vol. i. pp. 454-9, 465-9.

Writings of Jonathan Edwards," prefixed to an edition of his works published at London, in two volumes, in 1840. His views are brought out in the following passages :—

"We dislike the second term, 'imputation of Adam's sin,' because the word *imputation* is apt to suggest the idea of an *arbitrary transfer* of the guilt and consequent punishment of one moral agent to *another* moral agent, whose *moral condition* is essentially different. But this is not what is meant by it. If we could suppose one of the descendants of Adam born *without* this depraved bias, and actually, when master of his own actions, persevering in unbroken obedience to the law of God, then the imputation of Adam's guilt would be considered by Calvinists quite as absurd and as unjust as our opponents profess now to consider it. *All that is meant* by the 'imputation of Adam's sin,' is that, as in the original constitution of things, Adam and his posterity were linked together by an inseparable union, as the root of a tree and its branches ; and as the moral state of the latter (as well as their state in every other respect) was affected by that of the former, so it was reasonable that Adam should be treated as the federal head of his race. They are so far *one* as to warrant similarity of treatment. In this hypothesis, the moral state of his descendants is not the *consequence* of the imputation of Adam's sin, but presupposed as the *reason* of such imputation, and as *prior* to it in the order of nature. They are treated as he is because they are presupposed to be, and are *really*, morally like him. Thus, the great, and we may say the sole difficulty, is to reconcile it with justice, that the destinies of our race should be linked in a chain of mutual dependence with those of our first father ; that not only our physical condition (a fact universally admitted), but that our moral condition should take its complexion from his own ; that as he was we should be ; that if he fell, and, as a consequence, became mortal, we should fall with him, and become mortal too. Such a constitution, however, of course, presupposes the state of Adam's descendants to correspond with his own ; and the imputation of Adam's sin *means nothing more* than that they are treated as Adam was, simply because they are virtually in the same condition with him. According to this doctrine, therefore, the *real* difficulty is not to reconcile the imputation of sin and guilt where there is no sin and guilt at all (for that is not the case supposed), but to vindicate the reasonableness of a constitution by which one being becomes depraved by his dependence on another who is so, or by which the moral condition of one being is remotely determined by the moral condition of another. Such is the doctrine when freed from all theological technicalities, and the more we consider it, the more we shall perceive that the sole difficulty is the one we have mentioned.

"Such is the explication of the doctrine of Original Sin, which, it will be seen, does not, *as is so often represented*, imply the arbitrary imputation of the guilt of one moral agent to another in no sense guilty ; and then an equally arbitrary infliction of punishment. But, presupposing the moral state of Adam's descendants to resemble his own, and to necessitate, therefore, the same treatment, it represents it as just to deal with us as in our great progenitor, as virtually one with him, as grafted on his stock, as bound up in his destinies.

"It will be seen by the defence we have just made, that we should not choose to attempt to vindicate, by direct argument, that constitution by which the moral destinies of one being are, in fact, intrusted to the keeping of another. This is one of the mysteries about which, in our present state, it is in vain to reason. The difficulty is to be met simply by appealing, in the first instance, to the facts which prove such a constitution, and then by showing that the very same difficulty presses on any hypothesis that can be adopted on this subject, and, indeed, may be objected to all the proceedings of God towards this lower universe—*consequently* can never be conclusive against the Calvinistic doctrine of Original Sin."*

Mr Rogers is rather stating his doctrine than expounding and defending it; and for this, as well as for other reasons, it would be out of place to enter here upon a full discussion of it. But there are some obvious reflections suggested by these extracts, which we may state, without enlarging upon them. It is a somewhat peculiar procedure on the part of Mr Rogers, virtually to give his definition or description of the imputation of Adam's sin, as if it were the only true and sound one, and that which was generally adopted by Calvinistic divines. Mr Rogers adopts the mediate and consequent imputation of Placæus,—a view which is neither accordant with the natural ordinary meaning of the word, nor with the doctrine that has been held by the generality of orthodox theologians. His whole statement is plainly fitted to convey the impression that this,—and this alone,—is, and should be, recognised as the true Calvinistic doctrine, any other notion which the word imputation might suggest, and which may have been put forth in some quarters, being merely an unwarranted misrepresentation, repudiated by the judicious friends of the doctrine itself. Now, this is certainly a very erroneous impression concerning the actual facts of the case; for it can scarcely be disputed, that the doctrine of immediate and antecedent imputation, which he brings in as if it were merely a misrepresentation of opponents, and which he himself misrepresents, especially by the application of the word "arbitrary,"—an epithet which Arminians are so much in the habit of brandishing against all the doctrines of Calvinism,—has been explicitly maintained by the great body of the ablest Calvinistic divines who have flourished since Placæus's time.

---

* Essay xl.-xlii.

The doctrine concerning the imputation of Adam's sin is not to be settled, as Mr Rogers seems to assume, by laying down an arbitrary definition, warranted neither by the natural proper meaning of the words, nor by the prevailing *usus loquendi* among theologians. It can be determined only by an examination of Scripture, by ascertaining what it is that Scripture asserts or indicates concerning the actual relation subsisting between Adam and his descendants—the real bearing of his first sin upon the moral condition of his posterity. Placæus, the great champion, if not the inventor, of Mr Rogers's notion of imputation, undertook to show that there was nothing in Scripture to warrant any other idea of what might be called the imputation of Adam's sin to his posterity, except this, "that because of the sin inherent in us from our origin, we are deserving of being treated in the same way as if we had committed that offence."* But most Calvinistic divines have maintained that this position, though true so far as it goes, does not embody the whole truth; that Scripture gives us somewhat fuller and more definite information upon the subject, and warrants us to believe that Adam was constituted the covenant-head, or federal representative, of his posterity—God having resolved to make the trial or probation of Adam the trial or probation of the human race; that thus they sinned in him, and fell with him in his first transgression; and that thus the sin and misery of their natural condition assumes the character of a penal infliction, to which they are subjected because involved in the guilt of Adam's first sin imputed to them, or put down to their account. Whether Scripture does warrant and require us to believe this is a question on which there is room for a difference of opinion. If it does not, then we must fall back upon the mediate or consequent imputation of Placæus and Mr Rogers. But, if we were satisfied that this is the true state of the case, we would scarcely be contented with " disliking," as Mr Rogers confesses he does, " the term, imputation of Adam's sin;" nor would we attempt to explain it away by an arbitrary and unwarranted definition; we would reject it altogether as improper and unsuitable, fitted only to convey an erroneous impression.

Mr Rogers has not entered into any examination of the scriptural grounds by which this question should be determined, and

---

* " Theses Salmur." P. i. p. 206.

neither can we, at present, advert to them. We can only assert that, for above two hundred years past, the generality of the most eminent Calvinistic divines have contended, that the doctrine of immediate and antecedent imputation is taught in the natural and obvious meaning of the apostle's statements in the 5th chapter of the Epistle to the Romans, and is only confirmed by the most thorough, searching, critical investigation of their import; while it is also in full accordance with the whole history of God's dealings with the human race, and with the principles by which they have been regulated,—and especially with the great principle of covenant-headship and federal representation, so plainly exhibited in God's arrangements with respect to the recovery, as well as the ruin, of mankind. We have admitted, that the great doctrine or fact of the transmission from Adam and the actual prevalence among all his descendants, of a depraved moral nature, is of more intrinsic and fundamental importance, in itself and its consequences, viewed both theoretically and practically, than any particular tenet as to the cause, or ground, or *rationale* of this state of things can be. But this does not, in the least, affect our obligation to ascertain and to proclaim all that Scripture makes known to us on the subject. We admit, also, that the evidence of this great fact from Scripture, confirmed as it is by the testimony of observation and experience, is more varied, abundant, and conclusive than can be adduced in support of the doctrine of the imputation of Adam's sin, as it has been usually held by Calvinists. But the evidence for this doctrine is, we believe, sufficient and satisfactory; and, if so, men are bound to receive it. It certainly cannot be legitimately set aside by any thing but a disproof of the scriptural evidence on which it is professedly based; and this, we are persuaded, has not been and cannot be produced.

Mr Rogers represents it as a great advantage of his virtual denial of imputation, by resolving it into what is only mediate and consequent upon the existence of depravity as an actual feature of human nature, that it leaves only one difficulty unsolved—viz., "to vindicate the reasonableness of a constitution by which one being *becomes* depraved by his dependence on another;" and he plainly insinuates that any other doctrine upon the subject must be attended with additional and more formidable difficulties.

The substance of the only answer he attempts to this difficulty is, that the matter of fact as to man's natural condition is conclusively established by its appropriate evidence, and must therefore be received as true, and, of course, consistent with God's attributes and moral government, however great may be the difficulties attaching to it. This answer we admit to be quite sufficient and satisfactory; but we contend that the doctrine of imputation in the only true and fair sense of the word,—the doctrine of immediate and antecedent imputation,—does not introduce any additional difficulty into the investigation of this subject, and upon the whole rather tends to diminish or alleviate the admitted difficulty, than to strengthen or aggravate it. It is a principle of the greatest value and importance in the consideration of the difficulties attaching to speculations on religious subjects,—and especially in dealing with the objections commonly directed against Calvinism,—that the difficulties or objections really apply, not to particular doctrines or representations, but to actual facts or results, which are admitted, or can be proved, to exist or to take place under God's moral government. This principle applies equally to the views generally held amongst us with respect to the fall of mankind in Adam, and their salvation through Christ. The great, the only difficulty, in the one case is, that all men come into the world with morally depraved natures, which certainly and invariably involve them in actual violations of the divine law, and thus subject them to punishment; and in the other case, that of the whole human race thus involved in sin and misery, some only are saved from this condition and the rest perish, while this difference in the result cannot be fully explained by anything in men themselves, or by anything they have done or can do, but must be referred ultimately to the good pleasure of God. These are actual facts or results which can be conclusively proved, and must therefore be admitted to be true. It is with the fall alone we have at present to do; and here the great, the only real difficulty, is the universality of depravity with its certain and invariable consequences. This we undertake to prove to be an actual matter of fact. If its truth be denied, we must stop, and before proceeding farther, we must establish it, for it is the great fundamental position with respect to the moral condition of mankind. But it is admitted by all Calvinists,—and we have to do at present only with differences subsisting among them,—differences which we are persuaded do not and cannot seriously affect, either in the way of alleviation or aggravation, the difficulties attaching to the admitted fact.

Some Calvinists,—agreeing in this with those more evangelical Arminians who admit the great fact of the universal native depravity of mankind,—contend that, beyond establishing the reality of the fact, Scripture gives us no farther information on the subject, except this, that this depravity was transmitted by Adam to all his posterity, and that it is in some way or other to be traced to the relation subsisting between him and his descendants. They stop here, because they think that Scripture goes no farther, and because they have a vague notion,—which Mr Rogers appears to sanction,—that to go any farther would involve them in new and additional difficulties ; though there really can be no greater difficulty than what stands out palpably on the face of the fact itself. They usually allege, that Scripture makes known to us no other relation as subsisting between Adam and the human race, except that they are all his natural descendants; while in connection with this they admit, that God had established a constitution or arrangement, in virtue of which all Adam's descendants were in point of fact to have the same moral character into which he fell by his first sin. This constitution or arrangement of God, in virtue of which Adam transmitted to all his descendants the same depravity of moral nature which he brought upon himself, is of course admitted by all who, upon the authority of revelation, believe in the depravity of the human race. But it manifestly does not furnish,— or appear or profess to furnish,—any explanation or solution of the one great difficulty; which consists essentially in this, that God appears to be represented as the author or cause of the sin and misery of mankind. The admission of this divine constitution is really nothing more in substance than an assertion of the matter of fact, as a matter of fact; and then tracing the fearful result, directly and immediately, to a purpose and appointment of God. The view held by a certain section of Calvinists, from Placæus to Mr Rogers,—denying the imputation of Adam's sin in any fair and legitimate sense of the expression, and reducing it to a mere name or nonentity;—implies, that Scripture makes known to us no other relation, no other kind of unity or identity, as subsisting between Adam and the human race, except that of progenitor and posterity, —the unity or identity of a father with his descendants ; and this is simply asserting, in another form, the mere fact of the actual transmission of a depraved nature, as the result of a constitution or arrangement which God has established. This view of the matter leaves the difficulty just where it found it. It interposes nothing whatever between the result and the exercise of the divine sovereignty; it does nothing whatever towards explaining or vindicating that divine constitution or arrangement under which the result has taken place. At the same time, it is to be remembered, that it is universally admitted that this relation of progenitor and posterity,— this species of oneness or identity, does subsist between Adam and his descendants,—that it is in no way inconsistent with the more strict and definite views of imputation which have been held by the generality of Calvinists,—and that in so far as it can be made available or useful in the exposition of this subject, this advantage belongs equally to those who believe, and to those who deny, the generally received doctrine of imputation; while those who deny it have nothing else whatever to adduce in explanation or defence of their position.

If Scripture gives us no farther information upon this subject, then we must stop here, and,—in dealing with the objections of opponents,—take our stand upon the position, that the fact of the fall and the depravity of the human race has been conclusively proved, and must therefore be received as true. This ground is common to all who admit depravity, and it is sufficient to dispose of the difficulty. But Calvinists in general have contended, that Scripture does give us some additional information upon this subject; and that this additional information,—while certainly not furnishing a solution of the difficulty, which all admit to be insoluble,— introduces no additional difficulty, and not only does not aggravate the difficulty admitted to exist, but rather tends to alleviate it. The peculiarity of the doctrine of imputation,—immediate and antecedent imputation,—as held by the generality of Calvinists, consists in this, that it brings in another relation besides that of mere natural descent, as subsisting between Adam and his posterity,—another species of oneness or identity between them, viz., that of covenant headship or federal representation. Their doctrine is, that God made a covenant with Adam, and that in this covenant Adam represented his posterity, the covenant being made not only for him but for them,—including them as well as him in its provisions. The proper result of this was, that, while there was no actual transfer to them of the moral culpability or blameworthiness of his sin, they became, in consequence of his failure to fulfil his covenant engagements, *reï*,—or incurred *reatus*, or guilt in the sense of legal answerableness,—to this effect, that God, on the ground of the covenant, regarded and treated them as if they themselves had been guilty of the sin whereby the covenant was broken, and that in this way they became legally involved in all the natural and penal consequences which Adam brought upon himself by his first sin. Now this doctrine,—viewing it merely as a hypothesis, and independently of the actual support it receives from Scripture,—neither introduces any new difficulty into the investigation, nor aggravates the difficulty which all admit to exist. It does not in any respect make more sinful or miserable the actual condition of the human race as a reality or matter of fact, and it does not ascribe anything to God which appears more liable to objection or more incapable of explanation, by bringing His agency more closely into contact with the actual result of the sin and misery of mankind. On the contrary, it rather tends to alleviate the difficulty, and to throw some light upon this mysterious transaction,—by bringing it somewhat into the line of the analogy of transactions which we can comprehend and estimate, and illustrating its accordance with great general principles, which are exhibited, not only in God's ordinary providence, but specially and emphatically in the scheme of salvation by a Redeemer.

The great difficulty of course is to explain how, consistently with God's attributes and man's responsibility, the human race could come to be placed in a condition of sin and misery, without any apparent adequate ground in justice for their being so treated. And we think it by no means unlikely, that to a man reflecting upon this state of things as an ascertained reality,—even while he knew nothing of the information given as concerning it in Scripture,—the idea might occur, that the best and most satisfactory way of getting to anything like an explanation of it would be, if it could be shown to be of the nature of *a penal infliction upon the human race*,—an evil that had come upon them as a punishment of actual sin committed. There is no great difficulty in believing, that the moral depravity of Adam's own nature was a penal infliction upon him, through the withdrawal of the divine Spirit,—a punishment to which he was justly subjected on account of his first sin; and we cannot but feel, that if this idea of legal responsibility could in any way be introduced, and could in any measure be applied to the human race as a whole in connection with Adam, it would tend somewhat to alleviate or lighten the difficulty attaching to this mysterious and incomprehensible subject. Now, this is precisely what Scripture, according to the views of the defenders of the ordinary Calvinistic doctrine of imputation, does in the matter; this is the very service it renders, by leading us to believe, that God resolved to make the trial or probation of Adam the trial or probation of the human race,—that the covenant which He made with Adam comprehended all his posterity,—and that it laid a foundation for a legal or federal oneness or identity between him and them. The doctrine that Adam was the federal head or representative of his posterity in the covenant, lays a foundation for the imputation,—the immediate and antecedent imputation,—to them of the guilt or *reatus* of his first sin; and this imputation furnishes a ground for dealing with them as if they had committed that sin themselves, and thus involving them in the penal results which Adam brought upon himself by his own sin. There are thus interposed several steps between the actual moral character and condition of mankind and the mere sovereign purpose and agency of God; and these steps interposed, while they do not solve the difficulty, do not introduce into it any additional darkness or perplexity. On the contrary, being in accordance with analogies furnished by God's ordinary providence and by human jurisprudence,—as well as by the arrangements of the scheme of redemption,—they tend somewhat to relieve and satisfy the mind in the contemplation of this great mystery.

There are many persons,—and Mr Rogers is evidently one of them,—who have a strong prejudice against this doctrine of the imputation of the guilt or *reatus* of Adam's first sin to his posterity, as if it brought in some new and additional difficulties into the investigation of this subject,—as if it were the most mysterious and incomprehensible dogma of ultra-Calvinism, one which all moderate and reasonable Calvinists must repudiate. But if the considerations we have hinted at were duly weighed, this unfounded prejudice might possibly be removed; and it might be expected, that all men who admit the total depravity of human nature as an actual feature of man's condition, of which they can give us no account or explanation whatever, would be more likely to yield to the weight of the evidence,—quite sufficient, we think, though not overwhelming,—which Scripture furnishes in proof of the doctrine, that " the covenant being made with Adam, as a public person, not for himself only, but for his posterity, all mankind, descending from him by ordinary generation, sinned in him, fell with him in his first transgression."

Among the three different classes or sections into which we divided those divines, who,—while admitting the universal depravity of the human race,—declined to admit the orthodox doctrine of imputation, one consisted of those who rejected the ordinary orthodox phraseology, yet so far deferred to the authority of Scripture as to receive, though in a confused and inconsistent way, some part of the doctrine which they professed to reject. This has appeared most prominently and palpably among the New England Congregationalists and some of the New School Presbyterians in the United States; though there have been frequent indications of it among men who were fond of deviating from the old beaten paths, and aspired to be thought reasonable, moderate, and liberal. This is a curious and important feature of the controversy, and furnishes some interesting materials in confirmation of the old orthodox faith. An admirable specimen of what can be done in this department will be found in a crushing exposure, by Dr Hodge, of Princeton, of the inconsistency and confusion exhibited by Professor Moses Stuart, of Andover, in his commentary upon the Epistle to the Romans.*

We have dwelt so long upon these two subjects, that we must be very brief upon the remaining two; and, indeed, must confine ourselves to a mere statement as to what Calvin's sentiments upon

---

* Hodge's *Essays and Reviews*, p. 49.

On this subject of imputation, as well as on the former one of the controversy between the Supralapsarians and the Sublapsarians, the best exposition of the whole matter, and the best defence of the generally received orthodox doctrine, in a compendious form, and in books easily accessible, will be found in Turretine and De Moor. Turretine, Loc. ix. and Qu. ix., and De Moor, c. xv. s. 32, tom. iii. pp. 260–287. De Moor, as usual, gives numerous references to authorities. He gives also a very choice and valuable collection of extracts from standard divines in exposition and defence of the orthodox doctrine. There is a great deal of important matter, both argumentative and historical, on various departments of this controversy, in a very valuable series of articles on original sin and the doctrine of imputation contained in the first series of the " Princeton Essays." Almost every thing that can be said in defence of mediate and consequent imputation and in opposition to imputation, in the only fair and legitimate sense of it as generally held by Calvinistic divines, will be found in Placæus's treatise already referred to.

these two topics really were, without digressing into the more general history of the controversies concerning them.

III. It has been contended very frequently, and very confidently, that Calvin did not sanction the views which have been generally held by Calvinistic divines, in regard to the extent of the atonement,—that he did not believe in the doctrine of particular redemption, that is, that Christ did not die for all men, but only for the elect, for those who are actually saved,—but that, on the contrary, he asserted a universal, unlimited, or indefinite atonement. Amyraut, in defending his doctrine of universal atonement in combination with Calvinistic views upon other points, appealed confidently to the authority of Calvin; and, indeed, he wrote a treatise entitled, " Eschantillon de la Doctrine de Calvin touchant la Prædestination," chiefly for the purpose of showing that Calvin supported his views about the extent of the atonement, and was in all respects a very moderate Calvinist. Daillee, in his "'Apologia pro duabus Synodis," which is a very elaborate defence, in reply to Spanheim, of Amyraut's views about universal grace and universal atonement, fills above forty pages with extracts from Calvin as testimonies in his favour. Indeed, the whole of the last portion of this work of Daillee, consisting of nearly five hundred pages, is occupied with extracts, produced as testimonies in favour of universal grace and universal atonement, from almost every eminent writer, from Clemens Romanus down to the middle of the seventeenth century; and we doubt if the whole history of theological controversy furnishes a stronger case of the adduction of irrelevant and inconclusive materials. It was chiefly the survey of this vast collection of testimonies, that suggested to us the observations which we have laid before our readers in our discussion of the views of Melancthon.*

It is certain that Beza held the doctrine of particular redemption, or of a limited atonement, as it has since been held by most Calvinists, and brought it out fully in his controversies with the Lutherans on the subject of predestination; though he was not, as has sometimes been asserted, the first who maintained it. It has been confidently alleged that Calvin did not concur in this view, but held the opposite doctrine of universal redemption and

---

* *Supra*, p. 205.

unlimited atonement. Now it is true, that we do not find in Calvin's writings explicit statements as to any limitation in the object of the atonement, or in the number of those for whom Christ died; and no Calvinist, not even Dr Twisse, the great champion of high Supralapsarianism, has ever denied that there is a sense in which it may be affirmed that Christ died for all men. But we think it is likewise true, that no sufficient evidence has been produced that Calvin believed in a universal or unlimited atonement. Of all the passages in Calvin's writings, bearing more or less directly upon this subject,—which we remember to have read or have seen produced on either side,—there is only one which, with anything like confidence, can be regarded as formally and explicitly denying an unlimited atonement; and notwithstanding all the pains that have been taken to bring out the views of Calvin upon this question, we do not recollect to have seen it adverted to except by a single popish writer. It occurs in his treatise "De vera participatione Christi in cœna," in reply to Heshusius, a violent Lutheran defender of the corporal presence of Christ in the eucharist. The passage is this:—"Scire velim quomodo Christi carnem edant impii pro quibus non est crucifixa, et quomodo sanguinem bibant qui expiandis eorum peccatis non est effusus."* This is a very explicit denial of the universality of the atonement. But it stands alone,—so far as we know,—in Calvin's writings, and for this reason we do not found much upon it; though, at the same time, we must observe, that it is not easy to understand how, if Calvin really believed in a universal atonement for the human race, such a statement could ever have dropped from him. We admit, however, that he has not usually given any distinct indication, that he believed in any limitation as to the objects of the atonement; and that upon a survey of all that has been produced from his writings, there is fair ground for a difference of opinion as to what his doctrine upon this point really was. The truth is, that no satisfactory evidence has been or can be derived from his writings, that the precise question upon the extent of the atonement which has been mooted in more modern times, *in the only sense in which it can become a question among men who concur in holding the doctrine of unconditional personal election to everlasting life,* ever exercised Calvin's mind, or was made by him

---

* Tractatus Theologici. Opera, tom. p. 731.

the subject of any formal or explicit deliverance. The topic was not then formally discussed as a distinct subject of controversy; and Calvin does not seem to have been ever led, in discussing cognate questions, to take up this one and to give a deliverance regarding it. We believe that no sufficient evidence has been brought forward that Calvin held that Christ died for all men, or for the whole world, in any such sense as to warrant Calvinistic universalists,—that is, men who, though holding Calvinistic doctrines upon other points, yet believe in a universal or unlimited atonement,—in asserting that he sanctioned their peculiar principles.

It is true that Calvin has intimated more than once his conviction, that the position laid down by some of the schoolmen, viz., that Christ died " sufficienter pro omnibus, efficaciter pro electis," is sound and orthodox in some sense. But then he has never, so far as we remember or have seen proved, explained precisely in what sense he held it, and there is a sense in which the advocates of particular redemption can consistently admit and adopt it.* It is true also, that Calvin has often declared, that the offers and invitations of the gospel are addressed by God, and should be addressed by us, indiscriminately to all men, without distinction or exception; and that the principal and proximate cause why men to whom the gospel is preached finally perish, is their own sin and unbelief in putting away from them the word of life. But these are principles which the advocates of particular redemption believe to be true, and to be vitally important; and which they never hesitate to apply and to act upon. It is quite fair to attempt to deduce an argument in favour of the doctrine of a universal atonement, from the alleged impossibility of reconciling the doctrine of an atonement, limited as to its objects or destination in God's purpose or intention, with the universal or unlimited offers and invitations of the gospel, or with the ascription of men's final

---

* When the subject of the extent of the atonement came to be more fully and exactly discussed, orthodox Calvinists generally objected to adopt this scholastic position, on the ground that it seemed to imply an ascription to Christ of a *purpose or intention* of dying in some sense for all men. For this reason they usually declined to adopt it as it stood, or they proposed to alter it into this form,—Christ's death was sufficient for all, efficacious for the elect. By this change in the position, the question was made to turn, not on what Christ did, but on what His death was; and thus the appearance of ascribing to Him personally a purpose or intention of dying, in some sense, for all men, was removed.

condemnation to their own sin and unbelief. But as the generality
of the advocates of a limited atonement deny that the inconsistency of these two things, or the impossibility of reconciling them,
can be proved, and profess to hold both, it is quite unwarrantable
to infer, in regard to any particular individual, that because he
held the one, he must be presumed to have rejected the other.
And there is certainly nothing in Calvin's general character and
principles, or in any thing he has written, which affords ground
for the conclusion, that the alleged impossibility of reconciling
these two things, would,—had he been led to investigate the matter
formally,—have perplexed him much, or have tempted him to
embrace the doctrine of universal atonement, which is certainly
somewhat alien, to say the least, in its general spirit and complexion, to the leading features of his theological system. And
this consideration is entitled to the more weight for this reason,
that this difficulty is not greater than some others with which he
did grapple, and which he disposed of in a different and more
scriptural way,—or rather, is just the very same difficulty, put in a
different form, and placed in a somewhat different position.

There is not, then, we are persuaded, satisfactory evidence that
Calvin held the doctrine of a universal, unlimited, or indefinite
atonement. And, moreover, we consider ourselves warranted in
asserting, that there is sufficient evidence that he did *not* hold this
doctrine; though on the grounds formerly explained, and with
the one exception already adverted to, it is not evidence which
bears directly and immediately upon this precise point. The
evidence of this position is derived chiefly from the two following
considerations.

1st. Calvin consistently, unhesitatingly, and explicitly denied
the doctrine of God's universal grace and love to all men,—that is,
omnibus et singulis, to each and every man,—as implying in some
sense a desire or purpose or intention to save them all; and with
this universal grace or love to all men the doctrine of a universal
or unlimited atonement, in the nature of the case, and in the
convictions and admissions of all its supporters, stands inseparably
connected. That Calvin denied the doctrine of God's universal
grace or love to all men, as implying some desire or intention
of saving them all, and some provision directed to that object, is
too evident to any one who has read his writings, to admit of
doubt or to require proof. We are not aware that the doctrine

of a universal atonement ever has been maintained, even by men
who were in other respects Calvinistic, except in conjunction and
in connection with an assertion of God's universal grace or love to
all men. And it is manifestly impossible that it should be otherwise. If Christ died for all men,—*pro omnibus et singulis,*—this
must have been in some sense an expression or indication of a
desire or intention on the part of God, and of a provision made
by Him, directed to the object of saving them all, though frustrated
in its effect, by their refusal to embrace the provision made for
and offered to them. A universal atonement, or the death of
Christ for all men,—that is, for each and every man,—necessarily
implies this, and would be an anomaly in the divine government
without it. No doubt, it may be said, that the doctrine of a universal atonement necessitates, in logical consistency, a denial of the
Calvinistic doctrine of election, as much as it necessitates an
admission of God's universal grace or love to all men ; and we
believe this to be true. But still, when we find that, in point of
fact, none has ever held the doctrine of universal atonement without holding also the doctrine of universal grace,—while it is
certain that some men of distinguished ability and learning, such
as Amyraut and Daillee, Davenant and Baxter, have held both
these doctrines of universal atonement and universal grace, and
at the same time have held the Calvinistic doctrine of election ;
we are surely called upon in fairness and modesty to admit, that
the logical connection cannot be quite so direct and certain in the
one case as in the other. And then this conclusion warrants us
in maintaining, that the fact of Calvin so explicitly denying the
doctrine of God's universal grace or love to all men, affords a more
direct and certain ground for the inference, that he did not hold
the doctrine of universal atonement, than could be legitimately
deduced from the mere fact, that he held the doctrine of unconditional personal election to everlasting life. The invalidity of the
inferential process in the one case is not sufficient to establish its
invalidity in the other ; and therefore our argument holds good.

2d. The other consideration to which we referred, as affording
some positive evidence, though not direct and explicit, that Calvin
did not hold the doctrine of a universal atonement, is this,—that
he has interpreted some of the principal texts on which the advocates of that doctrine rest it, in such a way as to deprive them of
all capacity of serving the purpose to which its supporters commonly

apply them. If this position can be established, it will furnish
something more than a presumption, and will almost amount to a
proof, that he did not hold the doctrine in question. As this point
is curious and interesting, we may adduce an instance or two in
support of our allegation. In commenting upon 1 Tim. ii. 4,
" Who will have all men to be saved, and to come to the knowledge
of the truth," Calvin says:—"Apostolus *simpliciter* intelligit nullum
mundi vel populum vel ordinem a salute excludi, quia omnibus sine
exceptione evangelium proponi Deus velit. Est autem evangelii
prædicatio vivifica, merito itaque colligit Deum omnes pariter
salutis participatione dignare. At de hominum generibus, non
singulis personis, sermo est; nihil enim aliud intendit quam prin-
cipes et extraneos populos in hoc numero includere." Again, in
commenting upon 1 John ii 2, " And He is the propitiation for our
sins, and not for ours only, but for the sins of the whole world,"
he says :—" Qui hanc absurditatem (universal salvation) volebant
effugere, dixerunt sufficientur pro toto mundo passum esse Christum, sed pro electis tantum efficaciter. Vulgo hæc solutio in
scholis obtinuit. Ego quanquam verum esse illud dictum fateor,
nego tamen præsenti loco quadrare. Neque enim aliud fuit consilium Joannis quam toti ecclesiæ commune facere hoc bonum.
Ergo sub *omnibus* reprobos non comprehendit, sed eos designat qui
simul credituri erant, et qui per varias mundi plagas dispersi erant."
He gives the very same explanation of these two passages in his
treatise on " Predestination."[*] Now this is in substance just the
interpretation commonly given of these and similar texts, by the
advocates of the doctrine of particular redemption; and it seems
scarcely possible, that it should have been adopted by one who did
not hold that doctrine, or who believed in the truth of the opposite
one.

Let it be observed, that our object is not to show, that we are
warranted in adducing the authority of the great name of Calvin
as a positive testimony in favour of the doctrine of particular redemption,—of a limited atonement,—as it has been generally held
by Calvinistic divines; but rather to show, that there is no adequate
ground for adducing him, as has been done so frequently and so
confidently, on the other side. To adduce Calvin as maintaining
the doctrine of particular redemption, could scarcely, upon a full

---

* Niemeyer, pp. 259 and 286.

and impartial survey of the whole circumstances of the case, be regarded as warrantable. It is evident that he had never been led to examine this precise question, in the form which it afterwards assumed in controversial discussion, and to give an explicit deliverance upon it. He seems to have attached little or no importance to any definite doctrine about the extent of the atonement. In his "Antidote" to the earlier sessions of the Council of Trent, he passes by without comment or animadversion the fourth chapter of the sixth session, although it contains an explicit declaration that Christ died for all men; and he does this not tacitly, as if *per incuriam*, but with the explicit statement,—"tertium et quartum caput non attingo,"—as if he found nothing there to object to. He was in no way sensitive or cautious about using language, concerning the universality of the offers and invitations, or,—in the phraseology which then generally prevailed, the promises of the gospel,—and concerning the provisions and arrangements of the scheme of redemption, which might have the appearance of being inconsistent with any limitation in the objects or destination of the atonement. And it is chiefly because the great body of those who have been called after his name,—even those of them who have held the doctrine of a definite or limited atonement, —have followed his example in this respect, believing it to have the full sanction of Scripture, that Daillee and others have got up such a mass of testimonies from their writings, in which they seem to give some countenance to the tenet of universal redemption, even at the expense of consistency. But this is no reason why Calvinists should hesitate to follow the course, which Scripture so plainly sanctions and requires, of proclaiming the glad tidings of salvation to all men indiscriminately, without any distinction or exception, setting forth, without hesitation or qualification, the fulness and freeness of the gospel offers and invitations,—of inviting, encouraging, and requiring every descendant of Adam with whom they come into contact, to come to Christ and lay hold of Him, with the assurance that those who come to Him He will in no wise reject. The doctrine of particular redemption,—or of an atonement limited, not as to its sufficiency, but as to its object, purpose, or destination,—does not, either in reality or in appearance, throw any greater obstacle in the way of preaching the gospel to every creature, than the doctrines which all Calvinists hold, of the absolute unconditional election of some men to eternal life, and of

the indispensable necessity and determining influence of the special agency of the Holy Spirit in producing faith and conversion.
The difficulty of this whole subject lies in a department which
belongs to God's province, and not to ours.   He has imposed upon
us the duty of making Christ known to our fellow-men, not only
as able, but as willing and ready, to save unto the uttermost all
that come unto God by Him; and this duty we are bound by
the most solemn obligations to discharge, without let or hindrance,
without doubt or hesitation; assured that God, while exercising His
own sovereignty in dealing with His creatures, will, in His own
time and way, fully vindicate the consistency and the honour of
all that He has done Himself, and of all that He has required us
to do in His name.

IV. The only other topic to which we referred,—as one in regard to which it has been made matter of discussion what Calvin's
views were, and whether he did not come short of the accuracy
and precision exhibited by Beza, and the generality of later Calvinists,—is the doctrine of justification.   Some Arminians have
gone so far as to allege, that Calvin held their fundamental distinguishing principle upon this subject,—that, viz., of the imputation of faith as a substitute for, or in the room and stead of, a
perfect personal righteousness, as the ground of a sinner's forgiveness; in distinction from, and in opposition to, the doctrine
of the imputation of Christ's righteousness through the instrumentality of faith.   But no evidence has been produced from his
writings in support of this allegation, sufficient to entitle it to
examination.   It has also, however, been alleged, and with much
greater plausibility, that he held justification to consist solely in
pardon or remission of sin, without including in it, as the generality of Calvinists have done, the distinct additional idea of the
acceptance of men as righteous; and that, as a natural consequence, he did not admit the distinction, which has also been held
by most of his followers,—between the passive righteousness of
Christ, or His vicarious sufferings, as more immediately the ground
of our pardon,—and His active righteousness, or perfect obedience
to the law, as more immediately the ground of our acceptance and
title to heaven.   With respect to the first of these points,—viz., his
making justification to consist solely in pardon or remission,—it is
undeniable, that he has repeatedly made statements in which this

is asserted *in terminis*. But the meaning and bearing of these
statements have been somewhat misconceived, from not attending
to the leading object which he had in view in making them, and
to the import of the tenet against which he was arguing. His
chief object in laying down this position, was to deny and exclude
the popish doctrine of justification, which makes it comprehend
not only remission, but also regeneration. And the sum and substance of what he meant to inculcate, in laying down the position
that justification consisted only in remission, was just this, that it
did *not* comprehend, as the papists maintained, a change of character, but merely a change of state in relation to God and to His
law. That he did not mean to deny, and that he really believed,
that justification included acceptance as a distinct element from
forgiveness,—separable from it in thought, though always united
with it in fact,—and that he based the one as well as the other
solely upon the righteousness of Christ imputed through faith, can
be clearly established from his writings. Indeed, this may be said
to be put beyond all doubt, by the following very explicit commentary upon the apostle's statement,* that "Christ is made unto us
righteousness," or justification, "quo intelligit (apostolus) nos ejus
nomine acceptos esse Deo, quia morte sua peccata nostra expiaverit,
et ejus obedientia nobis in justitiam imputetur. Nam quum fidei
justitia in peccatorum remissione et gratuita acceptione consistat,
utrumque per Christum consequimur." This statement is far too
precise and explicit to admit of being explained away, and it is
quite conclusive as to what were Calvin's views upon the point now
under consideration.

It may be worth while to advert to another expression which
Calvin sometimes used when treating of this subject,—an expression which confirms the accuracy of the account we have given of
his sentiments, but which in itself is not strictly correct, as was
indeed brought out in the course of the subsequent controversies.
Calvin repeatedly speaks of justification as consisting in the remission of sins and the imputation of Christ's righteousness.
There can be no reasonable doubt that, when he used this form
of expression, he meant by the imputation of Christ's righteousness just acceptance, or positive admission into the enjoyment of
God's favour,—the bestowal of a right or title to eternal life, as
distinguished from and going beyond mere forgiveness. In any

---

* 1 Cor. i. 30.

other sense, and, indeed, in the strict and proper meaning of the
expression, the statement is inaccurate. The imputation of
Christ's righteousness, correctly understood, is to be regarded as,
in the order of nature, preceding *both* remission and acceptance,—
and as being the ground or basis, or the meritorious or impulsive
cause of these *two* results,—that to which God has a respect when
in any instance He pardons and accepts a sinner.

As to the distinction between the passive and the active righteousness of Christ,—the first regarded as more immediately the
ground of our pardon, and the second of our acceptance,—this does
not appear to be formally brought out in the writings of Calvin.
It is to be traced rather to the more minute and subtle speculations,
to which the doctrine of justification was afterwards subjected;
and though the distinction is quite in accordance with the analogy
of faith, and may be of use in aiding the formation of distinct
and definite conceptions,—it is not of any great practical importance, and need not be much pressed or insisted on, if men heartily
and intelligently ascribe their forgiveness and acceptance wholly
to what Christ has done and suffered in their room and stead.
There is no ground in anything Calvin has written for asserting,
that he would have denied or rejected this distinction, if it had
been presented to him. But it was perhaps more in accordance
with the cautious and reverential spirit in which he usually conducted his investigations into divine things, to abstain from any
minute and definite statements regarding it. Much prominence
came to be given to these distinctions between forgiveness and
acceptance, and between Christ's passive and active righteousness,
in the Lutheran church; and it is interesting to notice, that down
till about the middle of last century,—when everything like sound
doctrine and true religion were swept away by the prevalence of
rationalism,—not only these distinctions, but the whole of the scriptural doctrine on the subject of justification, were strenuously
maintained by the Lutheran theologians. Very few Calvinistic
divines have rejected the distinction between forgiveness and acceptance, though many have been disposed to pass over or omit
the distinction between Christ's passive and active righteousness.
The most eminent Calvinistic divines, who have maintained that
justification consists only in remission of sins,—thus denying or
ignoring the generally received distinction between forgiveness
and acceptance, and rejecting the imputation of Christ's' active

righteousness,—were Piscator and Wendelinus, who both belonged to the German Reformed Church, the former of whom flourished near the beginning, and the latter about the middle, of the seventeenth century. The general reasonings on which these men based their peculiar views, are of no force, except upon the assumption of principles which would overturn altogether the Scripture doctrines of substitution and imputation. The question resolves into this,—Whether we have sufficient evidence in Scripture for these distinctions? And in the discussion of this question it has, we, think, been shown that the scriptural evidence is sufficient; and that those who deny this, demand an amount of evidence, both in point of quantity and of directness and explicitness, which is unreasonable.

But many eminent divines have been of opinion that the controversies which have been carried on upon this subject, have led some of the defenders of the truth to press these distinctions,— especially that between Christ's passive and active righteousness,— beyond what Scripture warrants, and in a way that is scarcely in keeping with the general scope and spirit of its statements. There is no trace of this excess, however, in the admirably cautious and accurate declarations upon this subject in the Westminster Confession; where, while pardon and acceptance are expressly distinguished as separate elements in the justification of a sinner, they are both ascribed, equally and alike, to the obedience and death of Christ, without any specification of the distinct places or functions which His passive and active righteousness hold in the matter.

" Those whom God effectually calleth He also freely justifieth ; not by infusing righteousness into them, but by pardoning their sins, and by accounting and accepting their persons as righteous ; not for anything wrought in them, or done by them, but for Christ's sake alone ; not by imputing faith itself, the act of believing, or any other evangelical obedience to them as their righteousness, but by imputing the obedience and satisfaction of Christ unto them, they receiving and resting on Him and His righteousness by faith, which faith they have not of themselves, it is the gift of God."*

This statement contains a beautifully precise and exact repudiation of popish and Arminian errors, and assertion of the opposite truths, upon the subject of justification; but it wisely abstains from giving any deliverance, directly or by implication, upon those more minute points which are less clearly indicated in Scripture,

---

* C. xi. s. 1.

and have been made subjects of controversial discussion among
Calvinists. The same wisdom and caution are exhibited in dealing with this topic in the corresponding portions of the catechisms.
In the Larger Catechism, pardon and acceptance are both based,
equally and alike, upon " the perfect obedience and full satisfaction of Christ;" and in the Shorter Catechism, while they are
still distinguished from each other, they are both declared to be
based upon " the righteousness of Christ, imputed to us and received by faith alone." The danger of yielding to any excess, or
undue minuteness, of exposition upon this subject, and at the same
time the necessity and importance of maintaining the whole truth
regarding it, as sanctioned by Scripture, are very clearly and judiciously enforced by Turretine, with his usual masterly ability.*

The general subject which we have been surveying might
suggest some reflections fitted to be useful in the study of theology
and of theological literature, bearing especially upon the two
topics—of the use and application of testimonies from eminent
writers as authorities upon controverted questions,—and the value
and importance of definite and precise statements in the exposition
of the doctrines of Christian theology.

In almost all theological controversies, much space has been
occupied by the discussion of extracts from books and documents,
adduced as authorities in support of the opinions maintained; and
there is certainly no department of theological literature in which
so much ability and learning, so much time and strength, have
been uselessly wasted, or in which so much of controversial unfairness has been exhibited. Controversialists in general have
shown an intense and irresistible desire to prove, that their peculiar opinions were supported by the fathers, or by the Reformers,
or by the great divines of their own church; and have often
exhibited a great want both of wisdom and of candour in the
efforts they have made to effect this object. It is indeed very
important to ascertain, as far as possible, the doctrinal views which
have prevailed in every country where theology has been studied,
and in each successive generation since the canon of Scripture
was completed. And it is a gratifying feature in the condition of
the church, that so much attention has been given in modern
times,—especially on the Continent,—to the full and scientific

---

* Loc. xiv. Q. xiii. s. 11, 12.

treatment of the history of doctrines. The history of opinion can always be turned, by competent persons, to good account in the investigation of truth. It is important also to ascertain fully the views held even by individuals, who have exerted an important influence on their own and subsequent ages,—epoch-making men as they have been called,—such as Origen, Augustine, Abelard, Aquinas, Luther, Calvin, Arminius, and Socinus. Some deference is due to the opinions of men who have brought distinguished gifts and graces to bear on the study of theology. But no deference that may be shown to the opinions of men, should ever be transmuted into submission to authority, properly so called; as if it ever could be of essential importance, or of determining influence, to ascertain what other men believed on matters which are revealed to us in God's word. No document has ever been prepared by uninspired men, which did not exhibit some traces of human imperfection,—not indeed always in actual positive error, yet in something about it defective or exaggerated, disproportionate or unsuitable,—exhibited either in the document itself, or in its relation to the purpose it was intended to serve. There is no man who has written much upon important and difficult subjects, and has not fallen occasionally into error, confusion, obscurity, and inconsistency; and there is certainly no body of men that have ever been appealed to as authorities, in whose writings a larger measure of these qualities is to be found than in those of the Fathers of the Christian church. We have never read anything more wearisome and useless than the discussions which have been carried on between Romanists and Protestants, especially divines of the Church of England, concerning the opinions of the Fathers of the early ages. Never have ability and learning been more thoroughly wasted, than in those endless debates, in which so much pains have been taken, to bring out the meaning of passages in the Fathers, which really have no meaning, or no meaning that can be ascertained,—which in many cases their authors, if they could be called up and examined, would be unable to explain intelligibly; and to harmonise the confusion and reconcile the inconsistencies which abound in their works. It was right and important indeed to show conclusively and once for all, that the Romanists are not warranted to appeal to the early church, in support of their leading peculiar opinions; and the conclusive evidence which has been produced in proof of this position, it may be necessary occasionally to refer to. But beyond this, elaborate discussions of the meaning of particular passages in the Fathers, should in general be now regarded as nothing better than learned lumber. Occasions indeed do sometimes occur in theological literature where something of this kind may be called for. And we think that there was a *dignus vindice nodus*, and that an important service was rendered to the cause of truth, when Dr Goode, the Dean of Ripon, undertook and endured the *labor improbus* of proving—as he has done unanswerably, in his "Divine Rule of Faith and Practice,"—that the Tractarian appeal to the authority of the Fathers and also of the great Anglican divines, was characterised by the same incompetency and unfairness which have usually marked the conduct of Romish controversialists. *

In adducing extracts from eminent writers in support of their opinions, controversialists usually overlook or forget the obvious consideration, that it is only the mature and deliberate conviction of a competent judge upon the precise point under consideration, that should be held as entitled to any deference. When men have never, or scarcely ever, had present to their thoughts the precise question that may have afterwards become matter of dispute,—when they have never deliberately examined it, or given a formal and explicit deliverance regarding it,—it will usually follow, 1st, That it is difficult if not impossible to ascertain what they thought about it,—to collect this from incidental statements, or mere allusions, dropped when they were treating of other topics; and, 2d, That their opinion about it, if it could be ascertained, would be of no weight or value. A large portion of the materials which have been collected by controversialists as testimonies in favour of their opinions from eminent writers, is at once swept away as useless and irrelevant, by the application of this principle. The truth of this principle is so obvious, that it has passed into a sort of proverb,—" auctoris aliud agentis parva est auctoritas." And yet controversialists in general have continued habitually to disregard it, and to waste their time in trying to bring the authority of

---

* It is but right, however, to remember that unfairness in this matter, has been sometimes exhibited also by the friends of truth. It is a very humbling and mortifying exposure which has been made by Mr Isaac Taylor, in the Supplement to his Ancient Christianity, of inaccuracy in dealing with quotations from the fathers, exhibited in the authorised Homilies of the Church of England.

eminent writers to bear upon questions which they had never examined; and have not scrupled, in many cases, to have recourse to garbling and mutilation, in order either to silence testimonies or to make them speak more plainly. The opinion even of Calvin, upon a point which he had never carefully examined, and on which he has given no formal deliverance, is of no weight or value, and would scarcely be worth examining; were it not that so much has been written upon this subject, and that his views upon many points have been, and still are, so much misrepresented.

In dealing with authorities, then, it is necessary to ascertain, whether the authors referred to and quoted have really formed and expressed an opinion upon the point, in regard to which their testimony is adduced. It is necessary further to collect together, and to examine carefully and deliberately, the whole of what they have written upon the subject under consideration, that we may understand fully and accurately what their whole mind regarding it really was, instead of trying to educe it from a hasty glance at partial and incidental statements. And in order to conduct this process of estimating and applying testimonies in a satisfactory and successful way, it is also necessary, that we be familiar with the whole import and bearing of the discussion on both sides, as it was present to the mind of the author whose statements we are investigating. Without this knowledge, we shall be very apt to misapprehend the true meaning and significance of what he has said, and to make it the ground of unwarranted and erroneous inferences. We have seen how necessary it is in order to understand and construe aright Calvin's statements about imputation and justification, to know in what way these subjects were discussed at the time among Romanists as well as among Protestants; and many other illustrations of the necessity of a thorough acquaintance with the whole question in all its aspects, and of the errors arising from the want of it, might easily be adduced from this department of theological controversy. To manage aright this matter of the adduction and application of testimonies or authorities requires an extent of knowledge, a patience and caution in comparing and estimating materials, and an amount of candour and tact, which few controversialists possess, and in which many of them are deplorably deficient. This is not indeed a department of investigation which can be regarded as possessed of any great intrinsic importance, with a view to the establishment of truth. But it has always occupied, and it is likely to continue to occupy, a prominent place in theological literature, and it is therefore of some consequence that it should be conducted judiciously, accurately, and honourably.

Much more important than this subject of authorities and testimonies, is the other topic suggested by the survey in which we have been engaged, viz., the increasing fulness, exactness, and precision of deliverances on doctrinal matters, as the result of controversial discussion. The great lessons suggested by the investigation in which we have been engaged, and suggested, indeed, by the whole history of the discussion of all such questions, are, 1st, The obligation to improve the controversies which have sprung up in the church, for aiding in the formation of clear and accurate, precise and definite, opinions upon all topics of doctrinal theology, up to the full extent which Scripture, correctly interpreted and reasonably and judiciously applied, may be fairly held to sanction; 2d, The danger and mischief of laying down explicit deliverances, and indulging in elaborate controversies, about minuter matters which are not revealed to us, and which Scripture really furnishes no materials for determining; and, 3d, The necessity of great caution and much wisdom in introducing into symbolical books, and thereby imposing, as articles of faith or terms of communion, even true positions of a minute and definite description; which may possess no great intrinsic importance as connected with the development of the scheme of salvation, or which may derive their importance from temporary or local discussions. These, of course, are just truisms admitted by every one. Everything depends upon the right application of them to particular cases and topics, and this requires thorough and comprehensive knowledge, great soundness and discrimination of intellect, and much careful and deliberate investigation,—qualities which are very rare, and which especially are very seldom found in combination with each other.

In regard to each of these three positions, there are temptations and dangers on both sides,—great risks both of defect and of excess; and one chief means fitted, with the divine blessing, to guard against error in these matters, both on the right hand and on the left, is a comprehensive survey of the history of past discussions, and a sincere and impartial determination to turn it to the best account, with a view to the ascertaining of truth and the determining of the church's duty. It is an imperative obligation, attaching to every man, according to his means and opportunities, to acquire as accurate and complete a knowledge of the contents of divine revelation as he can. And next to the diligent and prayerful study of the word of God itself, in the unwearied and impartial application of all legitimate apparatus and auxiliaries, a comprehensive and discriminating investigation of past discussions, conducted by competent parties, affords the best means of discharging this duty and securing this result. Wherever men of ability, learning, and integrity, have brought their minds to bear upon the investigation of divine truth,—and especially when, by the collision of men of this stamp, the sifting analytic process of controversial discussions has been brought to bear upon the subjects examined,—materials are provided, which, by men who have not themselves been involved in the controversies, may be turned to the best account, in forming an accurate estimate, first, of the truth, and then, secondly and separately, of the importance, of the points involved. Men are bound to improve, to the uttermost, all their opportunities of acquiring the most clear, accurate, and exact knowledge of all the truths revealed in the sacred Scriptures ; and some men, in seeking to discharge this duty, have been honoured by the Head of the church to contribute largely to diffuse among their fellow-men more correct, definite, and comprehensive views of Christian doctrine than had prevailed before, and to show that these views were indeed sanctioned by the word of God.

The men who have been most highly honoured in this important department of work, were Augustine in the fifth century,—the Reformers of the sixteenth century, and especially Calvin, the greatest of them all,—and, lastly, the great Calvinistic systematic divines of the seventeenth century. The works of this last class of writers—such men as Francis Turretine, John Henry Heidegger, Herman Witsius, and Peter Van Mastricht—are based wholly upon the theology of the Reformation; but they carry it out to its completion, and may be said to form the crown and the copestone of theological science, viewed as an accurate, comprehensive, and systematic exposition and defence of the doctrines revealed in the word of God. We believe that these men have given an exposition of the doctrines which are made known to us in the sacred Scriptures, and which all men are bound to understand and believe, because God has revealed them, such as in point of clearness and fulness, accuracy and comprehensiveness, was never before equalled, and has never since been surpassed. In the writings of these men, and of others of the same class and period, we find, that almost every discussion raised for the last century and a half about the substance of theology—that is, about the doctrines actually taught in Scripture concerning all matters of universal and permanent importance, concerning God and man, Christ and the way of salvation, the church and the sacraments— is dealt with and disposed of,—is practically exhausted and conclusively determined. But it does not, by any means, follow from this, that the precise and definite statements, on doctrinal subjects, which the writings of these men present—although true in themselves and warranted by Scripture, as in general we believe them to be—should be embodied in symbolical books, and be thereby made terms of communion with a view to ordination to the ministry, and grounds of separation among churches. The duty of a church in settling her symbols, or arranging her terms of communion, is to be regulated by different principles from those which determine the duty of individuals, who are simply bound to acquire and to profess as much of accurate and distinct knowledge of truth as they can attain to, on all matters, whether important or not. When a church is arranging her terms of communion, other considerations, in addition to that of the mere truth of the statements, must be brought to bear upon the question, of what it is right, necessary, and expedient to do, or of what amount of unity in matters of opinion ought to be required. The principles applicable to this branch of the church's duty, have never been subjected to a thorough discussion by competent parties, though they are very important in their bearings ; and the right application of them is attended with great difficulty. Calvin would probably have made a difficulty about adopting precise and definite deliverances on some points, concerning the truth of which the great Calvinistic divines of the seventeenth century had no hesitation. But it will probably be admitted that he was qualified for the office of a minister in a Calvinistic church, even in this advanced nineteenth century.

The great general objects to be aimed at in this matter, though the application is, of course, the difficulty, are embodied in the famous maxim, which Witsius adopted as his favourite motto—" In necessariis unitas, in non necessariis libertas, in omnibus caritas."

CALVINISM AND ARMINIANISM.*

It has often been alleged that Calvinists are very pugnacious,— ever ready to fight in defence of their peculiar opinions. But a survey of the theological literature of this country for the last half century, gives no countenance to this impression. Much more has been published in defence of Arminianism than of Calvinism. Calvinists have scarcely shown the zeal and activity that might have been reasonably expected of them, either in repelling attacks that were made upon them, or in improving advantages that were placed within their reach. In the early part of the century, indeed, the "Refutation of Calvinism," by Bishop Tomline, was thoroughly refuted by Scott, the commentator, in his "Remarks" upon it, and by Dr Edward Williams, in his "Defence of Modern Calvinism." But since that time, Cople-

---

* *British and Foreign Evangelical Review.* July, 1858.

Essays on some of the Difficulties in the Writings of the Apostle Paul, and in other parts of the New Testament. Essay iii.—On Election. By RICHARD WHATELY, D.D., Archbishop of Dublin. Seventh Edition, enlarged. London, 1854.

The Primitive Doctrine of Election; or, An Historical Inquiry into the Ideality and Causation of Scriptural Election, as received and maintained in the Primitive Church of Christ. By GEORGE STANLEY FABER, B.D., Master of Sherburn Hospital and Canon of Salisbury. Second Edition. London, 1842.

A Treatise on the Augustinian Doctrine of Predestination. By J. B. MOZLEY, B.D., Fellow of Magdalen College, Oxford. London, 1855.

The Absence of Precision in the Formularies of the Church of England, Scriptural and suitable to a state of Probation. Bampton Lectures for 1855. By JOHN ERNEST BODE, M.A., Rector of Westwell.

An Exposition of the Thirty-nine Articles, Historial and Doctrinal. By E. HAROLD BROWNE, B.D., Norrisian Professor of Divinity in the University of Cambridge, and Canon of Exeter. Fourth Edition. London, 1858.

ston, Whately, Stanley Faber, and Richard Watson—men of deservedly high reputation—have all written against Calvinism, and some of them very elaborately, while no answer to any of them has been produced by its defenders. Whately and Richard Watson—the first from his sagacity and candour, exercised both upon matters of abstract reasoning and of philological investigation, and the second from the general soundness of his views upon original sin and regeneration, so different from the Pelagianism of the school of Whitby and Tomline—have made concessions, and thereby have afforded advantages, to Calvinists, of which they have hitherto failed, so far as we have noticed, to make any public use. The concessions of Watson are nothing but what every one who holds scriptural views of the moral state of human nature, and of the work of the Holy Spirit in changing it, must make; and such accordingly as have been made by all the more evangelical and antipelagian Arminians from Arminus downwards. But his attack upon Calvinism—forming the concluding portion of the second part of his "Theological Institutes," and published also in a small volume separately, as well as in the collected edition of his works,—is both from its great ability, and from the large amount of scriptural antipelagian truth which it embodies, deserving of special attention. It has been thirty years before the world, and it has not, so far as we know, been answered.

Dr Whately, Archbishop of Dublin, in his Essay upon Election—the third in the volume, entitled, " Essays on some of the Difficulties in the Writings of the Apostle Paul,"—has made some important concessions to Calvinists, both in regard to matters of abstract reasoning and philological exposition, which are eminently creditable to his sagacity and candour, but which they do not seem as yet to have turned to much account. There is really more of interest, and, in a sense, of something like novelty in these concessions of Dr Whately, than in almost anything that has been produced upon the subject of this great controversy in the present day. There is indeed nothing like novelty in the statements themselves to which we now refer. They express views which have been always laid down and insisted on by the defenders of Calvinism. The importance and the novelty are to be found only in the circumstance of their being brought forward by one who is not a Calvinist. Dr Whately, in the essay referred to, has admitted, in substance, that the arguments commonly adduced against the Calvinistic doctrine of election, derived from the moral attributes of God, apply as much to actual results occurring under God's providential government,—in other words, apply equally to the facts of the introduction and permanent existence of moral evil ;—and that the term election, as used in Scripture, relates, in most instances, to " an arbitrary, irrespective, unconditional decree." These are positions which have been always asserted, and have been often conclusively proved, by Calvinists ; but they have not usually been admitted by their opponents. And it may seem, at first sight, difficult to understand how any one could admit them, and yet continue to reject the doctrines of Calvinism.

We once had occasion[*] to refer to these positions of Dr Whately ; and, regarding him as an Arminian, we ventured to apply that designation to him, and to represent these positions as the concessions of an opponent. Dr Whately, it seems, does not believe or admit that he is an Arminian, and took offence at being so designated. In the last edition of the volume above referred to, he adverts to this matter in the following terms :—

"So widely spread are these two schemes of interpretation, that I have known a reviewer, very recently, allude to a certain author as " an Arminian," though he had written and published his dissent from the Arminian theory, and his reasons for it. The reviewer, on having this blunder pointed out, apologised by saying, that he had merely concluded him to be an Arminian, because he was not Calvinist, and he had supposed that every one must be either the one or the other ! It is remarkable that, by a converse error, the very same author had been, some years before, denounced as Calvinistic, on the ground that he was not Arminian."[†]

Dr Whately has acted from misinformation or misapprehension, in saying that the reviewer to whom he refers apologised for the blunder of representing him as an Arminian. The reviewer has never seen that there was any blunder in the matter, and is prepared to assert and to prove that, according to the ordinary acknowledged rules applicable to such questions, Dr Whately may be fairly called an Arminian, whether he perceives and admits that he is so or not; and that it is absurd to pretend, as he does, to be neither a Calvinist nor an Arminian.

---

[*] *North British Review*, vol. xvii. p. 482, Aug. 1852.

[†] Essay iii., On Election, sec. 2, note p. 68, 7th Edit.

There is no doubt a sense in which on this, as well as on most
of the leading questions in Christian theology, there is a three-
fold course open to men.   They may adopt Socinian as well as
Arminian or Calvinistic views on the subject of election, just as
on other great doctrines of the Christian system; but Socinianism
upon this point is not much brought forward nowadays, and was
therefore scarcely worth adverting to in an incidental and popular
allusion to existing differences.   Arminians and Socinians oppose,
with equal strenuousness, and upon substantially the same grounds,
the whole doctrines of Calvinists upon this subject.   They agree
with each other in all the main conclusions they hold in regard to
foreordination and election; so that all parties may really be ranked
under the two heads of Calvinists and anti-Calvinists.   The main
difference here between the Arminians and the Socinians is, that
the former admit, while the latter deny, the divine foreknowledge
of future events.   This is not a difference bearing directly upon
what is actually maintained under the head of predestination;
though it enters into, and has been largely discussed in connection with, the arguments in support of the one and the other side
of that question.   Indeed, some of the bolder and more candid of
the old Socinians acknowledge, that they denied the doctrine of
divine foreknowledge, chiefly because they were unable to see
how, if this were admitted, they could refuse to concede the Calvinistic doctrine of foreordination; while, at the same time, some
of the bolder and more candid of the old Arminians have made it
manifest, that they would gladly have rejected the doctrine of the
divine foreknowledge, if they could have devised any plausible
evasion of the scriptural evidence in support of it.   The admission
or denial of the divine foreknowledge,—though in itself a difference
of very great importance,—thus affects rather the mode of conducting the argument, so far as foreordination is concerned, than the
actual positions maintained by the opposite parties; though it has
often been brought into some of the more popular, but less accurate, forms of stating the point in dispute.   Arminians and
Socinians concur in denying all the leading positions held by
Calvinists on the subject of the divine decrees or purposes,—the
foreordination of all events,—and the absolute election of some
men to eternal life; and, practically, the great question is,—Is
the Calvinistic affirmation or the anti-Calvinistic negation of
these things true?   This being so, it is not strictly correct to

say, that the only antagonistic alternative to the Calvinistic doctrine of predestination is the Arminian one; because the fundamental Calvinistic position is denied equally by Arminians and Socinians; and the real question in dispute may be, and should be, stated in such a way as to omit any reference to the point of difference between the Arminians and the Socinians,—viz., the divine foreknowledge,—and to apply equally and alike to both sections of anti-Calvinists.

But while on this ground it must be admitted, that the antagonistic position to the Calvinistic doctrine is somewhat wider and more comprehensive than the Arminian one, as commonly stated by Arminians themselves; yet the Socinian denial of the divine foreknowledge is now so little brought under our notice, that there was really no call to take it into account in an incidental reference to the subject;—and there is no material inaccuracy in Calvinism and Arminianism being spoken of as the only really antagonistic positions.

It is not upon the ground which has now been adverted to, that Dr Whately objects to being called an Arminian, and tries to throw ridicule upon the idea that a man must be either an Arminian or a Calvinist. He is not a Socinian on this point; for he admits the divine foreknowledge of all events. He denies that he is an Arminian,—he denies that he is a Calvinist; and he denies that a man, though holding the divine foreknowledge of all events, and therefore not a Socinian, must be either a Calvinist or an Arminian on the subject of foreordination. He thus plainly gives us to understand that he holds a doctrine on this subject which is materially and substantially different both from Calvinism and Arminianism,—though he has not suggested any name by which to designate it. Now, we take the liberty of dissenting from all this; and we do not hesitate to affirm that Dr Whately is an Arminian; and further, that every man who has formed an intelligent and definite opinion upon this important controversy, and who repudiates the Socinian denial of the divine foreknowledge, must be either an Arminian or a Calvinist,—or rather must be an Arminian, if he refuses to admit the truth of Calvinism.

It may seem somewhat ungracious to refuse Dr Whately's own statement about his views, and to continue to maintain that he is an Arminian, when he himself repudiates the name. Most

certainly nothing ungracious is intended; the somewhat uncour-
teous form of the statement is the result of what was purely
accidental; and there are some important considerations, bearing upon the interests of truth, which seem to render it expedient
that the ground taken should be maintained. The allegation
that the Archbishop is an Arminian was introduced in the most
incidental way, and evidently under the influence of a feeling that
this was a position of notorious and undeniable certainty,—a position which no one could dispute, and of which no one would complain. We are neither convinced nor frightened by the somewhat
angry allusion made to this matter in the note above quoted from
him; and we think it may be fitted to throw light upon an important subject, not well understood, if we attempt to establish the
truth of the allegation. We have, of course, no doubt of the
integrity and sincerity of Dr Whately in abjuring the name of
an Arminian. We differ from him in opinion as to what is or
is not Arminianism, and as to what are the grounds and circumstances which warrant the application of this name; and these
are matters on which a difference of opinion may be expressed
without any want of personal respect being indicated. We think
we can prove, that Dr Whately's views upon the subject of
election are,—notwithstanding his important concessions to Calvinism, above referred to,—so accordant in substance with those
which have been generally known in the history of the church
as Arminian, and so different from those indicated by any other
recognised ecclesiastical designation, that it is perfectly warrantable to describe them as Arminianism.

We would scarcely have thought of taking the trouble of
attempting to prove this, had we not been persuaded that defective and erroneous views, on these matters, are very prevalent, especially among the clergy of the Church of England;
and that there is not a little,—in the present aspect of theological literature,—fitted to show the importance of trying to
diffuse accurate and definite views of the true *status quæstionis*
in regard to the topics involved in our controversy with the
Arminians.

Dr Whately is not the only eminent writer of the present day
who has advocated Arminianism, without being aware of this, and
even while repudiating it. The late Mr Stanley Faber,—who has
rendered important services in several departments of ecclesiastical

literature, and who was greatly superior to Dr Whately in theological erudition, though much inferior to him in sagacity and penetration of intellect,—published an elaborate work " On the Primitive Doctrine of Election," the second edition of which appeared in 1842. In this work he expounds three different theories on the subject of Election,—viz., Calvinism, Arminianism, and what he calls Nationalism, or the system advocated by Locke and Dr John Taylor. He labours to prove that all these three theories are erroneous,—opposed equally to the testimony of Scripture, primitive antiquity, and the symbolical books of the Church of England. He then brings forward a fourth theory, different from all these,—one which is neither Calvinism, nor Arminianism, nor Nationalism. This he calls Ecclesiastical Individualism,—meaning thereby an election of individuals to the privileges of the visible church,—to the enjoyment of the means of grace. This fourth theory,—as distinguished from and opposed to the other three,—he labours to establish as true, by an application of the three standards just mentioned. While Calvinism, Arminianism, and Nationalism, are all unfounded and erroneous, Arminianism is, in Faber's judgment, the farthest removed from the truth; or, as he expresses it,*—" Of the three systems, Arminianism has the *most* widely departed from aboriginal Christian antiquity" (including Scripture and the early fathers), " for, in truth, it has *altogether* forsaken it." Now, we are firmly persuaded, and think we can prove, that *both* the Nationalism which he rejects, and the Individualism which he upholds, are just in substance the very Arminianism which he denounces and abjures; that his Arminianism, Nationalism, and Ecclesiastical Individualism are really just one and the same system or doctrine, exhibited under slightly different aspects, and constituting the one only really antagonistic theory to Calvinism. Faber, we think, has utterly failed to distinguish between the essentials and the accidentals of the different systems which he has investigated. He has not penetrated beneath the surface. He has been entirely carried away by slight and superficial differences, while he has wholly failed to perceive intrinsic and substantial resemblances. The consequence is, that his " Primitive Doctrine of Election,"—though containing much interesting matter, which admits of being

---

* P. 292.

usefully applied,—is practically a mass of confusion; and can produce only error and misapprehension in the minds of those who are unacquainted with some of the more thorough and searching expositions of these important and difficult subjects.

If there be any truth in these statements,—if there be any fair ground for believing that Whately and Faber, the former most favourably representing the ability, and the latter the erudition, of the Episcopal Church of this country, are really Arminians, though they are not aware of it,—if these men are truly, in substance, teaching Arminianism, while they sincerely denounce and abjure it,—there must be some great misapprehension or confusion prevalent, which distorts and perverts men's views upon these subjects; and if any such state of things exist, it must be important, with a view to the interests of truth, that it should be pointed out and exposed.

The statements of Whately and Faber,—to which we have referred,—seem to be received as true, without any doubt or misgiving, in the great ecclesiastical denomination to which these authors belong; and we are not by any means confident that the generality of Scotch Calvinists, now-a-days, have sufficient knowledge of doctrinal theology to be able to detect the fallacy. The discussion of this subject extends greatly beyond what is personal to individuals, as affecting the accuracy of their statements. It really involves the whole question of the right settlement of the true *status quæstionis* in the great controversy about predestination. The settlement of the *status quæstionis* is always a point of fundamental importance in great doctrinal controversies. It is especially important in this one, where,—unless the state of the question is clearly settled and carefully and constantly attended to,—men are very apt to fight at random, to be dealing blows in the dark, and running some risk of wounding their friends. A right estimate of the accuracy of the statements of Whately and Faber, condemning and repudiating Arminianism, must be based upon an investigation of these two questions—1*st*, What is the real essential point of difference between Calvinists and Arminians on the subject of election? and 2*d*, Is there any real, definite, and important subject of controversial discussion involved in the exposition of election, and not disposed of by the determination of the fundamental question controverted between Calvinists and Arminians? It is only by settling and applying the first of these questions, that we can satisfactorily determine whether Whately and Faber,—and men holding such opinions,—may be justly designated as Arminians; and if, by a farther application of the results of the same inquiry, we can settle the second of these two questions in the negative, we thus establish the wider and more important conclusion, that men who intelligently investigate the subject of election, and form anything like a clear and definite opinion regarding it, must be substantially either Calvinists or Arminians, whether they perceive and admit this or not.

The consideration of these points, however, has a wider bearing than has yet been indicated. It is fitted to bring out some defects of considerable importance in the way in which this great class of theological topics have been usually discussed by divines of the Church of England. Doctrinal and systematic theology has not ordinarily been studied with much care by the clergy of that church; and the consequence of this has been, not only that crude, confused, and erroneous views upon doctrinal subjects abound in the writings of many of them, but also that the warrantableness and desirableness of vague and indefinite views upon these matters have found in them open and avowed defenders. The clergy of the Church of England, at the period of the Reformation, were generally, like most of the other Reformers, Calvinists, and continued to be so during the whole reign of Queen Elizabeth and the greater part of that of James VI. Since about the earlier part of the reign of Charles I., the great majority of them have ceased to be Calvinists, though many of these have refused, like Dr Whately, to be called Arminians, and some,— though not Calvinists,—have even declined to be called anti-Calvinists. These changes in the actual opinions of the clergy of the Church of England have taken place, while their symbolical books have continued unaltered upon doctrinal questions. Since the great body of the clergy have thus been at one time Calvinistic, and at another Arminian; and since probably, at all times, at least for two centuries and a half, there have been both Calvinists and Arminians among them, this has tended, in many ways, to produce great laxity and confusion of doctrinal views,—and has not only tended to produce this laxity and confusion in point of fact, but to lead men to justify its prevalence as a sound and wholesome condition of things. Calvinists and Arminians had equally to

show that their views were accordant with the Thirty-nine Articles;
and this almost unavoidably led, not only to a straining and tam-
pering with the language of the Articles, but even with the full
expression of their own personal convictions. Some have contended
that the Articles admitted only of a Calvinistic, others only of an
Arminian sense; while others have thought it more accordant
with the facts of the case, and with the honour of their church, to
maintain that they do not decide in favour of either doctrine, but
may be honestly adopted by both parties. The position that the
Articles are neither Calvinistic nor Arminian, distinctively, does
not differ very materially from the one that they are both. Some
have preferred to put it in this latter form; and this again has just
tended the more to deepen the confusion which has been introduced into the discussion.

We may give a specimen or two of what is a common mode
of speaking among the divines of the Church of England upon
this subject. Bishop Tomline concludes his "Refutation of
Calvinism" in these words:—"Our church is not Lutheran,—
it is not Calvinistic, it is not Arminian,—it is scriptural, it is
built upon the apostles and prophets, Jesus Christ being the
chief corner-stone." Dr Magee, the late Archbishop of Dublin,
—whom we regard as a far superior man to Tomline,—puts
the point under consideration in this way, in one of his
charges:—

"If any proof were wanting that our Articles are, as they profess to be,
of a comprehensive character, it would be found in this, that, of the contending parties into which our church is unhappily divided, each claims them as
its own. By those who hold the creed of Arminius, they are pronounced to
be Arminian; and by those who hold the creed of Calvin, they are pronounced
to be Calvinistic. The natural inference of the impartial reasoner would
be, that they are *neither*, whilst they contain within them what may be
traced to some of the leading principles of *both*. And this is the truth.
They are not enslaved to the dogmas of any party in religion. They
are not Arminian. They are not Calvinistic. They are *scriptural*. They
are *Christian*."*

In a note on this passage,† he asserts "that the doctrines
of the Church of England are not the doctrines of Calvinism, and
that the informed and intelligent clergy of that church are not

---

* Works, vol. ii. p. 428.   † P. 428.

the followers of Arminius." This has been a favourite mode of statement with very many Episcopalian divines, whom we believe to have been substantially Arminians, perhaps without their being aware of it. Some Episcopalians,—whose doctrinal views were sounder,—have, as we have hinted, been disposed rather to take the ground, that, without contradicting either Scripture or the English Articles, men might be both Calvinists and Arminians, or partly the one and partly the other. Statements to this effect, or something like it, have been produced from " Cecil's Remains" and from " Simeon's Memoir ;" and they have been employed by Professor Park of Andover, to countenance his ingenious attempt to involve important doctrinal differences in inextricable confusion, by distinguishing between the theology of intellect and the theology of feeling.*

There is, indeed, a distinction to be made between men's own personal convictions and their views as to the meaning and import of a symbolical document of public authority. It is quite possible to produce a deliverance upon the subject of election, which is neither Calvinistic nor Arminian,—that is, which is so general, vague, and indefinite, as to contain no decision of any of the points really controverted between the opposite parties. A church may think such an indefinite and indecisive statement the most suitable for a symbolical book,—may deliberately intend to include both parties within her pale,—and may so regulate her deliverances as not to make a definite opinion on the one side or the other a term of communion,—or what is virtually the same thing, a ground of separation. Very many of the clergy of the Church of England contend that this is realised in the Thirty-nine Articles. And it is quite possible that they may hold this to be an actual feature of these Articles, and approve of it as a right state of things for a church to exhibit in her symbols ; while yet they themselves, in their own personal convictions, may have decided the question in favour of the one side or the other. Tomline and Magee were Arminians as much as Whately and Faber, while maintaining that the Articles are neither Arminian nor Calvinistic ; and they might have taken this view of the Articles although they themselves had been Calvinists. But although the Episcopalian clergy may consistently maintain that the Articles

---

* Bibliotheca Sacra, 1852, No. v. pp. 209, 210.

are neither Calvinistic nor Arminian,—even while they themselves, in their own personal convictions, may have decidedly adopted the one view or the other,—yet there can be no doubt that the peculiar character of the Articles, and the kind of discussion which this has suggested or required, has tended largely to keep many Episcopalian divines in a state of great uncertainty and confusion in regard to this whole class of subjects. There being some plausible grounds for believing that subscription to the Articles did not require them to have their minds made up on the one side or on the other, very many have not thought themselves called upon to give the time and research necessary for forming a judgment on these difficult and arduous topics; and have preferred to exercise their talents rather in the way of trying to show that it was not only unnecessary, but very difficult and highly inexpedient and dangerous, to be forming a decided opinion, and to be giving an explicit deliverance, upon such matters. The title of the "Bampton Lectures" for 1855, by the Rev. John E. Bode,—and they form a very respectable work,—is this, "The Absence of Precision in the Formularies of the Church of England scriptural and suitable to a state of Probation." And this "absence of precision," which they regard as attaching to the public formularies, they too often extend to their own private personal convictions. This influence of the one upon the other has, no doubt, operated powerfully on the general state of thought and sentiment in the Church of England. But it ought not to have done so. There may be very good grounds why precise deliverances upon some doctrinal controversies should not be embodied in symbolical books; while yet it may be the duty of ministers to have formed for themselves a decided opinion regarding them. The reasons that satisfy many of the warrantableness and expediency of the "absence of precision in the public formularies," do not necessarily sanction the same quality as attaching to men's own personal convictions; though we fear that some notion of this sort is very prevalent among the clergy of the Church of England. Many have preserved and cherished the "absence of precision" in their own personal convictions; and in defending the propriety and expediency of this, they have introduced a vast deal of vagueness and confusion into the whole discussion.

This course has been adopted, and this tendency has been exhibited, chiefly by Arminians; and Arminianism certainly has got

the benefit of it.   Indeed, ignorance and confusion upon this subject always tend to the benefit of Arminianism.   Truth is promoted
by a thorough knowledge and a careful study of the subject in
hand, and by the clear and definite conceptions which are the
results of intelligence and investigation ; while any shortcoming or
deficiency in these respects tends to promote the prevalence of
error.   This holds true generally of all the ordinary subjects of
speculative inquiry.   It holds true pre-eminently of the leading
points involved in the controversy between Calvinists and Arminians.   There are vague, general, and indefinite positions about
the divine purposes and plans, and about the divine providence
and agency, in which both Calvinists and Arminians concur.   Calvinism may be said to involve, and to be based upon, a conversion
of these vague and indefinite positions into precise and definite
doctrines.   These doctrines the Arminians refuse to admit,—alleging that no sufficient evidence can be produced in support of
them, and that formidable objections can be adduced against
them.   They refuse to advance to the more profound and definite
positions, which may be said to constitute the distinctive features
of Calvinism ; and they insist that men should be satisfied with
those more superficial and indefinite views in which they and their
opponents agree.   We are not professing to give this as the formal *status quæstionis* in the controversy.   But this is an account
of the difference which is correct, so far as it goes ; and it illustrates
our present position, that imperfect and confused views upon these
subjects tend to injure truth and to advance error,—to damage
Calvinism and to favour Arminianism ; and this, too, even when
men's views may be so pervaded by ignorance and confusion, that
they do not themselves perceive this tendency, or do not really
mean to advance the object to which it leads.

It is one of the leading features or results of this vagueness
and confusion of thought upon these subjects, that there has commonly been a great tendency to multiply and exaggerate the differences of opinion which have been expressed regarding them ; as
if to convey the impression that there was a considerable variety
of views, out of which men were very much at liberty to make a
choice as they might be disposed.   As Arminianism is at the bottom of all this confusion, and as it is promoted chiefly for Arminian
objects, it has been common for divines of the Church of England
to magnify differences subsisting among Calvinists, and to repre-

sent each modification of sentiment that may have been brought out, as constituting a distinct and different doctrine. This process tends to increase the general mass of confusion attaching to the whole subject, and to excite a special prejudice against Calvinism, as if its supporters were divided among themselves on points of fundamental importance, and had not any uniform and well-settled position to occupy. We may refer to some historical illustrations of this feature of the controversy.

The first person, of any consequence, who openly taught Arminianism in the Church of England (not then known by that name) was Peter Baro, a Frenchman, who had held the office of Margaret Professor of Divinity at Cambridge for about twenty years. It was his teaching Arminianism, in opposition to the general doctrine of the Reformers, that occasioned the preparation of the famous Lambeth Articles in 1595,—a transaction, the history of which affords conclusive evidence of the general prevalence of Calvinism in the Church of England till the end of the sixteenth century. In 1596 he had to resign his office in the university because of his doctrinal views; and on that occasion he prepared a short exposition of his case, under the designation of " Summa Trium de Prædestinatione Sententiarum,"—the three doctrines being, 1st, Supralapsarian Calvinism; 2d, Sublapsarian Calvinism; and 3d, his own Arminianism—which he describes as the doctrine held by the Fathers who preceded Augustine, and by Melancthon and a few other Protestant divines; just as if the first and second differed from each other as much as they both differed from the third.

Arminius himself made large use of the same unfair mode of representation. In his *Amica Collatio* with Junius,—his predecessor in the chair of theology at Leyden,—he brings forward three leading doctrines upon the subject of predestination as prevailing among Protestants, and attempts to refute them in order to make way for his own. The three doctrines are, Supralapsarianism, which he ascribes, unwarrantably, to Calvin; Sublapsarianism, which he ascribes to Augustine; and a theory intermediate between them,—a sort of modification of Supralapsarianism,—which he ascribes to Thomas Aquinas.* In his famous " Declaratio Sententiæ," published in 1608, the year before his death, he brings

---

* Opera, p. 159.

forward again the same three opinions as contrasting with his own, though without associating them historically with the names of individuals. He puts first and most prominently, the highest Supralapsarianism, and dwells upon it at the greatest length. He admits, indeed, at last, that there is not any very material difference among these three doctrines,—all held by Calvinists. But he has taken care, in the first place, to have the controversial advantage of having conveyed the impression, that there is great diversity of sentiment among his opponents; and of having held up first and most prominently, in his account of their opinions, the highest Supralapsarianism,—the view against which it is easy to excite the strongest prejudice, while it has really been professed by comparatively few Calvinists. It is worth while to mention, as a curious specimen of elaborate controversial unfairness, that of the whole space occupied by the declaration of his judgment concerning predestination, Arminius devotes four-fifths to an exposure of high Supralapsarianism, leaving only the last fifth for the statement of the other two forms of Calvinism, and of his own anti-Calvinistic doctrine.

But we mean to confine ourselves for the present to our own country. The first elaborate Arminian work produced in England, after Laud's patronage had done something to encourage opposition to Calvinism, and after Bishop Montague had fairly broken the ice, was " An Appeal to the Gospel for the true doctrine of Divine predestination, concorded with the orthodox doctrine of God's free grace and man's free will, by John Plaifere, B.D." He held a living in the Church of England for a period very nearly corresponding to the reign of James VI. in that country, and is not to be confounded with Thomas Playfere, a Calvinist, who succeeded to the Margaret divinity professorship in Cambridge, when Baro lost it in consequence of his Arminianism.* John Plaifere begins his " Appeal" with a full and elaborate statement of five different doctrines upon the subject of predestination. The first, of course, is Supralapsarian Calvinism; the second is Sublapsarian Calvinism; the third is a sort of intermediate system between Calvinism

---

* Mr Goode, in his very valuable work, *The Doctrine of the Church of England as to the Effects of Baptism in the case of Infants,* has proved that *all* the theological professors, both Regius and Margaret, both at Oxford and Cambridge, for a period of at least fifty years from the accession of Queen Elizabeth, who have left any record of their opinions, were Calvinists, with the single dubious exception of Bishop Overall.—*Goode,* c. iii.

and Arminianism, propounded by Bishop Overall, and very similar to what was afterwards called Baxterianism; the fourth he represents as the doctrine held by Melancthon, by the Lutherans, and the Arminians; and the fifth and last is the opinion of Arminius himself, of the Jesuit defenders of *scientia media*, and, as he alleges, of all the fathers before Augustine. The first four he regards as erroneous, though in different degrees, while he admits that in all of them there are "some parts and pieces of truth, but obscure and mingled with defects." The fifth he adopts as his own, and defends it as true; though he has failed to point out any intelligible difference between this and the fourth. The substantial identity indeed of the fourth and fifth opinions is so obvious, that it is admitted, and the representation given is attempted to be accounted for, in the Preface to the republication of this work, in a "Collection of tracts concerning predestination and providence," at Cambridge in 1719.

The example set by Plaifere, in this the earliest formal and elaborate defence of Arminianism in the Church of England, has been largely followed down to the present day,—especially in the point of multiplying and magnifying differences, in order to excite a prejudice against Calvinism, and to shelter Arminianism in the confusion and obscurity. Bishop Burnet, in his Exposition of the Thirty-nine Articles, has manifested a good deal of candour and fairness. He was an Arminian, or, as he himself expresses it in his preface,—"I follow the doctrine of the Greek Church, from which St Austin departed and formed a new system." But he has distinctly admitted, in expounding the 17th article, that "it is not to be denied that the article seems to be framed according to St Austin's doctrine;" that "it is very probable that those who penned it meant that the decree was absolute;" and that "the Calvinists have less occasion for scruple" in subscribing than the Arminians, "since the article does seem more plainly to favour them." But what alone we have at present to do with is, that he follows the common Arminian course, by giving a distinct and separate head to Supralapsarianism. According to Burnet, there are four leading opinions on the subject of God's decrees or purposes, viz.:—1st, Supralapsarianism; 2d, Sublapsarianism; 3d, "That of those who are called Remonstrants, Arminians, or Universalists;" and 4th, "That of the Socinians, who deny the certain prescience of future contingencies."

Without further multiplying proofs of this, we come down to the present day. We have already stated Faber's classification of the leading doctrines upon this subject under the four heads of Calvinism, Arminianism, Nationalism, and Ecclesiastical Individualism,—the first three being, in his judgment, false, and Arminianism the worst,—while we maintain that three of them, including the fourth, which he defends as true, are just Arminianism, and nothing else.

There is a book which seems to be in great repute in England in the present day, which also illustrates the point we are now explaining. It is, "An Exposition of the Thirty-nine Articles, historical and doctrinal," by E. Harold Browne, B.D., Norrisian Professor of Divinity in the University of Cambridge. The third edition of it was published in 1856, and a fourth has already appeared, though it is a bulky 8vo of about 900 pages. We have done little more than dip into it; but we are satisfied that it is a highly respectable and useful book, embodying a large amount of information, and exhibiting a fair and candid spirit, though certainly not free from errors and inaccuracies. The Norrisian Professor begins his exposition of the 17th Article by an enumeration and brief statement of the leading theories which have been held upon the subject of predestination. According to this author, they are no fewer than *six*, viz.,— 1. Calvinism; 2. Arminianism; 3. Nationalism; 4. Ecclesiastical Election. Thus far he has fully followed Faber,—ecclesiastical election being just the election of individuals to outward privileges,—the elect being just virtually the baptized, and the election the visible church. The fifth theory he mentions is a somewhat unintelligible piece of complication, to which no designation is given; and the sixth is Baxterianism. This seems to be now, as indeed it has always been in substance, a favourite mode of representing the matter among the divines of the Church of England. Professor Browne's own opinions are not very explicitly brought out. He seems to think that the articles were expressed intentionally in such indefinite and general phraseology as to take in the adherents of several of the different theories. His own views seem to be very much the same as Faber's, while, at the same time, he concedes that there are some scriptural statements which do not easily admit of any other sense than a Calvinistic one.

Mozley's "Treatise on the Augustinian Doctrine of Predesti-

nation," is one of a different class, and of a higher order, both in
point of ability and general orthodoxy; while at the same time it
affords another specimen of that predilection for the "absence of
precision" on doctrinal questions, which has so generally characterised the clergy of the Church of England. It is a work of
very superior learning and ability, and is really a valuable contribution to our theological literature. This treatise is substantially
an exposition and defence of the Augustinian or Calvinistic view
of predestination; while at the same time the author seems determined, for some reason or other, to stop short of committing himself to a full and open assertion of the doctrine which he seems to
believe. He appears to be always on the point of coming out
with an explicit and unqualified assertion of Calvinism, when he
finds some excuse for stopping short, and leaving the subject still
involved to some extent, in obscurity and confusion. It would
almost seem as if Mr Mozley had some secret and inexplicable
reason for refusing to come out with an explicit profession of the
Calvinism to which all his convictions tend to lead him; and the
excuses or pretences he assigns for stopping short on the verge of
a full and open proclamation of this system, are of a very peculiar
and unreasonable kind. We refer to this very superior and remarkable book as another specimen, though in a somewhat peculiar
form, of the tendency of Church of England divines to exhibit and
to defend "the absence of precision," in discussing the points controverted between the Calvinists and the Arminians; and thereby
to involve the statement and exposition of this important subject
in obscurity and confusion,—qualities which always tend powerfully to promote the prevalence of Arminian error.

We have brought forward these historical notices to illustrate
the magnitude and the prevalence of what we believe to involve a
serious injury to doctrinal truth; and to show the importance of
attempting to settle, as precisely and definitely as possible, the
true state of the question,—the real meaning and import of the
main points controverted on the subject of predestination. This
is important, not so much in reference to the topic which has more
immediately suggested to us this investigation of it,—viz., determining the accuracy of the application of certain historical designations,—but chiefly in reference to the far higher object of
forming accurate and definite conceptions on the whole subject,
in so far as we have materials for doing so. We believe that it

can be proved, that men who admit the divine foreknowledge of all events, and who have formed a distinct and definite opinion on the subject of predestination, must be either Calvinistic or Arminian, whether they perceive and admit this or not; and that Whately and Faber may be fairly designated as Arminians, notwithstanding their honest repudiation of the name; inasmuch as they accord with the views commonly known as Arminian in every point of real importance, and differ from them only, if at all, on topics that are really insignificant. The determination of these questions must, from the nature of the case, depend upon the true *status quæstionis* between the contending parties; and there is no great difficulty in settling this,—although it is true that men, notwithstanding its paramount importance, often allow their minds to remain in a condition of great uncertainty and confusion regarding it.

In proceeding to consider this subject, we would begin with observing, that it tends to introduce obscurity and confusion into the whole matter,—that men in surveying it are apt, especially in modern times, to confine their attention too much to election,—that is, to the decrees or purposes and agency of God with reference to the eternal destinies of men;—without taking in predestination or foreordination in general,—that is, the decrees or purposes and agency of God with reference to the whole government of the world and all the actions of His creatures. The fundamental principle of Calvinism, as stated in the " Westminster Confession,"* is, " that God from all eternity did, by the most wise and holy counsel of His own will, freely and unchangeably ordain whatsoever comes to pass." If this great doctrine be true, and be validly established by its appropriate evidence, it includes and comprehends,—it carries with it and disposes of,—all questions about the purposes of God with respect to the eternal destinies of the human race. If it be true, that God hath foreordained whatsoever comes to pass, He must have predetermined the whole history and the ultimate fate of all His intelligent creatures. If it be true, that God hath eternally and unchangeably ordained whatsoever cometh to pass, it must also be true,—as being comprehended in this position,—that as the " Confession" goes on to say, " By the decree of God for the manifestation of His glory, some men and angels are

---

* C. iii., sec. 1.

predestinated unto everlasting life, and others foreordained to everlasting death." It serves some useful and important purposes bearing upon the apprehension and establishment of sound doctrine, to have regard to the import and evidence of the fundamental and comprehensive doctrine of predestination,—or of God's decrees in general; instead of confining our attention to the more limited topics usually understood to be indicated by the words election and reprobation. The decrees of God are usually understood as describing in general the purposes or resolutions which He has formed, and in accordance with which He regulates His own procedure, or does whatever He does in the government of the world. That God has, and must have, formed purposes or resolutions for the regulation of His own procedure in creating and governing the world, must be admitted by all who regard Him as possessed of intelligence and wisdom; and, therefore, the disputes which have been raised upon this subject appear to respect —not so much the existence of the divine decrees,—but rather the foundation on which they rest, the properties which attach to them, and the objects which they embrace. The main questions which have been usually discussed among divines concerning the divine decrees in general, or predestination in its widest sense, have been these,—1, Are the divine decrees or purposes in regard to all the events which constitute the history of the world conditional or not? and 2, Are they unchangeable or not? Calvinists hold that God's decrees or purposes in regard to every thing that was to come to pass are unconditional and unchangeable, while Arminians or anti-Calvinists deny this, and maintain that they are conditional and changeable. But while this is the form which the general question has commonly assumed in the hands of theologians, the real point in dispute comes practically to this: Has God really formed decrees or purposes, in any proper sense, with respect to the whole government of the world? It seems plain, —so at least Calvinists believe,—that it is unwarrantable to ascribe to a Being of infinite perfection and absolute supremacy any purposes or resolutions for regulating the administration of the universe, that should be left dependent for their taking effect, or being fully realised, upon the volitions of creatures; and liable to be changed according to the nature and results of these volitions. And this brings us back again to the simple but infinitely important and comprehensive question, Has God eternally and unchangeably foreordained whatsoever comes to pass? There is no difficulty in understanding the meaning of this question. The foreordination of every event implies, that God from eternity had resolved that it should come to pass, and had made certain provision for this result. And the real subject of controversy is just this, Has God foreordained, in this the only proper sense of the word, whatsoever comes to pass? All Calvinists say that He has; and all anti-Calvinists say that He has not. Arminians and Socinians equally deny this divine foreordination of all events; while Socinians also deny, but Arminians admit, that God foreknew or foresaw them all. The divine foreordination of all events must either be affirmed or denied,—all who affirm it are Calvinists, and all who deny it are anti-Calvinists; and if, while denying foreordination, they admit foreknowledge, then they may be fairly and justly described as Arminians, because this is the designation by which, for nearly two centuries and a half, the actual doctrinal position they occupy upon this fundamental and all comprehensive subject, has been commonly indicated.

Whately and Faber deny the divine foreordination, while they admit the divine foreknowledge, of all events; and therefore, according to the acknowledged rules and the ordinary practice by which this matter is regulated, they may, without any transgression of accuracy, or justice, or courtesy, be designated as Arminians.

But it was not this great doctrine of the foreordination of all events which Whately and Faber discussed, or seem to have had in their view. It comprehends indeed and disposes of the subject they discussed; and it is an act of ignorance or inconsideration, tending to involve the whole matter in confusion, that they did not take it into account. If they had been familiar with the whole subject in this its highest and widest aspect, and if they had seen that the settlement of the question of foreordination, as commonly discussed, disposes of the question of election, they would scarcely have ventured to deny that they were Arminians. But we must see what was their position in regard to the subject which they had under consideration, viz., election, or the doctrine of the purposes and procedure of God in regard to the ultimate destinies of the human race. What is Calvinism, and what is Arminianism, on this subject? The Calvinistic doctrine is this, that God from eternity chose or elected some men, certain definite individuals of the human race, to everlasting life,—that He determined certainly and infallibly to bring these persons to salvation by a Redeemer,— that in making this selection of some men and in resolving to save them, He was not influenced by any thing existing in them, or foreseen in them, by which they were distinguished from other men, or by any reason known to or comprehensible by us, but only by His own sovereign good pleasure, by the counsel of His own will,—and that this eternal decree or purpose He certainly and infallibly executes in time in regard to each and every one included under it. This is the Calvinistic doctrine of election; every Calvinist believes this, and every one who believes this is a Calvinist. The meaning of this doctrine, solemn and mysterious as it is, is easily understood; and men are Calvinists or anti-Calvinists according as they affirm or deny it. The grand question is,—Is this election,—such a choice of men to eternal life, on the ground of the good pleasure of God,—a reality, established by scriptural authority, or is it not? From the nature of the case it is manifest, that every thing of real importance hinges upon the reality of such an election as has now been described; and that the controversy, so far as it involves any thing vital or fundamental, is exhausted, whenever it is settled,—that is, practically, whenever a man has conclusively made up his mind, either that such an election is or is not revealed in Scripture. All men who are not Calvinists deny the reality of any such election on the part of God; and if while denying this, they admit that God foresaw from eternity the whole of the actual history of each individual of the human race, then they are Arminians,—and nothing but ignorance will lead them to object to this designation.

The fundamental principles of the Arminian doctrine upon the subject of election,—the leading features of the theory which has been always historically associated with that name,—may be accurately exhibited in the two following positions. 1st, That God made no decree,—formed no purpose,—bearing immediately and infallibly upon the final salvation of men, except this general one, that He would save or admit to heaven all men who should in fact believe in Jesus Christ and persevere till death in faith and holiness, and that He would condemn and consign to punishment all who should continue impenitent and unbelieving. And 2d, That if there be any act of God, bearing upon the ultimate salvation of particular men considered individually, which may be called in any sense an election, or decree, or purpose, it can only be founded on, and must be determined by, a foresight of their actual faith and perseverance.

The first of these is the true proper anti-Calvinistic position, held equally and alike by Arminians and Socinians ; and constituting manifestly the main substance of what must be held by every intelligent man who has not embraced Calvinism.   It implies that God did not make an election of particular persons to eternal life, and resolve to bestow upon them faith, holiness, and perseverance, in order to secure the end of this election ; but that He merely made choice of certain qualities or features of character, and resolved to treat them according to their proper nature, in whatever individuals they might turn out at last to be found. Having formed this general purpose to save those who might believe and persevere, and to condemn and punish those who might be impenitent and unbelieving, God virtually left it to men themselves to comply or not with the terms or conditions He had prescribed ;—having no purpose to exercise, and, of course, not in fact exercising, any *determining* influence upon the result in any case, whatever amount of assistance or co-operation He may render in bringing it about.   This must be in substance the ground taken by every one intelligently acquainted with the subject, who is not a Calvinist.   We could easily prove that this ground was taken by Arminius and his followers, and really formed the main feature of the discussion about the time of the synod of Dort.   The synod of Dort, in their deliverance upon the controversy raised by Arminius and his followers in opposition to the Calvinism of the Reformers, not only gave an exposition of the positive scriptural truth upon each of the five points, but also subjoined to these a rejection of the errors (*rejectio errorum*) which had been broached by Arminians; and upon the first of the articles, that on predestination, *the very first* of the Arminian errors which the Synod rejected and condemned was this, that " the will of God concerning the saving of those who shall believe and persevere in faith and the obedience of faith, *is the whole and entire decree of election unto salvation, and that there is nothing else whatever concerning this decree revealed in the word of God.*"*   Arminianism was funda-

---

* Acta Synodi, p. 78.   Hanov. 1620.

mentally and essentially a rejection of the Calvinism taught by
the great body of those whom God raised up and qualified as the
instruments of the Reformation. Its leading positions thus came
to be a denial of the Scriptural warrant for such a decree of
election as Calvinists usually advocate, and an assertion that the
whole of what is said in Scripture about a decree of election *bearing immediately upon the final salvation of men*, is exhausted by
the doctrine,—which, of course, all admit to be true,—viz., that God
has determined to save all who shall believe in Jesus Christ and
persevere to the end in faith and holiness, and to consign to
punishment all who continue impenitent and unbelieving.

The second position above laid down, states accurately the true
place and standing of the subject of the foreknowledge or foresight of faith and perseverance, about which so much is said in
the controversy between Calvinists and Arminians. We believe
that it is chiefly from want of clear and accurate conceptions of
the true logical position and relations of this matter of foreknowledge or foresight, that so many men are Arminians without being
aware of it; or rather that so many honestly but ignorantly repudiate Arminianism while they really hold it. The fallacy which
leads many astray upon this point is the notion, that the doctrine
that the divine decree of election, or the divine purpose to save
certain men, is based or founded only upon the foreknowledge
that these men will in fact believe and persevere, is an essential,
necessary part of the Arminian system of theology; and affords
a precise test for determining, both negatively and positively,
whether or not men are Arminians. This, though a very common
notion, and one not unnaturally suggested by some of the aspects
which this controversy has assumed, is erroneous. This matter
of foreknowledge does not intrinsically and logically occupy so
prominent and important a place in the controversy,—or at least in
that branch of it which concerns the settlement of the state of the
question,—as is often imagined. Its real place in this department
of the controversy is collateral and subordinate; and the practical
result of a correct view of its position, is, that while the founding
of election upon foreknowledge proves that a man is an Arminian,
the rejection of this idea is no proof that he is not. The fundamental position of Arminius and his followers was in direct opposition to the Calvinistic doctrine of the absolute election of some
men to everlasting life, based only upon the sovereign good plea-

sure of God. They held that this doctrine is opposed to the
testimony of Scripture and to right views of the divine character
and government.   But Arminians, while denying that God absolutely chooses some men to life in the exercise of His sovereign
good pleasure, admit, that He does infallibly foresee everything
that comes to pass,—that thus the history and fate of each individual of the human race were from eternity present to His mind,
and of course became in some sense the objects of His actings
and purposes;—and that, *on this ground and in this sense*, He
might be said to have resolved from eternity to save each individual who is saved.   The notion of an election to life originating
in and founded upon the foresight of men's character and conduct, is thus no necessary or fundamental part of the actual position which the Arminians occupy.   It is merely a certain mode of
expression into which they can, without inconsistency, throw their
leading doctrine; and the use of which involves something of an
accommodation or approximation to the language of Scripture,
and of their Calvinistic opponents.   Arminians virtually say to
their opponents,—" We wholly deny your doctrine of election to
life on the ground of God's sovereign good pleasure foreordaining
and securing this result; and the only sense in which we could,
consistently with this denial, admit of anything like an election
of individuals to life, is God's foreseeing and recognising this
result as a thing determined in each case by men's actual character.   An election to life in this sense and upon this ground is
undoubtedly a reality, a process which actually takes place,—and
we are quite ready to admit it, especially as it seems to accord
with and to explain those scriptural statements about election on
which you base your doctrine.   In short, if you will insist upon
something that may be called an election, at least in a loose and
improper sense, we have no objection to allow an election founded
on foresight, but we can concede nothing else of that sort."   This
is the true state of matters, and it brings out clearly the subordinate and collateral place held by the subject of foreknowledge
in the investigation of the state of the question.

Some Arminians are willing so far to accommodate themselves
to the scriptural and Calvinistic usage of language, as to admit
that, *in the sense now explained*, God had from eternity His own
fixed and unchangeable purposes in regard to the admission of
men individually into heaven; while others think it more manly

and candid to avoid the use of such language, *when their fundamental principle requires them so thoroughly to explain it away.* All that is implied in the election of any individual to eternal life, *in the only sense in which any one not a Calvinist can admit it*, is, that God foresees that that individual will in fact believe and persevere, and that on this ground—this being " the cause or condition moving him thereto"—He decrees or purposes to admit that man to heaven and to give him everlasting life.   The result is thus determined by the man himself,—God's decree (falsely so called) with respect to his salvation, being nothing but a mere recognition of him as one who, without His efficacious determining interposition, would certainly, in point of fact, comply with the conditions announced to him.   A decree or purpose based solely upon the foreknowledge or foresight of the faith and perseverance of individuals, is of course practically the same thing as the entire want or non-existence of any decree or purpose in regard to them. It determines nothing concerning them, it bestows nothing upon them, it secures nothing to them.   It is a mere word or name, the use of which only tends to involve the subject in obscurity and confusion.   Whereas, upon Calvinistic principles, God's electing decree in choosing some men to life is the effectual source or determining cause of the faith and holiness which are ultimately wrought in them and of the eternal happiness to which they at last attain.   God elects certain men to life, not because He foresees that they will repent and believe and persevere in faith and holiness, but for reasons no doubt fully accordant with His wisdom and justice, though wholly unknown to us, and certainly not based upon anything foreseen in them as distinguished from other men ; and then further decrees to give to these men, in due time, everything necessary in order to their being admitted to the enjoyment of eternal life, in accordance with the provisions of the scheme which His wisdom has devised for saving sinners.

But we are in danger of travelling beyond the consideration of the state of the question, and trenching upon the proper argument of the case.   Our object at present is simply to show that, although the idea of the foresight of men's faith and perseverance is commonly brought into the ordinary popular mode of stating the difference between Calvinists and Arminians, yet it does not really touch the substance of the point controverted, so as to be, out and out, a discriminating test of men's true doctrinal position.

It is rather a certain mode of speaking, by which Arminians endeavour to evade a difficulty, *and to approximate to scriptural language without admitting scriptural truth.*   When men say, as many
Arminians do, that the divine decree of election is based upon the
foresight of faith and perseverance, they are virtually saying that
there is no decree of election, in any proper sense of the word;— or,
what is practically the same thing,—that the whole and entire decree
of election is God's eternal purpose to save all who shall, in point
of fact, believe and persevere.   Foreknowledge thus does not
really affect the proper *status quæstionis*,—the real substance of
what is maintained on either side, or made matter of actual controversy; though it does enter fundamentally into the *argument
or proof*,—the Arminian admission of divine foreknowledge affording to the Calvinists an argument in favour of foreordination
which has never been successfully answered.

It is on such grounds as these that we contend that, while the
basing of election upon foreknowledge is a proof that men may be
justly described as Arminians, the declining or refusing to embrace
this idea is no proof that they may not be justly so designated.
We believe that erroneous and defective conceptions, on this point,
are one main cause why men are not aware that they are Arminians, and unwarrantably repudiate the designation.   There are
various reasons that lead men, who are really Arminians, to reject
this idea of an election founded on foresight.   Some think it more
manly and straightforward to declare openly that there is no such
thing as an election to eternal life, instead of grasping at what has
the appearance of being an election, but is not.   Others rather
wish to leave divine foreknowledge altogether in the background,
and to say as little about it as they can, either in the statement or
in the argument of the question.   Many, while admitting foreknowledge and denying foreordination, see the difficulties and inconveniences of attempting to connect them in this way.   The
attempt to found an election on foreknowledge brings out, in a
peculiarly palpable light, the fundamental objection of Calvinists
against the system of their opponents,—viz., that it leaves everything bearing upon the character and eternal condition of all the
individuals of our race undetermined, and indeed uninfluenced, by
their Creator and Governor, and virtually beyond His control; and
degrades Him to the condition of a mere spectator, who only sees
what is going on among His creatures, or foresees what is to take

place, without Himself determining it, or exerting any real efficiency in the production of it,—and who must be guided by what
He thus sees or foresees in all His dealings with them.   All this,
indeed, can be proved to be involved necessarily in the denial of
Calvinism ; but it comes out very plainly and palpably when Arminianism is put in the form of maintaining an election founded
on foresight, and on this account many Arminians shrink from
that mode of representation.   For these reasons, many who zealously maintain what is really the essential characteristic feature of
Arminianism, dislike and avoid the basing of election upon foresight ; and as this mode of putting the matter is popularly regarded
as the distinctive mark of Arminianism, those who avoid and reject
it are very apt, when their acquaintance with these subjects is
imperfect and superficial, to regard themselves as warranted in
repudiating the designation of Arminians.

Faber has made it quite manifest that it was chiefly by some
confusion upon this point that he was induced to abjure Arminianism, while he really believed it ; and we suspect that this has
operated as an element, though perhaps not the principal one, in
producing the same result in the case of Archbishop Whately.
Faber has developed his views upon these points much more fully
than Whately, and it may tend to throw light upon the matter
under consideration, if we advert to his mode of representing it.
Faber entitles his work, "An Historical Inquiry into the Ideality
and Causation of Scriptural Election."   By the ideality of election, he means the investigation of the question as to what it is to
which men are said to be elected or chosen ; and by the causation
of election he means the investigation of the question as to what
is the cause,' or ground, or reason of God's act in so electing or
choosing them.   It is plain enough, from the nature of the case,
that there can be only two distinct questions of fundamental importance in regard to the idea of election,—viz., 1st, Did God choose
men only to what is external and temporal? or, 2d, Did He also
choose them to what is internal and everlasting?   In other words,
Did God choose men only to external privileges and opportunities,
not determining by any act of His, but leaving it to be determined
by themselves, in the exercise of their own free will, whether or
not they shall improve these means of grace, and, consequently,
whether or not they shall be saved? or, Did He choose them also
to faith, and holiness, and heaven, to grace and glory, resolving

absolutely to save those whom He had chosen, and to give them everything needful to prepare them for salvation, in accordance with the provisions of the scheme which He had devised and proclaimed? The cause of election must, in like manner, be resolved either into something in men, existing or foreseen, or into something in God Himself; and, if everything in men themselves be excluded from any causal influence upon God's act in election, this is evidently the same thing as tracing election to God's sovereign good pleasure,—to the counsel of His own will.

It is by the application of these two pairs of differences that Faber discriminates his four different doctrines on election, viz., Calvinism, Arminianism, Nationalism, and Ecclesiastical individualism,—taking some assistance also from another distinction of much inferior importance,—viz., that between an election of nations or masses of men collectively, and an election of individuals. Calvinism he represents as teaching, that the idea of election is God's choosing absolutely some men individually to eternal life, and that the cause of election is not anything in these men themselves, but only the sovereign good pleasure of God. As Calvinists, we have no objection to make to this representation. Faber rejects the Calvinistic idea of election, but approves of our view of its cause. Arminians, according to him, agree with the Calvinists in representing the idea of election to be a choosing of men individually to eternal life, but differ from them in representing the cause of this election to be the foreknowledge of men's character and conduct, or their faith and perseverance foreseen. And here we see the fallacy which involves the views of Faber and many others, upon this whole matter in confusion, and which we have already in substance exposed. It is only a great ignorance of the whole bearing and relations of the notion of basing election upon foresight, that could lead any man to assert, as Faber does, that Arminians agree with Calvinists in maintaining that the idea of election is that God chooses some men to eternal life. Beyond all question, the fundamental principle of Arminianism is just a denial of the Calvinistic doctrine, that God really, in the proper sense of the word, chooses some men to eternal life—a denial that such an election is sanctioned by Scripture; while the idea of representing foreknowledge as the ground of election, is merely a collateral subordinate notion, having something of the character of an afterthought, and forming no part of the real substance or essential features of the actual position maintained. Arminians deny out-and-out that Scripture reveals any real election by God of some men to eternal life,—while they often add to this denial a statement to this effect, that if there be anything in Scripture which seems to indicate an election of some men to eternal life,—anything resembling or approximating to the Calvinistic idea of election,—it can be only an election based upon a foresight of men's character, which is manifestly, as intelligent and candid Arminians admit, no election at all. But, after the explanations formerly given, we need not dwell longer upon this point. Arminians then are, according to Faber, unsound, both in regard to the idea of election, in which, it seems, they agree with Calvinists; and in regard to the cause of it, in which they differ from them.

Let us attend now to what he says about the two other schemes, which are different from both of these. The third is what he calls Nationalism,—a doctrine taught by John Locke, Dr John Taylor of Norwich, and Dr Sumner, the present Archbishop of Canterbury, in his book on Apostolical Preaching. It is this, that the election spoken of in Scripture is merely a choice made by God of nations or masses of men to form His visible church, and to enjoy the outward means of grace; and that the cause of this election is the sovereign good pleasure of God, who gives to different ages and countries the enjoyment of the means of grace, or withholds them, according to the counsel of His own will. Here Faber thinks the causation right; it being resolved, as in the case of Calvinism, into the good pleasure of God. He thinks the ideality partly right and partly wrong; right in so far as it represents election as being only a choice to outward privileges and means of grace, and not, as Calvinists and Arminians concur in holding, a choice to salvation and eternal life; and wrong, in so far as it implies that election has for its object, not individuals, but nations or communities. The fourth theory which he expounds, and which he labours to prove to be altogether, both in ideality and causation, accordant with the sacred Scriptures, with primitive antiquity, and with the symbolical books of the Church of England, he calls by the name of Ecclesiastical Individualism. In point of causation, it agrees with Calvinism and Nationalism, in resolving the cause of election into the good pleasure of God. In regard to ideality, it agrees with Nationalism in the fundamental point of representing election as a choice of men only to the communion of the visible church and to the enjoyment of the means of grace, and not to anything implying or securing salvation; while it differs from it only in the insignificant point of making the objects of election individuals instead of nations.

It thus appears why it is that Faber represents Arminianism as the most erroneous of the three erroneous doctrines. Arminianism is erroneous both in point of ideality and of causation; whereas Calvinism and Nationalism are both right in point of causation, and Nationalism is only partially and slightly wrong in point of ideality. It must also be very plain, we think, from the explanation which has been given, that Faber,—while condemning and abjuring Arminianism, with, we have no doubt, perfect sincerity,—is himself an Arminian, and nothing else. The fundamental principle of Calvinists is, that God has absolutely chosen some men to salvation, resolving to give them eternal life, and of course infallibly executing this purpose. The fundamental principle of Arminians and of all who are not Calvinists, is and must be, that God has made no such decree,—formed no such purpose; —that He has not chosen any men to eternal life, or to anything which implies or secures it, but only to that which is in itself external and temporary, though, if rightly improved, it avails to men's salvation,—viz., the communion of the visible church and the enjoyment of the means of grace. Faber repudiates the fundamental principles of Calvinism; he strenuously contends for the fundamental principle of Arminianism; and therefore he may be justly called an Arminian.

The subject may also be illustrated in this way. Election is frequently spoken of in Scripture, and ascribed to God. Men are bound to understand the Scriptures, and they should investigate and ascertain what is there meant by election. Calvinists admit that election and cognate words are used in Scripture in a variety of senses. They admit that God, in fact, chooses nations and chooses men individually to the enjoyment of the means of grace; and that this choice of nations and individuals to external privileges is described in Scripture by the name of election, and is ascribed to the good pleasure of God. Thus far all parties are agreed. The distinctive principle of Calvinism is that, while election is used in Scripture in these senses,—to describe these processes,—it is also used in a higher and more important sense, to describe a process in which God, out of His own good pleasure, chooses some men to eternal life, and to the certain improvement as well as the outward enjoyment of the means of grace; and by which, therefore, He secures their salvation. God determines the outward privileges enjoyed by nations and individuals,—it is admitted that whatever He does in time He resolved from eternity to do,—and therefore He may be said to have chosen from eternity nations and individuals to the outward privileges which they come in time to enjoy. Nationalism and Ecclesiastical Individualism are thus both true so far as they go. No Calvinist denies either the one or the other. They both describe realities,—processes which actually take place under God's moral government,—which He resolved from eternity to carry through, and which are sometimes indicated in Scripture by election and cognate words. This is certainly true. The question is, Is it the whole truth? Is there, or is there not, another and higher sense in which the word election is used in Scripture, as descriptive of an act of God bearing directly and conclusively upon the salvation of men? Calvinists maintain that there is; Arminians and all other anti-Calvinists maintain that there is not; *and this is indeed the one essential point of difference between them.* Nationalism and Ecclesiastical individualism,—or the choice of nations and individuals to the means of grace,—though true so far as they go, viewed as descriptive of actual realities, are yet, when represented as embodying the whole truth, or as exhausting the senses in which election is used in Scripture, just a denial of the fundamental principle of Calvinism, and an assertion of the fundamental principle of Arminianism; and therefore both Nationalists and Individualists are equally and alike, at least when they admit foreknowledge, Arminians, and nothing else.

In the exposition of the scriptural meaning of election, the ground taken by Calvinists is this, that whatever other acts of God, bearing in any way upon the salvation of men, are or may be described by this name, there is an election spoken of in Scripture, of which the three following positions can be established :—1st, That it is not founded upon any thing in men (foreseen or existing) as the cause or reason why they are chosen, but only on God's own sovereign good pleasure. 2d, That it is a choosing of individuals, and not merely of nations, or masses of men collectively. And 3d, That it is directed immediately not to anything merely external and temporary, but to character and final destiny; that it is a choosing of men to eternal salvation, and does certainly and infallibly issue in that result in the case of all who are included in it. Calvinists believe that there is an election spoken of in Scripture, of which these three positions can be established; and it is the maintenance of all this that makes them Calvinists. But the question with which at present we are chiefly concerned, is,—What is the Arminian mode of dealing with these three positions? and what mode of dealing with them entitles us to call men Arminians?

With regard to the first of these positions, the more candid and intelligent Arminians admit, that there is an election spoken of in Scripture, which is founded not on anything in men, but only on the good pleasure of God. Some Arminians have denied this notwithstanding the clearest scriptural evidence. But these have not been the most reputable and formidable advocates of Arminianism. There is nothing in their Arminianism that should prevent them from admitting this, and it is only the misapprehension and confusion which we have already exposed about the bearing and relations of the idea of foreknowledge or foresight, that could lead any one to suppose that this admission involved them in inconsistency, or afforded any presumption that they were not Arminians. Arminians, indeed, must repudiate—in order to preserve anything like consistency,—*an election to eternal life*, founded only on the good pleasure of God, and not on anything in men themselves. If there were any such election as this, it could be founded only upon a foresight of faith, holiness, and perseverance. But rejecting any proper election to eternal life, there is nothing to prevent them from admitting an election of men to what is external and temporary, founded only on the good pleasure of God. Whately and Faber both admit what is sometimes called arbitrary or irrespective election; but as it is only an election to outward privileges,—which men may improve or not as they choose,—the admission does not afford even a presumption that they are not Arminians, although they seem to think it does.

The second position, viz., that there is an election spoken of in Scripture, the object of which is not nations or masses of men collectively, but men individually, does not of itself determine anything of much importance. Calvinists admit that there is an election of nations spoken of in Scripture; and many Arminians admit that there is also brought before us in the Bible an election of individuals as distinguished from masses. If the only election spoken of in Scripture be an election of masses or communities,— and this, of course, is the distinctive tenet of those who are called Nationalists,—it follows that the election could be only to what was external and temporary, that is, to outward privileges. And it is this plainly which has commended the notion to a certain class of Arminians. Finding it conceded, that there are instances in Scripture in which the election spoken of is applied to nations, they have bethought themselves of employing this notion for the purpose of shutting out Calvinism altogether, by showing that there is no other election,—no election of individuals,—spoken of in Scripture; and consequently that scriptural election is only to outward privileges. Nationalism, then, so far from being a different doctrine from Arminianism, is merely a form or aspect in which Arminianism may be embodied, with something like a show of an argument in support of it. The maintenance of Nationalism proves that men are Arminians, while the denial of it,—in other words, the admission that Scripture speaks also of an election of individuals,—is no proof that they are not.

The truth is, that the hinge of the whole question turns upon the third position above stated as maintained by Calvinists in regard to the meaning of election,—viz., that Scripture does tell us of an absolute and unchangeable election of some men to eternal life, an election which infallibly secures to these men grace and glory. The only conclusive proof that a man is not an Arminian, is the proof that he holds this fundamental principle of Calvinism. If men do not admit this great distinctive principle of Calvinism, *they must maintain*, that the election spoken of in Scripture is only an election to what is external and temporary,—that is, to privileges or opportunities which men may improve or not as they please. It is impossible to examine an Arminian commentary upon the scriptural statements concerning election, without seeing that the one grand object aimed at is just to establish, *that there are none of them which prove a real election to grace and glory*, and that they may be all explained so as to imply nothing more than an election to outward privileges. All the leading Arminian divines have taken,—and from the nature of the case could not avoid taking,— this ground, in dealing with the scriptural argument on the subject of election; and every one who takes this ground is thereby conclusively proved to be an Arminian. They may concede to Calvinists the first two of the positions we have laid down in regard to the scriptural meaning of election,—that is, they may admit that there is an election spoken of in Scripture which is founded only on the sovereign good pleasure of God, and which has respect to men individually, and not merely to nations or masses. They are quite consistent in their Arminianism, and have quite a sufficient basis on which to rest it, so long as they deny the third position, and maintain the converse of it; and by occupying this ground they prove themselves to be Arminians. This is precisely the case with Faber and Whately. They both deny that Scripture gives any sanction to a real election of some men to faith and holiness, to grace and glory, and therefore they are not Calvinists. They both maintain that the only election spoken of in Scripture is an election to outward privileges and opportunities, which men may improve or not, according to their own good pleasure; and therefore (since at the same time they admit foreknowledge) they may be most warrantably held to be Arminians.

From the explanation which has been given it must, we think, be very evident, that Nationalism and Individualism as explained by Faber, instead of being, as he represents the matter, two distinct doctrines on the subject of election, different both from Calvinism and Arminianism, are just two devices for evading the scriptural evidence in support of the former, and for assisting to furnish a scriptural argument in favour of the latter. There is very little real intrinsic difference between these two Arminian devices for answering the Calvinistic argument and evading the testimony of Scripture; for, on the one hand, an election of nations must be an election only to outward privileges; and, on the other hand, outward privileges are usually,—in the ordinary course of God's moral administration,—bestowed rather upon nations or communities than upon individuals. Some Arminians prefer the one and some the other of these two modes of disposing of the Scripture testimony in favour of Calvinism; while others again think it best to employ both methods, according to the exigencies of the occasion. The two together form the great staple of the scriptural argument of the whole body of Arminian divines; and it has been no uncommon practice among men to employ the one or the other mode of evasion, according as one or the other seemed to afford the more plausible materials for turning aside the argument in favour of the Calvinistic doctrine of election, derived from the particular passage which they happened to be examining at the time. Dr Whately takes the ground, directly and at once, that the election ascribed to God in Scripture is not an election to faith and salvation, but only to outward privileges or means of grace, which men may improve or not as they choose; while Dr Sumner, the present Archbishop of Canterbury, takes the other ground, and maintains that scriptural election is a choice not of individuals but of nations; and thus, of course, comes round to the same inevitable Arminian position, by a slightly different and somewhat more circuitous process.*

We are almost ashamed to have dwelt so long, and with such reiteration, upon these matters. But when we find it gravely put forth by such a writer as Faber, that Calvinism, Arminianism, Nationalism, and Ecclesiastical Individualism, indicate four different theories upon the subject of election,—Arminianism being at once more erroneous in itself, and yet nearer to Calvinism, than either of the other two; when we find the same views of the general import of these alleged theories brought out by one at

---

* Dr Whately has adverted to and explained the difference between himself and Dr Sumner in the Introduction to his Essays; and as the passage establishes the accuracy of the representation we have given of the views of both parties, we shall quote it: " I have been informed that some of the hearers of the discourse, of which the third Essay contains the substance, understood the argument in s. 2 to be merely a repetition of Archbishop Sumner's in his valuable work on ' Apostolical Preaching.' Such a misapprehension is, I trust, less likely to take place in the closet; but to guard against the possibility of it, it may be worth while here to remark, that though *I coincide with Archbishop Sumner in his conclusion*, the arguments by which we respectively arrive at it are different. The distinction which he dwells on, is that between *national* and *individual* election; that on which I have insisted is, the distinction between election to certain *privileges* and to *final reward;* he, in short, considers principally the *parties* chosen, whether bodies of men, or particular persons: I, the things to which they are chosen: whether the *offer* of one conditionally.' '(Introduction. p. xix.) And in a footnote to the third section of the Essay itself, he again adverts to the difference in this way (p. 75), "The view here taken of election some have hastily supposed to be at variance with that of Archbishop Sumner in his ' Apostolical Preaching,' while others have no less erroneously supposed them identical." The views of the two Most Reverend Primates on the subject of the scriptural meaning of election are certainly neither at variance nor identical. But the difference between them is very small; and they are both most thoroughly accordant with the fundamental principle of the Arminian doctrine upon this subject. Indeed, the two together form the most ordinary and familiar commonplace of the general current of Arminian writers in dealing with the scriptural evidence.

present holding the office of a professor of divinity in the University of Cambridge, in a work which seems to be in great repute, having gone through four editions in the course of the last seven or eight years ; and when we reflect upon the various indications presented, that these views of Faber and Professor Browne pass current as undoubted truths among many of the clergy of the Church of England ; we cannot but believe that ignorance, misapprehension, and confusion, are widely prevalent upon these subjects, and that there is an imperative call to attempt to dispel this thick darkness,—while at the same time we cannot but feel that it may probably not be easy to effect this. We have surely said enough to prove, 1*st*, That there are just two really distinct theories upon this subject which, with substantial historical accuracy, may be called Calvinism and Arminianism,—that the great point which forms the proper subject of controversy between Calvinists and Arminians is the existence or the non-existence,— the affirmation or the negation,—of a real decree, or an absolute purpose of God, formed from eternity, orginating in His sovereign good pleasure, choosing some men to eternal life, and effectually securing that these men shall have grace and glory. 2*d*, That it is a thorough fallacy to represent Arminianism,—as is done by Faber and Professor Browne,—as countenancing any proper decree or purpose of God really bearing upon the salvation of men,—a fallacy arising from the want of a right perception of the true bearing and relations of the idea of foreknowledge or foresight, as it has been brought into the discussion of this subject. And, 3*d*, That Nationalism and Individualism, instead of being theories differing from Arminianism, are just forms or aspects of it,—or rather, perhaps, attempts at arguments in support of it. All who believe that Scripture establishes the existence of such an election as is described in the first of these positions, are Calvinists ; and all who deny this, provided they at the same time admit the divine foreknowledge, are Arminians. When tried by this,—the only really sound and searching test,—Faber and Whately are undoubtedly Arminians ; and there is no violation of historical accuracy, or of substantial justice, in applying to them that designation, notwithstanding that they, through misapprehension, disclaim it.

Dr Whately, in his latest work, " The Scripture Doctrine concerning the Sacraments," has a remark which bears upon this matter, and may require to be adverted to. He says there,* "it is utterly improper that any should be called either by themselves or by others, 'Calvinists,' who dissent from any part of what Calvin himself insists upon as a necessary portion of his theory;" and upon this principle he would probably contend that it is "utterly improper to call him an Arminian," since he dissents from "some part of what Arminius insists upon as a necessary portion of his theory." Personally, we have no objection to the principle of the rule indicated by Dr Whately. We could not, even if so disposed, escape from the imputation of being Calvinists, by alleging that we dissent from any part of what Calvin insisted upon as a necessary portion of his theory, though we do dissent from some of his opinions. But in regard to the application of Dr Whately's remark to his own case, we venture to affirm, 1st, That the rule which he lays down about the application of such designations is unnecessarily and unwarrantably stringent; and, 2d, That even conceding the soundness of this stringent rule, we are perfectly warranted in calling him an Arminian.

1st, The rule is unduly stringent. This matter must be settled, —for there is no other standard applicable to the point,—by considering the practice of the generality of divines of different denominations. Now, there can be no doubt that it is a common and usual thing for divines to apply such designations as those under consideration, in a wider and more indefinite way than Dr Whatley's rule would sanction. Calvinism, Arminianism,. and similar names, are generally employed to indicate,—not so much the actual views held by Calvin, Arminius, and others,—but rather the general system of doctrine which these men did much to bring out and to commend, even though it may have been considerably modified in some of its features by the discussion to which it has been subsequently subjected. Controversy, conducted by competent persons usually leads,—though it may be after an interval, and even after the removal of the original combatants,—to clear up and modify men's views upon both sides ; and yet, for the sake of convenience, the same compendious designations may still be retained. The general practice of divines sanctions this use of these names,—though it is manifest that they must often be employed in a somewhat vague and ambiguous way,—there being no

---

* Note, p. 13.

precise or definite standard to which reference can be made, in order to determine their proper meaning and import. This unavoidable vagueness and uncertainty in the use and application of those words, leaves much room for carping and quibbling when men are disposed to evade or escape from a difficulty. But even with this drawback, there is much convenience in the use of such designations; the general usage of theologians sanctions it; and it is trifling to make an outcry about any matter of this sort, unless in a case of gross and deliberate unfairness. Calvin and Arminius must not be held responsible for any opinions which they have not themselves expressed. Still, there is no great difficulty in distinguishing between their personal opinions and the leading features of the systems of theology to which their names have been attached, as these seem to be logically related to each other, and as they have been commonly set forth by the most eminent divines of either denomination. Arminius never positively and decidedly renounced the Calvinistic doctrine of the certain perseverance of believers; but no one has ever had any hesitation about calling the denial of this doctrine Arminianism, upon these grounds—1st, That logically it forms a natural, necessary part of the Arminian system of theology, although Arminius himself did not perceive this, and did not insist upon it as a necessary portion of his theory; and 2d, That historically, the doctrine of perseverance has been denied by the great body of those divines who, ever since Arminius's time, have been called after his name. It is true, on the one hand, that men of sense do not suppose that these designations,—even when applied in a way which general usage warrants, —afford of themselves anything like a proof either of the truth or the falsehood of the doctrines to which they are attached; and it is also true, on the other, that men of sense will not raise an outcry about the application of one of these designations to themselves, if their views agree in the main with the general system of doctrine to which this designation has been usually applied. We would not object to be called Calvinists, though we differed much more widely from Calvin's own views than we do, nay, even though we dissented from some point which "Calvin himself insisted upon as a necessary portion of his theory," so long as we held the fundamental distinguishing principles of that scheme of theology with which his name is usually associated.

But 2d, Though Dr Whately's rule is unduly stringent, still

its fair application does not prove the unwarrantableness of calling him an Arminian. Not only does he hold all the fundamental
distinguishing principles of the system of theology which has been
generally known in the history of the church under the name of
Arminianism, as expounded by the generality of the most eminent
divines who have accepted that name for themselves,—but he
does not dissent from any part of what Arminius himself insisted
upon as a necessary portion of his theory ;—nay, he does not dissent from Arminius, or from the general body of Arminian divines,
in any doctrine of real importance. Arminius was very unwilling
to bring out, honestly and explicitly, his peculiar opinions. It
was only in 1608, the year before his death, that he was induced
to come out with a profession of his doctrines ; and even then his
conduct was not very manly and straightforward. We have four
different statements, more or less explicit, prepared by him in
that year, of his sentiments upon predestination. They are to
be found in his works.* We are unable to perceive any material
difference between the views of Arminius,—as there stated,—and
those of Dr Whately; and we are confident that no such difference
can be established. Dr Whately, in asserting that he is neither
a Calvinistic nor an Arminian, must be understood as intending
to affirm, that he differs in some points of real importance, not so
much from the opinions of Calvin and Arminius, as from the
leading views on the subject of election that have commonly been
held by Calvinistic and Arminian divines. He probably also intended, in making this statement, to convey the idea, that his views
lay somewhere between the one system and the other,—or, in other
words, that he neither went so far in one direction as the Calvinists, nor so far in the opposite direction as the Arminians. If this
was his intention,—as it seems to have been,—the fact would only
show how imperfect is his knowledge of these matters. For it is
evident, that in so far as anything like a material difference from
Arminius could be pointed out, it is to be found principally in
this direction, that Arminius retained *more* of the doctrines generally held by Calvinists than Dr Whately has done. But whatever there be in this, it is certain that he holds the whole substance
of what has been well known in the history of the Protestant

---

* His works in Latin (Leyden edition of 1629), at pp. 119, 138–45, 943,
and 951; or in Nichol's Translation of
the Works of Arminius, vol. i. pp.
529, 681–699, and vol. ii. pp. 698 and
718.

church for the last two centuries as Arminianism, as opposed
to Calvinism, and differing somewhat from Socinianism, on this
subject; and that therefore we are fully warranted, by the ordinary, reasonable, and convenient practice of theologians, to call
him an Arminian. We must be careful, indeed, to ascribe to him
no opinions which he has not professed or acknowledged. But he
has no right to demand that, because he has a dislike to the designation Arminian, we must have recourse to circumlocution in indicating his theological position, when he is utterly unable to
prove, that calling him an Arminian involves inaccuracy or injustice, or implies any deviation from the mode of dealing with
such topics which is sanctioned by the ordinary practice of theologians.

Faber having written a book upon the subject of election,—and
having there brought out his views fully and elaborately,—has
made it manifest what were the grounds that led him to believe
that he was not an Arminian; and we have had no difficulty in
pointing out the source of the fallacy in his case. Whately has
referred to this matter only incidentally; and has not gone into
any formal or elaborate exposition of the different theories which
have been held regarding it. In this way, while he has afforded
us abundant ground for believing that he is an Arminian, and
for calling him by that name, he has not told us explicitly or in
detail what are the grounds on which he considers himself warranted to repudiate the designation. Our views upon this point
must therefore be inferential, and, to some extent, conjectural.
We think there are some indications, in his statements upon the
subject of election, showing that he was, to some extent, misled
by the same fallacy about the relation between election and foreknowledge, which we have exposed in the case of Faber. They
both concur in rejecting the Arminian interpretation of Rom. viii.
29, " whom He did foreknow, He also did predestinate to be con-
formed to the image of His Son;" and of 1 Pet. i. 2, " Elect
according to the foreknowledge of God;"—denying, as Calvinists
do, that these passages afford a warrant for basing election upon
foresight.* And there are other indications,—though none, so far
as we remember, of a very explicit kind,—that Whately concurred
with Faber in rejecting altogether the idea of basing election upon

* Faber, pp. 232 and 344-5; Whately, p. 67, Ed. 7th.

foresight; and in imagining that, in rejecting this idea, he was abjuring the fundamental, distinctive principle of Arminianism. We have said enough, we think, to show that any such notion can originate only in a very defective and superficial knowledge of the intrinsic merits of this great controversy.

We have had occasion to refer to some points on which Dr Whately has expressed opinions different from those held by the generality of Arminians. These we have always regarded as eminently creditable to him, especially as we could not but view them as the concessions of an opponent. It is probably on these differences that he founds his warrant and right to deny that he is an Arminian. We think it proper to advert to these points of difference, not merely for the purpose of showing that they afford no ground for his abjuring the designation, but for the more important object of bringing out the valuable concessions thus made to Calvinism, by one whom we must still take the liberty of calling an Arminian.

The first point of this nature which we would notice we have already adverted to. It is one which only partially comes under the present head, as the same concession has been made by many Arminians. It is this, that Dr Whately distinctly admits, that the word election, as used in Scripture, "relates, in most instances, to an arbitrary, irrespective, unconditional decree;" and shows that those who endeavour to answer the Calvinistic argument founded upon the Scripture passages where election and its cognates occur, *by denying this,* are incapable of maintaining the position they have assumed.* There are some Arminians who are so afraid of admitting anything that might be called " arbitrary, irrespective, or unconditional" in God's purposes or procedure in regard to men, that they labour, in spite of the strongest opposing evidence, to exclude everything of this nature from every passage in Scripture where the words occur. But Dr Whately, and many of the more sagacious and candid Arminians, admit that this mode of dealing with the matter is unnecessary and unwarrantable. They could not indeed believe in any arbitrary, irrespective, unconditional decree of God bearing directly upon men's salvation, and exerting a determining influence upon the result. And, as we have fully explained, the fundamental, distinctive

---

* Pp. 78–80.   Edition Seventh.

principle of all anti-Calvinists,—Arminians included,—is just to deny that any such decree was or could be formed. But there is nothing in point of consistency to make it impossible for Arminians to admit an arbitrary, irrespective, and unconditional election, provided it be an election,—not to faith and salvation, to holiness and heaven, to grace and glory,—but only to what is external and temporary, to outward privileges or means of grace; it being still dependent on men's free will to improve or not their opportunities, and thus to attain or not to eternal life. Any such thing as an election to salvation could, upon anti-Calvinistic principles, be based only upon a foresight of what men individually would actually be and do; and in fairness and reason this could not properly be called an election. *But an election to outward privileges or means of grace might be based upon the sovereign good pleasure of God, as it exerts no efficacious determining influence upon men's eternal destiny.* Dr Whately denies the existence of any real election of some men by God to eternal life, and admits only an election to the means of grace. This is a conclusive proof that he is an Arminian;—and the proof is not in the least affected by his admission, that this election of some, whether nations or individuals, to outward privileges, is " arbitrary, irrespective, and unconditional,"—in other words, is founded on the sovereign good pleasure of God, and not on anything existing, or foreseen, in men themselves.

Some of the other concessions which Dr Whately has made to Calvinists are points in which he has few or none of the Arminians to countenance him, and they are therefore all the more creditable to his sagacity and candour; while at the same time we may say of them, in general, that they cannot be of any avail in proving that he may not be warrantably called an Arminian; inasmuch as they do not affect the state of the question, or the real meaning and import of the actual positions held on either side, and controverted between the two parties, but only the force and value of some of the arguments employed in conducting the contest.

The second,—and in some respects the most important,—of these concessions, is the admission that the arguments commonly adduced against Calvinism, derived from the moral attributes and government of God, are unsatisfactory and invalid; and that the grand difficulty of this whole subject applies to every system, inasmuch as it attaches to the facts,—admitted by all,—of the introduction and permanent continuance of moral evil. His views upon these subjects are brought out not only in his "Essay on Election," but also in what he has said in connection with the Discourse of his predecessor, Archbishop King on Predestination, which he has republished, with Notes and an Appendix, in the later editions of his "Bampton Lectures." He has fully adopted, as had been previously done by his friend Bishop Copleston, in his "Inquiry into the Doctrines of Necessity and Predestination," the leading principle expounded in King's famous Discourse. The principle is in substance this (we are not called upon to go into any details upon the point), that we know too little about God and the divine attributes and perfections, to warrant us in drawing conclusions from them as to the divine procedure—that the divine attributes, while infinitely superior in degree, are—though called by the same names,—not the same in kind as those which we ourselves possess,—that our knowledge of them is almost wholly, if not altogether, analogical;—and that, therefore, we are not entitled to draw inferences or conclusions, about the divine procedure from the divine power and knowledge, or from the divine justice and holiness, as we would from the same qualities in men. There is as much truth in this general principle, as to lay a good ground for condemning mnch presumptuous and ill-founded speculation, which has been brought to bear upon the discussion of this subject. But the principle is surely carried too far, when it is laid down so absolutely that our knowledge of God's attributes is wholly analogical, and does not warrant any inferences as to the mode of the divine procedure. The incomprehensibility of Jehovah,—the infinite distance between a finite and an infinite being,—should ever be fully recognised and acted on. But Scripture and right reason seem plainly enough to warrant the legitimacy and propriety of some inferences or conclusions as to God's procedure, derived from the contemplation of His attributes. King developed the leading principle of his Discourse for anti-Calvinistic purposes; and Copleston brought it forward,—to use a favourite phrase in the present day,—in the same dogmatic interest. Their object was to wrest, by means of it, from the hands of Calvinists, the formidable arguments usually adduced against Arminianism, derived from God's power, knowledge, and wisdom, which are often spoken of as His natural attributes.* Dr Whately, with superior sagacity and candour, sees and admits that this principle, if true and sound, is equally available for wresting from the hands of Arminians the arguments they have been accustomed to adduce against Calvinism, derived from what are often called God's moral attributes, His holiness, justice, and goodness. The great staple of the argument against Calvinism has always been, that the procedure which it ascribes to God is inconsistent with the holiness, justice, and goodness which all attribute to Him. If the argument derived from this source must be thrown aside as unwarrantable and invalid,—and Whately concedes this as necessarily involved in the fair application of King's principle,—Arminians are stripped of by far the most plausible things they have to adduce. They may still, indeed, consistently retain their leading position upon other grounds. They may still deny the fundamental principle of Calvinism, though deprived of what has been always felt to be the most formidable argument against it ; and this is, indeed, just the position occupied by Dr Whately. He still holds that there are good and sufficient grounds for rejecting the Calvinistic doctrine, though he declines to make any use of the common argument against it, derived from God's moral attributes. The abandonment .of this argument as unsatisfactory, does not produce any change in the actual doctrines he maintains. The position he occupies may be, and in point of fact is, the very same as that of those who continue to believe in the validity of the old favourite anti-Calvinistic argument; and as the abandonment of this argument does not make him less anti-Calvinistic, so neither can it afford any evidence

---

* The adoption and recommendation of King's Discourse by Bishop Copleston, gave rise to some discussion, the principal opponent being the Rev. E. W. Grinfield, in his " Vindiciæ Analogicæ." We have not seen the works published in this controversy, and our knowledge of them is derived mainly from an able review of them by the Rev. Richard Watson, published originally in the *Wesleyan Methodist Magazine*, and republished in the seventh volume of the collected edition of his works. It would seem, from Watson's statements, that Grinfield succeeded in convincing Copleston, that there were some views of this matter which he had not sufficiently attended to, and that his commendation of King's principle ought to have been much more cautious and qualified. The truth is, that Arminianism is much more dependent than Calvinism upon *inferences* derived from the consideration of the divine attributes. Watson himself, who was much superior to Copleston as a theologian, was quite well aware that Arminianism would lose much more than it would gain by the establishment of King's principle, and he took part decidedly with Grinfield in opposing it.

that he is not an Arminian. We must, therefore, continue to regard Dr Whately's abandonment of King's principle of the common argument from God's moral attributes, as the concession of an opponent, due to the force of truth; while we are not called upon to attach the same weight to his continued adherence to the ordinary Arminian ground of the invalidity of the argument in favour of Calvinism, derived from God's natural attributes. Calvinists do not, in general, admit the soundness of King's principle. They think they can establish the invalidity of the Arminian argument from the divine perfections upon other and more specific grounds; and thus they profess to be able to show, that they are warranted in accepting the concession of Dr Whately, as to the utterly precarious and uncertain character of the argument against Calvinism, from its alleged inconsistency with God's moral attributes; without at the same time needing to renounce the argument in favour of Calvinism and against Arminianism, derived from the consideration of His natural attributes.

The substance of this important concession is also presented by Dr Whately, in a more definite and specific form. He virtually admits that the arguments which have been commonly adduced against Calvinism on account of its alleged inconsistency with God's moral attributes, really apply to and tell against actual facts, —undoubted realities occurring under God's moral government,— that they thus prove too much, and therefore prove nothing;—in short, that the real difficulty is not anything peculiar to Calvinism, but just the introduction and the permanence of moral evil—an awful reality, which every system must equally deal with and in some way dispose of. It is admitted, that whatever God does in time He resolved from eternity to do; and if so, no peculiar or additional difficulty attaches to His eternal decree or purpose, as distinguished from that attaching to its execution in time, or to what God actually does in determining men's character and destiny. Whatever takes place in time God resolved from eternity to produce or to permit; and the fact of its occurrence proves that there was nothing in His character to prevent Him from producing or permitting it; and, of course, nothing to preclude His having resolved from eternity to produce or permit it. By following out these obvious considerations, Calvinists have proved that the great difficulty in this whole subject is just the permanent existence of moral evil under God's administration; and, as this is admitted on both sides to be an actual reality, the difficulty suggested by the contemplation of God's moral attributes is thus proved to be one which Calvinists and Arminians are equally bound, but, at the same time, equally unable, to solve. All this has been proved to demonstration by Calvinists, times without number; and it manifestly removes out of the way by far the most formidable and plausible objections by which their system has ever been assailed. Anti-Calvinists have never been able to devise a plausible answer to this line of argument, so subversive of their favourite and most effective allegations. But not one of them has ever, so far as we remember, conceded its truth and soundness so fully and frankly as Dr Whately has done. This concession is so important in itself, and so honourable to him, that we must present it in his own words:—

" Before I dismiss the consideration of this subject, I would suggest one caution relative to a class of objections frequently urged against the Calvinistic scheme—those drawn from the conclusions of what is called Natural religion, respecting the moral attributes of the Deity ; which, it is contended, rendered the reprobation of a large portion of mankind an absolute impossibility. That such objections do reduce the predestinarian to a great strait, is undeniable ; and not seldom are they urged with exulting scorn, with bitter invective, and almost with anathema. But we should be very cautious how we employ such weapons as may recoil upon ourselves. Arguments of this description have often been adduced, such as, I fear, will crush beneath the ruins of the hostile structure, the blind assailant who seeks to overthrow it. It is a frightful, but an undeniable truth, that multitudes, even in Christian countries, are born and brought up under such circumstances as afford them no probable, even no possible, chance of obtaining a knowledge of religious truths, or a habit of moral conduct, but are even trained from infancy in superstitious error and gross depravity. Why this should be permitted, neither Calvinist nor Arminian can explain ; nay, why the Almighty does not cause to die in the cradle every infant whose future wickedness and misery, if suffered to grow up, He foresees, is what no system of religion, natural or revealed, will enable us satisfactorily to account for.

" In truth, these are merely branches of the *one* great difficulty, *the existence of evil*, which may almost be called the *only* difficulty in theology. It assumes indeed various shapes ; it is by many hardly recognised as a difficulty ; and not a few have professed and believed themselves to have solved it ; but it still meets them,—though in some new and disguised form,—at every turn ; like a resistless stream, which, when one channel is dammed up, immediately forces its way through another. And as the difficulty is one not *peculiar to any one* hypothesis, but bears equally on all alike, whether of revealed or of natural religion, it is better in point of prudence as well as of fairness, that the consequences of it should not be pressed as an objection against any." *

" I cannot dismiss the subject without a few practical remarks relative to the difficulty in question (the origin of evil).

" First, let it be remembered, that it is not peculiar to any one theological system; let not therefore the Calvinist or the Arminian urge it as an objection against their respective adversaries; much less an objection clothed in offensive language, which will be found to recoil on their own religious tenets, as soon as it shall be perceived, that both parties are alike unable to explain the difficulty. Let them not, to destroy an opponent's system, rashly kindle a fire which will soon extend to the no less combustible structure of their own.

" Secondly, let it not be supposed that this difficulty is any objection to revealed religion. Revelation leaves us, in fact, as to this question, just where it found us. Reason tells us that evil exists, and shows us, in some measure, how to avoid it. Revelation tells us more of the nature and extent of the evil, and gives us better instructions for escaping it; but why any evil at all should exist, is a question it does not profess to clear up; and it were to be wished that its incautious advocates would abstain from representing it as making this pretension; which is in fact wantonly to provoke such objections as they have no power to answer." †

These views are, of course, familiar to intelligent Calvinists, as furnishing what they regard as a satisfactory answer to the most plausible objections of their opponents; their soundness is now for the first time fully conceded by a very able Arminian; and this concession, so honourable to him, may be expected to put an end to the coarse and offensive declamation in which Arminians have commonly indulged on this branch of the argument, and which has usually formed a very large share of their whole stock in trade as polemics.

The only other concession made by Dr Whately to Calvinism which we mean to notice is one connected with its alleged practical application. It has always been a favourite allegation of Arminians, that the Calvinistic doctrine of election tends to lead men to be careless about the improvement of the means of grace and the discharge of practical obligations, on the ground,—as they represent the matter,—that the result in each case is already provided for and secured irrespective of these things. The answer to this allegation is in substance, that it is not only consistent with,

---

* Essays, pp. 83, 84.　　　　| † Bampton Lectures, 3d edition, Appendix, p. 555.

but that it constitutes an essential part of, the Calvinistic doctrine, that God has foreordained the means as well as the end, and *has thus established a certain and invariable connection de facto between them.* This doctrine of the foreordination of the means as well as of the end, not only leaves unimpaired, to second causes, the operation of their own proper nature, constitution, and laws, but preserves and secures them in the possession of all these. It thus, when viewed as a whole, establishes most firmly the actual, invariable connection between the means and the end; and in its legitimate application, is at least as well fitted as any other doctrine can be, to keep alive, in the minds of men, a deep sense of the reality and certainty of this connection. All this Calvinists have conclusively proved, times without number; but Arminians have never been willing to concede it, since it completely disposes of a favourite objection, which, upon a partial and superficial view of the matter, appears very formidable. But Dr Whately admits the validity of the Calvinistic answer to the Arminian objection,— that is, he admits that the Calvinistic doctrine of election, *when the whole doctrine is taken into account and fully and fairly applied,* does not tend to exert an injurious influence upon the improvement of the means of grace and the discharge of practical obligations; while, at the same time, he tries to make a point against Calvinism, by labouring to show that by the same process by which Calvinists prove their doctrine to be harmless or innocent, it can be proved to be entirely useless, and to admit of no practical application whatever.

" It has indeed been frequently objected to the Calvinistic doctrines, that they lead, if consistently acted upon, to a sinful, or to a careless, or to an inactive life; and the inference deduced from this alleged tendency, has been, that they are not true. But this is a totally distinct line of argument, both in premises and conclusion, from that now adverted to ; and I mention it, not for the purpose either of maintaining or impugning it, but merely of pointing out the distinction. Whatever may be, in fact, the practical ill tendency of the Calvinistic scheme, it is undeniable that many pious and active Christians, who have adopted it, have denied any such tendency,—have attributed the mischievous consequences drawn, not to their doctrines rightly understood, but to the perversion and abuse of them ;—and have so explained them to their own satisfaction, as to be compatible and consistent with active virtue. Now if, instead of objecting to, we admit, the explanations of this system, which the soundest and most approved of its advocates have given, we shall find that, when understood as they would have it, it can lead to *no* practical result

whatever. Some Christians, according to them, are eternally enrolled in the
book of life, and infallibly ordained to salvation, while others are reprobate
and absolutely excluded : but as the preacher (they add) has no means of
knowing, in the first instance at least, *which* persons belong to which class ;
and since those who are thus ordained, are to be saved through the *means* God
has appointed ; the offers, and promises, and threatenings of the gospel are to
be addressed to all alike, as if no such distinction existed. The preacher, in
short, is to *act* in all respects, as if the system were not true.

" Each individual Christian again, according to them, though he is to
believe that he either is, or is not, absolutely destined to eternal salvation, yet
is also to believe that *if* his salvation is decreed, his holiness of life is also
decreed ;—he is to judge of his own state by " the fruits of the Spirit " which
he brings forth : to live in sin, or to relax his virtuous exertions, would be an
indication of his not being really (though he may flatter himself he is) one of
the elect. And it may be admitted, that one who does practically adopt and
conform to this explanation of the doctrine, will not be led into any evil by it ;
since his conduct will not be in any respect influenced by it. When thus
explained, it is reduced to a purely speculative dogma, barren of all practical
results."*

There is here no abandonment of his anti-Calvinistic position,—
nothing that should lead either himself or others to believe that
he is not an Arminian,—but there is a very explicit abandonment
of a favourite and plausible Arminian objection against Calvinism ;
and this important concession by such an opponent, is one of which
Calvinists are well entitled to take advantage. We cannot enter
upon any exposition of the practical application of the Calvinistic
doctrine of election, for the purpose of answering Dr Whately's
allegation,—that, by the very same process of explanation by which
Calvinism escapes from the positive objection of having an
injurious or dangerous tendency, it is proved to have no practical
application whatever, but to be a mere useless barren speculation.
We think we could prove that this notion is a confusion and a
fallacy ; and that it can be without much difficulty traced to this
cause, that he has not here made the same full and candid estimate,
as on some other branches of the argument, of the whole of what
Calvinists are accustomed to advance in explaining the practical
application of their doctrine, but confines his observation to some
of the features of the subject, and these not the most important
and peculiar. We think we could prove that it is this alone which
gives plausibility to his attempt to show, that the Calvinistic

---

* Essays, pp. 85-87.

doctrine of election, when explained by its more intelligent advocates in such a way as to escape from the imputation of having an injurious tendency, is deprived of all practical effect or utility whatever, and that we should act in all respects as if the doctrine were not true.

In these various ways,—and in one or two other points of less importance,—Dr Whately has made valuable concessions to Calvinism. In doing so he has been guilty of no inconsistency,—and we insinuate no such charge against him ; for his deviations from the course pursued by other anti-Calvinists affect,—not the meaning and import of any of the main positions actually held,—but only the validity of some of the arguments commonly adduced in the course of the discussion. He, no doubt, believes that he can still produce sufficient and satisfactory evidence against the Calvinistic doctrine of election,—though he has felt himself constrained to abandon, as unfounded, the objections commonly adduced against it from its alleged inconsistency with the divine character and government, and from its supposed injurious practical tendency. We regard these concessions as eminently creditable both to his head and to his heart, to his ability and his courage, to his sagacity and his candour. We value them very highly as contributions,—though not so intended,—to the establishment of what we reckon important scriptural truth. They have undoubtedly the advantage of being the concessions of an opponent; for Dr Whately admits that he is opposed to Calvinism, though he seems anxious to impress the conviction that he is equally opposed to Arminianism. We so highly admire the ability and candour Dr Whately has shown in the discussion of these topics, and we are so grateful for the valuable concessions he has made to what we reckon truth, that we would most willingly abstain from saying any thing that was disagreeable to him, except in so far as a regard to the interests of truth might require this. But we cannot retract the assertion that he is an Arminian. Were the matter, indeed, now to begin again *de novo*, we might avoid the use of this expression, knowing, as we now do, that he dislikes it, and feeling that we could express otherwise, by a little circumlocution, all that we meant to convey by it. But having been led to use the expression, in all simplicity, without imagining that it could be objected to or complained of,—and feeling confident that we can defend the perfect warrantableness of its

application to Dr Whately,—it would be an injury to truth to
retract it, or to refuse, when called upon, to defend it. In one
aspect, indeed, it is a matter of no importance whether Dr
Whately, or any man, may or may not be warrantably called an
Arminian; for the application of such terms, even when fully
warranted by ordinary usage, settles nothing about the truth or
soundness of doctrines. But when a question as to the application
of the name comes up in such a form, and is attended with such
circumstances, as virtually to involve the whole question of what
is Arminianism, and wherein does it differ from Calvinism ? or,
what is the true *status quæstionis* in the great controversy between
Calvinists and Arminians on the subject of Election ? then the
importance of the matter is manifest. Dr Whately's unexpected
denial that he is an Arminian, plainly raised the questions, what
is Arminianism, and in what respect does it differ from Calvinism ?
and whether there be any distinct and definite position that can be
taken upon the subject of election differing materially from both ?
The works of Faber and Professor Browne seemed to us to indicate
the existence of a great amount of misapprehension and confusion
as prevalent upon these questions among the clergy of the Church
of England; and suggested to us the desirableness of taking
advantage of Dr Whately's groundless repudiation of the charge
of being an Arminian, for giving some such explanation of the
state of the question as we have attempted. Faber has brought
out fully and distinctly the sources and the grounds of the misapprehension under which he, and no doubt many others, have been
led to abjure Arminianism while really believing it; and Dr
Whately is just as clearly and certainly an Arminian as Faber
was; but he has not brought out formally and in detail the
grounds on which he considers himself entitled to deny that he is
so. We have, in consequence, not ventured upon any explicit
allegations as to the origin and the cause of the strange fallacy
under which he labours in repudiating Arminianism as well as
Calvinism; but we have examined all the leading points in which,—
so far as we remembered,—he has deviated from the common course
of sentiment and expression among Arminian writers; and we
have shown, we think, that these deviations,—while highly honourable to him, and very valuable concessions to us,—imply no disbelief or denial of the fundamental distinctive principles of
Arminianism, and, indeed, do not affect the true state of the

question between the contending parties, but only the soundness and validity of some of the arguments adduced on the opposite sides respectively.

There is one other feature of Dr Whately's mode of dealing with this subject to which we must refer, though we scarcely know what to make of it. It is brought out in the following passages :—

"It is on these principles, viz.—That the first point of inquiry at least ought to be, What doctrines are *revealed* in God's word, and that we ought to expect that the doctrines so revealed should be, not matters of speculative curiosity, but of *practical* importance—such as "*belong* to us that we may do them;"—it is in conformity, I say, with these principles, that I have waived the question as to the *truth or falsity* of the Calvinistic doctrine of election, inquiring only whether it is *revealed*." *

"I am far from thinkly harshly of predestinarians, or of deciding that their peculiar doctrines are altogether untrue ; though, to me, they do not appear, at least, to be either *practical* or *revealed* truths. I do not call on them to renounce their opinions as heretical, but merely to abstain from imposing on others as a necessary part of the Christian faith a doctrine which cannot be *clearly* deduced from Scripture, and which there is this additional reason for supposing *not* to be revealed in Scripture, that it cannot be shown to have any practical tendency." †

"I wish it, then, to be distinctly understood (1) that I do not impute to any one opinions which he disclaims, nor am discussing any question as to what is inwardly *believed* by each, but only as to what is, whether directly or obliquely, *taught* ; and (2) that I purposely abstain, throughout, from entering on the question as to what is *absolutely true*, inquiring only what is or is not to be received and taught as a portion of *revealed gospel truth*. For no metaphysical dogma, however sound and capable of philosophical proof, ought to be taught as a portion of *revealed truth*, if it shall appear that the passages of Scripture that are supposed to declare it, relate in reality to a different matter. 'I would wish it to be remembered,' says Archbishop Sumner, 'that I do not desire to argue against predestination as believed in the closet, but as taught in the pulpit.' " ‡

And the same general idea is repeated, without the addition of anything else to explain it, in his last work, on the "Doctrine of the Sacraments." ‖

It is not easy to understand what Dr Whately meant by such statements as these. They surely indicate something very like confusion, vaccillation, and inconsistency. It would almost seem

---

* Pp. 84-5.   ‡ P. 96.
† Pp. 90, 91.   ‖ P. 13.

from them as if he had something like a latent sense that Calvinism, though not taught in Scripture, could yet be defended upon such grounds,—in the way of general reasoning of a philosophical or metaphysical kind,—as scarcely admitted of an answer; so that he shrunk from any formal deliverance on the question of its actual truth or falsehood. We do not wonder much at something like this state of mind being produced, especially in one who discerned so clearly, and who proclaimed so manfully, the weakness of some of the leading anti-Calvinistic arguments based upon topics of an abstract or metaphysical kind. We believe that the arguments in favour of Calvinism, derived from reason or general considerations, are just as triumphant,—viewed as a mere appeal to the understanding,—as the arguments from Scripture; and we do not wonder that there should occasionally be men who, while rejecting Calvinism, should have felt greater difficulty in disposing of the metaphysical than of the scriptural proof. This seems to be the case with Dr Whately. He appears to have something of the feeling, that on the field of general abstract discussion, he would not like to face a Calvinist; and that this department of the argument he would rather leave in abeyance than fairly grapple with. But, as we have said, we do not know well what to make either of the meaning or the consistency of some of his statements upon this subject. We must in fairness judge of his theological position, chiefly from the views he has expressed as to the meaning and import of the teaching of Scripture; and here, certainly, his position is not negative or ambiguous. He teaches explicitly and unequivocally, that the Calvinistic doctrine of election is *not* taught in Scripture; and he teaches further, that the only election which Scripture sanctions, is an election to outward privileges or means of grace, and not to faith, holiness, and heaven. This should settle the whole question with all who believe in the authority of Scripture; and the position here maintained is not only anti-Calvinistic, but may, when accompanied with an admission of the divine foreknowledge of all events, be warrantably and fairly designated as Arminian.

We are unwilling to quit this subject without some reference, however brief, to the objections by which the Calvinistic doctrine of election has been commonly assailed. The leading practical lessons, suggested by a survey of the controversy, for guiding men in the study of it, are such as these:—1*st*, That we should labour to form a clear, distinct, and accurate apprehension of the real nature of the leading point in dispute,—of the true import and bearing of the only alternatives that can well be maintained with regard to it. 2*d*, That we should familiarise our minds with definite conceptions of the meaning and the evidence of the principal arguments by which the truth upon the subject may be established, and the error refuted. 3*d*, That we should take some pains to understand the general principles at least applicable to the solution, or rather the disposal (for they cannot be solved) of the difficulties by which the doctrine we have embraced as true may be assailed. And, 4*th*, That we should then seek to make a wise and judicious application of the doctrine professed, according to its true nature, tendency, and bearing, and its relation to other truths; without allowing ourselves to be dragged into endless and unprofitable speculations in regard to its deeper mysteries or more intricate perplexities, or to be harassed by perpetual doubt and difficulty. A thorough and successful study of the subject implies the following out of all these lessons, and this conducts us over a wide and arduous field. It is on the first only of these four points we have touched,—one on which a great deal of ignorance and confusion seem to prevail. Of the others, the most important is that which enjoins a careful study of the direct and positive evidence that bears upon the determination of the main question on which the controversy turns. The strength of Calvinism lies in the mass of direct, positive, and,—as we believe,—unanswerable proof that can be produced from Scripture and reason, confirmed by much that is suggested by experience and the history of the human race, to establish its fundamental principles of the foreordination of whatsoever comes to pass, and the real and effectual election of some men to eternal life. The strength of Arminianism lies—not in the direct and positive evidence that can be produced to disprove Calvinistic foreordination and election, or to establish anti-Calvinistic non-foreordination and non-election,—but mainly in the proof, that God is not the author of sin, and that man is responsible for his own character and destiny; and in the inference that since Calvinism is inconsistent with these great and admitted truths, it must be false. This view of the state of the case shows the importance of being familiar with the direct and positive evidence by which Calvinism can be established, that we may rest on this as an impregnable foundation. But it shows also the importance of being familiar with the way and manner of disposing of the plausible and formidable difficulties on which mainly the Arminians found their case. These difficulties,—that is, the alleged inconsistency of Calvinism with the truths, that God is not the author of sin, and that man is responsible for his conduct and fate,—lie upon the very surface of the subject, and must at once present themselves even to the most ordinary minds; while, at the same time, they are so plausible, that they are well fitted to startle and to impress men, especially if they have not previously reflected much upon the subject. We do not intend to adduce the direct and positive evidence in support of the Calvinistic doctrine; but a few brief hints may help a little to show that the difficulties attaching to it, are, though not admitting of a full solution, yet by no means so formidable as at first sight they appear to be; and at any rate furnish no sufficient ground in right reason for rejecting the body of direct, positive, unanswerable proof by which the fundamental principles of Calvinism can be established. The following are some of the most obvious yet most important considerations bearing upon this matter, that ought to be remembered and applied, and especially that ought to be viewed in combination with each other, as parts of one argument upon this topic.

1st, When the same objections were advanced against the same doctrines as taught by the Apostle Paul, *he* manifested no very great solicitude about giving them a direct or formal answer; but contented himself with resolving the whole difficulty into God's sovereignty and man's ignorance, dependence, and incapacity. "Nay but, O man, who art thou that repliest against God? Shall the thing formed say to him that formed it, Why hast thou made me thus?" He knew that the doctrines were true, because he had received them by inspiration of the Holy Ghost; and we know that they are true, because he and other inspired men have declared them unto us. This should satisfy us, and repress any great anxiety about disposing of objections based upon grounds, the investigation of which runs up into matters, the full comprehension of which lies beyond the reach of our natural faculties, and of which we can know nothing except from the revelation which God has given us.

2d, It is utterly inconsistent with right views of our condition and capacities, and with the principles usually acted upon in regard to other departments of Christian theology,—as, for instance, the doctrine of the Trinity,—to assume,—as these objections do,—that we are entitled to make our actual perception of, or our capacity of perceiving, the consistency of two doctrines with each other, the test or standard of their truth. We do not pretend to be able to solve all the difficulties connected with the alleged inconsistency between the peculiar doctrines of Calvinism, and the truths that God is not the author of sin, and that man is responsible for his character and conduct, so as make their consistency with each other plain and palpable to our own minds or the minds of others; but we cannot admit that this affords any sufficient reason why we should reject one or other of the doctrines, provided each separately can be established upon competent and satisfactory evidence.

3d, The difficulties in question do not apply to the Calvinistic system *alone*, but bear as really, though not perhaps at first view as palpably, upon every system of religion which admits the moral government of God, the prevalence of moral evil among His intelligent creatures, and their future eternal punishment. Indeed, it is easy to show, that the leading difficulties connected with every scheme of doctrine virtually run up into one great difficulty, which attaches, and attaches equally, to them all, viz., the explanation of the existence and prevalence of moral evil ; or,— what is practically the same question, in another form,—the exposition of the way and manner in which God and men concur (for none but atheists can deny that in some way or other they do concur) in forming men's character and in determining men's fate. This subject involves difficulties which we cannot, in our present condition, fully solve ; and which we must just resolve into the good pleasure of God. They are difficulties from which no scheme of doctrine can escape, and which every scheme is equally bound, and at the same time equally incompetent, to explain. Men may shift the position of the one grand difficulty, and may imagine that they have succeeded at least in evading it, or putting it in abeyance or obscurity ; but with all their shifts and all their expedients, it continues as real and as formidable as ever. Unless men renounce altogether, theoretically or practically, the moral government of God, the prevalence of moral evil, and its eternal punishment, they must, in their explanations and speculations, come at length to the sovereignty of God, and prostrate their

understandings and their hearts before it, saying with our
Saviour, " Even so, Father, for so it hath seemed good in Thy
sight;" or with the great apostle, " O the depth of the riches
both of the wisdom and knowledge of God! how unsearchable
are His judgments, and His ways past finding out! For who hath
known the mind of the Lord? or who hath been His counsellor?
Or who hath first given to Him, and it shall be recompensed to
Him again? For of Him, and through Him, and to Him, are all
things; to whom be glory for ever.   Amen."*

* Rom. xi. 33-36.

CALVINISM,

AND THE

DOCTRINE OF PHILOSOPHICAL NECESSITY. *

In his "Discussions," Sir William Hamilton makes a theological demonstration, of a somewhat imposing kind. It is contained in the following passage :—

"Averments to a similar effect might be adduced from the writings of *Calvin*, and certainly nothing can be conceived more contrary to the doctrine of that great divine than what has latterly been promulgated as Calvinism (and, in so far as I know, without reclamation), in our Calvinistic Church of Scotland. For it has been here promulgated, as the dogma of this church (though in the face of its Confession as in the face of the Bible), by pious and distinguished theologians, that man has no will, agency, moral personality of his own, God being the only real agent in every apparent act of His creatures ; in short (though quite the opposite was intended), that the theological scheme of the absolute decrees implies fatalism, pantheism, the negation of a moral governor, as of a moral world. For the premises, arbitrarily assumed, are atheistic, the conclusion, illogically drawn, is Christian. Against such a view of Calvin's doctrine and of Scottish orthodoxy, I for one must humbly though solemnly protest, as (to speak mildly) not only false in philosophy, but heretical, ignorant, suicidal in theology."†

This strange passage was intended as a deadly assault upon Dr Chalmers, and upon the views which he had promulgated upon

* *British and Foreign Evangelical Review.* January 1858.
"Discussions on Philosophy and Literature, Education and University Reform." By Sir WILLIAM HAMILTON, Bart. Second Edition, 1853.
† Discussions, p. 628.

the subject of philosophical necessity. The doctrine here so vehemently denounced cannot, from the nature of the case, be any other than that commonly called the doctrine of philosophical necessity ; and though many will regard what is here said as very unjust and unfair, if viewed as applied to that subject, there is manifestly no other to which these statements can have any appearance of applying. When it is settled that the doctrine which Sir William here denounces is that of philosophical necessity,—and that, of course, the pious and distinguished theologians who are here held up to scorn are Dr Chalmers, and all who, professing like him to receive the Westminster Confession, have concurred with him in maintaining the doctrine of necessity as taught by Jonathan Edwards,—men will be able to understand something more of the import and object of the passage.

We do not of course intend to plunge into the *mare magnum* of the general subject of philosophical necessity as connected with " absolute decrees," " fatalism," " pantheism," " negation of a moral governor," etc., on which Sir William here declaims. The general subject brought before us by these statements is the most perplexing and mysterious that has ever occupied the mind of man. No one acquainted with the discussions which have taken place regarding it, can fail to have reached these two conclusions :—1st, That everything of any worth or value that can be said upon the subject, has been said in substance a thousand times ; and, 2d, That after all that has been said, there are difficulties and mysteries connected with it which never have been fully solved, and which manifestly never will be fully solved,—at least until men get either more enlarged mental faculties, or a fuller revelation from God. The practical result of the adoption of these conclusions,— which must have forced themselves upon all who have intelligently surveyed this subject,—is to render men rather averse to unnecessary discussions regarding it,—to make them less anxious about answering objections and clearing away difficulties,—and more willing to rest upon those fundamental principles which constitute the direct and proper evidence of what seems to be the truth upon the point. This state of mind and feeling,—the reasonable result of a deliberate survey of the discussions which have taken place upon the matter,—is sanctioned also by the example of the Apostle Paul, who, when the same objections were brought against his doctrines as have in all ages been brought against Calvinism, resolved the whole matter into the inscrutable sovereignty of God and the ignorance and helplessness of man, instead of directly and formally grappling with the objection. Sir William Hamilton's own views upon the subject are of a kind fitted to discourage,—if not to preclude, discussion ; especially discussion conducted in the way of bringing the opposite doctrines face to face, and trying to make an estimate of the comparative force of the objections against them. His views are briefly indicated in the following passages :—

" The philosophy, therefore, which I profess, annihilates the theoretical problem,—How is the scheme of liberty or the scheme of necessity to be rendered comprehensible ?—by showing that both schemes are equally inconceivable ; but it establishes liberty practically as a fact, by showing that it is either itself an immmediate *datum*, or is involved in an immediate *datum*, of consciousness." *

" *How* the will can possibly be free must remain to us, under the present limitation of our faculties, wholly incomprehensible. We are unable to conceive an absolute commencement ; we cannot, therefore, conceive a free volition. A determination by motives cannot, to our understanding, escape from necessitation." †

" *How*, therefore, I repeat moral liberty is possible in man or God, we are utterly unable speculatively to understand. But practically, the *fact*, that we are free, is given to us in the consciousness of an uncompromising law of duty, in the consciousness of our moral accountability." †

" Liberty is thus shown to be inconceivable, but not more than its contradictory necessity ; yet though inconceivable, liberty is shown also not to be impossible. The credibility of consciousness, to our moral responsibility, as an incomprehensible fact, is thus established." ‡

" This hypothesis alone accounts for the remarkable phenomenon which the question touching the *liberty* of the will—touching the *necessity* of human actions, has in all ages and in all relations exhibited. This phenomenon is the *exact equilibrium* in which the controversy has continued ; and it has been waged in metaphysics, in morals, in theology, from the origin of speculation to the present hour, with unabated zeal, but always with undecided success." §

It appears from these statements that Sir William, by his own admission, has thrown no new light upon this subject ; and that he claims credit for scarcely anything more than bringing out clearly, by an application of the doctrine of the conditioned, that there are, and must ever be, insoluble difficulties attaching to it.

---

* Reid's Works, p. 599, note.
† " Discussions," p. 624.

‡ " Discussions," p. 630.
§ " Discussions," pp. 631, 632.

Our present purpose does not lead us to advert to the grounds on which Sir William based his conclusion, or to the accuracy of the language in which his views are expressed. It is enough, in the mean time, that we direct attention to the fact, that he proclaims the existence of insoluble difficulties as attaching to this subject; and that he admits that he has made, and can make, no positive contribution to the explication of it. In substance, he leaves us on this whole subject of liberty and necessity very much in the position indicated in the remarkable and often quoted passage of Locke : " I cannot have a clearer perception of anything than that I am free, yet I cannot make freedom in man consistent with omnipotence and omniscience in God, though I am as fully persuaded of both as of any truth I most firmly assent to; and therefore I have long since given off the consideration of that question, resolving all into the short conclusion, that if it be possible for God to make a free agent, then man is free, though I see not the way of it." *

We have no material objection to offer to the substance of the statements quoted above from Locke and Sir William Hamilton ; but it may be worth while to notice how it is that they concur in this view as there brought out, although the one was a Necessitarian and the other was a Libertarian. Locke, though a Pelagian in theology, was a Necessitarian in philosophy,—that is, he held that doctrine of philosophical necessity, or that view of the laws which regulate men's mental processes and determine their volitions, against which Sir William declaims in the passage on which we are commenting. Sir William, on the contrary, makes here a sort of profession of Calvinism. He stands forth as the champion of Calvinistic orthodoxy, against the errors of its ignorant and injudicious friends ; and he gives something like evidence both of intelligence and integrity in dealing with this subject, by laying down the important position, that " the great articles of divine foreknowledge and predestination are both embarrassed by the selfsame difficulties."† But, notwithstanding this, he was in philosophy a Libertarian ; for, though he sometimes talks as if he thought it impracticable to decide between the opposite opinions, he at other times expresses a decided preference for the Libertarian view; and in the passage under consideration, he denounces, in no measured

---

* Locke, vol. iii. p. 487, folio edition, 1751. | † " Discussions," p. 627.

terms, the doctrine which is the contradictory correlative of it. The liberty or freedom for which Locke contended, was nothing more than actual moral responsibility for our actions; which he did not admit to be precluded, either by the doctrine of God's omniscience and omnipotence, or by the doctrine of philosophical necessity, though he was unable to explain how it could be reconciled with these doctrines. Sir William, on the other hand, was not tied up by any of his opinions to so limited a view of what liberty or freedom is, and would no doubt say that by the liberty which he claimed for man, he meant not merely actual moral responsibility, —which all admit,—but also that anti-necessitarian view of the laws that regulate man's mental operations, which has been supposed by many to be necessary as a basis for responsibility. But though he would say this, if necessary, and could do so consistently, it clearly appears, from a careful examination of the statements we have quoted from him, that he, like Locke, practically identifies liberty with actual moral responsibility ; and virtually admits, that the only thing which is really established by the testimony of consciousness, and *which is to be maintained at all hazards*, is our moral accountability, or the obligation "of an uncompromising law of duty." Most necessitarians,—including, of course, all the theologians whom Sir William denounces,—assert man's moral responsibility as fully and readily as their opponents ; and if it be merely the fact of moral accountability which man's consciousness establishes,—as Sir William virtually admits,—then the whole matter still resolves itself into the old and very perplexing question, as to what kinds or degrees of liberty are necessary to moral responsibility, and what kinds and degrees of necessity are inconsistent with it. Necessitarians, in general, have no hesitation in admitting the truth of Sir William's statement,[*] that it is the testimony of our consciousness, "that we are, though we know not how, the true and responsible authors of our actions, not merely the worthless links in an adamantine series of effects and causes." Necessitarians admit this, and undertake to prove, that there is nothing in the doctrine of philosophical necessity which can be shown to preclude either the actual reality, or the conscious sense, of this, as a feature in man's condition. Sir William virtually admits that it is only our actual moral responsibility to which the direct testi-

---

[*] P. 624.

mony of consciousness applies; and he has not entered anywhere, so far as we remember, into a deliberate and formal investigation of the nature and grounds of the liberty which is necessary to moral agency. By the denunciations, indeed, on which we are animadverting, and which, as we have explained, must be intended to apply to the doctrine of philosophical necessity as taught by Edwards and Chalmers, Sir William has identified himself with the Libertarian view; and has thus, whether he so intended it or not, virtually declared in favour of what has been commonly called the liberty of indifference, and the self-determining power of the will; for whatever he might say about the inconceivableness both of liberty and necessity, he would not, we presume, have denied that the one was the contradictory of the other, and that, therefore, the one was a reality, and the other was not.

But though Sir William has denounced the doctrine of philosophical necessity, and has, thereby, by plain implication, asserted a liberty of indifference and the self-determining power of the will, he has not entered into anything like argument against necessity, or in favour of liberty, beyond simply referring to the testimony of consciousness, in proof that we are responsible for our actions. This mode of dealing with it is unworthy of a philosopher, and wholly undeserving of notice as a call to enter upon a discussion of the general subject. "It has been here promulgated," he assures us, "as the dogma of this church ('our Calvinistic Church of Scotland'), by pious and distinguished theologians, *that man has no will, agency, moral personality of his own*, God being the only real agent in every apparent act of His creatures." Persons unacquainted with what has been going on in Scotland for the last generation, would be disposed to ask, with amazement, who are the pious and distinguished theologians who have put forth such offensive statements as Sir William ascribes to them? Those who are cognisant of the state of matters amongst us, are well aware that no theologians have ever promulgated this "dogma;" while they must know also that the only persons whom Sir William *could* have had in his eye, were Dr Chalmers and those who concurred with him in advocating the doctrine of philosophical necessity. These men certainly never intended to teach this; and they have made no statements bearing the slightest resemblance to those here put into their mouths. But Sir William, it seems, was of opinion that the doctrine of philosophical necessity implied all this, or led to it by logical sequence; and upon this ground he thought himself warranted in proclaiming to the world,—without furnishing to us any means of knowing the true ground of his assertion,—that pious and distinguished theologians in the Church of Scotland have promulgated the doctrine, " that man has no will, agency, moral personality of his own, God being the only real agent in every apparent act of His creatures." After this we are not in the least surprised that he goes on to tell us, that these men taught that "the theological scheme of the absolute decrees implies fatalism, pantheism, the negation of a moral governor as of a moral world." He admits, indeed, that " quite the opposite was intended;" but still he thinks himself entitled to charge them with teaching fatalism and pantheism; and intimates, further, in the immediately following sentence, that they can escape from atheism only by gross logical inconsistency.

In adverting to this charge of fatalism, pantheism, atheism, etc., we do not need to take into account what Sir William has here introduced into his statement about " the scheme of the absolute decrees." Sir William plainly did not intend to bring these charges against the scheme of the absolute decrees, simply as such, by whomsoever held; for, indeed, he professes to be writing here as a Calvinist, a champion of Calvinism, and, of course, an advocate of "the scheme of absolute decrees." And then, again, in so far as Dr Chalmers and other theologians may have assumed, that the scheme of the absolute decrees necessarily implied or drew with it the doctrine of philosophical necessity, this is just the point where we venture to think that their views are untenable, as we shall afterwards more fully explain. Sir William evidently intended, by the phraseology he has employed, to tell us that those of whom he was speaking regarded the scheme of the absolute decrees as implying the doctrine of philosophical necessity; and that, in his judgment, this doctrine of necessity, as held by them, implied fatalism, pantheism, atheism, etc. We cannot deny that Sir William had good grounds for ascribing to them the belief that the doctrines of the absolute decrees and of philosophical necessity are necessarily connected with each other; and we cannot defend the accuracy of this belief. But we do not need to take any of these topics into account in judging of Sir William's statement now under consideration. That statement is in substance this,—that some pious and distinguished theologians of the Church of Scotland have recently been teaching that man has no will, agency, moral personality of his own,—God being the only real agent in every apparent act of His creatures,—and that this is fatalism, pantheism, atheism; while the only ground he could have adduced for these heavy charges,—if he had been called upon to establish them,—was, that Dr Chalmers and some others had taught the doctrine of philosophical necessity as a part of their Calvinism, and that, in *his judgment* this doctrine necessarily implied all the fearful things which he had laid to their charge. The practice of adducing such charges, upon such grounds, and in such circumstances, is repudiated and denounced by every fair controversialist.

It is always a very unworthy procedure to describe a doctrine to which we are opposed, merely by consequences which we think deducible from it, but which its supporters disclaim; and then to attempt to run it down by attaching to it offensive nicknames. But there are some things which make it peculiarly unwarrantable to employ this process in regard to such a doctrine as that of philosophical necessity. Not only is it true that the doctrine has been maintained and defended by a large proportion of the ablest and best men that ever lived,—by many of the highest names in philosophy as well as in theology; but, from the nature of the case also, viewed both in its intellectual and in its moral aspects, there are considerations which aggravate the unreasonableness of attempting to dispose of it in such a way. The subject is one of great difficulty and intricacy; and this should have been felt to be a reason against attempting to scout it from the field of fair discussion by a dashing misrepresentation and a far-fetched inference. The question virtually resolves, as we have seen, into the investigation of the nature and grounds of the liberty and necessity that are consistent with, or indispensable to, moral agency; and nothing but utter incapacity or gross carelessness can prevent men from seeing that this is a subject of extreme difficulty, and one which no man, whatever be his standing or his pretensions, is entitled to treat in an offhand and reckless way. It is impossible for any man to reflect deliberately upon the ideas of liberty and necessity, —as applied, on the one hand, to the volitions of the divine mind and of other pure and holy beings, as for instance the glorified saints in heaven,—and as applied, on the other hand, to classes of men who have been subjected to most unfavourable moral influences, and have now sunk into deep moral degradation, but are still admitted to be responsible,—without seeing that there are profound mysteries connected with this matter which cannot be settled, as many seem to suppose, merely by laying it down that liberty is liberty, and that necessity is necessity, and that the one absolutely and universally excludes the other.

Liberty and necessity, manifestly, may be both predicated of the divine will, and of the will also of some classes of responsible creatures. If this be so, then we must have distinctions in the senses in which these words are applied,—precise specifications of the different senses in which they may be affirmed or denied respectively, of differently constituted and of differently circumstanced beings, all possessed of the capacity of moral agency. It is plain that liberty, in some sense, is not necessary to moral agency, and that necessity in some sense does not preclude it; and if so, there must be some difficult and intricate points to be examined and disposed of before the question between liberty and necessity can be determined; if it is to be decided by an application of the only standard to which Sir William refers, viz., their bearing respectively upon the point of responsibility. We do not profess to discuss this subject,—we merely wish to point out the unreasonableness of the way in which Sir William deals with it; and to explain why it is that there is nothing in what he has said about it, that calls for or requires any investigation of the general subject on the part of those whose views he has condemned.

There has always been a strong tendency, especially among the Libertarians, to attempt settling this controversy by dwelling upon inferences and practical consequences, supposed to flow from the opposite doctrines, instead of carefully examining the proper evidence directly applicable to the question of their truth and falsehood.* The question involved in this controversy is properly one of fact, and belongs to the province of psychology. It is a right and a safe rule for beings of our limited mental powers, and

---

* "The charge of fatalism and pantheism is sometimes met in the same style of argumentation, and the account is balanced by raising the cry of *Pelagian and Arminian* heresy. But it is quite as important, and, in most cases, far more easy, to determine whether a proposed doctrine is *true* or *false*, than to settle the question whether it is most nearly allied to Fatalism or Arminianism, to Pantheism or Pelagianism." (An Inquiry respecting the Self-determining Power of the Will, or contingent Volition, by Jeremiah Day, President of Yale College, p. 171.) This work contains a valuable defence of Edwards' views, published in 1838.

of our very inadequate capacity of tracing consequences, that we should make up our minds chiefly from an examination of the proper intrinsic evidence directly applicable to the subject under consideration, instead of attaching much weight to alleged inferences or consequences. The reasonableness of this general principle of procedure is peculiarly manifest when the consequence mainly founded upon is, that a particular doctrine overturns man's moral responsibility, and when this allegation is controverted by men of unquestionable ability and good character. When a body of men of this description assert, and undertake to prove, that the allegation, that a doctrine held by them overturns man's moral responsibility, and leads to fatalism and atheism, is unfounded; when they proclaim their belief in the existence and moral government of God, and their consciousness and recognition "of an uncompromising law of duty," and can appeal, in proof of the sincerity of this profession, to the general tenor of their own character and conduct; when they can further appeal to classes and communities who have received this doctrine, and yet have equalled any other sections of men in obedience to the divine will and in the discharge of moral duty; when such a state of things as this is presented, the allegation of an atheistic and immoral tendency becomes a practical absurdity, which should be left to those who are incapable of arguing the question upon its own proper merits, and which, even when brought forward by those who are capable of higher things, is scarcely worthy of notice. Calvinists, or Necessitarians,—against whose views this objection has been commonly adduced,—have perhaps wasted too much time and strength in elaborating a formal and direct answer to it. They might, we are disposed to think, have done more to establish them, by giving greater attention to the investigation of the materials by which the proper truth or falsehood of the contending theories,—apart from their alleged tendencies and consequences,—might be determined. Locke spoke like a true philosopher when, in the context of the passage formerly quoted, he said, "If you will argue for or against liberty *from consequences*, I will not undertake to answer you." Sir William, on the contrary, has descended to a mode of representation which should really have been left to those who are unable to reason, and are capable only of lavishing abuse. *

---

* We have much pleasure in supporting the strong disapprobation | here expressed of Sir William's mode of procedure, by the authority of the

Another curious peculiarity in Sir William's mode of dealing with this subject is, that his misrepresentation about moral responsibility, fatalism, atheism, etc., is directed only against the doctrine of philosophical necessity; while he gives us distinctly to understand, by the plainest implication, that no such objections can be substantiated against the doctrines of Calvinism. He is here professing to be a Calvinist, and to be defending genuine Calvinism against the misrepresentations of Dr Chalmers and others, who, while professing to believe in Calvinism, do not understand it so well as he,—who indeed corrupt the Calvinistic system by teaching the doctrine of philosophical necessity as a part of it. Sir William's heavy charges against these men are, of course, based not upon the Calvinism which he professes to hold in common with them, but upon the philosophical necessity which they taught as a part of their Calvinism, but in which he differs from them. In other words, he professes to believe, as every Calvinist does, that God hath foreordained whatsoever comes to pass, and he sees nothing in this doctrine that tends to overthrow moral responsibility and to bring in fatalism; while these alarming consequences attach to the doctrine of philosophical necessity—a doctrine which, as held by those whom he was denouncing, *could be nothing else* than an effectual provision made by God for bringing about the results which in His " absolute decrees" He had predetermined to bring to pass.

Upon the ground of considerations derived from these various sources,—viz., the general character and standing of this subject of liberty and necessity viewed historically as a topic of controversial discussion,—the special views of Sir William Hamilton regarding it,—and the very peculiar character of that passage of his which is more immediately under our consideration,—we do not consider ourselves called upon, and we do not intend, to enter upon the more general aspects of the great subject which is here brought

---

following weighty and most apposite statement of Sir James Macintosh :— "There is no topic which requires such strong grounds to justify its admission into controversy, as that of moral consequences; for, besides its incurable tendency to inflame the angry passions, and to excite obloquy against individuals, which renders it a practical restraint on free inquiry, the employment of it in dispute seems to betray apprehensions derogatory from the dignity of morals, and not consonant either to the dictates of reason or to the lessons of experience. The rules of morality are too deeply rooted in human nature to be shaken by every veering breath of metaphysical theory." — *Edinburgh Review*, vol. xxxvi. p. 255.

under our notice. We do not intend to deal with Sir William's two principal positions, viz. :—1. That the doctrine of philosophical necessity is " in the face of the Bible ;" 2. That it overturns men's moral responsibility, and leads to fatalism and atheism. Sir William has not given us any evidence or argument in support of these two positions. He has said nothing here upon the subject but what might just as well have been said by the most ignorant person that ever railed against Calvinism. We deny both these positions, though we do not mean to assert their contradictories. We do not believe that there is anything in the Bible that either proves or disproves the doctrine of philosophical necessity. We have never seen any satisfactory evidence that it tends to immorality and atheism.

There, is, however, another statement made by Sir William in the passage on which we are animadverting, which,—though relating to a point of inferior intrinsic importance,—is perhaps more likely to be believed by ordinary readers, and thereby to do mischief, while at the same time it involves a great personal injustice,—viz., that this doctrine is contrary to the teaching of Calvin,—is a corruption of pure Calvinism,—and more specifically, is " in the face of the Confession of Faith" of " our Calvinistic Church of Scotland." This was probably intended by Sir William to be the real gravamen of the charge against Dr Chalmers, that he had taught a doctrine opposed to the symbolical books which he had subscribed. This is a serious charge, and a favourite one with Sir William. He repeated it somewhat more calmly, though still not without plain indications of unphilosophical vehemence, in a note to the sixth volume of the collected edition of Professor Dugald Stewart's works. This note, which is as follows, was published in 1855 :—

" The Scottish Church asserts, with equal emphasis, the doctrine of the absolute decrees of God and the doctrine of the moral liberty of man. The theory of Jonathan Edwards touching the bondage of the will is, on the Calvinistic standard of the Westminster Confession, not only heterodox but heretical ; and yet we have seen the scheme of absolute necessity urged by imposing authority, and even apparently received with general acquiescence, as that exclusively conformable to the recognised tenets of our ecclesiastical establishment."*

It is the more needful to advert to this charge, because the leading idea on which it is based has been countenanced also by

* P. 402.

Professor Stewart, in a passage published for the first time by Sir William himself in 1854 in his edition of the "Dissertation on the Progress of Philosophy," forming the first volume of the collected works. Stewart's statement upon the subject, which is written with the calmness of a philosopher, and conveys no personal attack, is inserted by Sir William as a passage "restored" from the author's manuscript in the note M.M.,* and is as follows :—

"In the Confession of Faith of the Church of Scotland (the articles of which are strictly Calvinistic), the freedom of the human will is asserted as strongly as the doctrine of the eternal decrees of God. 'God (it is said, chap. iii.) from all eternity did, by the most wise and holy counsel of His own will, freely and unchangeably ordain whatsoever comes to pass. Yet so as thereby neither is God the author of sin, *nor is violence offered to the will of the creatures,* nor is the liberty or contingency of second clauses taken away, but rather established.' And still more explicitly in chap. ix, 'God hath indued the will of man with that natural liberty, that it is neither forced, nor by any absolute necessity of nature determined, to do good or evil.'"

Stewart here plainly sanctions the general idea on which Sir William's charge against Edwards and Chalmers is founded, and quotes those portions of the Confession which he regards as establishing his position. Such a charge, brought forward in such circumstances, and resting upon grounds which may appear not altogether destitute of plausibility to ill-informed persons, demands consideration ; and this brings us back to what we really intended to have been the main subject of this discussion. We believe the charge to be utterly groundless ; while at the same time we do not altogether approve of the aspects in which Edwards and Chalmers have represented this matter. Our views upon this point may be embodied in two plain propositions, and we do not mean to attempt more at present than briefly indicating the grounds on which we think they may be established. 1st, There is nothing in the Calvinistic system of theology, or in the Westminster Confession of Faith, which *precludes* men from holding the doctrine of philosophical necessity. 2d, There is nothing in the Calvinistic system of theology, or in the Westminster Confession, which *requires* men to hold the doctrine of philosophical necessity. By establishing the first of these positions, we vindicate Edwards, Chalmers, and other pious and distinguished theologians, from the charge which Sir William has adduced against them of corrupting Cal-

* P. 575.

vinism, and contradicting the Westminster Confession. By
establishing the second, we vindicate Calvinism from the servitude
which the views of Edwards and Chalmers seem to impose upon
it, of being obliged to undertake the defence of a doctrine which,
—whether true or false,—belongs, after all, to the department of
philosophy rather than of theology, and ought to be left to be disposed of upon its own proper philosophical grounds.

First, then, we say that there is nothing in the Calvinistic
system of theology, or in the Westminster Confession, which precludes men from holding the doctrine of philosophical necessity.
We have hitherto spoken of this doctrine chiefly incidentally,
assuming that its general nature and import are well known; but
it may be proper now to state more formally what is meant by it.
The advocates of this doctrine maintain that there is an invariable
and necessary connection between men's motives and their volitions,—between objects of desire and pursuit as seen and apprehended by them and all their acts of volition or choice; or that
our volitions and choices are invariably determined by the last
practical judgment of the understanding. Libertarians admit
that men's volitions or choices are, ordinarily and in general, determined by motives as seen and apprehended by the mind; but
deny that there is a law regulating our mental processes, by which
this determination of volitions by motives is rendered invariable
and necessary. On the contrary, they maintain, in opposition to
this, and as the only alternative, that the will has a liberty of indifference, whereby, irrespective or in disregard of any motives
that may be presented to it, it may remain *in equilibrio*; that it may
determine or put forth a volition or choice, either in accordance
with or in opposition to the motives presented to it, and that it
can do this in the exercise of an inherent self-determining power
of its own. The invariable and necessary influence of motives in
determining volitions,—and a liberty of indifference, combined with
a self-determining power in the will itself,—are thus the opposite
positions of the contending parties on this question. The dispute
manifestly turns wholly upon a question as to what is the law
which regulates those mental processes that result in, or constitute, volitions or choices; and this is properly and primarily a
question in philosophy, the materials for determining which must
be sought in an appeal to consciousness, and in an application of
the data which consciousness furnishes. This statement of the

real nature of the point in dispute, is surely fitted to suggest at
once the improbability of the necessitarian view telling so powerfully upon great theological questions, and leading to such fearful
consequences, as Sir William Hamilton alleges.

We have to show that men who have embraced the Calvinistic
system of theology, and subscribed the Westminster Confession,
are not thereby precluded from maintaining this view of the law
which regulates our volitions, commonly and justly described as
the doctrine of philosophical necessity. It may be proper, in the
first place, to advert to the authority of Augustine and Calvin,
unquestionably the two highest names in theology. Professor
Stewart, in the passage which immediately precedes that quoted
above,—and which is to be found in the former edition of the Dissertation, as prefixed to the " Encyclopædia Britannica," *—says
that " Augustine has asserted the liberty of the will in terms as
explicit as those in which he has announced the theological dogmas
with which it is most difficult to reconcile it, nay, he has gone so
far as to acknowledge the essential importance of this belief as a
motive to virtuous conduct ;" and then he gives a quotation from
Augustine in support of this statement. Sir William has asserted
that " nothing can be conceived more contrary to the doctrine of
that great divine (Calvin), than what has latterly been promulgated as Calvinism in our Calvinistic Church of Scotland,"—
meaning, as is manifest, the doctrine of philosophical necessity.
He has given no quotations or references in support of this position, though he would have had no difficulty in producing extracts, which, to those who had never read Calvin, would have
appeared to establish it. But the true views of Augustine and
Calvin upon this subject, are not to be learnt from a few isolated
passages. They can be correctly understood only upon a deliberate and comprehensive survey of their whole position. If it
be true, as Stewart alleges, that Augustine has expressly asserted
the liberty of the will, it is at least as true that he has often
explicitly denied it. He asserts it in some senses and denies it in
others; and he has not always taken due care to explain fully
the sense in which he was employing the phrase for the time,
and to adhere to this sense throughout. And accordingly, in the
great controversy between the Jansenists and the Jesuits as to

* 7th Edition, p. 267.

what Augustine's theological doctrines were, there is no point in regard to which the Jesuits have been able to make out nearly so plausible a case as in support of Stewart's position, that Augustine asserted the liberty of the will. On this, however, as on every other point, the Jansenists gained the victory,—though not quite so decisively as upon the other departments of the controversy. It has been proved that Augustine held, and held as great scriptural doctrines, that man before the fall had liberty or freedom of will,—in this sense, that he was able to will and to do good as well as to will and to do evil; that he entirely lost this liberty of will by the fall; that fallen man in his unrenewed state has not liberty of will, or has it only,—in this sense, that he is still fully responsible for what he does as being a free moral agent, acting voluntarily or spontaneously; and that when men's wills have been renewed by God's grace, and they are restored again to liberty of will,—in this sense, that they are now again able to will and to do good as well as evil,—it is still true that God requires of them what they are not able to perform. It can be proved that Augustine held all these views in regard to the liberty of the will; while it cannot be proved that he has given any deliverance whatever upon the only point involved in the controversy about philosophical necessity. All this, which can be proved in regard to Augustine, is equally true of Calvin, the main difference between the two cases being this, that Calvin has more fully and carefully than Augustine, explained the different senses in which the will might be said to be free and not free,—that he has adhered more closely in treating of this subject to precise and definite phraseology, carefully explained and consistently applied, —and that he has never spoken of free will without affording, to careful readers, abundant materials for understanding in what sense he employed it, and especially for satisfying themselves that he did not hold liberty in any sense inconsistent with necessity, as understood in the present controversy.

In Calvin's most important and masterly treatise, "De Servitute et Liberatione Humani Arbitrii," he has fully brought out his views upon this subject, and has furnished ample materials for establishing all we have said concerning him. A considerable portion of this treatise is occupied with an elaborate investigation as to what were Augustine's views upon this point,—and a conclusive proof, in opposition to his popish antagonist Pighius, that

Augustine, with occasional looseness and inaccuracy of expression, held the same views in substance which he and his fellow Reformers had promulgated. We may briefly advert to one or two points, indicating plainly enough the leading features of the views of Augustine and Calvin upon this matter. There is one very striking and pithy saying of Augustine's, in speaking of the fall, which Calvin repeatedly quotes with approbation, viz.: "Homo libero arbitrio male usus et se perdidit et ipsum,"—man, by making a bad use of his free will, lost both himself and it,—a statement which throws a flood of light upon the whole system of doctrine which these great men taught upon this subject. Another statement of Augustine's, which Calvin repeatedly quotes with approbation, and which was applied by them, both to renewed and unrenewed men, is, "Jubet Deus quæ non possumus ut noverimus quid ab ipso petere debeamus,"—God requires of us what we cannot perform, in order that we may know what we ought to ask from Him. We give only one other brief extract from the treatise above referred to. "I have always declared that I have no wish to fight about the name (of free will), if it were once settled that *liberty* ought to be referred not to the power or capacity of choosing equally good or evil, but to spontaneous motion and consent. And what else mean the words of Augustine? He says, 'The will is free, but only to evil. Why? because it is moved by delight and its proper appetite.' He adds afterwards, 'But this will which is free for evil because it is delighted with evil, is not free for good, because it has not been emancipated.' To which Calvin subjoins, 'all this is so accordant with my doctrine, that you might suppose it had been written for the defence of it.'* Luther and his followers, who had at first made some very absolute and exaggerated statements in the way of denying free will altogether, came afterwards to attach much importance to a distinction between man's freedom in things external, civil, and moral, and his freedom in things properly spiritual, and they embodied this distinction in the Confession of Augsburg.† Calvin admitted the truth and reality of this distinction, though he did not regard it as of much importance in a

---

* Calvini Opera, tom. ix. p. 141; Amstel, 1667. He touches upon the same topic also in the Institutes, B. ii., C. ii. s. 8 and 9, and c. iii. s. 13 and 14.

† Art. xviii.

theological point of view. But while admitting that man has a
power or freedom in things outward and merely moral which he
has not in things spiritual, he has given no indication that he
thought that even, in regard to the former class of subjects, man
has a liberty of indifference, or his will a self-determining power.
In the 2d chapter of the 2d Book of the Institutes, he has given
a very striking and eloquent description of what man can effect
by the exercise of his powers as brought to bear upon outward
and natural things, and upon arts, literature, and philosophy, as
compared with the blindness and uselessness of the unaided
understanding in religious matters. But neither here has he said
anything which implies that he denied the doctrine of philosophical
necessity, or ascribed to the will of man any liberty or capacity
inconsistent with it.

In short, neither Augustine nor Calvin entertained or discussed the psychological question as to what the laws are which
regulate men's mental processes, and determine their volitions.
The liberty and necessity of which they treated, and which in
different sentences they affirmed and denied, referred to something
very different from, and much more important than, this. From
their denials of liberty and free-will, we would not be warranted
in asserting that they held the doctrine of philosophical necessity ;
and neither, on the other hand, is any one entitled to infer, from
their assertions of liberty and free-will, that they denied that doctrine. And this, indeed, is really the substance of what is true,
and can be established, not only of Augustine and Calvin, who
have been honoured more than any other uninspired men to bring
out correctly the scheme of divine truth,—but of Calvinistic
divines in general, and among the rest, of the authors of the
Westminster Confession.

Professor Stewart evidently knew very little about this matter
in its theological aspects. But he writes modestly and cautiously.
The only statement he makes about Augustine is literally true,
though it is not the whole truth, and is certainly, in the sense in
which alone it can be established, quite irrelevant to the object he
had in view. That "nothing can be conceived more contrary to
the doctrine of" Calvin than the doctrine of philosophical necessity, as taught by Edwards and Chalmers,—and this is what Sir
William Hamilton *must* have intended to assert,—is a position for
which no evidence has been or can be produced ; and it is scarcely

possible that he could be ignorant that he had no materials whatever for establishing it.

We proceed now to the more important and pressing part of the case, that which professes to deal with the teaching of the Westminster Confession. Upon this point Stewart asserts, in almost the very same terms which he had employed in speaking of Augustine, that in the Confession the freedom of the human will is asserted as strongly as the doctrine of the eternal decrees of God;" and quotes two passages, the one from the 3d and the other from the 9th chapter in support of this position. He evidently meant to assert that the Confession, though teaching strict Calvinism on the subject of foreordination, taught also the Libertarian view on the subject of the will, as opposed to the doctrine of philosophical necessity. But both his general statement, and his proofs derived from the Confession, manifestly labour under all the difficulties and drawbacks connected with the ambiguity of the phrase, "the freedom of the human will," which is the subject of his proposition. The "freedom of the will" may be understood in a variety of senses, and on both sides of the controversy would be either affirmed or denied, according as it might be explained. It is plain enough from the context in what sense Stewart understood it, and meant it to be understood; but still the vagueness and ambiguity of the expression in itself gives the appearance of greater weight to his proofs than they possess. Sir William has not defined what the doctrine is against which he declaimed so vehemently in his "Discussions;" but it is quite plain, that what he had in view was, and could be nothing else than, the doctrine of philosophical necessity, as held by Dr Chalmers; and this he pronounced to be "in the face of the Confession as in the face of the Bible." In his more recent note in the 6th vol. of Stewart, he brings it out somewhat more definitely as "the theory of Jonathan Edwards touching the bondage of the will;" and this he pronounces to be "on the Calvinistic standard of the Westminster Confession, not only heterodox but heretical." It looks like an unfair attempt to excite prejudice, that in the next clause in which he repeats his attack upon Dr Chalmers, he should speak of it as "the scheme of *absolute* necessity, urged by imposing authority." But not to dwell upon this,—especially as it is notorious that Dr Chalmers' views upon this subject were avowedly identical with those of Edwards,—we are fully warranted in laying

it down, that Sir William has asserted, that the doctrine of philosophical necessity, as taught by Edwards and Chalmers, is "in
the face of the Confession,"—"is on the Calvinistic standard of the
Westminster Confession, not only heterodox but heretical." This
is a definite statement. It involves a serious charge. Is it true?

There is surely a considerable antecedent improbability that
the views of Edwards and Chalmers should be opposed in an important point to the Confession, and that Sir William Hamilton
should have been the first and only person to discover and proclaim this. Dr Chalmers had repeatedly professed his public adherence to the Confession as the confession of his faith. He, of
course, believed that he believed it, and that his teaching was in
full accordance with its statements. The ministers of the church
to which he belonged,—who had all themselves subscribed the Confession,—found nothing in his teaching opposed to it. The question
was once put formally and explicitly by Dr Erskine to Edwards,
whether he could subscribe the Westminster Confession, and he
in reply declared his readiness to do so.* But still it is not impossible that these men may have been wholly wrong in this matter,
and that Sir William may have been right. In publicly adducing
so serious a charge, he ought in fairness to have distinctly specified
the grounds on which it rested. He has not done so. But the
passages quoted by Stewart are manifestly those on which the
charge *must* rest; although something might also be made of a
passage in the 5th chapter upon Providence, and of the statements
which assert or imply, that our first parents were left to the freedom of their own will, and enjoyed before the fall a liberty of will
which we do not possess.

The first passage is taken from the 3d chapter; it is as fol-

* We subjoin the passage, though well known, because it is curious and interesting:—" You are pleased, dear sir, very kindly to ask me, whether I could sign the Westminster Confession of Faith, and submit to the presbyterian form of church government; and to offer to use your influence to procure a call for me to some congregation in Scotland. I should be very ungrateful if I were not thankful for such kindness and friendship. As to my subscribing to the substance of the Westminster Confession, there would be no difficulty; and as to the presbyterian government, I have long been perfectly out of conceit of our unsettled, independent, confused way of church government in this land, and the presbyterian way has ever appeared to me most agreeable to the word of God, and the reason and nature of things; though I cannot say that I think that the presbyterian government of the Church of Scotland is so perfect, that it cannot, in some respects, be mended." (P. 163, Memoir of Edwards, prefixed to the London Edition of his works in two large volumes, 1840.)

lows :—" God, from all eternity, did by the most wise and holy counsel of His own will, freely and unchangeably ordain whatsoever comes to pass, yet so as thereby neither is God the author of sin, nor is violence offered to the will of the creatures, nor is the liberty or contingency of second causes taken away but rather established."

Every one must see, and no Calvinist has ever disputed, that if it be indeed true that God has unchangeably foreordained whatsoever comes to pass, this certainly implies that liberty, in some sense, as predicated even of men's violitions and actions, is excluded ; and that necessity, in some sense, is established. This being tacitly conceded as undeniable, the latter part of the above section of the Confession is directed to the general object, of disclaiming or shutting out certain extreme views as to the inferences which some might deduce from this great doctrine of universal foreordination. All that is here expressly asserted is, that the three things here specified do not follow from foreordination. But we admit that the passage may be held in fairness to imply, that the things here specified not only do not follow from predestination, but are in themselves bad, or false, or impossible. The latter part then of the passage may be paraphrased thus: "It may be thought that this doctrine of foreordination makes God the author of sin, but however plausible this allegation may be, we do not admit its truth ; we deny that God is the author of sin, and we deny that it is a just inference from foreordination that He is so. It may further be alleged plausibly, that by this universal and unchangeable foreordination violence is offered to the will of the creatures, and that the liberty or contingency of second causes is taken away ; but we deny that violence is or should be offered to the will of the creatures, or that the liberty or contingency of second causes is taken away by foreordination or by any thing else; and, on the contrary, we hold that the liberty or contingency of second causes is rather established by it." Now there is here no mention of, or reference to, the doctrine of philosophical necessity. The only doctrine mentioned here is that of foreordination; and in addition to stating it and asserting its truth, the substance of what is said about it is, that while it may suggest plausible, it furnishes no solid, grounds for the inference, either that God is the author of sin, or that violence is offered to the will of the creatures. The only way therefore in which this section of the Confession can bear upon the proof, that the doctrine of philosophical necessity is heretical, is this,— this proves that it is wrong that violence be offered to the will of the creatures, the doctrine of philosophical necessity offers violence, etc., and therefore it is here condemned. But the Confession furnishes no materials that bear, or even seem to bear, upon the proof of the minor proposition about the nature, tendencies, and result of the doctrine of philosophical necessity. This proposition is not more self-evident,—nay, it is not even more plausible,—than the one that by foreordination violence is offered to the will of the creatures. It is not to be assumed as true. It must be proved by distinct and independent materials, for nothing of this sort is to be found in the Confession. Edwards and Chalmers have no hesitation in applying to their doctrine of necessity what the Confession applies to foreordination,—viz., that thereby neither is God the author of sin, nor is violence offered to the will of the creatures. And there is certainly nothing in the Confession that can be pleaded either to the effect of precluding them from taking this ground, or of throwing any difficulty in the way of their maintaining it. Indeed, the only correct sense of what is meant by " offering violence to the will of the creatures" is not, com- pelling them to will in a certain way,—for that is impossible and inconsistent with the nature of will as will,—but compelling them to do what their will abhors. We will present the view generally taken upon this point by Calvinists in the words of John Knox, in his masterly treatise on predestination, which having been re- published in the fifth volume of Mr Laing's admirable edition of his collected works, will soon, we hope, become better known amongst us than it has hitherto been. " I affirm that God worketh all in all things according to the purpose of the same His good will, and yet that He useth no violence, neither in compelling His creatures, neither constraining their wills by any external force, neither yet taking their wills from them, but in all wisdom and justice, using them as He knoweth most expedient for the mani- festation of His glory ; without any violence, I say, done to their wills, *for violence is done to the will of a creature when it willeth one thing and yet by force, by tyranny, or by a greater power, it is compelled to do the things which it would not."*

----

* Pp. 143, 144.

This is the proper meaning of the words, this is the recognised sense of the statement, among Calvinistic writers; and, therefore, the portion of the Confession founded on by Stewart, not only contains nothing in the least adverse to the doctrine of philosophical necessity, but nothing that has even the appearance of being so. For even the opponents of this doctrine will scarcely allege, that it implies that violence is offered to the will of the creatures, in the sense in which that has now been explained. In order to warrant such an allegation, it would be requisite that there should be a denial of the liberty of spontaneity, or the power of doing freely and spontaneously what we will or choose to do. And not only have all the supporters of philosophical necessity uniformly ascribed to men a liberty of spontaneity; but the opponents of that doctrine have admitted that this liberty of spontaneity is perfectly consistent with it, while they hold it to be insufficient as the basis of moral responsibility.

Mr Stewart seems to indicate, by his italics, that he regarded the clause on which we have been commenting, about "violence offered to the will of the creatures," as embodying the strength of his case. But if he had been familiar with the way in which these topics have been discussed among theologians, he would probably have been of opinion that the third point referred to, viz., "the liberty or contingency of second causes," furnished an argument quite as plausible, especially when viewed in connection with the fuller statement upon the same subject, contained in the 5th chapter on Providence, sec. 2. "Although, in relation to the foreknowledge and decree of God, the first cause, all things come to pass, immutably and infallibly, yet, by the same providence, He ordereth them to fall out according to the nature of second causes, necessarily, freely, or contingently." The third chapter states the substance of what Scripture teaches concerning God's decrees,—that is, His purposes or determinations formed from eternity as to all that was to come to pass in time. This fifth chapter gives the substance of Scripture teaching as to God's providence,—that is, as to all that He does in time for carrying into effect the purposes which He had formed from eternity. God having foreordained whatsoever comes to pass, provision is made for securing all the results so ordained and determined. And all who hold the Calvinistic doctrine on the subject of foreordination must, in consistency also, receive the common Calvin-

istic doctrine on the subject of providence, or the government
which God is ever exercising over all His creatures and all their
actions. Against the doctrine of foreordination, men are very
prone to adduce the objections,—that it makes God the author
of sin,—that it offers violence to the will of the creatures,
—and that it takes away the liberty or contingency of second
causes. These objections, seem to apply with equal plausibility,
to the doctrine of providence as to that of predestination; and
Calvinists deal with these objections, in both cases, in the same
way, by admitting that these consequences would be fatal to Calvinistic doctrines if it could be conclusively proved that they were
necessary consequences; and by asserting and undertaking to
prove that these consequences do not necessarily follow from their
doctrines, or at least that this cannot be established. We have
nothing to do at present with the allegation that the Calvinistic
doctrines of predestination and providence make God the author
of sin. We have already explained the meaning and bearing of
the allegation about violence being offered to the will of the creatures; and proved that it is utterly inadequate for the purpose for
which Stewart adduced it,—that it has no bearing whatever upon
the question whether Edwards' doctrine of philosophical necessity
is or is not opposed to the Confession. In regard to the third
point, we have nothing to do directly with the contingency, but
only with the liberty, of second causes. What is said about this,
and how does it bear, if at all, upon the question under consideration ? God has foreordained whatsoever comes to pass, and He
has made provision,—for securing that every thing which He had
before ordained should be actually brought about. This might
appear, and has indeed been alleged, to involve or require the
establishment of an absolute, universal, and indiscriminate
necessity or fatalism, as comprehending and controlling, equally
and alike, all agents and events. But Calvinists deny that
this follows from their doctrines. These doctrines no doubt
imply that, in relation to the foreknowledge and decree of
God the first cause, all things do come to pass immutably and
infallibly, and thus they certainly establish necessity and
exclude liberty in some sense; yet they do not take away the
liberty of second causes, and they leave it open to God to cause
all things to come about according to the nature of these second
causes, necessarily, freely, or contingently. In other words, Cal-

vinists maintain that God, in executing His decrees in providence, brings about different classes of events in a way that is in full accordance with their own distinct, proper natures,—bringing to pass necessary things necessarily, free things freely, and contingent things contingently. This, of course, implies that there are under God's government free agents, who are dealt with in all respects as free agents, according to their proper nature, and the actual qualities and capacities they possess. As free agents they act freely; and although, if the doctrine of the foreordination of all things be true, there is a necessity in some sense attaching to all their actions, this does not preclude their having also a liberty attaching to them, in accordance with their general character and standing, as being free, in contradiction from necessary, agents. Among these free agents—in whom the liberty of second causes is maintained and preserved,—notwithstanding the control which God exercises over all their actions in order to execute His decrees, are of course men, rational and responsible beings. God has made them rational and responsible, and He has endowed them with at least such freedom or liberty as is necessary to responsibility. He ever deals with them in accordance with the qualities and capacities which He has bestowed upon them. He does not deal with them as He does with the material creation or with the irra tional animals. Although ever infallibly executing His decrees, He leaves them in the full possession of the rationality, responsibility, and liberty which He has bestowed upon them.

No one acquainted with the ground taken in discussions upon this subject by the Calvinistic divines of the seventeenth century, can have any doubt that this is the meaning of the statement under consideration, and that this was all that these words were intended to express; 'and if so, then it is manifest that they just throw us back upon the question, to be decided upon its own proper grounds, as to the nature, species, and foundations of the liberty which men actually possess,—while they afford us no materials whatever, direct or indirect, for determining the question, whether or not this liberty is to be held as precluding the doctrine of philosophical necessity. Edwards and Chalmers of course held that men are free agents,—that they are in some sense possessed of a free will, which neither the predestination nor the providence of God annihilates or supersedes; and if so, they could have no difficulty in subscribing these portions of the Confession.

But perhaps the portion of the Confession which has most the appearance of something like hostility to the doctrine of philosophical necessity, is that which Stewart quotes from the beginning of the 9th chapter, which treats of " free will." The statement is this, " God hath endued the will of man with that natural liberty that it is neither forced, nor by any absolute necessity of nature determined to good or evil." This is plainly intended as a general description of the human will, or rather of some leading features of it, applicable to the will at all times, and amid all the changes which in some respects it has undergone. There is, it is here asserted, a certain natural liberty with which God has endued the will of man, and which it ever retains, and must retain, as essential to its proper nature. But it must be observed, that this is not a full definition or description of the will as a power or faculty of man, such as might be expected in a philosophical treatise giving an account of the human mind. The Confession professes to give a summary of what is taught in Scripture, and no one has ever imagined that Scripture contains materials for enabling us to give a full description of the will as a faculty of man, and to determine, directly and at once, between the two opposite theories of liberty and necessity. The Scripture affords materials for determining questions about the will only in some of its theological bearings. And accordingly it must be noticed that the Confession does not here speak generally of its being determined, but only of its being determined *to good or evil*. These words, " to good or evil," are a constituent part of the only affirmation here put forth. It is not a statement about the grounds and causes of the ordinary determinations of the will, or of volitions in general, but about *determinations to good or evil*,—that is, about volitions which involve a choosing between good and evil, or a preference of the one of these to the other. The general object of the whole chapter was to unfold the different aspects which man has presented in his fourfold state, as to freedom or liberty of will *in choosing between good and evil*. To the freedom or bondage of man's will, with reference to choosing between good and evil, as possessed and exhibited in four different conditions, the four following sections of the chapter are devoted ; and the first section was evidently intended to be introductory to the exposition of this general topic in its different stages. So that, viewed in its connection with what it introduces, it may be fairly regarded as amounting, in substance, to a statement to this effect,—that though man at different stages of his history—unfallen, fallen, renewed, glorified—has had his will determined to good and also determined to evil, *this result* is not to be ascribed in *either* case to force, or to any absolute necessity of nature, as that would be inconsistent with the natural liberty with which God has endowed the will. This was the aspect in which, principally,—we might almost say exclusively,—both the Reformers of the sixteenth, and the great Calvinistic divines of the seventeenth, century contemplated the subject of free will; and it is in this sense alone, we are convinced, that the compilers of the Westminster Confession intended to expound it.

But though we are satisfied of the sufficiency of the grounds on which this limitation of the import of the statement can be defended,—a limitation which of itself deprives it of all legitimate bearing upon the question of philosophical necessity,—we do not concede that our argument is dependent upon the establishment of this. Even if the statement be held to apply to the determinations of the will in general, instead of being limited to determinations which make a choice either of good or evil,—according to the moral character of the prevailing tendency of man's nature for the time;—still the language here employed is quite sufficient to remove from the minds of necessitarians all hesitation about accepting it. No necessitarian has any hesitation about repudiating force, or an absolute necessity of nature, as regulating the determinations of the will; and though libertarians may allege that the doctrine of philosophical necessity implies that the will is determined by force or by an absolute necessity of nature, yet they cannot establish this; while necessitarians openly and explicitly deny it, and cannot be convicted of any error or inconsistency in doing so. Nothing stands out more palpably on the face of the whole discussions which have taken place upon this subject, than these two facts, 1st, That Calvinistic necessitarians have always admitted that determination by force,—or as they usually called it, by constraint, or coaction, or compulsion,—is inconsistent with free agency and moral responsibility; and, 2d, That they have always contended, that there is nothing about the necessitarian view that gives any countenance to the idea that the will is determined by force. They have always contended that liberty or freedom—as opposed to all force or coaction—is indispensable, and must ever be maintained on all sides.   Indeed, the controversy between libertarians and necessitarians has often been made to turn upon this precise question, whether a liberty of spontaneity, as opposed to all force or coaction, all constraint brought to bear from without,—a liberty this which all necessitarians hold and which libertarians generally admit that they can hold consistently,—be or be not sufficient for moral responsibility.   Calvin says* "If liberty is opposed to coaction (or force) I confess and constantly assert that the will is free, and I reckon him a heretic who thinks otherwise.   If it is called free in this sense,—because it is not forced or violently drawn by an external movement, but is led on *sua sponte*, I have no objection to this.   But because men in general, when they hear this epithet applied to the will of man understand it in a very different sense, for this reason I dislike it."   Edwards himself says, speaking of the Stoics, whose Fate had been objected to him as identical with his necessity : "Whatever their doctrine was, if any of them held such a fate as is repugnant to any liberty consisting in our doing as we please" (the liberty of spontaneity as opposed to all force or coaction from any external cause), " I utterly deny such a fate.   If they held any such fate as is not consistent with the common and universal notions that mankind have of liberty, activity, moral agency, virtue and vice, I disclaim any such thing, and think I have demonstrated that the scheme I maintain is no such scheme."†   Turretine lays down six different senses in which liberty and necessity may be affirmed or denied respectively of man, or his will ; and—what is a curious, and with reference to our present argument, an important, coincidence,— he selects from the six the two species of necessity specified and repudiated in the Confession,—viz., that arising from force, and that arising from necessity of nature, or physical necessity,—and admits that these are contrary to the nature of the will and to moral responsibility, and are therefore to be rejected ; while, at the same time, he strenuously advocates other kinds of necessity, and among the rest, that based upon the last judgment of the practical intellect, which is just the same thing as the doctrine of philosophical necessity as taught by Edwards and Chalmers.

This fact is really conclusive upon the question we are now considering,—a question which just amounts in substance to this,—

* De Libero Arbitrio, p. 215. | † Part iv., sec. vi.

Does a denial of the determination of the will *by force or by an absolute necessity of nature,—understood in accordance with the views and language of the Calvinistic divines of the seventeenth century,—involve or imply a denial of the doctrine of philosophical necessity?* That the repudiation of determination by force does not imply this, has already been proved, and is, indeed, perfectly manifest. There is more doubt as to what is meant by necessity of nature, and as to what this might suggest about the point in dispute. A "necessity of nature," and still more an "absolute necessity of nature,"—the phrase used in the Confession,—seems to describe something much more intrinsic and fundamental, bearing more upon the essential qualities or constituent elements of will as will, —as a power or faculty essentially distinguishing those who have it from those who have it not,—than anything involved in the controversy about philosophical necessity, which merely respects one of the laws that regulate the determination of the volitions. And accordingly, on investigating the *usus loquendi* upon this point of the Calvinistic divines of the seventeenth century,—which must be the standard for the interpretation of the Westminster Confession,—we find that by necessity of nature, as applied to this matter of the will, they meant a necessity arising from, or connected with, those essential qualities of the will, in virtue of which it becomes one of the main things that distinguish men from mere material objects, and from the irrational animals. It is the nature of the will of man, that it implies the possession and exercise of a rational, deliberate, unconstrained, spontaneous choice. Without this, will would be no will; and without will, in this sense, man would not be a responsible being, and would sink to the level of mere matter, or of the beasts that perish. Calvin distinctly admitted that "a liberty or freedom from necessity, in the sense of coaction or compulsion, did so inhere in man by nature that it could not in any way be taken away from him." This point of the natural liberty with which God has endowed the will of man, is thus explained by Turretine, with his usual masterly ability :—

"Cum ergo ratio formalis libertatis non posita sit in indifferentia, non potest alibi quæri, quam in *lubentia rationali;* per quam *homo facit quod lubet prævio rationis judicio:* Ut hîc necessario duo conjungenda veniant ad eam constituendam. 1. τὸ προαιρετικὸν, ut quod fit, non fiat cæco impetu, et bruto quodam instinctu sed ἐκ προαιρέσεως, et prævio rationis lumine, et intellectus practici judicio. 2. τὸ ἑκούσιον, ut quod fit sponte et libenter fiat et sine coactione.

" Hanc autem esse rationem formalem liberi arbitrii, ex eo non obscure colligitur, quod *omni, soli,* et *semper* conveniat. Ita ut nullum sit agens liberum, vel creatum, vel increatum, in quo duo isti characteres non deprehendantur : nec ad tempus tantum, sed semper, ut positâ lubentiâ istâ rationali ponatur libertas, et sublatâ tollatur. Unde sequitur adjunctum esse inseparabile agentis rationalis, quod illud in quovis statu comitatur, ut non possit esse rationale, quin eo ipso sit liberum, nec spoliari queat libertate, quin privetur etiam ratione. Quod evincit etiam liberum arbitrium absolutè spectatum et in genere Entis nunquam ab homine tolli posse in quocunque versetur statu." *

And then, with regard to the different kinds of liberty and necessity that are, or are not, consistent with these views of the nature of the will, he selects,—as we have mentioned,—just the two specified in the Confession, as excluded absolutely and universally by right views of the essential qualities of the will,—viz., force and necessity of nature, or physical necessity. Force, or coaction, or compulsion, by an external power or pressure, needs no explanation ; and the other—the necessity of nature, or physical necessity, in conjunction with force, just as it is put in the Confession— Turretine explains in this way :—

" Ut duo sunt præcipui characteres Liberi Arbitrii, in quibus ejus ratio formalis consistit, 1. ἡ προαίρεσις, ut quod fit, prævio rationis judicio fiat, 2. τὸ ἑκούσιον, ut quod fit, sponte et sine coactione fiat : prior ad intellectum, posterior ad voluntatem pertinet : Duæ etiam necessitatis species cum eâ pugnant. Prima est *necessitas physica et bruta,* Altera *necessitas coactionis;* illa προαίρεσιν tollit, ista verò ἑκούσιον. Nam quæ fiunt ex necessitate physica ab agentibus naturalibus, ad unum naturâ et sine ratione determinatis, non possunt censeri fieri libere, id est prævio rationis lumine ; et quæ fiunt per vim et coacte, non possunt dici sponte fieri. *Et de his nulla inter Nos et Adversarios est controversia.* Hoc tantum obiter monendum Bellarminum † et alios ex Pontificiis Nostros calumniari, dum illis imponunt, quod sentiant libertatem a coactione sufficere ad constitutionem liberi arbitrii ; Quia præter illam requirunt etiam immunitatem a necessitate physica ; Et si quando dicunt hominem a coactione, non a necessitate liberum esse ; *necessitatis* voce non intelligunt eam quæ dicitur *physica,* de qua nulla erat controversia, et quæ satis per se excluditur, tum conditione subjecti, quod est rationale, tum ex actibus judicandi et volendi, qui cum ea sunt ἀσύστατοι ; sed necessitatem dependentiæ, servitutis, et rationalem.

" Sed si duæ istæ necessitatis species, a nobis commemoratæ, cum libero arbitrio pugnant ; non eadem est ratio aliarum, quæ cum eo subsistere possunt, et quibus non tam destruitur, quam conservatur et perficitur, quod sigillatim quoad quatuor necessitatis species ante notatas ostendi **potest**." ‡

---

* Loc. x. Qu. iii. s. 10 and 11.   ‡ Qu. ii., s. 5 and 6.
† Lib. 3 De Gratia et Lib. Arbit. c. 4.

And one of these four species of necessity, which are not inconsistent with the natural liberty of the will, or with moral agency, is that which forms the subject of our present discussion; in explaining which Turretine says that the nature of the will is such, "*ut non possit non sequi ultimum intellectus practici judicium.*" He says farther, in explanation of the same views :—

"Unde *Tertio* sequitur, Cum Providentia non concurrat cum voluntate humana, vel per *coactionem*, cogendo voluntatem invitam, vel *determinando physicè*, ut rem brutam et cæcam absque ullo judicio, sed *rationaliter*, flectendo voluntatem modo ipsi convenienti, ut seipsam determinet, ut causa proxima actionum suarum proprio rationis judicio, et spontanea voluntatis electione, eam libertati nostræ nullam vim inferre, sed illam potius amicè fovere. Quia duæ istæ tantum sunt necessitatis species, quæ libertatem perimunt, et cum ea sunt *ἀσύστατοι, necessitas naturalis, et coactionis;* Cæteræ, quæ oriuntur, vel a decreto Dei, et causæ primæ motione, *vel ab objecto et judicio ultimo intellectus practici*, tantum abest ut libertatem evertant, uteam magis tueantur, quia flectunt voluntatem, non cogunt, et faciunt ex nolente volentem. Quisquis enim facit sponte quod vult ex rationis judicio et pleno voluntatis consensu, id non potest non libere facere, etiamsi necessario faciat, undecunque fluat illa necessitas, sive ab ipsa rei existentia, quia quicquid est, quando est, necessario est, *sive ab objecto mentem et voluntatem efficaciter movente* [which is just philosophical necessity] sive a causâ prima decernente et concurrente [that is, divine predestination and providence]."*

We have had the less hesitation about laying before our readers these quotations from Turretine, because, in plain terms, they settle conclusively the question which we have undertaken to discuss; in other words, they establish, beyond dispute, the position, that the repudiation in the Confession, of the determination of the will by an absolute necessity of nature does not,—any more than the repudiation of determination by force,—preclude the maintenance of the doctrine of philosophical necessity. Libertarians may still assert that they regard the doctrine of philosophical necessity, as implying a determination of the will by force or by a necessity of nature; but they have no right to thrust their inferences or constructions upon their opponents, or to make these inferences the standard of what their opponents are to answer for. The allegation, that the doctrine of philosophical necessity is, in the face of the Confession,—especially when it is adduced as a personal charge,—must be proved by him who makes it. It can be

----

* Loc. vi. Qu. vi. s. 7.

proved only by producing from the Confession statements which, according to the ordinary recognised meaning of the words, or the known intention of the authors of the document, import a denial or rejection of the doctrine in question. The quotations we have produced from Turretine *prove*, that, tried by the views and the language of the Calvinistic divines of the seventeenth century, —the proper standard applicable to this matter,—the 1st section of the 9th chapter of the Confession, *contains nothing inconsistent with the doctrine of philosophical necessity.* The statement there made was meant to be introductory to a description of the changes which man has experienced, or is to experience, in regard to free will in his fourfold state ; and it was just intended to embody in substance a declaration to the effect, that whatever changes had occurred, or might occur, in the history of man in this respect, the essential features of his will or power of volition had continued unchanged ; that nothing had ever taken place either of an external or internal kind, which interfered with his deliberate and spontaneous choice, or with his moral responsibility ; that though, as is afterwards explained, man's will in one condition or period of his history had been determined to good, and in another condition or period to evil, this determination to good or evil did not arise from force, or from an absolute necessity of nature ; for that, if the determination to good or evil had originated in either of these causes, this would have been inconsistent with the nature of will as will, or with its essential feature as the characteristic of a rational and responsible being,—viz., a deliberate and spontaneous power of choice. The determination of man's will to good or evil by the application of external force, or by any necessity arising from the natural structure and inherent capacity of the power of volition, are expressly shut out. There is no appearance of the exclusion going beyond this ; and if so, the doctrine of philosophical necessity is untouched.

We could produce, if it were necessary, evidence from other authors that this was the sense in which the expressions under consideration were generally employed by the Calvinistic divines of the seventeenth century. We shall give only two brief extracts from Dr Owen, one of the very few names in theology entitled to stand side by side with Turretine,—extracts in which, it will be observed, that he uses the words " outward coaction" and " inward natural necessity," in the same sense in which the almost identical expressions are used in the Confession; and plainly intimates, that it is quite sufficient, in order to moral responsibility, to exclude these two species of necessity, and to retain the deliberation and spontaneity which are inconsistent with them. They are taken from his " Display of Arminianism; being a discovery of the old Pelagian idol Freewill, with the new goddess Contingency."

" Yet here observe, that we do not absolutely oppose free will, as if it were *nomen inane*, a mere figment, when there is no such thing in the world, but only in that sense the Pelagians and Arminians do assert it. About words we will not contend. We grant man, in the substance of all his actions, as much power, liberty, and freedom as a mere created nature is capable of. We grant him to be free in his choice, from all outward coaction or inward natural necessity, to work according to election and deliberation, spontaneously embracing what seemeth good to him. Now, call this power free will or what you please, so you make it not supreme, independent, and boundless, we are not at all troubled." And again, " We grant as large a freedom and dominion to our wills, over their own acts, as a creature subject to the supreme rule of God's providence, is capable of. Endued we are with such a liberty of will as is free from all outward compulsion and inward necessity, having an elective faculty of applying itself unto that which seems good unto it, in which it is a free choice, notwithstanding it is subservient to the decree of God."*

The greatest and best known names among the Calvinistic divines of the seventeenth century thus furnish us with satisfactory evidence, that the leading principle laid down in the Westminster Confession concerning the natural liberty of the will, does not exclude, and was not intended to exclude, the doctrine of philosophical necessity; and of course affords no evidence whatever that Jonathan Edwards' theory touching the bondage of the will is heretical.

The only thing else in the Confession that can be supposed to have any bearing upon the position taken up by Mr Stewart and Sir William Hamilton, is the statement, that our first parents were left to the liberty of their own will, and that in the exercise of this liberty they sinned and fell.

In the section immediately following that on which we have been commenting, and intended to describe how this matter stood in regard to the first period of man's history,—the first department of his fourfold estate,—it is put in this way, " Man in his

---

* C. xii. vol. x. pp. 116, 119.

state of innocency had freedom and power to will and to do *that which is good and well pleasing to God,* but yet mutably so that he might fall from it." This is a very important feature of the theology of the Reformers and of the Calvinistic divines of the seventeenth century, and it has been too much overlooked, as we shall afterwards explain, by Edwards and Chalmers ; but it has no bearing whatever upon the subject of philosophical necessity. The comprehensive doctrine, that man before the fall had freedom or liberty of will in the exercise of which he sinned,—that by his fall into a state of sin he lost this freedom,—and that men now in their natural state have it not, but are through regeneration to regain it, —was during the sixteenth and seventeenth centuries reckoned a leading feature of Calvinism. But for nearly a century past it has, chiefly through the influence of the writings of Edwards, been too much thrown into the background ; although a chapter in the Westminster Confession has been devoted to the exposition of it. This doctrine, of course, implies that there is a freedom or liberty of will which man may have notwithstanding God's decrees foreordaining whatsoever comes to pass,—notwithstanding His providence exercised in regulating and controlling all events,—and notwithstanding any general laws which may have been impressed upon men's constitution for regulating their mental processes, and especially, for determining their volitions. Calvinists have always held that all these things,—viz., the foreordination and providence of God, the general structure and framework of man's mental constitution, and the general laws that determine his volitions,— were unaffected by the fall ; that they stood in the same relation to the first sin of Adam as to any sins subsequently committed by him or his posterity ; and that they stood in the same relation to what was good in our first parents as to what is good in regenerate men upon earth. All these things being the same both before and after the fall, it follows, that the liberty of will which they ascribed to man unfallen, and which they denied to man after he fell,—as well as the necessity, or bondage, or servitude which they ascribed to the will of men as they now come into the world,—must be wholly different in their nature and source from liberty and necessity, in any of the senses in which they are usually made subjects of discussion among philosophers. And there is no difficulty in ascertaining what this difference is. It stands out palpably on the face of their system of theology. The liberty of will which they ascribed to man unfallen, was the effect of the tendency of his moral nature to what was good in virtue of his original righteousness, so that he could perfectly do God's will; while at the same time he possessed that capacity mutably so that he might fall. The necessity, or servitude, or bondage, which they ascribed to the will of fallen man, consisted in the loss of the liberty above described, and in the actual prevailing tendency of his moral nature to evil because of the depravity which had overspread it, so that he could no longer will good but could only will evil. The liberty which they thus ascribed to man in his original condition, they regarded as entirely lost by the fall, and as having now no existence in men in their natural condition, or until restored, in some measure, by divine agency in regeneration.

Liberty and necessity, in this sense and application, are entirely different in their whole nature and grounds, from liberty and necessity in the sense in which the position of Stewart and Hamilton has respect to them. The old Calvinistic divines,—including the authors of the Westminster Confession,—all held, that the foreordination and providence of God precluded liberty and established necessity in some sense; but in a sense quite different from that in which they are regarded as dependent upon righteousness or depravity of nature. Many Calvinists have regarded the foreordination and providence of God as establishing, or at least countenancing the doctrine of philosophical necessity, and as, of course, shutting out liberty of indifference, or the self-determining power of the will. But no intelligent Calvinist ever existed, who thought that there was anything in the doctrines of Calvinism, individually or collectively, which threw any difficulty or obstacle in the way of men embracing and maintaining the doctrine of philosophical necessity.

For this reason we have not thought it necessary to dwell upon any alleged inconsistency between the general principles of Calvinism and the doctrine of philosophical necessity. Mr Stewart does not allege any such inconsistency. Sir William himself rather insinuates than asserts it. The passages adduced from the Confession by Mr Stewart to prove his position, that the freedom of the human will (meaning thereby the libertarian as opposed to the necessitarian view of this matter), is asserted there, are not those which contain anything distinctively Calvinistic; but are statements which merely bear directly upon freedom or liberty in some sense or other. Of Sir William's bolder and more explicit assertions, that the doctrine of philosophical necessity " is in the face of the Confession as in the face of the Bible," and that "the theory of Jonathan Edwards touching the bondage of the will is, on the Calvinistic standard of the Westminster Confession, not only heterodox but heretical," he has not attempted to produce any evidence. We regret this. For we are very confident that no learning and ingenuity could have invested with plausibility a position so untenable. It is quite plain that the only passages in the Confession which have any appearance of affording countenance to his assertions, are just those which are referred to by Mr Stewart. We have adduced and considered all the passages in the Confession which could by possibility give any appearance of countenance to Sir William's charge of heresy against Edwards ; and we have shown that when these passages are interpreted according to the proper meaning of the words, and according to the recognised opinions and the established *usus loquendi* of the Calvinistic divines of the seventeenth century, every trace of the evidence which certain expressions in them might seem to furnish in support of the charge, disappears ; and that the accusation stands out in its true character as utterly groundless.

Sir William, by alleging that Edwards' doctrine, when tried by the standard of the Confession, was not only heterodox but heretical, became bound to do a great deal more than merely produce a proof, that there is a statement in the Confession which, when carefully examined and strictly interpreted, is inconsistent with it. This, if he could have produced it, would have been enough to entitle him to pronounce the doctrine heterodox or erroneous. But the way in which he " signalizes" the distinction between heterodox and heretical, shows that he was quite conscious that he ought to do more than this. According to the received meaning of the word heretical as distinguished from heterodox, he was not entitled to apply this epithet to Edwards' doctrine, unless he was prepared to show, that it ran counter to a statement occupying a place of prominence and of importance, and to establish this by evidence of commanding clearness and cogency. Heresy, as distinguished from mere heterodoxy, implies a palpable and decided difference in degree both with respect to the magnitude and prominence of the error, and the cogency of the evidence by which its erroneous character can be established.

Even if the doctrine of philosophical necessity could be proved to be erroneous, it could not, if tried by a Calvinistic standard, be regarded as an error of such serious magnitude as to warrant the designation of a heresy. No Calvinist believing in the divine foreordination of all events can possibly think the doctrine of philosophical necessity a great and serious error, or regard it as heretical. He may possibly believe the doctrine to be erroneous —to be destitute of sufficient proof. But if he be really an intelligent Calvinist, he must see that all the leading objections against it tell equally against the Calvinistic doctrines which he holds, and that it harmonises well with his whole system of theology.

What is true of a Calvinist is true, *mutatis mutandis*, of a Calvinistic creed. There may be nothing in the Confession to furnish direct evidence in support of the doctrine of philosophical necessity—we do not believe that there is; there may even be statements in the Confession that are inconsistent with it and exclude it—we have proved that none such have been or can be produced; but the allegation of heresy as implying, in all fairness, palpable and clearly proved opposition to the Confession in a point of vital importance, is perfectly preposterous.

There is nothing, then, in the Westminster Confession that need occasion difficulty to any necessitarian, acquainted with the way in which these subjects were discussed by the Calvinistic divines of the seventeenth century. If convinced of the truth of the doctrine of philosophical necessity,—whether upon the ground of the evidence directly and properly applicable to it as a psychological question, or on the ground of its appearing to be logically deducible from the theological doctrines of God's foreordination and providence,—there is nothing in this conviction that need prevent him from assenting to the Westminster Confession, for assuredly there is nothing in that document which either is or was intended to be inconsistent with it. Mr Stewart's statement that the freedom of the human will is asserted in the Confession is true in one sense, though not in that in which he meant it. Sir William's assertion that Edwards' doctrine about the will is, when tried by the standard of the Confession, heretical, is not only destitute of all solid foundation, but is disproved by every fair and reasonable consideration bearing upon the settlement of the point in dispute.

We must **now** advert briefly to the second position we laid down,

—viz., that there is nothing in the Calvinistic system of theology
or in the Westminster Confession which *requires* men to hold the
doctrine of philosophical necessity ; or in other words, that a man
may conscientiously assent to the Westminster Confession although
he should reject that doctrine.   Edwards and Chalmers seem to
have regarded the doctrine of necessity as an indispensable part of
their Calvinism.   They have not, indeed, formally laid down this
position and attempted to prove it.   They have rather assumed it
as if it were self-evident ; and usually write as if it were a matter
of course, that men holding the Calvinistic doctrines of predestination and providence must also hold their doctrine of necessity.
Dr Chalmers, speaking of the philosophical doctrine of necessity
and the theological doctrine of predestination, says, " It is one and
the same doctrine in different aspects and with different relations ;
in the one view with relation to nature, and in the other view with
relation to God."   And again, " Let the doctrine of philosophical
necessity, or, *theologically speaking*, the doctrine of predestination,
be as firmly established as it may," etc. *

We are not prepared to concur in this identification of the
philosophical doctrine of necessity with the theological doctrine of
predestination.   We regard it as unwarrantable and injurious.
We are not satisfied that the doctrine of necessity can be deduced,
in the way of logical consequence, from the doctrine of predestination.   The doctrine of necessity, held in combination with the doctrine of the providence of God as the creator, the upholder, and
governor of the world, affords a proof of the doctrine of predestination ; for if such a system as necessity implies has been established by God, and is constantly superintended and controlled by
Him, this must have been done for securing the accomplishment of
His purposes ;   and He must be actually executing His decrees, or
carrying into effect His determinations, in those volitions which
are the certain or necessary results of the constitution of nature,
in its relation to the laws of man's thinking, feeling, and acting.
But while the doctrine of necessity, if established, clearly and
directly confirms the doctrine of predestination, it is not so clear
that the doctrine of predestination affords ground for inferring or
deducing the doctrine of necessity. Predestination implies that
the end or result is certain, and that adequate provision has

---

* *Institutes of Theology*, vol. ii. pp. 357, 366, 367.

been made for bringing it about. But it does not indicate anything as to what must be the nature of this provision in regard to the different classes of events which are taking place under God's government, including the volitions of rational and responsible beings. Were we in the condition of being able to prove, that God *could not* have foreseen and foreordained the volitions of rational and responsible beings, and made effectual provision for accomplishing His purposes in this most important department of His government, without having established the system of necessity,—without having settled in accordance with that doctrine the internal laws which regulate men's volitions,— this would prove that predestination established necessity, so that every predestinarian was bound in consistency to be a necessitarian. But we have not materials to warrant us in maintaining, that God could not have certainly accomplished all His purposes in and by the volitions of responsible beings, unless He had established the scheme of necessity. And if so, there is a hiatus in every process by which we attempt to establish a logical transition from predestination to necessity, which cannot be filled up. Predestination and necessity manifestly harmonise with and fit in to each other. Sir William's insinuation that necessity is a corruption of pure Calvinism is preposterous. Every intelligent Calvinist must be disposed to regard the doctrine of necessity with favour, as having a large amount of antecedent probability attaching to it. He must see, that there is no serious objection to the doctrine of necessity that does not equally apply to predestination ; and that the doctrine of necessity, if established, gives some confirmation to the doctrine of predestination, and throws some light upon the means by which God executes His decrees or accomplishes His purposes, so far as the volitions of responsible beings are concerned. All this is true and very evident. A predestinarian can scarcely avoid, perhaps, having a leaning to the doctrine of necessity ; but unless he can find some argument or process of reasoning which warrants him in asserting that God *could not* have made effectual provision for accomplishing His purposes in this department except by means of the state of matters which necessity implies, he cannot pass *directly, in the way of inference,* from the one doctrine to the other.

From the nature of the case, the truth of the doctrine of necessity is properly and primarily a question in philosophy. It respects directly only the laws which regulate men's mental pro-

510 CALVINISM, AND THE [Essay IX.

cesses and determine their volitions. In order to settle it, we
must look within ourselves, and survey our own mental operations.
The materials that legitimately bear upon the decision of it, must be
all derived from consciousness; though, of course, they may branch
out into argumentations based upon the data which consciousness
furnishes, and may thus pertain to the department of metaphysics as
well as psychology. The Bible does not tell us any thing about the
causes or principles that ordinarily regulate or determine men's
general exercise of their natural power of volition. It affords us
no materials for ascertaining whether the laws that determine our
volitions presuppose the libertarian or the necessitarian theory.
It leaves all such questions to be determined by an investigation
of the evidence naturally and appropriately applicable to them,—
that is, by an examination of man himself, of his mental constitution and ordinary mental processes. And not only does the Bible
not determine any such psychological and metaphysical questions
directly, but it does not teach any doctrines which, indirectly or
by consequence, require or necessitate us to take a particular side,
in any of those questions which have been controverted among
philosophers upon philosophical grounds. If philosophers should
profess to deduce—from a survey of men's mental constitution,—
conclusions which contradict any doctrine revealed in Scripture,
this should be attended to and answered; and no great difficulty
has ever been experienced in dealing with allegations of this sort.
If they should profess to find, on a survey of men's mental constitution, grounds for adopting certain views concerning the liberty
or bondage of the will, which would preclude or shut out the
scriptural doctrines, that God has foreseen and foreordained whatsoever comes to pass,—or that He is ever exercising a most wise,
holy, and powerful providence over all His creatures, and all
their actions,—or that fallen man,—man as he is,—hath wholly
lost all ability of will to any spiritual good accompanying salvation,—it would be needful and not difficult to expose the unsoundness of these views, or the falsehood of the inferences deduced from them. But unless men profess to have established
something inconsistent with these theological doctrines, we do
not know that there is any particular theory concerning the
will or the laws that regulate its operations, deduced upon philosophical grounds from an examination of men's mental constitution
and processes, which can be proved to be inconsistent with any

statement in the word of God, or with any of the doctrines taught there, and which must therefore, on scriptural and theological grounds, be rejected.

Calvinists, in general, when they have been led to attend to this particular subject, have adopted necessitarian views, as harmonising most fully and obviously with their theological convictions. But this has not been universally the case. Some Calvinists have rejected the doctrine of philosophical necessity, and much larger numbers have declined to give any decisive or explicit deliverance concerning it. Some Calvinists have held that the theological doctrines of predestination and providence lead, by necessary logical sequence, to the doctrine of philosophical necessity. But it cannot be proved that either the certainty or immutability of the event, or the agency of God in providence in regulating and controlling men's volitions, necessarily requires or implies this necessity; or would be certainly precluded, by a liberty of indifference, or the self-determining power of the will. No doubt, the doctrine of necessity affords some assistance in forming a conception as to how it is that God accomplishes His purposes and controls our volitions without interfering with the essential qualities of the will or with our moral responsibility; while the self-determining power of the will seems to involve this matter in serious difficulties. But it is, we think, unwarranted and presumptuous to assert, that even a self-determining power in the will would place it beyond the sphere of the divine control, —would prevent Him in whom we live, move, and have our being, who is everywhere and at all times present in the exercise of all His perfections, who searcheth the heart and trieth the reins of the children of men, from superintending and directing all its movements according to the counsel of His own will. And unless this unwarranted and presumptuous position be taken up, it seems impossible to prove, that there is any thing in the Calvinistic system which makes it indispensable for its supporters, in point of logical consistency, to adopt the doctrine of philosophical necessity. Until this position be established, it is still open to Calvinists as to others, to examine the question as between liberty and necessity upon its own proper psychological and metaphysical grounds; and to adopt the one side or the other, according as they may think that the evidence for the one or the other, derived from an investigation into man's mental constitution, preponderates.

We have not ourselves, in the course of this discussion, indicated any opinion upon the precise point involved in the controversy between the libertarians and the necessitarians; and we really cannot say that we have formed a very decided opinion in favour of either side. Upon the whole, we regard the evidence in favour of the doctrine of philosophical necessity as preponderating. In order to dispose of this doctrine satisfactorily, it seems necessary that the argument of Edwards in favour of it, and against the self-determining power of the will, should be answered. We have never seen this done, and we scarcely think that it can be done. We have read lately the ablest and most elaborate answer that has been given to Edwards, viz., "Tappan's Treatise on the Will." But we have not been convinced by it that Edwards has failed in establishing his leading position; on the contrary, Tappan's failure has rather confirmed us in the conviction that Edwards cannot be answered. But the only point with which we have to do at present is this, that we do not hold ourselves tied up to take either the one side or the other, by anything contained in the sacred Scriptures, in the Calvinistic system of theology, or in the Westminster Confession of Faith.

Sir James Mackintosh, in an article upon Stewart's "Preliminary Dissertation,"* asserted the identity of the subjects of necessity and predestination,—agreeing in the main with the views indicated by Edwards and Chalmers, but going so far as to say explicitly, that "it is not possible to make any argumentative defence of Calvinism which is not founded on the principles of necessity." He became convinced, however, of the unsoundness of this view of the closeness of the connection between the theological and the philosophical doctrine, and retracted it in a note subjoined to his own Preliminary Dissertation. He says there† that "more careful reflection had corrected a confusion common to him with most writers upon these subjects." But he now goes into the other extreme; and besides, introduces some additional confusion, which it may be proper to correct. He now brings in, in connection with this matter, the distinction between Sublapsarian and Supralapsarian views; and asserts that "Sublapsarian predestination is evidently irreconcilable with the doctrine of necessity," but that "the Supralapsarian scheme may be built upon

---

* *Edinburgh Review*, vol. xxxvi.   † Note O, p. 423.

necessitarian principles." Although Mackintosh had not, in all probability, turned over so many theological books as Hamilton, he was well acquainted with theological subjects. But the statement which we have quoted from him is certainly inaccurate. The reason he assigns why Sublapsarian predestination is irreconcilable with necessity is, that the Sublapsarians admit that men had free-will before the fall, which he thinks Supralapsarians cannot do. The inaccuracy of this notion must be evident from the explanation given in the former part of this article, as to the real nature, import, and grounds of the freedom of will which man had before the fall, and which he lost by sin. *The free will which has been represented as possessed by man before the fall and as lost by sin, has no connection whatever with the discussion about philosophical necessity, and may be, and has been held equally by Sublapsarian and Supralapsarian Calvinists.*

It is much to be regretted that Stewart, Mackintosh, and Hamilton, should have all concurred in putting forth erroneous representations upon this subject. The errors of such men it is an imperative duty to point out and to correct. But it is still more imperative to point out the oversights or errors of men who are much higher authorities upon theological matters, such as Edwards and Chalmers. We have already explained the grounds on which we hold the assumption by these great men of the identity, or the necessary connection, of the theological doctrine of predestination and of the philosophical doctrine of necessity, to be unwarranted. We have indicated, though very briefly and imperfectly, the considerations by which we think it can be shown, that the Calvinistic doctrines of predestination and providence, as taught in Scripture, do not either include, or necessarily lead to, the doctrine of necessity; and may be fully expounded and applied by men who refuse to admit, or who even positively reject, that doctrine. The doctrine of necessity, when once established, leads by strict logical sequence to predestination, unless men take refuge in atheism. But it does not seem to follow *e converso*, that the doctrine of predestination leads necessarily to the doctrine of necessity; as men may hold, that God could certainly execute His decrees and infallibly accomplish His purposes in and by the volitions of men, even though He had not impressed upon their mental constitution the law of necessity, as that by which its processes are regulated and its volitions determined.

We would now advert, very briefly, to the injurious tendency and consequences of this assumed identity or necessary connection of the two doctrines,—the theological and philosophical. It tends to throw into the background the true scriptural, theological doctrine of necessity,—the doctrine of the servitude or bondage of the will of fallen man,—man as he is,—to sin because of the depravity which has overspread his moral nature. Not that Edwards or Chalmers have denied or rejected this doctrine. This would certainly have been heresy; for the doctrine is very prominently and explicitly asserted in the Westminster Confession. It is, indeed, plainly involved in what they were accustomed to teach concerning the entire corruption and depravity of human nature; and they would have had no hesitation in admitting this, and in professing their belief in the doctrine as a portion of God's revealed truth. Still, it is palpable that the doctrine of the bondage of the will of man to sin, because of depravity, has no prominence whatever in their writings when they treat of the doctrine of philosophical necessity. This we regard as an evil; and we have no doubt that it is to be ascribed to the fact of their minds being engrossed, when they contemplated man's natural condition, by the idea of a necessity of a different kind, but of far inferior importance in itself, and resting upon lower and more uncertain grounds.

The practice of distinguishing, in the exposition of this subject, between the freedom of man's will in his unfallen and in his fallen condition, and indeed of viewing it distinctively with reference to the different stages or periods of his fourfold state,—as unfallen, fallen, regenerate, or glorified,—has prevailed in the church in almost all ages. These views were fully brought out and applied by Augustine. They had a place in the speculations of the schoolmen, as may be seen in Peter Lombard's Four Books of Sentences,* and in the commentaries upon it. They were embraced and promulgated by the whole body of the Reformers, both Lutheran and Calvinistic. They have a prominent place in the writings of the great systematic divines of the seventeenth century. They have a prominent place in the Westminster Confession,—the 9th chapter, entitled "Of free will," being entirely devoted to the statement of them. And what is in some respects

* Lib. ii., Dist. 25.

peculiarly interesting, the doctrine of the loss of man's free will
by the fall, and of the servitude of the will of fallen man to sin
because of depravity, was held by Baius, Jansenius, and Quesnel,
and their followers,—the best men and the best theologians the
Church of Rome has ever produced;—and in them was condemned
by papal bulls,—a fact which confirms our conviction, that this is
one of the great cardinal doctrines of Scripture, which may be
said to have the support of the concurrent testimony of the universal Church of Christ,—of the great body of those whom Christ
has enlightened and sanctified. This servitude or bondage of the
will of man to sin because of depravity, was the only necessity
which the great body of the most competent judges in all ages
have regarded as being taught in Scripture as a portion of God's
revealed truth, or as being necessary for the full exposition of the
other cognate doctrines of Christian theology. This necessity now
attaching to the human will they regarded as a property of man,
viewed not simply as a creature, but as a fallen creature,—not as
springing from his mere relation to God as the foreordainer of all
things and the actual ruler and governor of the world, nor from
the mere operation of laws which God has impressed upon the
general structure and framework of man's mental constitution,—
but from a cause distinct from all these, that is, from the depravity, or prevailing aversion from God and tendency to evil, superinduced upon man's character by the fall. If this be indeed the
scriptural view of the bondage of man's will, it ought surely to be
openly proclaimed, and pressed prominently upon our attention, instead of being overlooked or thrown into the background, in favour
of another kind of necessity, as it certainly is in the writings of
Edwards and Chalmers on that subject. They would, no doubt,
have admitted the doctrine and defended it, if it had been pressed
upon their attention; but, in point of fact, they have scarcely ever
adverted to it. It seems to have been in their minds absorbed or
thrown into the background, and kept out of view, by the more
general subject of liberty and necessity in the form in which it
has been commonly discussed by philosophers; and in which it is
held to apply to man at all times, and irrespectively of his history
and position as fallen and sinful. In Edwards' great work on the
"Freedom of the Will," there is no reference to this distinction
between the liberty of the will in man unfallen and in man fallen,
or to the bondage of the will of fallen man to sin because of de-

pravity. It contains only an elaborate proof of the doctrine of philosophical necessity, as opposed to a self-determining power of the will and a liberty of indifference, with an answer to the objections commonly adduced against it. This we cannot but regard as a serious defect; while, at the same time, it is important to observe, that his proof of the compatibility of the philosophical doctrine of necessity with responsibility and moral agency, is at least equally applicable to the defence of the scriptural and theological doctrine of man's inability because of depravity to will anything spiritually good; and especially the great principle which he has so conclusively established, viz., "that the essence of the virtue and vice of dispositions of heart, and acts of the will, lies not in their cause but in their nature." The influence of the writings of Edwards has tended greatly to throw this important scriptural doctrine of the bondage of the will of man to sin because of depravity into the background; and Dr Chalmers having in this respect walked very much in his footsteps, has thrown the influence of his wonderful powers and great name into the same scale. Edwards and Chalmers have not gone in face of the Confession, or afforded any plausible ground for stamping upon them the brand of heresy. But they have certainly in their engrossment with this philosophical doctrine of necessity, about which the Confession of Faith says nothing, left out of view an important theological doctrine, to which the Confession gives prominence; and which certainly ought to have a distinct and definite place assigned to it in the exposition of the scheme of Christian theology.

Not only, however, has the theological doctrine of the servitude of the will of man to sin, or the inability of man in his natural condition to will anything spiritually good because of depravity, been thrown into the background by the undue exaltation of a merely philosophical topic; but the impression has been produced, that the maintenance of some of the leading and peculiar doctrines of Christianity is most intimately connected with, or rather dependent upon, the establishment of certain philosophical theories; and this impression is neither true nor safe.

Edwards and Chalmers seem always to assume that the theological doctrine of predestination, and the philosophical doctrine of necessity, are identical, or at least are so connected, that they must stand or fall together; and the impression thus produced is fitted to lead men to regard the proof or evidence of the one doctrine as bound up with, or dependent upon, the proof or evidence of the other. And we cannot but deprecate this result, as fitted to elevate the doctrine of necessity to a place and influence to which, however fully it may be established as true by its own appropriate evidence, it has not, and cannot have, a rightful claim; and as fitted also to lay upon the scriptural doctrine of predestination a burden or servitude to which it cannot be legitimately subjected. The Calvinistic doctrine of predestination has a sufficiently strong foundation in direct evidence, both from reason and Scripture, to maintain itself in opposition to all inferential objections to it,— and there are really no others,—and to bear up along with it every position, theological or philosophical, that can be really *proved* to be involved in or deducible from it. But still, as it is a doctrine which usually calls forth strong prejudices, and is assailed by plausible objections, it is right that we should beware of attempting to burden it with any weight which it is not bound to carry; or representing it as obliged to stand or fall with a doctrine so much inferior to it, at once in intrinsic importance, and in the kind and degree of evidence on which it rests.

It has never been alleged that there is anything in the Westminster Confession, apart from its statement of the great doctrines of Calvinism, which seems to require men to hold the doctrine of philosophical necessity; so that this point does not require any separate treatment.

Before quitting this subject, we would like to give some little explanation of the remaining portion of the 9th chapter of the Westminster Confession on free will. The chapter, as a whole, is a very remarkable and impressive,—we might almost call it eloquent,—statement of the scriptural truths bearing upon this subject, through all the leading stages in the eventful history of man, or of the human race. We have already considered the first section, setting forth the general doctrine of the natural liberty of the will, which it must always retain, and which it could not lose without ceasing to be will, viewed as an essential quality of a rational and responsible being; and excluding the determination of it to good or evil by force or by any absolute necessity of nature. Although the will has a natural liberty which prevents it from being determined to good or evil by such causes or influences as would manifestly exclude deliberate choice and spontaneous agency, yet it has, in point of fact, at different periods or in different conditions, being determined both to good and to evil. To each of the four great eras in this matter, or the different aspects in man's fourfold state, one of the four remaining sections in this chapter is devoted. To the first of these, or section 2d,—describing man's freedom of will in his state of innocency,—we have already adverted, and we need not now dwell upon it. The 3d section,—describing the condition of men as to free will in their natural fallen state,—is in some respects the most important, as bringing out a leading and most influential feature in the character of all men as they come into the world; and it is most intimately connected with the subject we have been discussing, in as much as it describes the only necessity which the Scripture represents as attaching to man by nature, and the only necessity therefore which can be held as needful to be taken into account, in expounding the general scheme of Christian doctrine. It is this :—" Man, by his fall into a state of sin, hath wholly lost all ability of will to any spiritual good accompanying salvation, so as a natural man being altogether averse from that good, and dead in sin, is not able by his own strength to convert himself, or to prepare himself thereunto." The fundamental proposition here is, that man hath wholly lost all ability of will to any spiritual good accompanying salvation; and the remainder of the statement is intended, partly to indicate the leading ground on which this doctrine rests, viz., that a natural man is altogether averse from spiritual good and dead in sin,—and partly to bring out the great practical conclusion which results from it, viz., that he is not able by his own strength to convert himself, or to prepare himself thereunto. The fundamental doctrine is, that man, by his fall into a state of sin, hath wholly lost all ability of will to anything spiritually good; and, of course, is in entire bondage or servitude to sin, that is, to his own natural sinful dispositions or tendencies. The question is,—Is this really the view which the word of God gives us of man's natural condition and capacities in regard to spiritual objects and results? and this question is to be decided by a careful investigation and application of all the scriptural statements and principles bearing upon the subject. Does the Scripture teach us that man, in his natural condition, and antecedently to his becoming the subject of the gracious operations of God's Spirit, cannot really will anything spiritually good? and, more especially, that he is unable to will to turn from sin unto God, or to prepare himself for so turning? It seems plain enough that this doctrine is involved in, or clearly and certainly deducible from, that of the complete and entire corruption or depravity of human nature. The doctrine of original sin or of native depravity,—in the sense in which it is held by orthodox divines,—implies that man, in his natural condition, has no tendency or inclination towards what is spiritually good,—that all his tendencies or inclinations are towards what is evil,—and that he does and can do nothing which is really pleasing and acceptable to God. If he is wholly averse from all good and wholly inclined to all evil, it would seem that he cannot will any thing good; because the will or power of volition must be determined and characterised by the general tendency or disposition of the moral nature of the being who possesses and exercises it. God can and must always will what is good, because His moral nature is essentially and unchangeably holy. Man in his unfallen state could always will what is good, or as the Confession says, had freedom and power to will and to do what was acceptable to God, because he was possessed of a pure and holy moral nature, endowed with original righteousness. And upon the same ground, because man now has a wholly depraved or corrupted nature, without any original righteousness, he has no ability of will to any thing spiritually good.

This doctrine of the utter bondage of the will of men to sin because of depravity, or of the inability of men in their natural fallen condition to will or to do any thing spiritually good, is not entirely dependent for its scriptural evidence upon its being involved in, or necessarily *deducible*, from the doctrine of the entire and total, and not merely partial or comparative, corruption of man's moral nature by the fall. For there are scriptural statements about men's natural state which bear directly and immediately upon the more limited topic of their inability to will what is spiritually good. Still the connection between the two doctrines is such as to remind us of the vast importance of being thoroughly decided in our convictions as to what Scripture teaches concerning the natural state of man as a fallen and sinful creature, and thoroughly familiar with the scriptural materials by which our convictions may be established and defended. It was a service of inestimable value which Edwards rendered to sound Christian theology, when, in his work upon "Original Sin," he so conclusively and unanswerably established from Scripture, reason and experience, the great doctrine—" that all mankind are under the influence of a prevailing effectual tendency in their nature to that sin and wickedness which implies their utter and eternal ruin." The conclusive demonstration of this " great Christian doctrine," or the unanswerable establishment of this great fact as an actual feature in the condition of all men, as they come into this world, entitles Edwards' work upon "Original Sin," notwithstanding some measure of obscurity and confusion on the subject of imputation, to be regarded as one of the most valuable, permanent, possessions of the Christian church.

The next stage in the history of the human race with respect to free will, viewed as being virtually the history of a man,—of one man,—at different periods (and this is the light in which the matter is really represented to us in Scripture), is thus described in the Confession.* " When God converts a sinner and translates him into the state of grace, He freeth him from his natural bondage under sin, and by His grace enables him freely to will and to do that which is spiritually good. Yet so as that by reason of his remaining corruption, he doth not perfectly, nor only, will that which is good, but doth also will that which is evil." Here, again, there is freedom of will ascribed to man in his regenerate state,—that is, an ability to will good as well as to will evil. In the regeneration of his nature the reigning power of depravity is subdued, and all the effects which it produced are more or less fully taken away. One of the principal of these effects was the utter bondage or servitude of the will to sin, because of the ungodly and depraved tendency of the whole moral nature to what was displeasing and offensive to God. This ungodly and depraved tendency is now in conversion, to a large extent, removed, and an opposite tendency is implanted. Thus the will is set free or emancipated from the bondage under which it was held. It is no longer subjected to a necessity,—arising from the general character and tendency of man's moral nature,—to will only what is evil, but is now able also freely to will what is good ; and it does freely will what is good, —though from the remaining corruption and depravity of man's nature,—it still wills also what is evil. It is not emancipated from the influence of God's decrees foreordaining whatever comes to

---

* Sec. iv.

pass. It is not placed beyond the control of His providence,—whereby in the execution of His decrees He ever rules and governs all His creatures and all their actions. It is not set free from the operation of those general laws which God has impressed upon man's mental constitution, for directing the exercise of his faculties and regulating his mental processes. But it is set free from the *dominion* of depravity; and thereby it is exempted from the necessity of willing only what is evil, and made equally able freely to will what is good. It has recovered, to a large extent, the only liberty it ever lost; and it is determined and characterised *now*,—as it had been in all the previous stages of man's history, both before and after his fall,—by his general moral character and tendencies;—free to good, when man had the image of God and original righteousness, but yet mutable so that it could will evil,—in bondage, when man was the slave of sin, so that it could will only evil and not good,—emancipated, when man was regenerated, so that it could freely will good as well as evil, though still bearing many traces of the former bondage and of its injurious effects; —and finally, to adopt again the language of the Confession, in closing the admirable chapter on this subject, " to be made perfectly and immutably free to good alone in the state of glory."

The extract from Sir William Hamilton, on which chiefly we have been commenting, occurs in connection with a discussion embodying some important and valuable truth,—truth which admits of an obvious application to the exposition and defence of Christian, and especially of Calvinistic, doctrines. He declares his satisfaction in being able to show, that his doctrine of "the conditioned" harmonises with the general spirit of divine revelation, by inculcating humility in our speculations in the investigation of truth because of the imperfection and limitation of our faculties,—by showing the unwarrantableness and absurdity of making our capacity of distinctly conceiving and fully comprehending doctrines, the measure or standard of their absolute truth, or of their consistency with each other; and the perfect reasonableness of believing upon sufficient grounds, things which in some respects are beyond our grasp, and cannot be fully taken in or comprehended by the exercise of our faculties when brought directly to bear upon them. Now all this is very important truth in connection with the exposition and defence of the great doctrines of revelation, and especially of the profound and mysterious doc-

trines of Calvinism.   Sir William has not here put forth any
thing which is not in substance to be found in the writings of
theologians, and which, indeed, has not been brought forward
more or less fully, and established more or less conclusively, by
every intelligent defender of Calvinism.   But it is not very common to find matter of this sort in the writings of philosophers ;
and Sir William, by giving it his sanction, has done a real service
to the cause of truth and orthodoxy.   He could not, however, let
this topic pass without indulging himself in some characteristic
statements to which it may be proper briefly to advert.   In his
usual spirit he labours to convey the impression, that these views
about the limitation of our faculties, and the bearing of this upon
the discussion of mysterious doctrines, have not in general been
understood and applied aright by theologians.   He seems half
inclined to insinuate, that these principles were little known till
he promulgated them.   But this was rather too absurd ; and accordingly he feels constrained to make the following concession :
—" It must, however, be admitted, that confessions of the total
inability of man to conceive the union of what he should believe
united, are to be found, and they are found not perhaps less frequently, and certainly in more explicit terms, among Catholic than
among Protestant theologians."*   It is certainly quite true, as is
here asserted, that such statements " are to be found,"—and indeed
they constitute a perfectly familiar commonplace,—among orthodox theologians.   The alleged greater explicitness of Catholics than
Protestants in stating these principles, is a mere *gratis dictum*,
which has no foundation in the realities of the case.   This statement seems to have been hazarded for the mere purpose of usher-
ing in a quotation from Cardinal Cajetan, which,—though about
the best thing ever written upon the subject,—Sir William felt
confident was wholly unknown to theologians now-a-days.   He
described the quotation as " the conclusion of what, *though wholly
overlooked*, appears to me as the ablest and truest criticism of the
many fruitless, if not futile, attempts at conciliating the ways of
God to the understanding of man, in the great articles of divine
foreknowledge and predestination (which are both embarrassed by
the self-same difficulties) and human free will."   Sir William
describes the passage as " wholly overlooked," notwithstanding its

---

* Discussions, p. 627.

superlative merits.   Now it so happens that we remember two instances,—and there are in all probability more,—in which this very
quotation from Cajetan had been produced and commended by
eminent writers,—one of them being no other than Bayle, who so
often furnishes passages to "persons of ordinary information."
Gisbertus Voetius, one of the best known names in the theology
of the seventeenth century,—a man who was, at least, as thoroughly versant in the literature of theology as Sir William was
in that of philosophy, and who knew as much of the literature of
philosophy as Sir William did of that of theology,—has quoted
with approbation a part of this passage from Cajetan, in a "Dissertatio Epistolica de Termino Vitæ,"* originally published in
1634, and republished at Utrecht in 1669 in the Appendix to the
5th volume of his " Selectæ Disputationes." The passage in Bayle
is to be found in the second part of his " Response aux Questions
d'un Provincial,"† where the extract from Cajetan is given as
quoted with approbation by an eminent Dominician theologian,
Alvarez, in a "Treatise de Auxiliis Divinæ Gratiæ." Sir William,
then, was mistaken in representing this passage in Cajetan as
" wholly overlooked." We do not suppose, indeed, that it was
suggested to him by Voet or Bayle, for we rather suspect,—especially as the passage after all contains nothing very extraordinary,
—that it was produced and paraded in the honest belief that no
one knew anything about it but himself.

It may be worth while to mention, that the discussion in connection with which this passage is introduced by Bayle, is very
similar to that in which Sir William brings it in. Bayle was
doing on that occasion just what Sir William did in the immediately following part of his Appendix,—viz., collecting what he calls
" Testimonies to the limitation of our knowledge from the limitation of our faculties."   Bayle had often spoken very much to the
same effect as Sir William has done, about the reasonableness and
obligation of believing when we cannot know and fully comprehend.   But this, coming from Bayle, was suspected of being intended to undermine the foundations of a rational faith; and to
amount, in substance, very much to the same thing as Hume's
well-known sneer about our holy religion being founded not on
reason but on faith.   Bayle defended himself against these

---

* P. 107. | † Chap. 161, Œuvres, vol. iii. p. 837.

charges in the 2d and 3d of the " Eclaircissemens," subjoined to
his Dictionary ; and more formally and elaborately, in the second
part of his " Reponse aux Questions d'un Provincial." He was
contending then against M. Jacquelot, who was a minister of the
French Protestant Church, and after the revocation of the Edict
of Nantes, settled as minister of the French Church in Berlin.
Jacquelot wrote a series of three works against Bayle ; and,
though he was a man of real ability, he certainly gave his skilful
adversary some advantage over him, by taking ground which, in
the present day, we would describe as too rationalistic. Several
other eminent men took part in the controversy, especially La
Placette, who, after the revocation of the Edict of Nantes, became
minister of the French Protestant Church at Copenhagen. Different grounds were taken by the different combatants in opposing Bayle ; and then some interesting discussions arose among
themselves, as to the best ground to be taken in dealing with the
great sceptic. The controversy thus, viewed as a whole, became
extremely curious and interesting. We cannot dwell upon it ; and
can only remark, that Bayle had no difficulty in producing from
many eminent men, both theologians and philosophers, quotations
which certainly seemed very much the same in substance with his
own statements, however different they might be in spirit and
object ; and that these quotations are in some instances identical
with, and in general very similar to, those which Sir William has
collected as " Testimonies to the limitation of our knowledge from
the limitation of our faculties."

CALVINISM,

AND ITS

PRACTICAL APPLICATION.*

———◆———

ONE of the leading forms which, in the present day, aversion to divine truth exhibits, is a dislike to precise and definite statements upon the great subjects brought before us in the sacred Scriptures. This dislike to precision and definiteness in doctrinal statements, sometimes assumes the form of reverence for the Bible,—as if it arose from an absolute deference to the authority of the divine word, and an unwillingness to mix up the reasonings and deductions of men with the direct declarations of God. We believe that it arises,—much more frequently and to a much greater extent,—from a dislike to the controlling influence of Scripture,—from a desire to escape, as far as possible without denying its authority, from the trammels of its regulating power as an infallible rule of faith and duty. It is abundantly evident, from the statements of Scripture as well as from the experience of every age and country, that men, in their natural condition, unrenewed by divine grace, have a strong aversion to right views of the divine character and of the way of salvation, or to the great system of doctrines revealed to us in the Bible ; and are anxious to escape from any apparent obligation to believe them. The most obvious and

---

* *British and Foreign Evangelical Review.* October, 1861.
"Essays on some of the Difficulties in the Writings of the Apostle Paul."

Essay III. On Election. By RICH-ARD WHATELY, D.D., Archbishop of Dublin. Seventh edition. London. 1854.

effectual way of accomplishing this, is to deny the divine origin and authority of the sacred Scriptures,—their title and their fitness to be a rule of faith or standard of doctrine. And when men, from whatever cause, do not see their way to do this plainly and openly, they often attempt it, or something like it, in an indirect and insidious way, by distorting and perverting the statements of Scripture—by evading their fair meaning and application,—or by devising pretences for declining to turn them to full account as a revelation of God's will to men, or to derive from them the whole amount of information about divine and eternal things which they seem fitted and intended to convey.

It has been the generally received doctrine of orthodox divines, and it is in entire accordance with reason and common sense, that we are bound to receive as true, on God's authority, not only what is "expressly set down in Scripture," but also what, "by good and necessary consequence, may be deduced from Scripture;"* and heretics, in every age and of every class, have, even when they made a profession of receiving what is expressly set down in Scripture, shown the greatest aversion to what are sometimes called Scripture consequences,—that is, inferences or deductions from scriptural statements, beyond what is expressly contained in the mere words of Scripture, as they stand in the page of the sacred record. Some interesting discussion on the subject of the warrantableness, the validity, and the binding obligation of Scripture consequences took place, in the early part of last century, among the English Presbyterians, when some of them had been led to embrace Arian views. With the dishonesty which the history of the church proves to have been so generally a marked characteristic of heretics and men of progress, those of them who had really, in their convictions, abandoned the generally received doctrine of the Trinity, professed, at first, to object only to the unscriptural terms in which the doctrine was usually embodied; declaimed about freedom of thought and ecclesiastical tyranny; and denounced all Scripture consequences as unwarrantable and precarious,—while they were, of course, quite willing to subscribe to the *ipsissima verba* of Scripture. But the progress of the discussion soon showed that these were hypocritical pretences; and that the men who employed them had deliberately adopted opinions in

---

* Westminster Confession, c. i. s. 6.

regard to the Father, the Son, and the Holy Spirit, which have been generally repudiated by the church of Christ, and which could no more be brought out fully and distinctly as opposed to what they reckoned error, *in the mere words of Scripture*, than the sounder views which they rejected.

Upon the occasion to which we have referred, the repudiation of Scripture consequences, and the opposition to precise and definite views on doctrinal subjects, were directed chiefly against the doctrine of the Trinity. In the present day, these views and tendencies are directed chiefly against the doctrine of a real vicarious atonement for the sins of men, and against the peculiar doctrines of the Calvinistic system of theology. Not that the true scriptural doctrine of the Trinity is more relished by men of rationalistic and sceptical tendencies, than it was in former times. It is not so. But men of this stamp seem generally, now-a-days, to be disposed to favour the attempt to evade or explain away this great doctrine, by adopting a kind of Platonic Sabellianism; and employing this as a sort of warrant for using not only the *ipsissima verba* of Scripture, but even a great deal of the language which has been commonly approved of by orthodox divines, as embodying the substance of what Scripture teaches upon this subject. The doctrine of the atonement stands in this somewhat peculiar predicament among the great fundamental articles of revealed truth, that it was never subjected to a thorough, searching, controversial discussion till the time of Socinus. The consequence of this is, that,—though there is satisfactory evidence that it was held in substance by the universal church ever since the apostolic age,—there is a considerable amount of vagueness and indefiniteness, and a considerable deficiency of precise and accurate statement upon it, in the symbols of the ancient church and in the writings of the Fathers; and that even in the Confessions of the Reformed churches,—there being no controversy on this topic with the Church of Rome,—it is not brought out so fully and precisely as most of the other fundamental doctrines of the Christian system. These facts have tended somewhat to encourage the practice, so common in the present day, of explaining away the true doctrine of the atonement, by concealing it in vague and indefinite language, under the pretence of repudiating Scripture consequences and adhering to the *ipsissima verba* of revelation. The leading presumption, so far as mere human authority is concerned, in opposition

to these latitudinarian tendencies, is this,—that they virtually resolve into a defence of Socinianism; and that Socinus and
his followers have been always regarded, both by the Church of
Rome and by the great body of the Protestant churches, as
deniers and opposers of the great fundamental principles of the
scheme of revealed truth, and as unworthy of the designation of
Christians.

The doctrines of Calvinism are, as might be expected, dealt
with in this rationalistic and sceptical age, very much in the same
way as the doctrines of the Trinity and the atonement. It is, indeed, only in the Calvinistic system of theology, that the doctrines
of the proper divinity and vicarious atonement of Christ, and of
the agency of the Holy Spirit, are fully developed in their practical
application. Arminians admit the doctrines of the divinity and
atonement of Christ, and the agency of the Spirit, into their
system of theology. But they do not fully apply them in some
of their most important practical bearings and consequences. And,
more especially, the general principles of their system preclude
them from admitting, the certain and infallible efficacy of these
great provisions in securing the results which they were intended
to accomplish. If the eternal and only-begotten Son of God
assumed human nature into personal union with the divine; if He
suffered and died as the surety and substitute of sinners, that He
might satisfy divine justice and reconcile us to God; and if, as
one leading result of His mediation, He has brought into operation
the agency of the third Person of the Godhead in order to complete the work of saving sinners; it seems a certain and unavoidable
inference, that such stupendous arrangements as these must
embody a provision for certainly effecting the whole result contemplated, whether that result was the salvation of all, or only
of a portion, of the fallen race of man. Now, the Arminian system of theology not only does not exhibit any provision adequate
to secure this result, but plainly precludes it; inasmuch as it is
quite possible, for anything which that system contains, that the
whole human race might perish,—that no sinner might be saved.
Arminianism thus tends to depreciate and disparage both the
work of Christ and the work of the Spirit, in their bearing upon
the great object they were intended to accomplish, the salvation of
sinful men. It is only the Calvinistic views of the work of Christ
and of the Holy Spirit, that are free from the great fundamental

objection to which we have referred, of making no adequate provision for securing the result intended.

The Calvinistic doctrines, in regard to the work of Christ and
the agency of the Spirit, are thus in beautiful harmony with the
other departments of that system of theology,—with those doctrines which are commonly regarded as the special peculiarities of
Calvinism. It is, we are persuaded, in some measure, because of
the vague and indefinite position in which the other departments
of the Arminian system require its adherents to leave the subjects
of the work of Christ and the work of the Spirit,—viewed in their
relation to the practical result contemplated,—that they have been
able to retain a profession of the divinity and atonement of Christ
and of the agency of the Spirit, notwithstanding the rationalism
on which the Arminian system of theology is really based. The
tendency of Arminianism is to throw the work of the Son and of
the Spirit, in the salvation of sinners, into the background, and to
lead to vagueness and indefiniteness in the statement of the truth
concerning them; while, in regard to those great doctrines which
Calvinists and Arminians hold in common, in opposition to the
Socinians,—as well as in regard to the peculiar doctrines of their
own system,—Calvinists hold clear, precise, and definite opinions.
This, in right reason, ought to be held to be a presumption of
their truth; although with many, especially in the present day, it
is held to furnish a plausible argument against them. Calvinism
unfolds most fully and explicitly the whole system of doctrine
revealed in the sacred Scriptures. It brings out most prominently
and explicitly the sovereign agency of God, the Father, the Son,
and the Holy Ghost, in the salvation of sinners; while it most
thoroughly humbles and abases men, as the worthless and helpless
recipients of the divine mercy and bounty.

Calvinism thus comes into full and direct collision with all the
strongest tendencies and prepossessions of ungodly and unrenewed
men; and has, of course, been assailed with every species of
objection. It cannot, indeed, with any great plausibility, be
alleged, that it is founded only on Scripture consequences,—that
is, inferences or deductions from scriptural statements. For
Calvinists undertake to produce from Scripture, statements which
directly and explicitly assert all their leading peculiar doctrines;
and if the Calvinistic interpretation of these statements be just
and well founded, it is plain that their fundamental principles are

directly and explicitly sanctioned by the word of God. The case
is very different with their opponents. Arminians, of course,
undertake to show that the statements founded on by Calvinists
are erroneously interpreted by them; and that, when rightly
understood, they furnish no adequate support to Calvinism. But
they scarcely allege that there are any scriptural statements which
directly and explicitly either assert Arminianism, or contradict
Calvinistic doctrines. The defence of Arminianism, and the
opposition to Calvinism, are based chiefly upon inferences or
deductions from Scripture statements; and statements, too, it is
important to remark, which do not bear directly and immediately
upon the precise points controverted. The scriptural argument
for Arminianism and against Calvinism, consists chiefly in a proof,
that God is holy, and just, and good; that He is not the author
of sin, and is not a respecter of persons; that men are responsible
for all their actions, and are justly chargeable with guilt and
liable to punishment, when they refuse to obey God's law and to
believe in the Lord Jesus Christ; and then, in the inference or
deduction, that the undeniable truth of these views of God and
man excludes Calvinism, and establishes Arminianism. This is
really the substance of the scriptural argument for Arminianism
and against Calvinism; while it is scarcely alleged by Arminians,
that there are any scriptural statements which directly and
immediately disprove or exclude the doctrines of Calvinism. On
the other hand, it is contended by Calvinists, that their views are
not only directly and explicitly asserted in many scriptural statements, but are also sanctioned by inferences or deductions from
scriptural views of the attributes and moral government of God,
and of the natural condition and capacities of man.

But though on these grounds, and by these processes, an impregnable argument can be built up in favour of Calvinism, yet
it has many formidable difficulties to contend with. The views
which it unfolds of the attributes and moral government of God,
of the natural condition and capacities of man, and of the way of
salvation as regulated and determined by these views of what God
is and of what man is, are utterly opposed to all the natural notions and tendencies of ignorant and irreligious men; and the
very clearness, definiteness, and precision with which all these
views are brought out and applied, are felt by many, especially
in the present day, as strengthening and aggravating all the ob-

jections against them. The leading objections against Calvinism,
—though based principally upon inferences or deduction from
admitted truths,—are so obvious as to occur at once to every one,
whenever the subject is presented to him; and they are possessed
of very considerable plausibility. They are just in substance
those which the Apostle Paul plainly gives us to understand
would certainly, and as a matter of course, be directed against
the doctrine which he taught. The apostle had laid down and
established the great principle, "It is not of him that willeth, nor
of him that runneth, but of God that showeth mercy,"—"He
hath mercy on whom He will, and whom He will He hardeneth."
He then assumes that, as a matter of course, this principle would
be objected to,—that men's natural notions would rise up in re-
bellion against it. "Thou wilt say then unto me, Why doth He
yet find fault? For who hath resisted His will?"*—which is just,
in plain terms, alleging that the apostle's doctrine made God the
author of sin, and destroyed man's responsibility. And the apostle,
in dealing in the following verses with this objection, makes no
attempt to explain away the doctrine which he had laid down, or
to back out of it; he does not withdraw or qualify the outspoken
Calvinism which he had so plainly enunciated, and substitute for
it the smooth and plausible Arminianism, which would at once
have completely removed all appearance of ground for the objection. On the contrary, he, without qualification or hesitation,
adheres to the doctrine he had stated; and disposes of the objection just as Calvinists,—following his example,—have always done,
by resolving the whole matter into the unsearchable perfections
and the sovereign supremacy of God, and the natural ignorance,
helplessness, and worthlessness of man.

The whole substance of what has been, or can be, plausibly
alleged against Calvinism, is contained in the objection, which the
apostle expected to be adduced against the doctrine he taught;
and the whole substance of what is necessary for defending Calvinism, is contained in, or suggested by, the way in which he disposed of the objection. But the subject has given rise, in every
age, to a great deal of ingenious and elaborate speculation; and
this speculation has been frequently of a very unwarranted, presumptuous, and even offensive description,—the presumption and

---

* Rom. ix. 19.

offensiveness being principally, though we admit not exclusively, exhibited on the side of the Arminians. We do not intend to enter upon a general discussion of the great leading objections which have been adduced against the Calvinistic system of theology, and of the way and manner in which these objections should be dealt with and disposed of. We have already indicated briefly, the leading considerations which should be brought to bear upon this subject, and which, when expounded and applied, are quite sufficient to dispose of all the plausible,—and, at first sight, apparently formidable,—objections that are commonly adduced against Calvinism; and thus to show, that the whole of the strong, positive evidence in support of it,—founded both on direct and express statements of Scripture, bearing immediately upon the points controverted, and also on clear and satisfactory inferences or deductions from the great general principles unfolded there, concerning God and man, the work of the Son and the Spirit, and the way of salvation,—stands untouched and unimpaired, and ought to command the assent and consent of our understandings and our hearts. We mean to confine ourselves, in a great measure, to a consideration of some misapprehensions which have been put forth in the present day, in regard to the practical application of Calvinism; and to an attempt to show that these misapprehensions arise from partial, defective, and erroneous conceptions on this whole subject.

There is only one topic connected with the more speculative aspects of the question, on which we wish to make some observations, viz., the connection between election and reprobation,—as it is often called,—and the use which the Arminians commonly attempt to make in controversial discussion of the latter of these doctrines. We had occasion, formerly, to censure the course of procedure usually adopted by the Arminians in this matter. But we think it deserving of somewhat further discussion,—as this will afford us an opportunity of exposing a very unfair, but very plausible, controversial artifice, which we fear has done much injury to what we believe to be the cause of God and truth.

It is the common practice of theologians,—though there are some diversities in this respect,—to employ the word predestination as comprehending the whole of God's decrees or purposes, His resolutions or determinations, with respect to the ultimate destiny, the eternal condition, of mankind; and to regard election and reprobation as two divisions of the subject, falling under the general head of predestination, and exhausting it. Election comprehends the decrees or purposes of God in regard to those of the human race who are ultimately saved; while reprobation is commonly used as a general designation of His decrees or purposes in regard to those men who finally perish. It is admitted by Arminians as well as Calvinists, that God decreed or resolved from eternity to do whatever He does or effects in time; and conversely, that whatever He does in time He from eternity decreed or resolved to do. This is not, on the part of the Arminians, any thing tantamount to an admission of the great fundamental principle of Calvinism,—viz., that "God from all eternity did, by the most wise and holy counsel of His own will, freely and unchangeably ordain whatsoever comes to pass;"* for they hold that many things come to pass,—such as the actions of free and morally responsible beings,—of which God is not the author or cause. These things, Arminians allege, God does not do or effect; and consequently He did not from eternity resolve to do or effect them. But whatever God really does or effects in time, whatever comes to pass by His agency, so that He is to be regarded as the author or efficient cause of it, they admit that He must be regarded as having from eternity decreed or resolved to do or effect. It is important to remember that intelligent Arminians concede this general principle; for it is very common among the lower class of Arminian writers, to talk as if there was some special and peculiar difficulty in the *eternity* of the divine decrees or purposes, beyond and in addition to what is involved in the execution of them in time. But this is a mere fallacy, intended to make an impression upon the minds of unreflecting men. It cannot be disputed, that whatever God does or effects in time, He from eternity decreed or resolved to do or effect; and there is plainly no greater or additional difficulty, no deeper or more inexplicable mystery, attaching to the eternal purpose to do a thing—to effect a result,—than to the actual doing or effecting of it in time. If God does or effects any thing in time,—such as the production of faith and repentance in the heart of a moral and responsible being, there can be no greater difficulty, so far as concerns either the character of God or the capacities of men, in His having resolved, from

* Confession, chap. iii. s. 1.

eternity, to effect this result. Whatever God really does in time, He not only *may*, but He *must*, from eternity have resolved or determined to do.

Arminians do not deny this general principle; but they are commonly disposed to throw it into the background, or at least to abstain from giving it prominence; partly, in order to leave room for appealing to men's feelings,—as if there was something specially harsh and repulsive in the eternity of the decree as distinguished from the execution of it in time,—and partly, to keep out of sight the compound or duplicate evidence which Calvinists can produce from Scripture in support of their leading doctrines, by the legitimate application of this principle of the certain and necessary identity of the purpose and the execution of it. Whatever indications are given us in Scripture,—as to what God decreed or purposed, in regard either to those who are saved or those who perish,—go equally to establish what it is that He does in time in regard to these two classes respectively; and whatever information is given us as to what He does in time with reference to the salvation of men individually, equally indicates what we must regard Him as having from eternity determined to do. And thus the scriptural evidence bearing upon both of these topics, goes equally, and with combined force, to establish one great general conclusion, which is just the fundamental principle of the Calvinistic system of theology. But this by the way,—for we are not at present attempting a general discussion of predestination. We have adverted to this topic, chiefly for the purpose of reminding our readers, that the words election and reprobation may be used, correctly enough, as general designations, either of what God purposed from eternity to do, or, of what He does in time, in relation to the saved and the lost respectively; and that, so far as our present object is concerned, it is not necessary to have respect to this distinction between the eternal purpose and the execution of it.

Election, then, may be regarded as descriptive generally of what God purposed from eternity and does in time, in regard to the salvation of those who are saved; and reprobation as descriptive of what He purposed and does in regard to the fate of those who ultimately perish. And as those who are saved and those who perish comprehend all the individuals of the human race, it is evident, from the nature of the case, that election and reprobation must stand in a very close and intimate mutual relation ; so that, if we have full and accurate conceptions of the one, we must thereby necessarily also know something of the other.   Election, —taken in this wide and general sense,—is evidently a subject of much greater practical importance than reprobation ; and, accordingly, there is much fuller and more direct information given us about it in Scripture.   There is a great deal told us there about God's purposes and procedure with respect to those who are saved ; and there is very little, comparatively, told us about God's purposes and procedure with respect to those who perish.   We have, indeed, full information supplied to us, as to what it is that men must do to be saved,—as to what is required of them that they may escape God's wrath and curse due to them for their sins ; and we are assured, that those to whom this information is communicated, and who fail to improve it for their own salvation, are themselves responsible for the fearful result.   This information is of the last importance, and it is fully furnished to us in Scripture.   But beyond this, there is little told us in regard to those who perish ; very little, especially, in regard to any purposes or actings of God bearing upon their ultimate destiny as individuals.   We have much information given us in Scripture about God's purposes and actings in regard to those who are saved. We are told plainly of His eternal choice or selection of them for salvation, out of the human race all equally sunk in guilt and depravity ; of His absolute, unconditional determination to save these persons so chosen or selected, in accordance with the provisions of a great scheme, which secures the glory of the divine character, the honour of the divine law, and the interests of personal holiness ; and of the execution of this decree,—the accomplishment of this purpose,—by giving to these persons, or effecting in them, faith and regeneration, with all their appropriate results,—by watching over them with special care after these great changes have been effected,—by upholding and preserving them in the exercise of faith and in the practice of holiness,—and by preparing them fully for the inheritance of the saints in light. By the application of these principles, we are able to give a full account of the great leading features and events in the history of every soul that is saved, from the eternal sovereign purpose of God to save that soul till its final admission to glory.

Calvinists contend that all these principles are set forth very

directly and explicitly in the statements of Scripture; and, in this
state of things, common sense and common fairness plainly dictate,
that the first thing to be done is to investigate and ascertain,
whether or not Scripture sanctions them; and if the result of the
inquiry be a conviction that it does, to receive them as true and
certain, along with all that is involved in, or results from them.
Arminians, of course, deny that Scripture sanctions these principles, and endeavour to show the insufficiency of the grounds on
which scriptural support is claimed for them. But they often
prefer to conduct the discussion in a different way. They are
usually anxious to give priority and prominence to the subject of
reprobation; and having refuted, as they think, the Calvinistic
doctrine upon this subject, they then draw the inference or deduction, that since election and reprobation are correlatives, and
necessarily imply each other, the disproof of reprobation involves
a disproof of election. Their reasons for adopting this line of
policy in conducting the discussion, are abundantly obvious, and
somewhat tempting, but very far from being satisfactory or creditable. The Calvinistic doctrine of reprobation admits more easily
of being distorted and perverted by misrepresentation than the
doctrine of election; and of this facility many Arminians have not
scrupled to avail themselves. The awful and mysterious subject
of reprobation can likewise be easily presented in lights, which
make it appear harsh and repulsive to men's natural feelings; and
this is one main reason why Arminians are so fond of dwelling
upon it, and labouring to give it great prominence in the discussion of this whole matter. The injustice and unfairness of this
mode of dealing with the question, is established by the consideration already adverted to,—viz., that there is much fuller and more
explicit information given us in Scripture on the subject of election than of reprobation. If this be so, then it is plainly the
dictate of common sense and common fairness, that we should
investigate the evidence of the doctrine of election before we proceed to consider that of reprobation; and that we should not
allow the conclusions we may have reached, upon satisfactory
evidence, with respect to the subject that is more clearly revealed,
to be disturbed by difficulties with respect to a subject which God
has left shrouded in somewhat greater mystery.

Calvinists not only admit, but contend, that both as to their
import and meaning, and as to their proof or evidence, the doc-

trines of election and reprobation are closely connected with each
other; and that inferences or deductions with respect to the one
may be legitimately and conclusively derived from the other.   In
the nature of the case, God's purposes and procedure, in regard to
those who are saved, must affect or regulate His purposes and procedure in regard to those who perish; and the knowledge of the
one must throw some light upon the other.   Calvinists have always
maintained, that the whole of what they believe and teach upon
the subject of reprobation, may be deduced by undeniable logical
inference from the doctrine which they hold to be clearly taught in
Scripture on the subject of election; and that it is also confirmed
by the more vague and imperfect information given us in Scripture,
bearing directly upon the subject of the fate of those who perish.
No intelligent Calvinist has ever disputed the position, that election necessarily implies and leads to a corresponding reprobation.
No Calvinists, indeed, have ever disputed this; except some of the
weaker brethren among the evangelical churchmen in England,
who have professed to believe in Calvinistic election as plainly set
forth in their 17th Article, but who have declined to admit the
doctrine of reprobation in any sense.   We can sympathise with
the feeling which leads men to shrink from giving prominence to
this awful and mysterious subject,—and even with the feeling which
led to the omission of any formal deliverance regarding it, both in
the articles of the Church of England and in the original Scotch
Confession of 1560, though both prepared by Calvinists.   But
there is no reason why men, in their investigation of divine truth,
should not ascertain and state, and, when necessary, maintain and
defend, the whole of what is contained in, or may be deduced
from, Scripture on this as on other subjects.

Arminians, for controversial purposes, have frequently given
great and undue prominence to this subject of reprobation; and
some Calvinists, provoked by this unfair and discreditable procedure, have been occasionally tempted to follow their opponents
into a minuteness and rashness of speculation that was painful and
unbecoming.   But Calvinists in general,—while not shrinking from
the discussion of this subject,—have never shown any desire to
enlarge upon it, beyond what was rendered necessary by the importunity of their opponents; and have usually conducted the discussion under the influence of a sense of the imperative obligation
to keep strictly within the limits of what is revealed, and to carry

on the whole investigation under a deep feeling of reverence and holy awe. Very different have been the spirit and conduct of many Arminians in dealing with this mysterious subject. They often shrink from meeting fairly and manfully the great mass of direct and positive evidence which can be produced from Scripture in support of the Calvinistic doctrine of election. They prefer to assail it indirectly by an attack upon the doctrine of reprobation ; and they adopt this course because, as we have said, there is much less information given us in Scripture about reprobation than election ; and because it is easier to distort and misrepresent the Calvinistic doctrine upon the one subject than the other, and to excite a prejudice against it. No man of ordinary candour will deny, that a great deal of evidence,—which is at least very plausible,—has been produced from statements contained in Scripture, in support of the Calvinistic doctrine of election. And if this be so, Calvinists are entitled to insist, that men, who profess to be seeking the truth, and not merely contending for victory, shall, in the first place, deal with this direct and positive evidence, and dispose of it, by either admitting or disproving its validity ; and shall not, *in the first instance*, have recourse to any indirect, inferential, and circuitous process for deciding the point at issue. But this mode of procedure, though plainly demanded by sound logic and an honest love of truth, is one which Arminians rather dislike and avoid ; and hence the anxiety they have often shown to give priority and prominence to the subject of reprobation, and to attempt to settle the whole question about predestination by inferences deduced from it.

When the Remonstrants or Arminians were cited before the synod of Dort, they insisted that, under the first article which treated of predestination in general, the discussion should begin with an investigation of the doctrine of reprobation ; and when the synod, upon the obvious grounds of sound logic, common sense, and ordinary fairness, to which we have referred,—and which are fully set forth in the Judgments of the different Colleges of the Foreign Divines, embodied in the Acts of the synod,*—refused to concede this demand, the Arminians' loudly complained of this as an act of great hardship and injustice. The excuse they gave for making this demand was this : that the difficulties which they had

---

* Pp. 139–151.

been led to entertain in regard to the truth of the system of doctrine generally received in the Reformed churches, were chiefly connected with the subject of reprobation; and that if this point could be cleared up to their satisfaction, there might be some hope of the two parties coming to an agreement.   But this, besides being a mere pretence, was, upon the grounds which we have already adduced, plainly untenable upon any right basis of argument.   It is conclusively answered by the fair application of the considerations,—that there is much fuller and clearer information given us in Scripture about election than about reprobation; that Calvinists really hold nothing on the subject of reprobation but what is virtually contained in, and necessarily deducible from, what is plainly taught in Scripture on the subject of election; and that the scriptural evidence for the doctrine of reprobation is, mainly and principally, though not exclusively, to be found in the scriptural proof of the doctrine of election,—that is, in the fair and legitimate application of the views revealed to us as to what God has purposed and does with respect to those who are saved, to the investigation of the question as to what He has purposed and does, or rather has *not* purposed and does *not* do, with respect to those who perish.

This unreasonable, unfair, and discreditable mode of procedure, adopted by Episcopius and his associates at the synod of Dort, has been often since exhibited by Arminian controversialists, at least practically and in substance; though perhaps it has not been so explicitly stated and so openly defended, as upon that occasion. We may refer to two or three instances of this.

The first work that appeared in England, containing a formal and elaborate attack upon the Calvinistic system of theology, was published anonymously in 1633.*   Its author was Samuel Hoard,

---

* The work entitled, *Apello Evangelium; or, An Appeal to the Gospel*, by John Plaifere (who must not be confounded with Thomas Playfere, Davenant's predecessor as Margaret Professor of Divinity at Cambridge and a Calvinist), seems to have been written before Hoard's book, in 1628 or 1629, though it was not published till 1652, many years after the author's death.   Plaifere's *Appeal* is also a formal and elaborate attack upon Calvinism, and is, upon the whole, an abler and a fairer book than Hoard's. It contains the earliest attempt with which we are acquainted, to distort the meaning of the 17th Article of the Church of England to an Arminian sense, a topic with which Hoard did not venture to meddle.   Plaifere's *Appeal* was republished in a collection of " Tracts concerning Predestination and Providence." Cambridge 1719.

rector of Moreton, and its title was, " God's Love to Mankind
manifested by disproving His Absolute Decree for their Damnation." And, in accordance with this title, the work just consists of
an attack upon the Calvinistic doctrine of reprobation, grossly distorted and misrepresented ; without an attempt to answer the great
mass of direct and positive proof, which Calvinists have produced
from Scripture, in support of their doctrine of election. This work
of Hoard's had the honour of being formally answered by three
great theologians,—Davenant, Twisse, and Amyraut,—the diversity of whose views upon some points, while they agreed in the
main, gave, perhaps, to the discussion as a whole, additional interest and value. Davenant's answer to Hoard was published in
1641, and is entitled, " Animadversions written by the Right Rev.
Father in God, John, Lord Bishop of Sarisbury, upon a Treatise
entitled, ' God's Love to Mankind.'" Amyraut's answer to Hoard
was also published in 1641, and is entitled, "Doctrinæ J. Calvini
de Absoluto Reprobationis Decreto Defensio." Hoard's work had
been translated into Latin, and published at Amsterdam, under the
auspices of Grotius. Amyraut, who had incurred the suspicion of
orthodox divines, by advocating,—in his treatise on predestination,
published in 1634,—the doctrine of universal redemption, seized
this opportunity of showing that he zealously maintained the fundamental principles of the Calvinistic system of theology, by preparing and publishing a reply to this work, in defence of the
doctrine of Calvin. Twisse's reply to Hoard, though written
before any of the other answers, and, indeed, principally before
the publication of Hoard's work, which had been sent to him in
manuscript, was not published till some years after its author's
death. It is entitled, " The Riches of God's Love unto the Vessels of Mercy consistent with His Absolute Hatred or Reprobation
of the Vessels of Wrath." It was published in 1653, and was
licensed and recommended by Dr Owen, at that time Vice-
Chancellor of Oxford. The first sentence of Owen's prefatory
recommendation of Twisse's work, is admirably pertinent to our
purpose, and, indeed, brings out the only point with which we
have at present to do in connection with this matter. It is this :—

" Of all those weighty parcels of gospel truth which the Arminians have
chosen to oppose, there is not any about which they so much delight to try
and exercise the strength of fleshly reasonings, as that of God's eternal decree
of reprobation ; partly, because the Scripture doth not so abound in the de-

livery of this doctrine, as of some others lying in a more immediate subserviency to the obedience and consolation of the saints (though it be sufficiently revealed in them to the quieting of their spirits who have learned to captivate their understandings to the obedience of faith), and partly, because they apprehend the truth thereof to be more exposed to the riotous oppositions of men's tumultuating, carnal affections, whose help and assistance they by all means court and solicit in their contests against it."

These three replies to Hoard rank among the most important and valuable works in this department of controversial theology. But at present we have to do with them only in this respect, that they all fully expose the erroneous and distorted account which Hoard gives of what it is that Calvinists really hold upon the subject of reprobation; and bring out the absurdity and unfairness of giving so much prominence to this topic in discussing the general question of predestination,—instead of beginning with the much more important subject of election, about which we have much fuller information given us in Scripture; and then, when the doctrine of Scripture upon the subject of election has been investigated and ascertained, proceeding to apply this, in connection with the fewer and obscurer intimations given us directly concerning reprobation, in determining what we ought to believe regarding it. We may give two or three extracts on these points from Davenant, whom,—notwithstanding his somewhat unsound views as to the extent of the atonement,—we consider one of the greatest divines the Church of England has ever produced. He thus points out the unfairness of the title, and of the general scope and object, of Hoard's work, while admitting,—as, of course, every intelligent theologian must do,—that the election of some men necessarily implies a corresponding reprobation of the rest; and indicating, at the same time, the true use and application that should be made of the fact, that the 17th Article of the Church of England, though explicitly asserting the Calvinistic doctrine of election, makes no direct mention of reprobation.

" . . . Obliquely to oppose the eternal, free, and absolute decree of predestination or election, under colour of disapproving an absolute decree for any man's damnation, befitteth not any divine who acknowledgeth the truth of that doctrine which the Scriptures have delivered, St Augustine cleared, and the Church of England established in the 17th Article. But, if the author of this treatise had no other aim than the overthrowing of such an eternal decree of predestination and preterition, as is fondly supposed will save men whether they repent or not repent, believe or not believe, persevere or not persevere;

and such an absolute decree of reprobation as will damn men, though they should repent and believe, or will hinder any man from repenting or believing, or will cause and work any man's impenitency or infidelity ; we both wish, and shall endeavour together with him, to root such erroneous fancies out of all Christian minds."*

" The title of the book justly rejecteth an absolute decree for the damnation of any particular person : for such a decree was never enacted in God's eternal counsel, nor ever published in His revealed word. But for absolute reprobation,—if by this word be understood only that preterition, non-election, or negative decree of predestination, which is contradictorily opposed to the decree of election,—the one is as absolute as the other, and neither dependeth upon the foreseen difference of men's actions, but upon the absolute will of God. For if God from eternity absolutely elected some unto the infallible attainment of grace and glory, we cannot but grant that those who are not comprised within this absolute decree are as absolutely passed by, as the other are chosen. The decree of damnation therefore must not be confounded with the decree of negative predestination, which (according to the phrase of the school rather than of the Scripture) is usually termed reprobation. By which term of reprobation some understand only the denial of election or predestination. And because the negation is to be measured by the affirmation, unless we be agreed what is meant when we say, *Peter was predestinated before the foundations of the world were laid,* we can never rightly judge what is meant when, on the contrary, we avouch, *Judas was reprobated before the foundations of the world were laid.* Some others, under the name of reprobation, involve not only the negative decree of preparing such effectual grace as would bring them most certainly unto glory, but an affirmative decree also for the punishing of men eternally in hell-fire.

" So far forth as this author seemeth to oppose the absolute decree of predestination, and the absolute decree of negative reprobation or non-election, reducing them to the contrary foreseen conditions of good or bad acts in men, he crosseth the received doctrine of the Church of England. But if he intend only to prove that the adjudication of men unto eternal life or eternal death, and the temporal introduction of men into the kingdom of heaven, or casting of men into the torments of hell, are always accompanied with the divine prescience or intuition of contrary acts or qualities in those which are to be saved or condemned ; we hold it and acknowledge it a most certain truth. Yet we must here add, that predestination and preterition are eternal acts immanent in God the Creator, whereas salvation and damnation are temporal effects terminated unto the creature : and therefore the latter may be suspended upon many conditions, though the former be in God never so absolute.

" The treatise ensuing would have had much more perspicuity if the author had briefly and plainly set down what he understandeth by this word predestination or election, and whether he conceive it to be an absolute or a condi-

---

* P. 2.

tional decree. If conditional, he should have showed us with whom God conditioned, upon what terms, and where the conditions stand upon record. If he grant absolute predestination, his plea for conditionate preterition will be to little purpose, with those who understand that the absolute election of such a certain number doth *in eodem signo rationis* as absolutely imply a certain number of men not elected.

" The wisdom of our Church of England in the 17th Article layeth down the doctrine of predestination, and doth not so much as in one word meddle with the point of reprobation ; leaving men to conceive that the one is the bare negation or denial of that special favour and benefit which is freely intended and mercifully bestowed in the other. Would to God the children of this church had imitated the wisdom of their mother, and had not taken a quite contrary course, baulking the doctrine of predestination, and breaking in abruptly upon the doctrine of reprobation.

" I know not whether I should think him more defective, who in disputing about reprobation runneth out into impertinent vagaries, or him that undertaketh the handling of this question without premising and opening the true nature of predestination.

" And no man need fear but (with all that are judicious, religious, and loving their own salvation) that manner of handling this controversy will be best accepted, which so reduceth man's sin and damnation to himself, as withal it forgetteth not to reduce his justification, sanctification, glorification, not to any foreseen goodness springing out of man's free-will, but to the free mercy of God, according to His eternal purpose effectually working in men those gifts and acts of grace which are the means to bring them unto glory." *

" If *striving to lie close be a probable argument of a bad cause,* those who are afraid to deal with the more lightsome part of this controversy which concerneth election and predestination, and thrust themselves, without borrowing any light from this, into the other (which taken by itself is much more dark and obscure), are the men who strive to wrap themselves and others in an obscure and dark cloud. Our Church of England was more willing and desirous to set down expressly the doctrine of absolute predestination, I mean of predestination causing faith and perseverance, than it was of absolute negative reprobation, I mean of such reprobation as implieth in God a will of permitting some men's final impiety and impenitency, and of justly ordaining them unto punishment for the same : and yet the latter doth plainly follow upon the truth of the former. It was wisdom, and not Jewish or Turkish fear, which made our Church so clear in the article for absolute predestination, and yet so reserved in the other ; easily perceiving that predestination of some men cannot be affirmed, but non-predestination or preterition or negative reprobation (call it as you please) of some others must needs therewith be understood.

" Though *truth be best uncovered,* yet all truths are not of the same nature, nor alike profitable to be debated upon : yet for the truth of absolute repro-

* Pp. 4–7.

bation, so far forth as it is connected and conjoined with absolute predestination, when the main intent of the Remonstrants is by opposing of the former to overthrow the latter, it importeth those who have subscribed to the 17th Article not to suffer it to be obliquely undermined."*

"The opinion here aimed at, is the doctrine of absolute reprobation, concerning which all disputes are frivolous, if it be not first agreed upon what is understood by these two words, absolute reprobation.

"For the understanding whereof, observe first, what our church conceiveth under the term of predestination. If a decree of God first beholding and foreseeing certain particular persons as believing and constantly persevering unto the end in faith and godliness, and thereupon electing them unto eternal happiness, then we will grant that the Remonstrants (whom this author followeth) embrace the doctrine of the Church of England. But if, in our 17th Article, God in His eternal predestination, beholdeth all men as lying *in massa corrupta*, and decreeth out of this generality of mankind, being all in a like damnable condition, to elect some by His secret counsel, to deliver them from the curse and damnation by a special calling according to His eternal purpose, and by working in them faith and perseverance; then it is plain that the Remonstrants and this author have left the doctrine of the Church of England in the point of predestination, and therefore may well be suspected also in the point of reprobation, which must have its true measure taken from that other.

"Secondly, take notice, what the word absolute importeth when it is applied unto the eternal and immanent acts or decrees of the divine predestination. Not (as the Remonstrants continually mistake it) a peremptory decree of saving persons elected, whether they believe or not believe, nor yet a decree of forcing or necessitating predestinate persons unto the acts of believing, repenting, persevering, or walking in the way which leadeth unto everlasting life; but a gracious and absolute decree of bestowing as well faith, repentance, and perseverance, as eternal life, upon all those to whom, in His everlasting purpose, He vouchsafed the special benefit of predestination. And that God can and doth according to His eternal purpose infallibly work faith and perseverance in the elect, without any coaction or necessitation of man's will, is agreed upon by all Catholic divines, and was never opposed but by Pelagius. And this absolute intending of eternal life to persons elected, and absolute intending of giving unto such the special grace of a perseverant faith, is that absolute predestination which our mother the church hath commended unto us, and which we must defend against the error of the semi-Pelagians and Remonstrants, who strive to bring in a predestination or election wherein God seeth faith and perseverance in certain men going before predestination, and doth not prepare it for them in eternity by His special act of predestination, nor bestow it upon them in due time, as a consequent effect of His eternal predestination.

---

* Pp. 54–56.

"Thirdly, it is to be observed, that our church, in not speaking one word of reprobation in the article, would have us to be more sparing in discussing this point than that other of election; quite contrary to the humour of the Remonstrants, who hang back when they are called to dispute upon predestination, but will by no authority be beat off from rushing at the first dash upon the point of reprobation.

"But further, from hence we may well collect, that our church, which by predestination understandeth a special benefit out of God's mercy and absolute freedom, absolutely prepared from all eternity, and in time bestowed infallibly upon the elect, would have us conceive no further of the silenced decree of reprobation, than the not preparing of such effectual grace, the not decreeing of such persons unto the infallible attainment of glory, the decreeing to permit them through their own default deservedly and infallibly to procure their own misery. All this is no more than God Himself hath avouched of Himself, 'miserebor cui voluero, et clemens ero in quem mihi placuerit.' And that which the apostle attributeth unto God.*

"Fourthly, this non-prædestinatio, non-electio, præteritio or negativa reprobatio (for by all these names divines speak of it) doth as absolutely leave some out of the number of the predestinate, as predestination doth include others within the same number. And the number of both, formally and materially, is so certain, that the diminution or augmentation of either is, by the general consent of orthodox divines, condemned for an erroneous opinion: though the semi-Pelagians spurned against this truth. If under the name of absolute predestination any conceive a violent decree of God thrusting men into a state of grace and glory, and under the name of absolute reprobation, a violent decree of God thrusting men into sin and misery, let who will confute them: for their opinion is erroneous concerning the one, and blasphemous concerning the other. But under colour of opposing such imaginary decrees, to bring in a conditionate predestination, to exclude this negative reprobation, to settle them both upon provision of human acts, is opposite to the doctrine of St Augustine, approved anciently by the Catholic Church, and till this newfangled age, generally and commonly allowed and embraced both by the Romanists and by the Protestants."†

Arminians, in more modern times, have not been slow to follow the example set them by their predecessors, in the mode of dealing with this subject. Whitby, in his Discourse on the Five Points,—which, though not a work of any great ability, was for a century, and until superseded by Tomline's "Refutation of Calvinism," the great oracle and text-book of the anti-evangelical Arminians of the Church of England,—devotes the two *first* chapters to the subject of reprobation. But, perhaps, the folly and unfairness of the Arminian mode of dealing with this sub-

* Exod. xxxii. 19. Rom. ix. 15, 16, 17, 18. | † Pp. 126, 130.

ject, may be regarded as having reached its acme in John Wesley's treatise, entitled, "Predestination calmly Considered," which was published about the middle of last century, and is contained in the tenth volume of the collected edition of his works. Wesley, in this treatise, begins with proving,—what no intelligent Calvinist disputes,—that the election of some men to everlasting life, necessarily implies what may be called a reprobation of the rest, or, as he expresses it, that "unconditional election cannot appear without the cloven foot of reprobation."* And having established this, he straightway commences an elaborate and violent attack upon reprobation, which he describes as "that millstone which hangs about the neck of your whole hypothesis,"† without attempting to grapple with the direct positive scriptural evidence, by which the doctrine of unconditional election has been established. Dr Gill, in an excellent reply to this treatise, entitled "The Doctrine of Predestination Stated," truly describes it in this way:—"Though he calls his pamphlet 'Predestination calmly considered,' yet it only considers one part of it, reprobation; and that not in a way of argument but harangue, not taking notice of our argument from Scripture or reason, only making some cavilling exceptions to it."‡ Wesley, indeed, is so engrossed and excited by reprobation, that he calls out, in a sort of frenzy, "Find out any election which does not imply reprobation, and I will gladly agree to it. But reprobation I can never agree to, while I believe the Scripture to be of God."§ This mode of contemplating and dealing with the subject, is manifestly inconsistent with sound reason and an honest love of truth. The first duty incumbent upon Wesley, and upon all men, in this matter, was just to "find out" what Scripture taught upon the subject of election,—to receive its teaching upon that point with implicit submission,—and to follow out the doctrine, thus ascertained, to all its legitimate consequences. He tells us, indeed, that he could not find the Calvinistic doctrine of election in Scripture; but he has not explained to us how he managed to dispose of the direct positive evidence usually adduced from Scripture in support of it. And we venture to think, that if he had examined Scripture with due impartiality, without allowing himself to be scared by the bugbear of what he calls "the cloven foot of reprobation," he would have found, as Calvinists

---

* P. 209.   † P. 255.   ‡ P. 22.   § P. 211.

have done, *this* election to be taught there,—viz., that God from eternity, out of the good pleasure of His own will, elected some men, absolutely and unconditionally, to everlasting life; and that, in the execution of this purpose, He invariably and infallibly bestows upon these men that faith, regeneration, and perseverance, which He alone can bestow, and without which they cannot be saved. We admit that this election necessarily implies a corresponding reprobation; but we really believe nothing more upon the subject of reprobation than what the election plainly taught in Scripture necessarily implies,—viz., this, that God passes by the rest of men, the non-elect, and leaves them in their natural state of guilt and depravity, withholding from them, or *de facto* not conferring upon them, that special grace, which, as He of course well knows, is necessary to the production of faith and regeneration; and doing this, as well as ultimately punishing them for their sin, in accordance with a decree or purpose which He had formed from eternity. We find in Scripture an election which necessarily implies *this* reprobation; and, therefore, we believe both upon the testimony of God. We do not consider ourselves at liberty to agree to " any election," as Wesley says, but what we find taught in Scripture; and we regard ourselves as bound to agree to *this* election, because taught there, even though it necessarily involves all that we believe on the subject of reprobation.

But we have said enough, we think, to show the unreasonableness and unfairness of the course frequently pursued by the Arminians, in labouring to excite a prejudice against the doctrine of election, by giving priority and prominence to the discussion of reprobation; and to enforce the obligation of the duty plainly imposed by logic, common sense, and candour, to deal in the first place, deliberately and impartially, with the mass of direct and positive scriptural evidence which Calvinists adduce in support of their doctrine of election,—without being prepossessed or prejudiced by any inferences or deductions that may be drawn from it, whether warrantably or the reverse, or by any collateral and extraneous considerations. Without pretending to discuss this subject, we would like, before leaving it, to make a few explanatory remarks, in the way of guarding against misapprehensions and misrepresentations of the doctrine generally held by Calvinists regarding it.

The sum and substance of what Calvinists believe upon the

subject is this,—that God decreed or purposed from eternity to do what He actually does in time, in regard to those who perish as well as in regard to those who are saved; and that this is in substance, withholding from them, or abstaining from communicating to them, those gracious and insuperable influences of His Spirit, by which alone faith and regeneration can be produced, leaving them in their natural state of sin and misery, and then at last inflicting upon them the punishment which by their sin they have deserved. In stating and discussing the question about reprobation, Calvinistic divines are careful, as may be seen in the extracts quoted above from Davenant, to distinguish between two different acts, decreed or resolved on by God from eternity and executed by Him in time ;—the one negative and the other positive,—the one sovereign and the other judicial,—and both frequently comprehended under the general name of reprobation. The first of these, the negative or sovereign,—which is commonly called non-election, preterition, or passing by,—is simply resolving, to leave (and in consequence leaving) some men, those not chosen to everlasting life, in their natural state of sin and misery,—to withhold from them, or to abstain from conferring upon them, those supernatural gracious influences which are necessary to enable any man to repent and believe; so that the result is, that they continue in their sin, with the guilt of all their transgressions upon their head. The second act,—the positive or judicial,—is more properly that which is called in the Westminster Confession of Faith, "foreordaining to everlasting death," and "ordaining" those who have been passed by "to dishonour and wrath for their sin." God ordains no men to wrath or punishment except on account of their sin; and makes no decree, forms no purpose, to subject any to punishment, but what has reference to, and is founded on, their sin, as a thing certain and contemplated. But the first or negative act of non-election,—preterition, or passing by,—may be said to be absolute, since it is not founded on sin, and perseverance in it, as foreseen. Sin foreseen cannot be the proper ground or cause why some men are elected and others are passed by, for all men are sinners, and were foreseen as such. It cannot be alleged, that those who were not elected, and who are passed by in the communication of special supernatural grace, have always been greater sinners than those who have been chosen and brought to eternal life. And with respect to the idea which might naturally suggest itself,—viz., that final impenitence, or unbelief foreseen might be the ground or cause, not only of the positive or judicial act of foreordination to punishment and misery, but also of the negative act of preterition,—this Calvinists hold to be inconsistent with the scriptural statements which so plainly ascribe the production of faith and regeneration, and of perseverance in faith and holiness, wherever they are produced, solely to the good pleasure of God and the efficacious operation of His Spirit, viewed in connection with the undoubted truth that He could, if He had chosen, have as easily produced the same results in others; and inconsistent likewise with the intimations plainly given us in Scripture, that there is *something* in God's purposes and procedure, even in regard to those who perish, which can be resolved only into His own good pleasure, into the most wise and holy counsel of His will.

The leading objections against the Calvinistic doctrine of reprobation are founded upon misapprehensions and misrepresentations of its real import and bearings. The objections usually adduced against it are chiefly these; that it implies, 1st, That God created many men in order that He might at last consign them to everlasting misery; and 2d, That His decree of reprobation, or His eternal purpose concerning those who perish, is the proper cause or source of the sin and unbelief, on account of which they are ultimately condemned to destruction. Now Calvinists do not teach these doctrines, but repudiate and abjure them. They maintain that these doctrines cannot be shown to be fairly involved in any thing which they do teach upon this subject. The answer to both these objections, is mainly based upon the views we hold with respect to the original state and condition of man at his creation, and the sin and misery into which he afterwards fell. God made man upright, after His own image, in knowledge, righteousness, and holiness,—fitted and designed to glorify and enjoy his Maker; and this brings out the only true and proper end for which man was created. Calvinists have always not only admitted but contended, that there are important differences between the relation in which the divine foresight of the unbelief and impenitence of those who perish stands to the decree of reprobation, and that in which the foresight of the faith and perseverance of those who are saved stands to the decree of election; and between the way and manner in which these two decrees

operate in the production of the means by which they are executed,
—means which may be said to consist substantially in the character and actions of their respective objects. We cannot dwell
upon these differences. It is sufficient to say, that while Calvinists
maintain, that the decree of election is the cause or source of faith,
holiness, and perseverance, in all in whom they are produced;
they hold that the preterition of some men,—that is, the first or
negative act in the decree of reprobation, based upon God's good
pleasure, the counsel of His will,—puts nothing in men, causes or
effects no change in them, but simply leaves them as it found
them, in the state of guilt and depravity to which they had fallen;
while they admit, that the second or positive part of the decree of
reprobation,—the foreordination to wrath and misery, as distinguished from preterition,—is founded upon the foresight of
men's continuance in sin. God, in the purpose and act of preterition, took from them nothing which they had, withheld from
them nothing to which they had a claim, exerted upon them no
influence to constrain them to continue in sin, or to prevent them
from repenting and believing; and in further appointing them to
dishonour and wrath *for their sin,* He was not resolving to inflict
upon them any thing but what He foresaw that they would then
have fully merited.*

The considerations which have now been hinted at, are amply
sufficient, when expounded and applied, as they have been by

---

* We do not remember to have
read in any Calvinistic author, a more
precise, comprehensive, and yet compendious statement of the differences
between election and reprobation, than
is to be found in the "Medulla Theologica" of William Ames, or, as he is
commonly called in Latin, Amesius.
Ames was one of the acutest controversialists and ablest divines of the seventeenth century. He was an English
puritan, was driven into exile because
of his nonconformity, and became
professor of divinity at Franeker.
He has, in his various works, made
most valuable contributions to the
Popish, Puritan, and Arminian controversies. He thus states the views
generally held by Calvinists as to the
differences between election and re-

probation, embodying the chief points
on which the answers to the Arminian
objections to reprobation are based:
" Hinc prima imparitas rationis inter
electionem et reprobationem; in electione enim finis rationem habet non
tantum Dei gratia gloriosa, sed etiam
hominum ipsorum salus; in reprobatione vero damnatio in sese non habet
rationem finis aut boni (the only end,
properly so called, being, as the context explains, the manifestation of the
divine justice). In eo nihilominus
secunda imparitas est rationis inter
electionem et reprobationem, quod
electionis amor bonum creaturæ com-
municat immediate, sed reprobationis
odium bonum tantum negat, non in-
fert aut infligit malum, nisi merito
creaturæ intercedente. In isto actu

Calvinistic divines, to answer the objections of the Arminians,—
that is, the special objections which they usually adduce against
the doctrine of reprobation, as distinguished from the more general
objections commonly directed against the Calvinistic system of
theology as a whole; and to expose the injustice and unfairness
of the misrepresentations which they often give of our sentiments,
that they may give greater plausibility to their objections.

We have stated, that we do not mean to enter into the consideration of any of the great leading objections against Calvinism,
based upon its alleged inconsistency with the moral attributes of
God and the responsibility of man; or of the more abstract
theoretical speculations which have been brought to bear upon the
investigation of this subject. We propose to consider only some of
the misapprehensions that have been put forth, and some of the difficulties that have been started, in regard to its *practical application.*

There is one general form of misrepresentation which Arminians often employ in dealing with the doctrines of Calvinism.
It is exhibited in the practice of taking a part of our doctrine,
disjoined from the rest, representing it as the whole of what we
teach upon the point; and then showing that, thus viewed, it is
liable to serious objections and leads to injurious consequences.
It is by a process of this sort that they give plausibility to their
very common and favourite allegation, that the Calvinistic doctrine of predestination discourages or renders unnecessary the use
of means,—the employment of efforts, for the attainment of ends,

---

tertia est imparitas rationis inter
electionem et reprobationem quod
electio est causa non tantum salutis,
sed et omnium eorum quæ causæ
rationem habent ad salutem, reprobatio vero neque damnationis, neque
peccati quod meretur damnationem,
est proprie causa, sed antecedens tantum. Hinc etiam sequitur quarta
disparitas, quod ipsa media non habent
semper inter se rationem causæ et
effectus, permissio enim peccati non
est causa derelictionis, obdurationis,
punitionis, sed ipsum peccatum."
(Medulla Theologica, lib. i., c. xxv.,
De Predestinatione, pp. 109–110.)

Mastricht, one of the best of the great
systematic divines of the seventeenth
century, has very closely followed, or

rather has copied, in his discussion of
this subject, these statements of Ames
(Theoretico-practica Theologia, lib.
iii., c. iv., s. 6, p. 304).

Those who wish to follow out the
investigation of this subject, will find
abundant materials in the following
works, in addition to those which have
already been mentioned:—Turretine,
Theologia Elenctica, loc. iv., qu. xiv.,
sect. 1–17; Pictet, La Theologie
Chretienne, liv., viii., c. vi.; De Moor,
Comment. in Marck, Comp. c. vii.,
sect. 29, tom. ii., p. 96; Gill's Cause
of God and Truth, part iii., c. i., ii.;
Jonathan Edwards' Remarks on important Theological Controversies, c.
iii., sect. 35.

which we may be under an obligation to aim at, or influenced by a desire to effect,—that it tends to discourage or preclude the steady pursuit of holiness, the conscientious discharge of duty, and the diligent improvement of the means of grace. Now this common allegation is possessed of plausibility, only if it be assumed as the doctrine of Calvinists, that God has foreordained the end without having also foreordained the means; and when their true and real doctrine upon the subject is brought out in all its extent and completeness, the plausibility of the objection entirely disappears.

The doctrine of the Westminster Confession upon this point is this,—that by God's decree ordaining from eternity whatsoever cometh to pass, the liberty or contingency of second causes is not taken away but rather established,*—and that " although in relation to the foreknowledge and decree of God, the first cause, all things come to pass immutably and infallibly, yet by the same providence He ordereth them to fall out according to the nature of second causes, either necessarily, freely, or contingently ;"†— that is, necessary things,—things necessary from the nature or constitution which He has conferred on them, or the laws which He has prescribed to them,—He ordereth to fall out, or take place, necessarily, or in accordance with their constitution and laws ; and in like manner, He ordereth free things, as men's actions, to fall out or take place freely, and contingent things contingently, according to their respective natures and proper regulating principles. The Confession also teaches, with more special reference to men's eternal destinies,—" that as God hath appointed the elect unto glory, so hath He, by the eternal and most free purpose of His will, foreordained all the means thereunto.‡ And these means, of course, comprehend their faith, conversion, sanctification, and perseverance, *means indispensably necessary in every instance to the attainment of the end.* Now this doctrine of the foreordination of the means as well as the end,—a foreordination which not only leaves unimpaired to second causes the operation of their own proper nature, constitution, and laws, but preserves and secures them in the possession and exercise of all these,—is not only quite consistent with the Calvinistic scheme of doctrine, but forms a necessary and indispensable part of it. *No doctrine*

---

* C. iii. s. 1.   † C. v. s. 2.   ‡ C. iii. s. 6.

does or can establish so firmly as this the actual invariable connection between the means and the end ; and no doctrine is fitted to preserve in the minds of men so deep a sense of the reality and certainty of this connection. No Calvinist who understands the doctrine he professes to believe, and who takes it in and applies it in all its extent, can be in any danger of neglecting the use of means, which he knows to be fitted, in their own nature or by God's appointment, as means, for the attainment of an end which he desires to have accomplished ; because he must see, that to act in this way is *practically to deny* a part of the truth which he professes to hold,—that is, to deny that God has foreordained the means as well as the end, and has thus established a certain and invariable connection between them. Calvinists are in danger of being tempted to act upon this principle, only when they cherish defective and erroneous views of the doctrines which they profess to believe ; and, in like manner, it is only from the same defective and erroneous views of the true nature and the full import and bearing of the Calvinistic doctrine of predestination, that Arminians are led to charge it with a tendency, to lead men to neglect or disregard the use of appropriate or prescribed means, in order to the attainment of ends.

All this is quite clear and certain, and it is perfectly conclusive as an answer to the objection we are considering. But how do the Arminians deal with this answer to their objection? They commonly just shut their eyes to the answer, or disregard or evade it, and continue to repeat the objection, as if had not been, and could not be, answered. A very remarkable and honourable exception to this common policy of Arminians in dealing with this matter, has occurred in the present day in the case of Archbishop Whately. He has admitted that the word *election*, as used in Scripture, relates, in most instances, " to an arbitrary, irrespective, unconditional decree ;" and he has also admitted that the arguments commonly directed against Calvinism, from its alleged inconsistency with the moral attributes of God, ought to be set aside as invalid ; inasmuch as, in reality and substance, they are directed against facts or results, which undoubtedly occur under God's moral government, and must, therefore, be equally dealt with and disposed of by all parties. He has made a concession equally important to us, and equally honourable to him, upon the point which we are at present considering. He has distinctly ad-

mitted, that the common allegation of the Arminians,—that the
Calvinistic doctrine of predestination overturns the necessity of
means and efforts, and thereby tends to lead to a sinful, or to a
careless and inactive, life,—is unfounded; and is, indeed, disproved
by the application which all intelligent Calvinists make of this
essential part of their general doctrine—viz., that God has foreordained the means as well as the end, and has thereby established
and secured a certain and invariable connection between them.
He has, indeed, coupled this admission with the allegation,—that
by the very same process of argument and exposition by which,
as he concedes, Calvinism can be vindicated from the charge of
having an immoral or injurious tendency, by discouraging the
conscientious discharge of duty and the diligent improvement of
means,—it can be shown, that it admits of no practical application
whatever, but is a mere barren, useless speculation.   This allegation we propose now to consider,—and we hope to be able to show
that it is founded upon misconception and fallacy.   But before
doing so, it may be proper to give a specimen or two of the way
in which the topic we have been considering, is dealt with by
Arminians who have less sagacity and candour than Dr Whately.
We shall take our specimens from men who have sounder and
more evangelical views of some of the fundamental principles of
Christian theology than he has, and from whom, therefore, better
things might have been expected ;—John Wesley, the founder of
the Methodists, and Richard Watson, perhaps the ablest and most
accomplished theologian that important and useful body has yet
produced.

Wesley, certainly, was not a great theologian, and, in that
character, is not entitled to much deference. His treatise on
"Original Sin," in reply to Dr John Taylor, is, perhaps, his best
theological work,—and it is a respectable specimen of doctrinal exposition and discussion. Most of his other theological productions
are characterised by inadequate information, and by hasty, superficial thinking; and these qualities were most conspicuously manifested when he was dealing with the doctrines of Calvinism. His
leading objections to Calvinism he was accustomed to put, compendiously and popularly, in this form—" The sum of all this is
this : One in twenty, suppose of mankind, are elected; nineteen
in twenty are reprobated. The elect shall be saved, do what they
will; the reprobate shall be damned, do what they can."

The first part of this statement about the comparative number of the elect and the reprobate, the saved and the lost, though not very closely related to the subject at present under consideration, may be adverted to in passing, as suggesting a topic which Arminians often adduce in order to excite a prejudice against Calvinism, though it is really altogether irrelevant. A dogmatic assertion as to the comparative numbers of those of the human race who are saved, and of those who perish in the ultimate result of things, certainly forms no part of Calvinism. There is nothing to prevent Calvinists, as such, from believing that, as the result of Christ's mediation, a great majority of the descendants of Adam shall be saved; nothing that should require them to deny salvation to any to whom Arminians could consistently concede it. The actual result of salvation in the case of a portion of the human race, and of destruction in the case of the rest, is the same in both systems, though they differ in the exposition of the principles according to which the result is regulated and brought about. In surveying the past history of the world, or in looking around on those who now occupy the earth, with the view of forming a sort of estimate of the fate that has overtaken, or that yet awaits, the generations of their fellow-men, Calvinists introduce no other principle, and apply no other standard, than just the will of God plainly revealed in His word *as to what those things are which accompany salvation;* and consequently, if in doing so, they should form a different estimate as to the comparative result from what Arminians would admit, this could not arise from anything peculiar to them as holding Calvinistic doctrines, but only from their having formed and applied a higher standard of the personal character, that is, of the holiness and morality, which are necessary to prepare men for admission to heaven, than the Arminians are willing to countenance. And yet it is very common to represent Calvinistic doctrines as leading, or tending to lead, those who hold them, to consign to everlasting misery a large portion of the human race whom the Arminians would admit to the enjoyment of heaven.

Neither is there anything in Calvinism necessarily requiring or implying a more unfavourable view than Arminianism exhibits, of the ultimate destiny of those of the human race who die in infancy, without having given any palpable manifestation of moral character. Calvinists believe that no one of the descendants of

Adam is saved, unless he has been chosen of God in Christ before the foundation of the world, redeemed with Christ's precious blood, and regenerated by the almighty agency of the Holy Spirit. And while all Calvinists hold that many infants, baptized and unbaptized, are saved in this way, there is nothing in their Calvinism to prevent them from believing, that all who die in infancy may have been elected, and may be saved through Christ. They are not, indeed, so bold and dogmatic as their opponents, in pronouncing what is or what is not consistent with the divine character in this matter. They are more fully alive to the fair influence of the consideration, that this subject is, from its very nature, an inscrutable mystery, and that very little light is thrown upon it by any information given us in Scripture. Upon these grounds, Calvinists have thought it right to abstain from dogmatic deliverances upon this subject ; but many of them have been of opinion that there are indications in Scripture, though not very clear or explicit, which favour the idea, that all dying in infancy are elected and saved, and there is nothing in their Calvinism to prevent them from believing this.*

But this topic is only incidental to the statement of Wesley, which we proposed to consider. The main point of it is, that he asserts that the Calvinistic doctrine of predestination necessarily implies " that the elect shall be saved, do what they will, and the reprobate shall be damned, do what they can." Toplady published an excellent exposure of this offensive misrepresentation, based, of course, upon the principle which we have been explaining, that the means have been ordained, as well as the end. Wesley attempted to defend himself, in a small tract, called " The Conse-

---

* Wesley is very fond of harping upon this string, but he occasionally introduces some variations, by altering his numbers. This was pointed out by Toplady in his answer to " The Consequence Proved." " Observe, reader, how suddenly Mr Wesley's polemical weather-glass rises and falls. In his printed letter to the late truly reverend and amiable Mr Hervey, he charged that incomparable man and the Calvinistic party in general, with holding the reprobation of ' nine out of ten.' In March 1770, we were charged with holding as above, that ' nineteen in twenty are reprobated.' In February 1771, we were charged with holding the reprobation of 'forty-nine out of fifty.' And about five months after, the glass is sunk 30 degrees lower, and in ' The Consequence Proved' stands again at ' nineteen out of twenty.' Next spring I suppose it will rise to ninety-nine out of a hundred."—(Toplady's " More Work for Mr Wesley." Works, edition 1825, vol. v. p. 364.

quence Proved," contained in his collected works.* In this tract, he undertakes to show, that the sentence we quoted from him in introducing this topic, " is a fair state of the case, this consequence does naturally and necessarily follow from the doctrine of absolute predestination." His defence of himself just consists of a proof, which of course was very easy, that the Calvinistic doctrine implies, that the end in both cases was foreordained, and, therefore, infallibly certain,—of an *assertion*, that from this principle " the whole consequence follows clear as the noonday sun,"†—and of an attempt to excite odium against the doctrine of reprobation, by alleging that it necessarily produced or implied a putting forth of God's agency in the actual production of depravity and unbelief in those who perish. He does not venture to look even at the principle, that the means are foreordained as well as the end, or attempt to show the inconclusiveness of this principle as an answer to his allegation. He simply repeats his allegation with increased audacity, and asserts that the " consequence follows clear as the noonday sun." It is true that, in regard to the elect, the end is in each case foreordained, and of course their salvation is infallibly secured. But it is also true, that this is only a part of our doctrine,—that we hold also that the means are foreordained and secured as well as the end,—and that these means, as God has plainly declared, and as all men, Calvinists as well as others, admit and believe, are faith in Christ, repentance unto life, holiness, and perseverance. God has just as fully and certainly provided for securing these means, as for securing the ultimate end of salvation, in regard to every one of the elect; and has made provision for all this in a way fully accordant with the nature of the subject, viz., man as he is, with all his capacities and incapacities as they are. To suppose that any elect person should, in fact, continue till the end of his life in a state of ungodliness and unbelief, is to suppose an impossibility. Our opponents have no right to make this supposition, because our doctrine, when fully apprehended and fairly applied, not only does not admit of it, but positively and infallibly precludes it,—that is, *demonstrates and establishes its impossibility*. It is true, that all who are elected to eternal life shall certainly be saved. But it is also true, *and it is equally a part of our doctrine*, that all who are elected to eternal

---

life shall certainly repent and believe, and shall certainly enter on, and persevere, in a course of new obedience. We can thus hold, and in entire consistency with all our peculiar principles, that no man shall be saved unless he repent and believe, and unless he persevere to the end in faith and holiness. And in this way it is manifest that,—notwithstanding the truth of the doctrine, that all the elect shall infallibly be saved, and in perfect consistency with it,—all the obligations incumbent upon men to believe and to persevere in faith and holiness,—of whatever kind these obligations may be, and from whatever source they may arise,—and the consequent obligations to use all the means which, according to God's revealed arrangements, may contribute to the production of these intermediate results, continue, to say the least, wholly unimpaired.

The same principles apply, *mutatis mutandis*, to the case of the reprobate, though here, as we have explained, the subject is involved in deeper and more inscrutable mystery, and the information given us in Scripture is much less full and explicit; considerations which have generally led Calvinists to treat of it with brevity, caution, and reverence, while they have too often tempted Arminians to enlarge upon it presumptuously and offensively. We have already explained that Calvinists repudiate the representation which Wesley here gives of their doctrine of reprobation, as implying, that God's agency is the proper cause or source of the depravity and unbelief, on account of which the reprobate are finally consigned to misery.* They deny that they hold this, and that anything they do hold can be proved necessarily to involve this consequence. Calvinists believe that men, in their natural state of guilt and depravity, are not able, by their own strength, to repent and believe; and that God bestows only on the elect, and not on the reprobate, that special supernatural grace which is necessary, in every instance, to the production of faith, holiness, and perseverance. They admit that they cannot

---

* Ames has put, with admirable brevity and terseness, the substance of the views of Calvinists upon this subject, with a rejection of the leading Arminian misrepresentations, in this way :—De reprobatione nos non sumus admodum solliciti nisi quatenus consequitur ex electione. Positiva au- tem reprobatio ad exitium sine consideratione ullius inobedientiae non sequitur ex electionis doctrina. Neque de numero reproborum aliud inde sequitur, quam omnes illos qui tandem incurrunt damnationem aeternam, fuisse ab aeterno reprobatos. (Amesii Anti Synodalia Scripta, p. 37.)

give a full and adequate explanation of the consistency of these doctrines, with men's undoubted and admitted responsibility for their character and destiny. The doctrines of men's inability in their natural condition to repent and believe, and of the non-bestowal upon all men of the supernatural grace which is necessary to enable them to do so, are just statements of matters of fact as to what man is, and as to what God does, and can be fully proved to be true and real both from Scripture and observation ; and it is not a sufficient reason for rejecting these doctrines or facts, which can be satisfactorily established by their appropriate evidence, that we cannot fully explain how they are to be reconciled with the doctrine or fact of man's responsibility. All that is logically incumbent upon us in these circumstances is just to prove, that the alleged inconsistency cannot be clearly and conclusively established ; and this Calvinists undertake to do. And this being assumed, all that is further necessary in order to answer the Arminian objection,—as directed even against this most profound and mysterious department of the subject,—is to show, as can be easily done upon the principles already explained, that while men are responsible for not repenting and believing, there is nothing in our Calvinistic principles which precludes us from maintaining, that every man who repents and believes shall certainly be saved.

So far then from Wesley's assertion, that the Calvinistic doctrine of predestination necessarily implies, that " the elect shall be saved, do what they will, and the reprobate shall be damned, do what they can," giving " a fair state of the case," it is evident that we can maintain, in full consistency with all our peculiar principles, that no man shall be saved unless he repent, and believe, and persevere to the end in faith and holiness ; and that every man who does so shall certainly be admitted to the enjoyment of eternal life.

The other instance we have to adduce, of an evasion of the fair application of the doctrine, that the means are foreordained as well as the end, is connected, not with predestination, as bearing upon the eternal destinies of man, but with the wider subject of the foreordination of all events,—of " whatsoever cometh to pass ;" —and it is taken from Richard Watson, the great theologian of the Wesleyan Methodists. It occurs in a review, contained in the seventh volume of the collected edition of his works, of a volume of sermons by Dr Chalmers, published originally under the title

" Sermons preached in St John's Church, Glasgow." This volume
of sermons contains a masterly discourse upon Acts xxvii. 31,
" Paul said to the centurion and the soldiers, Except these abide
in the ship, ye cannot be saved;" and Mr Watson's review is
chiefly occupied with an attempt to answer it. Dr Chalmers'
discourse is virtually an exposition and defence of the Calvinistic
doctrine, that God hath unchangeably foreordained whatsoever
comes to pass. It is based upon the assumption, that the ultimate
result in this matter, viz., the preservation of the whole ship's
company, had been absolutely predicted and promised by God to
the apostle, and, of course, was infallibly and infrustrably certain ;
and it is mainly occupied with an exposition of the grounds which
bring out the consistency of the absolute certainty of the result
with the conditionality, contingency, or uncertainty which may
seem to be implied in the apostle's statement, that this result could
not be effected, unless another event, dependent apparently upon
the free agency of responsible beings, viz., the continuance of the
crew in the ship, had previously taken place. The apparent inconsistency of the absoluteness and unconditionality of the final
result,—decreed, predicted, promised,—with the seeming contingency or uncertainty of the intermediate step,—the continuance
of the crew in the ship,—is explained, of course, by the application of the principle, that God had foreordained the means as well
as the end; had foreordained, and made provision for certainly
effecting or bringing about, the continuance of the crew in the
ship, as well as the ultimate preservation of all who were on board.
There was then no strict and proper conditionality,—no real and
ultimate contingency or uncertainty,—attaching to this intermediate event. It was, equally with the ultimate result, comprehended
in God's plan or purpose ; and equally certain provision, adapted
to the nature of the case and the position and relations of all the
parties concerned, had been made for securing that it should come
to pass. The hypothetical or conditional statement of the apostle
does not necessarily imply more than this, that an indissoluble
connection had been established, and did really subsist, between
the two events, the one as a means and the other as an end. If
this connection really subsisted in God's purpose and plan, then
the apostle's hypothetical statement was true ; while it did not
imply or assume real or actual uncertainty as attaching to either
event, and was indeed fitted and intended, in accordance with the

natural and appropriate operation of second causes, to contribute to bring about the result which God had resolved should come to pass. The whole history then of this matter,—and all the different statements put on record regarding it,—are fully explained by the doctrine, that the means are foreordained as well as the end; while in their turn they confirm and illustrate that doctrine, and confirm and illustrate also the principle formerly explained, which may be regarded as an expansion and application of that doctrine,—viz., that " although in relation to the foreknowledge and decree of God, the first cause, all things come to pass immutably and infallibly, yet by the same providence He ordereth them to fall out according to the nature of second causes, either necessarily, freely, or contingently."

The apostle's hypothetical or conditional statement here, is to be explained and defended in the very same way as such statements as these,—" Except ye repent, ye shall perish ;" " Whosoever believeth shall be saved." These statements are virtually hypothetical or conditional in their form,—they assert an invariable connection between the means and the end,—and the existence of this connection is sufficient to show that they are true and warrantable. The statements, being thus true and warrantable in themselves, are fitted to lead men who desire the end, to adopt the means without which it cannot be attained; while they are not in the least inconsistent with the doctrine,—resting upon its own proper scriptural grounds,—that God alone can produce faith and repentance, and that He certainly and infallibly bestows them on all whom He hath chosen to salvation.

This is the substance of the common Calvinistic argument; and it is brought out by Dr Chalmers in this sermon in a very powerful and impressive way. How is it met by Mr Watson? He first of all tries to throw doubt upon the import and bearing of God's declaration to the apostle, of His purpose or resolution to save the lives of all who were in the ship. He says,* " The declaration was not that of a purpose, in the sense of a decree, at all, but of a promise." But this is really nothing better than a quibble. God had said to the apostle, " There shall be no loss of any man's life among you, but of the ship." This was both a purpose and a promise ; it was the one just as much as the other,

---

* Vol. vii. p. 246.

and it might also be regarded as a prediction ; for a prediction is just a revelation of a purpose which God has formed in regard to a thing yet future. The words plainly import a declaration of an absolute and unconditional purpose of God,—an explicit prediction and promise of a definite event as certainly future, as infallibly and inevitably to take place. And this is so clear and certain, that it must be taken as a fixed principle in the interpretation of the whole narrative. Nothing must be admitted which contradicts this ; and everything must, if possible, be so explained as to accord with it. Mr Watson ventures to say, that the history shows, that the apostle did not understand this as an absolute purpose on God's part ; for, "if he had, there was no motive to induce him to oppose the going away of the mariners in the boat." This is a melancholy specimen of what able and upright men are some-times tempted to do by the exigencies of controversy. That the apostle believed, upon God's authority, that it was His absolute, irrevocable, and infrustrable purpose, that there was to be no loss of life, is made as clear and certain as words can make anything. He had also been told, upon the same infallible authority, that it was a part of God's plan that the crew were to continue in the ship ; not as if this were a condition on which the ultimate result was really and properly suspended, but as an intermediate step, through means of which that result was to be brought about. He knew that this mean had been foreordained as well as that end ; and that thus a necessary connection had been established *de facto* between them. This is all that is *necessarily* implied in his hypo-thetical statement, " Except these abide in the ship, ye cannot be saved ;" and he was guided to put the matter in this form, because this was the provision best fitted in itself, and was also fore-ordained in God's purpose, for bringing about this intermediate event as a mean, and thereby effecting the end. Mr Watson holds that the continuance of the crew in the ship was a condition on which the result of the preservation of the lives of all was, strictly and properly speaking, suspended ; and infers from this, that there was no absolute purpose to save them. That there was an absolute purpose to save them, is,—to say the least,—much more clear and certain, than that there was any condition, strictly and properly so called, upon which the accomplishment of the result was suspended. And, independently of this, his argument is a mere quibble on the meaning of the word *condition*. He just

asserts, over and over again, that an absolute purpose is an unconditional purpose ; assumes that a condition is something on which
the result purposed or contemplated, is really suspended ; and then
infers, that, wherever there is a condition attached, there can be
no absolute purpose.   This is his whole argument ; and it is really
nothing better than a quibble, combined with a resolute determination, to refuse to look at the explanations and arguments which
Calvinists have brought forward in expounding and defending
their views upon this subject.

Calvinists admit that the terms " absolute" and " conditional,"
as applied to the divine decrees, are contradictory, or exclusive
the one of the other ; and that absolute and unconditional, in this
application of them, are synonymous.   But they deny, that there
are any divine decrees or purposes, or any predictions or promises,
which can, in strict propriety of speech, be called conditional ;
while they admit that there are senses in which the word " condition" may be loosely and improperly applied to them.   There are
few words, indeed, which admit of, and have been employed in,
a greater variety of senses and applications, than the word " condition."   So much is this the case, that Dr Owen, in treating of
the subject of the alleged conditions of justification, lays it down,
as a sort of canon or axiom, " We cannot obtain a determinate
sense of this word *condition*, but from a particular declaration of
what is intended by it wherever it is used."*   Accordingly, the
exposition of the ambiguity of this word " condition," with an
exact specification of the different senses in which it may be and
has been employed,—in relation to the divine purposes, predictions,
and promises,—forms one of the best known and most important
commonplaces in this controversy, and has been fully and largely
handled by all the leading Calvinistic divines.   But all this Mr
Watson resolutely ignores.   He just assumes that a condition is
a condition, as if it had only one meaning or signification ; and as
the apostle's statement plainly implies, that, in some sense or other,
the continuance of the crew in the ship might be called a condi
tion of the result of saving the lives of all ; and as Calvinists admit
this, he infers, that, as an absolute and a conditional purpose are
contradictories, God could not have formed and declared an absolute purpose in the matter ; and that, of course, notwithstanding

---

* " On Justification," c. iii. p. 156.   Original Edition.

anything which He had either foreordained or foreseen, the crew might have succeeded in their purpose of leaving the ship, and thus have frustrated the purpose, and prevented the result, which the apostle, speaking in God's name, had absolutely and unconditionally predicted. Calvinists do not deny that there is a loose and improper sense, in which the continuance of the crew in the ship might be called a condition of the saving of the lives of all on board; inasmuch as it was God's purpose or plan, that the one event should precede, and be a mean of bringing about, the other, —an indissoluble connection being thus established and secured between them. But they deny that the one was a condition of the other, in the strict and proper sense of that word. To represent it as a condition, strictly and properly so called, implies not merely that the ultimate result was suspended upon it,—for this, in a sense, might be said to be true, in virtue of the connection *de facto* established between them as means and end,—but also, that God could not make, or at least had not made, any certain and effectual provision for bringing it about; so that the first event, and, of course, the second also, was left in a position of absolute contingency or uncertainty, dependent for its coming into existence upon causes or influences over which God could not, or at least, did not, exert any effectual control. It is only when the word "condition" is taken in this, its strict and proper sense, that an absolute and a conditional purpose are contradictories; and, in this sense, Calvinists deny that a conditional purpose was ever formed in the divine mind, or was ever embodied in a divine prediction or promise. There are no conditions, properly so called, attaching to the divine purposes, predictions, and promises. God has, absolutely and unconditionally, foreordained certain ends or ultimate results; and He has, with equal absoluteness and unconditionality, foreordained the means,—that is, the intermediate steps or stages by which they are to be brought about. And the conditional or hypothetical form in which predictions and promises are often put in Scripture, simply implies the existence of a *de facto* connection, or inter-dependence of events, as means and end; and is intended to operate upon men's minds in the way of bringing about the accomplishment of ends, by leading to the use and improvement of the natural, ordinary, and appropriate means.

Mr Watson refers to the great principle, by which we answer

the Arminian objection about the practical application of the Calvinistic doctrine of predestination,—viz., that God has foreordained
the means as well as the end; but he does so merely for the purpose of throwing it aside as irrelevant and fallacious. He does
not venture to look it fairly in the face, or to realise its true import and bearing. He does not even attempt to point out either
its fallacy or its irrelevancy. He disposes of it just by repeating
his favourite axiom,—which is really the sum and substance of all
that he has been able to produce upon this important department
of the argument—" It follows, if the predestination be absolute,
that there are no conditions at all,"*—a position which we can
admit to be true as it stands, but the ambiguity and futility of
which, in its bearing upon this branch of the controversy, we think
we have sufficiently established.

The discussions in which we have been engaged, may serve to
illustrate the unfairness often practised by Arminians in basing
their objections upon defective and erroneous notions of the real
doctrines of Calvinism; and may be useful, also, in reminding
Calvinists of the importance, with a view at once to the defence
of truth against opponents, and the personal application of it in
their own case, of seeking to form full and comprehensive views
of the whole system of Christian doctrine, and of its different
parts in all their bearings and relations.

The misrepresentations and evasions which we have pointed
out in Wesley and Watson, are fair specimens of what is to be
found in the generality of Arminian writers, in treating of this
subject; and it is surely not wonderful that the penetration and
sagacity of Archbishop Whately,—though himself an Arminian,
—should have enabled him to perceive, and that his candour and
courage should have led him to proclaim, the folly and futility of
all this. He has, as we have explained, distinctly and fully admitted, that the doctrine that God has foreordained the means as
well as the end, and has thereby established a certain and indissoluble connection between them, as expounded and applied by
Calvinistic divines, furnishes a conclusive answer to the common
allegation, that Calvinism is injurious, in its moral bearing and
tendency, by leading men to neglect the discharge of duties and
the use and improvement of means. The Calvinistic argument,

---

* P 249.

indeed, upon this point, is so clear and conclusive, that the wonder is not, that Whately should have admitted it to be satisfactory,
but that Wesley, Watson, and Arminians in general, should have
denied it.   The admission, however, is not the less honourable to
Whately's sagacity and candour ; because, so far as we remember,
he was the first Arminian who fully and openly made this important concession.   If we could have believed that Whately's example, on this point, would have been followed by Arminians,—and
that they would have admitted, as he has done, that the common
allegation about the injurious moral bearing of Calvinism is
answered or neutralised by a fair application of the whole of what
Calvinists teach upon this subject, we would scarcely have taken
the trouble to expose the statements of Wesley and Watson.   But
the whole history of theological controversy prevents us from
cherishing this expectation ; and constrains us to fear, that the
generality of Arminian writers will continue to reiterate the old
objection, and to disregard, or evade the conclusive answer which
has been so often given to it.

Whately, as we have stated, while admitting that Calvinism
can be successfully vindicated from the charge of having an injurious moral tendency, maintains that, by the same process by
which this allegation is refuted, it can be proved that our doctrine
has no practical bearing or effect whatever, but is a perfectly useless, barren speculation.   His views upon this point are brought
out in this way : "It may be admitted that one who does practically adopt and conform to this explanation of the doctrine, will
not be led into any evil by it ; since his conduct will not be, in
any respect, influenced by it.   When thus explained, it is reduced
to a purely speculative dogma, barren of all practical results."
"It is not contended that the doctrines in question have a hurtful
influence on human conduct, and consequently are untrue ; but
that they have, according to the soundest exposition of them, no
influence on our conduct whatever ; and, consequently (revelation
not being designed to impart mere speculative knowledge), that
they are not to be taught as revealed truths."   "The doctrine is,
if rightly viewed, of a purely speculative character, not ' belonging to us' practically, and which ought not, at least, in any way
to influence our conduct."   "Taking the system, then, as expounded by its soundest advocates, it is impossible to show any
one point in which a person is called upon, either to act or to feel,

in any respect, differently in consequence of his adopting it."
" The preacher, in short, is to act, in all respects, as if the system
were not true."* The general principle here laid down, of judging, whether a doctrine be revealed or not, by an application of
the test, whether it be merely speculative, or have a practical
bearing upon conduct, is a very unsound and dangerous one.
Even though we were to concede the truth of his abstract position, that " revelation is not designed to impart mere speculative
knowledge,"—a position which is obscure and ambiguous, and the
truth of which, consequently, is, at least, very doubtful,—we
would still dispute the soundness and validity of the application
he makes of it as a test. If we have a revelation from God,
surely the right and reasonable course is, that we should do our
utmost to ascertain correctly the whole of what it teaches upon
every subject which it brings before us ; assured that, whatever it
reveals, it is incumbent upon us to believe and proclaim, and, in
some way or other, useful or beneficial for us to know. And, if
there be fair ground for believing that, in some sense or other,
" revelation is not designed to impart to us mere speculative knowledge," then we should draw from this the inference, that the doctrine which we have ascertained to be revealed, is not merely
speculative, but has,—more or less directly, and more or less obviously,—some practical bearing or tendency. The soundness of this
general inference is not in the least invalidated, by the difficulty
we may feel, in particular instances, in pointing out any very
direct or obvious practical application of which a doctrine admits.
Revelation was undoubtedly intended to convey to us what may
be called speculative or theoretical knowledge ; and though it
may be admitted, that the general and ultimate bearing and tendency of the whole system of revealed doctrine is to tell practically upon character and conduct, it does not follow that every
particular doctrine must have a direct, and still less an obvious,
practical application. Some doctrines may have been revealed
to us chiefly, or even solely, for the purpose of completing the
general system of doctrine which God intended to teach us,
and of aiding us in forming more clear and enlarged conceptions
of other doctrines of more fundamental importance ; without
having, by themselves, any direct and immediate practical bear-

---

* Essays, Second Series. Essay III., on Election, s. v. pp. 85-91, 7th Ed.

ing. Such doctrines might, with some plausibility, be ranked under the head of what Whately calls "mere speculative knowledge;" and yet, there is plainly no ground for regarding this as a proof, or even a presumption, that they have not been revealed, —if there be adequate ground, on a careful examination of the statements of Scripture, for believing that they are taught or indicated there. To set up our notions or impressions upon the question,—whether a particular doctrine, alleged to be revealed in Scripture, is purely speculative or has a practical influence upon conduct,—as furnishing anything like a test of the sufficiency of its scriptural evidence, is nothing better than presumptuous rationalism ; and is fitted to undermine the supreme authority, and the right application, of Scripture as the infallible standard of truth. Dr Whately, to do him justice, has exhibited a good deal of obscurity and confusion in treating of this point. He says,*—" I have waived the question as to the truth or falsity of the Calvinistic doctrine of election, inquiring only whether it be revealed ;" and then he goes on to assert, that " one of the reasons for deciding that question in the negative," is, that " the doctrine is, if rightly viewed, of a purely speculative character;" and, again,† "I purposely abstain, throughout, from entering on the question as to what is absolutely true, inquiring only what is, or is not, to be received and taught as a portion of revealed gospel truth." Now we may surely assume that, whatever is really taught in Scripture, is to be received as "revealed gospel truth;" and, if so, then this forced and arbitrary distinction between the absolute truth of the Calvinistic doctrine, and its claim as a revealed truth, entirely disappears. The whole question resolves into this, What saith the Scripture ? and this question must be determined upon its own proper grounds. If the Scripture sanctions the Calvinistic doctrine of election, then this establishes both its absolute truth, and its position and claims as a revealed truth. If the Scripture does not sanction it, then it is not to be received, either as true or as revealed ; for Calvinists, while maintaining that the fundamental principles of their system derive support and confirmation from the doctrines of natural theology, have never imagined that their doctrine of election, with all that it necessarily implies, could be conclusively proved to be true, except from the

---

* P. 85.   † P. 96.

testimony of Revelation. It would almost seem (for this is really the only supposition which can give anything like clearness or consistency to his statement), that he had a sort of vague notion,—a kind of lurking suspicion,—that the Calvinistic doctrine of election, though not revealed in Scripture, might or could be established by evidence derived from some other source,—might be true though not revealed. But this is a position which probably he will not venture openly to assume; and, therefore, we must continue to adhere to the conviction, that his statements upon this subject are characterised by obscurity and confusion.

We have thought it proper to animadvert upon the fallacious and dangerous notions which seem to be involved in Dr Whately's general views, upon the subject of applying the practical influence of doctrines as a test, not of whether they are true, but of whether they are revealed. But we have no hesitation in denying his more specific position, that the Calvinistic doctrine of election, when so expounded as to stand clear of any injurious tendency, has no practical bearing or effect, but is a mere useless, barren speculation. All that has been, or can be, proved upon this point is simply this, —that the practical application of the Calvinistic doctrine does not extend over so wide a sphere, and does not bear so directly upon certain topics, as has sometimes been alleged both by its supporters and its opponents.

The alleged practical tendencies and effects of Calvinism have always entered very largely into the discussion of this whole controversy. Objections to the truth of Calvinism, on the ground of its practical moral tendency, very obviously suggest themselves to men's minds, and carry with them a considerable measure of plausibility; and men professing to believe Calvinistic doctrines have occasionally spoken and acted in such a way as to afford some countenance to these objections of opponents. Considering the obviousness and the plausibility of these objections, and the prominent place they have usually occupied in the writings of Arminians, it is of great importance that we have it now conceded by so able an opponent as Whately, that they are utterly baseless. In discussing this subject of the practical tendency of their system, Calvinists have acted chiefly upon the defensive. They have usually contented themselves, in a great measure, with repelling these objections, and proving that they are destitute of all solid foundation; and having accomplished this, they have then fallen back again upon the direct and positive scriptural proof of their doctrine, as establishing at once its truth, its importance, and its practical usefulness. The two principal rules by which we ought to be guided in discussing this branch of the subject,—both with a view to the defence of our doctrine against opponents, and also to the discharge of the duty of making ourselves a right and profitable application of it,—are these ;—1st, That the whole of the doctrine, and all that it necessarily involves, be fairly and fully taken into account, and a due application made of every part of it ; and especially that it never be forgotten, that God's decrees and purposes, in reference to the eternal destinies of men, comprehend or include the means as well as the end, and thus provide for and secure an invariable connection in fact between the means and the end,—a connection which is not, and cannot be, in any instance dissolved ; and 2d, That we fully and freely admit and apply, at the same time, all *other* doctrines and principles which are established by satisfactory scriptural evidence, even though we may not be able fully to explain how they can be shown to be consistent with the peculiar doctrines of our system. A careful attention to these two rules will enable us easily and conclusively to repel the objections of our opponents ; and at the same time will effectually preserve us from falling into any serious error, in our own personal practical application of the doctrines we profess to believe.

This is quite sufficient for all merely controversial purposes. But it is due to Dr Whately,—who has shown so much candour and fairness in admitting the insufficiency of several arguments generally employed by the Arminians,—to advert somewhat more particularly to his allegation, that the Calvinistic doctrine of election, though admitted to be, when rightly and fully explained, harmless and unobjectionable, is shown by the same process to be a mere barren useless speculation, having no practical influence whatever ;—or, as he puts it, that " it is impossible to show any one point, in which a person is called upon either to act or to feel in any respect differently, in consequence of his adopting it." Calvinists do not profess to found much upon the practical application which may be made of their doctrine of election, as affording a positive argument in support of it. They are usually satisfied with proving from Scripture that it is true,—that it is revealed there as an object of faith,—and that, with respect to its practical application, it can be shown to be liable to no serious or solid objection. They admit, that it is not fitted or intended to exert so comprehensive and so direct an influence upon character and conduct, as the great fundamental doctrines revealed in Scripture, concerning the guilt and depravity of men in their natural state, the person and work of the Redeemer, and the agency of the Holy Spirit; and therefore should not hold so prominent a place as these in the ordinary course of public instruction. But they deny that it is a barren, useless speculation. They maintain that it has an appropriate practical influence, in its own proper place and sphere; and that this influence, in its own department, and whenever it comes legitimately into operation, is most wholesome and beneficial. There are, as all intelligent Calvinists admit, important departments of the duties imposed upon us by Scripture,—important steps which men must take in order to the salvation of their souls,—on which the Calvinistic doctrine of election has no direct practical bearing. It is upon a perversion or exaggeration of this fact, admitted by us, that the whole plausibility of Whately's allegation rests; and it will be a sufficient answer to the substance of his statements upon this subject, and may at the same time serve other useful purposes, if,—while indicating how far and in what sense his allegation is true,—we briefly point out some legitimate practical applications of this doctrine, which are peculiar to it, and which cannot be derived from any other source. In doing so, we shall restrict our attention, as Whately does, to the subject of predestination in its bearing upon the eternal destinies of men, without including the more comprehensive subject of the foreordination of whatsoever comes to pass; and shall of course now assume that the Calvinistic doctrine is true, and is held intelligently by those who profess to believe it. We hope to be able to show that Whately's error upon this point is traceable principally to this, that he has not here made the same full and candid estimate,—as in some other branches of the argument,—of the whole of what Calvinists usually adduce in explaining the practical application of their doctrine; and confines his observation to some of the features of the subject, and these not the most important and peculiar.

The Calvinistic doctrine of predestination casts important light upon the character and moral government of God, a knowledge of which may be said to be the foundation of all religion.

God makes Himself known to us by all that He does, and by all
that He permits to take place; and if it be true, that He has from
eternity formed certain decrees and purposes with regard to the
everlasting destinies of men, and is executing these decrees or purposes in time, and if He has made known to us that He has done
and is doing so,—this must, from the nature of the case, afford
important materials for knowing Him, and for understanding the
principles that regulate His dealings with His creatures.   Whatever He does or has purposed to do, must be in entire accordance
with all the attributes and perfections of His nature, and is thus
fitted to afford us materials for forming right apprehensions of
their true bearing and results.   We must form no conceptions of
the supposed holiness, justice, or goodness of God, or of the way
and manner in which these attributes would lead Him to act, inconsistent with what He has done or purposed to do.   On the
contrary, we must employ all that we know concerning His procedure, to regulate our views of His attributes and character.   It
is very common for men, especially those who reject the doctrines
of Calvinism, to frame to themselves certain conceptions of the
divine attributes, and then to deduce from them certain notions
as to what God must do or cannot do.   But this mode of reasoning is unphilosophical and dangerous,—unsuited to our powers and
capacities,—which manifestly require of us, that we should adopt
an opposite course of procedure, and form our conceptions of the
divine attributes from what we know of the divine purposes and
actions ; and at least admit nothing into our conceptions of God's
character, inconsistent with what we know that He has done
or has purposed.   The doctrine of predestination is to be regarded as serving a purpose, in this respect, analogous to that of
the fall of the angels,—an event which has occurred under God's
moral government, and is fitted to throw important light upon His
character.   The fact revealed to us, that some angels fell from
their first estate, and that all who fell were left to perish ir-
remediably, without any provision having been made for restoring
them, or any opportunity of repentance having been allowed to
them, refutes some of the conceptions which men are apt to form
in regard to the divine character; and it should be remembered
and applied, in the way of leading us to form juster conceptions
upon this subject than generally obtain among us.   The fact that
from the race of man,—all of them equally fallen and involved in

guilt and depravity,—God of His good pleasure has predestinated some men to everlasting life, and passed by the rest and left them to perish in their sins, suggests nothing concerning the divine character inconsistent with what is indicated by the history of the fallen angels; but, while, in so far as concerns those men who perish, it confirms all the views of God which the history of the fallen angels suggests, and which we are usually most unwilling to receive, it supplies, in the purpose to save some men with an everlasting salvation, a new and most impressive manifestation of the divine character and moral government, which could not, so far as we can see, have been furnished in any other way. It is important then that we should realise what the Calvinistic doctrine of predestination, *as a general truth revealed in Scripture*, represents God as having purposed from eternity, both in regard to those who are saved and those who perish; and that we should apply this, as a great reality, in forming our conceptions of God's character and moral government, that thus we may know Him as fully as He has made Himself known to us; and may be enabled to glorify Him, by cherishing and expressing emotions, corresponding in every respect to all the perfections which He possesses, and to all the principles which actually regulate His dealings with His creatures.

Dr Whately might probably call this " mere speculative knowledge." But this would be an abuse of language; for it is certain that all the knowledge which God has been pleased to communicate to us concerning Himself, concerning the perfections of His nature and the principles of His moral government, is both fitted and intended to exert a practical influence upon the feelings and conduct of men.

But, while it is thus plain that the Calvinistic doctrine of predestination,—contemplated simply as a truth about God revealed in Scripture,—is fitted to exert a general practical influence upon men's views and feelings; we have further to inquire, whether there be any direct personal application which men can legitimately make of it, in its bearing upon themselves singly and individually. And upon this question, the substance of what we believe to be true is this,—1st, That men cannot legitimately make any direct personal application of this doctrine to themselves individually unless and until they have good reason to believe that they themselves individually have been elected to eternal life,—that is, of course (for there is no other way of ascertaining this), good reason to believe that they have been enabled to receive and submit to Christ as their Saviour, and have been born again of His word and Spirit; and, 2d, that when men have come to believe, upon good grounds, that they have been elected, the personal practical application of the doctrine is most obvious and most wholesome.

Men cannot make any direct personal application of the doctrine of predestination to themselves individually, so long as they continue in their natural state of guilt and estrangement from God, and while they have not yet embraced the offers and invitations of the gospel and entered the service of Christ; and therefore, with reference to all the duties and obligations attaching to this condition of things, the doctrine is not to be taken into account, or to exert any direct practical influence. We admit, nay, we contend, that this doctrine has no immediate practical bearing upon the process of setting before sinners, and urging upon them, the commands and invitations addressed to them in connection with the scheme of salvation, or on the right regulation of their conduct in dealing with these commands and invitations. This arises manifestly from the very nature of the case. Preachers of the gospel are not only warranted, but bound, to address the offers and invitations of God's word to men indiscriminately, without distinction and exception; and having God's sanction and command for this, they should do it without hesitation and without restriction. God does this, in order that He may thereby execute the purpose which He formed from eternity concerning the everlasting destinies of men; and that He may do so in accordance with the principles of man's moral constitution, and with all his capacities and responsibilities; and ministers are bound to do this in God's name, just because He requires it at their hands. Those who have not yet submitted to, or complied with, the commands and invitations of the gospel, cannot, in their present state,—though they may know, and profess to believe, the general doctrine of predestination as a part of God's revealed truth,—know anything whatever bearing in any way upon the question, *whether they themselves individually have been elected or not;* and, therefore, they have no right to take any opinion or impression upon *this* point into account, in dealing with the commands and invitations which are addressed to them. As they can know nothing about it, they should, in the meantime, leave it out of view, and give it no practical weight or effect what ever. The general doctrine of predestination,—the truth that God has chosen some men to everlasting life, and has resolved to pass by the rest and to leave them to perish in their sins,—is taught in Scripture; and, therefore, all who have access to the Bible ought to believe it. But men are to apply and to act upon only what they do know; and as, at the time when they are in the condition of considering how they should deal with the commands and invitations of the gospel, addressed to them and pressed upon them, they cannot know whether they themselves have been elected or not, they are not at liberty to take either an affirmative or a negative opinion upon this point into account, and to act upon it as a reality,—as a thing known. The general truth, that God has elected some and passed by others,—which is the whole of the doctrine of predestination as taught in Scripture,—does not furnish any materials whatever for practically influencing their conduct in their present circumstances, or with reference to the point which they have at present under consideration, and with which they are bound to deal; and therefore their duty, in right reason, is just to abstain from applying it to the particular matter on hand, and to proceed at once to obey the command and to accept of the invitation addressed to them. Any other course of procedure, in the circumstance, is manifestly irrational, as resting upon no actual ground of knowledge; and, as the doctrine of predestination taught in Scripture does not rationally produce, or tend to produce, a hesitation or a refusal to accept of the offers and invitations of the gospel, so it is in no way legitimately responsible for this result, in any instance in which it may have been exhibited.

All this is abundantly evident; and though denied by most Arminians, who would fain represent the doctrine of predestination as throwing rational and legitimate obstacles in the way of men receiving and submitting to the gospel, it is admitted by Dr Whately, who makes it an objection to our doctrine, that " the preacher" (and, of course, also the hearer) " is to act in all respects as if the system were not true." This is not a correct representation of the state of the case. The preacher is bound to state the whole truth of God, as it is revealed in His word; and to urge upon every man to apply every truth according to its true nature and real import, viewed in connection with his actual circumstances. The doctrine of predestination, as we have seen, casts much light upon the character and moral government of God ;

and it must always be a matter of great practical importance, that men have full and correct views and impressions upon these points. Whenever they have learned this doctrine, they are bound to apply it, according to its true nature and all that it fairly involves. But at the time when they have not yet embraced the offers and invitations of the gospel, and are only considering how they should deal with them, they have not yet any materials whatever for applying it, in the way of bearing upon the question, whether they have been elected or not; and, therefore, so far as that point is concerned, they are to act,—not as Dr Whately says, as if the system or general doctrine of predestination were not true,—but merely (for this is evidently the true state of the case), as if it did not then, at that time, afford any materials for determining one particular question concerning themselves individually; and thus did not afford any materials for deciding upon the one point of how they should deal with the commands and invitations addressed to them. Thus far, and to this extent, it is true that neither preacher nor hearer can make a direct, personal, individual application of the doctrine; but this is very far from warranting Whately's assertion, that the doctrine does not admit of any personal practical application whatever.

For, men may come at length to know upon sound and rational grounds that they have been elected to everlasting life; and it is then, and then only, that the practical personal application of the doctrine to men individually is brought out. Arminians are accustomed to represent the matter, as if the belief of the general scriptural doctrine, that God has elected some men to life and passed by the rest, must necessarily include in it the means of knowing directly and immediately, what men individually have been elected, and what have been passed by; and they often insinuate, moreover, that all who profess to believe in the doctrine of election, imagine, upon the mere ground of the truth of this doctrine, and without any intermediate process, that they themselves have been elected. God might have revealed to us this general doctrine, and required us to apply it in the way of regulating our general conceptions of His character and moral government; and yet might have afforded us no materials for deciding certainly at any time, whether we individually had been elected or not. And in connection with this point, it is most important to remember, that He has not provided any materials from which any man upon earth can ever, without a special revelation, be warranted in drawing the conclusion, that he himself, or that any one of his fellow-men, has *not* been elected; and that consequently no man is ever warranted to act upon this conviction as certainly true of himself. Arminians are fond of representing the doctrine of predestination as fitted to throw men into despair, by making them believe that they are foreordained to everlasting death. But while the doctrine implies that this is true of some men, in the sense which has been explained, it does not contain in itself, or when viewed in connection with any materials which are within our reach, any ground to warrant any man to come to this conclusion with respect to himself. And, therefore, despair is not in any case the proper legitimate result of the application of this doctrine; but must arise, wherever it exists, from the perversion or abuse of it, or of some other principle connected with it. Men may, indeed, have abundant ground for the conclusion, that their present condition is one of guilt and depravity; and that, consequently, if they were to die now, they would inevitably be consigned to misery. But there is evidently nothing in this that affords any legitimate ground for the conclusion, that God has from eternity passed them by and resolved to withhold from them His grace. This was once the condition of all men; and many have been rescued from it who had gone to a fearful excess of depravity. If men, indeed, did or could know, that they had been guilty of the sin against the Holy Ghost, or of the sin unto death, they might then legitimately draw the inference, that their eternal doom was fixed, and could not be changed. But while we know the general truth, that such sins may be committed, there are no materials provided in Scripture, by the application of which any man is warranted in coming to the certain and positive conclusion that he has committed them. And, in like manner, while we know that God has resolved to leave some men to perish in their sin, we have no materials provided by which any man is warranted, while he is upon earth, in coming to the conclusion, that he belongs to this number; and consequently there is no legitimate ground in the doctrine of predestination, or in any other doctrine taught in Scripture, why any man should despair,—should renounce all hope of salvation,—should act as if his condemnation were unchangeably determined, and on this account should refuse to comply with the offers and invitations of the gospel.

But although no man while upon earth can have any good ground for despairing of salvation,—as if he had full warrant for the conclusion that he has not been elected,—men may have good ground for believing that they have been from eternity elected to everlasting life; and of course are called upon to apply this conviction, according to its true nature and bearings. This important point is thus admirably stated in the Westminster Confession:— "The doctrine of this high mystery of predestination is to be handled with special prudence and care, that men attending to the will of God revealed in His word, and yielding obedience thereunto, may from the certainty of their effectual vocation be assured of their eternal election. So shall this doctrine afford matter of praise, reverence, and admiration of God; and of humility, diligence, and abundant consolation, to all that sincerely obey the gospel."* No man has any ground to conclude that he has been elected, merely because Scripture teaches the general doctrine, that God has chosen some men to everlasting life. Other materials must be furnished and applied, before any man is warranted to cherish this conviction. Some change must be effected in him, which is a necessary or invariable accompaniment or consequence of eternal election, and which may thus test and establish its reality in reference to him. It is a part of our doctrine, that every man who has been elected to life from eternity, is in time effectually called, or has faith and regeneration produced in him by the operation of God's Spirit. No man has or can have any sufficient ground for believing that he has been elected, unless and until he has been enabled to believe in Christ Jesus, and has been born again of the word of God through the belief of the truth; and wherever these changes have been effected, this must have been done in the execution of God's eternal purpose; and thus, taken in connection with the Scripture doctrines of election and perseverance, they afford satisfactory grounds for the conclusion, that every one in whom they have been wrought, has been from eternity elected to life, and shall certainly be saved. It is only from the certainty of their effectual vocation that men can be assured of their eternal election. But all who have been effectually called, and who are assured of this by a right application of the scriptural materials bearing upon the point, are bound, in

---

* Chap. iii. s. 8.

the application of the doctrine of election, to believe that they have been elected, and to apply this conclusion according to its true nature and bearings.

The materials by which men may attain to certainty as to their effectual vocation are to be found, partly in Scripture, and partly in themselves; and by a right use of these materials, men may, under the guidance of the Holy Spirit, attain to a firm and well-grounded conviction upon this point; and thus arrive at decided conclusions, both with respect to God's eternal purposes in regard to them, and with respect to their own everlasting destiny. If they have fallen into error in the application of these materials, if they have been persuaded of the certainty of their effectual vocation without good grounds,—that is, if they believe that they have been effectually called when they have not,—then, of course, all their ulterior conclusions, about the certainty of their election and of their perseverance, fall to the ground; they, too, must be equally erroneous, and, therefore, can exert only an injurious influence. But the doctrine of election is not responsible for this error, or for any of the injurious consequences that may have resulted from it. The error was solely their own, arising either from ignorance of what Scripture teaches upon the subject of effectual calling, or from ignorance of themselves,—or from both. Such cases afford no specimen of the right and legitimate application, or the natural and appropriate tendency, of the doctrine of election, or of any doctrine that is connected with it. The full and legitimate application of this doctrine, is exhibited only in the case of those who have been effectually called,—who are persuaded of this upon solid and satisfactory grounds,—and who, from this fact, viewed in connection with the general doctrine of election taught in Scripture, have drawn the inference or conclusion, that they have been elected to everlasting life, and that they shall certainly persevere in faith and holiness unto the end, and be eternally saved.

And what is the natural and appropriate result of this state of mind,—of these views and convictions about our present condition and future prospects, and the whole procedure of God in connection with them? The legitimate result of this state of mind,—and consequently the right application of the doctrine, as soon as it comes to admit of a direct practical bearing on the case of men individually,—is not to encourage them in carelessness or indifference about the regulation of their conduct, about the discharge of their duty, as if the result were secured do what they might,—that is, as if God had not established an invariable connection between the means and the end, or had not left all the moral obligations under which men lie at least unimpaired. Dr Whately admits that our doctrine is not liable to any charge of injurious tendency on this ground. But it is surely manifest that it is fitted to exert, directly and positively, an important practical influence. When men, who have been effectually called, infer from their effectual vocation, established by its appropriate evidence, that they have been elected and shall certainly be saved ; and when they realize and apply aright all the views which are thus presented of their condition, obligations, and prospects,—of all that God has done and will yet do with regard to them ; the result must be, that the doctrine of election, or the special aspect in which that doctrine presents and impresses all the considerations, retrospective and prospective, which ought to influence and affect the mind, will afford, as the Confession says, "matter of praise, reverence, and admiration of God ;" inasmuch as it brings out, in a light, clearer, more palpable, and more impressive than could be derived from any other source, how entirely God is the author of our salvation and of all that leads to it,—of all that we have and all that we hope for,—how gloriously His perfections have been manifested in all that He has done for us,—and how supremely we should feel ourselves constrained to show forth His praises, and to yield ourselves unto Him. It must afford, also, "matter of humility, diligence, and abundant consolation to all who sincerely obey the gospel," most effectually bringing down every high thought and every imagination that exalteth itself,—filling with peace and joy in believing amid every difficulty and danger,—and keeping alive at all times a sense of the most profound and powerful obligation to aim supremely and unceasingly at the great object, to which God's electing purpose was directed,—on account of which, in the execution of that purpose, Christ gave Himself for us, and sent forth His Spirit into our hearts,—viz., that we should be holy and without blame, before Him in love, that we should be cleansed from all filthiness of the flesh and of the spirit, and be enabled to perfect holiness in the fear of the Lord, that we should be made meet for the everlasting enjoyment of His glorious presence.

When, then, men are assured of their eternal election,—as an inference or deduction from the certainty of their effectual vocation,—this suggests and inculcates views of God and of themselves, —of what He has purposed and done for them and of the relation in which they stand to Him,—of their past history, present condition, and future prospects,—which cannot be derived, at least in the same measure and degree, or of so definite and effective a character, from any other form or aspect in which these subjects can be presented; views fitted to cherish in the heart all those feelings, desires, and motives that constitute or produce true piety and genuine godliness, and thus to assimilate men's character and conduct on earth to the life of heaven.*

In a note subjoined to his " Essay on Election," † Dr Whately makes an ingenious attempt to get some countenance to his notion, that the Calvinistic doctrine of election has no practical effect or bearing, from the 17th Article of the Church of England; while, at the same time, he tries to undermine the testimony in favour of Calvinism, which has been derived from that Article; and it may tend to throw further light upon the subject we have been considering, if we briefly examine his statements upon this point. He begins with quoting, from one of his previous works, some observations upon the principles which have often regulated the composition, and should therefore regulate the interpretation, of public ecclesiastical documents or symbolical books. He dwells especially upon the idea, that these documents have been often the results of a compromise, among men who differed somewhat from each other in their opinions; and illustrates the bearing of this consideration upon the right mode of explaining and applying them. His general views upon this subject are very sound and judicious, and may be most usefully applied in the explanation of many important ecclesiastical documents; but we think he utterly fails in the attempt he makes to apply them to the 17th Article of his own church. We quote the whole of his statement upon this point, and we request our readers to give it their special attention:—

" Our 17th Article is a striking exemplification of what has been said; for it contains modifications and limitations in one part of what is laid down in another, such as go near to neutralise the one by the other.

" It begins by stating the doctrine of predestination, in a form which certainly may be, and we know often has been, understood in the Calvinistic

---

* For a masterly and exhaustive discussion of this subject, see Dr Owen's great work on the Holy Spirit, B. v., c. ii.:—" Eternal Election, a cause of and motive unto holiness."
† P. 97.

sense ; and then it proceeds to point out the danger of dwelling on that doctrine, if so understood, before curious and carnal persons ; of whom one may presume there will usually be some in any congregation or mixed company ; so that such a doctrine is seldom if ever to be publicly set forth. Next, it cautions us against taking the divine promises otherwise than as they are *generally* (generaliter) set forth in Scripture; that is, as made to *classes* of men,—those of such and such a *description*, and not to *individuals*. We are not, in short, to pronounce this or that man one of the elect (in the Calvinistic sense), except so far as we may judge from the kind of character he manifests. And lastly, we are warned, in our own conduct, not to vindicate any act as conformable to God's will, on the ground that whatever takes place must have been decreed by Him, but are to consider conformity to His *will* as consisting in obedience to His injunctions.

" If, then, some may say, this doctrine is (1) not to be *publicly set forth*, nor (2) applied in our *judgment of any individual*, nor (3) applied in our *own conduct*, why need it have been at all mentioned ?

" As for the comfort enjoyed from the ' godly consideration' of it by those who ' feel within themselves the working of God's Holy Spirit,' etc., it would be most unreasonable to suppose that this cannot be *equally* enjoyed by those who do *not* hold predestinarian views, but who not the less fully trust in and love their Redeemer, and ' keep His saying.'

" But the article is manifestly the result of a compromise between conflicting views ; one party insisting on the insertion of certain statements, which the other consented to admit, only on condition of the insertion of certain limitations and cautions, to guard against the dangers that might attend the reception of the doctrine in a sense of which the former passage is capable."

The views set forth in this passage may be considered in two different aspects :—1st, in their bearing generally upon the Calvinism of the Articles; and, 2d, in their bearing upon Whately's special allegation, that the Calvinistic doctrine does not admit of any practical application.

On the first of these topics, Whately seems to intend to insinuate, that the 17th Article, as it stands, was the result of a compromise between men holding different and opposite views on the subjects controverted between Calvinists and Arminians; some statements being put in to please or satisfy the one party, and some to please or satisfy the other. It is on the ground of some notion of this sort, that many have contended, that the theology of the Church of England is neither Calvinism nor Arminianism ; while others have embodied the same general idea, in a somewhat different form, by maintaining that it is both the one and the other. But there is nothing whatever to support the idea of any such compromise, either in the actual statements of the article itself, or in the historical facts as to the theological sentiments of its authors, and the circumstances in which it was composed. It must now be regarded as a conclusively established historical fact, —a fact about which there is scarcely room for an honest difference of opinion,—that the framers of the English articles were Calvinists, and of course intended to teach Calvinism; or at least could not have intended to teach anything at all inconsistent with it. And there is certainly nothing in the article itself to contradict or discountenance this conclusion, to which the whole history of the matter so plainly points. There is not one statement contained in the article, to which any reasonable and intelligent Calvinist ever has objected, or ever could have thought of objecting. How honest and intelligent men who are not Calvinists, can satisfy or pacify their consciences in subscribing it, is a mystery which we never have been able to solve. But with this we are not at present concerned. It is certain, that there is nothing in the 17th Article,—not a thought or idea,—but what is found in other Confessions undeniably Calvinistic, and in the writings of Calvin himself, and of all the ablest and most eminent Calvinistic divines. The framers of the English articles were no donbt moderate Calvinists, who were not disposed to give countenance to the more extreme and minute expositions of the subject in which some Calvinists have indulged; and who were anxious to guard against the practical abuses into which some unintelligent and injudicious persons have fallen in the application of the doctrine, and to which we admit the doctrine is obviously liable in the hands of such persons. But there is really not a shadow of ground for Whately's assertion, that "the article is manifestly the result of a compromise between conflicting views;" and the conclusive proof of this is, that there is nothing in it which would not naturally and at once suggest itself as a matter of course to any intelligent Calvinist, who wished to give a temperate and careful statement of his opinions. His statements about "modifications and limitations," "limitations and cautions," which one party insisted upon in order to neutralize something else; and about this party consenting to admit the leading and general position, which it is admitted has a very Calvinistic aspect, "only on the condition of the insertion" of these limitations and cautions to modify it, are a pure fiction,—utterly unsupported by anything either in the history of the article, or in the article itself. No man could have

made such statements, who was intelligently acquainted with the
writings of Calvinistic divines, which make it manifest, that such
cautions and limitations constitute a natural and familiar commonplace in the exposition of their system of theology. Not only are
the limitations and cautions in the article perfectly consistent with
Calvinism, but some of them are of such a nature as could only
have been suggested and required by a previous statement of Calvinistic doctrine; and thus afford a positive proof, that its leading
general statement is, and was intended to be, a declaration of the
fundamental principle of Calvinism.

It is but fair, however, to remark, that Dr Whately has not
here stated, precisely and explicitly, what were the " conflicting
views" which he considers to have been compromised in the article
by modifying and neutralizing limitations; and, that thus it may
be open to him to allege, in his own defence, that he did not mean
to deny the Calvinism of the article, or to assert that there is any
thing in it opposed to the views generally held by Calvinistic
divines; and that the " conflicting views," which he says were
compromised, referred only to minor points, in which Calvinists
might differ among themselves. If this should be pleaded in his
defence, then we have to say, that he ought to have made his
meaning and object more clear and definite than he has done;
and that the natural and obvious bearing of his statements, viewed
in connection with the common mode of discussing this topic
among a large class of Episcopalian divines, decidedly favours the
idea, that, by " conflicting views," he just meant the opposite
opinions of Calvinists and Arminians. If his statement about
" conflicting views" referred to points of inferior importance, in
which Calvinists might differ from each other, it is at once trifling
and irrelevant; and if it referred to the differences between Calvinists and Arminians, it is conclusively disproved, at once by all
that is known concerning the history and the authors of the article,
and by the fact that there is nothing in it but what is maintained
explicitly and unhesitatingly by the great body of Calvinistic theologians.

But we have to do at present, chiefly, with the attempt made
by Whately to get, from the 17th Article, support for his allegation, that the Calvinistic doctrine of election does not admit of
any practical application. The article consists of three divisions.
The first, and most important, is a general statement of the doc-

trine, which Whately says, " may be, and we know, often has been, understood in the Calvinistic sense ;" and which all Calvinists regard as a clear and accurate description of the whole process by which sinners are saved, in full accordance with the distinc tive features of their system of theology. The second division sets forth the practical application of this Calvinistic doctrine under two heads,—the first declaring the " sweet and pleasant" use that may be made of it by " godly persons," " as well because it doth greatly establish and confirm their faith of eternal salva- tion to be enjoyed through Christ, as because it doth fervently kindle their love towards God ;" and the second, warning against an abuse to which it may be perverted by " curious and carnal persons lacking (in the Latin *destituti*) the spirit of Christ," who, if they " have continually before their eyes the sentence of God's predestination," may be led thereby into despair and profligacy. The third and last division consists of two positions, which do not, indeed, quite so clearly and certainly suggest or imply the Cal- vinistic doctrine, as do the use and abuse under the second divi- sion, but which are at least perfectly consistent with it. They may, indeed, be called " limitations and cautions ;" since, in exact accordance with the principles we have already explained, they limit the sphere of the practical application of the doctrine, and caution against applying it to matters on which it has no proper or legitimate bearing. These two limitations or cautions are,— first, " we must receive God's promises in such wise as they be generally set forth to us in Scripture ;" and, second, " in our doings, that will of God is to be followed which we have expressly declared to us in the word of God."

It will be observed that Whately, in the quotation we have given from him, postpones the consideration of the first head under the second division, about the use or application that is, and should be, made of this doctrine by godly persons,—proceeds at once to the abuse of the doctrine condemned in the second head of the second division, and to the two limitations or cautions set forth in the third,—and, having endeavoured to extort from these three topics some support for his main allegation, he then returns to the explicit declaration of the article about the right use or practical application of the doctrine, and tries to dispose of it. The whole process is very curious, as a specimen of careful and elabo- rate sophistry, though it is certainly not very successful.

The way in which he turns to account the statement in the article, about the abuse that may be made of the doctrine by carnal and ungodly persons, is this : Upon the assumption that there will usually be some such persons in any congregation, he bases the inference that "such a doctrine is seldom, if ever, to be publicly set forth ;" and, from the application which he afterwards makes of this inference, in his summing up of the argument, it is plain that he wishes it to be received as suggested by, or involved in, the statement in the article itself ; as if it were intended to be taught there, at least, by implication. Now, it is surely manifest that there is nothing in the article which affords any appearance of ground for this inference. The liability of a doctrine to be abused by a certain class of persons, is certainly not a sufficient reason why it should be "seldom, if ever, publicly set forth ;" but only a reason why, when it is set forth, the right use and application of it should be carefully pointed out, and the abuse or perversion of it carefully guarded against. To ascribe to the compilers of this article, a notion of so peculiar a kind as that a doctrine, which they had set forth as a great scriptural truth, should seldom, if ever, be publicly taught, when they had not said this, or anything like it, and to do this upon a ground so palpably inadequate, is a kind of procedure which is wholly unwarrantable.

He then proceeds to the two limitations or cautions, set forth in the third and last division of the article ; and to the account which, in the first instance, he gives of their import and bearing, we have nothing to object. It is true, as he alleges, that the first of them implies that "we are not to pronounce this or that man one of the elect (in the Calvinistic sense), except so far as we may judge from the kind of character he manifests ;" and that the second implies, that we are, "in our own conduct, not to vindicate any act as conformable to God's will, on the ground that whatever takes place must have been decreed by Him, but to consider conformity to His will as consisting in obedience to His injunctions." These positions are true in themselves ; they are plainly implied in the concluding division of the article ; and they certainly limit, materially, the sphere of the practical application of the doctrine ; but we think it manifest, from the explanations which have already been submitted, that they are altogether irrelevant to Whately's leading allegation,—that the doctrine admits of no practical application whatever.

He then goes on to give the summing up of the preceding argument in this way: "If, then, some may say" (he evidently wishes it to be believed that men may say all this truly and justly), "this doctrine is (1) not to be publicly set forth nor (2) applied in our judgment of any individual, nor (3) applied in our own conduct, why need it have been at all mentioned?" The conclusion here, indefinitely and modestly indicated in the shape of a question, is evidently intended as equivalent to an assertion of his favourite position, that the Calvinistic doctrine of election, even if admitted to be true, is a mere barren speculation, destitute of all practical influence. The question in which his conclusion is embodied, is virtually addressed to the compilers of the articles; and it plainly involves a serious charge against them, for teaching this doctrine, when, in Whately's estimation, there was no need to mention it. Their answer to this charge would undoubtedly have been, that there was need to mention it—1st, because it was a portion of God's revealed truth; and 2d, because it had an important practical use or application in the case of godly persons, as they had fully set forth in the first head of the second division of the article. But let us advert to the three points in which he has summed up his argument, and which he represents as all sanctioned by the statements of the article, on which he had been commenting. The first is that "this doctrine is not to be publicly set forth." This he had previously put in the modified form, that "it is seldom, if ever, to be publicly set forth;" but now, when he is summing up his argument, and endeavouring to found upon this consideration a presumption (for he could scarcely regard it as a proof), in support of his conclusion, he drops the qualification, and makes the assertion absolute,—"the doctrine is not to be publicly set forth." We have already shown, that there is no ground for this assertion in any thing contained in the article. The statement that the doctrine is liable to be abused by a certain class of persons, affords no ground whatever for the inference which Whately deduces from it, even in its qualified form. It furnishes good ground, indeed, for the declaration of the Westminster Confession, that the "doctrine of this high mystery of predestination is to be handled with special prudence and care," but for nothing more; and with this, we have no doubt, the compilers of the Thirty-nine Articles would have been perfectly satisfied, as embodying all that they meant to teach upon this point.

The second and third points, viz., that this doctrine is not to
be applied, or does not admit of any practical application, either
in our judgment of any individual, or in the regulation of our
own conduct, are intended as a compendious statement of the two
limitations or cautions in the concluding section of the article.
These two points he had previously explained more fully and definitely, and, as we have admitted, correctly. But we do not
admit, that there is the same fairness and correctness in the more
indefinite and compendious statement of them, which he now gives
in his summing up. Our objection to his argument, founded upon
these two points was, that they merely limited the sphere of the
practical application of the doctrine of election, but did not prove
his allegation, that it had no practical application whatever. He
seems to have had a sort of indistinct apprehension of this radical
defect in his argument; and in his summing up he tries to conceal it, by putting these two points in the most indefinite and comprehensive form, so as to give them the appearance of covering
the whole ground, and thus leaving no room whatever for the
practical application of the doctrine. To say absolutely, and
without any qualification or explanation, that the doctrine is not
to be applied in our judgment of any individual or in our own
conduct, is to assert rather more than we can admit to be true in
itself, or sanctioned by the statements of the article; and rather
more than is implied in the more full and formal exposition of
these statements, which he himself had previously given. On
these grounds, we cannot but regard Whately's summing up of
his argument upon this subject, as exhibiting more of the sophist
than of the logician.

After having done what he could to find some materials in the
article to give positive countenance to his allegation, he comes at
last to consider what is there set forth about the use and application of the doctrine. This,—both from its position in the article,
and its more direct and immediate bearing upon the point in dispute,—ought, in fairness, to have been considered first. But
Whately evidently thought it expedient, to accumulate something
like evidence in support of his position, before he ventured to face
the statement which so explicitly and conclusively disproves it.
The way in which he attempts to dispose of this statement is this,
—" as for the comfort enjoyed from the ' godly consideration' of
it by those who ' feel within themselves the workings of God's

Holy Spirit,' etc., *it would be most unreasonable to suppose* that this cannot be equally enjoyed by those who do not hold predestinarian views, but who not the less fully trust in and love their Redeemer, and keep His saying." Now, upon this, we have to remark, 1st, that the article does most expressly ascribe a specific use,—a definite practical application,—to the godly consideration of this doctrine by truly religious persons; and, 2d, that there is nothing unreasonable in ascribing to it this use and application. The article expressly asserts, that "the godly consideration of predestination and our election in Christ is full of sweet, pleasant, and unspeakable comfort to godly persons;" and the ascription of this result to the "consideration" of this doctrine, is of itself a flat and explicit contradiction to Whately's position, which no sophistry or shuffling, and no accumulation of probabilities or presumptions, can evade or dispose of. The article further specifies the process by which the consideration of this doctrine produces this result of "unspeakable comfort to godly persons;"—viz., "as well because it doth greatly establish and confirm their faith of eternal salvation to be enjoyed through Christ, as because it doth fervently kindle their love to God." To allege that the article, in ascribing to this doctrine the production of unspeakable comfort, by confirming men's faith of their eternal salvation, and increasing their love to God, did not intend to state anything peculiar to this doctrine, but merely described what might be derived equally or as fully from the consideration of other doctrines, is plainly to charge the article with containing downright nonsense or unmeaning verbiage. And here we may remark by the way, that the manifest and exact accordance between the view given in the 17th Article of the Church of England, concerning the right use and application of the doctrine of "predestination and our election in Christ," with the representation given of the same subject in the Westminster Confession, which we have already explained and illustrated, furnishes a proof of the identity of the system of doctrine taught in these two symbols.

As to the alleged unreasonableness of ascribing any such use or application specifically to the Calvinistic doctrine of election, we have, we think, sufficiently refuted this in our general observations upon this subject. And, indeed, it is surely self-evident, that this doctrine, when intelligently and rationally applied by persons who have good grounds for believing that they have been elected to eternal life, must produce practical results upon their views and feelings,—results operating beneficially upon their character and conduct,—which cannot be derived equally, if at all, from any other source. We admit, indeed, that the practical results derived from the application of this doctrine are confined within a narrow sphere ; and do not bear directly upon the enjoyment of the great essential blessings of the gospel, or upon the production of the fundamental elements of Christian character. They do not bear directly upon justification and regeneration,—the essential blessings on which universally, and in every instance, the salvation of sinners depends. They are connected more immediately with what may be called the secondary, or subordinate blessings of the gospel,—" assurance of God's love, peace of conscience, and joy in the Holy Ghost." But these form no unimportant part of the gospel provision. They materially affect not only the " comfort of godly persons," but their growth in grace; and they operate powerfully in aiding their increase in holiness, and in securing their perseverance therein unto the end. Every sinner who has been justified and regenerated shall assuredly be saved. And we have no doubt, that many men have been made meet for heaven, and admitted to the enjoyment of it, who never, so long as they continued upon earth, understood or believed the Calvinistic doctrine of election. The specific practical personal application of the doctrine, by men individually in their own case, requires, indeed, as its necessary antecedents and conditions, not only that they have, in fact, been enabled to repent and believe in Christ, —that they have entered upon the way which leadeth to heaven, by embracing Christ as He is freely offered to them in the gospel, —but also, that they are assured, upon good and sufficient grounds, that this is their present condition. And we willingly concede, that not a few have been, by God's grace, brought into this condition, and at last admitted into the kingdom of glory, who never attained to a distinct " certainty of their effectual vocation," and, therefore, could not be rationally " assured of their eternal election;" and who, of course, could make no direct personal application of the doctrine of election to their own case, or derive from it the special spiritual benefit which it is fitted to impart. But we are persuaded, that all these persons lived somewhat beneath their privileges,— failed, to some extent, in walking worthily of their high and holy calling,—and came short, more or less, in fully adorning their

Christian profession, by their ignorance or unbelief of the information which God has given us in His word, concerning His sovereign purpose of mercy in Christ Jesus, in regard to all who are saved; an absolute and unchangeable purpose formed from eternity, and executed in time, by bestowing upon them all those things which accompany salvation, and prepare for the enjoyment of heaven.

We shall conclude with a few additional remarks suggested by the last section of the 17th of the Thirty-nine Articles. It is expressed in these words:—" Furthermore, we must receive God's promises in such wise as they be generally set forth to us in holy Scripture; and, in our doings, *that* will of God is to be followed which we have expressly declared unto us in the word of God." We have already said enough to show, that these two statements,—while they certainly limit or restrict the legitimate sphere of the personal practical application of the Calvinistic doctrine of election, and caution against the abuses which have been made of it,—contain nothing whatever, in the least, inconsistent with Calvinism; nothing but what is to be found in the writings of all Calvinistic divines. It is, indeed, a curious circumstance,—and it has been often referred to, in opposition to the attempts which have been made to deduce, from this portion of the article, an argument against the Calvinism of its leading position,—that the second and most important part of this statement, which virtually includes or comprehends the first, is expressed in the very words of Calvin;* while the first part of it is to be found, in its whole substance and spirit, in many parts of his writings. We concede to the Arminians, that the word *generally*, here, is not to be taken in the sense of *usually or ordinarily*, but is intended to indicate the character of the promises as set forth in Scripture in a general, indefinite, unlimited, unrestricted way. There is nothing in this, however, which renders any service to their cause. The word *promises* is to be taken here, as it was used by the Reformers in general, in a wider sense than that in which it is commonly employed in more modern times. The Reformers generally used this word as comprehending all the offers and invitations of the gospel addressed to men in general,—to sinners as such,—freely offering to them all the blessings of salvation, and inviting them

---

* Inst. lib. i. c. 17, s. 5.

to come to God through Christ, that they may receive and enjoy
these blessings.   In modern times, the word *promises* is commonly
taken in a more restricted sense, as descriptive of those scriptural
statements which are addressed specially to believers,—to those
who have already been united to Christ by faith,—and which
assume that this is their present position.   But the word, as used
in the article, plainly comprehends, and, indeed, has special reference to, what we now commonly call the offers and invitations of
the gospel, or those scriptural statements which tell the human
race of the provision which God has made for saving them; and
on this ground call upon them to turn from sin unto God, to believe in the Lord Jesus Christ, and to lay hold of the hope set
before them.   Now, the substance of what is taught in the article
is this, that these offers and invitations are set forth to us in Scripture in a general or universal form,—no restriction being made,
no exception being put forth, no previous qualification being required as a condition of accepting them,—and that we must deal
with, or apply them, in this their general or unrestricted character,
without bringing in, *at this stage*, either the general doctrine of
predestination, or its possible, but wholly unknown, bearing upon
individuals, in order to modify or limit the general scriptural
representations, or the manner in which they ought to be dealt
with.   *Here*, neither the general doctrine of predestination, nor
its imagined bearing upon individuals, has any proper place; or
can exert any legitimate practical influence.   The offers and invitations must be set forth as they stand, in all their unrestricted
generality, and should be dealt with unhesitatingly, according to
their natural and obvious meaning and import.   This is all that
is involved in the first part of the statement we are considering;
and, to all this, Calvinists have no hesitation in assenting.   They
set forth the general offers and invitations of the gospel addressed
to mankind at large, in order to lead them from darkness to light;
they do all this as freely and fully, as cordially and earnestly,
as any other class of theologians; and they think they can show,
that it cannot be proved that there is anything in all this inconsistent with the peculiar doctrines they hold.

We have said that the second part of this statement about the
"will of God" virtually includes the first part about the
"promises."   And the reason is this, that the promises,—that is,
the offers and invitations of the gospel,—virtually comprehend or

involve commands or injunctions, and of course impose duties and
obligations.   The offers and invitations of the gospel are intended
to lead men to repent and believe, by setting before them motives
and encouragements to persuade them to do so.   But they, at the
same time, include or imply a command, that those to whom they
are addressed, should receive them and deal with them, according
to their true nature and import.   God has made this their imperative duty, by explicit injunctions contained in His word.   "To
escape the wrath and curse of God due to us for sin, God *requireth*
of us faith in Jesus Christ, repentance unto life, with the diligent
use of all the outward and ordinary means whereby Christ com-
municateth to us the benefits of redemption."   It is true, indeed,
that the right mode of representing and applying the offers and
invitations of the gospel is of such transcendent importance, from
its direct and immediate bearing on the only process by which
sinners individually are saved, that it was proper to state it
distinctly by itself, and to give it the fullest prominence.   But it
is not the less true, that the substance of what ought to be said
upon this topic is virtually comprehended in the wider statement,
which the compilers of the articles expressed in the words of
Calvin, viz.,—"that, in our doings, that will of God is to be
followed which we have expressly declared to us in the word of
God."   The general import of this position is,—that our whole
conduct is to be regulated, in all matters bearing upon our relation
to God and our eternal welfare, by the laws, injunctions, or commands, which are imposed upon us in Scripture; and not by any
thing which we may or can know as to God's purposes or inten-
tions with respect either to ourselves or others, or with respect to
any events or results that may be anticipated.   This is manifestly
a sound principle; and no intelligent Calvinist has ever refused or
hesitated to assent to it, and to act upon it.   There have, indeed,
been great disputes between the Calvinists and the Arminians in
regard to the will of God,—*voluntas Dei;*—and the right exposition
of this subject may be said to enter vitally and fundamentally into
the controversy between them.   But the disputes do not turn upon
the point with which we have at present to do.   Calvinists agree
with Arminians in holding, that the exclusive rule of our duty,—
of what we are bound to do,—is that will of God which is plainly
set forth in His word in the form of injunctions or commands.
The language employed in the article,—"*that* will of God,"

naturally suggests the idea, that there is another will of God besides what is here described, or another sense in which the expression may be employed; and it is about this *other* will that a great deal of controversy has been carried on. We cannot enter on the consideration of this topic, though it is very important in itself, and though there are indications that it is very ill understood by some in the present day who call themselves Calvinists. We have room only for a few words, not upon the subject itself, but merely upon some of the terms commonly used in the discussion of it.

" *That* will of God which we have expressly declared to us in His word," and which is universally admitted to be the exclusive rule of our duty, is called by Calvinistic divines by a variety of designations. They call it *voluntas præcepti, voluntas revelata, voluntas signi, voluntas* ἐυαρεστιας. These are just four different designations for one and the same thing; presenting it in somewhat different aspects, but all of them equally intended to indicate *that* will of God which is set forth in His word by injunctions and commands, and constitutes the sole rule of our duty. But Calvinists have always contended that there is another will of God, indicated by events or results as they take place. They hold that all events are foreordained by God, and that, of course, all events, when they take place, indicate what God had resolved to bring about, or, at least, to permit; and may thus be regarded as being, *in some sense*, manifestations of His will. This will of God, by which He regulates events or results, is quite distinct from that will by which He imposes duties and obligations; and yet it must be admitted to be a reality,—to have an existence and an efficacy,—unless He is to be shut out, not only from foreseeing and foreordaining, but from determining and regulating, the whole course of events which constitute the history of the world. This will of God, also, Calvinists usually designate by four different names, corresponding, but contrasted, with the four applied to the divine will in the former sense. They call it *voluntas decreti, voluntas arcana, voluntas beneplaciti, voluntas* ἐνδοκιας. These, too, are just four different designations of one and the same thing,—viz., that will of God by which He determines events or results. And about the divine will, in this sense, there has been a good deal of discussion, an acquaintance with which is indispensably necessary to an intelligent knowledge of this great controversy.

Arminians usually deny that events or results, simply as such, are to be regarded as furnishing a manifestation of the divine will; and appeal, in support of this view, to the conditional form in which predictions and promises about future events are frequently put in Scripture,—the conditions attached proving, as they allege, that God had formed no absolute purpose to bring about a certain result, and thus showing that the actual result, when it does occur, is not necessarily to be regarded as being, in any sense, an indication of the divine will. The fundamental principle of Calvinism is, that God hath unchangeably foreordained whatsoever cometh to pass; and, if this principle be true, then there can be no strict and proper conditionality attaching to any events or results, as if their actual occurrence were really suspended upon causes or influences which God had not resolved to regulate and control. Calvinists, accordingly, deny that there is any true and proper conditionality in the divine predictions and promises; the conditional or hypothetical form in which they are often set forth in Scripture, being intended merely to indicate a fixed connection established in God's purpose between means and end, and being designed, by indicating this connection, to exert a moral influence upon the minds of men, and thereby to contribute to bring about the result contemplated. Arminians object vehemently to the distinction which Calvinists make between the preceptive and revealed or declared will of God, and what they commonly call His decretive and secret will—the will of His good pleasure—as if this were to ascribe to God two opposite and contradictory wills. But there is really no opposition or contradiction between them. His preceptive will, which is revealed or declared, stands out, as all admit, on the face of Scripture, in the injunctions or commands which constitute the only rule of our duty. But His decretive will,—*voluntas decreti*, or *beneplaciti*,—must also be admitted as a reality, unless He is to be excluded from the determination and control of events. And, when Calvinists call this will of decree or of good pleasure—by which He determines actual events or results—His secret will, as distinguished from His revealed or declared will, by which He determines duties and imposes obligations—they just mean, that it is in every instance (except where God has issued a prediction or a promise) utterly unknown to us, until the event takes place, and, by its occurrence, reveals or declares to us what God had resolved to do, or, at least, to permit.

And there is surely nothing in all this but the statement of an undeniable matter of fact. Unless it be denied that the divine will has a determining influence in bringing about events or results, we must introduce some distinctions into the exposition of this matter; and there is no difficulty in showing that the Calvinistic distinction between the preceptive or revealed, and the decretive or secret, will of God, is much more accordant with Scripture, and liable to much less serious objections, than the distinction which Arminians set up in opposition to it, between an antecedent or conditional, and a consequent or absolute, will,—made absolute, of course, only by the fulfilment of the conditions.

It has been stated of late, that the older Calvinistic writers maintained the conditional character of the prophetic announcements, in opposition to those who asserted their absolute and unchangeable fixedness; and that, by the distinction which they were accustomed to make between the secret and the revealed will of God, they meant a distinction between His real intention or decree, which is fixed and immutable, and His declared purpose, which may vary from time to time with the changeful conditions of man. We have never met with these views among the older Calvinistic writers; and we venture to assert, that such statements as these indicate very great ignorance and misconception, as to the grounds usually taken by Calvinistic divines in expounding and defending the fundamental principles of their system of theology. But we cannot discuss this subject, though it is naturally suggested by the statement on which we have been commenting. We think we have said enough to show that the concluding portion of the 17th Article not only contains nothing which has any appearance of inconsistency with Calvinism; but even furnishes a presumption that it was indeed the Calvinistic doctrine of predestination, and no other, which the leading portion of the Article was intended to set forth.

We have had repeated occasion, in dealing with such questions as these, to advert to the important and useful influence of controversial discussions, as exhibited in the history of the church, in throwing light upon the true meaning of Scripture, and the real import and evidence of the doctrines which are taught there. We have endeavoured to enforce the obligation, incumbent upon all men, to improve past controversies, for the purpose of aiding them in forming the most accurate, precise, and definite conceptions upon every subject which the Bible brings under our notice; and we have referred to the great Calvinistic systematic divines of the seventeenth century, as the best specimens of the improvement that may and should be made of the fruits and results of polemical discussion, in bringing out a correct and exact exposition of all the doctrines taught in Scripture, in their mutual bearings and relations. But everything is liable to abuse and perversion. There are everywhere dangers, both on the right hand and the left, to which men are exposed, from the weakness and imperfection of their faculties, and the corrupting influences from without and from within, that often tell upon the formation of their opinions and impressions of things,—tending to produce defect or excess, and frequently, even when there may not be much of positive error, leading to onesidedness of conception, in the direction either of narrowness or exaggeration. Though a man may be well versant in some departments of theological literature, we can scarcely regard him as entitled to the character of a theologian, unless he be familiar with the works of the great systematic divines of the seventeenth century, both Calvinistic and Arminian. But an addiction to the study of systematic theology, and to the perusal of systems, has,—unless it be carefully regulated,—its obvious and serious dangers, which ought to be diligently and assiduously guarded against. No one class of men are to be implicitly followed, as if they were in all respects models for our imitation, with reference to all the objects which we are called upon to aim at. No uninspired men, or body of men, have ever in the formation and expression of their opinions, risen altogether, and in every respect, above the influences of their position and circumstances.

Controversial discussions have a strong and invariable tendency to lead those who have been engaged in them, to form an exaggerated impression of the magnitude of the topics, about which they have exercised their faculties, and spent their time and strength, and for which they may have contended unto victory. And it is usually not until another generation has arisen, that men are enabled to gather up fully the fruits of the contest; and to apply its results to the formation of a sound and judicious estimate, not only of the truth, but of the importance of the questions involved in it, and of the best and most effective way of defending the truth and exposing the error. No intelligent and judicious Calvinist will probably dispute, that the great contro-

versy, which Arminius raised in the beginning of the seventeenth
century, produced the effect of bringing the peculiar doctrines of
Calvinism into a position of something like undue prominence,—
a greater prominence than they have in the Bible, or than they
ought to have, ordinarily and permanently, in the thoughts of
men, and in the usual course of pulpit instruction. We have no
doubt that the fair result of that great controversy was, to establish conclusively the scriptural truth of all the peculiar doctrines
of Calvinism. But it does not follow from this, that the Calvinists,
who so decidedly triumphed over their opponents on the field of
argument, entirely escaped the ordinary influence of controversy;
and succeeded in retaining as sound an estimate of the comparative
importance, as of the actual truth, of the doctrines for which they
had been led to contend. There can be no reasonable doubt, that
the peculiarities of Calvinism were raised for a time to a position
of undue prominence, and that there are plain indications of this
in some of the features of the theological literature of the seventeenth century. We cannot dwell upon this point; but we may
refer, as an illustration of what we mean, to the marked difference, as to the prominence given to the peculiar doctrines of Calvinism, between the Institutions of Calvin himself and the theological systems of the great Calvinistic divines to whom we have
referred. We have the highest sense of the value, for many important purposes, of these theological systems. But we cannot
doubt, that Calvin's Institutions is fitted to leave upon the mind
a juster and sounder impression, of the place which the doctrines
of Calvinism hold in the Bible, and ought to hold permanently
in the usual course of pulpit instruction, or in the ordinary
preaching of the gospel.

We have made these observations, not certainly because we
have an impression that there is a tendency among us generally,
or in any influential quarters, to give undue prominence to the
peculiar doctrines of Calvinism; but because it has been alleged
of late, that professed Calvinists do not now give so much prominence to their peculiar doctrines as was commonly assigned to
them in former times, and that this affords evidence that Calvinism
has been greatly modified, if not practically abandoned. Our
object is just to indicate, how the fact founded on, in so far as it
is a reality, may be accounted for, in perfect consistency with
what we believe to be true,—viz., that professed Calvinists are

still thoroughly persuaded of the scriptural truth of the peculiarities of Calvinism, and are resolved to maintain and apply them, according to their true nature and importance, in their due proportions, and in their right relations to the whole scheme of divine truth.

We wish to remind our readers, in conclusion, that we have not professed or attempted to discuss the general subject of predestination, or to deal with its most important and fundamental departments. A full investigation of the whole subject would naturally divide itself into four branches, viz. : 1st, The settlement of the true *status quæstionis*, the real points in dispute between the contending parties; 2d, The examination of the scriptural evidence, direct and indirect, explicit and inferential, in favour of Calvinism, and in opposition to Arminianism ; 3d, The objections commonly adduced by Arminians against our real and admitted doctrines ; and 4th, The practical application of Calvinism. With the second of these branches of the subject,—which is the most important and fundamental,—we have not attempted to deal at all ; and to the third we have referred only in a very brief and incidental way, without professing to discuss it. Our observations have been almost wholly restricted to the first and fourth of these divisions, including a consideration of the objections commonly adduced against Calvinism, which are based upon misconceptions and misrepresentations, of the true meaning and import, and of the practical application, of its doctrines.

THE REFORMERS,

AND THE

LESSONS FROM THEIR HISTORY.*

HAVING spoken at length of the character of the Reformers, we mean to make a few general observations that may be fitted to suggest some useful practical lessons from the subject. It might afford materials for some interesting reflections to notice the variety of gifts which God conferred upon the different Reformers individually,—bestowing upon one what another wanted, or did not possess in the same degree; and thus providing, notwithstanding the infirmities of human nature, for their cordial co-operation, to a large extent, among themselves, in their different spheres, and also for enabling them to advance most fully, by their united labours and efforts, the success of the common cause. This would afford an interesting illustration of the abounding goodness and manifold wisdom of God; but we must confine ourselves to some of those circumstances which were common to the Reformers in general, viewed as a class or body of men; and we remark, 1st, That the Reformers in general were men eminently distinguished at once for the strength of their natural talents, and the extent of their acquired learning. That this was indeed the case, is too evident to admit of dispute, and has never been questioned even by their bitterest enemies. They were men possessed of such distinguished talents as would have raised them to eminence and influence in any department of study or occupation to which they might have turned their attention; and their

---

* From Dr Cunningham's MS. Lectures on Church History.

writings and their labours abundantly establish this position. This was, of course, no merit of theirs, and affords no ground whatever why either they or others should boast. Its importance and value lie only in this,—that it is a matter of fact, that God selected, and qualified in other respects, for the work of restoring His truth and reforming His church, men whom He had gifted with very superior natural abilities. This was the Lord's doing, —this was the course which He pursued on that memorable occasion, and which He has ordinarily pursued in most important epochs, connected with the maintenance of His truth and the advancement of His cause. We are to look upon it as just what the Lord in His wisdom was pleased to do,—as a thing effected, and of course intended, by Him in His actual administration of the affairs of the church and the world. We are to regard it in this light, as an undoubted reality, intended by Him, like all that He does, to make Himself known, and to unfold and impress the principles of His moral government; and, viewing the fact in this aspect, to consider what are the lessons which it is fitted to teach. It should lead men, of course, to estimate aright mental power and vigour as a valuable gift of God, intended by Him to be used, and often employed by Him, in fact, in the advancement of His cause. This, however, is not a lesson which it is very necessary to inculcate; for although occasionally fanatical exceptions do appear, the general and ordinary tendency of men is to overestimate mere intellectual power, irrespective of the purposes to which it is applied,—the objects to which it is directed. Still, it is right to remember that God, by selecting as instruments for the restoration of His truth and the reformation of His church, men whom He had gifted with very superior intellectual powers, has thereby borne testimony to their value and importance,—has indicated the responsibility connected with the possession of them, and the purpose to which they ought to be chiefly applied; while He has, also, by the same fact, made it not only warrantable, but incumbent upon all, to aim at the cultivation and improvement of the intellectual powers which He may have conferred, as a distinct and definite object, in subordination to His glory, and as a means of fitting Christians more fully for doing something for the advancement of His cause.

The fact that the Reformers were also, in general, men of extensive acquired learning, admits of a more direct and obvious

practical application; as it reminds us of our obligation to improve
to the uttermost our opportunities of acquiring useful knowledge,
and encouraging us in the prosecution of this object by holding
out the expectation, that the more knowledge we may be able to
acquire, we may become the more useful in promoting His cause.

God having, in His wisdom, selected for the work of Reformation, men whom He had endowed, generally speaking, with very
superior natural powers,—and whom He had united, or resolved in
His own good time to unite, to Jesus Christ, by a true and living
faith,—inspired them with a desire to acquire all the knowledge
that might be useful in the prosecution of the work to which they
were destined; and so arranged, in His providence, the outward
circumstances in which He placed them, that they had the means
and opportunities of gratifying this desire. Thus He brought about
the actual result; that they became, in point of fact, extensively
learned in all matters connected with the work in which they
were to be engaged; while we find, also, that He was graciously
pleased to employ the learning which they had acquired, or rather
which He had bestowed upon them, as instrumental, *in its place*, in
contributing, in some measure, to the promotion of His cause.
The success of that cause is to be ascribed wholly to His own
agency,—the operation of His Spirit upon the minds and hearts of
men; but the full recognition of the agency of the Spirit as the
only real author of the whole success, does not preclude the propriety of attending to and marking the instrumentality employed,
as exhibited in the men who were the instruments of bringing
about the results, and in the various gifts as well as graces bestowed upon them and manifested in their work; and it is a fact,
and one that ought certainly to be noticed and improved, that
God, in selecting and preparing the instruments whom He was to
employ in introducing and extending the Reformation, took care
that they should be men who, speaking of them generally, had
become possessed of a share of knowledge and learning, connected
with all theological subjects, greatly superior to that of the great
body of those by whom they were surrounded. The circle of
science, in every department, was greatly more limited then than
it is now; and the amount of attainable knowledge, by means of
reading, greatly less. But the important consideration,—that
which involves a principle and teaches a lesson,—is, that the
Reformers were led to desire, and were furnished in providence

with the means of acquiring, a very large amount of the then attainable knowledge which was fitted to increase their influence and to promote their success, in establishing truth and in organising the church. Some of them held a very distinguished place among the scholars of the age in some departments of literature that were not exclusively professional. Calvin derived most important advantages, with reference to the special work to which he was afterwards called, and the talents and habits which it required, from his having been led in providence, in early life, to go through a course of study in law and jurisprudence in two of the most eminent French Universities. Melancthon and Beza were acknowledged as ranking among the most eminent Greek scholars of the period; and brought at once that refinement of taste and elegancy of style which an acquaintance with classical literature tends to produce, and at the same time great philological learning, to bear upon the interpretation of Scripture and the defence of divine truth. Almost all of them were well read in the works of the principal writers of Greece and Rome,—in the writings of the Fathers, and the history of the church,—and in the scholastic philosophers and theologians of the middle ages; and this comprehended nearly all the knowledge that was then generally accessible. All this knowledge they were enabled to acquire; they employed it in the work to which they were called; and they found that the possession and application of it contributed to promote the success of their labours. The lesson which this fact is fitted to teach, is, that we should estimate highly the value of learning, as a means of promoting the interests of truth and righteousness; and that we should feel it to be incumbent to acquire as much of knowledge and learning as opportunities will allow,—especially of that knowledge and learning which bears most directly and immediately upon the various departments of labour in which we may be called upon to engage for the advancement of Christ's cause.

In tracing the history of the lives of the leading Reformers, we find that there is scarcely one of them who had not opportunities afforded them in providence, at some period or other, of devoting a considerable portion of time to diligent and careful study. We find they faithfully improved these opportunities,— that they were in consequence able ever thereafter to bring out of their treasure things new and old, and were thus fitted for wider and more extensive usefulness. In one aspect, indeed, the truest and highest test of the usefulness of men who have honestly devoted themselves to the immediate service of God, may be said to be the number of souls whom they have directly been the instruments of converting. God has not unfrequently bestowed, in large measure, this highest usefulness upon men who were but slenderly furnished either with intellectual superiority or acquired knowledge ; and any man, however great his talents and acquirements who has received many souls for his hire, may well be satisfied with his usefulness and the reward of it. But independently of the consideration, that in all probability God has never employed any man as an instrument of extensive good in His church whom He has not made the direct instrument of converting some from the error of their ways and thereby saving their souls,—it must be observed that there is a test of usefulness, which may be regarded as *in some respects* even higher than this,—when men are enabled to contribute to the wide diffusion of great scriptural principles or truths,—the maintenance and success of a great scriptural cause,—or the infusion of spiritual health and vigour into a dead or languid church. And in these high and diffusive departments of Christian usefulness, the Lord has usually been pleased to employ the services of men who had received from Him, not only the gift of renewed hearts, but also of superior intellectual powers, and of extensive and varied knowledge. So at least it certainly was at the era of the Reformation ; and the fact that God then took care that those whom He meant chiefly to employ in this important work, did in fact acquire extensive learning, which they employed in His service, should teach the obligation incumbent upon all, of improving to the uttermost the opportunities afforded in providence of acquiring all useful knowledge, and the sinfulness of neglecting them.

But, in the second place, the history of the Reformers is fitted to teach a lesson, by exhibiting a striking example of unwearied activity and industry. They were not mere students and authors, they were diligent and laborious workers. As students, they acquired a large stock of learning ; as writers they have transmitted to us a great mass of valuable authorship ; while, at the same time, most of them had a great amount of ordinary practical work and business to attend to, and to discharge, in the different situations in which they were placed. Most of them were voluminous

authors, and have left behind them productions, the mere tran-
scription of which we, with our low standard of industry and
labour, are apt to think might be work for a lifetime. The works
of the different Reformers exhibit, of course, in different degrees,
evidence of care and elaboration in point of thought and diction,—
but they have almost all bequeathed productions which must have
occupied a great deal of time, and required a great deal of thought
and pains. And they were none of them retired students, with
leisure to devote their time unbroken to reading, reflection, and
composition. They were all busily engaged in the discharge of
important public duties, as professors and teachers, as pastors of
congregations, and organizers of churches; and in the ordinary
administration of ecclesiastical affairs. They had a great public
cause in hand, in the defence and maintenance of which they
were called upon to take a part; and this not only required of
them the publication of works through the press, but must have
entailed upon them a large amount of private correspondence and
of personal dealing with men. They did not, in general (Beza
was an exception), attain to a great age, but they lived while they
lived; and amid much to distract and harass them, they performed an amount of labour, physical and intellectual, the contemplation of which is usefully fitted to humble us under a sense of
our imbecility, inactivity, and laziness, and to stir up to more
strenuous and persevering exertion. Zwingle was cut off at the
age of forty-seven; and yet, besides doing a great deal of work,
not only as pastor and professor of theology in Zurich, but as
the leading Reformer (of the German portion) of Switzerland,
he has left us four folio volumes of well-digested, well-com-
posed matter, upon all the great theological topics that then occupied the public mind. And what a life was Calvin's! Though
he lived only fifty-four years, and struggled during a large
portion of it with a very infirm state of bodily health, and
with much severe disease, half his life was well-nigh spent before the Lord brought him to Geneva, and called him to engage
in the public service of His church. But how much was he enabled, during the remainder of his life, to do and to effect ! Though
engaged incessantly in the laborious duties of a pastor and professor of theology, he was called upon to give his counsel and advice, by personal applications and by written correspondence, upon
almost every important question, speculative or practical, that

affected the interests of the Reformed cause throughout Europe; and yet he has left many folio volumes (in one edition nine, and in another twelve) full of profound and admirably-digested thinking upon the most important and difficult of all subjects,—exhibiting much patient consideration and great practical wisdom, clothed in pure and classical Latin; forming also (for some of them were written in French, and several, as the "Institutions," both in Latin and French), in the estimation of eminent French critics, who had no liking to his theology or his ecclesiastical labours, an era in the improvement of the language of the country which had the honour to give him birth. We are too apt to think, in these degenerate times, that a reasonable and not very exalted measure of diligence and activity in some one particular department, whether of study or of practical labour, is all that can be fairly expected; but the example of the Reformers should show that it is possible, through God's grace, to do much more,—should teach a lesson of the value of time, and of the obligation to husband and improve it,—and constrain all to labour, with unwearied zeal and diligence, expecting no rest here, but looking, as they did, to the rest that remaineth for the people of God.

The third and last lesson suggested by the history and conduct of the Reformers is, the necessity and importance of giving much time and attention to the study of the word of God. The Reformers were all led by God, at an early period in their history, to give careful attention to the study of the sacred Scriptures; and they were guided by His Spirit to form correct views of the great leading principles which are there unfolded. They were led to continue ever after to study them with care and diligence; and they persevered in applying them to comfort their hearts amid all their trials, and difficulties, and to guide them in the regulation of their conduct. It is very evident, from surveying the history and the writings of the Reformers, that their strength and success,—both as defenders of divine truth and maintainers of God's cause,—and also as men engaged, amid many difficulties in the practical business of the church, and the world, and in the administration of important affairs,—arose very much from their familiar and intimate acquaintance with the word of God—the whole word of God. They were familiar with the meaning and application of its statements, and they were deeply imbued with its spirit. The word of God dwelt in them

richly, in all wisdom and spiritual understanding, and thus became
" a light unto their feet, and a lamp unto their path." It is an interesting fact, and is one proof and manifestation of their deep
and careful study of the word of God, that many of the leading
Reformers have left, amid their other voluminous productions
and abundant labours, commentaries upon the whole, or a large
portion of, the sacred Scriptures. We have eight or nine commentaries upon the whole, or large portions of, the Old and New
Testaments,—the productions of as many of the most eminent and
laborious of the Reformers; and this fact of itself, proves the
large amount of thought and attention which they were accustomed to devote to the study of them, and the great familiarity
which they had acquired with them. To write a commentary upon
the Scriptures, which should really possess any value or utility,
implies that they have been made the subject of much deep study
and much careful meditation, as well as fervent prayer for divine
direction. The commentaries of the Reformers, upon the sacred
Scriptures, are, of course, possessed of different degrees of value
and excellence,—according to the different gifts and qualifications
of the men, and the time and pains which they were able to bestow upon them; and here, as in every thing else connected with
the exposition and application of the whole truth of God, Calvin
towers far above them all; yet, as a whole, they fully vindicate
what we have said of their talents, learning, and general character;
and fully prove that they were eminently qualified for discerning and opening up the mind of God in His word, and that they
devoted a large portion of time and attention to investigating
the meaning of the sacred Scriptures,—to forming clear and
definite conceptions of the import of their statements,—and to
bringing them out for the instruction and improvement of
others. There is reason to fear, that, since the period of the
Reformation, the careful study of the word of God itself has
not usually received the share of time and attention which its
importance demands. There has always been, and there still is,
too much time and attention, *comparatively,* given to the perusal and study of other books connected with theological subjects,
and too little to the study of the inspired volume. We know, in
general, but little of the word of God as it ought to be known,—
and we are very much disposed to remain in contented ignorance
of what God has written for our instruction. We are dependent

for all true knowledge of the word of God upon the agency of the divine Spirit,—but that Spirit we are but little concerned to implore. We are dependent, also, for the attainment of this knowledge, upon our own personal study of the sacred Scriptures, —upon bringing all the powers of our minds to bear upon the investigation of their meaning,—and giving to this study no inconsiderable portion of our time and attention. But we almost all continue to be chiefly occupied with other pursuits, and with the perusal of other books, while but a fraction of our time is given to the study of the Bible; and this, too, often without much sense of the solemnity and responsibility of the occupation, and without even our ordinary powers of attention and application being brought into full and vigorous exercise. Now all this is, in the first place, a *sin*,—because it is the neglect and violation of a plain and undoubted duty; and *then* it has a powerful tendency to diminish the vigour and check the progress of the divine life in the soul, and to enfeeble and paralyze all efforts, in commending with efficacy and success, divine truth to others. The Lord was pleased to lead the Reformers to a careful study of His word, and to guide them to correct views of its leading principles. He qualified them largely for opening up and expounding its statements to others,—He led them to give much time and attention to this occupation, and made their labours, in this department, orally and by writing, the great means of their usefulness and success; and we may be assured, that it will be, to a large extent, through our capacity to open up and understand the whole mind of God, as revealed in His word,—a capacity to be acquired only by fervent prayer and by diligent and continued study of the inspired volume itself,—that we shall best grow in grace and in the power of Christian usefulness.

INDEX.